D1686702

Citizenship and Involvement in European Democracies

This unique study presents the results of a cross-national analysis of citizenship and participation among citizens in 12 European democracies.

Research on the future and quality of contemporary democracy is usually restricted to focus either on political participation, on particular aspects of citizenship, or on social activities, exclusively. This new book offers the first empirical investigation of the relationships both between social and political involvement, and between 'small-scale' and 'large-scale' democracies.

Citizenship and Involvement in European Democracies offers representative samples of the populations in a selection of European countries between 2000–2002, including: Denmark; Germany (East and West); Moldova; the Netherlands; Norway; Portugal; Romania; Russia; Slovenia; Spain; Sweden; and Switzerland. The leading contributors provide new theoretical insights and offer a broad conceptualisation of citizenship, stimulating the ongoing discussions about the problems and challenges of democratic political systems.

This book has a companion volume entitled *Social Capital and Associations in European Democracies* edited by William A. Maloney and Sigrid Roßteutscher (Routledge, 2006). Both volumes will be of great interest to students and researchers of European Politics, Comparative Politics and Sociology.

Jan W. van Deth is Professor of Political Science and International Comparative Social Research at the University of Mannheim, Germany.

José Ramón Montero is Professor of Political Science at the Autonomous University of Madrid and at the Center for Advanced Study in the Social Sciences, Juan March Institute, Madrid, Spain.

Anders Westholm is Associate Professor of Government at Uppsala University, Sweden.

Routledge research in comparative politics

1 **Democracy and Post-Communism**
   Political change in the post-communist world
   Graeme Gill

2 **Sub-State Nationalism**
   A comparative analysis of institutional design
   Edited by Helena Catt and Michael Murphy

3 **Reward for High Public Office**
   Asian and Pacific rim states
   Edited by Christopher Hood and B. Guy Peters

4 **Social Democracy and Labour Market Policy**
   Developments in Britain and Germany
   Knut Roder

5 **Democratic Revolutions**
   Asia and Eastern Europe
   Mark R. Thompson

6 **Europeanisation and the Transformation of States**
   Edited by Bengt Jacobsson, Per Lagreid and Ove K. Pedersen

7 **Democratization**
   A comparative analysis of 170 countries
   Tatu Vanhanen

8 **Determinants of the Death Penalty**
   A comparative study of the world
   Carsten Anckar

9 **How Political Parties Respond to Voters**
   Interest aggregation revisited
   Edited by Kay Lawson and Thomas Poguntke

10 **Women, Quotas and Politics**
   Edited by Drude Dahlerup

11 **Citizenship and Ethnic Conflict**
   Challenging the nation-state
   Haldun Gülalp

12 **The Politics of Women's Interests**
   New comparative and international perspectives
   Edited by Louise Chappell and Lisa Hill

13 **Political Disaffection in Contemporary Democracies**
   Social capital, institutions and politics
   Edited by Mariano Torcal and José Ramón Montero

14 **Representing Women in Parliament**
   A comparative study
   Edited by Marian Sawer, Manon Tremblay and Linda Trimble

15 **Democracy and Political Culture in Eastern Europe**
   Edited by Hans-Dieter Klingemann, Dieter Fuchs and Jan Zielonka

16 **Social Capital and Associations in European Democracies**
   A comparative analysis
   Edited by William A. Maloney and Sigrid Roßteutscher

17 **Citizenship and Involvement in European Democracies**
   A comparative analysis
   Edited by Jan W. van Deth, José Ramón Montero, and Anders Westholm

18 **The Politics of Foundations**
   A comparative analysis
   Edited by Helmut K. Anheier and Siobhan Daly

Citizenship and Involvement in European Democracies
A comparative analysis

Edited by Jan W. van Deth,
José Ramón Montero,
and Anders Westholm

Routledge
Taylor & Francis Group
LONDON AND NEW YORK

First published 2007
by Routledge
2 Park Square, Milton Park, Abingdon, Oxon OX14 4RN

Simultaneously published in the USA and Canada
by Routledge
270 Madison Ave, New York, NY 10016

Routledge is an imprint of the Taylor & Francis Group, an informa business

© 2007 Jan W. van Deth, José Ramón Montero, and Anders Westholm for selection and editorial matter; individual contributors, their contributions

Typeset in Baskerville by Wearset Ltd, Boldon, Tyne and Wear
Printed and bound in Great Britain by MPG Books Ltd, Bodmin

All rights reserved. No part of this book may be reprinted or reproduced or utilised in any form or by any electronic, mechanical, or other means, now known or hereafter invented, including photocopying and recording, or in any information storage or retrieval system, without permission in writing from the publishers.

British Library Cataloguing in Publication Data
A catalogue record for this book is available from the British Library

Library of Congress Cataloging in Publication Data
A catalog record for this book has been requested

ISBN10: 0-415-41231-5 (hbk)
ISBN10: 0-203-96575-2 (ebk)

ISBN13: 978-0-415-41231-5 (hbk)
ISBN13: 978-0-203-96575-7 (ebk)

Contents

List of figures	x
List of tables	xi
Notes on contributors	xv
Acknowledgements	xxi

1 **Introduction: citizenship, involvement, and democracy in Europe** 1
ANDERS WESTHOLM, JOSÉ RAMÓN MONTERO, AND
JAN W. VAN DETH

PART I
Civic orientations 33

2 **Trust in people, confidence in political institutions, and satisfaction with democracy** 35
SONJA ZMERLI, KENNETH NEWTON, AND
JOSÉ RAMÓN MONTERO

3 **Political confidence in representative democracies: socio-cultural vs. political explanations** 66
BAS DENTERS, OSCAR GABRIEL, AND MARIANO TORCAL

4 **Norms of good citizenship** 88
BAS DENTERS, OSCAR GABRIEL, AND MARIANO TORCAL

5 **Political and social tolerance** 109
JOSÉ MANUEL LEITE VIEGAS

viii *Contents*

PART II
Voluntary organisations and social networks   133

6   Associational involvement   135
LAURA MORALES AND PETER GEURTS

7   Explaining associational involvement   158
GABRIEL BADESCU AND KATJA NELLER

8   Social networks   188
HAJDEJA IGLIČ AND JOAN FONT FÁBREGAS

PART III
Small-scale democracy   219

9   Small-scale democracy: citizen power in the domains of everyday life   221
JØRGEN GOUL ANDERSEN AND SIGRID ROßTEUTSCHER

10   Small-scale democracy: the determinants of action   255
HANSPETER KRIESI AND ANDERS WESTHOLM

11   Small-scale democracy: the consequences of action   280
ANDERS WESTHOLM AND EMANUEL VON ERLACH

PART IV
Large-scale democracy   301

12   Political involvement   303
IRENE MARTÍN AND JAN W. VAN DETH

13   Political participation: mapping the terrain   334
JAN TEORELL, MARIANO TORCAL, AND
JOSÉ RAMÓN MONTERO

14   Political participation and associational involvement   358
KLAUS ARMINGEON

15   Participation and political equality: an assessment of large-scale democracy   384
JAN TEORELL, PAUL SUM, AND METTE TOBIASEN

16 **Conclusion: the realisation of democractic citizenship in Europe** 415
JOSÉ RAMÓN MONTERO, ANDERS WESTHOLM, AND
JAN W. VAN DETH

Bibliography 439
Index 463

Figures

1.1	Participating countries	17
2.1	Social trust, political confidence, and satisfaction with democracy	60
9.1	Incentives, actions, and consequences in small-scale democracy	229
9.2	Pathways of citizen action in small-scale democracy	248
10.1	Action and dissatisfaction	259
10.2	Action and perceived opportunities	263
10.3	Action and resources in the form of civic skills	265
12.1	A typology of citizenship	310
12.2	Political interest and importance of politics	312
12.3	Political involvement, political discussion, and media exposure	316
13.1	A typology of the modes of political participation	341
14.1	Causal relationship between organisational involvement and political participation	368–9
15.1	Political participation and social group inequality	394–5
15.2	Explaining participatory inequalities	400–1

Tables

1.1	Country characteristics	20–1
1.2	Survey characteristics	28
2.1	Principal component analysis of social trust	40
2.2	Level and dispersion of social trust	40
2.3	Principal component analysis of confidence in institutions	42
2.4	Level and dispersion of political confidence	43
2.5	Level and dispersion of satisfaction with democracy	44
2.6	Correlation between social trust and political confidence	45
2.7	Correlation between different measures of social trust and political confidence	48
2.8	Correlation between different measures of social trust and political confidence in Moldova, Romania, and Spain	49
2.9	Correlation between social trust and confidence in Parliament in Spain according to the CID and WVS studies	50
2.10	Correlation of social trust and political confidence with satisfaction with democracy	51
2.11	Multiple regression analysis of social trust	53
2.12	Multiple regression analysis of social trust including membership in different types of associations	55
2.13	Multiple regression analysis of social trust including different forms of associational involvement	56
2.14	Multiple regression analysis of confidence in political institutions	58
2.15	Multiple regression analysis of satisfaction with democracy	59
3.1	Principal component analysis of political confidence	69
3.2	Average political confidence scores by country	70
3.3	Socio-cultural and micro-political explanatory variables for confidence in institutions of representative party-democracy (OLS estimates)	76–7
3.4	Socio-cultural and micro-political explanatory factors for the difference between confidence in institutions of the *Rechtsstaat* and confidence in institutions of representative party-democracy (OLS estimates)	80–1

3.5	Multilevel analysis of political confidence with interactions (OLS estimates)	84
4.1	Patterns of good citizenship: results of principal component analysis per country	94
4.2	Average support for different citizen values	96
4.3	The explanatory power of four aspects of social capital (model 1) and of these aspects plus control variables (model 2) on the support for various components of good citizenship	100
4.4	Effects of four components of social capital (model 1) and of these components plus control variables (model 2) on overall support for civic values	104–5
5.1	Political exclusion and social discrimination	115
5.2	Political exclusion and selected political and socio-economic characteristics	116
5.3	Political exclusion of different social groups	120
5.4	Social discrimination against different social groups	121
5.5	Social discrimination against different social groups according to the World Values Surveys 1990 and 1999	123
5.6	Multiple regression analysis of political exclusion of extremist groups	127
5.7	Multiple regression analysis of political exclusion of stigmatized groups and ethnic minorities	128
6.1	Levels of associational involvement	138
6.2	Breadth of associational involvement	141
6.3	Patterns of activism in associations	142
6.4	Passive and active involvement in associations (involved respondents only)	143
6.5	Associational involvement beyond membership: when those who take part in activities, donate, and do voluntary work outnumber members	146
6.6	Active involvement in different types of associations (involved respondents only)	148
6.7	Correlations between social trust and different forms of associational involvement	151
6.8	Mean level of social trust and levels of associational involvement	152
6.9	Correlation between social trust and different forms of exclusive associational involvement	152
6.10	Correlations between social trust and degree of involvement in different types of associations	154
7.1	Explaining involvement in any type of association	170–1
7.2	Explaining involvement in spare time and sports associations	174–5
7.3	Explaining involvement in interest groups	176–7

7.4	Explaining involvement in socio-cultural associations	178–9
7.5	Explaining involvement in religious associations	180–1
8.1	Multiplicity of social networks	191
8.2	Regression analysis of network multiplicity	194
8.3	Regression analysis of involvement in different kinds of networks (pooled analysis)	195
8.4	Strength of social ties in voluntary associations	201
8.5	Strength of social ties in the workplace	202
8.6	Frequency of political discussion	206
8.7	Frequency of discussing politics in different kinds of voluntary associations in Spain and Switzerland	208
8.8	Regression analysis of political discussion	210–11
9.1	Index for perceived opportunities to influence by domain	231
9.2	Mean perceived opportunities to influence by domain and country	232
9.3	Mean dissatisfaction by domain and country	237
9.4	Probability of taking action by domain and country (percentages)	239
9.5	Probability of different types of actions by domain (percentages)	242
9.6	Probability of different types of actions by domain and country (percentages)	244
9.7	Probability of success (percentages)	247
9.8	Pathways of citizen action by domain and country (percentages)	250
9.9	Mean perception of procedural fairness by domain and country	252
10.1	Predicting action in working life (multivariate logistic regression)	267
10.2	Predicting specific types of action in working life (multivariate logistic regression)	271
10.3	Predicting action in child education (multivariate logistic regression)	272
10.4	Predicting action in healthcare (multivariate logistic regression)	273
11.1	Predicting the success rate of attempts to exercise influence (multivariate logistic regression)	283
11.2	Perceived opportunities as a function of experiences from attempts to exercise influence	286
11.3	Dissatisfaction as a function of experiences from attempts to exercise influence	289
11.4	Summary evaluation of small-scale democracy	292–3
11.5	The cumulation of participation in small-scale democracy	294
11.6	Relationship between participation in small- and large-scale democracy	296

xiv Tables

12.1	Relationships between political interest and importance of politics	313
12.2	A typology of political involvement	313
12.3	Distributions of the four types of citizenship (in percentages)	315
12.4	Behavioural expressions of political involvement related to the four types of citizenship	317–18
12.5	Impact of political involvement on social and political participation by country and type of citizenship	322–3
12.6	Antecedents of three types of citizenship (multinomial logistic regressions, log-odds ratios)	326–7
13.1	Levels of political participation (in percentages)	338–9
13.2	Principal component analysis of participatory activities for all 13 societies (pattern matrix with oblimin rotation)	344
13.3	Principal component analysis of the participation items by groups of countries (pattern matrix with oblimin rotation)	346–7
13.4	Levels of political participation in 13 societies	349
13.5	Country-level correlations between modes of political participation	350
13.6	Individual-level correlations between modes of participation by groups of countries	352–3
14.1	Levels of political participation by organisational involvement	359
14.2	A general model for explaining political participation	371
14.3	Top down (cleavage politics) model for explaining political participation	372
14.4	Social capital model for explaining political participation	375
14.5	Self-selectivity model for explaining political participation	378–9
15.1	Distortion of left–right placement through participation (OLS estimates)	388
15.2	Distortion of tolerance through participation (OLS estimates)	390
15.3	Summary evaluation of participation and political equality	406–7

Contributors

Jørgen Goul Andersen is Professor of Political Sociology and Director of the Centre for Comparative Welfare Studies, Aalborg University (Denmark). Coordinator of the Danish Election Studies and the Danish ISSP programme, and 1998–2003 board member of the Danish Democracy and Political Power Project. Author/co-author/editor of some 30 books on welfare state, political participation, and political behaviour, including *Citizenship and Democracy in Scandinavia* (with Jens Hoff, London: Palgrave, 2001).

Klaus Armingeon is Professor of Political Science at the University of Berne (Switzerland). His main research interest is on comparative politics, including institutions (in particular consociational structures and collective labour relations), policies (in particular economic and social policies), and political participation. Recent publications include *The Politics of Post-Industrial Welfare States* (ed. with Giuliano Bonoli, London: Routledge, 2006); *OECD and European Welfare States* (ed. with Michelle Beyeler, Cheltenham: Edgar Elgar, 2004); 'Swiss Worlds of Welfare' (with Giuliano Bonoli and Fabio Bertozzi), in *West European Politics* (2004), and 'The Effects of Negotiation Democracy, A Comparative Analysis', in *European Journal of Political Research* (2002).

Gabriel Badescu is Associate Professor of Political Science at the Babes-Bolyai University, Cluj-Napoca (Romania). His main research interests are political participation, civil society, and social capital in Eastern Europe. He has published in the area of quantitative methods and research design, political culture, and transitions to democracy in the former communist countries. Recent publication: *Social Capital and Democratic Transition* (ed. with Eric Uslaner, London: Routledge, 2003).

Bas Denters is Professor of Urban Policy and Politics and Director of Studies of the School for Public Administration at the University of Twente (the Netherlands). His research interests are urban politics and urban democracy. He received the Annual Award of the Dutch Political Science Association (NKWP) for the best publication in Dutch political science in 1987. He has published in *Quantity & Quality*, *European Journal for Political Research*, *Public Administration*, and *Government and Policy*. He is convener of the Standing Group for Local Government and Politics (LOGOPOL) of the European Consortium for Political Research (ECPR).

Joan Font Fábregas is Lecturer in Political Science at the Autonomous University of Barcelona (Spain) and Research Director at the largest Spanish Survey Research Center (CIS). His main research interests are turnout, new mechanisms of citizen participation, and associations in political life. He coordinates the Spanish CID research on associations and political activists and participates in the EU funded project Democratic participation and political communication in systems of multi-level governance. His recent publications include *Public Participation and Local Governance* (ed., Barcelona: ICPS, 2003) and 'Dangerous Coalitions for Small Parties: the Electoral Consequences of Government', in *South European Society & Politics* (2001).

Oscar W. Gabriel is Professor of Political Science at the University of Stuttgart (Germany). His main research fields are political attitudes and political behaviour, particularly social and political participation and electoral behaviour, and local politics. He was member of the research group that conducted the German Electoral Studies in 1998 and 2002 and is currently engaged in the National Coordinating Team of the German part of the *European Social Survey*.

Peter Geurts is Associate Professor of Research Methods at the School of Business, Public Administration and Technology of the University of Twente (the Netherlands), Department of Political Science and Research Methods (POLMT). He specialises in survey methods (design and analysis).

Hajdeja Iglič is Assistant Professor of Sociology and Researcher at the University of Ljubljana (Slovenia). Her research focuses on the analysis of social networks and social capital. She studied networks of Slovenian elites before and after democratic transition, and networks of the general population in their relationship to political participation and mobilisation. Her recent publications include: 'Trust Networks and Democratic Transition', in *Social Capital and Transition to Democracy* (ed. Gabriel Badescu and Eric M. Uslaner, London and New York: Routledge, 2003), and 'Trust, Governance and Performance: The Role of Institutional in Interpersonal Trust in SME Development', in *International Sociology* (with Andrej Rus, 2005).

Hanspeter Kriesi is Professor of Comparative Politics at the University of Zurich (Switzerland). His main research interests are in the comparative analysis of political mobilisation and democratic decision making.

He published widely in the area of Swiss politics, social movements, and direct-democratic decision-making. Currently he is the Director of the Swiss NCCR *Challenges to Democracy in the 21st Century*. His most recent book is *Direct Democratic Choice. The Swiss Experience* (Lanham: Lexington Books, 2005).

Irene Martín is Lecturer in Political Science at the Autonomous University of Madrid and has been researcher at the Juan March Institute (Spain). Her main research interests are political culture, especially in Spain and Modern Greece. She is currently undertaking research on education for citizenship. Her recent publications include 'Interest in Politics and the Political Culture Approach: The Case of the New Democracies of Southern and Eastern Europe', in *Political Culture in Post-Communist Europe – Attitudes in New Democracies* (ed. Detlef Pollack *et al.*, Aldershot: Ashgate, 2003).

José Ramón Montero is Professor of Political Science at the Autonomous University of Madrid and at the Center for Advanced Studies in the Social Sciences, Juan March Institute, Madrid. His main research areas are political participation, political parties, political culture, and electoral behaviour. He has been a member of the Standing Committee for the Social Sciences, European Science Foundation, and is currently a member of the Academia Europea and of the Scientific Advisory Board of the European Social Survey. Recent publications are *Political Parties: Old Concepts and New Challenges* (co-ed. with Richard Gunther and Juan J. Linz, Oxford: Oxford University Press, 2002), *Democracy in Modern Spain* (with R. Gunther and Joan Botella, New Haven: Yale University Press, 2004), and *Political Disaffection in Contemporary Democracies: Social Capital, Instituions, and Politics* (co-edited with Mariano Torcal, London: Routledge, 2006).

Laura Morales is Assistant Professor of Political Science at the Universidad de Murcia (Spain). Her interests lie, especially, in the areas of electoral behaviour and political participation. She is a member of the Spanish National Coordination team of the European Social Survey, and she currently coordinates the project LOCALMULTIDEM (funded by the 6th Framework Programme) on immigrants' participation and integration at the local level. Her book *Nations of Political Joiners?* (a revised version of her Ph.D. thesis, which was awarded with the ECPR and the Spanish Political Science Association prizes for the best Ph.D. thesis in 2004) will be published by ECPR Press in 2007.

Katja Neller is Research Assistant at the University of Stuttgart (Germany) where she coordinates the German national study of the European Social Survey (ESS). Her main research interests are political culture, political behaviour, and political participation. Recent publication (with Oscar W. Gabriel): 'Kandidatenorientierungen und Wahlverhalten bei den Bundestagswahlen 1994–2002', in *Wahlen und Wähler:*

Analysen aus Anlass der Bundestagswahl 2002 (ed. J.W. Falter, O.W. Gabriel, and B. Weßels, Wiesbaden: VS Verlag für Sozialwissenschaften, 2005).

Kenneth Newton is Professor of Comparative Politics at the University of Southampton (UK). His main research interests are comparative government and politics, especially the role of the mass media, mass attitudes and behaviour, and the social basis of operations of democracy. Recent publications include *The New British Politics* (Harlow: Longmans, 2004, 4th edition) and *Foundations of Comparative Politics* (with Jan van Deth, Cambridge: Cambridge University Press, 2005).

Sigrid Roßteutscher is a Reader in Politics at the University of Mannheim (Germany) and project director at the Mannheim Centre for European Research (MZES). Her main interest is in political, social and religious participation, values and social inequality, and in concepts of democracy, in particular recent theories about the role of associations and religion in contemporary democracy. She obtained her Ph.D. at the European University Institute (EUI) in Florence, Italy.

Paul E. Sum is an Associate Professor at the University of North Dakota where he teaches courses in Comparative Politics. His research addresses issues of political participation, civil society development, political party systems, and ethnic relations, especially in post-communist societies. He has recently published articles on these subjects in *East European Politics and Society* (2004), *Law and Social Inquiry* (2004), and *Romanian Journal of Society and Politics* (2005).

Jan Teorell is Associate Professor of Political Science at Lund University (Sweden). His main research interests are comparative democratisation, political participation, and political methodology. At the moment he is working on a research project studying the determinants of democratisation across the globe. His articles have been published in *Party Politics, Scandinavian Political Studies, Studies in Comparative International Development*, and *European Journal of Political Research*.

Mette Tobiasen has been a consultant at the Danish National Institute of Social Research since 2005. Before that she was Assistant Professor of Political Sociology at the Department of Economics, Politics, and Public Administration of Aalborg University (Denmark). Her main research interests were globalisation, democracy, and political participation. She has published in the area of political consumerism, political participation, and global citizenship.

Mariano Torcal is Professor in Political Science at the Pompeu Fabra University in Barcelona (Spain) and National Coordinator of the European Social Survey in Spain. He has published articles on the topics of political culture and political behaviour in major international journals such as *Comparative Political Studies, British Journal of Political Research*, and *International Journal of Public Opinion Research*. The American Political Science Association awarded him with Honorable Mention for the Gregory M. Luebbert Prize for best article in comparative politics of 1997. He recently published *Political Disaffection in Contemporary Democracies: Social Capital, Institutions, and Politics* (co-edited with José Ramón Montero, London: Routledge, 2006).

Jan W. van Deth is Professor of Political Science and International Comparative Social Research at the University of Mannheim (Germany). He was Director of the Mannheim Centre for European Social Research (MZES) and is a Corresponding Member of the Royal Netherlands Academy of Arts and Sciences. He was convenor of the international network Citizenship, Involvement, Democracy (CID) of the European Science Foundation and is national coordinator of the German team for the European Social Survey. Recent publications include *Foundations of Comparative Politics* (with Kenneth Newton, Cambridge: Cambridge University Press, 2005).

José Manuel Leite Viegas is Professor of Sociology, and Coordinating Researcher at the Sociological Research and Study Center (CIES) in Lisbon. His main research interests are political values and attitudes, political and social participation, electoral abstention, voluntary associations, and the participation of women in politics. Recent publications: *Crossroads to Modernity – Contemporary Portuguese Society* (co-edited, Oeiras: Celta, 2000), *Cidadania, Integração, Globalização* (co-author, Oeiras: Celta, 2001), *As Mulheres na Política* (co-edited, Oeiras: Celta, 2004) and *Democracia: Novos Desafios e Novos Horizontes* (Oeiras: Celta, forthcoming).

Emanuel von Erlach has finished his Ph.D. Thesis on the impacts of membership in associations on political engagement in 2005. He is currently working in the field of educational statistics at the Swiss Federal Statistical Office.

Anders Westholm is Associate Professor of Government at Uppsala University (Sweden). He has directed or co-directed the Swedish Studies of Citizenship ('medborgarundersökningarna') and the research programme Mechanisms of Democracy. He has also served in several government commissions of inquiry as well as in the SNS Democratic Audit of Sweden. His research interests include democratic auditing, political participation, ethnic integration, political socialisation, power elites, theories of electoral choice, and methodology. Aside from monographs and edited volumes, his work has also appeared in journals such as the *American Political Science Review, Journal of Politics, Comparative Politics, Electoral Studies*, and *Political Psychology*.

Sonja Zmerli is Teaching and Research Assistant at the University of Technology Darmstadt (Germany). Her main research interests are social capital and its political consequences as well as political involvement in comparative perspective. Recent publications: 'Politisches Vertrauen und Unterstützung', in *Deutschland in Europa* (ed. Jan van Deth, Wiesbaden: VS Verlag für Sozialwissenschaften, 2004) and 'Applying the Concepts of Bonding and Bridging Social Capital to Empirical Research', *European Political Science* (2003).

Acknowledgements

The area of social capital, citizenship, civil society, social involvement, trust, and, more generally, the chances and opportunities for improving citizens' involvement in democratic societies, represents one of the most controversial topics in the social sciences. Empirical research is only slowly developed and usually restricted to a single country or to rather narrow concerns, focusing either on political participation, particular aspects of citizenship, or social activities. By the end of 1998, researchers from Austria, Denmark, Germany, Great Britain, the Netherlands, Norway, Spain, Sweden, and Switzerland begun to cooperate in order to develop cross-national research in this area. On the basis of an extensive Swedish study on citizenship (coordinated by Anders Westholm, Uppsala) and a Dutch community study (by Jan W. van Deth and Monique Leijenaar, Nijmegen), an international comparative research design was developed, which permitted the testing of the complex relationships between social and political involvement. Only such an encompassing research design is capable of answering the crucial question of whether – and if so, to what extent – do modes of social involvement contribute to a qualitative and quantitative improvement of contemporary democracies. Comparatively speaking, there is ample reason to assume that the link between the 'social' and the 'political', between 'big' and 'small' politics exists in manifold contextual and institutional variations. However, little is known about such variations, and more importantly, how such variations might differently contribute to democracy.

Based on the idea that only close international collaboration could result in the empirical information required in this area, the network Citizenship, Involvement, Democracy (CID) supported by the European Science Foundation (ESF) was founded (coordinated by Jan W. van Deth, Mannheim; see www.mzes.uni-mannheim.de/projekte/cid/). In the first stage of the network participants included Jørgen Goul Andersen (Aalborg), Klaus Armingeon (Bern), Paul Dekker (Den Haag), Bas Denters (Enschede), Oscar W. Gabriel (Stuttgart), Peter Geurts (Enschede), Tore Hansen (Oslo), Hanspeter Kriesi (Geneva), William A. Maloney (Aberdeen), José Ramón Montero (Madrid), Ken Newton

(Essex), Sigrid Roßteutscher (Mannheim), Per Selle (Bergen), Jan Teorell (Uppsala), Lise Togeby (Aarhus), Mariano Torcal (Madrid), Peter A. Ulram (Vienna), Jan W. van Deth (Mannheim), Anders Westholm (Uppsala), and Paul Whiteley (Sheffield). Some of these colleagues left the project after the initial phase and new members joined the network. The list of participants who remained at the final phase is identical to the list of contributors to the two volumes published.

The research design developed by the network includes two major components: first, a survey of representative samples of the population in European countries in order to examine the general orientations and behaviour of citizens and, second, a study of voluntary associations in several European cities/communities in order to obtain information about the structure of this area and the opportunities for engagement. For both parts of the project similar research designs have been developed (including common core questionnaires) and implemented in a number of countries.

The two parts of the CID-project address similar questions about citizenship and involvement. The population project provides analyses of individual citizens' involvement. However, before much participation can take place, groups must exist as vehicles for citizen engagement. Thus the organisational study focuses on the collective opportunities and routes for social and political involvement. In essence, these two parts are joined at the hip; viewing the same phenomenon from slightly different angles. Although it is clear that the two parts are highly complementary, they differ in their research designs and empirical evidence. For that reason, the results are published in two volumes clearly focused on 'their' specific aims. Both volumes share the general concern with democratic citizenship and the comparative perspective; and both are based on collaborative efforts of international groups of scholars. In the first volume, the availability of high-quality survey data collected in 13 societies (Denmark, East and West Germany, Moldova, the Netherlands, Norway, Portugal, Romania, Russia, Slovenia, Spain, Sweden, Switzerland) offers a unique opportunity to study the political and social behaviour of citizens. The results of this part of the project are presented in the first volume, devoted to *Citizenship and Involvement in European Democracies: A Comparative Analysis* (edited by Jan W. van Deth, José Ramón Montero, and Anders Westholm). The organisational study in eight European cities (Aalborg, Aberdeen, Bern, Chemnitz, Enschede, Mannheim, Lausanne, Sabadell) and an additional 18 smaller communities or villages in Spain, Switzerland, East and West Germany makes it possible to study the structure of voluntary sectors and opportunities for participation and mobilisation in very different institutional and organisational contexts. The results of this part of the project are presented in the second volume, devoted to *Social Capital and Associations in European Democracies: A Comparative Analysis* (edited by William A. Maloney and Sigrid Roßteutscher).

Developing and carrying out a large and complicated international project completely depends on the willingness of many people to spend their time and energy to collaborate and to contribute to the collective efforts. We are very grateful to all participants in the various stages of our common undertaking. This international collaboration was highly facilitated by the recognition of the CID-project as an official ESF-Network. The support of the ESF enabled the group to meet frequently between 1999 and 2003, and ESF staff members joined the discussions at several meetings (Marianne Yagoubi, Caroline Eckert, Henk Stronkhorst). Additional support for meetings of our group, the Steering Committee, or the young scholars, was received from universities in Aberdeen and Mannheim, as well as from institutes in Madrid (Juan March Institute, and the Spanish Ministry of Science and Technology, grant SEC2002-10279-E) and Barcelona (Jaume Bofill Foundation). Furthermore, the Mannheim Centre for European Social Research (MZES) provided substantial resources and support at all stages of the project to smooth communication, to build extensive integrated data sets, to document the various tasks, and to prepare manuscripts.

The organisation and collection of data in each of the 13 societies and 26 European communities was made possible with a number of generous grants. Data collection and preparing the information for our analyses was accomplished with support of a number of national foundations and institutes: Denmark (Democracy and Power Study, conducted on behalf of the Danish Parliament), Germany (German National Science Foundation DFG, grant DE630/7-1), Moldova and Romania (International Research and Exchanges Board IREX under the auspices of the Black and Caspian Sea Collaborative Research Program, funded by the Starr Foundation), the Netherlands (Institute for Governance Studies at the University of Twente), Norway (Norwegian Research Council; Power and Democracy Group; Stein Rokkan Center), Portugal (Science and Technology Foundation; Ministry of Science and Technology; Institute for Sociological Research ISCTE), Russia (Bank of Sweden Tercentennary Foundation), Slovenia (Ministry of Higher Education, Science and Technology, grant J5-3039-0582-04), Spain (Ministry of Science and Technology, grant SEC2000-0758-C02, and Automous University of Madrid, grant 9/SHD/001), Sweden (Bank of Sweden Tercentennary Foundation, Mechanisms of Democracy programme), and Switzerland (Swiss National Science Foundation SNF). We are very grateful for this impressive list of generous grants which allowed us to carry out our project in so many distinct countries.

The successful completion of an international project dealing with questions about complex social and political developments depends on the help of very many people over a long period of time. We cannot list all the research assistants, secretaries, managers, and colleagues who made this project possible, but we are very grateful for the generous support that was provided to us without hesitation over so many years. Especially, we would like to thank Stephanie Stuck (Mannheim) and Peter Geurts (Enschede) for designing and developing the integrated data sets and harmonising the data from so many different countries and cities. Finally, we want to express our personal gratitude to the MZES and the University of Mannheim, to the Juan March Institute and the Spanish Ministry of Science and Technology (grant SEC2002-03364), and to the Mechanisms of Democracy programme (funded by the Bank of Sweden Tercentennary Foundation), which provided us with the resources to finish this project.

Jan W. van Deth, Mannheim
José Ramón Montero, Madrid
Anders Westholm, Uppsala

1 Introduction

Citizenship, involvement, and democracy in Europe

Anders Westholm, José Ramón Montero, and Jan W. van Deth

Our point of departure: the concept of citizenship

When the word 'citizenship' is encountered in everyday conversations, it typically refers to polity membership. A person is described as having, for example, German citizenship, if he or she is formally a member of the state of Germany. The conception of citizenship that we outline below is much broader, yet intimately related to the use of the word in everyday parlance.[1] The fact that, today, a person is ordinarily described as being a *citizen* rather than a *subject* of a certain country is not coincidental but intended to convey the notion that he or she enjoys *full* membership in the polity and an associated *bundle of legal rights*.

Some 300 years ago, the idea that there might be a set of universal citizen rights was still a revolutionary one. The progress made towards the bundle of rights that many of us take for granted today has been slow and cumbersome. In his now classical account of the history of citizenship, British sociologist T.H. Marshall (1950) distinguishes three major types of citizen rights: civil, political, and social. Civil rights protect individual freedom. They grant the liberty of the person, freedom of speech, thought, and faith, the right to own property, to conclude contracts, and the right to justice. As Marshall points out, the last is fundamental in the sense that without it, the others cannot be legally defended and asserted. Political rights give citizens a say about the decisions of the polity, most fundamentally by granting them the right to vote and candidate in public elections. Finally, social rights assure citizens a certain minimum of social welfare and security.

According to Marshall, these three types of rights were instituted in a particular order. In fact, he goes as far as to identify each of them with one century: civil rights were largely a product of the eighteenth century, political rights primarily developed during the nineteenth century, and social rights did not make a serious appearance until the twentieth century.

As Marshall himself makes clear, his account is mainly inspired by British history and encounters several exceptions already in the British case. One may note, for example, that in many European countries, reasonably complete civil rights were not granted to women until well into the nineteenth century, full suffrage not instituted before the beginning of the twentieth century, and decisive steps toward social rights – especially in the important realm of education – already taken in the nineteenth century. An additional, major specification is that a considerable number of countries in the eastern, central, and southern parts of Europe have, for shorter or longer periods, suffered backlashes in the twentieth century, particularly with respect to civil and political rights, through the establishment of communist, fascist, and other modern forms of dictatorships. As a coarse stylisation, Marshall's scheme nevertheless captures some essential features of the historical development.

While Marshall emphasises the growth of the *content* of the bundle of rights we associate with citizenship, he indirectly describes another line of expansion as well. The *number* of residents who qualify as citizens has gradually increased. Citizenship in the sense of legal rights has thus become more encompassing in two different ways: more rights and more citizens.

The expansion in the latter regard can be stylised in the same rough manner as the former. If, for the sake of simplicity, we exemplify by the development of political rights alone, we find that many European countries instituted full and equal male suffrage toward the end of the nineteenth, and beginning of the twentieth, century. Although the power of the assemblies elected by popular vote often remained limited, the extension of the franchise to the entire male population nevertheless represented a significant step away from aristocracy (the rule of the nobility) and plutocracy (the rule of the rich) towards 'andrarchy' (the rule of men).

With some notable exceptions, such as Switzerland and France, universal suffrage for both genders followed relatively soon after the introduction of full and equal male suffrage. The period between the two reforms was, as a rule, particularly short in countries where the first of them took place relatively late (early twentieth century). Occasionally, such as in Finland (1906), women even gained the right to vote at the same time as men.

The introduction of full and equal suffrage for all nationals obviously represents an important watershed. At no prior point in the history of the nation state had it been possible to place an equal sign between the subjects of a country and its citizens. From this point onwards, however, we find countries in which virtually all nationals enjoyed full citizen rights, and where the passport could, for the first time, serve as a symbol of equality (occasionally a threatening one, as in Vladimir Mayakovsky's 1929 poem about his Soviet passport).

Nevertheless, 'natiocracy' (the rule of the nationals) does not necessarily represent the end of the development towards extended citizenship. For example, the issue of cultural rights and multicultural notions of citizenship is currently at the fore in many countries with significant immigrant or native minorities (see, for example, Barry 2001). From the 1970s onwards, several countries have taken important steps toward what might be termed 'habitocracy' (the rule of the inhabitants) by extending the right to vote in certain types of elections and referenda to all non-temporary residents regardless of nationality (see Blais *et al.* 2001). The battle over precisely what rights should be considered an essential part of citizenship and who should be entitled to them thus remains a significant ingredient of philosophical as well as political debate.

The dynamics briefly outlined above are fully reflected in Marshall's conception of citizenship. In his own words:

> Citizenship is a status bestowed on those who are full members of a community. All who possess the status are equal with respect to the rights and duties with which the status is endowed. There is no universal principle that determines what those rights and duties should be, but societies in which citizenship is a developing institution create an image of an ideal citizenship against which achievement can be measured and towards which aspirations can be directed. The urge forward along the path thus plotted is an urge towards a fuller measure of equality, an enrichment of the stuff of which the status is made and an increase in the number of those on whom the status is bestowed.
>
> (Marshall 1950: 28–30)

Marshall is, in this case, still speaking primarily of legal rights. However, he eventually extends the idea of citizenship as an ideal 'against which achievement can be measured' in a direction of particular relevance for this book. By introducing the notion of *effective citizenship*, Marshall proceeds beyond citizenship as a legal concept and introduces it as a sociological one. The sociological understanding implies that, given a certain bundle of legal rights, citizenship is something that can be *realised* to a greater or lesser extent. This idea becomes manifest a few pages later when Marshall points out that civil rights:

> confer the legal capacity to strive for the things one would like to possess but do not guarantee the possession of any of them. A property right is not a right to possess property but a right to acquire it, if you can, and to protect it, if you can get it. But, if you use these arguments to explain to a pauper that his property rights are the same as those of a millionaire, he will probably accuse you of quibbling. Similarly, the right to freedom of speech has little real substance if, from lack of education, you have nothing to say worth saying, and no means of making yourself heard if you say it.
>
> (Marshall 1950: 34–5)

Marshall's main point is that social rights are an essential precondition for realising civil, as well as political, rights. However, he also emphasises that neither the presence of social rights nor the material benefits in which they may result are sufficient for the realisation of citizenship:

> Citizenship requires a bond of a different kind [than earlier societies], a direct sense of community membership based on loyalty to a civilisation which is a common possession. It is a loyalty of free men endowed with rights and protected by a common law. Its growth is stimulated both by the struggle to win those rights and by their enjoyment when won.
>
> (Marshall 1950: 40)

By introducing a 'sense of community' into his conception of citizenship, Marshall does in fact incorporate (although he never explicitly says so), all three of the proud principles associated with the French Revolution: liberty, equality, and fraternity. Liberty, because his ideal is that of full citizenship: citizens should have the capacity to realise the opportunities that they are granted by law. Equality, because his ideal is that of equal citizenship: citizens should have the same capacity to realise their ambitions. And fraternity because his ideal is that citizens share a sense of community: unless they do so, they are unlikely to be able to organise their society in such a way as to approach the ideals of liberty and equality.

It is a well-known fact, however, that the three principles are not always compatible with each other. Nor does Marshall try to hide the significant tensions that exist between them. One expression of these tensions is the rich variety of *normative* theories of citizenship. The resurgence of interest in these theories in philosophical circles (see, for example, Kymlicka and Norman 1995) and public debate bears testimony to the fact that the notion of citizenship remains an ideologically powerful one, less tarnished at the present time than the banners under which similar battles were fought during the 1970s and 1980s (Marxism and neoliberalism).

Conventionally, three or four major traditions are distinguished in the literature (see van Gunsteren 1994; Jones and Gaventa 2002). Each of them can be said to provide a response to the question of how we should choose, if and when, the various principles of citizenship run into conflict with one another.

The *liberal* tradition stresses freedom, especially negative freedom (i.e. freedom from undesired intervention by the state or fellow citizens) and equality of (legal) opportunity. The notion of community is very thin. However, the variation within this tradition is enormous. There is a wide gulf between the ideals expressed, for example, by Robert Nozick (1974) and Brian Barry (2001), although both can be said to be exponents of the liberal tradition.

There is but a fine line of distinction between some versions of liberal citizenship theory and the socialist, or rather *social-democratic*, tradition

(Marxism leaves little room for the idea of citizenship), which emphasises equality beyond equal (legal) opportunity as well as positive freedom (i.e. freedom in the sense of having sufficient resources to utilise legal opportunities). The importance of more than a very limited set of shared beliefs and values is also more heavily stressed than in the liberal tradition.

The *communitarian* tradition is, in its modern manifestations, directed against the liberal emphasis on individual autonomy, the social-democratic emphasis on the welfare state as a means of realising citizenship, and the focus within both traditions on rights at the expense of obligations. It stresses the importance of the community rather than the individual, of 'natural' communities (e.g. the family) rather than 'artificial' ones (e.g. the welfare state), and of the responsibilities implied by community membership rather than the right to self-realisation.

The *republican* tradition, finally, accentuates the political community as opposed to the cultural, historical, or 'natural' community emphasised by communitarians. The primary rights, obligations, loyalties, and practices associated with citizenship are those that have a direct link to the political system.

Our undertaking: a cross-national inquiry into the realisation of citizenship

The purpose of this book is not to argue the superiority of one of these traditions over the others as an ideal of citizenship. Nor is it to chart in detail the actual development of the formal rights associated with the notion of citizenship. Instead, our aim is to contribute part of the answer to a major question that should be of interest regardless which ideal of citizenship one prefers or the way such ideals are reflected in current law. That question, which constitutes the common denominator of this book, is directly inspired by Marshall's notion of effective citizenship.

As Marshall observes, many of the rights associated with citizenship provide us with opportunities but do not guarantee our ability to take advantage of them. The legal opportunities to associate with others in voluntary organisations and to participate in political life are of utmost importance but insufficient to ensure a flourishing civil society or a system of government in which every citizen's voice is properly heard. This, in turn, prompts our central question: to what extent are the ideals of citizenship – espoused but not ensured by legal rights – actually realised in various countries on the European continent?

Three issues immediately come to the fore once these general contours of our inquiry have been formulated. First, *what* specific aspects do we include in our study of the realisation of citizenship? Second, *where*, more specifically, do we study them? Finally, *how* do we supply the empirical information required? In the remainder of this introductory chapter, we address each element in this triad of issues: first, we provide an outline of the book and its individual contributions. Subsequently, we present our setting by describing some of the potentially important characteristics of the countries we study. In the final section, we furnish some central facts about the data at our disposal and the way we analyse them.

Before we move on to this, however, it is useful to outline in brief terms some significant characteristics in each of the three regards. Our data source consists of a cross-national survey, executed at the turn of the century (1999–2002) and covers the populations of 12 European countries. The survey includes three Nordic countries – Denmark, Norway, and Sweden – three countries from the central parts of the continent – Germany, the Netherlands, and Switzerland – the two countries on the Iberian Peninsula in the south-west – Portugal and Spain – and four countries located behind the former Iron Curtain in the east – Moldova, Romania, Russia, and Slovenia.

No more than 15 years ago, the eastern part of Germany fell behind that curtain as well. For analytical purposes, this impels us to treat Germany as two separate entities corresponding to the two parts – East Germany and West Germany – into which the country was divided for 45 years (1945–1990). We thereby gain the opportunity to systematically test the hypothesis that the differential experiences faced by the populations of the two parts during the period of separation still render them significantly different with respect to the characteristics we investigate. Technically speaking, we thus proceed as though we had a sample of 13 rather than 12 countries.

Our study of the realisation of citizenship includes four major components, each of which making up one of the four parts into which all but the introductory and concluding chapters of this book are divided: civic orientations, voluntary associations and social networks, small-scale democracy, and large-scale democracy.

The last two of these components may require a bit more in the way of conceptual explanations, and it is therefore useful to begin at that end. The distinction between small- and large-scale democracy, as well as the idea to make both of them part of the study of the realisation of citizenship, originates from prior work on Scandinavian countries, beginning with the Swedish study of citizenship carried out in 1987 (Petersson *et al.* 1989; see also Andersen *et al.* 1993; Petersson *et al.* 1998; Andersen and Hoff 2001).

While one can arrive at essentially the same ideas from several different ends, one useful starting point is the notion of autonomy. Autonomy in the sense of self-determination is intimately related to the ideals of citizenship. The struggle for citizenship rights has to a significant extent been a struggle to free individuals from the restrictions imposed by heteronomy, that is, from the rule of anyone but themselves.

The concept of autonomy can be applied to individuals as well as to groups of varying size. When we think of democracy, we may think primarily of a system of government in which the population of an entire country rules itself. However, the notion of democracy is not restricted to the nation state but extends to the supra-national level (e.g. the European Union) as well as the sub-national one (local government). We also recognise, as an indispensable part of democracy, the rights of citizens to freely associate with each other outside the state in order to govern themselves in certain respects (e.g. a sports club with respect to its athletic activities or a residents' association with respect to matters of joint concern in a residential area). Finally, yet importantly, we recognise the rights of individual citizens to a private sphere into which others are not allowed to intervene.

There are thus many different ways in which citizens can realise the ideal of democracy as autonomy. When, in the following, we speak of large-scale democracy, we have in mind the way relatively large groups of people (e.g. the inhabitants of a municipality and upwards) attempt to govern themselves with respect to matters of joint concern. When we speak of small-scale democracy, we think of how smaller groups or single individuals try to control events of prime concern to them.

Our study of *large-scale democracy* is to a considerable extent a study of political participation. Our definition of that concept (discussed in detail by Jan Teorell, Mariano Torcal, and José Ramón Montero in Chapter 13), retains two of the key elements of the classical definition provided by Verba and Nie (1972): participation refers to actions rather than mental dispositions, and it involves an intent to influence. In a third respect, however, our definition deviates. While the classical definition focuses on actions 'aimed at influencing the selection of government personnel and/or the actions they take' (Verba and Nie 1972: 2), our aims at actions purporting to influence collective outcomes or 'the authoritative allocation of values for a society' (Easton 1953: 134) regardless of whether those outcomes or that allocation is a matter of government decision-making or not.

As pointed out by Teorell, Torcal, and Montero in Chapter 13, Verba and Nie (1972) did in fact concur with this view in the abstract but chose to concentrate on government decisions as an approximation. We see little reason to maintain that restriction, in particular since it would force us to exclude types of actions that we find central to include, such as various kinds of consumer participation (or 'political consumption'), that is, attempts to influence collective outcomes via the market rather than public policy. In general, government decision-making constitutes but one way (albeit a very important one) in which citizens might influence collective outcomes of one kind or another, and we find it important to have the option of empirically investigating how they choose between the various options at their disposal.

Our measure of political participation or participation in large-scale democracy (we use the two terms synonymously) is based on an extensive list of pre-specified activities that might be used for the purpose of improving societal conditions or prevent them from getting worse (e.g. that of contacting a civil servant, working in a political party, or boycotting certain products). The list we use is more similar to that employed by the *Political Action* study (see e.g. Barnes *et al.* 1979; Jennings *et al.* 1990) and later investigations in the tradition it initiated, than to that employed by Verba and his colleagues (see e.g. Verba and Nie 1972; Verba *et al.* 1978; Verba *et al.* 1995).

Our study of participation in *small-scale democracy* starts, by contrast, from a different end. Following the design used in previous Scandinavian studies (beginning with Petersson *et al.* 1989), we investigate the attempts of citizens to control their own lives within a pre-specified set of social roles or domains. The roles (domains) we have singled out are those of being gainfully employed (working life), that of being a student (student education), that of being a parent of schoolchildren (child education), and that of being a patient or relative of a patient (healthcare). While several other roles would also motivate investigation within in a study like ours – for example that of being a resident (housing) or unemployed (barred from working life) – we do not hesitate to claim that those we investigate are sufficiently central to be of considerable interest.

Like political participation (as we define it), participation in small-scale democracy need not necessarily target on government decision-making. In an attempt to influence one's own situation – and/or that of fellow workers, students, parents, or patients – one may find many different outlets (see Chapter 9), including that of exit (e.g. changing from one job, school, or health clinic to another).

However, to the extent that it is directed towards government institutions, participation in small-scale democracy would indeed qualify as political participation, not according to our definition but according to the classical definition of Verba and Nie (1972). Within the mode of participation they label contacting, they distinguish between two different forms depending on whether the referent is general (concerns a large group) or particularised (concerns a small group or a single individual). In our conceptualisation, the first is an instance of participation in large-scale democracy and the latter an instance of participation in small-scale democracy.

The central differences between our perspective and the classical one as developed by Verba and Nie are thus twofold: first, the distinction between outcomes affecting large and small numbers of individuals is in our case a major rather than a subordinate one. Second, we do not, in either case, restrict our attention to activities targeted on government institutions but also consider alternative means of exercising influence.

A third arena of citizen activity that we find crucial to include in our inquiry is *voluntary organisations and social networks*. We refer to the activities of citizens in this arena as social participation. Such participation is considered important to the realisation of citizenship in many different ways. First, it offers citizens opportunities for self-government outside the state. Second, it provides opportunities for participation in small- as well as large-scale democracy by allowing citizens with common ideas or interests to articulate and put pressure behind their demands as well as to promote certain outcomes by means other than public policy (such as when environmental organisations seek to improve environmental conditions by directly influencing consumer behaviour). Third, it is presumed to help citizens acquire the civic skills they need in order to be efficient in their attempts to exercise influence (e.g. communication skills). Finally, it is presumed to stimulate the development of virtuous civic orientations (e.g. social trust), thereby indirectly promoting the quantity as well as quality of their participation in small- and large-scale democracy.

Like participation in small- and large-scale democracy, social participation can find many different outlets. An important ambition of our inquiry has been to capture its variegated expressions in a more complete and systematic fashion than most previous studies. In order to achieve that goal we developed a measurement instrument that allows us to gauge four distinct modes of involvement in voluntary organisations – membership, participation in activities, voluntary work, and donations – for no less than 27 specific types of organisation plus a residual category. The same instrument also indexes the extent to which the respondent has personal friends within each type of organisation. This core instrument is complemented by several additional measures focusing on participation in friendship and support networks outside organisational life as well as patterns of interaction between members of organisations and between colleagues at the workplace.

Unlike the other three parts of our book, the very first part focuses on dispositions rather than activities. More specifically, it highlights *civic orientations* as represented by social trust, political confidence, citizen norms, and tolerance. Social trust refers to the horizontal relations between fellow citizens and is considered a key element of the wider notion of social capital. Political confidence refers to the vertical relations between citizens and their government, that is, to the confidence citizens place in the institutions and actors by which they are ruled. Citizen norms refer to the citizens' own ideals of good citizenship. Tolerance refers to the willingness of citizens to respect the rights of others in a political sense and to abstain from discriminating against them in a social sense.

We certainly do not claim that these four types of dispositions exhaust the set of civic orientations that would merit investigation in a study like ours. At the same time, we do not think we have to excuse the presence of any of those we have singled out. All are presumed to be important, directly or indirectly, to the realisation of citizenship in terms of individual and collective action. To what extent they actually are of importance is, to a significant extent, part of our inquiry.

Furthermore, the four types of orientation mentioned here are of course not the only ones we find reason to consider in the course of analysis. Rather, they are the ones we have chosen to put centre stage by according each of them a separate chapter. Similarly, the particular characteristics on which we focus in each part of the book are obviously not studied in isolation from one another. On the contrary, a very central part of our undertaking is to examine the relationships between civic orientations, social participation, and participation in small- and large-scale democracy. With these general guiding posts in mind, we are now ready to consider the what, where, and how of our undertaking in greater detail.

Our contribution: an outline of the book

Part I: civic orientations

Inspired by the work of Robert Putnam (1993, 1995a, 1995b), the research community has, over the past decade, experienced a strong revival of interest in the notion of social capital. While ideas about social capital can be traced far back in history, most notably to Alexis de Tocqueville's *Democracy in America* (published as two volumes in 1835 and 1840), recent work has not only sought to remind us about prior thinking in the area but also to develop it into a more elaborate theory. Nevertheless, or perhaps precisely therefore, the question of exactly how the notion of social capital should be delimited and measured remains disputed. There seems, however, to be fairly widespread agreement that the concept should be defined on the basis of patterns of social relationships between individuals (i.e. social networks) and that a key element is social trust (i.e. the extent to which ordinary citizens trust one another). According to social-capital theories, social trust is a central element in a positive circle of relationships of crucial importance for democratic and effective government.

Current empirical knowledge about social trust is, to a large extent, based on a measure originally developed and employed by Elisabeth Noelle-Neumann for the purpose of describing the state of postwar German society in the wake of the traumatic experiences of the Nazi period. While Noelle-Neumann's empirical initiative was certainly a laudable one, the measure she designed was, like most others developed in the early days of survey research, relatively crude: a single question with dichotomous response alternatives. The fact that much of the recent work purporting to test elements of social-capital theory still relies on this measure, casts doubts upon the validity of many of the findings obtained.

In Chapter 2, Sonja Zmerli, Kenneth Newton, and José Ramón Montero re-examine the evidence using a doubly improved measure of generalised social trust, constructed by means of multiple indicators and employing items that allow respondents to express their views in a more precise fashion. After validating their index of social trust and describing its variation across the 13 societies included in our study, they explore its bivariate relationship with political confidence (or vertical trust) on the one hand and satisfaction with democracy on the other. In a multivariate framework, they subsequently examine the association with a number of other factors, in particular various forms of involvement in voluntary organisations. In some respects, they are able to confirm the results obtained in prior studies, thereby reducing uncertainty about the validity of past conclusions. In other respects, however, they find that the weak relationships reported in previous research are to a considerable extent due to poor measurement. Once a better measure is substituted, the results are much more in line with theoretical expectations. Irrespective of whether the findings fall in the first or the second category, they certainly deserve to be taken into account by anyone interested in the concept of social capital and its implications for political life.

The chapter that follows puts the spotlight on another central aspect of the general notion of trust. While Chapter 2 focuses on the horizontal aspect – the extent to which ordinary citizens trust one another – Chapter 3 singles out the vertical one – the extent to which they place confidence in government institutions and associated actors.

Based on the items included in the CID survey, Bas Denters, Oscar Gabriel, and Mariano Torcal identify three different objects of such confidence: the institutions of the 'Rechtsstaat' (rule of law), the institutions of representative democracy, and the actors of representative democracy. After describing how the three dimensions vary cross-nationally, they proceed to the question of how the variation can be accounted for. In so doing, they distinguish between socio-cultural explanations – represented by various forms of social capital as well as indicators of modernisation and value change – and micro-political explanations – represented by perceptions of performance and responsiveness, partisan and ideological factors, and a measure of 'videomalaise'. To the furthest extent possible, they also explore the impact of macro-political characteristics. Although the authors find some support for the socio-cultural explanation, they conclude that political factors are of greater importance in explaining individual as well as cross-national variations in political confidence.

As we already know, we are far from a universal consensus among political philosophers about precisely how the ideals of citizenship should be delineated. Nor do ordinary citizens necessarily agree on what it takes to be a good citizen. In Chapter 4, Bas Denters, Oscar Gabriel, and Mariano Torcal investigate the extent to which citizens themselves feel they have to live up to various ideals of citizenship appearing in philosophical and public debate. The results of initial dimensional analyses suggest that the degree of citizen support for these ideals can be summarised by means of three dimensions: the law-abidingness, solidarity, and critical and deliberative principles. While the authors find some interesting cross-national differences in the relative amount of support for these specific ideals, they also find all three to be fairly strongly endorsed by the public in all countries investigated.

In later parts of the chapter, Denters, Gabriel, and Torcal proceed to examine the relationship between support for the ideals of citizenship and indicators of social capital, such as social trust and associational involvement. While the results provide a modicum of evidence in favour of social-capital theory, they also indicate that its explanatory power is generally rather limited, and that it varies across countries as well as across different dimensions of citizenship ideals.

The extent to which the rights of citizenship are respected is not only a matter of how public authorities behave but also of how citizens relate to one another. If many citizens do not respect the political rights of minorities or socially discriminate them, the realisation of citizenship is likely to suffer no matter how well behaved the authorities are. In Chapter 5, José Manuel Leite Viegas examines the degree of political and social tolerance displayed by the populations of our 13 European societies. He finds significant cross-national variation in several different respects: in the overall amount of intolerance, in the direction of intolerance (i.e. the extent to which specific minorities, e.g. homosexuals, are exposed), and in the extent to which social intolerance exceeds its political counterpart. When trying to explain this pattern, Leike Viegas finds support for a model based on a combination of socio-economic development and democratic experience.

Part II: voluntary organisations and social networks

In view of the high value commonly attached to civil society and its presumed importance for the realisation of citizenship, a major ambition of our undertaking has been to provide a much more comprehensive view of organisational involvement than that supplied by previously available data. To our knowledge, the information offered by the CID survey is in this regard uniquely rich, not only in comparison with previous cross-national data but also measured to what is nationally available in most countries.

In Chapter 6, Laura Morales and Peter Geurts provide a comprehensive description of four different dimensions of involvement – membership, participation in activities, donations, and voluntary work – across 27 different types of organisations. For all four dimensions, they find considerable cross-national differences in involvement, the levels being far higher in the more established democracies. However, the smaller proportion of citizens involved in organisational life elsewhere tends to be relatively active, thereby reducing the segment displaying only limited involvement.

Towards the end of the chapter, Morales and Geurts follow up the analyses of Zmerli, Newton, and Montero in Chapter 2 by conducting an in-depth study of the relationship between social trust on the one hand and various dimensions of involvement across different types of organisations on the other. Their results should help lay to rest any remaining doubts about the magnitude of the statistical relationship between these two aspects of social capital.

In Chapter 7, Gabriel Badescu and Katja Neller proceed to the question of how variations in organisational involvement can be explained. The model they develop is based on six different types of explanatory factors: five on the micro level (social status and resources; social integration and networks; social orientations, norms and motivations; political orientations; and a residual set of factors that span the other categories) and one on the macro level (prior regime type). In subsequent empirical analyses, these factors are introduced in a systematic fashion based on how strong our reasons are to suspect that the causal relationship is reciprocal.

The dependent variables include a general measure of organisational involvement as well as involvement in four specific types of associations: spare time and sports associations, interest associations, socio-cultural associations, and religious associations. Badescu and Neller are thus able to examine how their results generalise across countries as well as different types of associations. The very comprehensive test they undertake should be of considerable interest to anyone interested in the roots of organisational involvement.

Chapter 8 complements the two previous chapters by examining social networks inside as well as outside organisational life. Hajdeja Iglič and Joan Font Fabregas begin their analysis by examining the multiplicity (or number of) networks to which any one citizen can potentially belong. In doing so, they consider four different types of networks: friendship networks, support networks, networks in organisational life, and workplace networks. The authors subsequently proceed to investigate the strength of social ties within the last two types. Finally, they consider the relationship between social networks and interpersonal political communication.

Clear cross-national differences are evident in all three regards. Interestingly, these turn out to parallel, in some important respects, the pattern obtained with respect to organisational involvement. Citizens in the more established democracies tend to have relatively broad social networks with comparatively weak ties, whereas those in the newer democracies are more prone to have relatively narrow networks with comparatively strong ties.

Part III: small-scale democracy

The realisation of citizenship is not merely a matter of how democracy operates on a larger scale but also of how individuals or small groups of citizens are able to influence their situation within various social roles and domains. In the first of three chapters on small-scale democracy, Jørgen Goul Andersen and Sigrid Roßteutscher introduce the concept and explain how it relates to democracy on a larger scale. They explain the rationale for our choice of the four specific domains we have singled out for empirical analysis – those of working life, student education, child education, and healthcare – and describe as well as motivate our choice of research design.

As Andersen and Roßteutscher point out, the latter includes not only a measure of the extent to which people take action within small-scale democracy and a specification of which actions they take but also measures of the incentives to, and consequences of, action. The authors describe how citizen action as well as the two types of incentives on which we focus – dissatisfaction and perceived opportunities to influence – are operationalised, and describe their variations across countries as well as domains. A parallel account is given with respect to the consequences of action, where the design incorporates a measure of the extent to which citizens were successful in their attempts to influence (i.e. had their wishes satisfied) as well as a measure of the extent to which they considered themselves fairly treated in procedural terms (i.e. received a fair hearing).

Finally, Andersen and Roßteutscher provide a first example of how these design elements can be combined by describing the pathways of citizen action. By means of these pathways, it becomes possible to interpret 'silence' – do citizens abstain from action because they are satisfied or because they lack the capacity to act? – as well as action (either voice or exit in the Hirschman 1970 sense) – are citizens powerful or powerless if they do take action?

In Chapter 10, Hanspeter Kriesi and Anders Westholm make a more systematic attempt to explain why citizens do or do not take action within small-scale democracy. Drawing on theoretical ideas developed in previous research on social movements and political participation, they develop and test a model based on three major components: dissatisfaction, perceived opportunities, and resources. In so doing, they also examine whether the three components combine in a multiplicative fashion (as suggested by social-movement theories) or in a complementary, additive way.

While all three components turn out to have significant effects, their impact varies considerably across countries. In some cases, dissatisfaction is of great importance whereas in others, perceived opportunities and resources are more consequential. The authors interpret the implications of these findings based on Dworkin's (1981) distinction between 'ambition sensitive' and 'endowment sensitive' systems.

In the third and final chapter on small-scale democracy, Anders Westholm and Emanuel von Erlach consider the consequences of action from several different points of view. First, they replicate some of the analyses in the previous chapter taking outcome rather than action as the dependent variable. Second, they investigate the feedback of the experiences citizens make in their attempts to exercise influence on dispositions affecting their propensity to try again. Third, they examine the macro-level implications of the micro-level patterns evidenced in Chapters 10 and 11, comparing the results across countries as well as different domains of small-scale democracy. Finally, they consider the degree of complex inequality (Walzer 1983) by examining how participation accumulates across different domains of small-scale democracy as well as across the divide between democracy on a smaller and larger scale.

Part IV: large-scale democracy

Our treatment of large-scale democracy begins by considering political involvement, defined as a property distinct from political participation, and operationalised as a combination of two factors: the extent to which citizens express a subjective interest in politics and the importance they attribute to it in their lives. One of the central ideas of Chapter 12, written by Irene Martín and Jan W. van Deth, is that the degree of political involvement, on the one hand, and the concepts of democracy (and of democratic citizenship), on the other, are closely related. Based on democratic theory, the authors develop a typology containing four ideal types – a decisionist, a liberal-representative, a participatory, and a unitary type – which they subsequently operationalise by means of their two indicators of political involvement.

After empirically validating their construction, and demonstrating that the distribution of types varies systematically across countries, they examine its relationship with social as well as political participation, asking questions about the magnitude as well as character of the participation associated with each ideal type and about the cross-national variability of the patterns evidenced. The main conclusion is that different kinds of political involvement should be empirically distinguished in consonance with the postulates of the different theoretical models of democratic citizenship on which the authors draw.

In Chapter 13, Jan Teorell, Mariano Torcal, and José Ramón Montero develop the definition of political participation used in this book. They describe how the concept is operationalised, how each indicator varies cross-nationally, and how the individual indicators can best be combined into different summary modes of participation. While the dimensional structure turns out to vary somewhat across different sets of countries, the authors find that a solution based on four different dimensions (in addition to voting) fits all countries reasonably well. They also show how the five different modes thereby identified – consumer participation, contacting, party activity, protest activity, and voting – can be fitted into a typology based on the channel of expression (representational versus extra-representational), the mechanism of influence (exit versus voice), and the scope of its aim (targeted versus non-targeted). The authors conclude by describing the substantial cross-national variation displayed by the five modes of participation as well as the extent to which they are correlated within as well as across countries.

In Chapter 14, Klaus Armingeon proceeds to investigate how each of the five modes of political participation can be explained. While many different explanatory factors are considered, the main question raised by the author focuses on the relationship between organisational involvement and political participation: why do citizens with a high level of organisational involvement also participate more in politics?

Armingeon develops and tests three potential answers to this question:

1   because they are mobilised by their societal segments and leaders (cleavage politics);
2   because their organisational involvement offers them a 'school of democracy', imparting skills, values, and attitudes favourable to partaking in politics (social-capital);
3   because they are predisposed to be participants or non-participants in social as well as political terms (self-selectivity).

The findings suggest that neither the first nor the second explanation enjoys much empirical support whereas the third does. The author thus concludes that the relationship between organisational involvement and political participation is largely a spurious rather than causal one.

Democratic citizenship entails equal rights to participate in politics. In the chapter that concludes our treatment of large-scale democracy as well as our empirical analysis as a whole, Jan Teorell, Paul Sum, and Mette Tobiasen examine the extent to which the actual distribution of participation in our 13 societies deviates from this norm. For each of the five modes of participation, they investigate the amount of attitudinal distortion (with respect to political ideology and tolerance) as well as the degree of group inequality (with respect to gender, age, education, and locality). They also consider the extent to which the group inequalities observed stem from differences in the factors that motivate action or those that induce the capacity for action. Finally, they examine how the degree of attitudinal distortion, group inequality, and incapacitation are related to one another and to the level of political participation across our sample of 13 societies.

While the resulting pattern is certainly not a simple one, a number of systematic tendencies can nevertheless be distinguished. One of them leads the authors to conclude on an optimistic note. The degree of equality tends to be positively rather than negatively related to the level of participation. A fuller measure of participation does seem to go hand-in-hand with a more equal one.

Our setting: 12 European countries

The remainder of this book examines the realisation of citizenship in 12 European countries based on the data provided by our cross-national population survey. Before we proceed to the survey and its results, however, we find it important to give a brief presentation of the specific set of countries on which we focus. While many readers are likely to be

Introduction 17

relatively familiar with at least some of these countries, few will possess encyclopaedic knowledge about them all. From our own personal experiences as members of the CID team, we believe that this remains true even if we confine ourselves to the rather elementary and limited set of facts provided below.

Obviously, we make no claims whatsoever to having exhausted the kind of country characteristics that are potentially relevant as background information for a study like ours. Our ambition is merely to provide at least a few pieces of information that might enhance the reader's appreciation of the results we present in subsequent chapters.

As shown by the map in Figure 1.1, the 12 countries at our disposal can be divided into four different clusters based on their geographical proximity to each other. At the northern end, we find the three *Scandinavian* countries: Denmark (DK), Norway (NO), and Sweden (SE). Immediately to the south of Scandinavia, we have three *central-European* countries: Germany (DE), the Netherlands (NL), and Switzerland (CH). From the south-western corner, we can add the two *Iberian* countries: Portugal (PT) and Spain (ES). At the opposite end, we find four *eastern-European* countries: Moldova (MD), Romania (RO), Russia (RU), and Slovenia (SI). The abbreviations listed in parentheses after each country correspond to the country codes issued by ISO (International Organisation for Standardisation). Many of them are likely to be familiar to the reader inasmuch as they correspond to the country codes that appear in Internet addresses. We use them systematically throughout this book whenever typographical space is at a premium, for example in tabular presentations. For the two

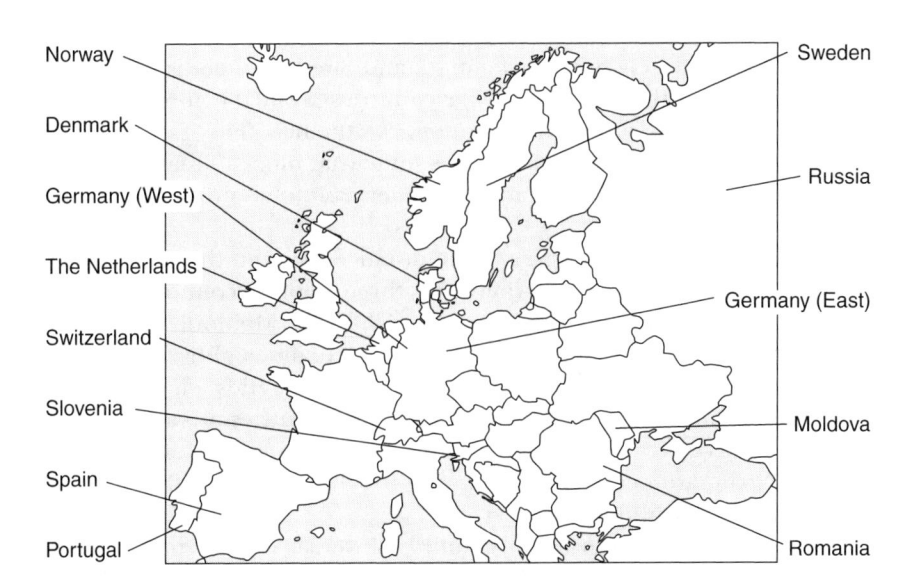

Figure 1.1 Participating countries.

parts into which we divide Germany, no ISO codes are available and we therefore substitute two of our own making: EG for East Germany and WG for West Germany.

Many of Europe's 44 countries are relatively small. Nine have less than one million inhabitants, 19 have 1–10 million, and another seven 10–20 million. Only nine surpass 20 million inhabitants. The 12 countries included in our study – about one-quarter of the entire population of European countries – tend to be somewhat larger than is typically the case (see Table 1.1). No less than four of them surpass the 20-million borderline, among them the two very largest countries in Europe: Russia (144 million) and Germany (82 million). None fall below 1 million inhabitants, whereas six are located in the 1–10 million and two in the 10–20 million range. Apart from failing to represent the very smallest countries, it is clear that our country sample is diverse in terms of population size and that this diversity is found not only in the sample as a whole but also within the four geographical clusters of countries described above. Only the Scandinavian countries are rather homogeneous in this respect.

In many other regards, however, geographical proximity goes hand-in-hand with homogeneity. A first example is provided by economic affluence and welfare as indicated by GNI per capita and life expectancy (see Table 1.1). The three Scandinavian countries are all among the most affluent in our sample. The very richest is currently Norway, whose per-capita GNI even surpasses that of Switzerland. A significant part of the explanation is the income generated by the Norwegian oil wells, which from the 1970s onwards has gradually propelled the country to the very top of the prosperity league.

With Switzerland following closely behind Norway, and Germany and the Netherlands closely behind Denmark and Sweden, there is not much to distinguish the three Scandinavian countries from the three central-European countries in terms of economic affluence. The gap between these two clusters and the Iberian one is somewhat more substantial: from an average of about US$30,000 in the former case to about US$13,000 in the latter.

Still more significant, however, is the distance between the Iberian and the eastern European cluster, where the three poorest countries have a per-capita income ranging from about US$500 (Moldova) to about US$2,000 (Russia). While the difference is actually slightly smaller in absolute terms than in the previous comparison, the ratios tell a different story. The Scandinavian and Central European countries are about twice as rich in terms of GNI per capita as the Iberian countries. However, Portugal and Spain are nevertheless from five to 30 times more affluent than Moldova, Romania, and Russia.

The fourth eastern European country, Slovenia, differs sharply from the other three by showing a GNI per capita on a par with that of Portugal. In fact, Slovenia is currently the most affluent of all countries behind the former Iron Curtain. Already prior to its emergence as an independent and democratic country, Slovenia was one of the most economically successful parts of eastern Europe and certainly the most prosperous region in the former Yugoslavian federation, to which it contributed considerably more in economic terms than it received.

Our observations regarding the magnitude of income differences are echoed by the figures for life expectancy (see Table 1.1). In the nine richest countries, the figure ranges from 76–80 years. In the three poorest, it drops to 66–70 years. Moldova, Romania, and Russia are, in this regard, distinctly different from the rest of our country sample.

With respect to education, however, their position is much less extreme (see Table 1.1). While the figures for Moldova, Romania, and Russia are noticeably lower than for the six richest countries, they tend to be above those for the Iberian countries, in particular Portugal, which lags behind considerably. While this may seem surprising in view of what we already know about economic performance and life expectancy, it is perfectly intelligible once we consider the policy differences between the former Iberian and eastern-European dictatorships.

As we turn from material welfare and human capital to cultural characteristics, we find another clear example of homogeneity within geographic clusters, coupled with heterogeneity between them, namely that of religion (see Table 1.1). The three Scandinavian countries are all predominantly Protestant, the three central-European countries all have significant proportions of Protestants as well as Roman Catholics, the Iberian countries, along with Slovenia, are predominantly Roman Catholic while the remaining eastern-European countries are largely Orthodox. That Slovenia deviates from its eastern-European neighbours as well as from the three religiously mixed countries further north is due to the fact that it was for many centuries ruled by the House of Habsburg (or other southern powers within the Holy Roman Empire of the German Nation), which mercilessly crushed any Orthodox or Protestant tendencies.

As far as religiosity rather than denomination is concerned, the three Scandinavian countries are all highly secularised, the figures for church attendance being among the very lowest in Europe (see Table 1.1). Except for East Germany and Russia, where the communist regime certainly had a good deal of success in its efforts to eliminate religion, all other countries in our sample show significantly higher levels.[2]

Once we proceed to questions of language and ethnicity, the picture becomes considerably more complicated. No less than seven of the 12 countries in our sample recognise more than one official language (see Table 1.1). At the top, we find Russia with 27 followed by Spain with five. Although Russian is certainly the main language in the Russian Federation and Spanish that in Spain, both countries recognise other languages as co-official within certain regions. In both cases, the presence of multiple

Table 1.1 Country characteristics

Characteristic	Scandinavia			Central Europe			Iberia		Eastern Europe			
	DK	NO	SE	CH	DE	NL	ES	PT	MD	RO	RU	SI
Population (millions)[a]	5	4	9	7	82	16	41	10	4	22	144	2
GNI/cap. (thousand USD)[a]	30.3	38.7	26.0	36.2	22.7	23.4	14.6	10.7	0.5	1.9	2.1	10.2
Life expectancy (years)[a]	77	79	80	80	78	78	78	76	67	70	66	76
Education (years)[b]	12.8	13.1	12.4	13.1	11.8 / 11.6	12.4	10.0	7.5	11.2	10.0	11.2	–
Dominant religion(s)[c]	P	P	P	P, R	P, R	P, R	R	R	O	O	O	R
Church attendance (%)[d]	8	8	9	24	30 / 7	22	33	34	29	45	8	35
Official languages[e]	1	3	1	4	1	2	4	1	4	1	27	3
Civil liberties (FH score)[f]	1	1	1	1	1	1	1	1	4	2	5	1
Political rights (FH score)[f]	1	1	1	1	1	1	1	1	3	2	5	1
Polity index (Polity IV)[g]	10	10	10	10	10	10	10	10	8	8	7	10
Beginning of current democratic era[h]	1915	1913	1921	1848 / 1990	1949 / 1990	1919	1977	1975	1991	1991	1991	1991
Year of independence or unification (if after 1800)[h]	–	1814 / 1905	–	–	1871 / 1990	–	–	–	1991	1880	–	1991
Member of the EU since	1973	–	1995	–	1951	1951	1986	1986	–	–	–	2004
Member of NATO since	1949	1949	–	–	1955	1949	1982	1949	–	2004	–	2004
Form of government[i]	M	M	M	FR	FR	M	M	R	R	R	FR	R
Election of head of state[j]	N	N	N	I	D	N	N	D	I	D	D	D
Power of head of state[k]	W	W	W	–	W	W	W	S	W	S	S	W
Parliamentary chambers[l]	1	1	1	2	2	2	2	2	1	2	2	2
Electoral system[m]	PL	PL	PL	PL	AMS	PL	PL	PL	PL	PL	PFPP	PL
Parties in parliament[n]	8/6	8/6	7/6	14/5	6/5	9/6	11/2	6/3	3/3	6/6	9/4	7/6
Public expenditure (%)[o]	38.7	37.1	43.2	27.6	33.3	46.9	34.2	39.8	n.i.	32.7	24.1	39.8

Notes

a   Figures for 2002 according to the World Development Indicators database of the World Bank, August 2004 edition (www.worldbank.org). GNI/capita is computed according to the World Bank's so-called Atlas method and expressed in August 2004 US dollars.
b   Mean number of years of full-time education according to the CID survey. For Germany, the upper figure is for the western part and the lower for the eastern. For Slovenia, information is not available.
c   O = Orthodox, P = Protestant, R = Roman Catholic.
d   Percentage attending church at least once a month according to the CID survey. For Germany, the upper figure is for the western part and the lower for the eastern.
e   DK: Danish; NO: Norwegian Bokmål (Book Language) and Nynorsk (New Norwegian) with Sami co-official in some municipalities; SE: Swedish is de facto the official language but not formally recognised as such; CH: French, Alemannisch (the Swiss form of German), Italian, and Rhaeto-Rhomansch; DE: German; NL: Dutch and Frisian; ES: Spanish and Basque, Catalan, and Galician co-official in some regions; PT: Portugese; MD: Moldovan (which, according to language specialists, is virtually identical to Romanian) with Gagauz, Russian, and Ukrainian co-official in some regions; RO: Romanian; RU: Russian with 26 other languages co-official in some regions; SI: Slovene with Hungarian and Italian co-official in some regions.
f   As rated for 2002 by Freedom House (www.freedomhouse.org) on a scale from 1 to 7. Countries with an average score for political rights and civil liberties of 1–2.5 are classified by Freedom House as 'free'. Those with an average of 3–5 are labelled 'partly free' and those with an average of 5.5–7 'not free'.
g   As rated for 2002 by the Polity index of the Polity IV data base (www.cidcm.umd.edu/inscr/polity) on a scale from −10 to +10, with high scores indicating more democratic and less autocratic regimes.
h   See the text for further details on the events associated with the years indicated.
i   FR = Federal Republic, M = Monarchy, R = Republic.
j   N = not elected, D = directly elected, I = indirectly elected.
k   W = weak, S = strong; Switzerland is a special case in that the president of the cabinet simultaneously serves as the president of the republic.
l   Norway has a so-called modified unicameral system. Once the parliament as a whole (the Storting) has been elected, it appoints one quarter of the representatives to the first chamber (the Lagting) and the remainder to the second (the Odelsting). Bills are processed by both chambers separately, but the Storting decides on other matters and also serves as a final resort for bills in the case of irresolvable disagreement between the chambers.
m   AMS = Additional Member System, PL = Party List, PFPP = Parallel First Past the Post.
n   Number of parties represented in parliament and, after the slash, number of parties commanding at least 5 per cent of the seats in the parliament as a whole (for unicameral systems) or its largest chamber (for bicameral systems). The figures are based on the situation at the end of 2004 as reported by the Parties and Elections in Europe database (www.parties-and-elections.de).
o   Average public expenditure 1995–1999 in per cent of GDP according to the Public Expenditure Cross Country Data of the World Bank (www1.worldbank.org/publicsector/pe/datasearch.cfm). For Moldova, no information is available.

official languages mirrors a considerable amount of ethnic heterogeneity as well as ethnic tensions, with the Chechenian and Basque cases being the most visible examples.

Moldova and Switzerland, both with four official languages, also represent instances of extensive ethnic diversity. While Moldovan (which language experts find difficult to distinguish from Romanian) is the main language in Moldova, and Alemannisch (the Swiss form of German, also known as Schwyzerdütsch) the main language in Switzerland, both countries have sizable minorities with other mother tongues (Gagauz, Russian, and Ukrainian in Moldova; French and Italian in Switzerland).

Norway recognises two forms of Norwegian, along with Sami in some municipalities. The most prevalent form is Bokmål (Book Language), produced and disseminated as a result of the long period of Danish rule. The other form, Nynorsk (New Norwegian) was constructed in the middle of the nineteenth century based on local Norwegian dialects, and was recognised as official in 1885. Its recognition created rather than eliminated political conflict inasmuch as each municipality (for administrative purposes) and school district (for educational) now had to choose between the two forms. The language issue remained rather salient for at least half a century, in particular since it was strongly correlated with social class as well as the urban–rural cleavage line. While symbolically significant, the Norwegian 'language barrier' is a minimal obstacle to practical communication. In fact, not only the two forms of Norwegian but also all major Scandinavian languages are so similar that Danes, Norwegians, and Swedes can (with only a small amount of practice) communicate freely with one another in 'Scandinavian'.

The Netherlands recognises Frisian (spoken by about 4 per cent of the population, mainly in Friesland between the North Sea and the IJsselmeer) as co-official with Dutch, and Slovenia recognises Hungarian and Italian as co-official with Slovene in some areas, in spite of the fact that both minorities are very small. The only numerically significant minorities in Slovenia originate from other parts of former Yugoslavia, and jointly account for about 10 per cent of the population.

The fact that five of the countries have but one official language obviously need not imply that they are completely homogeneous in ethnic terms. Romania has a sizable Hungarian minority and Germany, Portugal, and Sweden all have relatively large proportions of immigrants. So do several of the countries previously discussed (e.g. the Netherlands), which in turn implies that ethnicity is a salient issue in virtually all of the countries included in our study, albeit not in the same way or to the same extent.

An important precondition for a study like ours is the presence of, and respect for, the formal rights associated with citizenship. This is perhaps the one regard in which we would prefer all the countries in our sample to be perfectly homogeneous.

The actual state of affairs in virtually every country in the world is regularly reported by Freedom House as well as by the Polity IV database. Nine of our 12 countries reach top rank (1) on the seven-point civil liberties and political-rights indices offered by Freedom House. They also receive the highest score (10) on the 20-point Polity index provided by Polity IV. The remaining three, Moldova, Romania, and Russia, all deviate measurably from the ideal (see Table 1.1). For two of them, Moldova and Russia, the deviation is sufficiently large to place them in the category labelled 'partly free' rather than that labelled 'free' in the trichotomous classification used by Freedom House to summarise its two seven-point scales. In fact, with a score of five on both indices, Russia comes perilously close to falling into the third category, labelled 'not free'.

Note, however, that the standards applied by Freedom House are quite stringent, which tends to make differences between smaller and bigger offenders less visible. On the Polity index of the Polity IV database, which ranges from -10 to $+10$, Moldova, Romania, and Russia reach a score of $+7$ or $+8$. Without purporting to belittle the distance they still have to travel, we may note that they have come a long way from the position of countries like Kim Jong Il's North Korea (-9), Saddam Hussein's Iraq (-9), Robert Mugabe's Zimbabwe (-7), and Fidel Castro's Cuba (-7).

If our 12 countries, with greater or lesser right, all deserve to be called democracies, the period of time for which they have deserved that designation as well as the way they have reached it differs considerably. For five of the six countries in the first two geographic clusters – Denmark, Norway, Sweden, the Netherlands, and Switzerland – the road towards democracy was reasonably well in accord with Marshall's schematic account of the development of citizen rights (see the introductory section). In all five countries, a gradual expansion of political rights took place during the nineteenth century. In four of them, the last distinctive step – the extension of the franchise to women – was taken in the early 1900s, between 1913 and 1921 (see Table 1.1 for details).

The fifth country, Switzerland, is a special case in that it introduced universal suffrage for men about half a century earlier than the other four but lagged more than half a century behind them in introducing it for women. While all Swiss men gained the right to vote already in 1848, Swiss women had to wait until 1971 to receive the same right on the federal level and until 1990 in the last canton (the half-canton Appenzell Innerrhoden, where it took a federal court decision to break the last resistance).

According to Bock (2002: 156), the laggardness of Switzerland, in this regard (which it shares with France) is not coincidental: 'France and Switzerland were late-comers, not although they were the oldest male democracies in Europe but because they were'. In Bock's analysis, the fact that French and Swiss men won their right to vote early and without much resistance implied that French and Swiss women lacked the source of inspiration and natural allies (e.g. the labour movement) provided by later struggles for the right to vote in other countries. Whatever the reasons may be, however, neither the pioneering role of Switzerland in the one regard nor its laggardly behaviour in the other deserve to be forgotten when we consider when and how it ascended to democracy.

In Germany, the final country in the group of six so far discussed, universal male suffrage was in fact introduced at a rather early stage: at the time of the German reunification in 1871. However, as Bismarck noted, unification came about by means of 'blood and iron' rather than speeches and resolutions. During the next five decades, Germany thus remained autocratic with only limited elements of parliamentary rule. It took a lost war and a subsequent revolution before the democratic Weimar republic was introduced in 1918 (when women also gained the right to vote). The revolutionary manner in which it came about and the enormous economic difficulties it faced, paved the way for Hitler's 'Machtübernahme' in 1933, which in turn implied that democracy was interrupted until 1949 in the western part of Germany and until the 1990 reunification in the eastern part.

The remaining countries followed a line of development, which, in its very broad contours, resembles the German one: revolutions and/or other dramatic events brought about brief periods of democratic or almost democratic rule in the early 1900s (Portugal 1910–1926; Russia and, thereby, Moldova 1917; Romania 1923–1938; Spain 1931–1936; Yugoslavia and, thereby, Slovenia 1921–1928). The dictatorships that followed proved to be considerably more resilient than the German Nazi regime as well as the democratic regimes they replaced.

When these six countries finally joined West Germany in its return to democracy (Portugal in 1975, Spain in 1977, and the remaining four in 1991), the last, decisive step was another one than in the five countries previously discussed. While the peoples of Denmark, Norway, Sweden, the Netherlands, and Switzerland eventually won democracy by being granted the right to vote, those of Germany, Portugal, Spain, Moldova, Romania, Russia, and Slovenia ultimately won it by being granted the right to choose.

For Moldova and Slovenia, the transition to democracy was directly linked to their emergence as independent states. Neither country had previously enjoyed much of an independent existence. The closest predecessor of the current Moldovan state, the Duchy of Moldavia, was under the Ottoman Empire for many centuries and, from 1812, under Russian (later Soviet) or Romanian rule (between or during the world wars). As previously indicated, Slovenia was controlled by the House of Habsburg (or other powers within the Holy Roman Empire of the German Nation) until 1918 and was subsequently part of Yugoslavia.

Romania gained independence from the Ottoman Empire in 1880, and Norway from its union with Sweden in 1905. In the Norwegian case, however, the year in which the long period of Danish rule ended and the (involuntary) union with Sweden began (1814) is perhaps more significant, as indicated by the fact that Norway's national day is celebrated in commemoration of its constitution as an independent state on 17 May of that year. In reality, Norway enjoyed considerable autonomy long before its union with Sweden was dissolved.

All other countries in our sample have a long history as independent, albeit – in the German case – not always unified countries. The Holy Roman Empire of the German Nation was never a particularly coherent entity, and had already weakened considerably (following the 30-year war of 1618–1648) before it was dissolved by Napoleon in 1806. As we already know, Germany has subsequently been unified twice and divided once.

While the countries in our sample all deserve to be called independent, seven of them are currently members of the increasingly state-like association known as the European Union, and eight have military commitments to one another as members of NATO (see Table 1.1). Denmark, Germany, the Netherlands, Portugal, Spain, and (from 2004) Slovenia belong to both organisations. Sweden has joined the EU only, while Norway and (from 2004) Romania are NATO but not EU members.

Four of the five countries that took the gradual and peaceful road to democracy are constitutional monarchies (see Table 1.1). In the Danish, Norwegian, Swedish, and Dutch cases, the monarchy gradually surrendered its powers, and therefore survived. In Switzerland, this history could not repeat itself for the simple reason that the Swiss 'Eidgenossenschaft' had in effect ended its association with the Holy Roman Empire and become a federal republic already in 1499. Its very long history aside, the Swiss republic is also peculiar in the sense that there is no separate presidential office. The president of the cabinet (known as the prime minister in other countries) also serves as the president of the republic.

Among the other seven countries, only Spain remains a monarchy. Although (perhaps partly for that reason) it does not refer to itself as a federation, its regions have gradually come to enjoy considerable autonomy from the introduction of democracy onwards. Switzerland, Germany and Russia are unquestionably federations, with the federal element in Russia already present during the Soviet era.

For obvious reasons, the monarchies that remain alive today tend to be hereditary ones, and none of the five included in our sample consequently elects its head of state. Among the republics, the president is indirectly elected in two cases (Moldova, and, for obvious reasons, Switzerland) and directly elected in the other five. In only three countries, however, does the president enjoy a significant amount of political power (Portugal, Moldova, and Russia). In the remaining instances, the part played by the presidential office is largely ceremonial.

As expected, all three federal republics, along with Spain, have bicameral parliaments. So, however, do three additional countries: the Netherlands,

Romania, and Slovenia. All the others have unicameral systems, albeit a so-called modified one in the Norwegian case (see note to Table 1.1 for details). In nearly all cases, the parliament is elected by means of party lists in an essentially proportional fashion. The only two exceptions are Germany and Russia, both of which employ a mix of party lists and 'first past the post'. Germany has a so-called additional member system (AMS) whereas Russia employs a technique known as 'parallel first past the post' (PFPP).

As would be expected given the nature of their electoral rules, all the countries in our sample have multi-party systems. The number of parties represented in parliament ranges from three (Moldova) to 14 (Switzerland), the average coming close to eight (see Table 1.1). In some cases, however, these numbers provide rather deceptive indications of party fragmentation. Although represented in parliament, some of the parties are extremely small. If we consider only those which hold at least 5 per cent of the seats (in the larger chamber), the number drops from 14 to five for Switzerland, and from 11 to two for Spain. For the sample of countries as a whole, the number of significant (>5 per cent) parties ranges from two to six with an average just below five (see Table 1.1).

The countries that currently come closest to a two-party system are Portugal, Spain, and Moldova. In Portugal and Spain, the two largest parties received about 80 per cent of the votes and 90 per cent of the seats in the most recent elections. In neither case, however, does the largest party possess an absolute majority. In Moldova, politics is still dominated by the Communist Party, which obtained nearly 50 per cent of the vote and more than 70 per cent of the seats in the latest elections. Only two parties share the remaining seats. Russia currently has four parties with at least 5 per cent of the seats. The remaining countries all have five or six.

A rough indicator of the part played by politics in economic life as well as of the relative magnitude of welfare-state arrangements is public expenditure as a percentage of GDP (see Table 1.1). As expected, the three Scandinavian countries are all in the upper part of the distribution, with percentages slightly above (Sweden) or below (Denmark and Norway) 40 per cent. They are not alone however. With a public expenditure of 47 per cent, the Netherlands surpasses Sweden, while Portugal and Slovenia (40 per cent) are both slightly ahead of the other two Scandinavian countries. In only two countries does the figure fall below 30 per cent. These two certainly constitute an odd couple: a prime symbol of capitalism – Switzerland – together with a prime symbol of (past) communism – Russia. The latter is currently slightly ahead of the former in minimising public expenditure.

Our data source: the cross-national population survey

The results reported in this book are based on 12 surveys carried out in as many European countries at the turn of the century (1999–2002). The samples are all drawn to be representative of the adult population of each country, from 18 years of age (which in all countries is the point at which the right to vote is acquired) and upwards. Note that the populations sampled are not restricted to individuals who are, in a strictly legal sense, citizens of the countries studied but include all denizens (residents), irrespective of nationality. The number of cases at our disposal ranges from 990 for Slovenia to 4,252 for Spain (see Table 1.2). The per-country average, after dividing the German sample into two parts, is 1,725.

The responsibility as well as credit for having these surveys funded and executed rests with many different principal investigators, most of whom members of the ESF Network on Citizenship, Involvement, and Democracy (CID), as well as co-authors of this book and/or its CID companion volume.[3] These investigators all shared a willingness to include, as part of their respective surveys, a set of questions, the CID common core, asked in identical form in all countries. It is on the data obtained by means of this common core that the findings reported in this book are based.

The common core was worked out jointly by those members of the CID network who participated in its first four meetings (two in Mannheim, one in Uppsala, and one in Barcelona) from the autumn of 1998 to the autumn of 1999. Between meetings, a task force worked to resolve the many technical issues that arose in the process of developing the questionnaire instructions.[4] However, the general network meetings to which all members were invited took the important decisions regarding the content of the common core.

When searching for the best operationalisations of the concepts, we often took advantage of items asked in previous surveys on similar themes. A particularly frequent source of inspiration was the studies of citizenship previously conducted in Sweden.[5] Although we found little reason to reinvent the wheel, we did not hesitate to modify prior measures whenever we thought we had valid reason to do so. In many cases, we found it appropriate to alter pre-existing instruments in order to improve their fit to our conceptual needs, their suitability for cross-national comparisons, their validity and/or reliability in general, their cost efficiency, and their internal consistency (e.g. with regard to the response alternatives offered). The research instrument that resulted from our efforts – the CID common core questionnaire – is publicly available via the CID web site (www.mzes.uni-mannheim.de/projekte/cid).[6]

The common core was designed to require an average interviewing time of approximately 40 minutes, and the time estimates we have from subsequent pilot studies are well in line with that figure. It is thus a relatively large module, considerably more ambitious than those typically included in national surveys for providing a modicum of cross-national comparability (e.g. those of the Comparative Study of Electoral Systems, CSES). While the principal investigators were free to include additional questions, the common core universally accounted for a major share of

Table 1.2 Survey characteristics

Country	Year of data collection[a]	Method of data collection	Type of sample[b]	Available N of cases	Response rate (%)[c]
Denmark	1999	Face to face	Disproportionally stratified, SRS	1,640	61.7
East Germany	2001	Face to face	Multistage, stratified PPS	1,013	56.1
West Germany	2001	Face to face	Multistage, stratified PPS	1,991	55.2
Moldova	2001	Face to face	Multistage, stratified SRS	1,219	65.0
Netherlands	2001	Face to face	Multistage, disproportionally stratified	1,649	30.0
Norway	2001	Mail	Stratified SRS	2,297	47.1
Portugal	2001	Face to face	Multistage, stratified PPS	1,010	59.9
Romania	2001	Face to face	Multistage, stratified SRS	1,217	78.0
Russia	2000	Face to face	Multistage, stratified PPS	1,733	73.8
Slovenia	2001	Face to face	Multistage, stratified PPS	990	50.0
Spain	2002	Face to face	Multistage, disproportionally stratified	4,252	31.0
Sweden	2002	Face to face	Essentially SRS	1,271	61.8
Switzerland	2000	Phone and mail	Multistage, SRS	2,145	44.3

Notes

a In cases where the fieldwork spans two years, we indicate the year in which the predominant part of the field work was executed.
b SRS = Simple Random Sample, PPS = Probability Proportional to Size.
c The response rate is calculated as CN/SN, where CN is the number of responses collected and SN is the number of respondents originally sampled minus the number who have died or emigrated between the time of sampling and the time of data collection.

the total content of each survey. Consequently, the cross-nationally comparable information at our disposal is unusually rich.

In developing their national questionnaires, the principal investigators were not required to isolate the common core from the additional questions they wanted to ask inasmuch as that would have implied an unnatural and inefficient structure for each survey as a whole (e.g. because the additional questions were often thematically related to those in the common core). However, the investigators were asked to carefully consider and avoid any undesirable problems of comparability due to question order (e.g. by placing additional items inserted into a common core battery at the end of the battery and by not breaking up sequences of other intimately related sets of common core questions).

In most cases, the principal investigators were able to include the entire common core in their respective surveys. There are only two important exceptions. First, the Russian survey does not include the section on small-scale democracy and the Spanish survey only includes one of its four domains (working life). In both cases, the decision was unavoidable due to cost considerations combined with the restrictions imposed by research objectives outside the CID framework. Second, the Danish survey, which was the first to enter the field, was prevented from including a few items that were added to the common core when the preparation for fieldwork operations had already been completed in Denmark. In the Danish case, the loss of comparable information is marginal. In the Russian and Spanish case, it is more severely felt, but not of such a magnitude that it seriously limits the value of our analyses in the realm of small-scale democracy.

As a rule, the data were collected by means of face-to-face interviews (with other methods used only as a last resort, e.g. if the alternative was a complete refusal to participate). Again, there are two exceptions (see Table 1.2). In the Swiss case, it was not deemed realistic to obtain funding for, and execute, a survey based on face-to-face interviews due to the very high cost and (consequently) limited use of the method in Switzerland in recent years. Instead, the Swiss data were collected by means of telephone interviews combined with a follow-up mail questionnaire (so that questions presuming to visual communication via response cards could be asked in the most comparable form possible). In Norway, the survey first entered the field using face-to-face interviews. However, the survey house employed turned out to be unable to manage the task it had taken on. As a result, the original survey had to be abolished and (due to the consequent loss of financial resources) replaced by a mail questionnaire.

Although complete reliance on face-to-face interviews would obviously have been preferable, our analyses have given us very little reason to question the comparability of the Swiss and Norwegian data. In virtually all cases, the findings for these two countries are, in our view, well in line with what one might expect given the results for other countries. We think most readers will find reason to join us in that judgement. While neither the Swiss nor the Norwegian data are completely void of surprising deviations, they have given us no more reason to question them than the data for any other country. The case is particularly clear-cut with respect to Norway where our expectation of similarity with the other two Scandinavian countries are in many instances relatively firm, and we, in some cases, have the opportunity to compare our results with other Norwegian surveys based on face-to-face interviews. The findings have given us little reason for concern in either regard.

Many of the samples include elements of clustering. In addition, the individuals sampled are not always drawn with uniform probability and therefore carry different weight (see Table 1.2). Although advanced statistical techniques for handling sampling complexities of this kind are available, and although they are becoming increasingly easy to use, we have still found it necessary to fall back on the simpler procedures traditionally adopted by undertakings like ours.

To begin with, the estimates of statistical significance we report ignore the fact that the observations are not in all cases perfectly independent due to the presence of clustering. Consequently, the level of significance may be slightly overestimated. While we have no reason to think that the reported figures deviate more than marginally from the truth, the reader should still be aware about the presence and direction of the bias.

Second, we have chosen to employ the weights that make each sample fully representative of the respective population only in those instances when we report descriptive univariate statistics (e.g. the per-country means for a certain variable) or percentages for a classification based on one or more variables. In other cases, the samples are treated as though every individual carries the same weight.

The choice between weighting and not weighting cases that have been drawn with differential probabilities is largely a decision between two undesirable properties: bias and random error. If we weight, we eliminate the systematic bias that might otherwise exist but are likely to pay a price in terms of the amount of unsystematic error. If we abstain from weighting, we run a greater risk of bias but are likely to reduce random error. The rationale behind our decision to weight the sample for certain statistics (e.g. means and percentages) but not others (e.g. regression coefficients) is that we consider the risk of bias to be greater for the former than for the latter.

Many of the empirical analyses in this book rely on unstandardised coefficients of various kinds (e.g. unstandardised regression coefficients). In order to interpret such coefficients, the reader must be aware of the scale on which the variables involved are expressed. If, for example, the dependent variable is measured on a zero to ten scale and the independent variable on a zero to one scale, the absolute value of the unstandardised regression coefficient will be ten times greater than it would be if both variables were expressed on a zero to one scale.

Reporting, observing, and memorising information about the way each particular variable has been scored can be a rather tedious enterprise. The same holds for the task of evaluating the consequences: does that large coefficient really signify a sizable effect or is it merely a matter of how the variables in question have been scored?

For the reader's as well as our own convenience, we have therefore tried to standardise the scale employed. Unless information to the contrary is provided, all of our variables are scored on a zero to one scale. The minimal and maximal value that a variable logically speaking *could* take on is thus zero and one, respectively. This does not imply that the minimal and maximal values actually *observed* in our samples always reach those extremes. While we have chosen to standardise the scale itself, we have not standardised the empirically observed variables.

A couple of facilitating implications of our uniform scoring system are worth mentioning. First, if an ordinary regression coefficient takes on the value n, it implies that the expected change in the dependent variables amounts to $100n$ per cent of its logical range as we move from the logical minimum to the logical maximum on the independent variables (e.g. 50 per cent if the coefficient amounts to 0.50). Second, if one unstandardised regression coefficient is n times larger than another is, it implies that the effect of moving from the logical minimum to the logical maximum on the independent variable is n times greater in the former case. While we do not consider our scoring system to be a panacea for the vexing problem of comparing effects across variables or samples, we do think that it helps us, as well as readers, to digest the results in a more efficient manner than would otherwise have been the case.[7]

How the variables employed are operationalised in substantive terms is described in the empirical chapters that follow. In cases where the full question wording is not provided, the reader is referred to the common core questionnaire available on the CID website (www.mzes.uni-mannheim.de/projekte/cid).

However, let us conclude by briefly describing the operationalisation of two frequently used variables whose characteristics it would be somewhat tedious to repeat; namely age and education. Both are special cases compared to most other variables we employ in that they do not have a logical maximum. For age, we have made the scale approximately equivalent to those of other variables, by operationalising the variables as the number of years divided by 100. For education, which we measure as the total number of years in full-time education, the minimum score of 0 implies 0 years whereas the maximum score of 1 implies 25 or more years (i.e. we have truncated the distribution at 25 years, which in practice affects but a handful of respondents). For Slovenia, where the number of years in education is not available, we employ an eight-point level-of-education scale scored to range from zero to one.

Notes

1 To our knowledge, many languages provide but a single word for citizenship in the narrow as well as the wider sense. One exception is Danish, which distinguishes between '*statsborgerskab*' (the narrow meaning) and '*medborgerskab*' (the broader one).
2 To some extent, the low church attendance in East Germany might be explained by the fact that the percentage of Protestants is significantly larger than in West Germany.
3 The principal investigators are, for Denmark, Jørgen Goul Andersen (Aalborg University, Denmark); for Germany, Jan W. van Deth (University of Mannheim, Germany); for the Netherlands, Peter Geurts (University of Twente, Enschede, the Netherlands); for Portugal, José Manuel Leite Viegas (ISCTE and CIES, Lisbon, Portugal); for Moldova and Romania, Gabriel Badescu (Babes-Bolyai University, Cluj-Napoca, Romania); for Norway, Per Selle (University of Bergen, Norway); for Russia, Jan Teorell (Uppsala University, Sweden); for Slovenia, Hajdeja Iglič (University of Ljubljana, Slovenia); for Spain, José Ramón Montero (Autonomous University of Madrid, Spain); for Sweden, Anders Westholm (Uppsala University, Sweden); and for Switzerland, Klaus Armingeon (University of Bern, Switzerland).
4 The efforts of the task force were coordinated by Sigrid Roßteutscher (University of Mannheim, Germany). She was assisted by a team consisting of Jørgen Goul Andersen and Mette Tobiasen (Aalborg University, Denmark), and Jan Teorell and Anders Westholm (Uppsala University, Sweden). William A. Maloney (University of Aberdeen, UK) served as a consultant with respect to linguistic issues.
5 The Swedish studies of citizenship ('*medborgarundersökningarna*') have been conducted at Uppsala University by Olof Petersson, Anders Westholm, and Göran Blomberg in 1987 and by Anders Westholm and Jan Teorell in 1997. The items adapted for use in the CID common core are all derived from the 1997 study, but many are identical to those originally developed in 1987.
6 The English version of the questionnaire provided at the website was not developed for immediate use in any English-speaking country, but rather for translation into other European languages; therefore, we consciously opted for wordings that would minimise the likelihood of translation errors. As a result, the English used is sometimes less idiomatic than would otherwise have been the case.
7 The implications spelled out in this paragraph hold for any uniform scoring system. The 0–1 range, however, has one specific advantage over other natural alternatives, e.g. 0–10 or 0–100, in that it facilitates the interpretation of interaction effects. Consider the regression model $Y = a + bX + cZ + dXZ + e$. Provided that all variables are scored on a 0–1 range, the effect of X is b when Z is at its minimum (0) and $b + d$ when Z is at its maximum (1). Correspondingly, the effect of Z is c when X is at its minimum (0) and $c + d$ when X is at its maximum (1). No other scoring range makes the interpretation quite so simple.

Part I
Civic orientations

2 Trust in people, confidence in political institutions, and satisfaction with democracy

Sonja Zmerli, Kenneth Newton, and José Ramón Montero

Trust and politics

In claiming that 'Mutual trust lies at the heart of all political processes', the political philosopher John Dunn (1993: 641) reasserts a theme going back at least to Thomas Hobbes and John Locke, and coming from them to us through the writings of de Tocqueville, Simmel, Tönnies, Durkheim, Weber, Parsons, Coleman, and Luhmann.[1] In recent years, the theme has been reformulated in a powerful form by writers of the social capital school. According to them, social trust is the central element in a complex virtuous circle in which a set of attitudes, such as mutuality, reciprocity, and trust, are associated with social participation and engagement in community and civic affairs; these help to build the social and political institutions necessary for democratic and efficient governments; in turn, these create the conditions in which social and political trust can flourish. At the individual level, trust is the cornerstone 'habit of the heart', which is associated with a climate of social trust that enables citizens to cooperate with each other, build a common identity, and pursue common goals. At the structural level, effective community organisations, especially voluntary associations, are an essential part of the social framework necessary to build the social, economic, and political institutions of modern democratic society.

In this chapter, we focus on three core elements within this broad and complex set of claims: social trust, confidence in political institutions, and satisfaction with democracy. Within the exploratory goals assigned to this chapter, our aims are twofold. First, we will investigate the relationships between social trust and political confidence, on the one hand, and social trust and satisfaction with democracy, on the other. If social trust is an important foundation of politics, then those who trust should also be more likely to express confidence in the institutions of their government, parliament, the courts, the cabinet, the local government, the police, and the political parties. And if social trust is an important foundation of democratic government, then those who trust socially should be more likely to express satisfaction with the way democracy works in their country. Does the evidence suggest that social trust, confidence in political institutions, and satisfaction with democracy are associated in a mutually supportive way? Conversely, is the socially distrusting citizen also a politically disaffected and critical citizen who is suspicious of political leaders, disenchanted with political institutions, and dissatisfied with the workings of democracy (Norris 1999b; Putnam *et al.* 2000)? Second, we will examine the associations between those three core elements and some basic individual variables. Although the causal relations are not at all clear, the theory also argues that social trust, confidence in institutions, and satisfaction with democracy have common origins in attachment to the local community and participation in its affairs, especially involvement in its voluntary clubs and organisations.[2] In the last part of the chapter we therefore also look at the origins of those three elements. Are they linked by common associations with attachment to and participation in the local community and its voluntary organisations, or do they develop from different and separate circumstances?

Past research on these themes suggests that our two aims are not at all straightforward. In spite of its long and distinguished history, the theory linking trust, community attachment, membership of voluntary organisations, political confidence, and satisfaction with democracy has received only partial and qualified support from modern empirical social science, at least at the individual level. There is a substantial body of research finding that generalised social trust is not consistently or strongly associated with confidence in political institutions or satisfaction with democracy.[3] These works confirm Kaase's (1999: 13) conclusion that 'the statistical relationship between interpersonal trust and political trust is small indeed'. Nor has recent survey research uncovered a strong association between trust and civic engagement, or between trust and membership in voluntary associations. Uslaner (2001a: 572, 575), for example, has found 'no linkage between trust and most forms of civic engagement . . . Across a wide variety of surveys, the message is the same: in almost all cases, trust is not important for most forms of civic engagement'. Similarly, Hooghe (2003: 91–3) rejects the idea that interaction with others in a voluntary association leads to increasing levels of generalised social trust. Some argue that people are likely to join organisations because they trust the organisation to begin with (Newton 2001a: 207; but for a different view see Putnam 1993: 171–6; Putnam 1995b: 666), while others claim that participation in an organisation may reinforce particularised trust in people like themselves who join the organisation, but not generalised trust in different social types (Stolle 2001b).

There is some evidence of an association between trust and voluntary organisation membership, but it is weak and patchy, significant in some countries but not in others, among some social groups but not among others, and for some sorts of organisations but not for others. The evidence is not sufficiently robust to support the powerful claims of social capital theory.[4] At this point it is necessary to introduce an important methodological caveat. We should be careful to distinguish between 'bottom-up' individual level research that treats the individual as the unit of analysis, and 'top-down' aggregate, institutional, or cross-national research that compares countries. The 'rainmaker hypothesis' (Putnam *et al.* 2000: 26–7; see also Newton 2001a) argues that while social trust and political confidence may not be associated at the individual level, they should, at least, be associated at the cross-national, aggregate level. Although we have to deal with the empirical consequences of the presence or absence of an individual or aggregate-level relationship between trust and confidence, we do not have the space for trying to fully disentangle their interactions in this chapter. Just as rain falls on the just and the unjust alike, irrespective of their individual characteristics, so a general climate of social trust might benefit all citizens whether they, as individuals, are comparatively trusting or not. Social trust is a social or collective resource, and to some extent all may benefit from it, irrespective of their individual characteristics and whether they happen to trust or not.

Top-down research dealing with societies, institutions, or cross-national comparisons does support claims about the importance of trust for democracy insofar as they find an association between social trust and political confidence.[5] Nevertheless, it is still puzzling that only weak and patchy associations between social trust and political confidence have been uncovered at the individual level by survey research. Although there is no reason why social science results should necessarily be verified at the individual level, the absence of a strong individual association tends to undermine rather than support social capital theory. Since the Citizen, Involvement, Democracy (CID) survey uses more sensitive and reliable measures of trust than most other studies, we will investigate its association with political confidence and satisfaction with democracy in order to confirm or disregard the previous findings. Before we do so, however, we must start with some background comments about social trust, political confidence, satisfaction with democracy, and their measurement. We come to the conclusion that a great deal depends on the details of how these three elements are conceptualised and measured.

Social trust

The enormous importance attached to social trust is matched by fundamental disagreement about what it means (Lewis and Weingert 1985: 975; Misztal 1996: 9). After almost three decades of fairly intense theoretical and empirical work, the concept remains imprecise and confusing. Our approach to this conceptual tangle is threefold:

1   to produce a general working definition of trust;
2   to recognise that there are different types of trust, and work with what we believe is the most important type in modern society;
3   to show that the measures we use are reasonably reliable and valid.

Russell Hardin (1999: 24) has written that 'There is little point in arguing over the essential meaning of trust: It has no essential meaning. Rather, it has a variety of meanings that often conflict'. He goes on to define social trust in the following manner (1999: 26; emphasis in the original):

> To say that I trust you with respect to some matter means that I have reason to expect *you to act in my interest* with respect to that matter, because you have good reasons to do so, reasons that are grounded in my interest ... Your interest encapsulates my interest.

Trust is, therefore, 'encapsulated interest' (see also Hardin 1998: 12–15, and 2002, Chapter 1). To this extent, trust may be said to exist when *A* believes *B* will not knowingly or willingly do him harm, at worst, and will try to act in his interest and protect him, at best. This approach and definition has the merit of being close to the classical notion of trust as fidelity and promise-keeping, and to the modern usage of trust as having confidence or faith in others, and being able to rely upon them: I trust people when I think they will keep their word, and not mug, cheat, harm, lie to me, or exploit me. To trust means risking my interests in the hands of others. This is close to Hardin's (1998: 12–15) already mentioned definition of trust as 'encapsulated interest', to Gambetta's (1988b: 217) suggestion that trust is built upon the belief that others will act beneficially rather than maliciously towards us, and to Warren's assumption (1999b: 311) that trust involves shared interests and lack of malice.

There are clearly different types or dimensions of trust (Uslaner 2002: 52–6). *Particularised* trust in people we know is different from *generalised* trust in people we do not know. Social trust is different from political trust (Putnam 1995b; Newton 1999a: 179–80; Uslaner 2002: 54), and trust in people is different from confidence in institutions (Seligman 1997). In this chapter we are particularly interested in generalised trust, that is, thin trust in people we either do not know, do not know well, or who may not be much like us. This is the kind of trust best adapted to the circumstances of citizenship in modern, large-scale, heterogeneous, and impersonal societies, where weak ties are important (Granovetter 1973).[6] Particularised trust, sometimes known as thick trust, is more likely to be found in small face-to-face communities.

Despite the controversy about the nature and meaning of the concept of social trust, most survey research settles on the same question, or questions, to measure it. The standard question is: 'Generally speaking, would you say that most people can be trusted or that you can't be too careful in dealing with people?' This question, invented by Elisabeth Noelle-Neumann and first used in Germany in 1948, has been asked every year since then, making Germany the country with the longest social trust time-series in the world. The question was picked up by American researchers (including Almond and Verba (1963), in *The Civic Culture* study, and the 1960 presidential election survey), and has spread around the globe as a measure of general trust. In spite of that, however, there is some disagreement about whether the question is a particularly good one, either as a measure of particular trust, or as a measure of generalised trust. Nevertheless, evidence shows that it does work reasonably well. Analysing a survey that asked more than a dozen questions about whom or what people trust, Uslaner (2001a: 575; 2002: 54) found that the Noelle-Neumann question places heavy emphasis on trust in strangers, and concludes that the question does indeed measure generalised trust.[7]

In many cross-national studies (such as the World Values and Eurobarometer surveys), the standard general trust question is the only one used. However, Rosenberg (1956) devised a three-question item consisting of the original Noelle-Neumann question plus two others (tapping respectively helpfulness and fairness):

- Would you say that most of the time people try to be helpful or are they mostly looking out for themselves?
- Do you think that most people would try to take advantage of you if they got a chance or would they try to be fair?

Rosenberg and others have shown that the three-item scale forms a single measure of trust that is reasonably valid and reliable.[8] For this reason we have used the three-item Rosenberg scale in the CID surveys, and asked respondents to rate their trust, or lack of it, on an 11-point scale (0–10) for each single item.

Principal component analysis of the three questions on trust asked in the 12 nations and 13 societies (with the East Germans as the thirteenth society) covered in our study shows that they do, indeed, scale pleasingly in all of them (Table 2.1). The single component – known here as 'general trust' – explains between 59 and 78 per cent of the variance, showing that there is a single and strong underlying dimension. In spite of the theoretical argument about the concept of generalised social trust, therefore, the single component that emerges from this principal component analysis of the three item Rosenberg scale is a good and simple indicator of it. Table 2.2 ranks our 13 societies in terms of their mean score for the three trust items. It presents no surprises. The three Nordic countries are at the top of the table, and three of the East European countries together with Spain, East Germany, and Slovenia are at the bottom, with the Netherlands, Switzerland, Portugal, and West Germany in the middle range.

Confidence in political institutions

We agree with those scholars who argue that the word *trust* should be reserved for attitudes towards individuals, whereas *confidence* should apply to

Table 2.1 Principal component analysis of social trust

Country	General trust	Helpfulness	Fairness	Eigenvalue	Percentage of variance explained
Denmark	0.80	0.82	0.83	2.01	67
East Germany	0.87	0.90	0.89	2.35	78
West Germany	0.86	0.90	0.88	2.33	78
Moldova	0.76	0.87	0.86	2.08	69
The Netherlands	0.76	0.79	0.81	1.86	62
Norway	0.82	0.86	0.86	2.17	72
Portugal	0.87	0.87	0.85	2.23	74
Romania	0.79	0.84	0.84	2.03	68
Russia	0.79	0.80	0.80	1.91	64
Slovenia	0.79	0.80	0.80	1.90	63
Spain	0.81	0.80	0.79	1.92	64
Sweden	0.80	0.82	0.81	1.98	66
Switzerland	0.66	0.82	0.81	1.77	59

Table 2.2 Level and dispersion of social trust[a]

Country	Mean	Standard deviation	N
Norway	0.64	0.17	2,286
Denmark	0.64	0.17	1,639
Sweden	0.64	0.20	1,265
The Netherlands	0.63	0.15	1,639
Switzerland	0.61	0.18	1,647
Portugal	0.54	0.19	1,003
West Germany	0.52	0.21	1,989
Slovenia	0.45	0.19	989
East Germany	0.45	0.23	1,013
Spain	0.43	0.17	4,218
Russia	0.41	0.24	1,731
Moldova	0.36	0.21	1,215
Romania	0.36	0.23	1,208

Note

a The measure is an additive index (mean of valid scores) based on all three questions about social trust. The index ranges from 0 to 1. Countries are ordered by their mean social trust.

institutions.[9] While social trust belongs to the private sphere and is a feature of personal relationships based upon first-hand experience and knowledge, confidence belongs to the public, political sphere and is built upon second-hand sources, particularly the mass media (see Newton 1999a: 179). In the rest of the chapter we will thus follow the practice of talking about trust in people and confidence in institutions (or political confidence).

Although countless discussions have taken place about the meaning of trust, few analysts have concerned themselves with the concept of confidence. In its broadest sense, it refers to citizens' assessments of the core institutions of the polity (Lipset and Schneider 1983; Magalhães 2006; Chapter 3, this volume). To paraphrase Levi and Stoker (2000: 484–5), political confidence entails a positive evaluation of the most relevant attributes that makes each political institution trustworthy, such as credibility, fairness, competence, transparency in its policy-making, and openness to competing views. And to extrapolate from our treatment of trust, confidence in an institution entails the belief that it will not act in an arbitrary or discriminatory manner that is harmful to our interests or the nation's, but will treat us, and other citizens, equally, fairly, and justly. As a conceptual device, political confidence has been designed as a middle-range indicator of support between the specific political actors in charge of every institution and the overarching principles of democracy in which specific institutions are embedded in a given polity (Gabriel 1995: 361; Listhaug and Wiberg 1995: 299–302). As Newton and Norris (2000: 53) have written: 'confidence in institutions ... [is] the central indicator of the underlying feeling of the general public about its polity'.

As an empirical indicator, almost all studies follow the World Values and Eurobarometer practice of using the question:

- Please look at this card, and tell me for each item, how much confidence you have in them.

The items vary from one questionnaire to another. The CID questionnaire includes a set of ten public institutions, namely the police, civil service, courts, municipal boards, political parties, politicians, parliament, cabinet, and two international bodies, the European Union (EU) and the United Nations (UN). Because our concern is domestic politics, rather than international affairs, we have dropped the EU and UN from our analysis and concentrated on the eight internal institutions of government and politics.[10] Like the trust questions, the CID questionnaire asks respondents to rate their answers to the confidence questions on an 11-point scale, whereas the World Values and Eurobarometer surveys use a four-point scale.

Principal component analysis of responses to the eight questions reveals a single dimension in most of our countries (Table 2.3).[11] It thus seems that political confidence is all interconnected, in such a way that confidence in any one institution is likely to be repeated in all others.[12] In general, factor scores are relevant and have the correct sign, the percentage of variance explained is systematically high, and the KMO measures reveal an excellent degree of fitness for the interrelationships among the different institutions. That is, citizens are consistent and predictable in the confidence they express in different kinds of public institutions. Moreover, confidence levels in the different countries are very much as expected (Table 2.4), being highest in the old democracies, especially the

Table 2.3 Principal component analysis of confidence in institutions[a]

Confidence in	CH	DK	ES	EG	WG	MD	NL	NO	PT	RO	RU	SE	SI
Politicians	0.77	0.84	0.81	0.72	0.76	0.83	0.88	0.83	0.79	0.83	0.80	0.86	0.84
Cabinet	0.79	0.85	0.77	0.88	0.82	0.86	0.86	0.85	0.75	0.85	0.73	0.85	0.83
Parties	0.74	0.81	0.81	0.81	0.78	0.85	0.87	0.82	0.80	0.86	0.71	0.82	0.84
Parliament	0.83	0.87	0.86	0.88	0.85	0.89	0.87	0.88	0.81	0.89	0.81	0.87	0.86
Courts	0.72	0.69	0.75	0.76	0.70	0.87	0.70	0.74	0.72	0.83	0.75	0.71	0.78
Civil service	0.76	0.73	0.81	0.83	0.79	0.86	0.80	0.81	0.75	0.86	0.82	0.76	0.79
Police	0.66	0.57	0.64	0.72	0.60	0.73	0.65	0.64	0.57	0.73	0.74	0.62	0.72
Municipal board	0.69	0.71	0.62	0.70	0.71	0.75	0.69	0.74	0.56	0.74	0.68	0.72	0.70
Eigenvalue	4.43	4.64	4.65	4.98	4.56	5.53	5.06	5.04	4.19	5.46	4.59	4.87	5.08
Pct. variance explained	55	58	58	62	57	69	63	63	52	68	57	61	64
KMO[b]	0.87	0.87	0.88	0.90	0.88	0.91	0.91	0.90	0.85	0.91	0.90	0.90	0.89

Note

a Entries are loadings on the first component. Kaiser's criterion yields a unidimensional solution in all countries except Denmark.
b KMO is the Kaiser–Mayer–Olkin measure, which indicates to what extent the variables included in the model fit the underlying criteria. The values of KMO range from 1.0 (excellent fit) to 0.5 and less (poor fit).

Table 2.4 Level and dispersion of political confidence[a]

Country	Mean	Standard deviation	N
The Netherlands	0.61	0.14	1,631
West Germany	0.60	0.15	1,989
Denmark	0.59	0.16	1,637
Sweden	0.55	0.17	1,257
Switzerland	0.55	0.18	1,591
Norway	0.52	0.17	2,273
East Germany	0.52	0.18	1,011
Slovenia	0.49	0.21	983
Spain	0.47	0.18	4,101
Portugal	0.46	0.17	986
Romania	0.44	0.25	1,194
Moldova	0.34	0.22	1,215
Russia	0.33	0.21	1,723

Note
a The measure is an additive index (mean of valid scores) based on all eight questions about confidence in institutions. The index ranges from 0 to 1. Countries are ordered by their mean political confidence.

Netherlands, West Germany, and Denmark, and lowest in the new democracies, in particular Romania, Moldova, and Russia. This lends assurance in our political confidence measures.

Satisfaction with democracy

Table 2.5 shows the ranking of the CID societies according to how they score for our third main concept, satisfaction with democracy. There is general agreement about the best indicator to tap this variable. The CID survey uses the standard question employed in the Eurobarometer, ISSP, and World Values surveys. Like these, the CID survey also uses a four-point rating scale. The question reads:

- On the whole, are you very satisfied, fairly satisfied, not very satisfied, or not at all satisfied with the way democracy works in [name of country]?

The country results are as one would expect. Denmark, the Netherlands, Sweden, and West Germany are at the top of the table, Portugal, Slovenia, Romania, Russia, and Moldova at the bottom; the old, established democracies are high on the list, and the newer ones are low.

This distribution comes as no surprise particularly since the same pattern has been found in other studies over the last two decades (Schmitt 1983; Kuechler 1991; Klingemann 1999). In contrast with general agreement about question wording and the consistency of survey results, there is a good deal of dispute about how the results relate to democratic

Table 2.5 Level and dispersion of satisfaction with democracy[a]

Country	Mean	Standard deviation	N
Denmark	0.68	0.21	1,615
The Netherlands	0.65	0.20	1,598
Sweden	0.63	0.20	1,241
West Germany	0.62	0.22	1,964
Norway	0.57	0.19	2,186
Switzerland	0.57	0.22	2,103
Spain	0.55	0.22	4,072
East Germany	0.45	0.24	989
Portugal	0.44	0.24	965
Slovenia	0.42	0.22	942
Romania	0.32	0.24	1,161
Russia	0.31	0.25	1,441
Moldova	0.23	0.20	1,104

Note
a Satisfaction with democracy is measured on a four-point scale scored 0 to 1. Countries are ordered by their mean satisfaction with democracy.

support. Many scholars have questioned Easton's (1965: 267–8) classic distinction between diffuse and specific support, arguing that citizens do not perceive the difference and do not distinguish between basic support for democracy and the current performance of government, which means in empirical terms that the latter may be interpreted as a manifestation of the former.

The confusion between support for democracy and satisfaction with governmental performance has lead some to use inappropriate indicators or draw the wrong inferences from the data. Therefore, it is important to distinguish satisfaction with democracy, and measures of legitimacy (see Gunther and Montero 2004). Legitimacy may be considered to be 'the belief that, in spite of shortcomings and failures, the political institutions are better than any others that might be established' (Linz 1988: 65). In contrast, political contentment (Easton 1965: 406), or political discontent, lie on a different dimension, consisting of people's judgements of the day-to-day actions of political leaders and the operation of governmental institutions and processes (Kornberg and Clarke 1992: 20). Satisfaction with democracy thus comprises a set of perceptions relating to the ability of a given polity to solve problems that citizens consider to be particularly important. Political satisfaction, or dissatisfaction, arises from citizens' evaluations of the performance of the regime or authorities, as well as of their political outcomes, and expresses displeasure with a significant social or political object. In other words, political dissatisfaction is a general rejection of political objects that do not meet the standards that citizens set for them (Di Palma 1970: 30; Farah *et al.* 1979; Norris 1999b).

While democratic legitimacy or diffuse support of democracy tends to be fairly stable over time, dissatisfaction fluctuates in accordance with government policies, the condition of the society and economy, and the performance of key political institutions. And since it is focused on partisan political leaders and the governments they lead, it would not be surprising to find that, other things being equal, citizens supporting the party in government are more positive in their assessments than those who support opposition parties.

Social trust and political confidence

To examine the association between social trust and political confidence, we ran zero-order correlations between the factor extracted from the three-item Rosenberg trust scale and the factor extracted from the eight questions on confidence in public institutions. The CID results are unusual and surprising (Table 2.6). Contrary to almost all of the numerous studies published to date, and against all our expectations, there is a statistically significant zero-order correlation between social trust and confidence in institutions of government. The results are neither weak nor patchy. All the correlations are statistically significant at 0.001, and, moreover, they are substantively strong in almost all the societies except East Germany. The results are consistent and robust. Given the lack of any such findings in a large number of previous studies, these results are intriguing. And given their potential theoretical significance for social capital theory, they are worth investigating in greater depth.

Are these results simply a statistical artefact of our confidence factor? To eliminate this possibility, a second set of simple correlations was run,

Table 2.6 Correlation between social trust and political confidence[a]

Country	Pearson's r	N
Norway	0.39	2,151
The Netherlands	0.38	1,471
Romania	0.38	1,034
Denmark	0.37	1,519
Sweden	0.36	1,104
Switzerland	0.32	1,185
Moldova	0.29	1,040
Portugal	0.29	909
West Germany	0.28	1,916
Slovenia	0.25	891
Spain	0.24	3,505
Russia	0.23	1,298
East Germany	0.18	913

Note
a The measures correlated are the single factors extracted from the principal component analyses of social trust and confidence in institutions. All correlations are statistically significant at the 0.001-level. Countries are ordered by the strength of the correlation.

this time between the social trust factor and confidence in *each* of the eight separate political institutions. Since this gives us a total of 104 simple correlations (eight institutions in 13 societies), the results are not reproduced here, due to lack of space. But it is sufficient to say that 97 of the zero-order correlations are significant at the 0.001 level, four are significant at 0.01, two are significant at 0.05, and one alone is not significant. The results could hardly be clearer or more consistent: there appears to be a close association between social trust and confidence in political institutions in all 13 of the societies covered by this study.

We are therefore presented with a puzzle: contrary to previous research, we find a close, statistically significant, and often substantial association at the individual level between social trust and confidence in political institutions. Why is this? The answer does not seem to be found in the sequence of questions in the different questionnaires. While question order might affect the results to some extent, it is difficult to believe that it has such a strong effect.[13] There are two possible methodological explanations for the unusual findings.

1 *Number of indicators.* The CID questionnaire employs the full three-item Rosenberg trust scale, from which a single trust factor is extracted. Is this perhaps a better and more sensitive measure of generalised social trust than the single Noelle-Neumann question used in many other studies? Similarly, we have used factor scores for the eight questions on confidence in political institutions, while others have used a single questionnaire item, usually on confidence in parliament. Our measures are thus likely to be more refined and sensitive than others.

2 *Precision of indicators.* The CID questionnaire asks respondents to rate their answers on the three social trust questions on an 11-point scale. It is likely that this offers a more precise measure of trust than shorter rating scales.[14] As Krosnick and Fabrigar (1997: 144) have written, 'There are various reasons to believe that more scale points will generally be more effective than fewer ... More scale points permit a researcher to make more subtle distinctions among individuals' attitudes towards the same object. Thus, longer scales have the potential to convey more useful information'.

Due to lack of space we cannot fully investigate these possibilities, but we can at least point out some likely suggestions about the number and the precision of indicators. Some surveys (the World Values, for example) use a single social trust question and give respondents a dichotomised 'Yes/No' option in answering it.[15] The World Values study codes responses to the institutional trust (i.e. confidence) questions on a four-point scale, and many studies take as their indicator of political confidence the response to the single question about confidence in parliament. Is it possible that the full 11-point rating scale discriminates more sensitively for degrees of trust and confidence, and perhaps the three-item trust factor and eight-item confidence factor are better measures than the single questions used in other studies?

To test this possibility we re-ran our data, but this time in ways that increasingly approximate the type of measures and the rating scales used in other surveys. We change one variable at a time, so as to better identify what changes have what sorts of effects on the results. First, we use the usual single-item Noelle-Neumann social trust question (instead of the factor derived from the three-item scale) and correlate it with the confidence in institutions factor derived from the eight questions, both with the 11-point rating scale. Next, we employ the single social trust question on an 11-point scale and a single trust in parliament question, also on an 11-point scale. Third, we collapse the scales by using the single social trust question in dichotomised form and reducing the single confidence in parliament question to a four-point scale similar to that used by the World Values Surveys.[16] If it is correct that indicators and scales explain the difference between our results and others, then we would expect the correlations between social trust and political confidence to become smaller as we approximate the less refined measures and the narrower rating scales of other studies.

Table 2.7 shows that this is exactly what does happen. The correlations fall steadily as one moves from the most refined measures of the CID survey included in the first column to the least refined shown in the last column. East Germany is the only exception to this pattern. The correlations remain statistically significant in all cases of the final column, but nonetheless in a clear majority of eight of 13 societies they fall to half or less of their original size.

To check our results in a different way, we finally re-ran the Spanish, Moldovan, and Romanian data. The surveys in these countries happened to collect trust data from the same samples according to *both* the full CID format (the three-item Rosenberg trust scale and the eight questions about confidence in political institutions, both on a 0–10 rating scale) *and* the collapsed World Values format (a single social trust question coded 'Yes/No'). This enables us to check the results of the two sets of indicators used in the same surveys and applied to exactly the same respondents, thus allowing us to compare the results of each without making too many assumptions about how best to approximate World Values results by collapsing the CID rating scales.

The results shown in Table 2.8 confirm our previous expectations. The correlations fall steadily as we move down from the results of the most refined and sensitive factor scores for trust and confidence in the first row, to the least refined and sensitive figures shown in the last row. For example, in the Moldovan case (first column), the CID data show a correlation of 0.29 between social trust and confidence in political institutions;

Table 2.7 Correlation between different measures of social trust and political confidence[a]

Country	Full scales[b]		Single social trust question and political confidence factor[c]		Single social trust and confidence in parliament questions[d]		Collapsed single social trust and confidence in parliament questions[e]	
	Pearson's r	N	Pearson's r	N	Pearson's r	N	Pearson's r	N
Norway	0.39	2,151	0.32	2,155	0.26	2,231	0.21	2,231
The Netherlands	0.38	1,471	0.35	1,484	0.28	1,589	0.19	1,589
Romania	0.38	1,034	0.32	1,058	0.27	1,138	0.21	1,138
Denmark	0.37	1,519	0.34	1,542	0.30	1,620	0.24	1,620
Sweden	0.36	1,104	0.30	1,116	0.27	1,212	0.21	1,212
Switzerland	0.32	1,185	0.25	1,241	0.18	1,432	0.14	1,432
Moldova	0.29	1,040	0.25	1,079	0.20	1,162	0.18	1,162
Portugal	0.29	909	0.26	916	0.17	955	0.12	955
West Germany	0.28	1,916	0.22	1,919	0.21	1,965	0.14	1,965
Slovenia	0.25	891	0.19	905	0.18	967	0.17	967
Spain	0.25	3,435	0.16	3,496	0.16	3,743	0.12	3,743
Romania	0.23	1,298	0.15	1,323	0.15	1,636	0.11	1,636
East Germany	0.18	913	0.18	920	0.19	981	0.20	981
Weighted average correlations[f]	0.31	18,866	0.25	19,154	0.21	20,631	0.17	20,631

Notes

a All correlations are statistically significant at the 0.001-level. Countries are ordered by their coefficients in the *full scales* column.
b *Full scales* refers to the figures presented in Table 2.6, i.e. the social trust factor extracted from the three-item Rosenberg trust scale, based on 11-point ratings, and the factor extracted from the eight questions about public institutions, also based on 11-point ratings.
c *Single social trust question and political confidence factor* refers to a single social trust question, using 11-point ratings, and the factor extracted from the eight confidence questions, based on 11-point ratings.
d *Single social trust and confidence in parliament questions* refers to a single social trust question, using eleven-point ratings, and a single confidence in parliament question, also using eleven-point ratings.
e *Collapsed single social trust and confidence in parliament questions* refers to the measures described in table note *c* above, but with the first dichotomised and the second converted to a four-point scale so as to resemble the indicators used in the World Values Surveys. On the social trust question, values 0–6 were scored as 0 and 7–10 as 1. On the confidence in parliament question, 0–2 were scored as 1, 3–5 as 2, 6–8 as 3, and 9–10 as 4.
f *Weighted average correlations* are the sum of county coefficients multiplied by their Ns, and divided by the total N.

Table 2.8 Correlation between different measures of social trust and political confidence in Moldova, Romania, and Spain[a]

Measures correlated	Moldova		Romania		Spain	
	r	N	r	N	r	N
Social trust factor scores (three items) and political confidence factor scores (eight items)	0.29	1,040	0.38	1,034	0.25	3,435
Single 11-point social trust question and political confidence factor scores (eight items)	0.25	1,079	0.32	1,058	0.16	3,496
Single 11-point social trust question and single 11-point confidence in parliament question	0.20	1,162	0.27	1,138	0.16	3,743
Single 11-point social trust question and single confidence in parliament question on a four-point scale[b]	0.20	1,162	0.25	1,138	0.15	3,743
Single dichotomous social trust question and political confidence factor scores (eight items)	0.17	1,056	0.23	1,052	0.11	3,400
Single dichotomous social trust question and single 11-point confidence in parliament question	0.15	1,136	0.18	1,132	0.12	3,634
Single dichotomous social trust question and single confidence in parliament question on a four-point scale[b]	0.15	1,136	0.17	1,132	0.11	3,634

Notes
a All correlations are statistically significant at the 0.001-level.
b The 11-point confidence in parliament question was collapsed to four points as described in Table 2.7, note e.

but the same survey, using single questions and a 'Yes/No' scale for trust, and a four-point rating scale for confidence in parliament, shows a correlation of 0.15. Correspondingly, the Spanish results drop from 0.25 to 0.11. In the Spanish case, it is also worth noting that recoding the CID data to correspond with World Values measures produces results that are identical to those of the World Values study in 1999 and very close in 1990 (Table 2.9). Therefore, it is difficult to avoid the conclusion that the better the indicators and rating scales used to measure trust and confidence, the more likely they are to show a close association.[17] Conversely, the fact that previous research has not shown a consistently strong association between social trust and political confidence seems to be due to a combination of poor indicators and short rating scales.[18]

Social trust and satisfaction with democracy

If social trust is associated with political confidence, then perhaps it is also associated with satisfaction with democracy?[19] Data included in Table 2.10 confirm this association at the individual level. Not surprisingly, there is a close relationship between political confidence and satisfaction with democracy, since these are aspects of the same general type of political support. But the figures also show that the socially trusting are more satisfied with democracy. Although the figures vary quite substantially from one country to another, they are highly significant in all cases except East Germany.[20] It is noticeable, however, that the association between social trust and satisfaction with democracy is less consistent and less close (a result that might partly be due to the fact that the latter is measured on a four-point scale) than that between social trust and political confidence, and its coefficients are moreover less homogeneous across countries.

The conclusions to this part of the chapter are as simple and straightforward as they are statistically clear. The best, most reliable, and most

Table 2.9 Correlation between social trust and confidence in parliament in Spain according to the CID and WVS studies[a]

Survey	Pearson's r[b]	Kendall's tau[b]	N
CID	0.11**	0.10**	3,634
WVS (World Values Surveys)			
1999	0.11*	0.11*	1,109
1990	0.07*	0.06*	3,925
1981	−0.01	−0.00	2,106

Notes
a In all studies, social trust is measured by the same single dichotomous question. In the WVS study, confidence in parliament is measured by a single question using a four-point scale. In the CID study, confidence in parliament is measured by a single question using an 11-point scale, collapsed to a four-point scale as described in Table 2.7, note e.
b Levels of statistical significance: ** = 0.001, * = 0.01.

Table 2.10 Correlation of social trust and political confidence with satisfaction with democracy[a]

Country	Social trust and satisfaction with democracy		Political confidence and satisfaction with democracy	
	Pearson's r	N	Pearson's r	N
Denmark	0.23	1,586	0.45	1,529
East Germany	0.10	974	0.49	901
West Germany	0.16	1,957	0.48	1,922
Moldova	0.13	1,039	0.36	1,023
The Netherlands	0.20	1,581	0.44	1,467
Norway	0.21	2,162	0.45	2,079
Portugal	0.13	951	0.35	896
Romania	0.26	1,107	0.42	1,045
Russia	0.11	1,358	0.35	1,131
Slovenia	0.14	931	0.39	862
Spain	0.10	3,924	0.39	3,404
Sweden	0.22	1,215	0.50	1,108
Switzerland	0.19	1,482	0.40	1,236

Note
a All correlations are statistically significant at the 0.01-level and with one exception (East Germany, social trust) on the 0.001-level as well. For information on the measures used, see notes to Tables 2.5 and 2.6.

refined measures we have of social trust, political confidence, and satisfaction with democracy show that they are, indeed, associated with each other at the individual level at statistically significant levels. To this extent, our results are consistent with the claims of social capital theory as far as individual citizens are concerned.

Social trust, political confidence, and satisfaction with democracy: multivariate analyses

So far we have presented only bivariate correlations. Do our findings stand up to the more searching test of multivariate regressions? And what do these tell us about the origins of our dependent variables? In the last section of the chapter we will try to answer these questions with three basic multivariate regressions on social trust, political confidence, and satisfaction with democracy. For the selection of independent variables we have relied on a combination of theoretical, empirical, and pragmatic considerations. To begin with, we have taken into account some of the many recent attempts to provide empirical explanations of any one of our three dependent variables, most of them working with survey data at individual level, and only sporadically analysing the complete set of reciprocal relationships these variables may have among themselves. Although the range of models and the operational variables in these studies are quite disparate, many of them contain a common core for explaining sources of social trust that include at least personality characteristics of individuals (life satisfaction), participation in voluntary associations (membership, activism, or a compound measure), and their linkages, attachments or identifications with some type of community.[21] With respect to the origins of political confidence, recent studies have often focused on social capital or social psychological explanations (including social trust) and political or institutional theories (including either aggregate or individual level variables, such as satisfaction with democracy).[22] Finally, the sources of satisfaction with democracy have been analysed with a mixture of variables measuring party choice and party preferences, confidence in government and trust in political leaders, political attitudes and institutional features, economic performance and assessment of public policies, citizens' expectations, and years of democracy.[23]

In selecting our independent variables, we have also kept in line with the exploratory nature of this chapter. Rather than providing a systematic theoretical and empirical account of the sources of social trust, political confidence, and democratic satisfaction, our aim is to confirm whether the multivariate analysis maintains the exceptionally strong and consistent relationships among those indicators found through bivariate correlations. To do this, we compiled a selection of variables covering different degrees of associational involvement, life satisfaction, attachment to the local community (neighbourhood or village) and the municipality, population size of the locality in which the respondent lives, and exposure to television. As social background variables we have selected education, age, gender, and religious denomination. Most of the variables are self-explanatory.[24]

Table 2.11 shows the coefficients of the OLS regression on social trust. The results confirm our previous finding that social trust is strongly and consistently associated with confidence in political institutions across all countries at the individual level. But contrary to social capital theory, membership of voluntary associations rarely makes a significant appearance at all, confirming the results of many other studies.[25] However, life satisfaction, community attachment, and education are linked to social trust in most countries. It seems clear that satisfied, socially integrated, and educated people are more likely to trust, and that, consequently, both trust and life satisfaction tend to also be linked to education and status.[26]

No other variable makes a strong or consistent showing across all the nations. Satisfaction with democracy, age, gender, and the urban–rural continuum make sporadic appearances, and in some cases signs change to underline the weak and patchy nature of the results. It should also be noted that the regressions do not explain a great deal of the variance in social trust: they rarely manage to account for as much as a fifth, and more usually the adjusted R^2 is between 12 and 18 per cent. There are consistently strong statistical associations between trust, on the one hand, and political confidence, life satisfaction and community attachment, on

Table 2.11 Multiple regression analysis of social trust[a]

Predictor	CH	DK	ES	EG	WG	MD	NL	NO	PT	RO	RU	SE	SI
Political confidence	0.23***	0.31***	0.20***	0.23***	0.30***	0.21***	0.32***	0.28***	0.28***	0.25***	0.23***	0.30***	0.16***
Satisfaction with democracy	0.06**	0.05*	0.01	0.00	0.02	−0.07	0.02	0.04	0.02	0.10**	−0.02	0.09**	0.04
Associational membership	0.02	0.01	0.03**	0.02	0.06***	0.04*	−0.02	0.00	−0.02	−0.02	0.02	0.01	0.01
Life satisfaction	0.21***	0.12***	0.08***	0.11*	0.17***	0.26***	0.14***	0.11***	0.16***	0.14***	0.13***	0.08*	0.17***
Community attachment	0.11***	0.03*	0.04**	0.01	0.08**	0.09**	0.11***	0.07***	0.12***	−0.01	0.08**	0.07**	0.04
Size of locality	−0.03	−0.01	0.06***	−0.09**	0.05**	0.02	−0.02	−0.01	−0.04	−0.01	−0.02	−0.04	0.01
Exposure to television	−0.77	−0.12**	−0.07**	−0.03	−0.13	−0.01	0.01	−0.13***	0.05	0.02	0.02	−0.06	0.02
Education	0.05**	0.05*	0.09***	0.08*	0.09***	−0.04	0.08***	0.06***	−0.01	0.05	0.08**	0.10***	0.13***
Age	−0.06	−0.14***	−0.02	−0.10**	0.08**	−0.07	−0.10***	−0.13***	0.04	−0.10*	0.01	−0.16***	−0.10**
Gender (female)	0.02**	0.03***	0.01*	−0.03	−0.01	−0.01	−0.00	0.04***	−0.03	−0.01	0.04*	0.04*	0.03**
Religious denomination[b]													
Protestant	0.02*	R	–	−0.09***	−0.02**	–	0.00	R	–	−0.03	–	R	–
Catholic	R	–	R	−0.11***	R	R	R	−0.04	R	0.01	–	−0.06	R
Orthodox	–	–	–	–	–	R	–	−0.07**	–	R	R	–	–
Muslim	–	−0.02	–	–	0.00	–	0.01	–	–	−0.04	0.05	–	–
Other religion	−0.00	−0.00	−0.06*	0.06	0.02	−0.04	−0.00	−0.03	0.00	−0.15	−0.00	−0.05	−0.03
No religion	0.00	0.01	0.03***	R	−0.01	−0.03	−0.02	−0.02*	0.09	–	−0.01	−0.01	0.02
Adjusted R^2	0.214	0.191	0.120	0.079	0.166	0.174	0.212	0.246	0.125	0.177	0.109	0.179	0.118
N	1,126	1,488	3,135	879	1,853	770	1,220	1,812	803	914	1,040	1,081	836

Notes

a Entries are unstandardised regression coefficients. Levels of statistical significance: *** = 0.001, ** = 0.01, * = 0.05.
b The largest denomination constitutes the reference category (R). Denominations represented by too few cases to be distinguished are subsumed under 'other religion'.

the other, but they are not particularly successful in explaining a significant percentage of the variation in trust. But those results are no worse, and in most cases somewhat better, than most research of this kind (see Whiteley 1999: 42).

Given its relevance for social capital research, we might take a second look at the role played by voluntary organisations in generating social trust. First, there are many different kinds of voluntary association and, as Stolle and Rochon (2001: 144) have written: 'we expect that associations directed to different purposes will have different effects on the development of public social capital'. Second, membership is only one measure of voluntary activity, and perhaps other measures, such as participating in voluntary activity, or doing voluntary work in associations, might prove to be more productive of trust.

To what extent do different organisations and other forms of associational involvement have an impact on social trust? Tables 2.12 and 2.13 provide two rather eloquent answers.[27] In Table 2.12, we distinguish four types of voluntary associations (see Chapter 7, this volume) according to different criteria. Following Offe and Fuchs (2002: 192–9), spare-time, socio-cultural, and religious organisations belong to what they label as 'secondary or civic associations'; therefore, we should expect them to be better at producing social trust compared to interest, or 'tertiary', associations. Following Stolle and Rochon (2001: 154–5), interest and cultural associations, because of their purposes and degrees of inclusiveness, should be particularly productive of social trust. Moreover, religious organisations are treated separately on the grounds that trust is said to be associated with moral values (Uslaner 2002). And following both Putnam (2000) and Stolle (1998: 502), we might expect that associations fostering face-to-face interactions are much more likely to generate trust than those with passive or mediated forms of involvement.

However, none of these hypotheses are supported by any coefficient in Table 2.12. For every organisation and for every country, the coefficients are roughly the same as in the previous Table 2.11 – and most of them, moreover, are not significant (except for Spain and West Germany). With the partial exception of community attachment, the effects of other variables do not change appreciably. The same applies more generally to Table 2.13, which shows the effects of different forms of associational involvement on social trust, from membership to voluntary work and having friends in voluntary associations. With the exception again of Spain and West Germany, the contribution of these forms of engagement to social trust is usually small or insignificant. Only in these two countries, West Germany and Spain, is associational involvement a powerful predictor of social trust. In the other societies there is no pattern to suggest that face-to-face interaction in different types of organisations or distinct forms of associational involvement produce or strengthen social trust.

We now move from social trust to political confidence as our depend-

Table 2.12 Multiple regression analysis of social trust including membership in different types of associations[a]

Predictor	CH	DK	ES	EG	WG	MD	NL	NO	PT	RO	RU	SE	SI
Political confidence	0.22***	0.30***	0.20***	0.25***	0.31***	0.21***	0.32***	0.28***	0.29***	0.25***	0.23***	0.30***	0.17***
Satisfaction with democracy	0.07**	0.05*	0.02	0.02	0.01	−0.07	0.02	0.04	0.02	0.10**	−0.01	0.09**	0.04
Membership in													
Spare-time and sports clubs	0.00	0.01	0.02*	0.01	0.03**	0.00	0.02*	0.01	0.00	0.02	−0.04	0.00	0.02
Interest organisations	0.00	0.01	0.03***	0.01	0.00	0.04*	−0.02	0.00	−0.02	−0.01	0.02	0.00	0.00
Socio-cultural organisations	0.02	0.02*	0.02**	0.03	0.07***	−0.01	0.01	0.02	−0.01	0.01	0.03	0.04**	0.02
Religious organisations	−0.02	0.01	0.07***	0.06	0.03	0.03	−0.00	0.02	0.03	−0.04	−0.04	0.02	−0.04
Life satisfaction	0.20***	0.12***	0.07***	0.08	0.18***	0.26***	0.13***	0.10***	0.15***	0.14***	0.13***	0.07*	0.17***
Community attachment	0.11***	0.03	0.04**	0.02	0.06**	0.08**	0.10**	0.05***	0.12***	−0.01	0.08***	0.07**	0.04
Size of locality	−0.04	−0.01	0.06***	−0.11**	0.07***	0.02	−0.02	−0.00	−0.03	−0.00	−0.02	−0.03	0.01
Exposure to television	−0.92**	−0.09**	−0.07**	−0.05	−0.21**	−0.01	0.02	−0.14**	0.05	0.03	0.02	−0.04	0.02
Education	0.10*	0.13***	0.10***	0.21***	0.04	−0.05	0.08**	0.09***	−0.01	0.02	0.18***	0.16***	0.12***
Age	−0.07*	−0.12**	−0.03	−0.15***	0.06*	−0.07	−0.11***	−0.13***	0.04	−0.10*	−0.00	−0.15***	−0.10**
Gender (female)	0.02*	0.03***	0.01*	−0.02	−0.02	−0.01	−0.00	0.04***	−0.02	−0.01	0.04*	0.03**	0.03*
Religious denomination[b]													
Protestant	0.02	R	–	−0.10***	−0.01	–	0.01	R	–	−0.03	–	R	–
Catholic	R	–	R	−0.14***	R	–	R	−0.04	R	0.01	–	−0.06	–
Orthodox	–	–	–	–	–	R	–	−0.08**	–	R	R	–	R
Muslim	–	−0.00	–	–	0.00	–	0.01	–	–	−0.04	0.05	–	–
Other religion	−0.01	−0.02	−0.07**	0.04	0.03	−0.04	0.00	−0.04**	0.00	−0.16	−0.01	−0.05	−0.02
No religion	−0.00	0.01	0.03***	R	0.01	−0.04	−0.02	−0.02	0.08	–	−0.01	−0.01	0.02
Adjusted R^2	0.203	0.204	0.134	0.104	0.159	0.172	0.203	0.235	0.122	0.175	0.110	0.180	0.118
N	1,112	1,468	2,997	814	1,706	770	1,208	1,669	803	919	1,040	1,083	836

Notes

a Entries are unstandardised regression coefficients. Levels of statistical significance: *** = 0.001, ** = 0.01, * = 0.05.
b The largest denomination constitutes the reference category (R). Denominations represented by too few cases to be distinguished are subsumed under 'other religion'.

Table 2.13 Multiple regression analysis of social trust including different forms of associational involvement[a]

Form of involvement	CH	DK	ES	EG	WG	MD	NL	NO	PT	RO	RU	SE	SI
Involvement	0.06*	0.03	0.04***	0.02	0.06***	0.03*	−0.03	−0.02	−0.02	−0.01	0.02	−0.01	0.02
Membership	0.02	0.01	0.03***	0.02	0.05***	0.03*	−0.01	0.01	−0.02	−0.01	0.02	0.01	0.01
Activity	0.02**	0.03**	0.04***	0.02	0.07***	0.03	0.00	0.01	0.02	−0.02	0.01	0.01	0.01
Donation	0.02*	0.03***	0.03***	0.04	0.06***	0.02	0.01	0.02**	−0.01	−0.01	0.01	0.02	0.01
Voluntary work	0.02*	0.01	0.03*	0.02	0.07***	0.01	0.01	0.01	0.00	−0.02	0.02	0.03*	0.02
Friends	0.03**	0.01	0.03***	0.02	0.07***	0.02	0.02*	0.03***	−0.02	−0.02	0.01	0.02	0.02

Note
a These results are drawn from multiple regression analyses where the remaining independent variables correspond to the ones included in Tables 2.11 and 2.12. Entries are unstandardised regression coefficients. Levels of statistical significance: *** = 0.001, ** = 0.01, * = 0.05.

ent variable and perform the same regression analysis. As can be seen in Table 2.14, social trust, satisfaction with democracy, and attachment to the municipality appear in all the country equations, but trust is always significant at the highest level.[28] The robust association between social trust and confidence in political institutions is confirmed once more. Satisfaction with democracy is even more important; but its higher coefficients are only to be expected given that, conceptually, the two are closely related.[29] Attachment to the municipality is the third variable that appears strongly in all the country equations. It is interesting that, where social trust is concerned, it is attachment to the social unit, the community, that matters; but for the political measure of confidence, it is attachment to the political unit, the municipality, that counts. This suggests that social variables are most important for social trust, and political variables for political confidence (Newton 2001a; Anderson and LoTempio 2002). As Denters *et al.* (Chapter 3, this volume) make it clear in their much more comprehensive empirical analysis, both the socio-cultural and the political explanations of political confidence have some power, and should be seen as complementary rather than rival approaches; but the explanatory power of the political approach is considerably stronger.

The social trust and political confidence regressions also differ in that life satisfaction is closely related with trust, but not so closely associated with political confidence. Where Listhaug and Wiberg (1995: 319) found a positive though tenuous impact of life satisfaction on confidence levels, we find an association in only half the countries. As with social trust, membership of voluntary associations is unrelated to confidence.

The third set of regressions deal with satisfaction with democracy (Table 2.15). The coefficients tell much the same sort of story of mixed and scattered results, but with one significant difference. When distinct statistical models of satisfaction with democracy are run (not shown here due to lack of space), both social trust and confidence in institutions appear as strong variables in the equations *if* they are entered separately. But, when they are run in the same equation (as in Table 2.15), it is the confidence variable that retains its strong association with satisfaction, not the trust variable. Social trust is thus strongly associated with political confidence, and political confidence is strongly associated with democratic satisfaction. But social trust is not associated with democratic satisfaction independently of confidence. This suggests that the effect of social trust on satisfaction with democracy works through confidence in political institutions.

The satisfaction with democracy regressions also shows another interesting difference. While social trust and municipal attachment largely disappear from the scene, life satisfaction makes a reappearance in ten of the 13 equations. The results for the other variables are generally scattered, patchy, and once again, voluntary associations are insignificant (except in Portugal). Between 15 and 30 per cent of the variance is explained in each

Table 2.14 Multiple regression analysis of confidence in political institutions[a]

Predictor	CH	DK	ES	EG	WG	MD	NL	NO	PT	RO	RU	SE	SI
Social trust	0.19***	0.24***	0.20***	0.10***	0.13***	0.22***	0.25***	0.25***	0.20***	0.27***	0.15***	0.17***	0.16***
Satisfaction with democracy	0.25***	0.27***	0.26***	0.29***	0.25***	0.34***	0.25***	0.31***	0.22***	0.29***	0.25***	0.35***	0.31***
Associational membership	0.01	0.02	0.01	−0.00	0.02**	0.03	0.02	0.02	−0.00	0.02	−0.01	−0.01	0.01
Life satisfaction	0.00	0.03	0.05**	0.03	0.03	0.08**	0.02	0.08***	0.03	0.10***	0.08***	0.06**	0.03
Municipal attachment	0.13***	0.06***	0.09***	0.17***	0.13***	0.09***	0.07***	0.05***	0.09***	0.11***	0.06***	0.06**	0.15***
Size of locality	−0.00	0.02	−0.02	−0.05*	−0.05***	0.01	−0.05*	−0.02	0.02	−0.03	−0.05**	−0.00	−0.01
Exposure to television	0.01	−0.06	−0.02	0.07	0.10*	−0.11*	0.00	−0.03	0.13*	0.10	0.03	0.01	0.05
Education	0.06**	0.04*	0.03	−0.00	0.01	0.05	0.04**	0.04**	0.06*	−0.09*	−0.02	0.04*	0.05
Age	0.03	0.05	−0.05*	0.07*	−0.07***	0.02	0.00	−0.03	−0.06	−0.06	−0.14***	−0.04	−0.13***
Gender (female)	−0.00	−0.00	0.01*	0.02	0.02**	−0.04**	0.01	−0.01	0.01	0.01	0.01	−0.00	−0.01
Religious denomination[b]													
Protestant	−0.01	R	–	0.05*	0.01	–	0.01	R	−0.08	−0.03	–	R	–
Catholic	R	–	R	0.04*	R	–	R	0.01	R	0.01	–	−0.00	R
Orthodox	–	–	–	–	–	R	–	−0.05*	–	R	R	–	–
Muslim	–	−0.01	–	–	0.00	–	0.03	–	–	−0.04	0.01	–	–
Other religion	0.03	−0.03	−0.03	0.01	−0.02	−0.01	−0.01	−0.00	−0.05*	−0.12	−0.03	0.00	0.01
No religion	−0.04*	−0.02	−0.06***	R	−0.02	0.02	−0.01	−0.02*	0.05	–	0.01	−0.02	−0.01
Adjusted R^2	0.270	0.298	0.225	0.313	0.349	0.219	0.306	0.316	0.217	0.273	0.211	0.321	0.243
N	1,123	1,487	3,144	879	1,853	801	1,222	1,805	804	927	1,052	1,084	835

Notes

a Entries are unstandardised regression coefficients. Levels of statistical significance: *** = 0.001, ** = 0.01, * = 0.05.
b The largest denomination constitutes the reference category (R). Denominations represented by too few cases to be distinguished are subsumed under 'other religion'.

Table 2.15 Multiple regression analysis of satisfaction with democracy[a]

Predictor	CH	DK	ES	EG	WG	MD	NL	NO	PT	RO	RU	SE	SI
Social trust	0.11**	0.08*	0.02	0.00	0.02	−0.05	0.05	0.05	0.04	0.10**	−0.02	0.08**	0.05
Political confidence	0.50***	0.55***	0.47***	0.55***	0.65***	0.29***	0.64***	0.49***	0.51***	0.31***	0.43***	0.55***	0.41***
Associational membership	−0.00	0.01	−0.01	0.00	−0.02	−0.01	−0.03	−0.00	0.04*	0.03	0.00	−0.02	0.00
Life satisfaction	0.11**	0.14***	0.02	0.26***	0.13***	0.16***	0.11*	0.09***	0.06	0.18***	0.11***	0.10**	0.06
Municipal attachment	−0.02	−0.02	0.04*	0.01	0.09***	0.04	0.02	0.00	−0.03	0.03	0.02	0.00	0.05
Size of locality	0.04	0.01	0.01	0.01	0.02	−0.04	0.00	0.03**	−0.12***	0.03	−0.01	0.03	0.08***
Exposure to television4	−0.03	0.00	0.05	0.01	−0.09	0.04	−0.06	0.02	−0.05	0.03	−0.02	0.02	−0.0
Education	−0.00	0.06*	0.05*	−0.00	0.03	−0.02	0.03	−0.02	0.05	0.04	0.04	0.05*	−0.01
Age	0.08*	−0.06	−0.01	0.06	0.02	−0.04	0.08*	0.09***	−0.02	−0.12***	0.28***	0.12***	0.12***
Gender (female)	−0.00	−0.06***	−0.02	−0.03	−0.01	0.04**	0.00	−0.01	−0.03	−0.01	−0.00	−0.02	−0.00
Religious denomination[b]													
Protestant	−0.01	R	–	0.08***	0.01	–	−0.01	R	0.05	−0.07	–	R	–
Catholic	R	–	R	0.08**	R	–	R	−0.08**	R	0.01	–	0.07	R
Orthodox	–	–	–	–	–	R	–	−0.00	–	R	R	–	–
Muslim	–	0.03	–	–	−0.01	–	−0.02	–	–	0.03	0.01	–	–
Other	0.01	0.02	0.00	0.02	−0.01	−0.03	0.02	−0.03*	0.02	0.13	−0.02	0.02	−0.01
No religion	−0.04*	−0.01	−0.04**	R	−0.01	−0.04	−0.01	−0.01	0.01	–	−0.02	−0.01	−0.00
Adjusted R^2	0.179	0.234	0.152	0.297	0.246	0.175	0.209	0.220	0.148	0.218	0.181	0.281	0.175
N	1,123	1,487	3,144	879	1,853	801	1,222	1,805	804	927	1,052	1,084	835

Notes
a Entries are unstandardised regression coefficients. Levels of statistical significance: *** = 0.001, ** = 0.01, * = 0.05.
b The largest denomination constitutes the reference category (R). Denominations represented by too few cases to be distinguished are subsumed under 'other religion'.

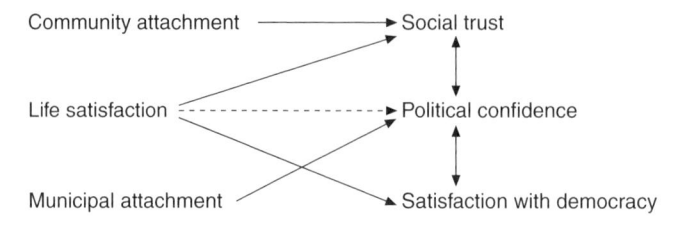

Figure 2.1 Social trust, political confidence, and satisfaction with democracy.

country, and most of the work is done by the single measure of political confidence.

The associations among our three main variables are summarised in Figure 2.1. Although the lines are merely indicative of associations that are consistently significant in all or in most of the CID countries, the picture presents an interesting pattern of relationships between social trust and political confidence, on the one hand, and between confidence and satisfaction with democracy, on the other. The three variables are related but in different direct and indirect ways, and have their origins in distinctive combinations of social and political circumstances. Confirming the correlations developed in previous sections of this chapter, the multivariate analysis shows that political confidence is the most important predictor of social trust in every CID country. Whereas political confidence also holds a systematic, consistent, and strong relationship with satisfaction with democracy, social trust is linked to the latter only by virtue of its association with life satisfaction, which in turn is associated with our three dependent variables (much less so for political confidence).

In other words, it seems that social trust is strongly associated with political confidence, and political confidence is strongly associated with democratic satisfaction; but social trust is not associated with democratic satisfaction independently of confidence. While attachment to the community is associated with social trust, it is attachment to the municipality that accompanies political confidence. None of our measures of involvement in voluntary associations play a significant or consistent role in the models. Neither membership, nor participation, nor donating money, nor doing voluntary work, nor having friends in voluntary associations has any impact on social trust (except in Spain and West Germany). The composite variable of associational involvement, which combines all these measures, performs even worse (still with the same German and Spanish exceptions).

Conclusions

Social trust is thought to be the central element in a complex virtuous circle in which a set of attitudes, including mutuality, reciprocity, and trust are associated with community involvement, especially with membership of voluntary associations and clubs, which, in turn, are linked to civic engagement and democratic political participation, which helps to build the social and political institutions necessary for democratic and effective government. Democracy and good government subsequently create the conditions in which social trust and political confidence can flourish, enabling citizens to develop their sense of citizenship and encouraging community involvement, civic engagement, and democratic participation, so completing the virtuous circle.

There are two main problems with this befitting theory. First, survey research, of which there are numerous studies available, shows that involvement in voluntary organisations has only a weak connection with generalised social trust. The same research shows that, by and large, voluntary activity has only a weak connection with political attitudes and behaviour, including confidence in political institutions and satisfaction with democracy. The results are much the same whether one takes passive membership of one or more associations as the measure of voluntary activity, or whether one takes a stronger measure of active work and engagement in them. One can sometimes find evidence to support the theory, but it is usually weak, patchy, and far from robust enough to be convincing.

The results of the present research confirm this conclusion. They provide little support for the claim that membership of voluntary associations creates generalised social trust in others, and virtually no evidence at all of a link between membership and support for political institutions and democracy. In this sense, membership of voluntary associations seems to be irrelevant to citizenship, political involvement, and democracy.

The second problem with the theory linking generalised social trust with confidence in political institutions is that past research has invariably found no link at all between them at the individual level of analysis. Many studies, and once again there is a fair amount of them, conclude that it is not the case that those who trust their fellow citizens are also likely to have confidence in the institutions of democratic government.

In this respect, our own results are surprising. Contrary to previous empirical findings, we discover that social trust and confidence in political institutions *are* associated. The link between them is strong in all our 13 societies and maintains its statistical and substantive strength in regression analysis which takes account of other variables. Indeed, in the country regressions on social trust (see Table 2.11), confidence in political institutions is by far the strongest variable in each equation in 12 of the 13 societies. This is a surprising finding.

Given that no previous research shows a strong or consistent association between social trust and confidence in political institutions, we must be cautious in drawing conclusions from our exceptional results. There are some valid reasons, however, for taking them seriously. The measures of trust and confidence used here may be more precise, sensitive, and reliable than most others, partly because we use social trust and political confidence factors drawn from a set of questions that scale, and partly because we use an 11-point rating scale for all questions.

Our findings have two implications. Methodologically, it seems advantageous to use batteries of scaleable items and 11-point rating scales (at least for social trust and political confidence), although this may make surveys more expensive and time consuming. Substantively, it seems clear that social trust and political confidence are, indeed, associated at the individual level, which is consistent with the hypotheses set forth by those social capital theorists who expect to find an association at both the individual and aggregate levels.[30]

A link at the individual level between social trust and political attitudes also has some important implications for the social origins of citizenship and democracy, but these are not entirely consistent with the theory outlined at the beginning of the chapter. This theory argues that patterns of social attitudes and behaviour (generalised social trust, membership of voluntary associations, and community attachment) will cluster together, and will be associated with another cluster of political attitudes and behaviour (civic attachment and engagement, confidence in political institutions, and satisfaction with democracy). Although we find some of these associations, the patterns are not nearly as tight or simple as the theory predicts. The evidence suggests that there are different, though overlapping, pathways leading to generalised social trust, on the one hand, and attitudes of confidence towards democratic institutions, on the other.

Basically, these pathways are threefold. First, social trust is most closely linked to life satisfaction and attachment to the local community, although it is also strongly associated with confidence in political institutions. In their turn, attachment to the community and social trust are not directly associated with satisfaction with democracy. Second, satisfaction with democracy is closely associated with confidence in political institutions, which, subsequently, is associated not with attachment to the community but with attachment to the municipality. And, finally, satisfaction with democracy is not directly linked with social trust or attachment to the community, although it is linked with a common third factor, life satisfaction, which appears to lie at the heart of the causal network.

The implications of these findings for citizenship, involvement, and democracy must be stated cautiously at this stage. The conclusion seems to be that *social* attitudes and behaviour form one cluster of variables, while *political* orientations and behaviour form another, with life satisfaction linking the two. The classical theory is part right and part wrong. Satisfaction with democracy is mainly rooted in political conditions, while social trust is mainly rooted in social conditions, with life satisfaction being a common source of both. Social trust is not the crucial variable linking social life with democratic satisfaction after all, although it is closely associated with confidence in political institutions. Membership of voluntary associations does not figure at all in the models of social trust or confidence in political institutions.

In short, the conditions of democratic activity and stability seem not to be as closely tied to the circumstances of community life as classical theory suggests. Involvement with and participation in the local community may have all sorts of benefits for both the community and its individual members, but its impact on democracy and its institutions seems to be indirect and comparatively weak. In this regard, our results question the extent to which democracy rests upon a vibrant community life. Be that as it may, the social roots of political life will be examined more closely in later chapters of this book.

Notes

1 It is neither necessary nor possible to cite the vast and rapidly increasing volume of work on social trust. For recent general commentaries see Luhmann 1979; Gambetta 1988a; Hardin 1991b, 1993, 1996, 1998, 2002; Putnam 1995b, 2000, 2002; Misztal 1996; Seligman 1997; Braithwaite and Levi 1998; Hollis 1998; van Deth *et al.* 1999; Warren 1999b; Dasgupta and Serageldin 2000; Sztompka 2000; Edwards *et al.* 2001; Dekker and Uslaner 2001; O'Neill 2002; and Uslaner 2002.
2 See Putnam 1995b; van Deth 1996; Brehm and Rahn 1997; Torcal and Montero 1999: 182; Newton 1999a: 171–4; Uslaner 1999: 128; Minkoff 2001; and Stolle and Rochon 2001.
3 See Wright 1976: 104–10; Craig 1993: 27; Putnam 1995b: 665; Orren 1997; Hall 1999; Newton 1999a: 179–80; Newton and Norris 2000: 62–6; Newton 2001a; and Delhey and Newton 2003.
4 See, for example, Dekker and van den Broek 1995; van Deth 1996; Brehm and Rahn 1997; Knack and Keefer 1997: 1281–3; Newton 1999a; 1999b; 2001a; Torcal and Montero 1999; Whiteley 1999: 40–1; Booth and Richard 2001: 50; Stolle and Rochon 2001; Paxton 2002; and Uslaner 2002: 128–35.
5 See Putnam 1993: 111–15; Inglehart 1997; Knack and Keefer 1997; Newton and Norris 2000; Newton 2001a; Paxton 2002; Uslaner 2002: 217–48; Rothstein and Stolle 2003; and Delhey and Newton 2003.
6 For two distinct and yet complementary analyses of the varieties of trust, see Newton 1999b: 14–20 and Offe and Fuchs 2002: 191–4.
7 There is also some intriguing, though entirely inconclusive, evidence that the trust measure does actually correspond to the likelihood of citizens acting in a trustworthy manner. A small experiment in which wallets with money in them were 'lost' in various cities around the globe shows that the wallets were more likely to be turned over to the police in cities with a higher trust rating as measured by the standard trust question (see Knack and Keefer 1997: 1257). Similarly, the experiment conducted by Yamagishi (1988) found a correspondence between trusting attitudes and trusting behaviour.
8 While Rosenberg called his scale a misanthropy scale, it clearly loads heavily on trust, and might just as easily be called a trust scale. In fact, Rosenberg himself labelled it as a 'faith-in-people' scale in his 1956 and 1957 articles. On the other hand, it should be mentioned that in the United States the General Social Survey has been also using the three–item Rosenberg trust scale, but with only two possibilities of response (Yes/No); see Brehm and Rahn 1997: 1008 and Uslaner 2002: 68–74.

9 See, for example, Luhmann 1979: 39, 1988b; Giddens 1990: 114; Seligman 1997: 16–22; Offe 1999: 44–5; and Hardin 2000: 33–5. For a contrary position, see Paxton 1999: 105–6.
10 A principal component analysis of all ten institutions (domestic and international) produces either a single political confidence factor, or two of them, one of which loads heavily on internal institutions, and the other on international ones; see also Denters *et al.*, Chapter 3, this volume.
11 This is not so only in Switzerland, Portugal, and West Germany, where two factors break down quite neatly into confidence in the institutions of politics and government (politicians, party, the cabinet) and non-political public institutions (courts, civil service, police, and municipal boards). But since these three deviating cases are just at the borderline based on the Kaiser criterion (the first factor explains 52–59 per cent of the variance, and the second only 13–18 per cent), we work with the one-factor solution in this chapter.
12 This finding is consistent with the results of other research; see, for example, Listhaug 1998; Norris 1999b: 222; Bouckhaert and van de Walle 2001; and Christensen and Laegrid 2002.
13 It is true that, while question order is generally consistent in the common core questionnaires of the 13 CID surveys, it varies in different countries from one survey to another, and from one counting to another in other surveys. But this survey and country variability is unlikely to account for the consistently weak and statistically insignificant results of the associations between trust and confidence in almost all of the other surveys.
14 There is still another potential explanation. Given the natural propensity of 11-point rating scales, it is conceivable that respondents who see themselves as 'middle of the road' types, or as 'radicals' on the fringe of society and politics, might have consistently marked the same points on the rating scale and, therefore, gave a degree of spurious association to their responses. We are grateful to Willem Saris for making this point.
15 As already indicated, the wording of the WVS question is, 'Generally speaking, would you say that most people can be trusted, or that you can't be too careful in dealing with people?'
16 We are grateful to Michael Braun, ZUMA Mannheim, for having provided us with important assistance in this regard.
17 In experiments using the Multi-Trait, Multi-Method approach for the CID social trust questions, undertaken for the European Social Survey pilots (which happened to have exactly the same indicators) in the Netherlands and Great Britain, Saris and Gallhofer (2003: 10) found that 'the forced choice two point scale is definitively worse in both countries than the 11 point scale with respect to validity'.
18 Rothstein (2002: 320) reports a similar experiment in four Swedish surveys conducted yearly since 1996 with similar positive results.
19 See Putnam 1993 and Inglehart 1997: 180–7. However, Uslaner (2002: 218) questions whether 'democratic societies are trusting societies'. It should be mentioned that both Uslaner and Inglehart base their conclusions on cross-national comparative data, not on the kind of individual data that this chapter is concerned with.
20 In Spain, however, where the Pearson's *r* coefficient reaches the same value as in East Germany, the high level of statistical significance is probably due to the high number of cases.
21 See, for instance, Whiteley 1999, which adds some individuals' normative beliefs and moral codes; Delhey and Newton 2003, which adds satisfaction with democracy, other personality traits, and networks of friends; and Freitag 2003, which adds moral values and confidence in political institutions.

22 See, for example, Listhaug and Wiberg 1995, which adds ideology, political interest, postmaterialism, and subjective life satisfaction; Newton and Norris 2000, which adds voluntary activism; Rohrschneider and Schmitt-Beck 2003, which adds political values; and Brehm and Rahn 1997, which provides a structural model of confidence in government, social trust, and civic engagement.
23 See, for instance, Clarke *et al.* 1993; Anderson and Guillory 1997; Anderson 1998 (which also takes social trust into consideration); Anderson and Tverdova 2001; and, from a complementary perspective, Mishler and Rose 2001a.
24 In Tables 2.11 to 2.13 we explore, among other things, also the effect of three different aspects of social involvement. Table 2.11 depicts the influence of being a member in any of the voluntary associations listed in the CID questionnaire. The impact of *membership* in different types of organisations (presented and discussed in greater detail in Chapter 7) is analysed in Table 2.12. Finally, in Table 2.13 we present the effects of distinct components of associational involvement (namely, whether the respondent is a member, has participated in any activity, donated money, done voluntary work, and has personal friends within an organisation; see also Chapter 6, this volume). *Life satisfaction* is an 11-point scale indicating to what extent the respondent is satisfied with his or her life as a whole. *Community attachment* and *municipal attachment* are 11-point scales indicating to what extent the respondent is attached to the neighbourhood or village (a social entity), on the one hand, and the municipality or town (a political entity), on the other. *Size of locality* ranges from rural to big city (more than 500,000 inhabitants). *Exposure to television* is based on the average number of hours per day the respondent spends watching television.
25 See, for example, among many others, Newton 1999a: 179–84, 2001a: 211–12, and Newton and Norris 2000: 65 for the lack of relationships between social trust and political confidence; and Putnam 1995a: 73; Stolle 1998: 522; Torcal and Montero 1999: 184; and Stolle and Rochon 2001: 131 for the association between social trust and membership of voluntary organisations; see also Whiteley 1999: 39 and Freitag 2003: 957–8 for findings similar to ours.
26 See on those points Brehm and Rahn 1997: 1019; Whiteley 1999: 39; Uslaner 2002: 84–6; Wuthnow 2002: 86; and Delhey and Newton 2003: 110–11.
27 See Chapter 6, this volume, for a more detailed analysis.
28 For reasons of space we do not present the regression on political confidence that shows its association with attachment to the community to be weaker than attachment to the municipality.
29 Although Holmberg (1999: 113) has claimed that the relationship between confidence in political institutions and satisfaction with democracy is spurious, it does not seem to be the case in spite of their conceptual closeness.
30 Cross-national empirical research results, based on data of the recently released first round (2003) of the European Social Survey, confirm this strong and consistent relationship between social trust and political confidence at the individual level in 21 European countries (Zmerli 2004).

3 Political confidence in representative democracies
Socio-cultural vs. political explanations

Bas Denters, Oscar Gabriel, and Mariano Torcal

Introduction

In the past 25 years political scientists have repeatedly claimed the emergence of a crisis of political confidence amongst western publics. In the 1970s, for example, the postwar era of unprecedented economic growth, prosperity, and security came to an end and neo-Marxists, neo-Liberals, and neo-Conservatives alike, claimed that the economic decline and ever-increasing, contradictory public demands would lead to a major crisis of political confidence in the western world (Crozier *et al.* 1975; Kaase and Newton 1995).

The breakdown of the communist regimes in central and eastern Europe, the subsequent third wave of democratisation, and the economic recovery of the 1990s may have marked the beginning of an era of greater public confidence in political institutions and actors. Nevertheless, these events did by no means go hand-in-hand with a declining concern amongst political scientists about this public confidence. At the end of the 1990s, political scientists reported the appearance of the 'critical democrat'. According to many scholars, contemporary political culture is characterised by a combination of strong support for democratic ideals, on the one hand, and critical attitudes towards democratic practice on the other (Montero *et al.* 1997; Klingemann 1999; Norris 1999a, 1999c; Montero and Torcal 2006).

In this chapter we will first describe the public's confidence in political institutions and actors in 13 contemporary European democracies. Moreover, we will try to enter the debate on alternative explanations of political confidence. This is not only important for understanding changes in political confidence over time, but also provides an explanation for cross-national variations in contemporary levels of political confidence in Europe. In the relevant literature we find two basic lines of argument. On the one hand, some analysts claim that political confidence is rooted in *socio-cultural factors*. In other words: the result of long-term processes of socialisation. In the tradition of Alexis de Tocqueville (and, more recently, Lerner 1958; Almond and Verba 1963), it is argued that networks of civic cooperation provide a training ground for the values, norms, and civic skills necessary for a healthy democracy. In this contemporary debate, Robert Putnam (1993 and 2000) employed the concept of *social capital* to argue for the democratic effects of networks and civic virtues. In his view, declining levels of social capital are a major factor underlying increasing public disenchantment with the government.[1] In this volume, Zmerli *et al.* (Chapter 2) also report results that show a significant and consistent relationship between social trust, as part of the cultural component of social capital (Putnam 1993: 167), and confidence in institutions.

On the other hand, many social scientists have recently claimed that variations in levels of political confidence might predominantly have *political origins*. These political origins are rather diverse. First, they pertain to people's subjective assessments of government performance, their sympathy for the incumbent government, and other personal political outlooks (micro-political factors). Second, these factors also pertain to macro-political factors, especially the characteristics of political institutions (Listhaug and Wiberg 1995; Nye and Zelikov 1997; McAllister 1999; Miller and Listhaug 1999; Katzenstein 2000; Newton and Norris 2000; Magalhães 2006).

The socio-cultural and political approaches have been perceived as rival explanations (Mishler and Rose 2001b). In this chapter, we will regard them as complementary and will consider the relative importance of socio-cultural and political factors as an empirical question. First we will discuss the importance of some socio-cultural explanations, confirming the impact of social trust (see Chapter 2, this volume). Second we will show the role of political factors in explaining micro and macro variations in institutional confidence.

In the first section we will deal with the concept and measurement of political confidence. Based on this we will provide a description of levels of political confidence in our 13 societies and 12 countries. This analysis will show that the level of confidence differs considerably for various forms of confidence and that it varies substantially across our cases. After this descriptive analysis we will provide a more detailed theoretical discussion of the two types of explanation (socio-cultural and political). This theoretical discussion will provide the basis for the empirical analyses in the rest of the chapter. In our empirical analyses we will begin with an assessment of the explanatory power of the two models. Subsequently we will try to explain the variations – for different forms of confidence and for different countries – that we found in our descriptive analyses.

Political confidence: concept and measurement

Political confidence refers to citizens' attitudes towards the core institutions and key actors of the political regime (Gamson 1968: 1–19; Hart

1978: 19–31; Lipset and Schneider 1983).[2] Several distinctions are important for people's political confidence. First, many authors have divided the concept between political orientations towards political actors (confidence in political *actors*) and towards political institutions (confidence in political *institutions*).[3] A second important distinction pertains to institutions which characterise contemporary democracies, and institutions that represent the *Rechtsstaat* (loosely translated as 'the constitutional state'). As shown in the empirical analyses of Gabriel *et al.* (2002: 177–82), the national parliament, the government, the political parties, and the civil service are seen by the public as representative of the central decision-making agencies of a modern state, while the courts, together with the police, represent the *Rechtsstaat*.[4] Therefore, we will not only have to distinguish between the confidence in public institutions and in political actors, but also between the key actors and institutions of a liberal democracy and the hierarchical institutions of the *Rechtsstaat*. To measure political confidence in the CID project we have included a ten-point scale, measuring confidence in and/or approval of the set of seven potential objects of confidence:[5]

1 Actors in a representative party-democracy:

　1.1 Political parties;
　1.2 Politicians.

2 Institutions in a liberal democracy:

　2.1 Parliament (legislative power);
　2.2 The cabinet (executive power).

3 Institutions of the *Rechtsstaat*:

　3.1 The civil service;[6]
　3.2 The courts;
　3.3 The police.

　The dimensional analysis of our data reveals a high degree of interconnection between these items, suggesting a one-dimensional solution (see also Chapter 2, this volume). These results clearly indicate that various forms of confidence are closely related. A more detailed analysis, in which we relaxed the non-correlation restriction between factors, reveals, however, a more differentiated pattern that reflects the above threefold distinction of forms of confidence (see Table 3.1). One dimension pertains to confidence in the key democratic actors (political parties and politicians), a second dimension represents the institutions of representative democracies (parliament and cabinet), and a third pertains to the institutions of the *Rechtsstaat*.

　The results of the country-by-country dimensional analyses present a very similar structure. Consequently we have decided to only display the results of the aggregate analysis. Correlations among the factors are high, especially

Table 3.1 Principal component analysis of political confidence[a]

Confidence in	Factors		
	1	2	3
Parties	**0.83**	−0.13	−0.07
Politicians	**0.88**	0.06	–
Cabinet	0.00	**−0.79**	0.02
Parliament	0.08	**−0.80**	0.05
Courts	−0.04	−0.11	**0.79**
Civil service	0.10	−0.16	**0.60**
Police	0.02	0.08	**0.83**

Note

a Principal axis analysis based on pooled data with the number of factors preset to three (pattern matrix after oblimin rotation). The presentation order of the factors follows the presentation order in the text and does not correspond to the size of the eigenvalues of the factors.

between the institutions and actors of the political regime. In fact, in the Netherlands, Portugal, Sweden, and West Germany, these two dimensions remain together; and in Russia and Slovenia, confidence in political parties presents loadings on both of these factors. The country-by-country pattern matrix for the institutions of the *Rechtsstaat* is more stable. This observation, together with the lower correlation of this factor with the two other factors, indicates the distinctiveness of this third dimension of political confidence.

Based on a combination of theoretical arguments and empirical evidence, we therefore maintain our distinction between the three objects of political confidence and have accordingly created three indices: confidence in actors (political parties and politicians); confidence in democratic institutions (parliament and cabinet); and confidence in institutions of the *Rechtsstaat* (courts, civil service, and police). We have created an index for each dimension with the average confidence per set of relevant items on a scale with a theoretical range of zero to one.

Comparative levels of political confidence

The comparative levels of the three dimensions of political confidence allow for a number of preliminary conclusions (see Table 3.2). First it seems clear that confidence in the institutions of the *Rechtsstaat* is higher than confidence in democratic institutions, in all countries with the exception of Russia and Moldova (very low in both cases). Moreover, for all countries, the degree of confidence in democratic actors is lower than the two other forms of confidence. Citizens of all democracies tend to have least confidence in political parties and politicians, whereas the confidence in the institutions of the *Rechtsstaat* is highest in all but two of our countries.

Second, with regard to the comparative levels of confidence across

Table 3.2 Average political confidence scores by country[a]

Country	Confidence in actors of representative party-democracy	Confidence in institutions of representative party-democracy	Confidence in institutions of the Rechtsstaat
The Netherlands	0.55 (0.16)	0.58 (0.16)	0.63 (0.15)
West Germany	0.48 (0.19)	0.58 (0.19)	0.68 (0.17)
Denmark	0.50 (0.19)	0.54 (0.21)	0.69 (0.16)
Sweden	0.46 (0.19)	0.55 (0.22)	0.64 (0.18)
Switzerland	0.41 (0.21)	0.56 (0.22)	0.62 (0.2)
Norway	0.40 (0.19)	0.51 (0.21)	0.61 (0.19)
East Germany	0.40 (0.21)	0.50 (0.23)	0.62 (0.19)
Slovenia	0.38 (0.24)	0.48 (0.24)	0.55 (0.23)
Portugal	0.32 (0.21)	0.46 (0.21)	0.52 (0.20)
Spain	0.35 (0.22)	0.45 (0.22)	0.49 (0.19)
Romania	0.33 (0.27)	0.43 (0.29)	0.48 (0.27)
Moldova	0.28 (0.24)	0.35 (0.26)	0.35 (0.25)
Russia	0.25 (0.22)	0.36 (0.25)	0.34 (0.26)
Average for established democracies (above dashed line)	0.47	0.55	0.64
Average for new democracies (below dashed line)	0.28	0.43	0.47
Average for all countries	0.38	0.48	0.55

Note

a Countries are ordered by the average score for all three types of political confidence. Figures in parentheses are standard deviations.

countries, it is evident that confidence is highest in the established democracies (the Netherlands, West Germany, Denmark, Sweden, Switzerland, and Norway) and lower in the so-called 'new democracies' (East Germany, Slovenia, Portugal, Spain, Romania, Moldova, and Russia). Among the 'new democracies' only East Germany reveals levels of confidence that are somewhat similar to those observed in the established democracies. The average confidence in the new democratic institutions is 0.43, while this average reaches 0.55 for the traditional democracies. The difference is also significant for confidence in politicians and political parties; in new democracies the level of confidence is only 0.28, whereas in the old democracies it equals 0.47. Notably, the differences in the confidence in the institutions of the *Rechtsstaat* between the two groups of countries are not as clear as expected. In fact, if we ignore the scores for Moldova and Russia, the confidence-levels are quite similar to those observed in long-established democracies (0.63 and 0.64, respectively).

Third, the levels of the public's political confidence in Russia and Moldova, two former communist countries, are substantially lower than in all other countries. Apart from this there are no clear differences between former communist and non-communist countries. Romania displays similar confidence levels to Spain and Portugal, and Slovenia has even slightly higher confidence levels than the southern European democracies. Finally, the ranking of countries according to the levels of confidence is practically the same for the three dimensions of confidence.[7]

Explaining political confidence

A number of different hypotheses have been used to explain political confidence. Following our previous distinction, we divide these into two main groups: socio-cultural and political explanations. We will now enter a more detailed discussion of each of these two approaches.

Socio-cultural explanations

Socio-cultural explanations have focused on the importance of political socialisation from early childhood through to people's inclusion in social networks, particularly in family and among peers (Almond and Verba 1963; Easton and Dennis 1969). Putnam (1993 and 2000) and other advocates of the *social capital* approach are considered to be prominent contemporary representatives of such an explanation. In our subsequent discussion we will begin with an explanation of this line of argumentation. An important alternative social explanation is provided by the theory of *individual modernisation and value change* (e.g. Inglehart 1977; Klingemann and Fuchs 1995: 17–22). In the next sub-sections we will discuss these two alternative socio-cultural explanations.[8]

The social capital model

The social capital model is based on the idea that political confidence is a reflection of social trust. The most important current exponent of this approach is Robert Putnam (1993, 2000), although other scholars have also contributed to an explicit formulation of the various linkages between social engagement and social trust, with citizens' political beliefs (Newton 1999b; Norris 1999a).[9] For Norris and Newton, the gist of the social capital argument implies that patterns of social interaction are not only related to citizens' trust in each other,[10] but also to citizens' political confidence (Newton 1999b: 17; Norris 1999b: 21–2). In Newton's (1999a: 179) words, political confidence and social trust are considered to be 'different sides of the same coin'. From this perspective, *political* confidence is at least to some extent a by-product of *social* trust and exogenous to the political system (cf. Mishler and Rose 2001b: 31).[11]

But Putnam's concept of social capital not only includes social trust; it also refers to people's integration in social networks. In order to determine the impacts of social capital on various forms of political confidence, we will have to investigate the effects of people's participation in these networks. On this basis we will be able to establish the roles that either of these components of social capital may play in an explanation of political confidence and the relative impact of these variables on political confidence.[12] These general formulations, however, need to be specified since *the type of involvement* in organisations varies. Voluntary associations offer a large number of different roles to people interested in social activity. Various types of involvement can be distinguished – ranging from mere membership to participation in activities and the development of personal friendship ties[13] (see Chapters 6 and 7) – and these may have different effects on citizens' confidence in institutions. Associational involvement, however, may not be the most important factor (Newton 1999b). Participation in working life, for example, may be as, or even more, important than associational involvement. Therefore, we will also examine the effects of employment.

Individual modernisation and value change

An alternative explanation that focuses on social developments and socialisation is related to theories of individual modernisation and value change (Inglehart 1977; Kaase and Marsh 1979: 37–41; Dalton 1988: 241–2; Klingemann and Fuchs 1995: 17–22; Kaase and Newton 1995: 40–9). Individual modernisation (Fuchs and Klingemann 1995: 12) refers to changes in both the personal skills of citizens and to changes in people's value orientations: more specifically, the rise of post-materialist value orientations (Inglehart 1977). These changes in skills and value orientations are thought to have some important consequences.[14] They may result in a process of citizens' 'cognitive mobilisation' that generates demands regarding new issues (e.g. environmental protection, peace, integration of minorities) as well as participatory demands. Furthermore, value change leads to the adoption of new standards in the evaluation of political objects. Politicians are no longer evaluated on the basis of their contribution to economic prosperity, security, and other material goals, but according to whether or not they act responsively regarding the 'new demands'. A failure to meet the demands of a more exacting public is likely to result in a decline in political confidence (Inglehart 1979 and 1990; Fuchs and Klingemann 1995: 17, hypotheses 7, 8, and 9).

One of the implications of individual modernisation is that citizens will assume a more active role in the political system, and will become more mature and less deferent towards traditional hierarchical authorities. This process is expected to be especially damaging for some institutions of the *Rechtsstaat*. Inglehart (1999: 243–5) hypothesises that such effects are likely to be especially pronounced among well-educated people and among representatives of the younger generations. Therefore, we will take respondents' education and age into consideration. Since the modernisation and value change approach also emphasises the role of social factors and citizens' political socialisation (development of new value orientations), we have subsumed this approach under the 'socio-cultural' explanations.

Political explanations: micro-politics

Recent theoretical developments and empirical research indicate that the origins of change and distinctive cross-national levels of political confidence may not be as apolitical as social explanations of political confidence imply. A number of different political explanations have been proposed (Norris 1999a). Some of these are micro-political, and focus on citizens' political experiences. Others are macro-political, and focus on the nature of the institutional context. In this section we will discuss some of the theoretical arguments underlying such micro-political approaches. This does not, however, imply that we will totally ignore possible institutional explanations. In the second half of this chapter we will also explore the potential for macro-level, institutional explanations.

Micro-political approaches focus on the political orientations of citizens. These approaches are all based on the presumption that political confidence is not primarily a product of social forces and socialisation in early life, but the result of contemporary political experiences and a person's current political orientations (Denters 2002: 809). Building on earlier work (Crozier *et al.* 1975; King 1975), the current literature has reconsidered the importance of various aspects of citizens' actual political orientations (Fiorina 1999; Norris 1999a; Pharr and Putnam 2000):

1   Evaluations of governmental performance;
2   Evaluations of political responsiveness;
3   Representation of one's preferred party in government and voter's ideology;
4   Impact of television.

EVALUATIONS OF GOVERNMENTAL PERFORMANCE

According to Miller's (1974b) classic study, citizens' lack of confidence in the institutions of government may be the result of extended periods of frustrated expectations, resulting from inadequate institutional performance. In this view, low levels of political confidence are not so much related to the government's objective achievements, as to the gap between actual performance and citizens' expectations (e.g. Miller and Listhaug 1999: 212–16). This generates a widespread feeling that the government fails to respond to public needs and expectations.[15] In our empirical analysis we will consider the impact of people's overall satisfaction with the way in which the democratic system is functioning in their country.[16] We expect that the more satisfied people are with the workings of the democratic system, the more politically confident they will tend to be.

EVALUATIONS OF POLITICAL RESPONSIVENESS

In a representative democracy, the perceived responsiveness of political officeholders may be a crucial determinant of citizens' political confidence, especially for their confidence in the democratic actors and institutions (Lipset and Schneider 1983). Notably, responsiveness is considered by many as a defining characteristic of democracy (e.g. Pitkin 1967). There is some debate whether perceived responsiveness reflects recent experiences with current institutions or whether it is the result of political socialisation. There is at least some evidence (e.g. Denters and Geurts 1998), however, that suggests that perceptions of responsiveness are not primarily sediments of political socialisation in early life, but are based on recent political experiences.[17]

REPRESENTATION OF ONE'S PREFERRED PARTY IN GOVERNMENT AND VOTER'S IDEOLOGY

Two important clusters of political factors affecting political confidence pertain to the representation of one's preferred party in government, and citizens' ideological preferences. With regard to the former, Holmberg (1999: 117–18) formulated the *home-team* hypothesis;[18] suggesting that political trust 'goes up among people who's preferred party is in the Cabinet and goes down among people whose party is out of the ruling circle'. Although Holmberg does not find evidence in support of this hypothesis, other studies have typically produced corroborative evidence. This is not only the case for studies focusing on confidence in political officeholders (e.g. Craig 1993: 37–8), but also for studies of confidence in political institutions (e.g. Norris 1999c: 232).[19] In addition to this, citizens' ideological (left–right) orientation may provide further political clues for their attitudes towards the current government and governmental policies, as well as subsequent assessments of the trustworthiness of political actors and institutions (Newton and Norris 2000: 65).

IMPACT OF TELEVISION

Finally, several scholars blamed the erosion of political confidence on the extensive coverage and notoriety of political scandals in the mass media, which influenced public opinion and caused increasing detachment from the institutions, and politics in general (Robinson 1976; Lipset and Scheider 1983; Wattenberg 1986; Dogan 1997). In her review of the so-called 'videomalaise' literature, Norris (2000) suggests that there may be direct effects of television exposure on political support. As she (2000: 238) summarises the argument underpinning the direct effect:

> Television coverage of politics is thought to encourage viewers to become cynical and disenchanted with their institutions of government because its focus on exposing government scandals and corruption, revealing insider strategies, and dramatizing political conflict.[20]

Political confidence: assessing the impact of two models

We will now analyse the effects of the various categories of explanatory variables on political confidence. Even though the level of confidence varies for the three forms of confidence, the explanations for these three manifestations proved to be rather similar. Our main conclusions do not differ from one form of political confidence to the other. Therefore, we have decided to only present the results for one aspect of political confidence, i.e. confidence in political institutions (parliament and cabinet).[21]

A first major conclusion that can be drawn from Table 3.3 is that both the socio-cultural explanation and the political explanation of political confidence are valid. Therefore, the two approaches should not be perceived as rival but as complementary (cf. Mishler and Rose 2001b). Even so, we can conclude that, despite the relevance of the socio-cultural variables, the explanatory power of the political approach is somewhat higher.

Among the socio-cultural factors, social trust is clearly and consistently the most powerful factor in explaining political confidence. Social trust has a statistically significant effect on political confidence, irrespective of the form of political confidence for all of our countries, with the exception of Portugal. This result is in line with other findings in this volume (see Chapter 2), that indicate the relevance of social trust in explaining political or institutional confidence, even after controls for other relevant variables.[22] However, it is also evident that the effects of other aspects of social capital (as measured by various forms of associational involvement) are not systematically related to political confidence. If there is an impact

Table 3.3 Socio-cultural and micro-political explanatory variables for confidence in institutions of representative party-democracy (OLS estimates)[a]

Type of explanation and predictor	NL	WG	DK	SE	CH	NO	EG	SI	PT	ES[b]	RO	RU[b]	MD[c]
Socio-cultural explanations													
Social capital													
Social trust	0.15***	0.17***	0.17***	0.08**	0.12***	0.18***	0.10***	0.11**	0.06	0.10***	0.17***	0.17***	0.11*
Membership in organisations	−0.01	−0.02	0.02	−0.01	−0.01	−0.00	0.00	0.03	0.01	0.02	−0.10	−0.04	0.06
Friends in organisations	−0.19**	0.06	0.12	0.26***	0.07	−0.06	0.10	−0.01	0.14*	0.21	0.93	−0.08	−1.55
Active in organisations	0.02	0.01	0.01	−0.01	0.01	0.03	0.02	−0.03	−0.02	−0.04*	0.13	0.01	0.04
Gainfully employed	0.00	−0.02	−0.02	−0.02	−0.02	−0.00	0.03*	0.02	−0.02	−0.01	0.00	−0.04**	0.02
Modernisation and value change													
Materialism	−0.00	0.15***	0.04	0.04	0.16***	−0.02	0.16**	0.27**	0.02	–	0.15	–	0.07
Post-materialism	0.15***	−0.06	0.10***	0.08**	−0.01	−0.10**	−0.05	−0.10	0.07	–	0.04	–	0.03
Age	0.01	−0.05	0.11***	0.03	0.13**	0.00	0.02	−0.21***	−0.09	−0.02	−0.09	−0.17**	−0.24***
Education	0.05*	0.04	0.10***	−0.04	0.17***	0.06*	−0.23***	0.10	0.07	−0.07***	−0.04	−0.09	−0.00

Micro-political explanations

Satisfaction with democracy	0.20***	0.21***	0.30***	0.34***	0.27***	0.32***	0.37***	0.28***	0.26***	0.22***	0.30***	0.21***	0.28***
Perceived responsiveness	0.21***	0.22***	0.20***	0.29***	0.27***	0.30***	0.15***	0.27***	0.10**	0.25***	0.27***	0.29***	0.16***
Preferred party in cabinet	0.02**	0.04***	0.07***	0.07***	0.02	0.06***	0.04**	0.09***	0.07***	0.09***	0.17***	0.03*	0.09***
Ideology	−0.14	−0.01	−0.05**	−0.04	−0.04	−0.03	0.05	0.03	−0.02	0.17***	0.02	0.00	0.06
TV exposure	0.02	0.15	0.02	0.04	0.20	−0.12**	0.11	0.08	0.23*	0.01	0.21*	0.03	0.72***
Constant	0.12***	0.20***	−0.10*	0.09	−0.04	0.02	0.15*	0.07	0.20**	0.18***	0.02	0.32***	0.07
R^2	0.28	0.26	0.35	0.38	0.30	0.38	0.33	0.30	0.22	0.29	0.39	0.22	0.19

Notes

a Countries are ordered by the average level of political confidence (see Table 3.2). Levels of statistical significance: *** = 0.001, ** = 0.05, * = 0.1.

b Some factors are not included because data were not available in the country dataset.

c In Romania and Moldova, there is serious multicollinearity with regard to the three different aspects of organisational involvement we distinguish. The VIF values for 'membership in organisations' are 6.14 for Romania and 7.23 for Moldavia while those for 'active in organizations' are 6.96 and 10.0 respectively. To investigate the impact of this multicollinearity problem, we removed one of the three variables at fault ('active in organisations'). This led to a substantial reduction of the VIF values (to values just above 1.0) but left the parameter estimates virtually unchanged for all predictors outside the sphere of organisational involvement. Hence, the main conclusions remain valid in spite of the multicollinearity problem.

of these structural components of social capital, it is an indirect effect that runs through social trust (or other factors).[23]

In addition to the relevance of social trust, the results also testify to the relevance of materialist and post-materialist value orientations. The exceptions are Portugal, Romania, and Moldova. We should, however, be aware that the effects of these value orientations are neither as strongly nor as consistently related to the various forms of political confidence across our selection of countries as social trust.

Irrespective of the importance and consistency of some of the socio-cultural variables, these factors are by no means the best predictors of political confidence. The results consistently show how important *micro-political variables* are for our understanding of political confidence. Citizens' assessments of democratic performance and institutional responsiveness are the best predictors of political confidence. Despite a much lower general impact, the cabinet representation of one's preferred party (the home-team hypothesis) is also significant for all countries apart from Switzerland. Citizens' ideological orientation is only modestly relevant.[24]

Finally, our results are by no means confirmative of the *videomalaise argument*. In this respect, we think that Norris (2000: 239) is correct when she concludes that 'watching television is not consistently associated with indicators of political confidence, undermining the contention that broadcasting is to blame for the decline in confidence.'

Differences in levels of confidence

The first major conclusion we drew in the previous section was that the explanations for all three aspects of political confidence were rather similar. However, in our descriptive analyses we also found (see Table 3.2 above) considerable differences in the levels of confidence in the political actors, the democratic institutions, and the confidence in the institutions of the *Rechtsstaat*. What causes these differences in levels of confidence? To answer this question we created two new dependent variables. For each individual respondent we computed two difference scores: one pertaining to the difference between someone's confidence in political institutions and one's confidence in parties and politicians; the other pertaining to the difference between confidence in the institutions of the *Rechtsstaat* and in the political institutions tout court (cabinet and parliament). Our expectation is that the variations in the confidence levels are likely to have distinctly political origins. In other words, we expect that the previously discussed micro-political factors are the major *explanans* for these differences in support levels. This expectation is based on the observation that conceptually representative institutions (i.e. the parliament or the cabinet) relate to formal structures and not to specific officeholders or incumbents. This is more predominantly the case for the institutions of the *Rechtsstaat* (i.e. the courts, the police, and the army). However, political actors are most closely related to the specific officeholders. We can therefore expect especially political factors that relate to citizens' evaluations of government and the presence of one's preferred party in government to explain the differences in the confidence levels.

To test this expectation we regressed the two new dependent variables on the same factors as we have used previously. Table 3.4 presents the results for one of these two variables, the difference score between confidence in the institutions of the *Rechtsstaat* and the institutions of representative democracy.[25] These results reveal two patterns: first, they show that the differences in the confidence scores are, to a large extent, due to the impact of the political variables, especially satisfaction with democratic performance and representation of one's preferred party in government. The results also indicate that there is no consistent systematic effect for any of the social-capital factors. These findings were essentially reproduced in the analysis of the other dependent variable (difference in confidence between political institutions and actors), and provide corroboration for our theoretical assumptions.

Second, the table shows that the difference in levels of confidence (between the institutions of the *Rechtsstaat* and the political institutions) is partly the result of citizens' value orientations. In six of the 11 countries for which we have information about citizens' value orientations, we found a significant effect of one or both of the value factors (materialism or post-materialism). In five of these six cases, this was in the expected direction: endorsement of materialist values has a positive effect on confidence in traditional, hierarchical institutions. This effect is not reproduced for the other dependent variable.[26]

Therefore, taking aside the effect of value orientations from the relatively high level of support for institutions of the *Rechtsstaat*, the micro-political variables are the major explanatory factor for the differences in levels of confidence in different political objects. Neither social trust nor associational involvement has a consistent effect on such differences.

Cross-national variations: the potential role of macro-political variables

Whereas the previous political explanations focused on citizens' subjective orientations towards the political world, macro-political explanations may help us to explain cross-national variations in political confidence. These macro-political explanations concentrate on 'objective' characteristics of the political world. We may thus refer to these approaches as either contextual or macro-political. There are several factors that may be used in such macro-political explanations. For example, McAllister (1999) used indicators for the *actual* economic performance of governments in explaining variations in political confidence. Many other scholars have focused on institutional explanations (Weil 1989; Miller and Listhaug

Table 3.4 Socio-cultural and micro-political explanatory factors for the difference between confidence in institutions of the *Rechtsstaat* and confidence in institutions of representative party-democracy (OLS estimates)[a]

Type of explanation and predictor	NL	WG	DK	SE	CH	NO	EG	SI	PT	ES[b]	RO[c]	RU[b]	MD[c]
Socio-cultural explanations													
Social capital													
Social trust	0.05	−0.10	0.00	0.08**	0.07*	0.03	−0.03	0.06	−0.01	0.02	0.11**	−0.02	0.02
Membership in organisations	0.02	−0.01	0.01	0.01	−0.02	0.01	−0.02	0.04	0.03	0.01	0.03	0.01	−0.08
Friends in organisations	0.01	−0.01	−0.02	−0.10	−0.03	0.03	0.01	0.05	0.02	−0.20*	−0.35	0.29	1.46*
Active in organisations	0.01	0.02	−0.01	−0.01	0.04	0.01	−0.01	−0.07*	0.02	0.03	−0.05	−0.01	0.09
Gainfully employed	−0.01	0.01	0.03***	0.00	0.03	0.00	0.01	0.00	−0.01	−0.01	−0.00	0.03*	0.00
Modernisation and value change													
Materialism	0.12***	−0.08**	0.13***	0.07	0.08	0.16***	0.07	0.03	0.22**	—	−0.01	—	−0.02
Post-materialism	−0.08*	0.13***	−0.10***	−0.07	−0.10*	−0.03	0.08	0.09	−0.21***	—	0.07	—	0.01
Age	0.08*	0.01	−0.07*	−0.02	−0.04	0.02	−0.01	0.20***	0.07	0.05**	0.12	0.20***	0.32***
Education	0.01	−0.09***	−0.07**	0.02	−0.02	−0.03	−0.00	−0.05	−0.01	0.04**	−0.03	−0.08	−0.06

Micro-political explanations

Variable														
Satisfaction with democracy	−0.05**	0.01	−0.10***	−0.09***	−0.14***	−0.07***	−0.13***	−0.11***	−0.04	−0.05***	−0.07	0.04	0.07	
Perceived responsiveness	−0.04*	−0.15***	−0.10***	−0.12***	−0.16***	−0.14***	−0.13***	−0.13***	−0.02	−0.08*	−0.06***	−0.05	−0.01	0.04
Preferred party in cabinet	−0.02**	−0.03***	−0.05***	−0.08***	−0.00	−0.04***	−0.05***	−0.03	−0.09***	−0.06***	−0.10***	−0.04**	−0.07***	
Ideology	0.02	0.03	0.05**	0.01	0.08**	0.05***	−0.04	0.13***	0.04	−0.08***	0.06	0.08**	−0.00	
TV exposure	0.00	0.03	−0.01	−0.21*	0.09	0.08	−0.07	0.11	0.07	0.01	−0.01	−0.06	−0.26***	
Constant	−0.02	0.18	0.27***	0.19***	0.12	0.01	0.15**	−0.17*	0.01	0.07***	−0.06	−0.13***	−0.11	
R^2	0.03	0.09	0.12	0.11	0.10	0.10	0.13	0.11	0.10	0.08	0.10	0.06	0.14	

Notes

a The dependent variable is confidence in institutions of the *Rechtsstaat* minus confidence in institutions of representative party-democracy. Countries are ordered by the average level of political confidence (see Table 3.2). Levels of statistical significance: *** = 0.001, ** = 0.05, * = 0.1.

b Some factors are not included because data were not available in the country dataset.

c In Romania and Moldova, there is multicollinearity with regard to aspects of associational involvement ('Friends', 'Active involvement', and 'Membership'), resulting in coefficients close to or even over 1.00. The main conclusions of the Chapter, however, in no way depend of the biased estimations for the effects of these factors.

1990; Listhaug and Wiberg 1995; Morlino and Tarchi 1996; Anderson and Guillory 1997; Magalhães 2006). A variety of political-institutional factors have been identified as potentially relevant. Norris (1999c: 232), for example, has focused on the degree of liberty and political freedom, the party system, and, to a lesser degree, on decentralisation of the state and parliamentarism/presidentialism.

Although such macro-political explanations are often persuasive, an empirical assessment of their validity is hampered by the limited number of countries in our analysis. This implies that we are confronted with a situation of many potentially interesting institutional variables and a small N. Despite the restriction, we carried out an exploratory analysis aimed at gauging the potential of a macro-political explanation of political confidence. We started this exploration with a two-stage analysis of the additional explanatory power that country-level variables can have when we take all relevant non-political and political variables at the individual level into account. In the first stage we analysed a micro-level model including all relevant non-political individual level variables alongside a set of country-dummy variables (results not shown). This analysis suggests that country-dummy variables are significant and relatively strong predictors of various forms of political confidence. In the second stage we included the two most important micro-political factors (satisfaction with democratic performance and perceived responsiveness): the impact of the country-dummy variables on political confidence was substantially reduced. This attenuation was especially pronounced for the confidence in the actors and institutions of representative party-democracy. For the third dependent variable (confidence in institutions of the *Rechtsstaat*), a substantial impact of country dummies remain for Portugal, Spain, Moldova, and Russia. The initial results indicate that micro-political variables are capable of explaining much of the cross-national differences in levels of political confidence, particularly for citizens' confidence in political actors and democratic institutions. In other words, there is very little room for pure macro-level explanations, regardless of the nature of such macro-level accounts (e.g. institutional, economic, or cultural) of cross-country variations in political confidence.[27]

Of course, this still leaves the possibility that the effect of some of the micro-political variables, for example perceived responsiveness on political confidence, varies for different countries. In order to establish such an effect, we should inspect the significance of the effect of interaction terms that model the joint effect of the country-dummy variable and the relevant micro-political variable. In principle, such interactions could occur with any of the previously discussed individual level factors. Here we concentrate on two potential interactions: a macro-factor with the perceived institutional responsiveness and a macro-factor with citizens' satisfaction with democratic performance. Rather than introducing country dummies (which would lead to a jumble of interaction terms), we classified countries according to an aspect of their national political culture – i.e. their level of political confidence. On the basis of this criterion we distinguished three groups: high-confidence (Denmark, the Netherlands, Sweden, Switzerland, and West Germany); medium-confidence (Norway, East Germany, and Slovenia); and low-confidence systems (Spain, Portugal, Romania, Moldova, and Russia). In the first stage of our analysis we have entered the significant non-political micro-level factors alongside the macro-political factor (see Table 3.5).[28] The results indicate that the two dummies are significant, despite the loss of country-specific information due to the clustering of countries into three groups. In the second stage of this interaction analysis, we added the individual political variables, as well as the interactions of these variables with the dummies.[29] As can be seen in Table 3.5, the introduction of the micro-political factors, and the interaction terms at the second stage of the analysis, results in an important reduction of the impact of the country-grouped dummy variables. This effect occurs for both democratic actors and institutions and, as might have been expected to a lesser extent, for the confidence in the institutions of the *Rechtsstaat*.

The results also indicate that, for two of the confidence variables, we find a statistically significant interaction effect for both sets of interaction terms. For confidence in political actors and confidence in the institutions of the *Rechtsstaat*, we observe that the relation of micro-political factors to political confidence is stronger (significant and positive) in countries with lowest levels of confidence. In the case of confidence in representative institutions, we only find a statistically significant interaction for satisfaction with democracy and medium levels of confidence.

Of course, we do not know whether it is actually the level of national political confidence or an associated factor that accounts for such interaction effects. On the basis of previous research there is a whole range of institutional (see Fuchs *et al.* 1995; Anderson and Guillory 1997), cultural, and political-historical factors (Torcal 2003, 2006) that might account for such a macro-level effect.[30]

Conclusions

In this chapter we have looked into the usefulness of the socio-cultural and the political approaches for our understanding of various forms of political confidence. Our analyses have shown that, with regard to individual variations, both these models contribute to our understanding. Among the socio-cultural variables, social trust is a consistent and quantitatively important factor to explain people's confidence, confirming similar findings in Chapter 2 of this volume. As already discussed, this finding is not in line with previous research.[31] Other aspects of social capital (associational participation and social connectedness) do not have a direct effect on political confidence. In addition to the relevance of

Table 3.5 Multilevel analysis of political confidence with interactions (OLS estimates)[a]

Predictor	Actors of representative party-democracy		Institutions of representative party-democracy		Institutions of the Rechtsstaat	
	Stage 1	Stage 2	Stage 1	Stage 2	Stage 1	Stage 2
Social trust	0.25***	0.19***	0.25***	0.11***	0.23***	0.13***
Age	−0.04***	−0.06***	−0.05***	−0.08***	0.01	−0.01
Education	0.01	−0.03**	0.00	−0.02**	−0.04***	−0.04***
Cabinet representation of own party	0.01***	0.01***	0.07***	0.07***	0.01***	0.01*
Ideology	−0.01	−0.02**	0.01	−0.00	0.04***	0.03***
High confidence countries	R	R	R	R	R	R
Medium confidence countries	−0.08***	−0.02	−0.04***	−0.02	−0.04***	−0.02
Low confidence countries	−0.11***	−0.09**	−0.08***	−0.00	−0.17***	−0.17***
Perceived responsiveness	—	0.32***	—	0.24***	—	0.12***
Satisfaction w. democratic performance	—	0.20***	—	0.27***	—	0.21***
Responsiveness × High confidence	—	R	—	R	—	R
Responsiveness × Medium confidence	—	−0.02	—	0.03	—	0.00
Responsiveness × Low confidence	—	0.03*	—	0.02	—	0.10***
Satisfaction × High confidence	—	R	—	R	—	R
Satisfaction × Medium confidence	—	−0.01	—	0.05*	—	0.02
Satisfaction × Low confidence	—	0.03*	—	−0.01	—	0.06***
Constant	0.36***	0.20***	0.41***	0.24***	0.51***	0.40***
R^2	0.16	0.33	0.15	0.32	0.24	0.36
N	11,363	10,955	11,380	10,970	11,392	10,985

Note

a Levels of statistical significance: *** = 0.001, ** = 0.05, * = 0.1. Empty cells indicate that a variable was not included in the first stage of the analysis; R indicates the reference category for a set of dummy variables.

social trust, the results also testify to the relevance of materialist and post-materialist value orientations. However, we should be aware that the effect of such value orientations is not nearly as important as people's social trust.

In addition to these socio-cultural variables, our results indicate that an explanation of political confidence is not complete unless we consider the effect of micro-political factors. The most important of these factors are citizens' satisfaction with democratic performance, their perception of the responsiveness of politicians, and whether their preferred party is represented in government. These findings suggest that, for a better understanding of political confidence, we need both socio-cultural and micro-political factors. The two models should therefore not be considered as rival explanations: both can be combined into one integrated theory of political confidence. This by no means implies that both sets of explanatory variables are also equally important. Our results clearly show that the explanatory power of political factors exceeds the importance of the socio-cultural variables. This is true for the analyses of individual level variations in political confidence. The micro-political factors, however, allow us to explain differences in the levels of confidence for various forms of political confidence and contribute to our understanding of cross-national variations in levels of political confidence. Moreover, these factors are also capable of explaining much of the cross-national differences in levels of political confidence, especially for citizens' confidence in the actors and the institutions of representative party-democracies. Finally, some exploratory analyses have shown that it may sometimes be worthwhile to include macro-political factors in an analysis of political confidence. Before embarking on further research into such micro-macro links, it is probably useful to develop more sophisticated theories about the micro-macro linkages. Because of the dozens of suggested macro-factors and the innumerable potential interaction effects, renewed theoretical reflection will have to prevent such macro-orientated research degenerating into an endless data-fishing exercise.

Notes

1 Almond and Verba (1963) and others (e.g. Nie *et al.* 1996) have also stressed the importance of education.
2 In line with Zmerli *et al.* (Chapter 2, this volume), we avoid the use of the term *trust* when linked to institutions; see also Luhmann (1988a: 102) and Hardin (2002: 172).
3 For example, Norris (1999b), in her fivefold classification of support (building on Easton 1975), has distinguished between confidence in regime institutions and confidence in political actors. From this it is also evident that political confidence is an important component of political support.
4 A rather similar distinction has been suggested on the basis of the results of principal component analyses conducted on data from the World Values Study (Döring 1992; Torcal 2002).

5 We have asked people to 'tell how strongly you personally trust each of these institutions' (0 indicates no trust at all; 10 indicates very strong trust). This measurement is not based on assumptions about particular considerations that people may use when making assessments about the trustworthiness of these institutions (Levi and Stoker 2000: 498).
6 Conceptually the similarity between the institutions of the *Rechtsstaat* is their involvement in law-enforcement. From this perspective the civil service (as a 'Weberian' bureaucracy) may also be conceived of as an institution of the *Rechtsstaat*.
7 The rank-order correlation for the three dimensions are in the range between 0.87 and 0.96.
8 This modernisation approach also addresses the role of schools and education as another important social institution in addition to voluntary associations.
9 The following theoretical argument therefore cannot be seen as a literal translation of the models outlined by any of these authors. Moreover, although scholars like Norris and Newton have tried to contribute to the development of the social capital approach into a coherent model, we should not necessarily consider these authors as advocates of the social capital approach.
10 The direction of causality is not immediately evident here. Putnam (1995b: 666) claims that 'causation flows mainly from joining to trusting'. And Newton (1999b: 16–17) has argued that causality may be the other way around.
11 For the moment we hypothesise that this will be true for all forms of political confidence. In our empirical analyses we will be able to verify this. In these analyses we will employ the social trust index as developed in Chapter 2.
12 Our focus is not on the relationship of involvement to social trust and vice versa; such an analysis is beyond the scope of our chapter.
13 Membership in organisations was scored 1 if the respondent was a member of any organisation and 0 if not. Activity in organisations was scored 1 if the respondent had participated in activities organised by, or done voluntary work for, any organisation during the past 12 months and 0 if not. Friendship ties within organisations was scored 1 if the respondent had personal friends within an organisation in which he or she was involved and 0 if not. See Chapter 6, this volume, for further information on the measurement instruments used in order to capture various types of organisational involvement.
14 In emphasising the importance of skills, this alternative approach also stresses the importance of education in citizens' political socialisation. Ever since Easton and Dennis (1969) the relevance of education has been emphasised.
15 Clarke *et al.* (1993); Muller and Seligson (1994); and Pharr and Putnam (2000: 23). Other empirical studies have found evidence to support this view (e.g. Listhaug 1995; Listhaug and Wiberg 1995; Nye 1997: 8–10; Miller and Listhaug 1999; Newton and Norris 2000; and Denters 2002).
16 According to Torcal (2002) and Linde and Ekman (2003), this is also a good indicator of satisfaction of the incumbent performance and is highly related with party preferences. This was measured by a single question: 'On the whole, are you very satisfied, fairly satisfied, not very satisfied or not at all satisfied with the way democracy works in [name of country]?' This item was subsequently recoded to have a theoretical rage between 0 and 1.
17 The measure is based on two items: 'How many opportunities do ordinary people have to present their opinions to politicians?' And, 'How much weight do politicians attach to opinions presented to them by ordinary people?'. We have created an index representing the respondent's mean position on both items and transformed it as to have a theoretical range between 0 and 1.
18 This proposition has a long history that goes back to the well-known Citrin (1974) and Miller (1974a and 1974b) debate; see also Miller 1979.

19 We have established the composition of the incumbent government in each of the 12 countries at the time of the data-collection and subsequently have used citizens' party-identification to determine whether or not they were supporting an opposition or a governmental party.
20 In this chapter we shall concentrate on the direct effect of this factor, since we are not interested in an explanation of social capital per se. To determine the direct effect we have established citizens' exposure to television, by computing the average number of hours per week watching television on 0 to 1 scale.
21 Although the basic results were rather similar, the effect of having one's preferred party in government is, for obvious reasons, slightly stronger for the reported model than in the models for the two other aspects of political confidence.
22 In Chapter 2, Zmerli *et al.* attribute the lack of relationship between social trust and confidence in institutions (political confidence) detected in preceding studies to measurement error.
23 Since we are not interested in the precise relations between the various components of social capital, we shall not go into any such possible indirect effects.
24 In the light of the literature, this limited impact may be considered as a surprise (Fiorina 1999; Newton and Norris 2000). But there is some evidence that ideology has a largely indirect effect through associated variables like the cabinet representation of one's preferred party and satisfaction with democratic performance (see also Linde and Ekman 2003: 401).
25 For reasons of space we did not include the table with results for the other dependent variable. When appropriate we will discuss some results in the text and the footnotes.
26 With regard to the other dependent variable (results not shown) we find that in the Netherlands, West Germany, Denmark, Switzerland, Norway, and Slovenia, higher-educated respondents have a higher confidence in democratic institutions (when compared to their confidence in the political actors).
27 Once again, for lack of space we have not included the results of these analyses in tabular form.
28 In the regression model we included this factor as a set of dummy variables. We used the high-confidence category as the reference category in the regression model.
29 In the second stage model we left the interaction of the dummies with the countries with highest confidence levels as the reference category.
30 One such a politico-historical factor might be the democratic tradition of a country. The classification of countries in terms of the level of confidence is strongly correlated with this factor. In the high-confidence group all countries are established democracies, whereas Norway is the only country in the medium and low confidence categories that is not a new democracy.
31 We will not dwell on this in order not to duplicate the extensive discussion already undertaken in Chapter 2.

4 Norms of good citizenship

Bas Denters, Oscar Gabriel, and Mariano Torcal

Introduction

Normative political theorists have argued about good citizenship for centuries. From Aristotle to Alexis de Tocqueville and Walter Bagehot, civic virtues such as rationality, moral obligation to pursue the common good, social engagement, and political activism have been interpreted as prerequisites of a good society and a good polity (see, for example, Almond 1980; Walzer 1989). There is, however, still no generally acknowledged, uncontested model of good citizenship, even after centuries of philosophical and academic debates.

In recent years the citizenship debate, previously a purely philosophical and academic issue, has evolved into an important topic of the public discourse. Once representative democracy was established and the basic political and civil rights conquered, citizens began to question their role and their involvement, as well as their capacity to influence and control governments and public policies. The debate on the quality of those democracies and citizenship has begun. This discourse was driven by the process of societal modernisation that has resulted in greater individual autonomy and provided more and more citizens with the intellectual resources to define their place in society and in the democratic system. Moreover, globalisation and transnational migration have added to the diversity of outlooks on socio-political life in modern European societies. At the same time, we hear pleas in the public debate to restore people's responsibility. With the decline of the traditional welfare state, citizens are expected to become more actively involved in resolving their personal problems as well as engaging themselves in the production of goods and services that were previously provided by the authorities. These expectations are based on a conception of citizenship in which people should not only be concerned with their private affairs, but should feel a moral obligation to contribute to the promotion of the common good.

Whether or not contemporary citizens are willing and able to take on such responsibilities is a matter of debate (see, for example, Klages 2000a, 2000b). Social scientists have expressed divergent ideas regarding the potential consequences of modernisation. On the one hand some analysts have emphasised the emancipative effects. Ronald Inglehart, for example, has pointed out that the value change that accompanies modernisation will provide the basis for a new, more participatory, type of social and political order and citizenship. On the other hand, scholars have indicated that people's willingness to accept traditional norms such as compliance, discipline, and thinking of others may be declining in an age of increasing individualisation (for example, Noelle-Neumann 1978). Likewise, Putnam (1995b, 2000) has stated concerns about the disappearance of the 'Civic Generation', and Münkler (1997: 153) has pointed out that, due to the recent social, political, and economic changes, many people fear that 'good citizenship' might become extinct (see also Walzer 1991).

In this chapter, we will examine how mass publics in western and eastern Europe perceive good citizenship. We will start with the assumption that a pluralism of civic norms, entailing a coexistence of different conceptions of good citizenship, is characteristic for modern societies (Sniderman *et al.* 1996). In this contribution we will focus on three notions of citizenship (similarly to Conover and Searing 2002; Rose and Pettersen 2002): a traditional elitist model (core norm, *law-abidingness*); a liberal model (core norm, *deliberation*); and a communitarian model (core norm, *solidarity*). Pluralism of civic norms, however, does not necessarily imply cultural fragmentation. The coexistence of norms may take many different forms. At the individual level, citizens might endorse either a particular 'pure' conception of citizenship (for example, a predominantly communitarian view) or mixture of norms stemming from different conceptions. At the societal level, normative pluralism might imply anything ranging from widespread consensus over a particular pattern of norms (either one of the 'pure' types or a particular mixture) to the prevalence of dissent between advocates of divergent normative conceptions of citizenship. Empirical research of the type we have conducted is expected to show how European mass publics perceive citizenship.

In this chapter we will address two main questions. First, we will look into the consequences of value pluralism. We will start this exploration by examining whether, in the hearts and minds of the members of European mass publics, the various notions of citizenship have been incorporated in a more or less integrated belief system or whether these notions constitute 'pure' – mutually exclusive and competing – philosophies. In the latter case of cultural fragmentation, we should find no or only weak positive correlations between the different individual value orientations and we should be able to classify most individuals as 'believers' in one or another 'pure' belief system. In the second section, we shall deal with such individual level questions. We can, however, also observe such patterns of integration and fragmentation at the aggregate level. In the third section, we will therefore ask similar questions about the attitudinal patterns that are characteristic for each of our nations. On the basis of such analyses we will be able to answer the question as to whether value pluralism results in cultural fragmentation, where at the individual and/or the aggregate level we find evidence of fragmented belief systems.

After these descriptive analyses we will turn to a second question that pertains to one of the main threads in this book: what is the democratic relevance of social involvement and social trust? In the final section of this chapter, we will look into the question as to whether particular civic norms go hand-in-hand with social involvement and social trust.

Concepts and the structure of individual orientations

Concepts

Before we begin our empirical investigation it is necessary to determine the key components of the various concepts of citizenship typical of the western tradition. According to Conover *et al.* (1991: 805; italics added), 'citizenship is a fundamental identity that helps situate the *individual* in *society*'. The status of the citizen is defined in two fundamental relations: the relation between the individual and the other members of his/her society; and the relation between the individual and his/her institutions of government (e.g. Prior *et al.* 1995: 5–6). Notions of citizenship specify the principles according to which these two relations should be conceived in order to realise a good society.

In their *Civic Culture*, Almond and Verba (1963: 337f.) presented a model of citizenship integrating two different and partially contradicting elements of the citizen's relation to the political authorities. In order to meet the requirements of democratic politics, citizens should be politically interested, active, self-conscious, and critical, but at the same time loyal, trusting, and deferential.[1] On the one hand, political authorities need discretion in order to perform their task of making and implementing authoritative decisions in an effective way. On the other hand, the more they are trusted and the more people behave as loyal subjects instead of self-conscious citizens, the higher the risk of abuses of political power by officeholders. Thus, in addition to loyalty, a critical sense and activism are required for effective democratic checks on political power. Clearly, the first segment of the civic role is rooted in a *traditional-elitist view of democracy*. Regarding the critical activist component of citizenship, the literature provides a number of different views.

In a *liberal interpretation* (Kymlicka and Norman 1995: 297–8), general virtues such as law-abidingness and loyalty should go hand-in-hand with critical and deliberative values: that is, political virtues such as the ability to question authority and a willingness to engage in the public discourse.[2] Within liberal theory there is some debate about the normative weight of this component. Whereas Kymlicka and Norman (1995) stress the importance of public engagement and the development of a critical attitude towards the authorities, someone like Walzer (1995: 158–9) presents a different view: 'To live well is not to make political decisions or beautiful objects; it is to make personal choices ... And the market within which the choices are made ... largely dispenses with politics; it requires at most a minimal state'.

Whereas the previous notions of citizenship focus on the relation of individuals with their government, *communitarians* emphasise the importance of members of the community towards one another. Voluntary associations of citizens are perceived as the breeding ground of civic virtues. In his discussion of the communitarian tradition, Putnam (1993: 86–91; Conover and Searing 2002) highlights the importance of orientations like solidarity, community participation, and tolerance. Such principles are reflected in a communitarian notion of *good citizenship*, that specifies norms regarding the *individual and collective actions* perceived as legitimate and the rights and duties of *citizens as 'good members'* of a society, 'entitled to whatever prerogatives and encumbered with whatever responsibilities are attached to membership' (Walzer 1989: 211). The communitarian view stresses the notion of *active participation* in *social life* as the core element of good citizenship (Walzer 1989: 216–18) and *civic virtues* such as solidarity and being socially active for the good of the society (Kymlicka and Norman 1995: 294–7). According to Conover *et al.* (1991: 802), communitarians favour a model of citizens:

> who are not so much *autonomous individuals making private choices*, as *social and political people whose lives are intertwined* ... Such 'communal' citizens share with their neighbours' common traditions and understandings, which form the basis for their public pursuit of a common good ... Communal citizen identities are 'thick' – such citizens not only have the right to participate in public affairs but also are expected to do so actively for the community's sake and for their own ... Individual rights tend to drift to the background where they are regarded as contextually defined. Duties, by contrast, are brought forward because they involve responsibilities that are to be welcomed rather than shunned.

Finally, the *participatory model* emphasises active political participation as the key element of citizenship which 'enlarges the minds of individuals, familiarises them with interests which lie beyond the immediacy of personal circumstance and environment, and encourages them to acknowledge that public concerns are the proper ones to which they should pay attention' (Oldfield 1990: 184; cit. in Kymlicka and Norman 1995: 292–3). According to Kymlicka and Norman, '*civic republicanism*' is a variant of the participatory model, conceiving participation as a value in itself rather than as a means of civic education. The rationale behind this view is that playing an active role in social and political life is morally superior and more rewarding than restricting oneself to the pursuit of private pleasures. Walzer (1995: 155) assesses active participation in a collective setting as the common denominator of a participatory interpretation of citizenship: 'To live well is to be politically active, working with our fellow citizens, collectively determining our common destiny ... for the work itself, in which our highest capacities as rational and moral agents find expression'. The participatory view of citizenship was very popular in the late 1960s and early 1970s (Habermas 1961; Pateman 1970), but is still endorsed by theorists like Barber (1984) and Mansbridge (1980).

This short review of the most prominent notions of good citizenship reveals several things. First, civic virtues consist of rather abstract principles which cannot be easily operationalised for the purpose of empirical analyses. Second, when it comes to specific political norms or virtues, we cannot overlook a considerable overlap among competing conceptions of good citizenship. Law-abidingness, for example, is shared by traditional elitists, liberals, and communitarians; and solidarity is common to the advocates of the participatory model and communitarians.

The norms of good citizenship: structures of citizen views

Only recently have there been attempts to link normative theories of good society and good citizenship to empirical research (for example, Staub 1989; Conover *et al.* 1991; Nie *et al.* 1996; Gabriel *et al.* 2002: 68–96; Rose and Pettersen 2002). The CID surveys contain a set of items tapping various components of civic orientations, thus enabling an empirical study of the ideas of good citizenship prevailing in various European countries. These items were a sub-set of a broader battery of 16 items of a Swedish survey in which four sub-dimensions of citizenship were identified (Petersson *et al.* 1998).[3] On the basis of our limited sub-set of items we were not able to replicate the exact results obtained in the Swedish study. Therefore, we had to focus on only three of the four sub-dimensions: law-abidingness, critical and deliberative principles, and solidarity.

With regard to our theoretical discussion in the previous section, we would expect to find three distinct but related dimensions of citizenship rights and duties. In order to examine whether or not this theoretical distinction would be empirically valid in the countries in our sample, we conducted an exploratory principal component analysis of six items that, according to the criterion of face validity, could be considered as representations of good citizenship.[4] Theoretically, we would expect to find either a coherent one-dimensional 'syndrome' of good citizenship or, alternatively, several distinct, but interrelated, sub-dimensions referring to the key norms of solidarity, critical and deliberative principles, and law-abidingness (Kymlicka and Norman 1995: 294–6; Rose and Pettersen 2002).

First of all, the loadings on the un-rotated first factor (results not reported) show that there is a common notion of good citizenship

Norms of good citizenship 93

underlying the items selected for analysis. However, a closer examination of the data included in Table 4.1 suggests a more differentiated pattern with *three* factors standing for the theoretically expected *sub-dimensions of the idea of good citizenship*. Three of the sub-dimensions stipulated by Rose and Pettersen (2002) were identified in the factor analysis: law-abidingness (not evade taxes, obeying laws), solidarity (solidarity, think of others), and critical and deliberative principles (form own opinion, be self-critical). Although these sub-dimensions will be treated separately in subsequent analyses, both the initial, un-rotated, factor solution and the correlations among the three factors underline that they belong to a common syndrome.

The general pattern described so far is prevalent (with relatively minor deviations) in most, but not all, countries. If we take into account that there was only a limited number of items available we can say that the three-factor solution worked out reasonably well. The results for Switzerland and Slovenia reflect the theoretically expected pattern of loadings of the six items on the three factors. Moreover, with minor deviations this pattern was also found in Sweden, Denmark, Norway, West and East Germany, and Russia (where the item 'being self-critical' had a double loading on both the critical and deliberative principles and the solidarity factor), the Netherlands (where the item 'show solidarity' had a double loading on the critical and deliberative principles and the solidarity factor), and Romania (where 'being self-critical' loaded on the solidarity dimension but, contrary to our expectations, not strongly on the critical and deliberative principles factor). Stronger deviations were found in Spain (where not only the item 'being self-critical' had a double loading on both the critical and deliberative principles and the solidarity factor; but where unexpectedly 'show solidarity' loaded on the law-abidingness factor) and in Moldova (where 'being self-critical' loaded on the solidarity dimension but not strongly on the critical and deliberative principles factor; and notably, 'form own opinion' produced a double loading on the critical and deliberative principles factor and the law-abidingness factor). The strongest deviations occurred in Portugal, where it was impossible to replicate the general pattern described so far.

In conclusion, however, the pattern of loadings of the six items on the underlying dimensions of citizenship provides empirical support for the theoretical expectations. 'Being self-critical' appears to be the only item not neatly fitting into the expected pattern due to its frequent double loadings. It also becomes obvious that this item is associated with both communitarian (solidarity) and liberal interpretations of citizenship (critical and deliberative principles). Although this finding is not in line with our expectations, we should point out that it matches Putnam's notion of good citizenship that entails communitarian as well as liberal principles. In almost all remaining instances, the items roughly show the loadings we would have expected from a theoretical point of view (Putnam 1993:

Table 4.1 Patterns of good citizenship: results of principal component analysis per country[a]

Factor and country	Think of others	Show solidarity	Obey laws	Not evade taxes	Form own opinion	Be self-critical
Solidarity						
Denmark	**0.66**	**0.54**	−0.02	0.11	−0.06	**0.34**
East Germany	**0.84**	**0.49**	0.02	0.03	−0.09	**0.33**
Moldova	**0.85**	**0.46**	−0.00	0.02	**0.45**	**0.74**
The Netherlands	**0.62**	**0.36**	−0.00	0.03	−0.13	0.24
Norway	**0.78**	**0.45**	−0.01	0.03	0.00	**0.49**
Portugal	**0.78**	0.12	−0.07	0.06	0.02	**0.73**
Romania	**0.89**	**0.37**	0.04	−0.03	0.04	**0.59**
Russia	**0.91**	**0.37**	0.00	−0.02	−0.03	**0.42**
Slovenia	**0.78**	**0.49**	0.01	−0.01	−0.10	0.13
Spain	**0.89**	0.27	−0.02	−0.03	−0.08	**0.36**
Sweden	**0.62**	**0.44**	0.02	0.10	−0.06	**0.40**
Switzerland	**0.66**	**0.50**	0.02	0.06	−0.09	0.23
West Germany	**0.86**	**0.59**	−0.03	0.06	−0.06	**0.38**
Critical and deliberative principles						
Denmark	−0.04	0.00	0.11	−0.04	**0.59**	**0.36**
East Germany	−0.07	0.18	0.19	−0.14	**0.90**	**0.55**
Moldova	−0.14	0.06	−0.02	−0.00	**0.39**	0.12
The Netherlands	−0.03	**0.31**	0.04	−0.03	**0.76**	**0.56**
Norway	−0.14	0.16	0.01	0.00	**0.62**	**0.31**
Portugal	−0.15	0.09	−0.12	0.07	**0.45**	0.14
Romania	−0.16	0.18	0.01	0.00	**0.66**	0.24
Russia	−0.09	0.20	0.01	−0.03	**0.75**	**0.36**
Slovenia	−0.07	0.20	0.00	−0.02	**0.86**	**0.58**
Spain	−0.10	0.15	0.02	−0.01	**0.76**	**0.37**
Sweden	−0.09	0.08	0.08	0.01	**0.62**	**0.41**
Switzerland	−0.07	0.19	−0.03	0.06	**0.62**	**0.55**
West Germany	−0.13	0.17	0.07	−0.04	**0.76**	**0.47**
Law-abidingness						
Denmark	0.04	0.11	**0.73**	**0.65**	0.13	−0.06
East Germany	0.01	0.16	**0.64**	**0.74**	0.09	−0.09
Moldova	0.01	0.22	**0.90**	**0.72**	0.10	−0.06
The Netherlands	0.09	0.03	**0.74**	**0.71**	0.08	−0.03
Norway	0.06	0.12	**0.70**	**0.74**	0.06	−0.05
Portugal	0.06	**0.40**	**0.90**	**0.62**	**0.45**	−0.04
Romania	0.04	0.09	**0.69**	**0.76**	0.11	−0.06
Russia	−0.01	0.13	**0.77**	**0.81**	0.02	0.04
Slovenia	0.01	0.07	**0.78**	**0.85**	0.04	−0.01
Spain	0.07	**0.30**	**0.83**	**0.77**	0.10	−0.04
Sweden	0.06	0.18	**0.72**	**0.77**	0.13	−0.18
Switzerland	0.07	0.04	**0.79**	**0.61**	0.13	−0.09
West Germany	0.06	0.04	**0.79**	**0.78**	0.10	−0.07

Note

[a] Entries are factor loadings (pattern matrix after oblimin rotation). Loadings equal to or higher than 0.30 are in bold. In cases where all loadings with absolute values greater than 0.30 on one component are negative (i.e. in East Germany for solidarity and in the Netherlands, Norway, Russia, and Switzerland for law-abidingness), the signs of the loadings have been reversed for ease of interpretation.

86–91). On the basis of these results, we will differentiate between the three aforementioned notions of citizenship in the remaining sections of this chapter.

As was expected, the correlations among the three factors in all countries turned out to be moderately strong.[5] This indicates that, in the hearts and minds of larger parts of the national mass publics, the various notions of citizenship go hand-in-hand. Apparently, citizens do not consider the norms implied in the conceptions of citizenship incompatible. Another test for the fragmentation hypothesis is to consider how many people adhere to an integrated conception of citizenship, in which *all three* values (criticism and deliberation, solidarity, and law-abidingness) are considered important. Our analyses (not reported in a table) indicate that an absolute majority of the citizens in the countries of our survey confirm the importance of *all three* clusters of citizenship values. The percentage of people that endorse all three values simultaneously is highest in Denmark (80 per cent). But even in the lowest-ranking countries – Switzerland and Romania (55 per cent) – a comfortable majority of the population consider all three citizen values as important. Like the results of the factor analysis, this suggests that, at the level of individual citizens, there is no widespread cultural fragmentation.

The distribution of the ideas of good citizenship

If we now turn to the aggregate level of analysis, we can ask to what extent the citizens of particular national political communities differ in their beliefs about good citizenship. This question is of interest for two reasons. First, within a political community there should be a considerable degree of *consensus* over key norms and values of citizenship (as a core element of a system's political culture). From this perspective, it is important to see whether, in modern societies, such a consensus still exists (Sniderman *et al.* 1996; Tetlock 2002). Second, many observers have claimed that the *level of support for civic norms* is cause for concern. In the western world, former civic norms are supposed to be eroding, while the post-communist central and eastern European societies apparently still lack a civil society tradition and are facing problems in creating a civic culture (Putnam 1993 and 2000; further references may be found in Stolle 2003).

Notwithstanding such rhetoric of crisis, the three sets of civic norms are surprisingly widely endorsed in *all* societies under observation (Table 4.2).[6] On a scale that runs from zero to one, the support scores for law-abidingness vary between 0.71 (in the Netherlands, West Germany, Switzerland, and East Germany) and 0.89 (in Romania). For critical and deliberative principles, the scores vary between 0.70 (in Portugal) and 0.83 (in Denmark and Sweden); and for solidarity, between 0.63 (in West Germany) and 0.75 (in Romania).[7] These consistently high scores indicate

Table 4.2 Average support for different citizen values[a]

Country	Citizenship values		
	Solidarity	Law-abidingness	Critical and deliberative principles
Romania	0.75	0.89	0.77
Sweden	0.71	0.84	0.83
Denmark	0.73	0.80	0.83
Slovenia	0.71	0.78	0.82
Norway	0.73	0.76	0.79
The Netherlands	0.71	0.73	0.80
Russia	0.64	0.81	0.78
Moldova	0.69	0.81	0.73
Spain	**0.74**	**0.75**	**0.72**
Switzerland	0.64	0.72	0.79
East Germany	0.64	0.71	0.79
West Germany	0.63	0.71	0.77
Portugal	**0.70**	**0.73**	**0.70**
Total	0.70	0.77	0.77

Note

a Scales range from 0 to 1. Countries are ordered by the average support for all three values.

that in all countries the public considers the three value orientations as almost equally important components of civicness.

Nevertheless, the level of support varies for these sub-dimensions. Public support for the norms of law-abidingness and for criticism and deliberation is clearly even more widespread than the support for solidarity. This is not surprising, since, as Rose and Pettersen (2002) rightly argued, the former two values and norms are also part of a liberal interpretation of citizenship, whereas solidarity is a distinctive element of a 'thick', communitarian interpretation of citizenship.

From a comparative perspective, there are no clearly defined clusters of countries where the public embraces a particular concept of good citizenship (for example, a predominantly liberal conception). Support for solidarity is most widespread in countries as different as Romania and Slovenia, on the one hand, and Denmark, Norway, and Sweden, on the other. For law-abidingness, Romania, Russia, and Moldova rank highest alongside Denmark and Sweden. Likewise, the value of critical and deliberative attitudes is broadly supported not only in Sweden, Denmark, and the Netherlands, but also in Slovenia and East Germany. This indicates that levels of support for civic norms in some of the post-communist countries, particularly in Romania and Slovenia, are almost as high as in some of the traditional western European democracies like Sweden and Denmark. At the other end of the scale, some long-standing democracies in the west (notably, Switzerland and West Germany) rank relatively low on both the solidarity and the law-abidingness scales. Given the vast differences in the political history over the last half century of these countries, these results are striking.

However, we should not overlook the still prevalent differences between the west and the east. If we establish a rank-order of the three components of citizenship per country, we find an interesting picture. First, there is a cluster of nations (the regular printed countries in Table 4.2) in which the public gives the highest priority to critical and deliberative principles, followed by law-abidingness and solidarity. This rank-order can be found in all traditional western European democracies with the sole exception of Sweden. Two of the most westernised post-communist publics, East Germany and Slovenia, join this group. A second group, where law-abidingness ranks first and critical and deliberative values second, consists of three post-communist nations (Russia, Romania, and Moldova, plus Sweden, which are italicised in Table 4.2). Finally, there is a third pattern which is to be found in the two southern European democracies where the three different notions of citizenship are almost equally widespread and law abidingness prevails only slightly (bold printed in Table 4.2). It is tempting to interpret this pattern in terms of the various national political traditions. The position of Sweden, however, clearly points to the necessity of caution in interpreting such patterns.

Civic norms, social involvement, and social trust

Theoretical considerations

We now turn to our second question: what are the relations between various components of social capital and civic norms? In the previous section we have already indicated that people's involvement in social networks (and ensuing social trust) may also play a key role in civic norms. The name of Alexis de Tocqueville is inextricably bound to this line of reasoning. In his analysis of nineteenth century American democracy, he pointed to the important role of voluntary associations in the development of democratic virtues. In a de Tocquevillean spirit, both the *theory of neo-pluralism* and research on *political culture* have perceived voluntary associations as training grounds for democracy (Kornhauser 1960; Almond and Verba 1963; for a concise summary, see Stolle 2003). More recently, the role of voluntary associations in the dissemination of civic virtues was underlined in the debate on *social capital* from a similar point of view.[8] In Robert Putnam's (1993: 89–91) words:

> The *norms and values* of the civic community are embodied in, and reinforced by, distinctive social structures and practices ... Internally, associations instil in their members habits of cooperation, solidarity, and public spiritedness ... Externally, what twentieth century political

scientists have called interest articulation and interest aggregation are enhanced by a dense network of secondary associations ... According to this thesis, a dense network of secondary associations both embodies and contributes to effective social collaboration. Thus ... in a civic community of associations of like-minded equals contribute to effective democratic governance.'

The effects of social involvement may be both directly and indirectly linked to *social trust*. Putnam sees social trust as a 'beneficial side-effect' of social involvement (for example, Putnam 1993: 173–4; see also, Offe 1999; Gabriel *et al.* 2002; Stolle 2002). Without social trust, communitarian citizenship is inconceivable: 'Interpersonal trust is probably the moral orientation that most needs to be diffused among people if republican society is to be maintained' (Poggi as quoted approvingly by Putnam 1993: 89). Therefore, support for a communitarian or republican interpretation of citizenship can be regarded as a product of voluntary activity and of social trust. However, the causal order among those variables is open to question. On the one hand, we may assume that social involvement is the determinant of civic norms and values. On the other, it is equally plausible that becoming active in voluntary associations and developing feelings of trust to one's fellow citizens can be regarded as typical attitudes and behaviours of people strongly endorsing civic norms and values.

Based on these general assumptions, organisational involvement, social trust, and civic values and norms should be positively related. Therefore it should not come as a surprise that, in Robert Putnam's (1993: 86–91) account of civic virtues, solidarity, trust, and associational involvement are considered as parts of a general syndrome, which Putnam named 'social capital'. Accordingly, people strongly involved in the voluntary sector and people who trust their fellow citizens should support civic norms and values more strongly than others – non-joiners and non-trusters (Gabriel *et al.* 2002; Stolle 2003).

As indicated in the previous chapter of this book, however, these general formulations need to be specified. *The type of involvement* (mere membership, being active, and having friends) in organisations, for example, may vary. Different types of associational engagement may have different effects upon the acquisition of civic virtues. Our general assumption is that membership matters as such, but that a *closer involvement* (either having personal friends in such organisations or active membership and voluntary work) has a greater effect in terms of civic virtues (Gabriel and Kunz 2000; Stolle 2003).[9]

Empirical results

In order to test this assumption, we will now turn to the data. Following the underlying research question, we will treat the three dimensions of citizenship as dependent variables, while we include four aspects of people's social capital in the analysis as explanatory factors. The included aspects of social capital are social trust and three aspects of organisational involvement: membership, activity, and friendship ties within organisations.[10] These explanatory variables were simultaneously included in a multiple regression model (model 1). In a second step, additional variables (education, age, church affiliation, left–right self-placement, and television-exposure) that, in previous research, have often been considered as relevant predictors of civic virtues were introduced (model 2).[11] This second step is aimed at getting a more complete picture of the impact of social involvement and social trust on civic values and norms while other relevant factors are held constant.[12]

In the following pages, we will show the results of separate analyses for the three dimensions of citizenship, that is, law-abidingness, solidarity, and critical and deliberative principles. The focus here is not on the impact of each of the four aspects of social capital separately, but on two more general questions. How important are the four aspects of social capital *taken together* in explaining people's conceptions of good citizenship (model 1)? And how relevant are these aspects of social capital when we take alternative explanations into account (model 2)? In a subsequent section we will turn to the more detailed question about *which elements* of social capital are important in shaping people's civic attitudes.

How relevant is social capital to the various components of citizenship?

According to the results presented before, citizenship is a multifaceted concept, including the traditional norms of law-abidingness, solidarity, and criticism and deliberation. In this section we will try to clarify to what degree the various components of citizenship are linked to the four important aspects of social capital.

As shown in Table 4.3, critical and deliberative principles are only weakly related to social capital in most societies under observation. In no single country was it possible to explain more than 10 per cent of the variance by invoking interpersonal trust and social involvement. If we are even more lenient and take 5 per cent as our criterion, the four aspects of social capital only seem to have an impact in East Germany, Norway, Romania, and West Germany. As a first conclusion, it seems reasonable to state that social capital is not particularly relevant to promote citizens' critical and deliberative virtues. Including variables such as education, media use, age (year of birth), and so on, does not greatly change the situation. More than 10 per cent of the variance is explained in Romania and West Germany, but, in general, the explanatory power remains poor.

Roughly the same applies to law-abidingness, where the results for

Table 4.3 The explanatory power of four aspects of social capital (model 1) and of these aspects plus control variables (model 2) on the support for various components of good citizenship[a]

Country	Critical and deliberative principles			Law abidingness			Solidarity		
	Social capital (model 1)	With controls (model 2)	ΔR^2	Social capital (model 1)	With controls (model 2)	ΔR^2	Social capital (model 1)	With controls (model 2)	ΔR^2
Denmark	0.034***	0.046***	0.012	0.030***	0.067***	0.037	0.076***	0.145***	0.069
East Germany	0.080***	0.070***	−0.010	0.037***	0.081***	0.044	0.047***	0.135***	0.087
Moldova	0.000	0.004	0.004	0.000	0.021***	0.021	0.000	0.002	0.002
The Netherlands	0.035***	0.068***	0.033	0.055***	0.115***	0.060	0.010***	0.046***	0.036
Norway	0.053***	0.056***	0.003	0.093***	0.156***	0.063	0.111***	0.169***	0.058
Portugal	0.033***	0.078***	0.045	0.037***	0.064***	0.027	0.038***	0.062***	0.024
Romania	0.056***	0.106***	0.050	0.018***	0.070***	0.052	0.032***	0.067***	0.035
Russia	0.010*	0.016*	0.006	0.016***	0.064***	0.058	0.019***	0.051***	0.032
Slovenia	0.001	0.026**	0.026	−0.003	0.017*	0.020	0.001	0.026**	0.025
Spain	0.043***	0.057***	0.014	0.013***	0.086***	0.073	0.027***	0.051***	0.024
Sweden	0.060***	0.079***	0.019	0.051***	0.123***	0.072	0.049***	0.106***	0.057
Switzerland	0.031***	0.065***	0.034	0.025***	0.139***	0.114	0.027***	0.099***	0.072
West Germany	0.080***	0.109***	0.049	0.037***	0.103***	0.066	0.180***	0.238***	0.058

Note
a Entries are adjusted R^2s. Levels of statistical significance: *** = 0.01, ** = 0.05, * = 0.1.

model 1 meet the 5 per cent criterion in the Netherlands, Norway, and Sweden. Contrary to the findings on criticism and deliberation, introducing additional variables (particularly age and religion) leads to a substantial increase of explained variance. For model 2, five countries pass the 10 per cent hurdle (Switzerland, the Netherlands, Norway, Sweden, and West Germany), and six more meet the 5 per cent criterion (Denmark, East Germany, Spain, Portugal, Romania, and Russia). Only in Moldova and Slovenia does model 2 fail to meet the 5 per cent criterion.

Finally, the baseline social capital model accounts for more than 10 per cent of the variance in the support for solidarity in West Germany and Norway; in Denmark, this model explains more than 5 per cent. Again the introduction of control variables results in an increase in the explanatory power. In five countries the second model explains more than 10 per cent (Denmark, East Germany, Norway, Sweden, and West Germany), and in five more countries the 5 per cent hurdle is surpassed (Switzerland, Spain, Portugal, Romania, and Russia).

On this basis we can draw several conclusions. First, social capital in its own right is only a weak predictor of people's support for civic values; this is true for all three dimensions of civic values. Second, our analyses indicate that, especially for law-abidingness and solidarity, the introduction of control variables improves the explanatory power of the model. Third, we can conclude that, with regard to the latter two dimensions, the models perform best in some (though not in necessarily all) of the established western democracies.

What factors affect civicness?

In the previous section we have seen that adding control variables results in a substantial increase in the explained variance of the regression models (this is the case for all three dependent variables, though to a varying degree). Table 4.3, however, did not tell us much about the causal effects of the various components of social capital and the other variables in the analysis. We do not know which – if any – of the respective components are responsible for the total effect of social capital. Neither do we know whether the effects of the social capital factors remain significant after the introduction of the control variables. In order to simplify the analysis we have focused on a composite index that measures people's overall support for the three distinct, though correlated, components of good citizenship.[13] The higher the score on this composite measure, the more supportive people are of various components of good citizenship.

EXPLANATORY POWER

If we consider the evidence from Table 4.4, we see that, in terms of the proportion of explained variance, the results for model 1 (social capital components only) are far from impressive. In Norway and in West Germany, more than 10 per cent variance is explained and in four more countries (Denmark, East Germany, the Netherlands, and Sweden) the percentage of explained variance exceeds 5 per cent. When we introduce control variables (model 2) the explanatory power of the model improves; in some countries substantially (e.g. in Switzerland), in others less so (e.g. in Moldova and Slovenia). In conclusion, the extended model explains more than 10 per cent of variance in eight countries (Switzerland, Denmark, East Germany, the Netherlands, Norway, Romania, Sweden, and West Germany). The countries where the model performs less well are all located in southern (Spain and Portugal) and eastern Europe (Moldova, Russia, and Slovenia). The combination of these results for models 1 and 2 suggest that social capital (in its own right and in combination with control variables) is a rather poor predictor of support for civic virtues in some (though not all: see the cases of East Germany and Romania) of the countries in eastern Europe and to a lesser extent in southern Europe.

THE EFFECTS OF SOCIAL CAPITAL

When we turn to the impact of various components of social capital, our analyses show that, of the four components of social capital under study, *social trust* turns out to be not only the strongest, but also the most consistent factor influencing people's overall support for civic values. This is true for both model 1 (without controls) and for model 2 (with controls). Only in Moldova and Slovenia does trust fail to have an impact on the dependent variable. Moreover, if compared to the effects of the other aspects of social capital, social trust is by far the strongest determinant of support for civic values. Trust turns out to have a relatively strong effect (≥ 0.10 in both models 1 and 2) in all the established western European democracies and in Portugal. In the other countries, the effects of trust are weaker (i.e. East Germany, Spain, Romania, and Russia) or absent (i.e. Moldova and Slovenia). This general pattern of results is obtained for both models (either with or without control variables). This indicates that factors like education and age (year of birth) do not eliminate the effect of social trust. These findings suggest that, at least to some extent, Putnam (2000: 137) was right when he claimed that 'trusting citizens are good citizens'.

If we turn to *organisational involvement* (either sheer membership, having friends, or active participation), we have already seen that the direct effects of these three components of social capital are eclipsed in their importance by the effects of social trust. This is not to say, however, that forms of organisational involvement are without any impact. In nine of the 13 countries we found statistically significant (but consistently weak) effects of one or more of the involvement variables, even after we controlled the effects of other variables. The exceptions are Moldova, Romania, Russia, and Sweden. Moreover, we observed that mere membership is only occasionally of importance (i.e. in the Netherlands, Norway, and Slovenia). Only when associations become a more-or-less important part of one's life (either by active participation or by having personal friends in associations), does membership gain some importance for people's support for civic virtues. We find such effects in Switzerland, Denmark, East Germany, Spain, the Netherlands, Portugal, Slovenia, and West Germany. In almost all instances, such effects survive after the introduction of control variables. This clearly implies that not just being a member in organisations counts, but that associations are only effectual if members are embedded in some dense personal networks of the voluntary sector. However, we should realise that, in terms of their direct effects on people's support for civic values, the importance of associational involvement is limited.

ADDITIONAL FACTORS

Social trust and involvement are not necessarily the only factors contributing to the support of civic norms. Some authors have pointed to the role of education (Nie *et al.* 1996), and others emphasise the importance of age, and the effects of (excessive) exposure to television (Putnam 2000: 216–76). Religion and left–right placement are also considered to be important factors (Putnam 2000). If we inspect the explained variance for model 2 in Table 4.4 (and in Table 4.3), we immediately see that, even after the introduction of additional factors, the improvement of the regression model in terms of its explained variance is only modest.

Examining the effects for each of these additional factors separately, we first find a consistent and relatively strong (in nine cases the coefficient exceeds 0.10) *age* (year of birth) effect, with the older age cohorts more strongly supporting civic norms than the younger ones. Second, the widespread assumption that *education* fosters support of norms of good citizenship values is not generally confirmed. Only in five instances (Switzerland, the Netherlands, Portugal, Romania, and West Germany) are the better educated indeed most supportive of civism. Third, contrary to Putnam's hypothesis, frequent *exposure to television* is not a systematic impediment for people's support of civic values. Only in Switzerland, Sweden, and West Germany is there some support for this hypothesis. In the other countries we either find no effect or even a positive effect of television exposure (Moldova, the Netherlands, and Romania). Fourth, church attendance is a consistent, though a rather weak, explanatory factor. Church attendants tend to be relatively supportive of civic values.

Table 4.4 Effects of four components of social capital (model 1) and of these components plus control variables (model 2) on overall support for civic values[a]

Country and model	Components of social capital				Control variables					Constant	R²	ΔR² model 2–model 1
	Social trust	Member in organisation	Friends in organisation	Active in organisation	Age (reversed scale)	Education	TV exposure	Church attendance	Left–right placement			
Denmark												
Model 1	0.19***	0.00	0.01	0.01	–	–	–	–	–	0.64***	0.071	–
Model 2	0.15***	–0.01	0.01*	0.00	–0.15***	0.01	0.04	0.06***	–0.06***	0.78***	0.111	0.040
East Germany												
Model 1	0.08***	0.00	0.05***	0.03*	–	–	–	–	–	0.65***	0.076	–
Model 2	0.06***	0.01	0.05**	0.02	–0.16***	–0.07*	–0.03	0.14***	–0.10***	0.81***	0.147	0.071
Moldova												
Model 1	0.02	0.03	–0.05	0.04	–	–	–	–	–	0.73***	0.000	–
Model 2	–0.04	–0.01	–0.05	0.05	0.00	0.02	0.20**	0.02	0.07**	0.68***	0.013	0.013
The Netherlands												
Model 1	0.13***	0.00	0.05***	–0.00	–	–	–	–	–	0.63***	0.057	–
Model 2	0.10***	0.02**	0.01*	0.01	–0.10***	0.10***	0.04*	0.05***	–0.06***	0.68***	0.103	0.046
Norway												
Model 1	0.28***	0.02***	0.01	0.01	–	–	–	–	–	0.55***	0.135	–
Model 2	0.24***	0.02**	0.01	0.01	–0.11***	0.00	0.00	0.08***	–0.10***	0.67***	0.189	0.054
Portugal												
Model 1	0.13***	0.00	0.05***	–0.00	–	–	–	–	–	0.62***	0.047	–
Model 2	0.15***	0.00	0.04***	–0.02	–0.08*	0.14***	0.11	0.08***	–0.06**	0.61***	0.083	0.036

Romania										
Model 1	0.10***	0.03	0.02	0.02	—	—	0.20***	0.76***	0.047	—
Model 2	0.09***	0.04	0.00	0.02	−0.08	0.18***	0.05**	0.65***	0.116	0.069
Russia										
Model 1	0.10***	−0.01	0.02	0.02	—	—	0.07	0.70***	0.017	—
Model 2	0.09***	0.02	0.02	0.01	−0.22***	0.01	0.05**	0.77***	0.054	0.037
Spain										
Model 1	0.07***	0.01	0.03***	0.02**	—	—	0.02	0.69***	0.034	—
Model 2	0.07***	0.00	0.04***	0.02**	−0.08***	−0.01	0.02	0.73***	0.066	0.032
Slovenia										
Model 1	0.00	−0.02	0.02	0.01	—	—	0.14	0.77***	−0.00	—
Model 2	0.03	−0.04**	0.00	0.04**	−0.10***	0.10	−0.03	0.79***	0.029	0.029
Sweden										
Model 1	0.17***	0.01	0.02**	0.00	—	—	−0.18***	0.66***	0.080	—
Model 2	0.12***	−0.00	0.01	0.00	−0.12***	0.03	−0.08***	0.80***	0.127	0.047
Switzerland										
Model 1	0.14***	−0.00	0.01	0.03***	—	—	−0.19***	0.61***	0.039	—
Model 2	0.11***	−0.01	0.01	0.02*	−0.24***	0.07***	−0.10***	0.77***	0.133	0.094
West Germany										
Model 1	0.15***	−0.02	0.07***	0.02*	—	—	−0.21***	0.58***	0.143	—
Model 2	0.16***	0.00	0.07***	0.00	−0.12***	0.04**	−0.07***	0.67***	0.203	0.060

Note

a Entries are adjusted R^2s. Levels of statistical significance: *** = 0.01, ** = 0.05, * = 0.1.

Such an effect emerges in all the nations under observation – with the exception of Moldova. Finally, in all western European democracies, East Germany, and Portugal, people's identification with a leftist position on an ideological left–right scale is positively related to support of civic values.[14] In Moldova, Romania, and Russia, we find the reverse effect: positions on the right are associated with support for civic values.

In addition to evidence for the important role of social capital, particularly trust and active participation or integration in voluntary associations, and in the shaping of civic attitudes, we have found three other major factors affecting civic attitudes: age, religion, and ideological orientation. Most of these results are well in line with Putnam's assumptions about the roots of good citizenship.

Conclusions

In this chapter we focused on two main questions. First, we asked whether the pluralism of social norms that is characteristic for modern societies results in cultural fragmentation. In answering this question we looked both at the structure of individual civic attitudes and at cross-national patterns of citizenship. After these descriptive analyses we turned to our second question that pertains to one of the main threads in this book: what is the democratic relevance of social involvement and social trust?

With regard to the first question, our findings suggest that moral pluralism has not resulted in cultural fragmentation. We found that, in the hearts and minds of citizens, the support for various citizenship norms are closely linked and that, in all countries analysed, widespread support for the norms of law-abidingness, criticism and deliberation, and solidarity exists. Moreover, we found that in each of our countries the majority of citizens internalised a fully-integrated concept of citizenship, based on simultaneous strong support for each of the three basic components of citizenship. These findings confirm the analyses of Klages (2000a and 2000b), who argued that a synthesis of traditional orientations like rule conformity and modern norms and values (for example, political activism) is typical for a contemporary civic society.

With regard to our second question, we find that social trust and forms of associational involvement make a modest contribution to the shaping of civic norms in many of the countries under analysis. If we look at the overall results, reported in Table 4.4, and the results for the sub-dimensions of solidarity and law-abidingness, it is clear that the relative impact of the social capital factors (and social trust in particular) in building support for civic values is greatest in various established western democracies. This finding is in line with the 'Tocquevillean model of civic virtue' (Newton 1999a): social involvement and its 'beneficial side-effect', are related to public support for solidarity.

Norms of good citizenship 107

From this perspective, the results for some of the eastern European countries are, however, somewhat puzzling. In the third section of this chapter we discovered that in Slovenia and Romania, for example, a large majority of the public supports norms like solidarity, law-abidingness, and criticism and deliberation. Such a result was not expected, given the clearly different social and political history of the respective nations during the second half of the twentieth century. In such societies the key mechanism of the 'Tocquevillean model', a flourishing civil society with a wide variety of voluntary organisations, is not yet fully developed.

However, as Newton (1999a) pointed out, there are other mechanisms that may provide social trust and civic virtues. These are mechanisms of social control in close-knit communities, or alternative institutions like the mass-media or schools; a set of mechanisms that may serve as vehicles for political socialisation. Both these mechanisms may provide part of an explanation for the eastern European findings. Whether or not this is actually the case is a matter for further investigation. If such speculations have some validity, they dramatically highlight the vulnerability of the cultural basis of democratisation in at least some of the eastern European countries. Ironically, in the coming years the process of modernisation and the renunciation of the cultural heritage of former communism may well erode public support for some of the norms and values that are at the core of democratic citizenship in western-style democracies. Since the post-communist nations in central and eastern Europe are still on the road to the formation of social capital, they will still need a considerable amount of time before having established alternative mechanisms for securing continuing public support for key values and norms of democratic citizenship.

Notes

1 In his analysis of the values of modern societies, Klages (1984) depicts a similar pattern by contrasting conformist (hierarchy, obedience, achievement orientation) to non conformist (self-actualisation, participation, equality) values.
2 In addition to such virtues, these authors also emphasise the relevance of other values: social virtues (open-mindedness and independence), and economic virtues (work ethic, and capacity to delay self-gratification).
3 The Swedish researchers labelled these dimensions participation, deliberation, solidarity, and law-abidingness. This division is closely related to the fourfold division between political participation, critical and deliberative values, solidarity, and law-abidingness that we identified in the discussion of normative theories of citizenship.
4 Accordingly, three factors were pre-selected before rotating the initial solution. We were well aware that we were actually violating the rule of having at least three items per factor because of our limited number of items. Therefore we should treat the results of the analysis as illustrative rather than as conclusive.
5 The correlations between these factors were -0.36 (solidarity with law-abidingness), -0.42 (law-abidingness with critical and deliberative principles), and 0.44 (solidarity with critical and deliberative values). Negative correlations

are due to different signs of the factor loading coefficients. Interpreted in a substantial sense, the three concepts of citizenship are positively correlated.
6 For this purpose we have computed three indices, one for each of the dimensions resulting from the previously reported factor analyses. Each index therefore is based on the sum score of two items. All items were rescaled so as to have a minimum of 0 and a maximum of 1. These three indices will also be used for subsequent analyses.
7 This is also confirmed by the relatively modest standard deviations for the mean support rates. For law-abidingness, with a mean score of 0.70, the standard deviation was 0.21; for criticism and deliberation, the mean was 0.77 and the standard deviation 0.18. And finally for solidarity, the mean was 0.70 and the standard deviation 0.20. If we look at comparable figures per country, we get similar results.
8 See Coleman 1988; Staub 1989; Putnam 1993, 2000; Verba *et al.* 1995; Feldman and Steenbergen 1996; Warren 1999a, 2001; Claibourn and Martin 2000; Dekker and Uslaner 2001; Gabriel *et al.* 2002; Hooghe and Stolle 2003b; and Stolle 2003.
9 In this chapter we will not analyse the potential effect of people's involvement in different types of organisations. Although previous work (for example, Putnam 1993; Foley and Edwards 1996; Cohen 1999; Putnam 2000: 31–115; Stolle and Rochon 2001; Stolle 2003) has shown that not all types of organisations will have the same impact on the transmission of civic virtues, a detailed analysis of this topic would be beyond the scope of this chapter.
10 Information on operationalisation is provided in Chapter 2 for social trust and in Chapter 3, note 13, for the measures of organisational involvement.
11 This may be seen as problematic, because there is likely to be reciprocal causality between the dependent and the independent variables. For our purposes, however, it is not necessary to get an *exact* estimate of the relative strengths of the reciprocal causal effects; therefore, we can ignore this complicating factor.
12 Therefore, the results of the extended models will be examined only:
    1 to see if controls affect the impact of our two key explanatory variables;
    2 to establish the relative explanatory power of these two factors vis-à-vis the control variables;
    3 to gauge the gains in additional explanatory power by introducing these additional factors.
13 The use of this composite index is justified by both the relative strength of the correlations between the three factors and by the basic similarities in the analytical results reported in Table 4.4. The composite index is computed as the average score of the three separate indices.
14 A low score indicates a position on the far left; a high score indicates a position on the far right.

5 Political and social tolerance

José Manuel Leite Viegas

Introduction

In the final quarter of the twentieth century, a considerable number of countries made the transition from totalitarian or authoritarian regimes to democratic government, particularly in southern Europe, eastern Europe, and Latin America. While the introduction of democracy does not automatically imply respect for the rules and the law that the constitutions stipulate, comparative empirical studies show that support for democracy has risen among the citizens of these new democracies (Klingemann 1999; Norris 1999b) as has the acceptance of basic democratic values (Dalton 1994; Thomassen 1995).

At first glance, we might think that tolerance would be included in these trends. After all, political tolerance springs naturally from the egalitarian and pluralistic principles of liberal democracy: respect for individual liberties, equality before the law, acceptance of diverse opinions and lifestyles, rejection of arbitrary conduct in complying with the law, and the endorsement of minority rights.

The problem, however, is in fact somewhat more complex. Democratic pluralism is based on the recognition that modern societies are heterogeneous and that social differentiation may entail positive results in terms of social and political progress. But the majority principle, another rule of democracy, may also jeopardise respect for the opinion and behaviour of less popular or minority groups in society, a risk that Alexis de Tocqueville ([1835, 1840] 2000) clearly emphasised. It was recognised early on that political intolerance is not restricted to non-democratic societies. It represents a serious problem, which has been analysed empirically in contemporary democracies, particularly in the postwar period.

Until the work of Sullivan *et al.* (1982), empirical analyses concurred with the thesis that political tolerance had tended to increase in democratic countries in the postwar period, mainly due to higher levels of education among their citizens (Stouffer 1955; Davis 1975; Nunn *et al.* 1978). Later studies confirm this tendency. They also confirm the importance of education and date of birth, both of which are of course associated with social and economic modernisation (Davis 1975; McClosky and Brill 1983; Sniderman *et al.* 1989; Wilson 1994; Thalhammer *et al.* 2001). This theoretical orientation, which we may term the 'standard theory', has been contested by the so-called 'revisionist' theory. Sullivan *et al.* (1982) question earlier results, in particular the seminal work by Stouffer (1955), based on what they consider to be a theoretical as well as methodological bias.

For the progenitors of the 'revisionist theory', 'tolerance implies a willingness to "put up with" those things one rejects or opposes' and, on a political level, 'it implies a willingness to permit the expression of ideas or interests one opposes' (Sullivan *et al.* 1982: 2). Consequently, the empirical analyses of discriminatory attitudes towards a single target group (in the American studies, a left-wing group), without considering how close the respondents were to this group, were not, strictly speaking, measuring tolerance but rather the lessening, in time, of the rejection of people with such ideological tendencies.

I believe, however, that these theories are flawed by a rationalistic positivism that is inconsistent with the real situation. Tolerance does not just develop after one gets to know another person and his or her ideas. It also involves a predisposition towards understanding someone else's motives and accepting them, albeit conditionally. The attempt to understand other people's ideas in their context and on the basis of their complex causality – 'the sober second thought', as some analysts term it – can mitigate the overall rejection of an individual or a group, with this process becoming an integral part of tolerance. It should be added that other empirical studies question the linear nature of the relationship between the degree of intolerance and the proximity to members of a given social group (Sniderman *et al.* 1989; Gibson 1992b).

In analysing attitudes of political tolerance, we are not simply dealing with a diversity of tastes in relation to distinctive social groups. If this were the case, we would be concealing the existence of exclusion and discrimination processes involving certain unpopular and minority target-groups. Political tolerance has to be measured according to the acceptance by the individual of the rights and liberties of people belonging to unpopular or minority groups, on equal terms with all other citizens. Political tolerance begins, therefore, in the sphere of citizenship.

My analyses in this chapter, however, will not focus only on political but also on social tolerance. The latter is defined as the extent to which acceptance in the various areas of social life is accorded to potential targets of discrimination such as political and religious extremists, people belonging to various types of stigmatised groups, and ethnic minorities. The rise of new phenomena or ones with new configurations or dimensions, such as AIDS, drug addiction, crime, terrorism, and ideological fundamentalism, and the increase in ethnic minority groups in developed societies have awakened feelings of insecurity and reinforced the stigmatisation of different social groups. These processes are known to nourish attitudes of intolerance. The question is how these new situations manifest themselves at the beginning of the twenty-first century with respect to attitudes of (in)tolerance in democratic societies, where social, cultural, and lifestyle differences are increasingly accepted.

In this chapter, attitudes towards political exclusion and social discrimination registered at a given moment are taken to be the product of two factors:

1   the beliefs and attitudes acquired during primary socialisation (Sears 1993: 121) or, in a more comprehensive formulation, the *habitus* (Bourdieu 1980: 88), that is, the symbolic and ideological structures generated during the experiences acquired in different life trajectories;
2   the impact of conjunctural problems (terrorism, drugs, crime, religious and political extremism), which largely depends on the level of information on these problems.

I also presume that the structure of beliefs and values acquired in socialisation and life trajectories will determine the different ways in which individuals perceive situations of insecurity and, in particular, their degree of tolerance. Where the willingness to accept social difference is limited, any aggravation in a target group's situation tends to provoke general attitudes of social exclusion and discrimination. As Sniderman *et al.* (1989: 4) put it: 'For the people only loosely attached to the value of tolerance, it can suffice that a group is out of the ordinary or merely unfamiliar to excite an intolerant response'. Where there is a greater willingness to accept difference, citizens respond to situations of insecurity in more selective ways: they might react to a given target group without serious repercussions on other target groups, and distinguish between social discrimination and political exclusion, for civic reasons as well as for reasons related to the perception of danger.

These ideas will guide the empirical analysis. I shall therefore seek to distinguish attitudes towards social target-groups that only differ in their socio-cultural characteristics or lifestyles, even if unpopular, from attitudes towards social target-groups that, on the other hand, are seen as a social threat. In the next section of this chapter, the levels of political and social intolerance in our sample of countries will be analysed in a comparative perspective. I will also present a theoretical framework of macro-social characteristics that will allow us to understand the cross-national differences in tolerance. In a subsequent section, I will attempt to explain measures of tolerance on the individual level by relating them to other aspects of social and political experiences and thinking.

A comparative analysis of political exclusion and social discrimination

Some scholars have advanced the economic development in modern societies as one of the preconditions for the establishment of democracy (Lipset 1960). From a more general point of view, there are other conditions for the institutionalisation of democratic values and governments: the social division of labour, functional interdependence, the creation of markets, free cooperation between people, the development of individual responsibility, the spread of scientific and technological knowledge, and a greater exchange on the individual as well as societal level (Lipset 1994). More open, pluralistic, and interdependent societies promote feelings of trust in others, which is generally accepted as a basis for tolerance.

This developmental point of view would not be complete without mentioning that, by destroying the old forms of integration in communities, capitalist development generates new forms of social and political inequality and exclusion. Relationships of integration and citizenship must therefore be interpreted, together with the often conflicting capitalist development and democratisation of the state (Marshall [1963] 1973). It is in this matrix of social relationships that the principles of liberalism, citizenship, and democracy have been created and broadened. But it is the latter aspects, these political principles, that more directly determine the levels of tolerance in a society. Democratic relationships institutionalise the interplay of peaceful discussion and deliberation between groups with differing ideas and interests. With the necessary respect for the political opinions of minorities, democratic relationships thus help to spread a culture of tolerance and participation (Muller and Seligson 1994).

Let us begin with an analysis of the factors of democracy and citizenship. The main idea that I intend to develop is clearly and concisely expressed by Peffley and Rohrschneider (2003: 5) who argue that 'citizens in a more stable democratic nation have more opportunities to practice or observe toleration through elections, pluralistic conflicts of interests, and this should increase citizens' appreciation of tolerance'. Within this framework, Peffley and Rohrschneider consider the 'number of years that the country has lived under a stable democratic regime' and whether the system is 'federal' or 'non-federal' as factors explaining political tolerance. The existence of a democratic regime and its durability over time will be an important dimension to consider. But it must be complemented by other democratic indicators. By necessity, a legal, democratic framework includes some of the requirements already mentioned – electoral competition, the freedom to oppose, and respect for the law – which, irrespective of the different democratic institutional formulae, immediately produce, to a certain extent, the effects in question. However, the effect on tolerance will also depend on the type of democratic institutions and the way they operate. Consequently, Peffley and Rohrschneider add federalism as another indicator of 'checks and balances' in the way democracy operates.

I will introduce yet another aspect of democratic functioning: the degree of political inclusion. It could easily be hypothesised that the greater the number of people involved in these processes, the more pronounced the effects of tolerance will be. In other words, tolerance will depend on how far the rights of citizenship go and how far they are effectively exercised. Therefore, my first hypothesis is that more enduring and inclusive democracies will show higher levels of tolerance.

This hypothesis involves two dimensions: the duration of democracy and the degree of political inclusion. The indicators used are:

1 the number of years uninterrupted democratic rule;
2 the average voter turnout in national parliamentary elections between 1945 and 2000 (only considering democratic elections);
3 the year in which women were given the right to vote.

I acknowledge from the outset that the last two indicators are not perfectly ideal. To begin with, political involvement cannot be reduced to electoral participation. Furthermore, formal inclusion could extend, for example, to the political rights granted to non-nationals or the ease with which they can acquire formal citizenship in their country of residence. In practice, however, the choice of indicators is largely dictated by availability.

The second hypothesis is related to socio-economic factors. As we know, the development of the welfare state succeeded in creating higher levels of education, social security, remuneration, and employment, minimising the effects of social exclusion that result from the process of development. With higher standards of living and higher levels of education, citizens tend towards values more centred on the individual and his or her well-being. In this context, we also find an increasing acceptance of different lifestyles (Inglehart 1977). A similar idea was presented already in Stouffer's seminal study of tolerance. According to Stouffer (1955: 236):

> great social, economic, and technological forces are operating slowly and imperceptibly on the side of spreading tolerance. The rising level of education and the accompanying decline in authoritarian child-rearing practice increase independence of thought and respect for others whose ideas are different.

Analyses of the processes of modernisation may incorporate, at a more specific level, different options of social development. Everything else equal, a high level of social integration is more likely in countries where it is supported by continuous public policies than in countries where it is not. The 'Nordic model' of the welfare state, which is inclined to address citizenship in all its aspects, in particular the political aspect, fosters participation more than the 'Continental' model, which tends to address the materialistic values of family security (Esping-Andersen 1991). My second hypothesis, which focuses on the end product of these policies, is that higher levels of social well-being and socio-economic integration promote tolerance.

Two aspects should be considered: the level of social development and well-being on the one hand, and the extent of integration as indexed by the levels of social marginalisation on the other. As a measure of the former, I employ the Human Development Index (HDI), which is in turn based on three indicators: life expectancy, education, and GDP. As a measure of the latter, I use the average rate of unemployment in the decade preceding our survey.

Certain technical reservations are in order with respect to the second of the two measures. The progenitors of the HDI refused to include it into their index on the ground that conditions of comparability are met only for countries within the OECD. In addition to this problem, data for the most recently established democracies cover only a few years. Despite these limitations, the indicator is included in the model, since it matches the theoretical concept.

Overall tolerance levels by country

I intend to analyse attitudes of political exclusion and social discrimination towards different social groups: extremist groups, stigmatised groups, and ethnic minorities. To monitor these attitudes, respondents were asked whether any of the social groups presented to them:

1   should be allowed to hold public meetings; and
2   would be acceptable as neighbours.

The groups included 'Christian fundamentalists', 'Islamic fundamentalists', 'left-wing extremists', 'right-wing extremists', 'racists', 'people with a criminal record', 'drug addicts', 'people with AIDS', 'homosexuals', 'immigrants', and 'people of a different race'.

The tendency to exclude politically and discriminate socially with respect to the entire set of groups is presented in Table 5.1, which indicates the mean number of groups mentioned on a scale ranging from 0 (no group) to 1 (all groups). Evidently, there are significant differences between countries with regard to political exclusion as well as social discrimination. In line with the results obtained by others (Gibson 1992a; Thalhammer *et al.* 2001; Peffley and Rohrschneider 2003), the macro-social characteristics of each country appear to exert a strong influence on overall levels of political and social tolerance. Comparing the two types of intolerance, the figures tend to be higher for social discrimination than for political exclusion, especially in Denmark, Sweden, the Netherlands,

Table 5.1 Political exclusion and social discrimination[a]

Country	Political exclusion	Social discrimination
Denmark	0.10 (0.16)	0.18 (0.18)
Portugal	0.15 (0.21)	0.17 (0.18)
Sweden	0.19 (0.20)	0.32 (0.23)
The Netherlands	0.21 (0.19)	0.29 (0.19)
Norway	0.22 (0.21)	0.34 (0.24)
West Germany	0.25 (0.23)	0.32 (0.26)
Spain	0.27 (0.22)	0.26 (0.28)
East Germany	0.29 (0.21)	0.31 (0.22)
Switzerland	0.32 (0.21)	0.37 (0.21)
Russia	0.38 (0.24)	0.40 (0.25)
Romania	0.43 (0.33)	0.44 (0.35)
Moldova	0.46 (0.35)	0.47 (0.36)

Note
a Means with standard deviations in parentheses. Countries are ordered and grouped by the degree of political exclusion. Slovenia has been omitted since only some of the required information was collected in that country.

Norway, West Germany, and Switzerland. In countries where political exclusion is more prevalent, this difference is not evident. We will return later to these variations. In any case, it is clear that the countries can be divided into three groups based on the level of political tolerance. The first group includes Denmark, Portugal, Sweden, the Netherlands, and Norway, the second West Germany, Spain, East Germany, and Switzerland, and the third Russia, Romania, and Moldova.

How do the two hypothesis fare based on this grouping? Table 5.2 shows the level of political tolerance along with the values of the political and socio-economic factors singled out by the hypotheses. Let us first consider the impact of the political characteristics. Switzerland excepted, all countries with a continuous democratic life of at least 80 years belong to the most tolerant group. The contrary holds true as well. The most recent democracies (less than ten years old) all belong to the group of least tolerant countries. Countries that are intermediate in terms of the duration of democracy (more than ten years but less than 80) are intermediate in terms of political tolerance as well, except for Portugal, which in spite of its relatively short recent democratic history falls into the most tolerant group.

The remaining political characteristics may shed some light on the deviant behaviour of the Portuguese and Swiss cases. Switzerland displays the lowest average turnout, and was the last country to give women the vote. These characteristics undermine the value of the first indicator (years of democracy) and may help explain why Switzerland belongs to the second rather than the first group in terms of political tolerance. While Portugal has a relatively high turnout, it is clear that an explanation

Table 5.2 Political exclusion and selected political and socio-economic characteristics

Country[a]	Political exclusion	Political characteristics			Socio-economic characteristics	
		Number of years as a democracy[b]	Average turnout (parliamentary elections 1945–2002, in %)[c]	Number of years since women were granted the right to vote[d]	Human Development Index[e]	Average rate of unemployment (1990s, in %)[f]
Denmark	0.10	80	86	87	0.926	7.1
Portugal	0.15	26	76	26	0.880	5.5
Sweden	0.19	+80	86	81	0.941	6.1
The Netherlands	0.21	+80	87	83	0.935	5.5
Norway	0.22	+80	80	89	0.942	4.7
West Germany	0.25	52	83	–[g]	–[h]	–[h]
Spain	0.27	23	74	71	0.913	19.1
East Germany	0.29	12	76	–[g]	–[h]	–[h]
Switzerland	0.32	+80	57	31	0.928	3.3
Russia	0.38	9	58	84	0.781	11.5
Romania	0.43	10	73	56	0.775	8.0
Moldova	0.46	8	73	9	0.701	11.1

Notes

a Countries are ordered and grouped by the level of political exclusion.
b In 2002 based on Freedom House data. For the newer democracies, the democratic area is considered to have begun when the new democratic constitution was adopted. For East Germany, the beginning of the democratic period is considered to be 1993, when the two Parliaments approved the bill of unification.
c For OECD countries, the information was obtained from IDEA (www.idea.int/vt/index.cfm). For Moldova and Romania, only the elections in the democratic period are considered. The values for East and West Germany were calculated on the basis of the values recorded in the different 'Bundesländer' for the elections in 1994 and 1998 (www.bunbeschlleiter.de/wahlen/ergeb94/e/t/land94913.htm).
d In 2002 based on data from the web site of the Inter-Parliamentary Union (www.ipu.org/wmn-e/suffrage.htm) and counted from the year in which the right was granted without restriction.
e The HDI was created within the United Nations Development Programme (hdr.undp.org). The figures refer to year 2000 and are provided by the 2002 report, pp. 149–52 (undp.org/2000/complete.pdf).
f These data are contained in the United Nations Development Programme report (2002) described in note e. Only OECD countries are included.
g Although women in Germany were given the right to vote in 1918, it is difficult to relate this fact to the two postwar Germanies.
h It was not possible to obtain separate figures for the two parts of Germany after unification.

of the Portuguese exception must take into account the impact of conjunctural factors, to which we will return later on.

Let us first, however, consider the impact of the last two political characteristics more systematically. The Netherlands, Denmark, West Germany, and Norway display the highest levels of voter turnout, all equal to or greater than 80 per cent. With the exception of West Germany, all belong to the most tolerant group. In Russia and Switzerland, turnout is notably lower, with the former belonging to the least tolerant group and the latter to the intermediate group. The countries that first granted women the right to vote, such as Norway (1913), Denmark (1915), Russia (1918), the Netherlands (1919), and Sweden (1921) belong, with the exception of Russia, to the most tolerant countries. The case of Russia illustrates the comparability problems associated with this indicator. In fact, we are comparing recognition of the right to vote in liberal democracies with its recognition in countries where democracy was non-existent. But the hypothesis is not compromised as it is based on three indicators. With regard to the other two, Russia remains in line with the conjecture.

Let us now proceed to the second hypothesis and the impact of socioeconomic characteristics. In descending order: the countries with HDI values above 0.9 are: Norway, Sweden, the Netherlands, Switzerland, Denmark, and Spain. With the exception of Switzerland and Spain, all belong to the most tolerant group of countries. Moldova, Russia, and Romania, all with HDI values of around 0.7, belong to the least tolerant group. Portugal registers an intermediate HDI value (0.880), which is not fully in line with its top position in terms of tolerance.

To shed some light on the exceptions, we may consider the second indicator: the average unemployment rate. The figure for Spain (19.1 per cent) is significantly higher than for any other country. In Portugal, by contrast, the unemployment rate is relatively low (third from the bottom). In both cases, a combined reading of the two measures (HDI and unemployment) helps to explain the position with respect to tolerance. The extremely low unemployment rate in Switzerland, however, makes the Swiss case even less intelligible than if it was on the basis of the HDI alone.

An analysis of the correlations between the rate of political exclusion and the political and socio-economic characteristics considered shows that only the HDI and the number of years as a democracy yield statistically significant coefficients (-0.82 with $p<0.01$ and -0.67 with $p<0.05$, respectively). If, in addition, we regress political exclusion on these two variables, only the HDI shows a statistically significant effect ($\beta=-0.10$; $p<0.003$; $R^2=0.68$).

In strictly statistical terms, we might thus conclude that a direct effect of the other political and socio-economic characteristics considered cannot be confirmed. Nor, however, are we in a position to rule out their importance. The fact that we are dealing with a limited number of cases obviously limits the reliability of the findings. A strict reading of the statistical results indicates that a direct effect can be confirmed for the HDI only. But we must not forget that the number of years as a democracy, when considered individually, correlates closely with the level of tolerance, and that the other factors singled out by our two hypotheses may be important as auxiliary explanations. It is evident that these hypotheses require more extensive testing before more definitive conclusions can be drawn.

Conjunctural factors and tolerance

Can we say, in view of the theoretical considerations and empirical findings presented above, that civil and political rights are no longer a problem in established democracies, as there is a consensus regarding the social and political acceptance of others, with all the diversity of social status, religion, and ideological and political orientation? Not exactly. Empirical research shows that attitudes of political intolerance persist in established democracies. There are even cases in which an increase has been recorded, as is confirmed in particular by the European Values Surveys (EVS) of 1990 and 1999 and the Euro Barometers of 1997 and 2000 (EB 47.1 and 50). The report from EB 50 (Thalhammer *et al.* 2001) states right at the beginning that attitudes toward minority groups have developed with contradictory signs since 1997. If, on the one hand, certain results revealed more positive attitudes towards minorities, in particular a rise in support for policies of integration for these social groups, there was, on the other hand, an increase in the fears of deterioration in public services, particularly in the area of social protection, with the causes being partly attributed to minority groups.

In a response to these apparently inconsistent patterns, Sniderman *et al.* (1989) established a distinction between 'principled' and 'situational' tolerance. For them, it is essentially a matter of distinguishing consistent attitudes with regard to principles of tolerance from situation-dependent expressions of (in)tolerance not based on an underlying set of principles. 'Situational tolerance' reveals itself in assessments that depend on the specific relationship between the majority and the different groups that are potentially subject to discrimination.

While it may not be necessary to actually think in terms of two different concepts of tolerance, these considerations lead to a hypothesis about the effects of conjunctural factors. A rise in insecurity and political conflict that the majority of citizens associate with a certain social group tends to increase political and social discrimination against that group. However, the impact will depend on the overall (and hence more 'principled') level of tolerance. In countries with high levels of intolerance, subjective perceptions of conflict and insecurity tend to increase discrimination against the target group without distinction. In countries with low levels of intolerance, the effects are more selective. They are most visible for rights that, supposedly, put citizens' security at risk, but are less evident with respect to other rights of the target group.

To test this hypothesis we need to disaggregate political exclusion and social discrimination results based on the target groups. The results are presented in Tables 5.3 and 5.4, where the individual groups are divided into four categories: ideological extremists, religious fundamentalists, stigmatised groups, and ethnic minorities.

With regard to my hypothesis, note to begin with that the percentages for social discrimination against 'drug addicts' are significantly higher than the corresponding percentages for political exclusion, except in those countries where the general level of intolerance is highest: Russia, Romania, and Moldova. In some cases, the differences are quite large: 52 percentage points for Norway, 44 for Sweden, 40 for the Netherlands, 28 for Denmark, 24 for West Germany, 25 for Spain and Switzerland, and 17 for Portugal. The same pattern is evident for 'people with a criminal record' and 'people with AIDS', although in these cases the differences are smaller. For 'homosexuals', 'immigrants', and 'people of a different race', the differences between political exclusion and social discrimination tend to be very small. In these cases people do not seem to think that their personal security is threatened.

This pattern seems to support my hypothesis. Before drawing any general conclusion, however, it is important to consider the results for the five extremist groups. Generally speaking, the order of the countries with regard to the political exclusion of 'Christian fundamentalists' and 'Islamic fundamentalists' is similar to that for political exclusion in general. However, the figures are generally higher than those for the target groups previously considered, particularly for 'Islamic fundamentalists'. If we compare the political exclusion rates for 'Islamic fundamentalists' with those for social discrimination, we find the values to be quite similar for Russia, Romania, and Moldova. In other countries, Portugal and Spain excepted, the rate of social discrimination is higher than that of political exclusion. Countries with relatively high levels of general tolerance seem reluctant to accept physical proximity to these religious extremists, although they are relatively ready to accept their participation in political life. Once again, the hypothesis is confirmed. Generally tolerant societies differ in their attitudes toward political exclusion and social discrimination.

With regard to the political exclusion of ideological extremists, the picture changes significantly. With regard to 'right-wing extremists' and 'racists', the exclusion rates are relatively high for almost all countries (Denmark and Portugal excepted), and the borderlines between the three groups of countries blurred.

It is worth reflecting on some particular situations. In Portugal, the political exclusion of religious and political extremists is low. Although the exclusion rate for 'racists' is higher than for other extremist groups, it is low in comparison with other countries. This explains the country's

Table 5.3 Political exclusion of different social groups[a]

Social group	CH	DK	EG	WG	ES	MD	NL	NO	PT	RO	RU	SE	SI[b]
Ideological extremists													
Left-wing extremists	49	10	41	37	42	45	36	25	9	45	16	21	33
Right-wing extremists	69	24	72	65	48	37	51	45	11	38	67	35	54
Racists	73	32	67	57	55	54	61	60	32	49	60	57	65
Religious extremists													
Christian fundamentalists	32	7	24	17	29	57	12	21	12	49	12	17	31
Islamic fundamentalists	47	20	33	31	52	55	29	34	20	55	50	26	47
Stigmatized groups													
People with a criminal record	31	4	32	24	17	58	11	27	17	43	50	27	–
Drug addicts	14	5	22	18	22	65	13	10	20	64	62	17	–
People with AIDS	6	2	6	6	6	49	3	3	10	10	26	2	–
Homosexuals	–	5	15	8	10	59	5	9	16	16	49	6	26
Ethnic minorities													
Immigrants	13	4	9	6	8	37	4	6	5	30	12	3	10
People of a different race	8	2	5	4	6	34	2	3	8	22	9	2	7

Notes
a Entries are the percentages of respondents who want to exclude individuals from the social group in question from participation in public life.
b For Slovenia, only partial information is available.

Table 5.4 Social discrimination against different social groups[a]

Social group	CH	DK	EG	WG	ES	MD	NL	NO	PT	RO	RU	SE	SI[b]
Ideological extremists													
Left-wing extremists	52	17	38	42	35	42	39	28	7	41	14	27	–
Right-wing extremists	69	37	73	71	42	35	59	53	8	36	60	47	–
Racists	73	40	61	61	50	53	69	63	34	47	50	64	63
Religious extremists													
Christian fundamentalists	41	13	25	21	24	58	16	30	10	47	13	26	–
Islamic fundamentalists	55	47	36	41	48	56	38	46	18	52	47	39	–
Stigmatized groups													
People with a criminal record	45	7	40	37	26	61	22	55	22	46	54	60	22
Drug addicts	39	33	33	42	47	70	53	62	37	66	80	61	52
People with AIDS	7	3	10	12	14	58	7	10	19	38	49	7	15
Homosexuals	14	5	13	12	9	61	5	11	17	58	54	8	24
Ethnic minorities													
Immigrants	10	2	9	7	10	39	5	12	2	31	12	6	9
People of a different race	4	10	6	7	7	36	4	6	10	26	10	5	6

Notes
a Entries are the percentages of respondents who reject members of the social group in question as neighbours.
b For Slovenia, only partial information is available.

position on the general scale of political tolerance. In addition, and in contrast to the pattern found in other countries, the rate of social discrimination against these particular groups is lower than the rate of political exclusion, except for 'racists'. These results seem to be consistent with my ideas about the effect of conjunctural factors on tolerance. In Portugal, there is little political conflict with either religious or political extremists, as illustrated by the absence of xenophobic political parties.

Switzerland also displays certain interesting peculiarities. The values for political exclusion and social discrimination are high not only for religious and ideological extremists, but also for individuals with a criminal record, which reveals the primacy of the values of order and security. For the other target groups, however, exclusion and discrimination rates are very close to countries with average levels of tolerance.

It may also be worthwhile to consider the development over time of social discrimination towards different target groups in order to clarify certain points and confirm others. For this purpose I have selected some countries from the EVS in 1990 and 1999 (Table 5.5). With regard to ideological extremism, there is a general trend towards increased social discrimination rates in all countries, except Portugal, where there has been a marked decrease, and Germany, where there has been a slight fall of 3 percentage points in the case of the extreme left. When it comes to 'drug addicts', the discrimination rates are high and relatively stable, again with the notable exception of Portugal. For all other target groups, the trend is towards a decrease in social discrimination, especially in Portugal, where there has been a fall of 20 percentage points for 'people with AIDS' and 26 percentage points for 'homosexuals'. These findings add to our understanding of the particularities of the Portuguese case.

A micro-level model of political tolerance

At various points in the previous section, I have hinted at individual-level characteristics favouring or inhibiting the development of tolerance. It is now time to provide a more systematic presentation of these factors for the purpose of constructing and testing a micro-level model of tolerance.

Let us begin with the dependent variable. According to well-established methodological principles, the more homogeneous the object to be explained, the more successful the explanation will be. The theoretical assumptions originally put forward and, to a certain extent, confirmed by the empirical results for different target groups favour a division of these groups into two main categories, the first containing extremist groups and the second stigmatised groups and ethnic minorities (see Table 5.3). My focus is on the political exclusion of these groups.[1] Hence, two dependent variables were constructed, one for each category of groups. Both variables indicate the mean number of groups excluded on a scale ranging from 0 (no group) to 1 (all groups).

Table 5.5 Social discrimination against different social groups according to the world values surveys 1990 and 1999[a]

Social group and year	Denmark	Germany	The Netherlands	Portugal	Spain
Left-wing extremists					
1990	6	51	47	30	25
1999	9	48	50	13	25
Right-wing extremists					
1990	7	62	52	28	28
1999	20	74	69	15	29
Muslims[b]					
1990	15	20	14	19	12
1999	16	13	12	8	11
People with a criminal record					
1990	28	27	28	57	37
1999	31	25	32	43	32
Drug addicts					
1990	54	60	72	61	56
1999	60	58	73	46	53
People with AIDS					
1990	9	28	15	45	34
1999	6	12	8	25	21
Homosexuals					
1990	12	34	11	52	29
1999	8	14	6	26	16
Immigrants/foreign workers[c]					
1990	12	16	9	10	9
1999	11	11	5	3	9

Notes
a Figures are percentages.
b The CID survey provides data on Islamic fundamentalists rather than Muslims.
c The CID survey provides data on immigrants. Foreign workers are not mentioned.

Regarding the independent variables, we should distinguish the long-term structural factors underlying the formation of basic predispositions about social and political life from conjunctural effects deriving from perceptions of social conflict.[2] With regard to the structural factors, the literature allows us to distinguish three main dimensions. The first focuses on socio-economic and socio-cultural levels of modernisation in industrial societies. The second covers social attitudes and identities, as expressed through people's perceptions and feelings about others and themselves (social identities). The third is more explicitly political and encompasses values, identities, and behaviour directly related to political life.

Among the factors within the first dimension, education and age (or generation) are most prevalent in the literature (Stouffer 1955; Nunn *et al.* 1978; Sullivan *et al.* 1982; Bobo and Licardi 1989; Sniderman *et al.*

1989). The reasons advanced for the importance of education are twofold. On the one hand, education puts people in touch with different ideas and different lifestyles. On the other hand, more educated people are better equipped to relate to abstract democratic norms in specific situations. Age (or generation), gender, place of residence (in our case operationalised on a scale from rural to urban), and church attendance are variables which belong to the same theoretical construct.

Within this set of variables, my hypothesis is that gender will not matter much (Thalhammer *et al.* 2001) but that we can expect higher tolerance among the well-educated, the young, the religious, and those living in an urban environment. These expectations refer primarily to the political exclusion of stigmatised groups and ethnic minorities. For the other dependent variable, my expectation is that these variables will wholly or partly lose their explanatory power.

With regard to the second dimension (social attitudes and identities), it was recognised at an early stage that perception of danger associated with a certain group contributed to intolerant attitudes towards this group. These effects, however, depended on the characteristics of the person. Stouffer (1955) referred to the optimistic characteristics of persons favouring tolerance, and McClosky and Brill (1983) considered flexibility and self-esteem to operate in a similar way. Within the fields of sociology and political science, the amount of trust placed in others (see Chapter 2) is somewhat analogous to the psychological constructs just mentioned. In their study on tolerance, Sullivan *et al.* (1982: 162) mention the relatively high correlation ($r = 0.20$) between social trust and tolerance. My hypothesis is that social trust has greater explanatory power with regard to the exclusion of stigmatised groups and ethnic minorities than with regard to the exclusion of extremist groups.

Within this dimension, I also consider the degree of attachment to one's religion and culture, for which a negative relationship with political tolerance is expected. As shown by several studies (e.g. Gibson and Gouws 2000), strong identifications with particular groups tend to boost intolerance with respect to other groups. However, it is conceivable that religious identification could increase the political tolerance of stigmatised groups and ethnic minorities. As long as extremist and fundamentalist threats to religion are not at issue, religious principles of social solidarity may be operating.

With regard to the third dimension finally, the macro-analysis carried out above underlined the importance of the political sphere in shaping attitudes of tolerance. In many micro analyses, acceptance of democratic values appears as the main explanation (Lawrence 1976; Sullivan *et al.* 1982). There is, however, a certain amount of controversy about the results obtained. For Prothro and Grigg (1960) and McClosky (1964), for instance, the empirical results do not indicate a relationship between acceptance of democratic standards and tolerance.

While no strictly equivalent indicators appear in my model, I do consider confidence in institutions (as operationalised in Chapter 2), that is confidence in political institutions and actors as well as institutions associated with the rule of law). My expectation is that trust in institutions favour tolerant attitudes with respect to both dependent variables.

Authoritarianism and dogmatism have often appeared in the literature as explanations of political intolerance (Stouffer 1955; Sullivan et al. 1982). While my model does not include anything strictly equivalent to these psychological constructs, I do consider the norms of good citizenship presented in Chapter 4. My hypothesis is that citizens stressing law-abidingness are more intolerant, particularly with regard to stigmatised groups and ethnic minorities. For those who emphasise solidarity, I expect the contrary, that is greater tolerance, at least for stigmatised groups and ethnic minorities. For those who underline the importance of criticism and deliberation, finally, a positive effect on tolerance might be expected for both dependent variables.

Ideological position has also been considered in the literature. The results indicate that liberals (in the United States) and people on the left (in Europe) tend to be more tolerant (Sniderman et al. 1989; Thalhammer et al. 2001). However, some European studies have pointed to an increasing lack of ideological identification as well as a blurred understanding of the traditional notion of left and right (Schweisguth 1999). Nevertheless, my hypothesis is that those who place themselves to the left are more tolerant toward stigmatised groups and ethnic minorities. However, I expect little explanatory power with regard to extremist groups, since in this case, the threats to democratic principles will tend to neutralise primary inclinations of tolerance.

With respect to political involvement, early results pointing to a positive and significant relationship (Stouffer 1955) have later been contested. With other variables controlled, in particular education, Nunn et al. (1978) found that political involvement had little impact. Nevertheless, the matter certainly merits further testing. The measure I use is the extent to which people discuss politics, and my hypothesis is that those who do so more frequently are less prone to political exclusion, particularly with respect to stigmatised groups and ethnic minorities.

With regard to conjunctural factors, migratory flows in Europe and the spread of drugs and AIDS have produced new minority and stigmatised groups. This situations may breed perceptions of insecurity, which in turn might favour the rise of intolerant movements. The same sense of insecurity may partly explain the increased political exclusion of extremist groups in traditionally tolerant countries. To explain attitudes towards groups that pose a supposed threat to people's security, we have only one variable, that is, the amount of exposure to information about politics and social affairs obtained through newspapers, radio, and television. My hypothesis is that a higher level of political tolerance is to be expected among those who receive more information, at least with regard to stigmatised groups and ethnic minorities. For the other dependent variable, my expectations are the reverse.

The results of my analyses are presented in Tables 5.6 (extremist groups) and 5.7 (stigmatised groups and ethnic minorities). Note to begin with that, for most countries, the variance explained is lower for the first dependent variable than for the second. This is in line with my general hypothesis that many of the predictors are likely to have less impact for extremist groups than for stigmatised groups and ethnic minorities. Even in the latter case, however, a predominant part of the variance remains unexplained.

Another general pattern is that the results show a considerable amount of variation across countries. This is true with regard to the proportion of variance explained as well as with regard to the impact of the individual predictors. As we shall see, this does not mean that the effects are generally inconsistent or out of line with my hypotheses. But the extent to which a particular effect is present varies considerably across countries.

In some cases, however, there are indeed signs of inconsistency in the sense that the same predictor shows a positive and statistically significant effect in some countries but a negative one in others. Among these is the very first predictor: the size of the locality in which the respondent lives. For the first dependent variable, the effect of living in a more urban environment is negative (as hypothesised) in five countries but positive in three others, all of which located in eastern Europe (East Germany, Romania, and Russia). For the second dependent variable, the three significant are all negative, but the expectation that place of residence would matter more for this aspect of tolerance than for the first is hardly borne out.

In line with our expectations, gender does not have much impact. In five out of 24 cases, there is a weak but statistically significant difference, usually indicating slightly greater tolerance among women. As far as age is concerned, the expected pattern of greater intolerance among older citizens manifests itself with a fair amount of regularity. The effect is statistically significant, and sometimes fairly strong, in 14 cases, all but one of which (Portugal for the second dependent variable) showing the expected sign.

The results for education, on the other hand, are surprisingly mixed. For stigmatised groups and ethnic minorities, statistically significant effects are found in only four instances, all of which carrying the expected sign and some reaching respectable strength. For extremist groups, the effect is significant in five instances, but in all but one of these (Norway), education is positively rather than negatively associated with the rate of political exclusion.

The effect of church attendance, finally, resembles that of gender. It is statistically significant in only three of 24 cases, two of which showing the expected sign.

Table 5.6 Multiple regression analysis of political exclusion of extremist groups[a]

Predictor	CH	DK	EG	WG	ES	MD	NL	NO	PT	RO	RU[b]	SE
Size of locality	−0.04	−0.08**	0.11*	−0.11***	0.06*	−0.15***	0.12	−0.02	−0.13***	0.11*	0.05*	−0.14***
Gender (female)	0.01	−0.02	−0.02	0.00	−0.03	0.04	−0.01	−0.02	−0.05*	−0.01	−0.05**	−0.01
Age	0.15*	0.00	0.15*	0.26***	0.03	0.00	0.23***	0.06	−0.00	0.12	0.12*	0.04
Education	0.01	0.02	0.33***	0.15**	−0.01	0.20	0.09	−0.25***	0.11	0.21*	0.22***	−0.01
Church attendance	−0.06	−0.02	0.05	−0.01	−0.02	−0.05	0.00	−0.09**	0.00	0.11	0.11***	−0.04
Religious attachment	0.02	0.01	−0.20***	−0.07	−0.04	0.08	−0.04	0.02	0.02	−0.02	–	0.00
Cultural attachment	0.05	0.00	0.10*	0.09	0.13**	0.16	0.07	0.08*	−0.01	−0.12	–	0.05
Social trust	−0.06	0.01	−0.10*	−0.11*	−0.15***	−0.08	−0.03	−0.12*	−0.17***	0.02	0.01	−0.17**
Confidence in institutions	0.02	−0.15**	0.20**	0.06	−0.08	−0.26***	−0.19**	−0.16**	0.08	−0.02	−0.11**	−0.06
Good citizen: solidarity	−0.08	0.10*	−0.14*	−0.15***	0.07	0.06	0.16	−0.05	−0.00	−0.08	−0.01	0.08
Good citizen: law-abidingness	0.05	−0.03	−0.02	0.17***	0.06	0.06	−0.10	0.07	−0.03	0.38***	0.03	0.04
Good citizen: deliberation	−0.01	−0.04	0.13	0.13**	−0.06	0.03	0.10	0.00	0.03	−0.06	0.01	−0.08
Left–right placement	0.07	0.08*	−0.03	−0.10	0.09*	−0.03	0.06	0.03	0.02	0.07	0.06	0.09
Political discussion	0.04	0.00	−0.04	0.02	0.07**	0.06	0.15***	−0.09*	0.06	0.08	0.09***	0.01
Media exposure	0.09	−0.02	0.08	−0.13***	0.03	0.15*	0.04	0.15**	0.10*	0.06	0.01	0.03
Adjusted R^2	0.01	0.01	0.10	0.05	0.02	0.06	0.05	0.04	0.05	0.05	0.06	0.02
N	1,071	1,489	780	1,582	2,672	730	1,179	1564	772	874	1,469	1,033

Notes

a Entries are unstandardised regression coefficients. Levels of statistical significance: *** = 0.001, ** = 0.01, * = 0.05. *Size of locality* ranges from 0 (rural area) to 1 (city with more than 500,000 inhabitants). *Gender* is a dummy variable scored 1 for female. *Age* and *education* are operationalised as described in Chapter 1. *Church attendance* ranges from 0 (never) to 1 (several times a week). *Religious* and *cultural attachment* are both 11-point scales scored to range from 0 (no attachment at all) to 1 (very strong attachment). *Social trust* and *confidence in institutions* are operationalised as described in Chapter 2. The *good citizen* measures are operationalised as described in Chapter 4. *Political discussion* is a four-point scale ranging from 0 (never) to 1 (often). *Media exposure* is an additive index ranging from 0 to 1 and based on three five-point scales indicating how often the respondent reads the political contents of a newspaper, listens to or watches the news on the radio or TV, and listens to or watches programmes about politics and social affairs on the radio or TV. *Left–right placement* is an 11-point scale scored to range from 0 (far left) to 1 (far right). To avoid excessive loss of cases, respondents for which left–right placement was missing were placed in the middle of the scale. Slovenia is excluded from the analysis due to problems of comparability.

b Two of the predictors are missing from the Russian data set.

Table 5.7 Multiple regression analysis of political exclusion of stigmatised groups and ethnic minorities[a]

Predictor	CH	DK	EG	WG	ES[c]	MD	NL	NO	PT	RO	RU[b]	SE
Size of locality	−0.07	−0.01	−0.01	−0.06**	0.01	−0.09*	−0.04	0.00	−0.14***	0.03	0.01	−0.02
Gender (female)	−0.04**	−0.01	−0.04*	−0.01	−0.01	0.06*	−0.01	0.00	−0.01	−0.04	0.01	−0.01
Age	0.31***	0.05*	0.03	0.20***	0.11***	−0.09	0.07*	0.26***	−0.15*	0.08	0.22***	0.14***
Education	−0.28***	−0.03	−0.06	0.06	−0.03	−0.00	−0.05	−0.15***	−0.30***	−0.00	−0.05	−0.15***
Church attendance	−0.00	−0.00	0.07	−0.05*	0.01	−0.10	−0.01	−0.03	0.03	0.05	—	0.00
Religious attachment	0.06*	0.02	−0.10***	0.02	0.04*	0.08	0.01	0.05**	0.06	0.09	—	−0.02
Cultural attachment	0.09**	−0.02	0.11***	0.07*	0.07**	0.26***	0.07**	0.02	0.03	−0.14	0.02	0.05
Social trust	−0.16***	0.01	−0.09**	−0.16***	−0.10***	−0.15*	−0.07*	−0.14***	−0.07	−0.04	−0.09**	−0.15***
Confidence in institutions	−0.04	−0.10***	−0.10*	0.20***	−0.03	−0.10	−0.12**	−0.03	−0.02	0.06	−0.08*	−0.06
Good citizen: solidarity	0.04	−0.02	0.16***	−0.14***	−0.03	0.04	0.06	−0.04	−0.05	−0.10	0.05	−0.00
Good citizen: law-abidingness	0.03	0.04*	0.12**	0.10***	0.03	0.15	−0.05	0.02	0.01	0.34***	0.00	0.07*
Good citizen: deliberation	−0.22***	−0.02	−0.21***	−0.02	−0.11***	−0.01	−0.02	−0.10***	−0.00	−0.15**	0.00	−0.12**
Left–right placement	0.08*	0.05	0.20***	0.06	0.12***	0.03	0.04	0.05*	0.02	0.04	0.05	0.05
Political discussion	0.04	−0.03*	0.02	−0.08**	−0.01	0.00	0.01	−0.01	−0.01	0.03	0.02	−0.01
Media exposure	−0.05	−0.00	−0.08*	−0.14***	−0.01	0.13*	−0.04	−0.06	0.13***	−0.01	0.02	−0.04
Adjusted R^2	0.17	0.04	0.10	0.17	0.08	0.09	0.04	0.13	0.08	0.02	0.03	0.12
N	1,071	1,489	780	1,582	2,672	745	1,179	1564	772	912	1,469	1,033

Notes
a See note to Table 5.6.
b Two of the predictors are missing from the Russian data set.

Let us now proceed to the second of our three general theoretical dimensions, that is, social attitudes and identities. For religious attachment, statistically significant effects are visible in only five cases, four of which refer to the second of the two dependent variables. Three of these effects are positive, indicating a greater rate of exclusion among respondents with strong religious attachment. Notably, the other two cases, where the effect is negative, both pertain to East Germany.

For cultural attachment, the pattern is somewhat stronger as well as more consistent. Nine of the effects are statistically significant, all of which in the expected direction. Six of them refer to the second dependent variable. However, the most important factor within this general dimension is undoubtedly social trust. In this case, 15 effects are statistically significant, all of which having the expected negative sign. Again, most of them (two-thirds) refer to the second rather than the first dependent variable.

The first representative of the third, more explicitly political, dimension is confidence in institutions. The pattern in this case is not quite as strong and consistent as for social trust, but still readily discernable. Eleven of the effects are statistically significant and nine of them have the expected negative sign. The two deviations are East Germany on the first dependent variable and West Germany on the second. Note that in this case a slightly larger proportion of the significant effects (six of 11) refer to the first rather than the second dependent variable.

With respect to the three norms of good citizenship, those regarding law-abidingness and criticism and deliberation both have a moderate but consistent impact. Seven of the effects are statistically significant in the former case, six in the latter. All carry the expected sign, positive for law-abidingness and negative for criticism and deliberation. All but two of them (both for law-abidingness) refer to the second rather than the first dependent variable.

For solidarity, the pattern is weaker as well as less consistent. Only four of the effects are statistically significant (two for each dependent variable) of which three carry the expected negative sign. The deviating case is East Germany with regard to the second of the two dependent variables.

Left–right placement displays a picture fairly similar to that of law-abidingness. Six of the effects are statistically significant and all carry the expected positive sign. Two-thirds of them refer to the second rather than the first dependent variable.

The impact of political involvement as measured by the frequency of political discussion is not nil but quite inconsistent. While six of the effects are statistically significant, only half of them carry the expected negative sign. The positive effects (for the Netherlands, Russia and Spain) all pertain to the first rather than the second dependent variable.

Regardless of whether we see it in the light conjunctural effects, as I did in my theoretical discussion above, or take it to be yet another indicator of political involvement, the pattern for political media exposure is very similar to that for political discussion. While eight of the effects are statistically significant, five of them carry a positive rather than negative sign. In this case, positive effects are found for the first (Moldova, Norway, and Portugal) as well as the second (Moldova and Portugal) dependent variable.

Conclusions

I have demonstrated that there are significant differences between the countries studied with regard to the level of political and social tolerance. Two hypotheses regarding the impact of political and socio-economic factors were advanced to explain the level of political tolerance across countries. Although the measures at our disposal represent a simplification, they indicate that the level of tolerance is closely associated with social development and well-being on the one hand, and the duration of democracy on the other.

We can divide the theoretical positions on tolerance into two camps. Based on theories of modernisation, the first argues that the process of development produces greater tolerance. The second, relying on the most recent information on conflicts in relation to certain social groups and the increase in xenophobia, claims that intolerance in democratic societies is rising, contradictory to the supposed structural trends. My response was not to take sides in a dichotomous fashion but to try to specify the conditions under which these positions are defensible. The theories of modernisation are correct if we consider groups that represent other cultures, social characteristics, and lifestyles, but are not perceived as a social danger. My group-by-group analysis of political exclusion and social discrimination as well as my attempts to explain political exclusion on the micro-level helps to buttress this conclusion.

Although our data represent but a single point in time, they could nevertheless bear witness to the effect of new forms of insecurity on the rate of social discrimination. Among other things, I have shown that the most tolerant countries discriminate socially against certain target groups to a greater extent than they exclude them politically, in particular with respect to 'drug addicts', 'people with a criminal record', and 'Islamic fundamentalists'. In these countries, attitudes of rejection are more selective and can be assumed to coincide with perceived insecurity. In the most intolerant countries, rejection is equally strong in the political as in the social domain, revealing what we could call low structural tolerance.

It also proved worthwhile to consider the absolute rejection levels for different target groups. With respect to political exclusion, the groups most strongly rejected are 'right-wing extremists', 'racists', and 'Islamic fundamentalists'. In these cases, the differences between countries are very small, with the exception of Denmark and Portugal, where the rejection levels are noticeably lower. At the other end of the scale, the groups least commonly excluded are 'people with AIDS', 'immigrants', and 'people of a different race', although in Moldova, Romania, and Russia the rate of political exclusion of these groups remains high. These results are consistent with my hypothesis that the effect of perceptions of insecurity with regard to certain social groups depends on the overall level of tolerance. In countries that are generally more tolerant, the impact is selective. It does not extend to all target-groups and implies a distinction between social discrimination (which is higher) and political exclusion.

With regard to the micro-level model of political exclusion, I decided to divide the different target groups into two categories: extremist groups on the one hand and stigmatised groups and ethnic minorities on the other. The regression analyses produced complex, varied but nevertheless systematic results. To begin with, and as conjectured, the proportion of variance explained tends to be lower for the first dependent variable than the second. Further, the results show considerable variation across countries with respect to the variance explained as well the impact of specific predictors. None of them has a clear effect across the board. Quite a few, however, show a significant impact in the expected direction in a substantial subset of countries.

In outlining the model, I distinguished between three dimensions as far as the long-term, structural factors are concerned. The first focuses on levels of modernisation, the second on social attitudes and identities, and the third on more explicitly political characteristics.

Among the predictors belonging to the first dimension, age (or generation) provides the strongest pattern, with the elderly being significantly more intolerant in more than half of the cases. Somewhat surprisingly, the impact of education is not quite as visible. Furthermore, the direction of the effect varies with the dependent variable: negative with respect to the exclusion of stigmatised groups and ethnic minorities but usually positive with respect to the exclusion of extremist groups. The remaining predictors within the first dimension – size of locality, gender, and church attendance – tend to show but weak and/or inconsistent effects.

As far as the second dimension is concerned, the strongest predictor is social trust, which has a significant effect in the expected (negative) direction in well above half of the cases. Cultural attachment also shows the hypothesised (positive) effect in a relatively large number of instances whereas the impact of religious attachment is rather weak and inconsistent.

With respect to the third dimension, finally, confidence in institutions, degree of support for the norms of criticism/deliberation and law-abidingness, respectively, and left–right placement all display quite consistent effects in the expected direction (negative for the first two, positive for the others) in a moderately large number of instances. For the third norm of good citizenship, solidarity, as well as for political involvement in the form of political discussion and media exposure, the pattern is weaker and/or less consistent.

Notes

1 Regression analyses were also carried out for social discrimination against these two categories of groups. Inasmuch as they do not add much to the results, they are not presented.
2 This is a classical distinction in sociology and is cited in many studies on tolerance (see for example, Marcus *et al.* 1995: 15). There are also authors who overestimate the importance of situational factors either in general (Downs 1957; Converse 1964) or in some specific analyses (McClosky 1964; McClosky and Brill 1983).

Part II
Voluntary organisations and social networks

6 Associational involvement

Laura Morales and Peter Geurts

Introduction

The right of citizens to assemble and to unite in associations is a well-acknowledged and cited prerequisite for democracy. However, it is one thing to *have* the right and another to *exercise* it. Is it important to what extent citizens actually make use of this fundamental democratic right and how that use is distributed among them? During the last decade, social scientists have sparked a vivid debate about the virtues of associational involvement for democracy, for the economy and for society as a whole.[1] Researchers have provided several reasons why citizens' participation in associations is relevant.[2]

Involvement in associations is thought to be related to democratic attitudes and orientations, participatory behaviour, and knowledge about issues of public interest. On the one hand, involvement in associations might well have an effect on the set of attitudes and orientations citizens hold. Associations have often been portrayed as *schools of democracy* inasmuch as they can promote positive feelings towards other social and political institutions (political trust, legitimacy, interest in politics, etc.), towards other individuals (social trust), and towards oneself as a politically capable actor (feelings of efficacy).[3] It is argued that this is due to the spillover effects of interacting with other trusting people, and the sense of efficacy and confidence that may result from successful interaction with political institutions (see, for example, Brehm and Rahn 1997; Stolle 1998).[4] On the other hand, associational involvement can also have effects on individuals' behaviour. Many scholars have argued that involvement in associations foster political discussion and participation, since they tend to politicise members through the opportunities to exchange information they provide while at the same time providing the necessary skills and knowledge to interact with political institutions (see Almond and Verba 1963; Erbe 1964; Olsen 1972; Verba *et al.* 1978; Cohen and Rogers 1992; Rosenstone and Hansen 1993; Verba *et al.* 1995; Leighley 1996; van Deth 1997).[5] Additionally, to the extent that associations can be used as resources for mobilisation, citizens involved in them are more likely to participate in politics. Associations are cooperative networks, but they can also induce cooperation beyond their boundaries.

In addition to the potential effects of associational involvement, some researchers argue that participation in associations is a structural indicator of the existence of stocks of social capital. Associations facilitate repeated cooperation and can be used for productive ends. Beyond the social capital debate however, associational involvement is one of many indicators of social (and political) integration. *Caeteris paribus*, individuals who are involved in associations will be more integrated in the social and political life that surrounds them than citizens who have no contact whatsoever with associations. Associations contribute to the integration of citizens within their communities, allowing them to exercise their citizenship more fully. On this basis, Cohen and Rogers (1992), Rogers and Cohen (1995), and Hirst (1994) argue that associational involvement is of intrinsic democratic value since it helps citizens acquire information relevant for their public action, provides them with opportunities for deliberation, and increases their self-government.

Finally, associational involvement can also have important distributional implications. Associational involvement is in itself a resource and frequently affects the allocation of resources and the distribution of power. Thus, if this behaviour is not equally distributed across social categories, participation in associations might contribute to increased social and political inequalities or, at best, reproduce the unequal representation of interests and preferences in the public sphere (see Verba and Nie 1972; Verba *et al.* 1995; and Schlozman *et al.* 1999). Nevertheless, associational involvement may show a more complex relation with participatory inequalities, since they can serve to equalise public action by providing additional resources to the less resourceful. In fact, the effects of associational involvement on political (in)equality can be related to the degree to which individual resources determine certain types of political action (Verba *et al.* 1978: 130 ff.). Thus, associational affiliations might help to equalise the vote, but have the opposite effect on more demanding forms of political participation.

In summary, the existing body of research brings up many interesting questions related to associational involvement. The first set is fundamentally descriptive and refers to the degree to which citizens are integrated in their communities through associations. To what extent are citizens involved in associations? In what types of associations are they most commonly involved, and what is the nature of their involvement? How do these patterns vary across countries? A second set of questions focuses on the factors that enable us to understand the different patterns of associational involvement. Which factors prompt some citizens to get involved in associations? Which factors determine the type of associations they choose? And, more importantly, are these factors the same across countries, or are they context-specific? Finally, some of the most crucial issues focus on the effects of participation in associations. Are citizens in organizations more trustful, efficacious, and confident in institutions? Are they more likely to participate in politics? Is this true for all types of associations and across all countries? Does organisational involvement promote or impede political equality?

Some of these questions have been addressed in previous chapters. Others will be analysed in those that follow. The main purpose of this chapter is to provide an overview of the patterns of associational involvement found in our 13 European societies. However, we will, also explore the relation between different forms of associational involvement and one of its presumed spillover effects: that on social trust.

The first section provides a discussion of the instruments used to measure associational involvement. The second section proceeds to an overview of the different patterns and forms of associational involvement. In the following section we propose a scale of associational involvement and use it to analyse our survey results. The fourth section examines in greater detail how the various forms of involvement vary across types of associations and how the constitutive goods of associations are related to the predominance of active versus passive forms of involvement. The last section explores the extent to which different kinds of associational involvement is related to social trust. The chapter concludes with a discussion of the findings and their implications.

Measuring associational involvement

One of the main contributions of the Citizenship, Involvement, and Democracy (CID) project lies in the innovative measurements of associational involvement. The dataset covers a spectrum of 27 associational types (plus one residual category), the most detailed break-down available so far. For each of them, we have information about several different types of involvement: membership, participation in activities, donations, and voluntary work.[6]

This approach to the measurement of associational involvement is very demanding both from the point of view of the respondent and from the point of view of the survey designer and the analyst.[7] On the other hand, several studies have shown measurement issues to be crucial for comparative inquiries of associational engagement. The items usually employed in order to capture such engagement may underestimate, in particular, the more informal ways of involvement.[8] As shown in Table 6.1,[9] asking about membership only generally underestimates the degree to which citizens are involved in associations. More importantly, the magnitude of this underestimate is not constant across countries, since some nations (especially Portugal, Slovenia, Spain, Norway, and Switzerland) show a higher proportion of citizens who are involved in associations without being members.

Table 6.1 Levels of associational involvement[a]

Country	Any involvement	Membership	Activities	Donations	Voluntary work	N
Norway	96	88	58	66	45	2,297
Switzerland	95	86	54	66	41	1,647
Denmark	93	92	70	43	44	1,640
Sweden	92	90	68	46	50	1,271
The Netherlands	87	84	54	41	31	1,649
West Germany	71	68	60	28	42	1,991
Slovenia	63	53	33	39	21	1,005
Portugal	58	43	34	35	22	1,010
East Germany	55	51	42	20	26	1,013
Spain	49	42	32	23	16	4,252
Russia	28	25	16	6	11	1,733
Romania[b]	20	20	15	9	9	1,217
Moldova[b]	20	20	14	8	12	1,219
Average	64	59	42	33	28	–
Standard deviation	28	28	20	20	14	–
Ratio maximum/minimum	4.8	4.6	4.9	11	5.6	–

Notes

a Percentages of respondents who are involved in the specified way in at least one association. The averages and standard deviations are calculated from the table values and, thus, give equal weight to all countries. Countries are ordered by the percentage of respondents showing any involvement in associations.

b The use of a slightly modified version of the measurement instrument in Moldova and Romania implies that involvement is equivalent to membership for these two countries.

It also becomes evident that focusing on volunteering as an indication of active forms of involvement – as, for example, in the World and European Values Surveys – implies an underestimate. As we expected, those who take part in activities organised by associations far outnumber those who engage in voluntary work. Again, cross-national differences are substantial. In Denmark, Germany, and Spain the percentage of citizens who participate in activities is several times higher than the percentage who do voluntary work.

Furthermore, the importance of these measurement issues becomes evident when we consider the percentage of respondents who are involved in associations only by means of participating in activities or donating money (results not shown). On average, the proportion of such citizens amounts to 1 and 3 per cent, respectively. Although this may seem a limited proportion, cross-national variations are again notable. In countries such as Portugal, Slovenia, and Spain, dismissing these two forms of involvement implies ignoring more than 10 per cent of all involved citizens.

In summary, this improved way of measuring associational involvement contributes considerably to a more accurate picture of this phenomenon. It is especially useful for cross-national comparisons, since it limits the potential biases introduced by the traditional narrow conception of involvement as measured by membership and voluntary work only. The explicit measurement of multiple forms of engagement in associations allow us to analyse the gradation of citizens' organisational involvement more accurately.[10]

Associational involvement: an overview

Previous research has already shown that levels of associational involvement vary greatly across countries (Curtis *et al.* 1992, 2001; Wessels 1997; van Deth and Kreuter 1998; Morales 2001, 2002, 2004). However, as we have indicated, prior information regarding these cross-national differences is mostly limited to levels of membership, and in very few cases (the World Values Surveys) to voluntary work in associations. How do European citizens differ in the extent and type of involvement in associations? Table 6.1 shows the general levels of associational involvement in 13 European societies, as well as the forms this involvement takes: membership, participation in activities, donations, and volunteering.

European countries do indeed differ substantially in the degree to which their citizens are involved in associations. The proportion showing any type of involvement varies from 96 per cent in Norway to 20 per cent in Romania and Moldova.[11] This means that the proportion is about five times larger in the first country than in the latter two. The ratio of maximum to minimum involvement becomes even larger when we consider individual types of involvement. It is particularly large for donations.

In Norway and Switzerland, citizens are more than ten times more likely to donate money to associations than in Russia.

Another important aspect is that countries showing unusually high or low levels of involvement in associations tend to do so for all forms of involvement. Thus, Norway, Switzerland, Denmark, and Sweden invariably show high levels regardless of which form of involvement we look at, while Russia, Romania, and Moldova constantly show the lowest percentages. Hence, the general pattern for Scandinavian and Swiss citizens is one of high involvement, while some Eastern European nationals are minimally engaged in associations.[12] Among the former countries, Denmark and Sweden are outstanding for their active citizenry, whereas the Norwegians and the Swiss show remarkably high levels of donations.

Given the vast array of associational types listed in the questionnaire, we can get an impression of the *breadth* of citizens' associational involvement by counting the number of types in which they are engaged. This is of special interest because, *caeteris paribus*, citizens who are only involved in one type of association are exposed to a narrower range of social and political stimuli than those who are involved in several. Table 6.2 gives an indication of the breadth of involvement for each form of engagement. Again, cross-national patterns are consistent with previous results. Where citizens are more frequently involved in associations, they also tend to be involved in a wider range of associations. Conversely, in countries where citizens are rarely involved in associations, their involvement tends to be of limited breadth.

In most countries the average number of associational categories in which citizens are involved is very close to the number in which they are members. However, Norway and Switzerland deviate substantially from this pattern. Once more, we see that the behaviour of Norwegian and Swiss citizens is remarkable when it comes to donating money. On average, citizens in these two countries contribute financially to at least two different types of associations, often without possessing membership in the recipient organisation.[13]

Active versus passive forms of associational involvement

So far we have described general patterns of involvement in associations, and the specific forms this involvement takes. However, some of the most interesting hypotheses related to this type of behaviour claim that associational involvement is currently limited, for the most part, to relatively passive forms of engagement. Citizens are said to be chequebook participants,[14] clients or passive supporters. In this regard, the nature of associational involvements is thought to be transforming.[15] To the general decline in associational involvement, some authors argue, we have to add a decline in the level of commitment of those who still get involved in associations. Putnam (2000, Chapter 3) contends that, while the number of associations

Table 6.2 Breadth of associational involvement[a]

Country	Involvement		Membership		Activities		Donations		Voluntary work		N
	Mean	S.d.	Mean	S.d.	Mean	S.d.	Mean	S.d.	Mean	S.d.	
Norway	5.0	3.7	2.8	2.1	1.3	1.8	2.0	2.5	0.9	1.5	2,297
Switzerland	5.1	3.8	2.9	2.5	1.3	1.7	2.2	2.7	0.8	1.5	1,647
Denmark	3.7	2.5	3.3	2.2	1.5	1.6	0.9	1.4	0.7	1.1	1,640
Sweden	3.5	2.3	3.0	2.0	1.4	1.5	0.9	1.3	0.9	1.2	1,271
The Netherlands	3.9	3.1	3.0	2.4	1.1	1.4	1.0	1.6	0.6	1.1	1,649
West Germany	1.6	1.6	1.4	1.4	1.1	1.2	0.5	0.9	0.7	1.0	1,991
Slovenia	1.4	1.7	1.0	1.3	0.6	1.0	0.7	1.1	0.3	0.8	1,005
Portugal	1.2	1.5	0.7	1.1	0.5	0.9	0.7	1.2	0.3	0.8	1,010
East Germany	1.0	1.4	0.9	1.1	0.7	1.2	0.3	0.7	0.4	0.9	1,013
Spain	0.9	1.4	0.6	1.0	0.4	0.9	0.4	0.8	0.2	0.6	4,252
Russia	0.4	0.8	0.3	0.7	0.2	0.6	0.1	0.4	0.1	0.5	1,733
Romania	0.3	0.8	0.3	0.8	0.2	0.6	0.1	0.4	0.1	0.5	1,217
Moldova	0.4	1.5	0.4	1.5	0.2	0.6	0.1	0.4	0.2	0.5	1,219
Average	2.2		1.6		0.8		0.7		0.5		
Standard deviation	1.8		1.2		0.5		0.7		0.3		
Ratio maximum/minimum	17.0		11.0		7.5		22.0		9.0		

Note

[a] Entries are the average number of types of associations in which the respondent is involved. As in Table 6.1, countries are ordered by the percentage of respondents showing any involvement in associations. The maximum value is 28.

is steadily increasing in the United States, new organisations are increasingly 'memberless' and generally little more than mailing lists. Jordan and Maloney (1997) have described a similar process in the United Kingdom: the strong emergence of *protest businesses* within the new-social-movements sector.[16] Thus, active involvement in associations, which is a better indicator of the existing stocks of social capital, is thought to be plummeting.

While our data do not allow us to explore the claims around this declining trend, we are able to assess the degree to which inactive forms of involvement are indeed dominant. As we have seen, the CID survey includes questions on different forms and degrees of associational involvement. This means that, for each individual, we can ascertain what type of involvement they engage in. With the information on membership, participation in activities, and voluntary work, we are able to construct a scale of citizens' associational involvement that spans the range from completely uninvolved to activist.[17]

As shown by the results in Table 6.3, passive forms of involvement are not as prevalent as one would expect from previous research. This is particularly so for the 'client-type' form of involvement. This form of involvement is more frequent, relative to other types, in countries with medium to low levels of associational involvement such as Portugal, Russia, and Spain.

Cross-national patterns appear more clearly if we consider only those citizens who are involved in associations, as in Table 6.4. In all countries,

Table 6.3 Patterns of Activism in associations[a]

Country	Uninvolved	Passive member	Client	Volunteer	Active member	Activist	N
Norway	8	27	2	2	25	36	2,297
Switzerland	9	28	3	2	25	33	1,647
Denmark	7	21	0	0	29	42	1,640
Sweden	9	21	0	0	22	47	1,271
The Netherlands	14	28	1	1	30	26	1,649
West Germany	30	8	1	1	20	41	1,991
Slovenia	44	20	1	3	16	17	1,005
Portugal	51	13	3	3	14	17	1,010
East Germany	47	11	2	1	16	25	1,013
Spain	55	12	2	1	16	14	4,252
Russia	72	10	1	1	6	9	1,733
Romania	80	4	0[b]	0[b]	6	9	1,217
Moldova	80	5	0[b]	0[b]	5	11	1,219

Notes
a Passive member = member only; client = activities only; volunteer = voluntary work only; active member = membership plus activities; activist = membership plus activities plus voluntary work. As in Table 6.1, countries are ordered by the percentage of respondents showing any involvement in associations.
b For Moldova and Romania, these results should be interpreted with caution due to the use of a slightly modified version of the measurement instrument in these two countries.

Table 6.4 Passive and active involvement in associations (involved respondents only)[a]

Country	Passively involved	Actively involved	N
Norway	34	66	2,196
Switzerland	38	62	1,570
Denmark	23	77	1,522
Sweden	24	76	1,166
The Netherlands	35	65	1,443
West Germany	15	85	1,352
Slovenia	44	55	631
Portugal	42	58	582
East Germany	23	77	551
Spain	36	64	2,056
Russia	43	57	485
Romania[b]	23	77	242
Moldova[b]	23	77	243

Notes
a Entries are percentages. As in Table 6.1, countries are ordered by the percentage of respondents showing any involvement in associations.
b In Moldova and Romania, active involvement is probably overestimated due to the slightly modified version of the measurement instrument used in these two countries.

citizens actively involved in associations outnumber those passively involved. Moreover, levels of involvement do not appear to be strongly related to the level of activity among those involved. If indeed there is any relationship at all, countries where citizens are more frequently involved in associations tend to have a larger share of passive as opposed to active involvement.[18] But since the relationship is weak and the overall level of involvement so much higher in the countries of northern and central Europe than it is elsewhere, these countries nevertheless show substantially higher levels of organisational activity in the population as a whole.

In summary, associational involvement of all types is more frequent in the northern and central than in the southern and eastern European countries. In the former case, citizens are more prone to engage in associations and they do so in more diverse ways. Finally, although the organisations citizens join certainly tends to outnumber those in which they actively participates, the majority of those engaged in organisations are active participant in at least one of them. Therefore, passive forms of associational involvement are by no means dominant in the societies we study.

Types of associations and forms of involvement

Now that we have explored the interrelations between different forms of associational involvement, a further question emerges: do patterns of involvement substantially vary with the type of association considered?

The type of association that attracts by far the greatest proportion of citizens is the sports club.[19] In the Scandinavian countries about half of the adult population is involved in some way in such an organisation. Only eastern European countries like Russia, Romania, and Moldova show very low levels of involvement in this case. Trade unions also attract large numbers of citizens, especially in Scandinavia and eastern Europe, where they are the most popular type of organisation. Automobile organisations are a special case, since they are invariably limited to membership and their leverage is restricted to a few countries (the Netherlands, Switzerland, and, to a lesser extent, Germany and Norway). Among the least populous types of associations are lodges and service clubs along with immigrants' organisations.

Despite these common patterns, we find remarkable national peculiarities. With no less than 59 per cent involvement, primarily through donations, humanitarian and human-rights organisations are extremely popular in Norway. A parallel case is charities in Slovenia. Residents' associations are particularly strong in Scandinavia and the Netherlands and consumer organisations (often co-ops) are very popular in Sweden and Denmark. Environmental organisations and animal rights groups have found fertile ground in Switzerland and the Netherlands, while the more classical professional organisations are doing particularly well in Norway and Switzerland.

Sports clubs are at the top not only in terms of overall involvement but also in terms of activity. Between 10 and 35 per cent of the citizens in our national samples engage in some activity organised by sports or outdoor clubs. Other recreational associations, such as cultural societies and hobby clubs, are also successful in engaging citizens in their activities. The same is true about certain other types of organisations as well, such as trade unions and religious organisations.

Involvement via donations is relatively common in many European societies. As we saw in Table 6.1, this form of engagement is particularly widespread in northern and central Europe. In many cases, it is strongly concentrated to certain types of associations. Humanitarian or human rights organisations compete with the more traditional charities and social-welfare associations for the first position in terms of attracting donations. Humanitarian groups are preferred by citizens in Norway and Sweden, while charities are more frequent recipients in most other countries. Strong evidence of what has been termed *chequebook participation* – that is, a high level of donations combined with a low level of involvement in other regards – is found for environmental organisations and animal rights groups in Switzerland and the Netherlands and humanitarian aid or human rights organisations in Norway.[20] Nonetheless, sports clubs and associations for medical patients also receive widespread citizen financial support in Scandinavia and Switzerland. The same is true about religious groups in Norway, Switzerland, the Netherlands, and Portugal.

Voluntary work is a much more uncommon form of associational involvement and quite concentrated to specific types of associations, predominantly sports clubs but also cultural societies, charities, hobby clubs, residents' groups, and religious organisations. The precise extent to which these organisations attract volunteers varies across countries: cultural societies are particularly strong loci of voluntary work in West Germany, charities in Switzerland, and residents' organisations in all three Scandinavian countries.

How involvement patterns vary across different types of associations is shown in Table 6.5, which is restricted to the types of associations in which those who take part in activities, donate, and do voluntary work outnumber members in at least one country. Some interesting cross-national patterns emerge. Youth associations have a particularly high proportion of active involvement (participation in activities and voluntary work) in most northern and central European countries. Many of the new social-movement organisations (e.g. environmental, animal rights, peace, and humanitarian or human-rights organisations) receive a large share of the donations in many European societies. This is particularly so in Norway, Switzerland, Sweden, and the Netherlands, where donators outnumber members in almost all of these organisations. In general, however, this pattern is most pronounced for the organisations that focus on fellow citizens who are less well off (associations for charity or social welfare, medical patients, and the disabled). Two partial exceptions in this regard are Portugal and East Germany, whose citizens show high levels of active involvement in these organisations and are even more likely to volunteer their work than to become members.

A further question that arises is whether patterns of involvement are consistent across theoretically-defined clusters of associations. In other words, are any of the typologies of associations appearing in the literature useful for the purpose of understanding how citizens engage in associations? Different typologies of associations may be helpful for different purposes. Hence, the strategy employed when creating such a classification will have to vary depending on the final objective.[21] In our case, we are looking for distinctions that might be related to different types of involvement. To that end, we argue that one of the main aspects that might help us distinguish different involvement patterns across associations are their goals. According to the character of the goals associations primarily pursue (their constitutive goals), we may distinguish between associations that primarily pursue individual or private goods and associations that primarily aim at obtaining collective goods.[22]

The distinction between associations according to the type of good pursued is certainly not a new one. Boix and Posner (1996) use it for the purpose of arguing that it is reasonable to expect different effects of each type of association on the production of social capital. Similarly, Warren (2001) employs a typology of constitutive goods in his discussion of the

Table 6.5 Associational involvement beyond membership: when those who take part in activities, donate, and do voluntary work outnumber members[a]

Type of association	NO	CH	DK	SE	NL	WG	SI	PT	EG	ES	RU
Youth associations	A/D/V	A/D	A/V	A/V	–	A	–	–	A	–	–
Environmental organisations	D	D	–	D	–	–	–	–	–	–	–
Associations for animal rights	D	D	–	–	D	–	–	–	D	–	–
Peace organisations	D	D	–	D	D	–	–	–	–	–	–
Humanitarian aid or human rights organisations	D	D	D	D	D	D	–	–	D	D	–
Charity or social-welfare organisations	D	D	D	D	D	D	D	D	D	D	–
Associations for medical patients	D	D	D	–	–	–	–	D/V	V	D	–
Associations for disabled	D	D	D	D	D	–	D	D	V	D	–
Parents' associations	A	–	–	–	–	–	–	–	–	–	–
Cultural societies	A	–	–	–	–	–	–	A	–	–	–
Immigrants' organisations	–	–	–	–	A	–	–	–	–	–	–
Religious or church organisations	–	–	–	–	–	–	A	D	–	–	–
Women's organisations	–	–	–	–	–	A	–	–	–	–	–
Associations for war, victims, veterans, or ex-servicemen	D/V	–	–	–	–	–	–	–	–	–	–

Note

a Only associational categories with patterns which deviate from the typical dominance of membership are shown. Letters indicate those cases where those who take part in activities (A), donate (D) and/or do voluntary work (V) significantly outnumber members. Moldova and Romania are excluded from this analysis since the slightly modified version of the measurement instrument used in these two countries implies that questions about participation in activities, donations, and voluntary work were asked of members only. As in Table 6.1, countries are ordered by the percentage of respondents showing any involvement in associations.

theoretical expectations we might have about the democratic effects of different types of associations, although the classification of goods he proposes is not identical.[23] In line with Warren's (2001) approach, we put forth this bipolar distinction with the theoretical expectation that it will imply different patterns of involvement.

We thus expect associations that pursue private goods to prompt more active forms of involvement, since the acquisition of private goods is most likely related to organisational activity itself. For organisations that pursue collective goods, by contrast, incentives for activism should be smaller. As Hardin (1991a) argues, the dilemma of cooperation in modern societies is increasingly being solved through individual economic contributions due to the expansion of the middle class, which can afford to resort to this form of collective action.

Table 6.6 shows the proportion of those involved in each associational category who are also actively involved (participate in activities and/or do voluntary work). To a large extent, the results are in accordance with our expectations. Let us for simplicity focus mainly on those associational categories that clearly correspond to the ideal types of private versus public good seekers. For example, lodges and service clubs as well as cultural, sports, and hobby associations are for the most part first and foremost private-good producers. In line with our expectations, they show the highest proportion of active involvement in most countries. In most of these associations, more than half of those involved are active. At the opposite end, associations that primarily pursue public goods, such as organisations for human rights, environmental issues, charity and social welfare, animal rights, medical patients, or the disabled, tend to have relatively low proportions of active involvement (peace organisations excepted). Involvement in these associations is often limited to membership and economic contributions. These are probably the associations that best represent the classical public-cause mail-order organisations.

Beyond these general patterns, some country-specific patterns emerge. We see that German citizens are more inclined to be active in the associations they engage in. In those countries where the overall level of involvement is lowest, such as Russia, Romania, and Moldova, the number of observations per associational type is often smaller than 15. We therefore have reasonable reliably estimates for a limited portion of categories only. However, with the exception of trade unions, investment clubs, and welfare and charity associations in Russia, all associational categories in these three countries show a predominance of active involvement. In these countries, even associations that seek collective goods can count on active supporters. The opposite end is probably best represented by Switzerland and the Netherlands, where involvement in associations is often limited to membership and/or donations.

In general terms, we can draw two main conclusions from these analyses. First, the distinction between associations according to their

Table 6.6 Active involvement in different types of associations (involved respondents only)[a]

Type of association	NO	CH	DK	SE	NL	WG	SI	PT	EG	ES	RU	RO	MD	Average
Women's	0.86	0.51	–	0.85	0.80	1.00	–	–	–	0.85	–	–	–	0.81
Lodge/Service	1.00	0.51	1.00	0.84	(0.38)	–	n.i.	(0.93)	–	n.a.	n.r.	–	–	0.78
Cultural	0.66	0.53	0.78	0.86	0.63	0.92	0.74	0.88	0.98	0.78	0.71	(0.94)	0.80	0.77
Sports	0.61	0.61	0.85	0.82	0.66	0.92	0.59	0.66	0.93	0.67	0.67	–	–	0.75
Other hobbies	0.55	0.50	0.78	0.77	0.67	0.92	0.57	0.77	0.99	0.75	–	–	–	0.73
Immigrants'	1.00	0.50	–	–	0.45	0.82	–	–	–	(0.87)	–	–	–	0.73
Parents'	0.73	0.48	0.80	0.66	0.53	0.98	0.61	0.61	0.87	0.63	0.84	0.70	0.91	0.72
Youth	0.53	0.48	0.88	0.81	0.62	0.86	0.49	0.66	(1.00)	0.71	–	–	–	0.70
Religious	0.46	0.44	0.63	0.83	0.42	0.89	0.72	0.57	0.77	0.61	–	0.81	–	0.68
Political parties	0.39	0.43	0.65	0.55	0.41	0.86	0.41	0.88	0.89	0.78	0.55	0.66	(1.00)	0.64
Residents'	0.41	0.44	0.50	0.44	0.39	0.97	0.69	(0.80)	(0.87)	0.62	0.72	0.63	0.86	0.62
Pensioners'	0.34	0.38	0.46	0.64	0.44	0.92	0.44	–	0.89	0.70	(0.76)	(0.53)	–	0.59
Farmers'	0.39	0.50	0.56	0.39	(0.31)	0.72	0.53	–	–	0.56	–	(0.88)	0.91	0.57
Business/Employers'	0.44	0.43	0.53	0.36	0.48	0.44	–	(0.53)	(0.75)	0.68	–	–	–	0.51
Peace	0.50	0.22	0.45	0.30	0.47	(1.00)	–	–	–	0.65	–	n.r.	–	0.51
Professional	0.40	0.35	0.35	0.40	0.37	0.59	0.54	–	0.76	0.50	–	–	–	0.47
Veterans	0.28	0.40	0.71	0.49	0.37	0.53	0.46	–	–	–	–	–	–	0.46
Investment clubs	1.00	0.36	0.20	0.31	0.40	–	n.i.	–	–	0.44	(0.47)	–	n.r.	0.45
Trade Unions	0.20	0.25	0.29	0.24	0.16	0.50	0.26	0.44	0.61	0.48	0.45	0.70	0.82	0.42
Disabled	0.19	0.11	0.30	0.30	0.35	0.58	0.27	0.09	(0.55)	0.41	0.68	–	–	0.35
Consumers'	0.47	0.09	0.11	0.09	1.00	–	–	(0.17)	–	0.47	–	–	–	0.34
Medical/health	0.08	0.19	0.14	0.33	0.18	0.83	0.46	0.13	0.72	0.33	–	–	–	0.34
Animal rights	0.24	0.09	0.15	0.13	0.08	0.47	(0.35)	(0.53)	0.83	0.46	–	–	–	0.33
Charity/social-welfare	0.26	0.23	0.18	0.22	0.32	0.54	0.24	0.22	0.48	0.32	(0.49)	–	–	0.32
Environmental	0.22	0.17	0.20	0.24	0.12	0.62	0.48	–	–	0.47	–	–	–	0.32
Humanitarian/Human Rights	0.11	0.14	0.25	0.19	0.16	0.42	–	(0.31)	0.41	0.31	–	–	–	0.26
Automobile	0.07	0.04	0.11	0.43	0.01	0.05	0.15	–	0.11	0.18	–	–	–	0.13

Note

[a] Entries are proportions of active citizens among all individuals involved in each type of association. A dash [–] indicates that the number of observations is below 15. Figures in parentheses are based on 15–19 observations. N.r. indicates that there are no reported observations and n.i. that the type of association was not included in the questionnaire for the country in question. Associational types are ordered by the average level of active involvement. As in Table 6.1, countries are ordered by the percentage of respondents showing any involvement in associations.

constitutive goals (private vs. collective goods) seems to be useful for the purpose of understanding patterns of involvement within associations. Associations that primarily seek private goods tend to promote active involvement to a higher degree, since the acquisition of the goods by the individual is directly related to his or her own active participation. Second, countries in which the overall level of involvement is high tend to have a greater proportion of passive involvement. Apparently, it seems difficult to get large proportions of citizens involved *and* active at the same time.

Associational involvement and social trust

Part of the increasing attention devoted to associational involvement in the last decade can be attributed to the lively debate about social capital initiated and inspired by the work of Putnam (1993, 1995a, 1995b, 2000). Followers of the social capital thesis argue that associations contribute to the creation of social capital thanks to the interaction that takes place within them. Associations are loci of repeated cooperation, facilitate information flows, and provide resources for action. Hence, associational involvement constitutes a privileged structural indicator of social capital. In addition associational involvement is regarded as an important source of other positive attitudes and behaviours. In particular, it is thought to generate social trust and other norms of reciprocity – the attitudinal or cultural component of social capital[24] – as well as to encourage participation in political matters. In this section we will explore to what extent different forms of involvement in associations might have the hypothesised effect as far as social trust is concerned.

There are several mechanisms that could lead to the creation of social trust based on associational involvements. Participation in associations could have a spillover effect thanks to the interaction with other trusting people, and as a consequence of positive experiences of cooperation with others. There is no denying that interaction and cooperation within associations creates norms of reciprocity and trust among individuals who share goals and interests. More contentious is the argument that these norms are extended outside the circles of acquaintances bonded by the association itself. Indeed, it is still unclear how participation in associations creates generalised social trust (Levi 1996). Some authors argue that this could come about through the extension of the social networks beyond the organisation and through the generalisation of particularised trust to all other citizens or, at least, to all similar citizens (see, for example, Brehm and Rahn 1997; Stolle 1998, 2001b).

On the other hand, it is quite possible to argue that the causal relationship between the behavioural and the attitudinal component of social capital could go in the opposite direction. In fact, it is plausible that trusting individuals are more prone to engage in associations, since some degree of positive feelings towards other fellow citizens is necessary to establish cooperation (Stolle 1998). In an extension of this line of reasoning, Putnam (2000: 137) suggests that social trust and associational involvement reinforce each other, thus creating a virtuous circle.

As indicated in Chapter 2, a considerable amount of research has already shown that the relationship between trust and associational membership is, at best, a weak one (see also Newton 1999a, 1999b, 2001b; Uslaner 2001a; Norris 2002). However, some scholars have discussed the common assumption that all types of associations should have the same ability to generate social trust (Eastis 1998; Seligson 1999; Diani 2000; Stolle and Rochon 2001). Further, Putnam (2000) argues that not all forms of associational involvement should be equally effective in generating social capital and trust. In his view, only active forms of participation in associations that guarantee face-to-face interaction will have the virtuous consequences. The richness of the CID data provides an excellent opportunity to further explore the hypothesised relationships between associational involvement and social trust. Since we do not have access to longitudinal information and limit ourselves to bivariate correlations, we will not be able to make any claims about the direction of causality but only about the strength of the statistical relationship.

Generally speaking, that relationship is indeed fairly weak (see Table 6.7). Except for West Germany and, to a much lesser extent, Spain and Switzerland, the correlation between social trust and different forms of associational involvement is almost negligible. In Romania and Portugal, no relationship seems to exist, not even for the most active forms of involvement. Thus, generally speaking, involvement in associations does not seem to have a great impact on the generation of social trust (or vice versa). Nevertheless, it is true, as Putnam (2000) contends, that active forms of associational involvement are in most instances more strongly related to trust than are passive forms (see Table 6.8).

Is this relationship really to be attributed to social interaction? As discussed in footnote 17, involvement in associations is cumulative: citizens who engage in the more active forms also tend to engage in the more passive ones. Thus, the greater social trust of the most active might not only be due to the virtuous consequences of personal interaction with co-members but could also be related to the greater social commitment of these citizens. To a certain extent, we can try to isolate the independent effect of personal interaction by singling out those respondents that are only engaged in one of the forms of associational involvement: donation, membership, participation in activities, or volunteering.

The results presented in Table 6.9 are quite illustrative.[25] Indeed, only Portugal and to some extent West Germany corresponds to the expected pattern of greater social trust among citizens who interact face to face within associations. In the Danish case, passive donors show higher trust levels than other involved citizens. In all other countries, active involvement in associations does not seem to produce or require different trust levels than passive.

Table 6.7 Correlations between social trust and different forms of associational involvement[a]

	Involved	Membership	Activities	Voluntary work	Organisational involvement scale	N
Norway	0.07**	0.09***	0.09***	0.08***	0.11***	2,264
Switzerland	0.10***	0.09***	0.11***	0.12***	0.14***	1,538
Denmark	0.09***	0.08**	0.12***	0.07**	0.12***	1,601
Sweden	n.s.	0.07**	0.12***	0.14***	0.14***	1,238
The Netherlands	0.08***	0.08**	0.08**	0.09***	0.10***	1,623
West Germany	0.23***	0.23***	0.26***	0.23***	0.27***	1,985
Slovenia	0.09**	0.07*	n.s.	0.07*	0.07*	964
Portugal	n.s.	n.s.	0.07*	n.s.	n.s.	990
East Germany	0.08**	0.08*	0.10**	n.s.	0.09**	1,004
Spain	0.14***	0.13***	0.14***	0.11***	0.14***	4,072
Russia	0.08***	0.08**	0.07**	0.08***	0.08**	1,651
Romania	n.s.	n.s.	n.s.	n.s.	n.s.	1,148
Moldova	0.08**	0.08**	0.08*	n.s.	0.08**	1,133
Average correlation	0.08	0.08	0.10	0.09	0.11	

Note

a Entries are product-moment correlations. Levels of statistical significance: *** = 0.001, ** = 0.01, * = 0.05, n.s. = not significant. As in Table 6.1, countries are ordered by the percentage of respondents showing any involvement in associations.

Table 6.8 Mean Level of social trust and levels of associational involvement[a]

Country	Not involved	↔	Passively involved	↔	Actively involved	F statistic	N
Norway	0.59	n.s.	0.62	***	0.65	13.03***	2,264
Switzerland	0.52	n.s.	0.59	***	0.63	16.61***	1,538
Denmark	0.58	n.s.	0.62	*	0.65	11.81***	1,601
Sweden	0.61	n.s.	0.60	***	0.66	10.19***	1,238
The Netherlands	0.55	n.s.	0.58	n.s.	0.60	7.70***	1,623
West Germany	0.45	n.s.	0.47	***	0.56	74.12***	1,985
Slovenia	0.43	*	0.46	n.s.	0.46	4.24*	964
Portugal	0.55	n.s.	0.52	n.s.	0.56	2.76 n.s.	990
East Germany	0.43	n.s.	0.45	n.s.	0.48	4.51*	1,004
Spain	0.41	***	0.44	**	0.47	46.03***	4,072
Russia	0.40	n.s.	0.43	n.s.	0.45	5.62**	1,651
Romania	0.35	n.s.	0.36	n.s.	0.36	0.23 n.s.	1,148
Moldova	0.36	n.s.	0.36	n.s.	0.41	4.17*	1,133
Average	0.48		0.50		0.53		

Note

a Levels of statistical significance of the pairwise mean contrasts are reported between the corresponding columns: *** = 0.001, ** = 0.01, * = 0.05, n.s. = not significant. As in Table 6.1, countries are ordered by the percentage of respondents showing any involvement in associations.

Table 6.9 Correlation between social trust and different forms of exclusive associational involvement[a]

Country	Only involvement is				N
	Donations	Membership	Activities	Voluntary work	
Norway	n.s.	n.s.	n.s.	n.s.	365
Switzerland	n.s.	n.s.	n.s.	n.s.	254
Denmark	0.16*	−0.17**	n.s.	n.s.	233
Sweden	n.s.	n.s.	n.s.	–	189
The Netherlands	n.s.	n.s.	n.s.	n.s.	334
West Germany	n.s.	n.s.	n.s.	0.15*	173
Slovenia	n.s.	n.s.	n.s.	n.s.	185
Portugal	−0.25***	n.s.	0.20**	0.28***	182
East Germany	n.s.	n.s.	n.s.	–	121
Russia	n.s.	n.s.	n.s.	n.s.	207

Note

a Entries are product-moment correlations. These analyses only include respondents who are involved in associations through one of these four forms of involvement. Moldova and Romania are excluded from the analysis due to the use of a slightly modified version of the measurement instrument in these two countries. Levels of statistical significance: *** = 0.001, ** = 0.01, * = 0.05, n.s. = not significant. As in Table 6.1, countries are ordered by the percentage of respondents showing any involvement in associations.

Similar conclusions can be drawn from the patterns in Table 6.10, which shows the correlation between social trust and the involvement scale (see Table 6.3 above) for each of several selected types of associations. Most of the cells indicate the absence of any statistically significant relationship. Nevertheless, some interesting patterns emerge. Increasing involvement in sports clubs and religious associations is often related to slightly higher levels of social trust. Similar results are also found in the case of trade unions and, albeit on a still weaker scale, for youth, charity, environmental, and humanitarian organisations as well as for political parties.

In summary, our results partially challenge Putnam's (2000) expectations. Generally speaking, active associational involvement does not seem to have much of a relationship with social trust; and to the extent that it does, it is visible only in some countries and for some associations. Thus, there is not much evidence to support the claim that associational involvement produces social trust (or vice versa).

Conclusions

The preceding section aside, the main purpose of this chapter is to provide a thorough descriptive account of the patterns of associational involvement in our 13 European societies. The measurement instrument included in the CID survey has enabled us to describe associational involvement in greater depth than in any prior cross-national study. The analysis of different forms of involvement – membership, participation in activities, voluntary work, and donations – as well as the extent to which they are found in different types of associations give us a more accurate and detailed picture of this important side of democratic citizenship than those previously available.

We can summarise our findings by means of two basic configurations. In the first, which is found in the well-established democracies of northern and central Europe, citizens are highly integrated into civil society. Nearly all citizens are involved in one way or another in at least one association, many in several. More than half of them are actively involved – that is, participate in activities or do voluntary work – in at least one association. In the second configuration, which applies to the newer democracies in eastern and southern Europe, the level of involvement is far lower, however measured. In many cases, the differences across the two groups of countries are dramatic. With respect to the breadth of involvement, the country at the top has levels roughly ten to 20 times higher than that at the bottom across all four forms of involvement (membership, participation in activities, donations, and voluntary work) as well as a combined measure (see Table 6.2).

With respect to the process of demand- and preference-representation, the first configuration is more apt to produce a more inclusive and less

Table 6.10 Correlations between social trust and degree of involvement in different types of associations[a]

Country	Sports	Youth	Charities	Religious	Trade unions	Political parties	Environmental	Humanitarian	N
Norway	0.05*	0.04*	n.s.	0.08***	0.08***	n.s.	n.s.	0.06**	2,264
Switzerland	0.06*	0.09***	0.11***	0.06*	n.s.	0.06*	n.s.	n.s.	1,538
Denmark	0.09***	n.s.	n.s.	n.s.	0.08***	0.06*	0.07**	0.07**	1,601
Sweden	0.10***	n.s.	n.s.	0.07*	0.11***	0.08**	n.s.	0.14***	1,237
The Netherlands	n.s.	0.06*	0.07**	0.08***	−0.05*	n.s.	0.07**	n.s.	1,623
West Germany	0.21***	n.s.	n.s.	0.08***	n.s.	n.s.	0.04*	n.s.	1,985
Slovenia	n.s.	n.s.	n.s.	n.s.	n.s.	n.s.	n.s.	n.s.	964
Portugal	0.10**	n.s.	n.s.	0.08**	n.s.	n.s.	n.s.	0.08*	990
East Germany	0.08**	0.07*	n.s.	n.s.	n.s.	n.s.	n.s.	n.s.	1,002
Spain	0.07***	0.06***	0.09***	0.11***	0.05***	0.07***	0.04*	0.06***	4,072
Russia	n.s.	n.s.	n.s.	n.s.	0.06**	n.s.	n.s.	n.s.	1,651
Romania	n.s.	n.s.	n.s.	n.s.	n.s.	n.s.	n.s.	n.s.	1,148
Moldova	n.s.	n.s.	n.s.	0.06*	n.s.	n.s.	n.s.	n.s.	1,125
Average	0.09	0.06	0.09	0.08	0.05	0.07	0.05	0.08	

Note

a Entries are product-moment correlations. Levels of statistical significance: *** = 0.001, ** = 0.01, * = 0.05, n.s. = not significant. As in Table 6.1, countries are ordered by the percentage of respondents showing any involvement in associations.

biased development. Most citizens are included in the system of interest-representation through their organisational involvement. The second configuration need not imply bias in representational terms but is more likely to do so, since only a limited few are organised and active. Surely, further research is required on this score. To what extent do these different configurations have substantial implications for the process of political representation? Does it matter for the proper representation of citizen interests that most or only a few of them are involved in associations?

Notes

1 We will not attempt to provide a detailed account of this debate here, but will limit ourselves to some of the basic lines of scholarly argument about the relevance and effects of associational involvement. A pertinent discussion of the literature is found in Warren 2001.
2 The reader should also note that we will concentrate on aspects related to individual behaviour. Thus, we are not dealing with the effects of associations *qua* organisations, but with the consequences and effects of individuals' involvement in associations.
3 The list of works that make some (or all) of these claims is endless, but some fundamental samples are to be found in Almond and Verba 1963; Cohen and Rogers 1992; Putnam 1993, 2000; and Verba *et al.* 1995.
4 The empirical foundation for these assumptions remains weak. See opposing views in Eastis 1998; Seligson 1999; and Diani 2000.
5 The empirical validity of these statements is still open for discussion as evidenced by other chapters in this book.
6 The common core of the CID questionnaire listed up to 27 associational categories plus an 'other associations' one, which were designed to cover all existing associations in Europe. In addition, national teams were allowed to incorporate further categories into the list if they deemed it necessary to cover the whole array of relevant associations present in their own countries. However, for the sake of presentation and comparability, all tables and analyses presented in this chapter have been done after collapsing those country-specific categories into one of the 28 common ones. In terms of question design, respondents were first presented with a list of associational types. For each type, they were then asked whether they were involved in the sense of being a member or having participated in activities, donated money, or done voluntary work during the past 12 months. If the answer was positive, they were asked specific questions about each of the four aforementioned forms of involvement. They were also asked whether they had personal friends in the organisation in question.
7 Most cross-national surveys ask about membership only. Some add voluntary work. The Eurobarometers usually measure associational involvement in terms of membership only, while the World Values Surveys also consider voluntary work. More details on measurement techniques across different surveys can be found in Morales 2002 and 2004.
8 See various interesting discussions about measurement issues pertaining to associational involvement in Baumgartner and Walker 1988; Smith 1990; Baumgartner and Leech 1998: 30–3; Andersen and Hoff 2001: Chapter 5; Morales 2002; and von Erlach 2002.
9 All results in this chapter have been produced with the cases weighted so as to correct for deviations from proportional representation. As a result, the data may be considered representative for each country. In addition, in all tables

the countries are ordered according to the percentage of citizens that are involved in associations in any way (membership, activities, donation, or voluntary work), from highest to lowest.
10 Certainly, this measurement instrument could be further improved, especially by considering the extent to which a certain form of involvement applies to multiple organisations of the same kind. As in virtually all surveys of which we are aware, respondents were asked about their involvement in a given set of types of associations, but they were not asked for the number of associations in which they are involved within each type. Thus, the recorded response of a citizen who reports membership in, for example, a sports club would be the same regardless of the number of sports clubs he or she holds membership in. For this reason, we should always keep in mind that we are, strictly speaking, not able to count the number of associations in which citizens are involved but only the number of associational types to which their involvement applies, and that the latter count will underestimate the former to an unknown extent. See Morales 2002 for an illustration of the importance of this aspect.
11 In this chapter, 'any involvement' implies a positive response to a question about membership, participation in activities, voluntary work, or donations with respect to at least one type of association.
12 See Howard 2003a for a detailed analysis of the weakness of civil society in post-communist Europe.
13 Other analyses (not reported here) show that these cross-national patterns hold even when we consider involved respondents only, although the cross-national differences are reduced.
14 That is, participation via donations only.
15 See Norris 2002: 3–9 for a summary of the 'decline of participation' arguments.
16 Jordan and Maloney (1997) do not make any longitudinal claim or any argument about a general decline in citizen involvement. What they do argue is that 'mail-order' organisations are not participatory vehicles and, as such, their increasing leverage does not promote greater citizen involvement nor participatory democracy.
17 Mokken scaling analyses (not reported here) show that these three forms of involvement are scalable in terms of difficulty and can thus be used for the purpose of constructing cumulative scales. This is true for all 13 surveys. Donations, however, deviate from the pattern formed by membership, participation in activities, and voluntary work. Although in almost every country a valid cumulative scale can be formed even when donations are included (the exception is Switzerland, where donations are not scalable at all), the position of donations on that scale varies considerably across countries. The three patterns that emerge are quite interesting. In Russia, East and West Germany, Romania, Moldova, and Sweden donating money is the least common form of involvement in associations. In Switzerland, Portugal, Slovenia, and Norway, donations are the second most frequent form of involvement, just behind membership. In Denmark, the Netherlands, and Spain, the ordering is the same as in the questionnaire itself: membership, participation in activities, donations, and voluntary work. We do not report the tables with the results of the Mokken scaling analyses here due to space constraints. The key indicators of validity and reliability of the tested scales are generally fulfilled (reproducibility above 0.90; scale rho and item rho are above 0.30). In addition, the monotonic homogeneity has been visually checked.
18 The correlation between percentage of uninvolved citizens and percentage of passive involvement is -0.10 ($N=13$). However, since the Romanian and Moldovan figures most probably over-represent active involvement, it is safer to conclude that there is no relationship between the two aspects of involvement.

19 Due to space restrictions, the raw tables are not reported here but can be found in Morales and Geurts 2004.
20 For example, 21 per cent of the Swiss citizens donate money to environmental organisations while only 14 per cent are members of such an organisation. Similarly, 51 per cent of the Norwegian citizens donate money to humanitarian/human rights organisations while only 17 per cent are members of such an organisation.
21 This is probably one of the main obstacles to the possibility of finding a 'unique' typology or taxonomy of associations that will suit all purposes. Attempts like that of Roßteutscher and van Deth (2002) are unfortunately limited by the fact that the distinctions that can be made according to the thematic concern of associations may not be useful for all purposes.
22 In our usage, 'collective goods' refers to pure public goods and common pool goods. Thus, our criterion for distinguishing between the two types of goods is, primarily, excludability from the consumption of the good. It is this excludability, or rather its impossibility, that introduces the 'free-rider' problem. The size of the club (see Buchanan 1965) or the rivalry for consumption is not decisive in our case.
23 In addition, Warren's (2001: 123–40) classification of constitutive goods (status, interpersonal identity, individual material, exclusive group identity, inclusive social, and public material) can be reduced, as he points out, to a dichotomy between private and public goods – or individual versus social, as he calls them.
24 There is an interesting debate in the literature as to whether social trust should be regarded as a general attitude or as a context-specific relational concept. See van Deth 2003 for an overview of several conceptualisations and measurements of social capital.
25 Table 6.9 shows the results for the subsample of respondents who are involved through but one of the four forms of involvement (membership, participation in activities, donations, and voluntary work). This increases the homogeneity with respect to the overall amount of involvement so as to better isolate the impact of the form of involvement.

7 Explaining associational involvement

Gabriel Badescu and Katja Neller

Introduction

Within democratic theory, there is a consensus that the quality of a democracy depends on the robustness of its associational life. It is assumed that associations have the potential to contribute to forming and enhancing the attitudes, knowledge and skills on which democratic practices are based (e.g. Putnam 1995b; van Deth 2002; Hooghe 2003). As indicated in Chapter 6 of this volume, there is a large and growing literature on these links between organisational life and democracy. According to three important claims appearing in that literature, involvement in organisations nourishes democratic attitudes, generates social trust, and fosters political participation. The empirical validity of these claims about the effects of organisational involvement is subject to analysis in earlier as well as later chapters of this book. In this chapter, however, we instead want to examine the causes of organisational involvement.

Associations speak on behalf of groups of citizens, thereby contributing to the aggregation and representation of individual preferences in the process of collective decision-making (see, for example, Foley and Edwards 1996). However, activists in associations are not always representative of the citizenry as a whole. In general, they tend to belong disproportionately to more advantaged groups. Consequently, the needs and priorities they express may give unequal consideration to the needs and orientations of all citizens (Verba *et al.* 1995; Skocpol 1999). At the same time, associations may reduce inequalities by providing resources, platforms, and training grounds that help the more disadvantaged to express their opinions.

The general aim of this chapter is to examine the factors explaining involvement in voluntary associations across 13 European societies. By examining a broad range of predictors, and by comparing their impact across different types of organisations, we try to contribute to the ongoing discussion on the distinctive characteristics that set the organisationally involved apart from other citizens. By probing for systematic variations with regard to the causes of organisational involvement in older versus newer democracies, we additionally try to assess whether political history has an impact not only on the quantity but also on the quality of organisational involvement.

In the next section of this chapter, we provide an overview of prior research on the determinants of associational involvement. In the subsequent section, we present the results of our own empirical analyses. In the concluding section, we summarise the main findings and discuss their implications.

How to explain associational involvement: an overview

Our presentation of the main hypotheses and findings of prior research is structured on the basis of five groups of possible determinants of associational involvement (the first four of which adapted from Gabriel *et al.* 2002):

1   general factors;
2   social status and resources;
3   social integration and networks;
4   social orientations, norms and motivations;
5   political orientations.

To these five, we add a special subsection on the particular characteristics of associations in east European countries and the way these characteristics can be expected to affect organisational involvement.

General factors

Two factors extensively discussed as possible determinants of organisational involvement are age and gender. We refer to them as general factors because they are expected to exert a kind of 'general' influence in various respects and do not fit neatly and unambiguously into any single one of the other groups of determinants (Gabriel *et al.* 2002). For example, age and gender could be seen as 'resources', but also as 'integration' factors.

Several studies show that the young as well as the old tend to be less involved in voluntary organisations than the middle-aged. This is often attributed to the physical hindrances of the elderly and the high 'mobility' of the young (Curtis *et al.* 1992; van Deth and Kreuter 1998). On the other hand, the elderly tend to have much free time to spare and a high level of social integration from at least some points of view. Further, Putnam (1995b: 675), with an emphasis on a generational rather than life-cycle perspective, claims that a whole 'civic generation, born roughly between 1910 and 1940' being more engaged and more trusting than the younger ones, is now disappearing.

Gender is taken into account because women are disadvantaged by traditional role patterns. They often remain responsible for the 'home' and may therefore be less integrated in a social or professional context promoting organisational involvement (see e.g. van Deth and Kreuter 1998).

Consequently, we will test the following hypotheses:

- Two alternative hypotheses for age:
    1. The young and the elderly are less likely to be involved in organisations than the middle-aged. Hence, a curvilinear relationship between age, membership and involvement can be expected.
    2. The likelihood of organisational involvement increases continuously with age. Hence a linear relationship can be expected.[1]
- Men are more likely to be involved in associations than women.[2]

Social status and resources

Given the strong relationship between organisational involvement and political participation (van Deth 1997, 2001a), it is not surprising that many of the factors that appear in explanations of political participation are also encountered in those that attempt to account for organisational involvement. Membership and activity in voluntary associations are often interpreted as direct effects of the socio-economic factors that have been considered the most important determinants of political participation since the late 1940s (Milbrath and Goel 1977). The common explanation of why higher status groups tend to have higher levels of organisational involvement is that they have the resources (time, money, contacts) and the verbal and cognitive skills to participate (Kohn and Schooler 1982; van Deth and Kreuter 1998; Gabriel *et al.* 2002).

Inequalities in socio-economic resources, such as income and education, are reproduced as inequalities in political and organisational participation. Citizens with higher levels of education and income are more likely to participate in voluntary organisations (Schlozman *et al.* 1999). Empirical findings also show that the middle class is clearly dominant in associational life. This pattern can be found, with minor variations, in many western societies (Richter 1985; Curtis *et al.* 1992; Dekker and van den Broek 1996; Gabriel *et al.* 2002).

Consequently, we will test the following hypotheses:

- Education is a resource for involvement in voluntary associations. Higher levels of education tend to be associated with higher levels of involvement.
- Income is another resource-related determinant of organisational involvement. Although the relationship may not be perfectly linear, the increase in involvement abating somewhat among the very rich, we expect the general tendency to be positive.[3]

Social integration and networks

The idea that citizens' involvement in associations depends on the degree to which they are socially integrated is not new (see, for example, Smith 1957). A low level of integration in social networks tends to be associated with low organisational involvement. The main argument is that organisational involvement is the result of prior integration in social networks. These networks provide a training ground for social skills as well as opportunities to exchange information with other people who share similar interests. The most important networks are those related to family, professional, and religious life (Gabriel *et al.* 2002: 104).

Having a family indicates a higher level of social integration. According to previous findings, parents of under-age children are more likely to be involved in associations. However, having a family might also imply a lack of time for organisational involvement.

Full-time workers are more strongly integrated than part-time workers, who are in turn more integrated than the unemployed. People altogether excluded from working life (e.g. pensioners and housepersons) form a special category, with a lower level of social integration (Curtis *et al.* 1992; Gabriel *et al.* 2002) but more time for voluntary activities (Putnam 1999).

Religious integration is of course particularly important for religious and social associations, but religion is also of interest as another network in which one can be more or less integrated. According to Wuthnow (1999: 333) 'active church-attenders are more likely to give money and time to voluntary organisations, including ones that have no evident connection to churches'.

Community size can also be placed in the context of integration. The effects of this factor are discussed for example by Curtis *et al.* (1992) and Putnam (2000). The lowest level of involvement in voluntary associations is likely to be found in the inner areas of big cities, while higher levels are typical for smaller communities. According to Putnam (2000), exceptions to this linear relationship are rural communities and towns with less than 10,000 inhabitants. The process of social integration is usually time-consuming. As a result, the longer the time of residence in a certain community, the higher the level of integration in the social networks of the respective village, town or city.

Media exposure does not fit exactly into our four groups of determinants. We decided to place it in the integration category since a large amount of media consumption (e.g. in the form of television watching) can be seen as indicating a lack of integration inasmuch as it takes time away from social activities. On the other hand, exposure to the political content of mass media may reflect an interest in politics and society, which is an indicator of social integration. Putnam's (1995b, 2000) claims regarding 'videomalaise' play an important role in the literature (see, for example, Norris 1996). He blames the decline of social capital on the spread of television as a dominant leisure-time activity. In his view, excessive television watching inhibits other social activities, leads to a loss of social trust through exposure to negative news, and promotes general pessimism and aggressiveness. Other researchers (e.g. Hall 1999) have not been able to find any linear relationship between the time spent watching television and the time spent on activities within voluntary associations.

Political media exposure is sometimes discussed as a factor promoting involvement in voluntary associations. Contrary to extensive (non-political) television-consumption, positive effects of exposure to the political contents of the media can be expected because people need information about society, social problems, collective actions, and organisations they could join as a prerequisite of involvement (see Brehm and Rahn 1997 with respect to newspapers).

Consequently, we will test the following hypotheses:

- Dense and diverse networks tend to favour a higher level of social integration, as well as attachment to the local community. As a consequence, we expect that people who are married or cohabiting, have under-age children, belong to a group of friends with whom they have contact on regular basis, attend religious services, have lived for a long time in the same place, and live in smaller localities, are more likely to be involved in associations.[4]
- Taking into account Putnam's findings, we want to consider an alternative to the last hypothesis: the relationship between community size and involvement could also be curvilinear, with people living in very small and rural communities and people living in big cities being less involved than others.
- We expect that people who work part-time are more likely to be involved in organisations than those who work full-time as well as those who are unemployed or not in the labour force, the reason being that part-time workers have more spare time than the former and a higher level of social integration than the latter.
- We also expect that those who follow the political contents of the media display a higher level of organisational involvement. On the other hand, we expect that the total amount of television watching is negatively associated with associational involvement once the effect of other factors – including political media exposure – is controlled.[5]

Social orientations, norms, and motivations

The hypothesis that a high level of social trust is related to involvement in associational life has received prominent theoretical attention and at least some empirical support (e.g. Putnam 1993, 2000; Brehm and Rahn 1997; Stolle 1998; Badescu 2003 with respect to east European countries). In some studies social trust is seen as an effect of associational involvement associations (e.g. Putnam 1993), in others as a prerequisite of getting involved (e.g. Inglehart 1990). Some researchers, such as Brehm and Rahn (1997: 1001–2.) combine the two points of view: 'The more citizens participate in their communities, the more they learn to trust others; the greater trust that citizens hold for others, the more likely they are to participate'. Recent evidence suggests that organisational involvement does not generate social trust but that people with a high trust level are more likely to become organisationally involved (Stolle 1998; Uslaner 2003).

When involvement is treated in an undifferentiated fashion, a certain amount of correlation is often found (e.g. Putnam 1993, 2000; Whiteley 1999). If different types of civic engagement are considered separately, trust is found to be rather strongly related to involvement in some associations but more weakly to involvement in others. In a study of associations in Sweden and Germany, Stolle argues that organisations that are 'more diverse, more engaged and those with weak ties, accommodate more trusting people' (1998: 521). In an analysis of the American public, Uslaner (2002) finds that trust is a strong predictor of involvement in cultural and business associations but has a weak impact on involvement in ethnic associations, and no impact at all as far as involvement in religious organisations are concerned.

Post-materialist value orientations are closely connected to values of political and social involvement and self-realisation. These factors can be assumed to influence involvement in voluntary associations in general, independently of whether the associations are of a newer or older type. People with a post-materialist value orientation are more likely to participate than others (van Deth 1996). Based on a different conceptualisation of value orientations formulated by Klages (see e.g. Klages and Gensicke 1999), a synthesis of values that endorse political and organisational participation and values that define volunteering as a chance for self-fulfilment rather than as a social or civic duty promotes involvement in voluntary associations (Gensicke 2001).

A factor rarely discussed in this context is that of tolerance towards other people (see Chapter 5). Some associations may stress ethnic or religious borders within a society, but we hypothesise that these kinds of organisations account for a minority of those involved in associational life. Therefore, it could be expected that people who are more tolerant towards others are more often engaged in associations.

The motivations and norms promoting involvement in voluntary associations can be characterised as a mixture of personal (ego-orientated), altruistic, and functional incentives (see, for example, Gaskin and Smith 1995). The effects of motivations and social norms are closely related to general value orientations. A description of social motivations and norms as well as related measures can be found in Gabriel and Kunz (n.d.). Two of the categories they suggest will be used in our analysis:

1   social motivations, for example altruism and solidarity with the disadvantaged;
2   social norms and pressures, that is, expectations of other social groups ('can't say no if someone asks you to take an active part in an organisation', Ajzen 1988).

Some of the items indexing 'what it takes to be a good citizen' (see Chapter 4) can be used to operationalise these factors. Consequently, we will test the following hypotheses:

- People with a higher level of social trust are more likely to be involved in associations. Although some associations may rely on particularistic trust (i.e. trust in people from the same group, defined, for example, by ethnicity or religion) which is sometimes negatively correlated with general social trust (Uslaner 2002), we expect an overall tendency for higher levels of general trust to correspond with higher levels of organisational involvement.[6]
- People who emphasise values and norms of solidarity and self-realisation are more likely to be involved in associations.[7]
- Tolerant people are more likely to be involved in associations.[8]
- People who hold associational activity to be an important virtue of good citizenship are more likely to be involved in organisations.

Political orientations

The effects of political orientations on organisational involvement are seldom debated or analysed. One reason for this research gap is the problem of causality. As already discussed with respect to social trust, the direction of the relationship between political orientations and organisational involvement is not clear. Most researchers concentrate on the effects of associational involvement on political participation and/or political orientations. However, other causal directions also seem plausible (for details see van Deth 1997). In this chapter, we will consider the effects of political interest, political efficacy, trust in institutions and satisfaction with democracy on organisational involvement.

Political interest can be seen as a sign of interest in society and therefore as an indicator of social integration. Political efficacy – that is, an optimistic view of one's own political capabilities (internal efficacy) and the responsiveness of political authorities (external efficacy) – is often regarded as a potential consequence of organisational involvement. However, it can also be considered as an incentive for such involvement: if somebody feels able to influence 'society' or 'politics', he or she is more likely to get involved in organisations opting for such goals. According to Dekker and van den Broek (1996), involvement in voluntary associations is positively correlated with political competence, but they do not take a stand with respect to question of causality. With respect to confidence in institutions, some scholars (for example Rothstein 2004) argue that low confidence in judiciary institutions makes involvement in collective action much more difficult.

There is a theoretical ambiguity in the discussion of this point in the literature: in general, feelings of political efficacy, confidence in institutions, and satisfaction with the way democracy works are believed to improve the capacity and motivation to get involved. People could feel unmotivated or incapacitated by a lack of political competence, a low level of confidence in institutions, or dissatisfaction with democracy. On the other hand, dissatisfaction with the political situation might also work as a motivation to act (see e.g. Norris 2002 and the analyses in Chapter 10), for example by getting involved in associations (see e.g. Berman 1997).

Consequently, we will test the following hypotheses:

- People interested in politics are more likely to be involved in organisations.[9]
- For political efficacy, confidence in judicial institutions, and satisfaction with democracy, we will consider two alternative hypotheses:

  1. that high levels produce a positive effect on organisational involvement;
  2. that low levels do so.[10]

Prior regime type: established democracies versus post-authoritarian and post-communist countries

Institutional frameworks can play an important role as determinants of the intensity and type of involvement. We want to take a closer look at the differences between the older democracies, the younger ones from southern Europe, and the ex-communist societies, by focusing on how the prior regime type affects the links between individual characteristics and organisational involvement.

A clear result from all comparative studies on European countries, including the one presented here (see the previous chapter), is that people from the former communist countries tend to be involved in associations to a lesser extent than elsewhere. Even when controlling for levels of economic well-being, political rights, civil liberties and 'civilisation', the presence or absence of a communist past is the most important factor for explaining the level of participation in civil society across countries (Smolar 1996; Howard 2003b). In analysing survey data for Russia and East Germany, Howard (2003b) finds that the main factors explaining the link between the communist past and the low level of civic engagement in the present are:

1 people's previous experiences with organisations, and particularly the legacy of mistrust of formal organisations that results from the forced participation in communist organisations;
2 the persistence of informal private networks that function as a substitute for, or alternative to, formal and public organisations;
3 the disappointment with the new democratic and capitalist systems today, which has led many people to avoid the public sphere.

Prior regime type is expected to cause variations among post-authoritarian regimes as well. According to Pérez-Díaz (1993) and Encarnación (2003), Spain appears to have more in common with the ex-communist countries than with other authoritarian regimes with respect to the development of civil society. This is a result of the particular effort of the Franco regime to suppress all autonomous organisations within civil society.

According to several scholars, associations in the post-communist societies are qualitatively different from those in the older democracies. Many authors believe that in the Balkan countries, in the countries representing the former members of the Soviet Union, and, to at least some extent, in other ex-communist countries, associations are of a different nature, having both determinants and effects not shared with western societies (Ash 2000; Kalb 2002). These differences are thought to arise from the fact that many of the associations in the east were created by international organisations, in line with the idea that the development of civil society is critical to democratisation and 'successful transition'. In many cases, these 'child' organisations remain dependent on their 'parents'. Organisations of this type tend to be only weakly anchored in local communities, and the motivations to get involved in them are not expected to be the same as for 'naturally grown' associations (Sampson 1996). Based on these considerations, we will examine the extent to which there are systematic differences between the explanations of organisational involvement that apply to older democracies, post-authoritarian countries and ex-communist countries.

- We expect that the shorter the tradition of autonomous voluntary associations in a society, the more likely it is that activity will be motivated primarily by private and individual rather than public and collective ends.[11] This is because lower performance of state institutions in newer democracies tends to give citizens more reason to act in order to protect personal interest. One expected consequence is that in these societies, differences between the involved and the uninvolved with respect to general attitudes and norms, such as social trust, tolerance, and solidarity are smaller than in the older democracies.
- We also expect that in the countries with the largest 'import' of associations – Moldova, Romania, and Russia – involvement in associations is disproportionately higher in urban areas, where associations were

set up with the help of foreign donors. Additionally, we expect a much higher effect of education than in the west.

East Germany is a special case among the former communist countries: It is one of the societies with a weak tradition of autonomous organisations, but at the same time, its unification with West Germany resulted in a faster and stronger process of building voluntary associations.

- The higher the similarity between East and West Germany, the more support we have for the idea of a fast pace of transformation. The cases of Spain and Portugal create a further test of the existence of a qualitative difference in organisational involvement as a result of prior regime type. If we can place them on a continuum between the older democracies, on the one side, and the former communist countries on the other, we have support for the idea that a qualitative difference exists and that it is persistent over time.

Results: explanations of organisational involvement

Any explanatory effort aimed at organisational involvement benefits from careful consideration of the specific kind of involvement at issue. As shown in the previous chapter, we can distinguish between several different forms of involvement (membership, donations, participation in activities, and voluntary work)[12] as well as between involvements in different types of organisations. An important initial step of our analysis was to design a set of dependent variables that summarise the vast array of data at our disposal in an efficient and meaningful way.

To that end, we followed a two-step strategy. First, we analysed three different involvement measures: a summary measure of involvement, a measure of membership alone, and a measure of other forms of involvement alone (donations, participation in activities, and voluntary work).[13] In each case, we considered a dichotomous measure as well as a count of the number of types of organisations in which the respondent was involved (cf. Tables 6.1 and 6.2 in the preceding chapter). Since our analyses show the various measures to have similar patterns of determinants, we focus in the following on the summary measure (number organisations in which the respondent is involved divided by the total number of organisations we asked about), but occasionally comment on the results for specific types of involvement.

Second, we analyse the determinants of involvement in different types of organisations. Previous research has shown that important differences can be found when different types of associations are compared. For our analysis, we will adapt and modify the classification of associations developed by Gabriel *et al.* (2002). Based on a broad range of empirical analyses, Gabriel *et al.* conclude that three dimensions of organisations should be separated:

1 leisure time and sports associations;
2 interest organisations;
3 social-cultural groups (including religious associations).

Considering the fact that religious organisations and religious attachment play a quite varied role in the 13 European societies we analyse, we decided to modify this classification and to form an additional category for religious and church associations. Hence, we will distinguish between four types of organisations:

1 *spare time and sports associations*, consisting of sports clubs, clubs for outdoor activities, hobby associations, and youth organisations;
2 *interest groups*, including trade unions and professional organisations as well as organisations for environmental concerns, animal rights, peace, humanitarian aid, medical patients, disabled people, pensioners, consumers, automobile owners, residents, immigrants, war victims, and women;
3 *socio-cultural associations*, including charity or social welfare, cultural, and parents' organisations as well as lodges or service clubs;
4 *religious associations*.[14]

Our independent variables are divided into two main groups, with those in the first assumed to be antecedent to those in the second in terms of causal order. The first group consists of gender, age, education, time of residence, size of locality, marital status, parenthood, and employment status. The second includes social trust, tolerance, self-realisation, solidarity, church attendance, membership in informal networks, political media exposure, number of hours of television watching, political interest, confidence in judicial institutions, satisfaction with democracy, political efficacy, and the extent to which activity in associations is regarded as a civic virtue. For each dependent variable and country, we analyse two different models: the first with the predictors in the first group only, the second with the predictors of both groups. Due to space constraints, we report the effect of the predictors in the first group for the first model only, although these predictors are included in both models.

Explaining involvement in any type of association

The first set of determinants discussed in our presentation of prior research above consists of general factors (gender and age), factors indexing socio-economic resources (education and income), and factors related to social integration (time of residence, size of locality, marital status, parenthood, and employment status). Let us now consider the actual effect of these factors.

As shown in Table 7.1 *men* tend to be involved in organisations to a greater extent than *women* in most countries. The exceptions are Denmark, where the opposite is true, and the Netherlands, Norway and Russia where the difference is not statistically significant. The effect of *age* is significant in the majority of countries and displays non-linear patterns. The young tend to be less involved in most countries, with the exceptions of West Germany, Portugal, Moldova, and Russia. The elderly tend to be just as, or less, involved than others, except in Moldova.

The level of *education* is one of the best predictors in each of the countries under study. The relationship is statistically significant and positive in every case. Assessing the effect of *income* in a comparative perspective proved to be highly problematic. Not only is the income measure we have difficult to compare across countries, it also tends to have relatively large amounts of missing data. In Portugal and Slovenia, only about half of the respondents reported their incomes. We therefore chose to report the results of regression models that do not include this variable. When income is included in the analysis, it has a significant effect in each of the countries under study.

Time of residence has a positive effect in Denmark, West Germany, Sweden and Switzerland, and no significant negative effect in any other case. *Size of locality* has no significant effect in most countries. Among the exceptions are West Germany, Norway, Portugal, and, to a lesser extent, Denmark, where the level of organisational involvement is higher in smaller localities than in larger ones. By contrast, in Russia and Slovenia, people from larger localities tend to be more involved, whereas in Romania the inhabitants of the largest towns are less involved than those living in other urban areas but more involved than those living in a rural environment. Our check for curvilinear effects of size of locality showed no significant relationships, except in the case of Romania.

Being *married* or *cohabiting* has a positive effect in a number of western countries but not in any of the former communist countries in the east. The presence of under-age *children* in the household does not have much of an impact on organisational involvement. The effect is positive and significant in only two instances (Denmark and Portugal) and negative in one (Moldova).

Being a *houseperson* has negative, but generally weak and often insignificant, effects in most countries. Sweden is the country where the effect is strongest. Having a *full-time job* has positive effects in most countries, but they are generally weak. The effect tends to be stronger in analyses where the dependent variable is membership alone rather than various organisational activities or our summary measure of involvement. A possible explanation is that a full-time job provides a good context for social integration but, at the same time, limits the time available for activity. People *working part-time* tend to fall between those with full-time employment and those without a job. The effect is positive in most cases, but statistically significant

Table 7.1 Explaining involvement in any type of association[a]

Predictor	CH	DK	EG	WG	NL	NO	SE	PT	ES	MD	RO	RU	SI
Gender (female)	0.00	0.01*	−0.01*	−0.01***	0.01	0.01	0.00	−0.01*	0.00	0.00	0.00	0.00	−0.01*
Age													
Young	−0.05***	−0.06***	−0.02*	0.00	−0.05***	−0.06***	−0.03**	−0.01	−0.02***	0.01	−0.01*	0.00	−0.02*
Old	−0.02	−0.03**	−0.01	0.00	−0.01	−0.03**	0.00	0.01	0.00	0.01*	0.00	0.00	−0.02*
Education	0.20***	0.18***	0.05***	0.04***	0.18***	0.08***	0.14***	0.06***	0.06***	0.03*	0.04***	0.04***	0.06***
Time of residence	0.03**	0.01*	0.00	0.01**	0.01	0.00	0.02	0.01	0.00	0.00	0.00	0.00	−0.01
Size of locality	−0.04*	−0.01*	−0.01	−0.03***	−0.02	−0.03***	−0.01	−0.04***	0.00	0.00	0.00	−0.00	0.02**
Married or cohabiting	0.02**	0.02**	0.00	0.01***	0.03	0.02***	0.02	0.00	0.01***	0.00	0.00	0.00	0.00
Children	0.00	0.02**	0.00	0.00	0.01	0.01	0.01	0.01**	—	−0.01*	0.00	0.00	0.01
Houseperson	0.00	−0.02	−0.01	−0.01	−0.01	−0.03	−0.06*	−0.01	−0.01	−0.01	0.00	−0.01*	−0.01
Employment													
Full-time job	0.02	0.02***	0.01**	0.01*	0.01	0.01	0.01	0.00	0.00	0.01*	0.01**	0.01***	0.00
Part-time job	0.02	0.02*	0.01	0.01*	0.02	0.01	0.01	0.01	0.00	0.01	0.00	0.00	0.01
Adjusted R^2	0.05	0.18	0.05	0.09	0.09	0.05	0.08	0.08	0.06	0.02	0.09	0.09	0.05
N	1,538	1,604	929	1,818	1,387	1,971	1,249	1,002	3,972	1,197	1,201	1,723	985

Social trust	0.02*	0.00*	0.00	0.03*	0.03	0.04	0.04*	0.01	0.02***	0.00	0.00	0.00	0.04
Tolerance	−0.04**	0.00	0.00	−0.03	0.06	−0.02	−0.02	−0.03	−0.01*	−0.01	0.00	0.00	−
Self-realisation	−0.01	−0.01	0.00	0.00	−0.08	−0.03	−0.03	−0.01	−	−0.02*	0.00	−	−0.03
Solidarity	−0.01	v0.00	0.01**	0.02*	0.03	0.00	0.00	−0.01	0.01***	0.02	0.01*	0.00	−0.02
Church attendance	0.03***	v0.03**	0.03***	0.04***	0.05***	0.05	0.05***	0.03***	0.01***	0.01	0.00	0.00	0.02
Informal contacts	0.02*	0.01***	0.03***	0.03***	0.03***	0.01	0.01*	0.02***	0.02***	0.02*	0.01**	0.01***	0.00
Political media exposure	0.04**	0.04**	0.04*	0.06***	0.08**	0.02	0.02	0.05***	0.02	−0.03	0.01	0.00	0.02
TV hours	−0.10	−0.03**	−0.09	−0.01***	0.07	−0.09	−0.09	−0.04	0.01	0.03	0.01	0.00	−0.09
Political interest	0.03**	0.01*	0.02**	0.02**	0.02	0.04	0.04**	0.03	0.05***	0.02*	0.01**	−	0.07***
Confidence in judiciary	0.00	0.00	0.00	0.00*	0.00	0.00	0.01**	0.00	0.01	0.00	0.00	0.00	0.00
Satisfaction with democracy	−0.01	−0.02	−0.02***	−0.05***	−0.04	−0.03**	−0.03**	0.00	−0.01**	0.01	0.00	0.00	0.00
Political efficacy	0.03**	0.01**	−0.02**	0.05	0.06	0.04***	0.04**	0.00	0.03***	0.01	0.00	0.02***	0.03
Activity as a virtue	0.05***	0.07***	0.06***	0.10***	0.08***	0.07***	0.07***	0.04	0.05***	−0.01	0.01***	0.01*	0.03*
Adjusted R^2	0.179	0.249	0.383	0.366	0.209	0.172	0.242	0.222	0.18	0.076	0.133	0.13	0.11
N	789	1,367	762	1,522	1,115	1,579	1,042	677	2,433	391	682	1,016	512

Note

a Entries are unstandardised regression coefficients. Levels of statistical significance: *** = 0.001, ** = 0.01, * = 0.05.

in only a few countries. An additional analysis restricted to those who are gainfully employed shows that people who have strong social ties to their colleagues and are actively involved in decision-making at the workplace, tend to display higher levels of associational involvement.

The second group of independent variables consists of general attitudes, orientations and norms, political attitudes, and several variables that reflect additional aspects of social integration. *Social trust* has an effect on organisational involvement only in the case of west European countries (and less so for membership than for other types of involvement). In no former communist society is the effect of trust significant and positive. There are several possible explanations for this difference. First, as Badescu (2003) has shown in the case of Romania, the standard measures of social trust tend to have validity problems, which could apply to other east European societies as well.[15] Second, not every kind of association benefits from a higher level of social trust (Uslaner 2002), and the type of groups that are associated with trust are less numerous in eastern European countries than in western ones.

Social tolerance shows non-significant effects in the majority of cases. In no country is the effect significant for more than one of the three dependent variables we have tried. People who favour norms and values of *self-realisation* do not generally differ significantly from those who do not. For *solidarity*, weak positive effects can be found in most countries, but they are statistically significant in less than half of the cases. Again, the effects tend to be weaker when the dependent variable focuses on membership alone. East Germany and Spain are the only countries with significant effects for all specifications of the dependent variable.

Political interest has positive and significant effects in most countries regardless of how the dependent variable is specified. The effects of confidence in judicial institutions are close to zero in the majority of cases, with the exception of positive coefficients in West Germany, the Netherlands, Norway and Sweden. People who are less *satisfied with the way democracy works* in their country tend to have a higher level of organisational involvement. This tendency is less clear in the case of the former communist societies (with the exception of East Germany). People, who think they have greater chances than others to present opinions to politicians and to make politicians take account of their opinions (*political efficacy*), are more involved in almost every country. Moldova and Romania are the exceptions to this pattern: neither confidence in judicial institutions, nor satisfaction with democracy, or political efficacy has significant effects here.

Church attendance is one of the strongest predictors in the majority of countries under study, with stronger effects on forms of involvement other than membership. East European countries however, display weaker relationships. It is notable that East Germany appears to be more similar to West Germany than to other post-communist societies. As hypothesised, churches seem to provide an effective context for social integration. In the next subsection, where we distinguish between involvement in church based associations and involvement in other types of associations, we will shed additional light on the link between church attendance and associational involvement.

People who belong to a *network of friends* tend to participate more in associations, in each country under study, with the exception of Slovenia. The relationships tend to be stronger in the west European countries.

Political media exposure tends to have fairly strong effects in the west but insignificant in the east. Is this difference due to the media or to the public in these societies? The fact that East Germany is more similar to other post-communist societies than to West Germany in this regard, suggests that the difference is not the result of having different media. A possible explanation may be found in the relatively low level of efficacy and the weak links between efficacy and participation in the eastern societies. Since the organisationally involved segments of the public in these societies see their possibilities to influence politicians as very limited, they have just as little incentive to follow the political news as those who are not involved. As to the hypothesised negative effect of the *time spent watching television*, we find that our data do not provide much in the way of support. Most of the effects are non-significant.[16]

The extent to which citizens regard *associational activity as a civic virtue*, by contrast, turns out to be one of the strongest predictors. Those who think that being active in organisations is an important prerequisite for being a good citizen show higher levels of involvement in each country under study. Again, there is a clear difference between west and east European countries. The weakest effects in western Europe are stronger than any of those in eastern Europe, although there is considerable support for the notion of organisational activity as a civic duty in the east European countries.

Explaining involvement in different types of associations

When we distinguish between different types of associations, some of the patterns evidenced deviate from those described in the previous section (see Tables 7.2 to 7.5). The impact of *gender* varies across the four types of organisations we consider. When it comes to spare time and sports associations and, to a lesser extent, interest groups, men are more involved in most cases. With regard to socio-cultural and, to a lesser extent, religious associations, it is the other way around. The effect of *age* shows a deviant pattern with respect to spare time and sports associations. The young, but also the elderly, tend to be most involved in this case whereas the middle-aged are at the top with respect to other types of associations.

Education has no significant effect on involvement in religious associations, except in Norway, Switzerland and Spain, where the effect is positive, and West Germany, where it is negative. For other types of

Table 7.2 Explaining involvement in spare time and sports associations[a]

Predictor	CH	DK	EG	WG	NL	NO	SE	PT	ES	MD	RO	RU	SI
Gender (female)	−0.05***	−0.01	−0.03**	−0.03	−0.01	−0.03***	−0.05***	−0.07***	−0.02***	−0.01	−0.01***	0.00	−0.05***
Age													
Young	0.06**	0.02*	0.04**	0.04	0.06**	0.02	0.04**	0.01	0.02***	0.03***	0.01**	0.02***	0.03**
Old	0.01	0.01	0.03*	0.01	0.04**	0.03*	0.03*	0.01	0.01*	0.01**	0.01	0.00	0.00
Education	0.06	0.12***	0.06**	0.12	0.08**	0.07	0.17***	0.07*	0.06***	0.02	0.02	0.04***	0.07***
Time of residence	0.06***	0.04***	0.00	0.02	0.03*	0.02	0.05*	0.01	0.01	−0.02*	0.00	−0.01	−0.03
Size of locality	−0.11***	−0.06**	−0.03	−0.04***	−0.06**	−0.06***	−0.07**	−0.05**	−0.00	−0.00	−0.00	−0.00	0.03
Married or cohabiting	0.02**	0.00	−0.01	0.03**	0.01	0.02**	0.00	0.00	0.00	−0.01*	0.00	0.00	−0.03***
Children	0.02	0.01	−0.01	−0.01	−0.01	0.03**	0.02	0.00	–	−0.01**	0.00	−0.00*	0.01
Houseperson	0.01	0.02	0.03	0.03**	0.00	−0.02	−0.03	−0.01	0.00	−0.01	0.00	−0.01	−0.01
Employment													
Full-time job	0.00	0.03**	0.03**	0.04***	0.01	0.00	0.02*	0.00	0.01*	0.00	0.00	0.00	−0.02
Part-time job	0.02	0.03	0.02	0.05***	0.00	0.01	0.01	0.04	0.01	0.01	0.01	0.00	0.01
Adjusted R^2	0.08	0.04	0.05	0.10	0.02	0.05	0.10	0.11	0.06	0.07	0.03	0.05	0.11
N	1,538	1,604	929	1,818	1,387	1,971	1,249	1,002	3,972	1,197	1,201	1,723	985

	1	2	3	4	5	6	7	8	9	10	11	12	13
Social trust	0.03	0.03	-0.01	0.02**	0.03	0.03	0.04	0.04	0.02*	0.01	0.01	0.00	0.06
Tolerance	0.00	-0.08	-0.02	-0.01	-0.05*	0.03	-0.02	-0.04	-0.01	0.00	0.00	0.00	—
Self-realisation	-0.02	-0.03	-0.04	-0.01	0.02	-0.05	-0.02	0.00	—	-0.02	0.00	—	-0.04
Solidarity	-0.06	-0.03	-0.01	0.02**	-0.07	0.00	0.00	-0.02	0.01	0.00	0.00	-0.01*	-0.03
Church attendance	-0.01	0.02	0.03	-0.01	-0.02	0.03	0.00	0.02	0.00	0.00	0.00	0.02**	0.02
Informal contacts	0.02**	0.02***	0.02*	0.05***	0.04***	0.05***	0.02**	0.09***	0.01***	0.00	0.01	0.01***	0.00
Political media exposure	0.07*	0.03	0.04	0.05	0.09**	0.06	0.02	0.09**	0.02	-0.02	0.00	-0.01	0.01
TV hours	-0.11	-0.18**	-0.05	-0.12	-0.02	0.02	-0.17	0.10	-0.02	0.02	0.01	0.03	0.03
Political interest	-0.03	-0.06*	0.02	0.03**	-0.05*	-0.01	0.04	0.00	0.02***	0.03	0.00	—	0.04*
Confidence in judiciary	0.05*	0.02	0.05	0.08***	0.04	0.02**	0.04	0.02	0.02	0.01	-0.01	0.01	-0.01
Satisfaction with democracy.	0.00	-0.01	0.01	-0.02	-0.03	-0.02	-0.03	0.02**	-0.01	0.00	0.00	0.01	-0.02
Political efficacy	0.04*	0.02	-0.03	-0.06	0.00	0.07***	0.02*	-0.01	0.03*	0.00	0.00	0.01	0.02
Activity as a virtue	0.16***	0.18***	0.15***	0.16***	0.13***	0.13***	0.18***	0.06***	0.05***	0.01	0.01*	0.00	0.04*
Adjusted R^2	0.178	0.116	0.209	0.271	0.077	0.109	0.183	0.213	0.085	0.079	0.034	0.079	0.137
N	786	1,368	777	1,529	1,124	1,567	1,041	673	2,433	381	681	1,016	512

Note

a Entries are unstandardised regression coefficients. Levels of statistical significance: *** = 0.001, ** = 0.01, * = 0.05.

Table 7.3 Explaining involvement in interest groups[a]

Predictor	CH	DK	EG	WG	NL	NO	SE	PT	ES	MD	RO	RU	SI
Gender (female)	0.00	0.00	−0.01**	−0.01***	0.01	0.00	0.00	0.00	0.00	0.00	−0.01*	0.00	−0.01
Age													
Young	−0.07***	−0.08***	−0.02**	−0.01**	−0.08***	−0.07***	−0.04***	−0.02**	−0.03***	0.00	−0.01***	−0.01**	−0.06***
Old	−0.03	−0.03**	−0.01	0.00	−0.02*	−0.03**	0.01	0.00	−0.01***	0.00	−0.01*	0.00	−0.03**
Education	0.21***	0.15***	0.05***	0.04***	0.18***	0.10***	0.11***	0.08***	0.05***	0.04***	0.07***	0.05***	0.05***
Time of residence	0.02	0.01	0.00	0.01	0.01	0.00	0.02	0.00	0.00	0.00	0.01	0.00	0.01
Size of locality	−0.01	−0.00	0.02	−0.01	−0.00	−0.02	−0.00	−0.01**	−0.01**	−0.01	−0.01	−0.00	0.02*
Married or cohabiting	0.02***	0.02***	0.00	0.01	0.03***	0.02***	0.02***	0.00	0.01**	0.00	0.00	0.00	0.01
Children	−0.01	0.01**	0.00	0.00	0.02*	0.01	0.01**	0.01*	–	−0.01	0.00	0.00	0.01
Houseperson	0.00	−0.04	−0.02	−0.02***	−0.01	−0.04	−0.06	0.00	−0.01***	−0.01	0.00	−0.01	−0.02
Employment													
Full-time job	0.03	0.03***	0.01	0.01**	0.03***	0.02***	0.01***	0.01*	0.00	0.02***	0.02***	0.02***	0.01*
Part-time job	0.02	0.02	0.00	0.00	0.02*	0.01***	0.01*	0.00	0.00	0.01	0.00	0.00	0.01
Adjusted R^2	0.05	0.11	0.04	0.07	0.10	0.09	0.09	0.06	0.04	0.05	0.12	0.11	0.08
N	1,538	1,604	929	1,818	1,387	1,971	1,249	1,002	3,972	1,197	1,201	1,723	985

Social trust	0.03	0.02	−0.01	−0.01	−0.02	0.01	0.02	0.01	0.02*	0.01	0.00	0.00	0.01
Tolerance	0.04	−0.03	0.01	0.01	−0.02	0.05	−0.02	−0.01	−0.01	0.00	0.00	0.00	—
Self-realisation	−0.01	−0.02	0.01***	−0.01	0.03	−0.06	−0.02	−0.01	—	−0.03	0.00	—	−0.03
Solidarity	0.05	−0.01	0.01	0.01	0.01	0.01	−0.03	−0.01	0.01***	0.02	0.01*	0.00*	0.02
Church attendance	0.02	0.01	0.00	0.01**	0.00	0.02	0.02	0.01	0.00*	0.01	−0.01	0.01	−0.01
Informal contacts	0.01	0.02**	0.02**	0.01**	0.02*	0.02**	0.01	0.00	0.01***	0.03**	0.01	0.01*	0.00
Political media exposure	0.12**	0.06	0.04**	0.05***	0.05***	0.08**	0.02	0.03**	0.03	−0.01	0.00	0.01	0.04
TV hours	−0.12	−0.07	−0.03	−0.05**	0.01	0.09	−0.05	−0.02	0.00	0.03	0.04	0.02	−0.06
Political interest	0.04	0.05*	0.01	0.03**	0.05	0.05**	0.05	0.04**	0.02***	0.02	0.02**	—	0.05**
Confidence in judiciary	0.00	0.01	0.00	−0.01	0.04***	0.01	0.06*	0.00	0.00	0.00	0.00	0.00	−0.03
Satisfaction with democracy	−0.02	−0.01	−0.03	−0.02	−0.06***	−0.05	−0.06**	−0.01	−0.01*	0.01	0.01	0.00	0.01
Political efficacy	0.07*	0.04	0.02	−0.01	0.05	0.08**	0.07**	0.01	0.04***	0.02	0.01	0.03**	0.03
Activity as a virtue	0.05	0.03*	0.07***	0.03***	0.09***	0.08***	0.09***	0.02	0.05***	−0.01	0.02**	0.01	0.03**
Adjusted R^2	0.099	0.117	0.217	0.147	0.146	0.140	0.139	0.120	0.137	0.094	0.146	0.129	0.095
N	789	1,367	762	1,522	1,115	1,579	1,042	677	2,433	391	682	1,016	512

Note

a Entries are unstandardised regression coefficients. Levels of statistical significance: *** = 0.001, ** = 0.01, * = 0.05.

Table 7.4 Explaining involvement in socio-cultural associations[a]

Predictor	CH	DK	EG	WG	NL	NO	SE	PT	ES	MD	RO	RU	SI
Gender (female)	0.02**	0.02***	0.01	0.02***	0.01	0.03***	0.01*	0.00	0.01***	0.00	0.00**	0.01***	0.01*
Age													
Young	−0.04**	−0.04***	−0.02*	−0.01	−0.05***	−0.05***	−0.05**	−0.01	−0.02**	0.01	−0.01	0.01*	−0.03***
Old	−0.01	−0.02	−0.02*	−0.01	−0.01	−0.02*	−0.01	0.01	0.01**	0.01	0.00	0.00	−0.02**
Education	0.27***	0.24***	0.03**	0.07***	0.19***	0.08***	0.25***	0.09***	0.10***	0.03**	0.04***	0.03**	0.07***
Time of residence	0.02	0.02*	0.01	0.03**	0.01	0.01	0.02*	0.00	0.01	0.01	0.00	−0.01*	−0.01
Size of locality	−0.01	−0.00	−0.01	−0.03*	−0.00	−0.03**	0.02*	−0.03**	−0.01	0.01	−0.01	−0.00	−0.00
Married or cohabiting	0.01	0.01	0.00	0.02***	0.00	0.02**	0.02*	0.01	0.02***	0.00	0.00	0.00	0.00
Children	0.01	0.02**	0.01	0.01	0.01	0.00	0.01	0.01*	–	−0.01	0.01	0.00	0.01
Houseperson	0.00	−0.01	0.01	−0.01	0.00	−0.01	−0.05	−0.01	−0.01*	−0.01	0.00	−0.01	−0.01
Employment													
Full-time job	0.00	0.00	0.01	0.00	−0.01	0.00	0.00	−0.01	0.00	0.01*	0.01	0.00	0.00
Part-time job	0.02	0.02*	0.03	0.02	0.01	0.01	0.03**	0.01	0.00	0.01	0.01	0.00	0.00
Adjusted R^2	0.06	0.10	0.02	0.04	0.05	0.07	0.08	0.03	0.06	0.03	0.05	0.04	0.04
N	1,538	1,604	929	1,818	1,387	1,971	1,249	1,002	3,972	1,197	1,201	1,723	985

	(1)	(2)	(3)	(4)	(5)	(6)	(7)	(8)	(9)	(10)	(11)	(12)
Social trust	0.08**	0.0***4	0.00	0.05***	0.03	0.03**	0.07	0.02	0.03**	0.00	0.00	0.03
Tolerance	−0.01	−0.02	0.00	−0.02**	0.03	0.01	0.01	−0.03*	−0.02*	0.00	0.00	–
Self-realisation	0.01	0.00	−0.02	0.00	0.00	−0.07	−0.01	0.02*	–	−0.01	–	0.03
Solidarity	0.05	0.01	0.01	0.02**	0.04**	0.05***	0.03***	0.00	0.06***	0.01	0.01	0.02
Church attendance	0.08***	0.04**	0.04***	0.06***	0.05***	0.01	0.10*	0.01	0.02**	0.03**	0.02**	0.07**
Informal contacts	0.02	0.02**	0.00	0.04***	0.03***	0.02***	0.02	0.01*	0.03***	0.01	0.01	0.01
Political media exposure	0.02	0.04	−0.01	0.04*	0.04	0.03	0.04**	0.07**	0.01	0.02*	0.00	0.00
TV hours	−0.16	−0.16*	−0.01	−0.07	0.02	−0.03	−0.23	−0.09**	0.01	−0.03	−0.02	−0.02*
Political interest	0.06	0.05*	0.04**	0.00	0.03*	0.01	0.03	0.03	0.04***	0.01	–	0.08***
Confidence in judiciary	0.00	0.00	−0.03*	0.00	0.00	−0.01	−0.02	−0.01	0.02*	0.01	0.00	−0.01
Satisfaction with democracy	−0.01	−0.02	−0.03**	−0.01	−0.03	−0.02	0.00	−0.01	−0.02**	0.00	0.00	−0.01
Political efficacy	0.06	0.05**	0.03**	−0.01	0.06	0.05	0.07**	0.02	0.04**	0.01	0.02**	0.03
Activity as a virtue	0.03	0.05***	0.05*	0.07	0.08	0.07***	0.05*	0.02	0.07***	0.01	0.01	0.04*
Adjusted R^2	0.121	0.158	0.130	0.182	0.142	0.127	0.155	0.090	0.122	0.022	0.054	0.094
N	789	1,367	762	1,522	1,115	1,579	1,042	677	2,433	391	682 / 1,016	512

Note

a Entries are unstandardised regression coefficients. Levels of statistical significance: *** = 0.001, ** = 0.01, * = 0.05.

Table 7.5 Explaining involvement in religious associations[a]

Predictor	CH	DK	EG	WG	NL	NO	SE	PT	ES	MD	RO	RU	SI
Gender (female)	0.03	−0.01	0.01	0.01	−0.01	0.04**	0.01	0.04**	0.01	0.00	−0.01	0.00	0.00
Age													
Young	−0.07**	−0.01	−0.06*	−0.04	−0.11***	−0.03*	−0.08**	−0.03	−0.05***	−0.01	−0.01	0.00	−0.01
Old	−0.05*	−0.01	−0.02	−0.02	−0.03	−0.02	−0.04	0.00	−0.04***	0.00	0.00	−0.01	0.00
Education	0.18**	0.04	0.03	−0.08*	0.06	0.17***	0.07	−0.07	0.06***	−0.02	0.04	0.01	−0.01
Time of residence	0.03*	−0.01	0.02	0.05*	0.00	−0.02	−0.01	0.03	0.01	−0.01	0.00	0.01	0.00
Size of locality	−0.02	−0.02	−0.04	−0.10***	−0.01	−0.03*	−0.08***	−0.13***	−0.00	−0.01	−0.04	−0.00	−0.00
Married or cohabiting	0.02	0.00	−0.02	0.01	0.02	−0.01	0.01	0.00	0.01	0.00	0.00	−0.01	0.00
Children	0.03	0.00	0.01	0.02	0.04	0.01	0.00	0.05*	–	−0.01	0.00	0.00	0.01
Houseperson	0.00	0.04	−0.03	−0.03	−0.03	0.07	−0.07	0.01	−0.02**	0.05**	−0.02	0.03**	0.02
Employment													
Full-time job	0.03	−0.01	0.01	−0.05*	−0.01	−0.01	−0.02	−0.01	0.00	0.01	−0.01	0.00	0.00
Part-time job	0.03	0.03	0.02	0.01	0.03	0.04	0.02	−0.04	−0.01	0.01	−0.03	0.00	0.00
Adjusted R^2	0.01	0.00	0.01	0.04	0.02	0.02	0.02	0.05	0.02	0.00	0.01	0.01	0.00
N	1,538	1,604	929	1,818	1,387	1,971	1,249	1,002	3,972	1,197	1,201	1,723	985

Social trust	0.01	−0.01	0.06*	0.03	−0.03	−0.02	−0.01	0.05	0.03**	−0.04	0.00	0.00	0.03
Tolerance	0.03	−0.05	0.00	−0.03	−0.12	0.05	−0.01	−0.01	−0.02	−0.01	0.02	0.00	–
Self-realisation	−0.10*	−0.01	0.06	0.01	−0.07**	0.01	−0.07	0.00	–	0.00	−0.01	–	0.02**
Solidarity	0.05**	−0.01	−0.09*	0.01	0.06	0.08**	0.10**	−0.09	0.03*	0.02	0.04*	0.00	−0.01
Church attendance	0.34***	0.28***	0.49***	0.28***	0.49***	0.57***	0.41***	0.31***	0.02***	0.12***	0.09***	0.02***	0.06***
Informal contacts	0.02	0.01	−0.01	0.06***	0.05**	0.01	0.00	0.09**	0.02	−0.02	0.03	0.01	0.01
Political media exposure	−0.14*	−0.07	0.04	0.01	0.01	0.00	0.04	0.08*	0.00	−0.03	0.01	0.00	0.00
TV hours	−0.48	0.01	−0.20	−0.27*	0.00	−0.04	−0.16	−0.25	0.01	−0.01	−0.09	−0.02	−0.10
Political interest	0.08	0.01	−0.06	0.01	0.05	−0.02	−0.04	−0.04	0.01*	0.02	0.03	–	0.08
Confidence in judiciary	0.03	−0.05	−0.04	−0.03	0.01	−0.03	0.07*	−0.12**	0.01	0.00	−0.04*	0.00*	−0.01
Satisfaction with democracy	−0.04	−0.01	−0.05	−0.05	0.00	−0.01	−0.05	0.06	−0.02	0.04	0.04*	0.00	−0.01
Political efficacy	0.00	−0.04	0.03	0.06**	0.02	0.04	0.04	0.09	0.03*	0.04	−0.02	0.02	0.03
Activity as a virtue	0.05	0.01	0.07*	0.13***	0.05	0.05*	−0.05*	0.15***	0.07	−0.01	0.01	0.01	0.03
Adjusted R^2	0.196	0.125	0.276	0.183	0.366	0.279	0.197	0.205	0.100	0.054	0.056	0.023	0.089
N	789	1,367	762	1,522	1,115	1,579	1,042	677	2,433	391	682	1,016	512

Note
a Entries are unstandardised regression coefficients. Levels of statistical significance: *** = 0.001, ** = 0.01, * = 0.05.

associations, the effects of education tend to be strong and positive. The *time of residence* is more important for involvement in spare time and sports associations as well as socio-cultural organisations than for involvement in the other two kinds of associations. The *type of locality* has a relatively strong effect for spare time and sports associations, a relatively weak effect for interest groups, and a medium effect for socio-cultural and religious associations. The effects of being *married or cohabiting* and of having underage *children* tend to be much weaker for religious organisations. Having a *full-time job* is more important with respect to spare time and sports associations as well as interest groups. The effect of having a *part-time job* extends additionally to socio-cultural groups. The effect of being a *houseperson* is not significant for any of the four types associations in most countries. This is the only clear deviation from the findings of Gabriel *et al.* (2002), who find this factor to have a major effect as far as involvement in interest groups are concerned.

Social trust has only weak effects in the case of the east European countries, including East Germany. For the west European countries, social trust tends to have positive effects on involvement in socio-cultural organisations and, to a lesser extent, spare time and sports associations. For interest groups and religious associations, the effect is close to zero in most cases. This result is in line with findings for the USA (see, for example, Uslaner 2002). Values of *tolerance* and *self-realisation* are weak predictors for all four types of organisations. The positive effects of solidarity are largely restricted to socio-cultural and religious associations.

Political interest has positive effects for interest groups and socio-cultural associations but virtually no effect for religious associations. For spare time and sports associations the effects are mixed: five are statistically significant of which two are negative (Denmark and the Netherlands) and three positive (West Germany, Spain, and Slovenia). With very few exceptions, the effects of *confidence in judicial institutions* are close to zero. As to *satisfaction with democracy*, those who are less satisfied tend to be more involved as far as interest groups and socio-cultural associations are concerned, at least in western Europe. However, this tendency is weak. It is statistically significant only in the Netherlands, Sweden, and Spain for interest groups and in East Germany and Spain for socio-cultural associations. People with a strong sense of *political efficacy* tend to be more involved as far as spare time and sports associations, interest groups, and socio-cultural associations are concerned. In Norway, Sweden, Switzerland, Spain, and Russia, there are statistically significant effects for at least two of these three types. For religious associations, by contrast, the effect is significant for West Germany and Spain only.

The effect of *church attendance* on organisational involvement is not confined to religious organisations. It extends to socio-cultural groups in most countries but not to spare time and sports associations or interest groups (with the exception of weak, yet statistically significant, effects in West

Germany, Spain, and Russia). The fact that church attendance stimulates involvement in non-religious associations supports the argument that churches provide an effective context for social integration.

People who belong to a *network of friends* tend to be more involved in spare time and sports associations, and, to a lesser extent, in interest groups and socio-cultural associations. The effects are weaker in the case of the ex-communist societies, and close to zero in Slovenia for all of these types of associations. The effect of belonging to an *informal network* of friends is close to zero for religious associations, with the exception of weak positive effects in West Germany, the Netherlands, and Portugal.

The positive effects of *political media exposure* do not extend to religious associations, where the pattern is weak and inconsistent. The amount of time spent watching television is rarely statistically significant for any of the four types of associations. However, the direction of the relationship tends to be negative as hypothesised, at least in western Europe.

The effects regarding *associational activity as a civic duty* differ in an interesting fashion across types of organisations. Those who think that being active in organisations is an important prerequisite of being a good citizen are more likely to be involved in all four types of associations, but the effect is particularly pronounced for spare time and sports associations. This is a puzzling result in view of the fact that organisations of this type are typically assumed to serve the individual and private goals of the participants (see the discussion in Chapter 6) more than the public ends primarily associated with norms of citizenship.

Our analyses indicate that the effect patterns are at least moderately consistent across countries. They also suggest, however, that there are certain systematic cross-national differences, particularly between western and eastern Europe. Investigating these differences might provide useful insights regarding the impact of society-level factors on organisational involvement. A set of cluster analyses reveals that the set of country clusters depend on the way in which distance between country profiles is conceptualised.[17] The overall conclusion based on these analyses is that the way individual level factors shape organisational involvement does not follow a clear divide between east and west or any other categorisation based on the age of the democratic regime. A relatively high degree of similarity between explanatory models of participation in Moldova, Romania, and Russia can be found. At the same time, however, the other countries do not show any strong and systematic difference from these three ex-communist societies. The age of the democratic regime seems to have a strong effect on the overall level of involvement, but the way it relates to the individual decision to be involved or not is less clear.

Conclusions

In this chapter, we have tried to examine the impact of a considerable number of factors assumed to play a significant role in explaining involvement in voluntary associations. By doing so, we are in a position to address three important issues. First, we can evaluate the relative importance of determinants of associational involvement. Second, we can judge to what extent people involved in associations are representative for the citizenry as a whole in their social and attitudinal characteristics. Third, we can assess the differences between the older democracies, the younger democracies from southern Europe, and the ex-communist societies.

Our analyses identified several micro-level variables with strong effects. These results show remarkable similarity across countries under study and support the idea of a general model for explaining organisational involvement. Countries with different socio-economic, cultural, and political characteristics as well as very dissimilar distributions of associational involvement have largely similar patterns of determinants. The fact that the explanatory factors have quite similar effects across countries supports the results beyond the limits of the thirteen societies under study.

Socio-economic resources and indicators of social integration as well as factors indexing social orientations, norms, and motivations prove to be important predictors of organisational involvement. The effects of resources and levels of social integration are consistent across the majority of countries. Middle-aged men with a high education and income are more likely to be involved in associations. Additionally, we found that people integrated in social networks are more involved than others. Those who spend more time at the place of work, in church, and with informal networks of friends tend to be more involved. In some of the countries, the same is true about those living in smaller localities. Among the indicators of social integration, being married or cohabiting and having underage children play a more important role for membership than for other forms of involvement. This finding suggests that these factors have a dualistic effect on involvement. While they tend to increase social integration, they also tend to limit the amount of time available for participation in organisational activities.

People, who read, listen to, or watch political news are more likely to be involved in associations. However, the effects are weak or non-existent in the post-communist countries. The expected negative effect of extensive television consumption found only weak support in the large majority of cases.

Political orientations turn out to have a considerable impact in many instances. People with a strong interest in politics, a strong sense of political efficacy, and high level of dissatisfaction with the way democracy work tend to be more involved in organisations. The only exceptions are the negligible effects of confidence in judicial institutions and the limited impact of political orientations more generally on involvement in religious associations.

Finally, the extent to which associational activity is regarded as a civic duty is among the strongest predictors. Those who think that being active in organisations is an important prerequisite of being a good citizen are more involved in associations. Our interpretation of the relatively high support for this norm in the east European countries coupled with its relatively weak effect on actual involvement in these countries is that norms supportive of activity are an unexploited resource rather than a constraint responsible for the slow development of the associational sector in the former communist societies.

Generally speaking, the results indicate that people who are active in associations are not representative of the citizenry as a whole with respect to socio-economic characteristics. Higher levels of education and income have direct effects on organisational involvement as well as effects mediated by attitudes. Is the fact that some groups have a disproportionate representation in associations a reason for concern about the way needs and priorities receive consideration in society? An encouraging finding is that in many of the countries under study, those who are active in organisations tend to express more solidarity with those in need and higher levels of trust than others. However, this tendency is much weaker in the east European countries. This result is in line with previous findings showing only weak differences in terms of factors like trust, tolerance, and solidarity between the involved and the uninvolved in Moldova and Romania (Badescu *et al.* 2004).

Although the determinants of involvement are largely consistent across different types of associations, there are several instances where the effects differ. The organisations that stand out most clearly from the others in this regard are the religious ones. Compared to other types of organisations, involvement in religious associations has a smaller number of significant determinants. The effects of gender, education, being married or cohabiting, having a full-time job, and having trust in others tend to be much less important. Only solidarity and, unsurprisingly, church attendance, tend to have an explanatory power on a par with that for other types of organisations. In other words, involvement in religious associations is less affected by socio-economic resources and social integration than other types of organisations. Therefore, they compensate, to some extent, for the lack of equal representation in other associational domains.

Our analyses also reveal a rather high degree of similarity between countries with different prior regime types. The way that individual-level variables shape organisational involvement does not follow a clear divide between the east and the west, or any other categorisation based on the age of the democratic regime. However, a particularly high degree of similarity between the patterns displayed by Moldova, Romania, and Russia can be found, which is not entirely due to the low level of involvement in these three countries. This finding provides some support for the idea that the 'naturally grown' associations differ in their recruitment patterns from those 'imported' as a result of international aid. However, the other countries do not show any strong and systematic deviations from these three ex-communist societies. Moreover, the fact that Spain and Portugal cannot be placed on a continuum between the older democracies on the one side, and the former communist countries on the other, suggests that prior regime type and the age of the democratic regime have a limited effect, at most, on the way individual-level determinants shape the propensity to get involved in voluntary organisations.

Notes

1 We operationalise age in a way that allows us to identify non-linear relationships. To allow our two dummy variables to capture these relationships as efficiently as possible, we allow the age intervals to vary across countries. Thus, the upper limit for 'young' is 30 in Moldova, Spain, and Romania, 50 in East Germany, the Netherlands or Slovenia, and 40 in all other countries. The lower limit for 'old' is 50 in Moldova, Spain, and Romania, 70 in East Germany, the Netherlands, and Slovenia, and 60 in all other countries. Using the same intervals across the board would underestimate the effect of age in some countries.
2 Men are coded 0 and women 1.
3 Education is operationalised as described in Chapter 1. Income refers to household income.
4 Time of residence ranges from 0 (two years or less) to 1 (11 years or more). Size of locality ranges from 0 (rural area) to 1 (large city). Parenthood is coded 0 for those with no child under 18 years of age and 1 for all others.
5 Media exposure is an additive 0–1 index based on the extent to which the respondents reads the political content of a newspaper, listens to or watches news programmes on the radio or television, listens to or watches other programmes about politics and social affairs on the radio or television, and uses the Internet to obtain information about politics and society. Television hours refers to the number of hours per day that the respondent watches television, divided by 24.
6 Social trust is an additive 0–1 index based on the three items described in Chapter 2.
7 Solidarity is an 11-point scale ranging from 0 for those who say it is not at all important to show solidarity with people who are worse off than themselves to 1 for those who say it is very important. Self-realisation is an 11-point scale ranging from 0 for those who would not like at all to live in a society which emphasises that people can achieve self-realisation to 1 for those who would very much like to live in such a society.
8 Tolerance is an additive 0–1 index based on six items measuring social tolerance (accept as neighbour, see Chapter 5) towards the following groups: 'immigrants', 'homosexuals', 'people with a criminal record', 'people of another race', 'people with AIDS', and 'drug addicts'.
9 Political interest is an additive 0–1 index based on items indicating the degree of interest in general, national, local, and international politics.
10 Efficacy is an additive 0–1 index based on two 11-point scales indicating the extent to which the respondents think they have smaller or greater chances

than others to present their opinions to politicians and to make politicians take account of their opinions. Satisfaction with democracy is a single item scored on a range from 0 to 1. With respect to confidence in institutions, we focus on confidence in judicial institutions, which is expected to be particularly important with respect to collective action. We thus use an additive 0–1 index based on two 11-point scales indicating the degree of confidence in the courts and the police. The effects of other forms of trust are similar or weaker in each case.

11 Badescu *et al.* (2004) found that, in Moldova and Romania, activity is frequently motivated by personal interest, especially by the need to acquire skills that are valued in the labour market. Such is the case even with respect to associations that seek to produce collective goods.
12 Membership refers to the current situation whereas participation in activities, donations, and voluntary work refers to the past 12 months.
13 Factor analyses show that in each country participation in activities, voluntary work, and donations can be approximated by a single dimension. The minimum share of the total variance explained by the first factor is 56 per cent (in Switzerland), the mean across all countries is 70 per cent, and the second factor has an eigenvalue of less than 1 for each country.
14 For each type of organisation, the dependent variable is defined as $(I + M + D + A + V)/5N$ where I, M, D, A, and V denote a count of the number of organisations of the type in question in which the respondent is involved, a member, a donator, active, and a volunteer, respectively, and N denotes the number of organisations of the type in question.
15 Badescu (2003) shows that respondents from Romania are influenced in their assignments of 'other people' as trustworthy or untrustworthy, not only by their level of social trust, but also by their level of particularistic trust, which both theoretically and empirically is not linked to organisational involvement.
16 We checked for curvilinear effects of time spent watching television. There are very few people who do not watch television at all. When those with 0 to 1 hours of watching are compared to others, the effect on participation is linear.
17 The clustering method we used is between-groups linkage based on squared Euclidean distance as well as product-moment correlations. For reasons of space, the analyses are not presented here.

8 Social networks

Hajdeja Iglič and Joan Font Fábregas

Introduction

It is widely accepted that social networks affect the way people participate in politics. Numerous studies have shown that networks of durable social ties such as friends and family, colleagues and neighbours, provide group boundaries and informal social organisations that underlie collective identities and actors. Political mobilisation follows the lines of social networks established in routine activities of everyday life, since they enable coordination and resource mobilisation (McCarthy and Zald 1977; McCarthy 1996).

At the individual level, social ties function as a recruitment mechanism. People are asked to participate in political activities of various sorts, from voting to donating and protesting, and their response to these recruitment efforts is affected by both their own individual political preferences and the strength and structure of social ties from which the request comes. This is what scholars have called 'micromobilisation contexts' (Snow *et al.* 1980; McAdam 1988; McAdam and Paulsen 1993).

Even when a direct request for participation is absent, social ties are important as the sites of person-to-person transmission of political information and preferences that occur during political discussion. Political discussion, which takes place on various social occasions, is an important vehicle of social influence, a process in which people change their political preferences in response to information they receive through communication with others (Huckfeldt and Sprague 1991, 1995). The two-step flow model (Katz and Lazarsfeld 1955) provided one of the earliest explanations regarding the importance of informal social communication in politics, and its interaction with the media and political campaigns.

Recently, social capital theory has argued for a role of social networks that goes beyond resource mobilisation, political discussion, and recruitment for participation. According to social capital theory, political action is rooted in the social networks of everyday life in as much as social life gives rise to feelings of trust, and norms of reciprocity among citizens (Putnam 1993, 2000). The feelings of trust, and norms of reciprocity that develop in the context of networks, are social resources which people bring into political arenas. The experience of trustworthy relations in the realm of social networks helps one to engage in cooperative behaviour, when it comes to political ties and networks, and affects the quality of public debate (Fishman 2004).

In this chapter, we focus on three aspects of social networks within this set of claims about the relationship between social networks and politics: the multiplicity of social networks in which people participate, the strength of social ties within different networks, and the frequency with which people engage in political discussion with their social ties. It is these three aspects of social networks that Gibson (2003: 96) considers crucial in determining the overall political potential of networks.

The *multiplicity of social networks* in which one is involved reflects the magnitude and diversity of one's social integration. It is expected that when people are members of a larger number of networks, their chances of being recruited to various kinds of political action increase, since each of the many social networks they belong to has the potential to turn into a political network and become an agent of political mobilisation. On the other hand, the exposure to multiple and diverse sources of recruitment can hinder the mobilising role of networks. Multiple involvements seem to reduce the structural availability (Snow *et al.* 1980) of people for political mobilisation and weaken the process of social influence while increasing individual autonomy.

The *strength of social ties* reflects one's personal commitment to various social networks. Stronger social ties are assumed to be more efficient in mobilising channels than weaker social ties, because people conceive political information coming from stronger social ties as more reliable than those originating from weaker ties. Stronger social ties also imply solidarity-related incentives for collective action, especially when they are embedded in a dense network structure. On the other hand, weaker social ties tend to reach further into the social structure and connect diverse social circles (Granovetter 1973).

Finally, people do various things with their interaction partners, from helping each other in matters of everyday life, to socialising and discussing politics. *Political discussion* can present a constitutive element of social relationships: among people who join political organisation and share their political interests, or as a by-product of primarily social relationships, in the case of friendship. Political discussion is expected to remain important for one's political behaviour even in the situation of increased individualisation of political decisions, when 'the politics of choice appears to be replacing the politics of loyalties' (Norris 2002: 4). However, we expect the role of political discussion to be less recruitment and mobilisation, and more political deliberation, moderation and consensus formation.

The aim of this chapter is to describe and explain the political potential of social networks – the multiplicity of networks, strength of social ties, and frequency of political discussion in 11 European societies, some of them old and others new democracies.[1] Further analyses of the impact of these factors on political participation can be found in Part IV of this book.

Additionally, this chapter provides evidence on the relationships between different aspects of networks: between multiplicity of networks and strength of ties, on the one hand, and strength of ties and political discussion on the other. The first relationship has been widely discussed in the social modernisation literature and more recently within the social capital theory under the notions of bonding and bridging aspects of social networks. The question is, whether an increase in the number of involvements and affiliations leads to weaker commitment in social ties. For the second relationship, the problem of political discussion is placed in the context of weaker and stronger social ties. We ask if the strength of ties affects the ability of networks to serve as sites for political discussion. The three aspects of social networks can thus be regarded as interrelated: the multiplicity of networks is assumed to affect the strength of social ties, and the strength of social ties is assumed to have an impact on the frequency with which people engage in political discussion.

For the purpose of this chapter, we use a broader notion of networks than the one used in Chapter 6 and Chapter 7, where networks are operationalised in terms of involvement in voluntary associations. The data collected in our survey provide a unique opportunity to look at a larger number of networks, which include associations and workplace-related networks as well as friendship and social support networks. In addition, the questionnaire was designed to measure the strength of social ties people maintain in these networks. It does so by asking people how often they actually engage in social support, sociability relations, and discussions of organisational matters with their fellow members and co-workers.

Multiplicity of social networks

The concept of multiplicity of networks refers to the number of networks in which people are involved. It suggests that people with multiple networks have a larger number of interaction partners, and that they are connected to very different networks. The overall measure of network multiplicity is defined as the sum of the different kinds of networks in which people are involved: networks established in the workplace,[2] and voluntary associations,[3] informal friendship networks,[4] and support networks.[5] We consider them as involved in the workplace and associational networks only in so far as they maintain a minimum level of interaction with co-workers and co-members. Table 8.1 provides information about cross-country differences in network involvement. It shows the total level of involvement as well as involvement in particular kinds of social networks. For the workplace and voluntary associations, it also shows the per-

Table 8.1 Multiplicity of social networks[a]

Country	Mean number of networks	Friendship networks (%)	Support networks (%)	Organisational membership (%)	Organisational networks (%)	Employed (%)	Workplace networks (%)	Not involved (%)	N
Switzerland	2.09	56	21	86	75	68	55	11	1,237
Norway	1.83	44	11	88	69	68	55	10	1,674
The Netherlands	1.70	40	22	84	60	57	47	15	1,520
Sweden	1.51	25	12	90	60	67	53	17	1,245
Slovenia	1.51	55	18	53	40	47	39	15	948
West Germany	1.32	25	9	68	60	53	40	24	1,969
East Germany	1.02	16	10	51	38	52	38	34	993
Spain	0.98	32	5	42	31	50	32	38	3,621
Portugal	0.82	17	7	43	29	67	29	48	966
Romania	0.80	7	25	20	17	36	30	45	1,141
Moldova	0.71	13	11	20	17	49	36	48	809

Note
a Countries are ordered by the average number of networks.

centage of the population involved in organisations and the workplace compared with the percentage of people actually taking part in the respective social networks.

The number of different kinds of social networks in which people are involved varies considerably across countries, from an average of two kinds of networks in Switzerland to less than one in Romania and Moldova. In general, people in the western European countries (Switzerland, Norway, Sweden, and the Netherlands) are members of a significantly larger number of networks than people in the southern (Spain, Portugal) and eastern European (East Germany, Romania, Moldova) countries. Sweden, Slovenia, and West Germany represent intermediate cases with their citizens being involved in about one and a half networks.

High network multiplicity in western European countries is a result of the fact that people are likely to be involved in informal and formal social contexts, meaning that formal and informal integration at the country level complement rather than substitute one another. This finding runs contrary to the traditional sociological idea of the weakening of social bonds, which says that integration in formal, associational networks should be regarded as a substitute for weak informal networks, in the sense that people who have lost the ability of spontaneous socialising and bonding with their friends and family now search for meaningful social ties in the context of associations and organisations (e.g. Wirth 1938; Tönnies [1887] 1955; Nisbet 1969). Instead, what seems to be true for most countries is that people who are generally open to establishing social ties with others, do so in formal and informal social contexts. Whether a certain individual focuses more on informal or formal networks depends on her life situation and personal style. Notably, in countries with a low multiplicity of networks, people stay away from formal and informal networks alike.[6]

In all countries, social networks that evolve in organisational contexts are a very important source of social ties. It might be that social ties that emerge in voluntary associations and the workplace are not as strong as friendship ties, but their potential role as creators of social capital is primarily in bringing much larger percentages of the population into contact with one another than is achieved through informal friendship networks.

The percentage of people not involved in any kind of network is inversely related to the multiplicity of networks. The general propensity of the population to get involved in various social networks, which we can observe in western Europe, increases both the average number of networks per person and the percentage of the population involved in at least one kind of network. In the southern and eastern European countries, between 30 and 50 per cent of the population is not involved in any network beyond a few very close ties. This is a large section of the population, especially if we compare it to the western European countries where the percentage of those uninvolved varies between 10 and 15 per cent.

Substantial cross-country differences in network multiplicity deserve closer examination. Especially important is the question of the factors that explain the generally low network involvement of people in the southern and eastern European countries. The comparison of causal models that explain network involvement in different countries will also reveal whether network involvement has different roots in different countries. We consider countries as social contexts that affect the general level of network involvement in two different ways: by determining the higher or lower level of involvement, and by interacting with individual level variables, thus affecting the underlying individual model of network involvement.

There is a plethora of models trying to explain network involvement. We include in the analysis the following three groups of factors: *social positions* (gender, education, age) that define major social groups which differ in the extent and nature of their network involvement, *opportunity structures* (residential mobility, size of locality, attending religious services) that relate to the opportunities for contacts and network formation and have been used in the sociological studies of modernisation and loss of community, and *cultural traits* such as trust[7] in people and attachment to collective identities, which gained prominence in recent studies of social capital.

One of the strongest predictors of network multiplicity is education[8] (Table 8.2). The number of networks in which people are involved increases with years of schooling. However, there are specific thresholds: obtaining a secondary education increases one's chances of being involved in friendship networks compared to those with primary education, while people with post-secondary education add to these informal contacts the formal ones established in voluntary associations and the workplace (Table 8.3).

Another strong predictor of network involvement, besides education, is employment.[9] Being employed largely increases one's chances of being involved in social networks. Almost 22 per cent of the population in Moldova, 18 per cent in East Germany, and 14 per cent in Spain, Portugal, and Romania are only involved in workplace-related networks. For them, the workplace is the only source of social ties beyond family and kin.

The impact of the other two background variables, age and gender, is much weaker, especially when controlled for education and employment. In most countries, men and women are included in the same number of networks. It is only in Portugal and Spain that women are included in about 10 per cent fewer networks than men. Differences between men and women are stronger when we look at specific kind of networks (Table 8.3) rather than the overall level of involvement. As seen in other studies, women are less likely to take part in associational networks, while they are more frequently included in communal support networks.[10] Significantly lower levels of women's involvement in associational networks are found

Table 8.2 Regression analysis of network multiplicity[a]

Predictor	CH	NL	NO	SE	WG	EG	ES	PT	SI	RO	MD
Gender (male)	0.01	−0.01	−0.03**	0.01	0.04***	0.04**	0.04***	0.11***	0.00	−0.00	−0.01
Age											
Below 30	−0.02	0.03	−0.01	−0.05**	0.04*	−0.04	−0.09	−0.04*	−0.01	−0.03	−0.02
Above 60	−0.03	0.01	−0.03*	−0.01	−0.04*	−0.04*	−0.01	0.01	−0.02	0.03	0.02
Education	0.21***	0.35***	0.07*	0.25***	0.16***	0.26***	0.20***	0.49***	0.23***	0.26***	0.23***
Employment	0.24***	0.24***	0.23***	0.24***	0.24***	0.17***	0.22***	0.13***	0.20***	0.29***	0.25***
Residential mobility	−0.02	−0.01	−0.00	−0.03	−0.01	−0.01	−0.02	−0.02	0.01	−0.01	0.01
Size of locality											
Big city	−0.02	−0.03	−0.02*	0.01	−0.04***	−0.02	−0.04***	−0.04	0.03	−0.03*	−0.02
Village	0.02	0.02	−0.02*	−0.01	0.05**	0.10***	−0.02	0.06**	0.04*	−0.03*	−0.03
Religiosity	0.06*	0.02	0.13***	0.11***	0.15***	0.19***	0.07***	0.17***	0.03	0.06*	0.03
Social trust	0.09**	0.11*	0.08**	0.10***	0.11***	0.01	0.15***	0.01	0.05*	0.06*	0.04
Attachment											
Local	0.11***	0.09*	0.11***	0.06*	0.12***	0.09*	0.01	0.04	0.01	−0.04	0.04
Global	0.02	−0.01	−0.02	0.01	0.07**	0.05*	0.08***	0.07*	0.07*	0.07*	0.06
Adjusted R^2	0.300	0.318	0.293	0.316	0.345	0.280	0.341	0.267	0.231	0.498	0.437
N	1,066	1,248	1,383	1,118	1,711	842	2,910	893	857	967	533

Note
a Entries are unstandardised regression coefficients. Levels of statistical significance: *** = 0.001, ** = 0.01, * = 0.05.

Table 8.3 Regression analysis of involvement in different kinds of networks (pooled analysis)[a]

Predictor	Network multiplicity		Organisational networks	Friendship networks	Support networks
	Model 1	Model 2			
Gender (male)	0.02***	0.01***	0.10***	0.00	−0.05***
Age					
Below 30	−0.01**	−0.02***	−0.04***	0.07***	−0.03***
Above 60	−0.01**	0.01	−0.01	−0.03***	0.01**
Education	0.26***	0.37***	0.49***	0.30***	0.10***
Employment	0.22***	0.22***	0.04***	0.01	−0.01
Residential mobility	−0.01***	−0.01**	−0.01	−0.02***	−0.03***
Size of locality					
Big city	−0.02***	−0.03***	−0.04***	0.00	0.01
Village	0.01**	0.01**	0.01	0.04***	0.00
Religiosity	0.09***	0.08***	0.21***	0.03**	0.07***
Attachment					
Local	0.05***	0.02**	0.12***	0.04***	0.01
Global	0.03***	0.02**	0.04**	0.01	0.05***
Social trust	0.10***	0.09***	0.24***	0.11***	0.05***
East Germany	−0.01	−	−0.05**	−0.17***	−0.04**
Moldova	−0.10***	−	−0.32***	−0.22***	−0.03***
The Netherlands	0.10***	−	0.03*	0.02	0.08***
Norway	0.09***	−	0.11***	0.02	−0.02
Portugal	−0.11***	−	−0.25***	−0.19***	−0.05***
Rumania	−0.08***	−	−0.34***	−0.28***	0.11***
Slovenia	0.10***	−	−0.08***	0.19***	0.054***
Spain	−0.04***	−	−0.29***	−0.05***	−0.08***
Sweden	0.03**	−	0.014	−0.15***	−0.01
Switzerland	0.16***	−	0.12***	0.17***	0.08***
West Germany	base	−	base	base	base
Social trust × (MD, PT, RO, SI)[b]	−0.06***	−	−0.14***	−0.07**	−0.09
Country level of social trust	−	0.59***	−	−	−
Adjusted R^2	0.404	0.346	0.209	0.123	0.048
N	16,835	16,526	18,719	22,054	19,621

Notes

a Entries are unstandardised regression coefficients. Levels of statistical significance: *** = 0.001, ** = 0.01, * = 0.05.
b Social trust multiplied by a dummy variable scored 1 for Moldova, Portugal, Romania, and Slovenia.

in particular in Spain, Portugal, East and West Germany, and Slovenia. In Romania and Moldova, both men and women exhibit very low levels of associational involvement, but the general pattern of gender differences is the same. In Switzerland, Norway, the Netherlands, and Sweden, where associational membership of women is relatively high, women added new associational involvements to support networks in which they were traditionally engaged, rather than replacing them.

Age differences in network multiplicity are small in most countries. The general trends are, first, that network multiplicity is somewhat lower among older people (over 60 years old), since they are less integrated in friendship and associational networks, although they more often take part in support networks. Second, we observe that younger generations (from 15 to 29 years old) are more often involved in friendship groups and less in support and associational networks in all countries. Middle-aged (from 30 to 60 years old) people have the highest network multiplicity, since they become highly involved in associational networks at the same time as maintaining a large part of their friendship networks. One can clearly observe life-cycle effects in this pattern. People change the kind of networks they belong to as they move through life, although this change is moderate.

Since the differences between young and middle-aged people are small,[11] one can hardly expect that they would hide significant generational effects as found by Putnam for the United States (2000: 248–57). However, the lack of significant differences between middle and older generations might indicate that the decline in network involvement, which is characteristic for older people, has been counteracted with a trend of generational decline among middle-aged people, resulting in lowering of the difference between the two groups. Table 8.2 shows that in most countries older people indeed have about the same level of network involvement as middle-aged people (most differences are small and not significant), which can be an indicator of the passing of the civic generations.

Another set of predictors included in the regression equation of network multiplicity are opportunity structures, measured by residential mobility, urbanisation, and secularisation. According to the established sociological argument (Wellman 1979; Fisher 1982), those who are not very mobile and who live in small towns and rural areas have very different opportunities for network creation than people who move frequently and live in large cities. The latter are embedded in egocentric or ego-anchored social networks consisting of dyads and triads that originate in different social settings. On the other hand, the stability of the social environment of the former group allows for more collectivistic and group-orientated networks that are cohesive and durable.

The effects of structural variables are fairly consistent across countries, although they are weak and often not statistically significant. Residential mobility[12] does indeed have a negative impact on social networks – those who are recent movers or have lived in their present housing for less than ten years are less involved in networks than those who are long-time residents. The two groups do not differ so much in the associational involvement, but in the integration in friendship and support networks.

Size of locality[13] also does not make a big difference in network involvement. People from big cities have somewhat smaller, and villagers somewhat larger, networks than those living in towns, although differences are mostly not statistically significant. Urbanisation decreases both associational involvement (especially in big cities) and involvement in informal networks (more predominantly in towns and cities compared to villages and rural areas).

The most important structural variable is church attendance.[14] People who frequently attend church are more likely to be integrated in associational and especially support networks. Participating in communal support networks is a very positive social consequence of one's active engagement with the church, although this social support often tends to be limited to people's immediate surroundings; their church and neighbourhood, rather than bridging various social groups, as noted by Uslaner (2001b).

The linkage between trust and social networks has been widely disputed. Some authors have argued that the relationship is strong, others that it is weak or even absent. The causal order of the variables is also unclear: trust is treated as a by-product of organisational and communal involvement (Putnam 2000; Brehm and Rahn 1997), as well as an important facilitator of group membership and network involvement (Stolle 1998).[15] The dispute about the relationship between networks and trust has partly to do with a lack of conceptual distinction between different kinds of trust: particular and generalised trust. Uslaner (2002) argues that networks and trust are strongly intertwined and form a reciprocal relationship in the case of particular trust, which is trust in people one meets and interacts with regularly in various social contexts, like neighbours, co-workers and co-members. In contrast, in the case of generalised trust the relationship is expected to be predominantly one-directional – from trust to networks, since such judgment is based less on concrete experience with others, and more on individual's moral orientations (Mansbridge 1999) and collective experiences with society and state (Offe 1999; Rothstein and Stolle 2001; Uslaner 2002).

The analysis shows that network involvement in general, and involvement in voluntary associations in particular, is positively related to generalised trust and that the impact of trust on networks is relatively strong.[16] Trusting people are involved in a larger number of networks. Social similarity of others does not seem to diminish this need for interpersonal trust, although the role of trust is indeed larger in associational than in friendship networks. Since associational networks bring together very different people, generalised trust is needed in order for them to interact and work together to reach common goals. On the other hand, friendship networks include people who have chosen each other in the first place, on the basis of social similarity and personal affinity.

The impact of generalised trust varies across countries. It is stronger in western than in eastern European countries and Portugal, as indicated by the interaction effect in model I of Table 8.3. How can we explain this differential effect of trust? One reason might be that the impact of trust on networks depends on the structure of network involvement. In countries where network involvement is heavily dependent on involvement in workplace networks (like in Portugal, Slovenia, East Germany, Romania, and Moldova), the role of generalised trust is small, since generalised trust is not linked with workplace involvement. In countries where people are also involved in other kinds of networks, especially in voluntary associations-related networks, the role of trust increases. This provides additional evidence for our argument that generalised trust is especially important for the formation of networks of weak ties characteristic for voluntary associations, which bring together rather dissimilar people, and less for 'structurally induced' networks of co-workers and strong ties of friendship, which connect similar people with regard to their social position, world-views and interests.

Since network formation is an interaction process, an individual's network involvement can be expected to result from both his own propensity for entering social relationships as well as from the propensity of his or her social environment to respond positively to such attempts. This interaction is expressed in Uslaner's (2001b: 108) argument that people who live among a lot of trusters may not actually become trusters, but may go along with the behaviour of trusters by getting involved in their communities. However, the opposite can also be expected: trusters who live in a low-trust environment might not be able to get involved in social interactions and networks as much as they would like to. In this case the social context in which they live constrains their network involvement. In our analysis we tested the explanatory power of trust conceived in both ways: as an individual resource and a contextual attribute (van Deth 2000, 2001b; Newton 2001a; Uslaner 2001b; Norris 2002).[17] The results for model II in Table 8.3, where the country level of social trust is included instead of country-specific intercepts, show that trust considered as a contextual attribute is among the strongest determinants of network involvement. Social networks are collective endeavours, and participation in networks depends largely on the contextual level of trust, which promotes or constrains network formation regardless of the individual level of trust.

The last variable included in the model is territorial identity. We expect that people who identify strongly with any territorial collectivity are more likely to join networks than those with low collective identification. The reason is that identification with collectivity makes spending time with other people and working for the common good more valuable, as shown by the many studies of social dilemmas (Brewer and Kramer 1986; Kollock 1998). The reverse relationship can also be expected: high involvement in social networks contributes to high identification with a territorial unit. Just as was emphasised in the discussion of interpersonal trust, this 'virtuous circle' is more plausible in the case of local than non-local (e.g. national, European, or world) attachments, since social networks are mostly local.

People with a stronger territorial attachment[18] are indeed more likely to be involved in multiple networks than those with a weak attachment. Again, there are important differences between countries with respect to what kind of territorial attachment leads to higher network involvement.[19] In the western European countries, including East Germany, it is attachment to neighbourhood and municipality that has a strong and significant impact on network involvement, which is in line with our expectation that local attachment is positively related to social networks. We suggest that local attachment and networks reinforce one another in this case. In contrast, in the eastern and southern European countries, local attachment is not conducive to social networks. For people from these countries, local communities (i.e. neighbourhoods and municipalities) are quite 'hollow', consisting of a weak social fabric, despite the fact that they feel attached to them in a stronger way than people in the western European countries.[20] In this case, strong collective identity does not seem to originate in rich networks, but rather in shared history and culture.

It is the non-local, and more 'global' attachments that help people from the southern and eastern European countries to engage in richer social networks. This is because identification with Europe and 'humanity as a whole' brings about a kind of universal morality not present in the local identities of these countries, according to which the social relations between people are regarded in a less competitive and more generous way. People who attach to more 'global' identities also form a kind of subculture, with a common goal to change (democratise) their countries. In order to realise this goal they network and participate in the voluntary associations.

In summary, the largest gap in network multiplicity has been found between the western European countries (Norway, the Netherlands, Switzerland) on the one side, and the eastern (Moldova, Romania) and southern (Spain, Portugal) European countries on the other. West Germany, Sweden, and Slovenia stand in between these two groups of countries. The strongest predictors of network multiplicity are education, employment, and generalised trust. Variables included in the model explain about 40 per cent of the variance in network multiplicity. While opportunity structures – urbanisation, mobility, secularisation – indeed work in the direction of network dissolution as suggested by many studies of modernisation, their impact is counteracted by the rising levels of education and higher degree of generalised trust. This model of network involvement holds across all countries. The only exceptions are very weak effects of generalised trust and attachment to local identity in the southern and eastern European countries compared to the western European countries.

Strength of ties

The findings on significant differences in network multiplicity across countries raise the following questions: how is people's involvement in larger or smaller numbers of networks related to the quality of social ties? Does a more extensive involvement in social networks in western European countries come at the expense of the strength of ties that connect people to one another? Or, is the smaller number of networks in southern and eastern Europe a sign of a general lack of social connectedness in these countries, which is also reflected in weaker social ties?

Strength of ties is one of the most prominent aspects of social networks. It refers to the quality of social ties in the sense that closer social ties indicate higher personal commitment and understanding, and stronger social influence. In our study we measured the strength of ties with four questions asking how often respondents do the following things with other members of organisations, clubs, and co-workers: help each other with practical matters outside organisational life, visit each other privately, and talk about problems concerning the organisation or its goals. This operationalisation of the strength of ties combines the notion of frequency of contact with the content of the ties (i.e. 'what people do with one another'). 'Helping' and 'visiting' both indicate very strong informal integration and a presence of sociability relations within organisations.[21] 'Talking about organisational problems' represents yet another dimension of organisational social structure,[22] which shows that social networks within organisations develop along the lines of social and task environments. People who often talk with others about organisational problems might be connected with sociability ties, but this is not necessarily the case. For this reason we treat 'helping' and 'visiting' each other as strong-tie content, and 'talking about organisational problems' as weak-tie content.

The strength of social ties[23] is especially high in Spain, Moldova, and Romania, in the workplace and voluntary associations alike (see Tables 8.4 and 8.5).[24] In these countries both dimensions of strength of ties, socialising (strong-tie content), and discussing organisational matters (weak-tie content), score high. With the exception of Portugal, we can say that countries with the smallest network multiplicity exhibit the highest average strength of ties in associations and the workplace. In addition to this, when we look at the percentage of highly integrated people within organisations,[25] these three are again among the countries with the highest score.

Table 8.4 Strength of social ties in voluntary associations[a]

Country	Mean for sociability ties	Mean for discussion ties	Mean for social ties combined	High involvement, % of members	N	High involvement, % of population	N
Spain	0.67	0.69	0.68	45	1,215	15	3,628
Moldova	0.63	0.69	0.66	46	220	13	809
Switzerland	0.55	0.63	0.59	35	1,015	22	1,726
Romania	0.55	0.59	0.57	33	227	7	1,141
West Germany	0.47	0.54	0.51	22	1,357	15	1,969
Slovenia	0.37	0.61	0.49	22	513	12	948
Norway	0.44	0.54	0.48	20	1,494	18	1,674
The Netherlands	0.46	0.52	0.48	29	1,290	24	1,520
East Germany	0.39	0.51	0.45	22	514	11	993
Sweden	0.38	0.46	0.42	18	1,131	16	1,245
Portugal	0.28	0.37	0.37	6	428	3	966

Note
a Countries are ordered by the average strength of social ties in voluntary associations.

Table 8.5 Strength of social ties in the workplace[a]

Country	Mean for sociability ties	Mean for discussion ties	Mean for social ties combined	High involvement, % of members	N	High involvement, % of population	N
Romania	0.65	0.78	0.72	54	362	17	1,141
Moldova	0.68	0.71	0.70	48	415	25	809
The Netherlands	0.54	0.83	0.69	47	807	25	1,520
Spain	0.62	0.74	0.68	47	1,454	19	3,628
Switzerland	0.51	0.76	0.63	39	1,238	28	1,726
Slovenia	0.44	0.82	0.63	38	423	17	948
Sweden	0.43	0.82	0.63	34	728	20	1,245
Norway	0.44	0.74	0.59	27	1,438	23	1,674
West Germany	0.41	0.53	0.47	14	877	6	1,969
East Germany	0.32	0.54	0.44	12	444	5	993
Portugal	0.22	0.28	0.25	3	527	3	966

Note
a Countries are ordered by the average strength of social ties in the workplace.

Among western European countries, which have generally high network multiplicity, the highest strength of ties is found in Switzerland. Workplace and voluntary associations in this county include a high percentage of people who are strongly integrated. Other western European countries exhibit moderate levels of strength of ties, some stronger in the case of the workplace, others in the case of voluntary associations. What contributes to the lower strength of ties in these countries, compared to Switzerland, is especially a lack of strong sociability ties.[26] Differences among countries with respect to weaker ties based on discussion are much smaller.

At a first glance, it seems as if strength of ties is negatively related to the multiplicity of networks. With the exception of Switzerland, the strength of ties is stronger in countries with lower network multiplicity. One can expect a negative relationship between strength of ties and network multiplicity on the basis that involvement in a larger number of social networks means that people spend less time with, and depend less on, the people they meet in each of the organisations. This results in less personal commitment and weaker social ties. Similarly, involvement in a larger number of networks can be expected to increase the diversity of people one interacts with. Since people tend to develop stronger ties with those similar to themselves, as has been shown in studies of friendship and homophily (McPherson and Smith Lovin 1987), those who are involved in multiple networks can again be expected to maintain, on average, weaker social ties since their interaction partners are more dissimilar. On the other hand, network multiplicity and strength of ties might be considered as indicators of an underlying personal trait in the sense that people who are more sociable and 'open for forming social ties' are both involved in a larger number of networks and connected with others with stronger social ties. If this is true, then the relationship between the two variables should be positive. Finally, strength of ties is expected to result from the active participation of people in organisations. Those who actively participate in the organisation are supposed to be more involved with their co-members (Knoke 1982).

The individual level analysis reveals that in all countries the strength of social ties, network multiplicity, and activism[27] in voluntary associations and the workplace are positively correlated (the correlations range from 0.109 to 0.478, across countries and social contexts). Especially strong correlations are found between network multiplicity and strength of ties, on the one hand, and activism and strength of ties, on the other. Thus, stronger social ties are indeed characteristic for those who are more open for forming social ties and are involved in larger number of networks, as well as for those who are actively involved in the life of organisations. There is no evidence that involvement in multiple networks reduces the strength of ties and personal commitment.

Despite the positive relationship between network multiplicity, activism, and strength of ties, people in the western European countries have a lower average strength of ties than those in eastern European countries and Spain, although they have higher levels of network multiplicity and activism. This is because, at any level of network multiplicity and activism, countries like Romania, Moldova, and Spain show higher average strength of ties.[28] Thus, individual level characteristics such as a general propensity for forming social ties, and active involvement in organisational life, factors that generally lead to a higher strength of ties, do not explain cross-country differences.

We suggest an explanation in terms of sociability style. Social networks in western Europe seem to be more individualised and selective,[29] meaning that people choose only specific co-members and co-workers as their strong ties. Social ties tend to be dyadic. They originate in a large number of social settings and across individuals' egocentric networks in the form of friendship relations by which they enrich social structure with bridging ties. By contrast, in the eastern and southern European countries people tend to establish strong ties with the whole group of people they meet in organisations and in the workplace. In this case, social networks are group-orientated, and their boundaries are determined by membership in collectivities.

That differences between countries, with respect to the average strength of ties in organisations, are more a matter of sociability style than a dissolution of a social bond is also supported by data showing that the proportion of the population that is highly integrated in the organisational contexts is about the same in the western European countries as in the eastern and southern European countries (Tables 8.4 and 8.5, right-side columns). This means that, on average, the lower strength of ties in organisations in the western European countries is due to the fact that the highly integrated core of organisational members is joined by a larger number of less integrated members, while in the eastern and southern European countries, organisations consist of a smaller number of members who are highly integrated. Thus, the capacity of people for bonding in organisations, as expressed in the proportion of the population that is highly integrated, is not much different across countries, but the character of organisations is clearly different. Organisational settings in the western European countries have a much sparser social structure compared to the southern and eastern European countries, where larger proportions of members are highly integrated. The involvement of people in organisations in southern and eastern Europe is of a more dichotomised type; they are either strongly integrated or not involved in networks at all. In western Europe, organisational networks bring larger number of citizens in contact with one another, through both weak and strong ties.

Thus, none of our expected patterns detailing how network multiplicity and strength of ties are related across European countries holds. Less network involvement in southern and eastern Europe is not related to generally weaker social ties and social anomy, but quite the contrary; to the lack of weak social ties and the predominance of strong ties in organisational networks. However, the high level of involvement found in the western European countries is also not related to the general dissolution of social bonds and social anomy, but rather to the co-existence of strong and weak social ties within organisational settings.

Political discussion

Political discussion is the last characteristic of social networks that we will discuss in this chapter. We perceive it as a content of social ties, which emerges during the interaction between people. The frequency with which people engage in political discussions is strongly related to their political interest, and this relationship has been elaborated in numerous studies of political behaviour. Yet, political discussion, as opposed to political interest, takes place in social relations and networks. People with a high level of political interest may or may not engage in political discussion, depending on the expectations and interests of people in their social environment. The social environment has the ability to constrain or promote the expression of political interest through political discussion. If citizens participate in organisations with an explicitly political agenda and thus find themselves in the company of people with a similarly high level of political interest, we can expect that their political interest translates into political discussion at a similarly high level. On the other hand, people may, under certain social conditions, consciously avoid discussing politics with others, or discuss it only with certain people. For example, Volker and Flap (2001) show that in socialist East Germany, discussing politics was exclusively a matter for very close social ties, due to the fear of political sanctions.

In our study, political discussion is measured with a general question: 'how often do you discuss political matters with others?' and more specific questions about the discussion of politics with family, friends, neighbours, co-workers, and co-members. The general level of discussing politics with others is highest in Switzerland, Norway, and the Netherlands, and lowest in Spain, Romania, and Portugal (Table 8.6). The correlations between measures of discussing politics are high (product-moment correlations range from 0.33 to 0.78, across countries). People who discuss politics frequently with their family and friends are also more likely to discuss it with their weaker social ties such as co-workers and co-members. This may be because the individual level factors that encourage or inhibit political discussion, such as political interest, education, gender, age, and early socialising experiences show consistent impact on individual involvement in political discussion across social contexts. Nevertheless, social context and context-specific networks matter. People are more inclined to discuss politics with some social ties than with others.

Table 8.6 Frequency of political discussion[a]

Country	Discussing politics with others			Discussing politics with particular others			
	Mean	Standard deviation	N	Mean for friends	Mean for co-workers	Mean for co-members	Mean for neighbours
Switzerland	0.65	0.31	1,647	0.57	0.51	0.41	0.28
Norway	0.61	0.25	2,297	0.58	0.60	0.34	0.29
The Netherlands	0.56	0.31	1,643	0.51	0.52	0.26	0.20
Sweden	0.52	0.29	1,257	0.45	0.50	0.26	0.22
East Germany	0.49	0.30	1,009	0.49	0.43	0.39	0.27
West Germany	0.47	0.28	1,969	0.48	0.39	0.39	0.24
Moldova	0.47	0.32	1,190	0.47	0.47	0.37	0.36
Slovenia	0.43	0.33	983	0.45	0.40	0.23	0.22
Spain	0.36	0.33	4,242	0.34	0.34	0.26	0.11
Romania	0.34	0.34	1,208	0.32	0.40	0.22	0.21
Portugal	0.30	0.30	1,005	0.31	0.27	0.17	0.14

Note

a Countries are ordered by the frequency of political discussion with others.

In all countries, family, friendship, and work-based networks are more important loci for political discussion than voluntary associations and neighbourhood. About one-third of the population discuss politics with their friends often, or at least sometimes. A similar percentage of people in employment discuss politics with co-workers. Almost three-quarters of respondents who are members of voluntary associations never or only rarely discuss politics with their co-members. This shows that the political potential of voluntary associations, measured by the frequency of political discussion among members is very weak, especially when compared to workplace and informal friendship networks. However, since voluntary associations are internally very diverse, one must look at the level of political discussion in different kinds of voluntary organisations.

The most politicised networks are found among people who are members of political parties.[30] They are followed by members of peace, environmental, and immigrants' organisations, and trade unions, which are all organisations in which politics features regularly on the agenda. The least politicised networks are found in organisations that serve various kinds of individual objectives of their members such as sports clubs, religious organisations, and associations for medical patients and addictions. Differences between countries with respect to politicisation of social networks are smaller in the case of 'political' organisations than 'non-political' ones. Thus, Spanish associational networks are, in particular, less politicised than Swiss ones when it comes to sports clubs, cultural, and religious organisations (see Table 8.7). When organisations are of a more 'political kind', Spanish networks are as politicised as Swiss ones. On the other hand, the generally high propensity of Swiss people to discuss politics with co-members does not depend much on the kind of the voluntary associations in which they meet. We can conclude that the higher politicisation of voluntary association-based networks in the Swiss case reflects, first of all, a generally higher level of political discussion among the organisational members, regardless of the kind of organisation they belong to, and second, a larger proportion of citizens being involved in organisations that are more explicitly concerned with political issues, such as political parties, trade unions, immigrants', peace, and environmental movements.

Is the frequency with which one discusses politics with others affected by social networks? As argued above, political discussion should be perceived as the content of social ties that depends not only on an individual's inclinations, but also on the social relations and networks in which he or she is involved. Social ties are channels through which political communication is conducted. These ties have the ability to constrain or enable this communication. The frequency of political discussion is expected to depend, first, on the quality of social ties (i.e. strength of ties), and second, on the kind of people brought together by social interaction (i.e. their similarity in political interest and views). People connected by stronger social ties are assumed to enter political discussion

Table 8.7 Frequency of discussing politics in different kinds of voluntary associations in Spain and Switzerland

Type of association	Spain			Switzerland		
	Average discussion frequency	Percentage who are members	N of members	Average discussion frequency	Percentage who are members	N of members
Political parties	0.67	2	102	0.62	12	195
Immigrants' organisations	0.58	1	15	0.50	3	41
Peace organisations	0.45	1	32	0.50	8	136
Environmental organisations	0.43	2	76	0.46	25	408
Trade unions	0.42	5	210	0.50	12	197
Cultural organisations	0.33	7	317	0.46	23	372
Housing organisations	0.35	4	159	0.46	14	223
Charity or social welfare organisations	0.26	11	457	0.46	35	579
Associations for medical patients/addicted	0.23	4	152	0.44	22	365
Religious or church organisations	0.24	4	187	0.47	19	311
Sport organisations and outdoor clubs	0.27	13	540	0.45	45	736
N			4,252			1,647

more frequently than those connected by weaker ties, because stronger ties include people who know each other well, while weaker ties carry uncertainty with respect to political preferences and orientations of interaction partners. People avoid political discussion in such uncertainty, because they do not want to turn otherwise neutral social relationships into conflicting ones. This line of argumentation is also used in explaining why political discussion is strongest among people who share political preferences and strong political interest.

The quality of social ties is measured with a battery of questions already discussed in the section about strength of ties. Again, we distinguish between strong-tie content (socialising with co-members) and weak-tie content (discussing organisational issues), and measure how often respondents relate to one another in various ways. Network composition was more difficult to measure, since we lack information about the actual people with whom one meets in the organisations. We can assume however, that when one is a member of a political party, environmental or peace movement, or immigrant organisation (e.g. more 'political kinds' of organisations), one is in contact with people who share ones political views.

Table 8.8 shows the results of multiple regression of political discussion with co-members on social networks (strength of ties and composition) and a range of other variables: interest in politics, political socialisation during childhood, and various individual attributes (gender, age, and education). The regression model is estimated only for those respondents who are involved in organisational networks.

As suggested by numerous studies of political behaviour, political interest has the strongest effect on political discussion. The comparison of model 1, which includes a measure of political interest, and model 2 with no such measure, shows that political interest is a strong direct predictor of political discussion and an important intermediary variable through which the effects of other variables such as political discussion during the childhood years and background variables are mediated. Political discussion during childhood years affects political discussion mostly through an individual's increasing political interest. The same is true for gender and education. Men and highly-educated people more frequently discuss politics with co-members because they have a stronger interest in politics than women and those less educated.

Very differently, the three network variables exhibit a direct effect on political discussion, independent of political interest. *Ceteris paribus*, people who are members of political organisations are more likely to discuss politics than those who are members of organisations with a less pronounced political profile. The same applies for the strength of ties. Integration in organisations promotes political discussion. In most countries, already the weaker version of strength of ties has a strong impact on political discussion, while sociability ties increase the likelihood

Table 8.8 Regression analysis of political discussion[a]

Model and variable	CH	NL	NO	SE	WG	EG	SI	ES	PT	RO	MD	All
Model 1												
Political interest	0.35***	0.29***	0.26***	0.28***	0.09**	0.07	0.16**	0.41***	0.33***	0.28***	0.65***	0.27***
Political socialisation	0.05	0.05	0.09**	0.10***	0.13***	0.15***	0.11**	0.06*	0.08*	0.13*	0.15	0.09***
Gender (male)	0.05**	−0.01	0.01	−0.02	0.03*	0.03	0.06*	0.07***	0.02	0.13*	−0.07	0.02***
Age												
Below 30	−0.05	−0.01	−0.08*	−0.02	−0.02	−0.01	−0.07*	−0.08*	−0.03	−0.03	−0.03	−0.04***
Above 60	−0.01	−0.02	−0.02	−0.03	0.03	0.02	0.03	0.07*	0.03	0.07	−0.15*	0.02
Education	−0.10	−0.15*	−0.11*	−0.002	0.09	0.06	0.21*	0.14**	−0.01	0.15*	−0.12	0.01
Strength of discussion ties	0.13***	0.18***	0.18***	0.16***	0.25***	0.29***	0.08*	0.06	0.10*	0.31***	0.22	0.16***
Socialising	0.11***	0.13***	0.11***	0.12***	0.04	0.18***	0.11**	0.11**	0.01	0.01	0.06	0.10***
Member of political organisation	0.10***	0.03	0.147***	0.12***	0.07*	0.09*	0.10**	0.13***	0.20***	0.23***	0.15*	0.11***
R^2	0.23	0.21	0.24	0.28	0.20	0.31	0.14	0.31	0.26	0.35	0.39	0.28
N	1,043	914	1,152	726	1,081	335	355	1,178	282	143	140	7,335

Model 2

Political socialisation	0.15***	0.12***	0.16***	0.17***	0.16***	0.16***	0.13***	0.14***	0.14***	0.17**	0.30***	0.15***
Gender (male)	0.07***	0.03	0.03	0.01	0.04*	0.04	0.07*	0.10***	0.04	0.14**	−0.01	0.04***
Age												
Below 30	−0.07*	−0.02	−0.09**	−0.03	−0.03	−0.01	−0.08*	−0.11***	−0.08*	−0.08	−0.07*	−0.06***
Above 60	0.05*	−0.01	0.01	0.00	0.04*	0.02	0.04	0.06*	0.05	0.08	−0.09**	0.02***
Education	0.04	−0.07	−0.06	0.13*	0.11*	0.09	0.28**	0.27***	0.17**	0.23*	0.27*	0.12***
Strength of discussion ties	0.13***	0.20***	0.20***	0.18***	0.26***	0.31***	0.08	0.10*	0.11*	0.36***	0.28*	0.18***
Socialising	0.13***	0.11***	0.10***	0.12***	0.04	0.18***	0.12*	0.09*	0.03	0.04	0.02	0.11***
Member of political organisation	0.14***	0.06*	0.18***	0.15***	0.08***	0.09**	0.12**	0.24***	0.32***	0.28***	0.28**	0.15***
R^2	0.16	0.15	0.21	0.22	0.20	0.30	0.13	0.20	0.17	0.30	0.22	0.25
N	1,043	914	1,152	726	1,081	335	355	1,178	291	143	142	7,360

Note

a Entries are unstandardised regression coefficients. Levels of statistical significance: *** = 0.001, ** = 0.01, * = 0.05. Country intercepts for model 1 (joint analysis of all countries): 0.06*** (EG), 0.05*** (WG), 0.05*** (CH), 0.01 (MD), 0.00 (NO, base category), −0.01 (PT), −0.02 (ES), −0.06*** (SE), −0.06*** (SI), −0.08*** (RO), −0.10*** (NL). Country intercepts for model 2 (joint analysis of all countries): 0.06*** (EG), 0.04*** (WG), 0.04*** (CH), 0.00 (NO, base category), −0.01 (MD), −0.02 (PT), −0.06*** (ES), −0.07*** (SE), −0.10*** (SI), −0.11*** (RO), −0.12*** (NL).

of political conversation. The alternative variables of social integration, such as generalised trust and attachment to either local or global identities, do not have any significant effect on political discussion.[31] It is social integration and networks within particular organisations, rather than broader social integration, which contribute to political discussion.

Despite this clear general pattern, important differences emerge between countries as to exactly how the causal mechanism works and what the explanatory power of particular variables is. We can distinguish between three groups of countries. The first group consists of Spain, Portugal, Romania, and Moldova. These are countries in which the general level of discussing politics with others is low, and political discussion strongly depends on the level of political interest. In the social context where over 70 per cent of the population express no interest in politics, even a small increase in political interest seems to have considerable consequences for one's political engagement and willingness to enter into political discussion. Schooling, which has almost lost the role of political education in western European countries, acts as an important promoter of political interest and consequently of political discussion. Yet another effective way of raising political interest and discussion in these countries is membership in 'political kinds' of organisations. This corresponds to the findings in Table 8.7, where we see that in Spain the kind of organisation one belongs to has a strong effect on political discussion. This is a result of the fact that members of 'political kinds of organisations' have a much higher level of political interest than members of other kinds of organisations. Additionally, the strong effect of membership in political organisations also reflects the fact that in a country with a generally low level of political interest and political discussion, it is difficult to find suitable partners for political discussion outside of political organisations. Political organisations in this case represent islands of political engagement amidst a population that is in general disinterested in politics.

In the second group of countries, which includes West and East Germany, and to a certain extent Slovenia, the impact of political interest on political discussion is relatively weak. Most of the effect of political interest is lost once we include other variables in the model, especially political socialisation during childhood and network variables. This means that political interest is very much nested in social networks, past and present. Political socialisation is very important in this respect. Its effect on political discussion goes well beyond political interest. People discuss politics as a social norm acquired in childhood, regardless of their own political interest. Present networks affect political discussion mainly through the variable of strength of ties. The strength of ties with which people are connected in organisations is a strong predictor of political discussion, especially their weaker component. Taking part in discussions about organisational problems contributes to the readiness of people to engage in political discussion. Except in Slovenia, education plays a much lesser role in promoting political discussion than in the previous group of countries.

In the third group of countries, consisting of Switzerland, Norway, the Netherlands, and to a certain extent Sweden, political interest and political discussion are moderately related. Most of the impact of political discussion during childhood years appears to be indirect, contributing to the rise of political interest, which affects present political discussion. In these countries, which are all characterised by a high level of political interest among the general population, the total impact of political socialisation, as well as the impact of background variables on political discussion, is relatively weak.[32] However, social networks matter. All three measures of networks contribute to people's propensity for political discussion, although the combined effect of strength of ties is stronger than the effect of network composition.[33] This means that in a society with a generally high level of political interest, people engage with others in political discussion as a by-product of their otherwise non-political conversation. When they avoid political discussion, it is not because there is nobody around them who would be interested in talking politics, but because they are not sufficiently integrated in organisations in order to engage in political conversation.

We can conclude that social networks matter for the frequency with which people engage in political discussion. Their impact is strong, significant, and largely independent from other variables. Both aspects of social networks, network composition and strength of ties, are crucial in this respect. People are more likely to discuss politics when they are in the company of other people with who share the same political interests. Here, political discussion takes place regardless of the strength of ties, and discussing politics might be considered a constitutive element of their relationships. On the other hand, where political discussion develops as a by-product of otherwise 'non-political' social relationships, stronger social ties help. This is especially important for those organisations that are not primarily concerned with politics.

Conclusions

We have analysed three aspects of social networks in Europe, which we suggest are crucial for understanding their political capacity: the number of social networks in which people are involved (i.e. network multiplicity), the strength of social ties in these networks, and the frequency with which networks act as vehicles for political discussion.

The 11 societies included in our study have quite different social networks. The data can be interpreted in the sense that some countries are characterised by stronger, and others by weaker, social networks. For example, networks formed in formal and informal social contexts appear to be complementary rather than opposing: countries where people belong to more organisations are also the countries where people engage in a larger number of informal networks, resulting in higher network multiplicity. This is particularly the case in western European countries, and less so in southern and eastern European ones. People in the western European countries are also more likely to engage in political discussion. On the other hand, the analysis of strength of ties reveals that organisational contexts in the eastern and southern European countries consist of a denser social structure. In these countries, a larger proportion of organisational members are very strongly connected with their co-members and co-workers, and the average strength of ties is higher. The analysis of different aspects of social networks thus suggests that differences between countries should be regarded as differences in type rather than strength of social networks. While at the individual level the number of network involvements and strength of ties are positively related, we observe a certain trade-off between network multiplicity and strength of ties at the country level. The larger openness of western European networks in the sense of the larger proportion of citizens included in networks, and higher number of network involvements per citizen, seems to be achieved by means of weak ties. These weak ties are not replacing but rather complementing strong ties, since we have not found any evidence for the general dissolution of ties in western European countries. Very differently, the network pattern we found in southern and eastern Europe can be best described in terms of closed networks, since people are involved in a smaller number of networks with a dense network structure.

However, not only multiplicity and strength of ties are related. Strength of ties also matter for political discussion, and both weaker and stronger versions of social integration (discussing organisational matters and socialising) contribute to the frequency with which people discuss politics. Social ties through which people get to know their interaction partners and develop a certain level of trust and familiarity are an important facilitating condition for the emergence of political discussion.

Voluntary associations are not the unique or even the most essential loci for network formation. In most countries, workplace and friendship networks are more important (more people involved and stronger social ties). However, our results suggest that even if associations are not the only, or the most important, source of social networks, they matter for political action well beyond their role as a top-down mobilisation agent. This is because they provide the social context within which people develop weaker or stronger social ties that promote political discussion among members, in addition to those motivated by the organisational leadership.

Our analysis also suggests that networks might play different roles in political mobilisation, depending on the type of network involvement. In line with the distinction between politics of choice and politics of loyalty, we presume that politics of loyalty should be more pronounced in countries where networks are closed, while politics of choice is characteristic for countries with open networks. With involvement of citizens in multiple networks and the weakening of the corporate basis of social ties, the role of social networks is less about direct recruitment and mobilisation, and more about political deliberation through political discussion.

Differences between countries in network involvement can be partly explained by variations in the composition of their populations. Among the most important individual level predictors of networks are education, employment, trust, and attachment to collective identities. However, the role of independent variables is often not identical in all countries (e.g. the role of trust or territorial attachment), showing that countries appear as relevant contexts, which shape the level as well as the relationship between causal factors and social networks.

Notes

1 Denmark and Russia are omitted from most of our analyses, although they are considered in other chapters. The reason is that for these two countries the data on social networks was not collected.
2 Work networks were measured with four questions asking how often respondents do the following things with their co-workers:

 1 help each other with practical matters outside organisational life;
 2 visit each other privately;
 3 talk about problems concerning the organisation or its goals;
 4 argue with one another.

 The response categories range from 'never' to 'rarely', 'sometimes', and 'often'. We consider respondents as involved in work networks if they even rarely engage in two of the four relations.
3 Voluntary associations-based networks were measured with the same set of questions as work networks. A respondent is considered to be taking part in organisational networks if he or she even rarely does two of the four things with his co-members: home visiting, helping in everyday matters, talking about organisational issues, and arguing.
4 Involvement in friendship networks was measured with the following question: 'Apart from formal organisations, do you belong to any group or network of friends or acquaintances with whom you have contact on a regular basis?' People answered this question with either 'yes' or 'no' (values 1 and 0 in the analysis). One should note that the question does not ask about very close friendship relations, which are usually dyadic ties. Instead, it asks about group embedded friendship relations, about sociability rather than intimate ties.
5 The information about informal support networks was obtained with the following question: 'Do you actively provide support for ill people or elderly neighbours, acquaintances and other people, without doing it through an organisation or club?' Respondents could choose among three answers: 'Yes, regularly', 'yes, occasionally', and 'almost never'. In the analysis the first answer was coded with 1 and the other two with 0.
6 It is only in three intermediate cases (Sweden, West Germany, and Slovenia) that involvement in one kind of network is much higher than the others. In West Germany and Sweden, involvement in associational networks is high,

while involvement in informal friendship networks is low, especially when compared with other western European countries. In Slovenia, the picture is reversed, with informal networks being a much more important locus of integration than associational networks.
7 On the relationship between trust and organisational involvement see also Chapters 6 and 7, this volume.
8 Education was measured by the number of years spent in school. It was transformed to range from 0 to 1, with value 1 meaning 25 years of education or more.
9 Employment was measured with the question asking about the employment status of the respondent. We consider someone as being employed if he:

1 works full-time;
2 works part-time;
3 is employed, but currently on leave of absence or parental leave;
4 is temporarily unemployed or not working for other reasons (less than six months).

Respondents received the value 1 if employed and 0 otherwise.
10 Lowndes (2002) argues that gender dynamics are crucial for understanding network involvement, because men and women generate social capital in different ways and get involved in very different kinds of social networks. Charitable endeavours (voluntary work) and informal sociability that evolves around child-care and community life are social capital forming activities that are distinctively female. On the other hand, men spend more time than women in social clubs and sports related activities (Lowndes 2002: 534).
11 The exception is Sweden, where younger people are much less involved, even in friendship networks.
12 People who are recent movers or have lived in their present housing for less than ten years are considered mobile (value 1), while those who have lived in their present housing for more than ten years are treated as long-time residents (value 0).
13 People are considered as living in a city if the place where they live is a city or suburb of a city with more than 200,000 inhabitants. We define their place of living as a town if it has more than 5,000 and less than 200,000 inhabitants, and as a village or rural area if it has less than 5,000 inhabitants.
14 Church attendance was measured with a question asking how frequently the respondent attends religious ceremonies. The answers range from 'several times a week', to 'once a week', 'at least once a month', 'several times a year', 'once a year', 'less than once a year', and 'never'.
15 The analyses of international data sets provide more evidence for the argument that trust enables network formation than vice versa. The effects of organisational membership and voluntary activity on trust are weak (Whiteley 1999), while trust is an important predictor of group membership (Uslaner 2003). Trusting other people can be understood to facilitate network creation, because people who trust are also more likely to enter new and 'potentially risky relationships' (Yamagishi 2001).
16 Trust in people is measured with the standard question: 'Generally speaking, would you say that most people can be trusted or that you can't be too careful in dealing with people?' The answers were coded on an 11-point scale from 0 to 10, and transformed to a range from 0 to 1.
17 We included in the regression analysis two measures of trust. For trust as an individual resource, we simply took the individual-level measure of trusting other people. Contextual trust was measured as the average generalised trust expressed by people in the respective country.

18 Territorial attachment was measured by asking people about how strongly they feel connected to:

1 neighbourhood;
2 municipality;
3 region;
4 country;
5 Europe;
6 humanity as a whole.

19 The distinction between local and global attachment was made on the basis of factor analysis results of six questions about attachment to different territorial units. Neighbourhood, municipality, and region score high on the first factor. Attachment to Europe and humanity as a whole form a second factor. Attachment to the nation state appears in both components with a relatively high loading, which is why we omitted this variable in the latter construction of indices. Local attachment is defined as an average attachment to neighbourhood and municipality, while global attachment is calculated as an average attachment to Europe and humanity as a whole. Both variables are transformed to range from 0 to 1. We do not use the information about regional attachment, although it clearly measures local attachment, because this variable has a lot of missing values in some countries.

20 In all countries, territorial attachment is related to education – higher education promotes global attachment, and lower education, local attachment. A generally lower level of education in the eastern and southern European countries thus contributes to a higher level of local attachment in these countries compared to western Europe.

21 The product-moment correlation between the two items ranges from 0.576 to 0.696, across countries.

22 Although the correlation between 'talking' and both sociability variables is relatively high, the principal component analysis which also takes into account the question of how often one argues with co-members and co-workers reveals two dimensions: the sociability dimension and discussion dimension. 'Talking' scores relatively high on both dimensions.

23 The composite measure of strength of ties is defined as the sum of the frequency with which people get involved in both kinds of social ties, sociability and discussing ties. It is standardised with a 0 ('never') to 1 ('often') scale.

24 Note that the strength of ties is defined only for those respondents who are members of voluntary organisations (or employed). The alternative approach would be to set the strength of ties for non-members of organisations (or non-employed) to 0. In this case the average strength of ties would reflect both the proportion of people included in organisations in a given country and the strength of ties maintained by those who are members.

25 People who are highly integrated in organisational or workplace networks are those who do one of the activities (socialising or discussing organisational matters) frequently, and the other activity at least sometimes.

26 The exception is the workplace in West and East Germany where discussion ties appear much less often than in other countries. In this case, the elaborate institutional structure of the workplace participation seems to constrain spontaneous interaction in the form of discussing organisational matters.

27 We operationalised activism in two different ways. First, respondents involved in voluntary associations were asked whether they have participated during the last 12 months in the activities organised by voluntary associations (see Chapter 6 for a more detailed discussion). We took the number of voluntary associations in which they actively participated as a measure of their activism.

Second, in order to obtain comparable measures of activism for voluntary associations and the workplace, we also used four questions asking how often the respondent does the following things as a part of his (her) activities in organisations and the workplace:

1 participate in decisions at a meeting;
2 plan or chair a meeting;
3 prepare or give a speech before a meeting;
4 write a text other than a private letter at least a few pages long.

We defined a measure of activism, for voluntary associations and the workplace alike, by taking the average frequency with which the respondent engages in these activities.

28 Actually, differences between countries in the average strength of ties are more pronounced at the lower levels of activism than the higher. When people are actively involved in three voluntary associations or more, differences almost disappear. Thus, it is mostly less active members of organisations who are more strongly integrated in organisations in Romania, Moldova, and Spain, compared to other countries. This is also reflected in the fact that in these countries the correlation between activism and strength of ties is weaker than in other countries. The same can also be observed for Switzerland, another country with high average strength of ties in voluntary associations.

29 Authors like Wellman (1979) and Fisher (1982) were some of the first who described personal networks found in the United States and Canada in terms of individualisation and selectivity.

30 In order to simplify the presentation of results, we limit this analysis to two countries only: Spain and Switzerland. They differ significantly with respect to the level of political discussion with co-members; Spain has a low (0.26) and Switzerland a high (0.41) frequency of discussing politics in voluntary organisations. Although Spain is not the country with the lowest level of political discussion, it is very suitable for comparison because of the large sample size, which allows for the analysis across different kinds of associations. In other countries with a low level of political discussion, many cells are empty.

31 Because the effects of these variables are small and statistically non-significant we do not include them in the models presented in Table 8.8.

32 The impact of education, when also incorporating the effect of political interest (model II) is close to zero, and when controlled for the effect of political interest (model I), it is negative. This means that education, on the one hand, contributes to political discussion as much as it increases political interest, while, on the other hand, it decreases political discussion by making people less dependent on politics due to the rising of the level of resources they control. As suggested by Hardin (1999), politics becomes less salient for shaping one's own life in the case of more resourceful citizens.

33 The role of the context (i.e. political versus non-political kinds of voluntary associations) is weak especially in Switzerland and the Netherlands. It is somewhat more important in Norway and Sweden.

Part III
Small-scale democracy

9 Small-scale democracy
Citizen power in the domains of everyday life

Jørgen Goul Andersen and Sigrid Roßteutscher

Introduction

Citizenship is not only about citizens' ability to influence the situation of the polities to which they belong, but also about their ability to control their own personal situation in everyday life. Although the efforts of citizens to exercise influence over their personal situation does not amount to political participation as defined in this book (see Chapter 13), it is nevertheless an important aspect of citizenship in its own right. In addition, it may have important implications for other, more directly political, realms of citizenship, e.g. by having a spill-over effect on political participation.

The following three chapters focus on what we have labelled participation in small-scale democracy, that is, the efforts of individual citizens to exert influence over their own life situation in important social roles. Four such roles were selected for investigation in our cross-national survey: that of being gainfully employed (the domain of working life); that of being a patient or close relative of a patient (the domain of healthcare); that of being a parent of school children (the domain of child education); and that of being a student (the domain of student education).

The concept of small-scale democracy is novel in the international participation literature. It presents a different perspective that also solves some of the puzzles encountered in the attempt to define and measure political participation. Therefore the first sections of this chapter will elaborate on the concept and measurement of small-scale democracy, present the historical and theoretical background, and discuss the delineation between small-scale and large-scale democracy. The remaining sections present the operationalisations and describe the main characteristics of small-scale democracy captured by our design: the incentives to take action, action itself, and its consequences. The two chapters that follow examine the relationships between these three characteristics as well as some others that call for attention in the context of small-scale democracy. Chapter 10 focuses on the causes of action while Chapter 11 considers its consequences.

Defining participation in small-scale democracy

By participation in small-scale democracy we mean actions taken by citizens in order to control their own personal situation. Such actions may take place in many different domains: for instance, parents may try to combat problems at their children's school, students may try to improve the training they get, patients may try to influence the medical treatment they receive, and employees may try to change their working conditions. These examples are selected from the domains covered by our cross-national survey. While these particular domains are certainly important, they do not purport to be more than a sample of the many significant situations where similar actions may take place.

The actions in question may take many different forms. In many cases, they might be carried out through informal channels, for example, via informal contacts with the person in charge. However, this is not a defining criterion. Participation in small-scale democracy may also involve the use of formal channels of participation (for example, work councils). It may also include contacts with government officials, as long as these contacts primarily concern the personal situation of the citizen in question rather than collective outcomes of broader scope.

This helps to solve one of the classic problems in delineating political participation. Some have chosen to include 'particularised contacts', that is, contacts with government official about personal concerns, in the definition of political participation since these contacts aim at influencing the actions of government personnel (Verba *et al.* 1978: 54). Others have excluded them from the definition on the grounds that they do not aim at influencing collective outcomes. The definition of political participation used in this book (see Chapter 13) follows the latter path. This, however, does not imply that we abstain from studying 'particularised' forms of participation. On the contrary, we devote far more attention to them than is commonly the case and do not stop short at the special (but important) case in which they involve interaction with government personnel. But we do so under another heading than that of political participation.

Small-scale democracy is concerned with tangible outcomes, that is, more with the implementation of policies in specific instances than with policy-making. Again, this is not a defining criterion. Political participation or, equivalently, participation in large-scale democracy may also focus on policy implementation, such as when citizens protest against the way the local school board has decided to implement national policy when it comes to, for example, teacher qualifications. What makes such protests an instance of political participation is that they are aimed at influencing collective outcomes affecting more than a very limited number of citizens. Although one can imagine a few borderline cases, the distinction is generally not difficult to apply.

Actions in small-scale democracy may often be purely individual in the

Citizen power 223

sense that they do not involve cooperation with others. However, this is not a defining criterion either. Voting as well as a number of other forms of political participation (e.g. signing petitions or donating money for political ends) are also individual acts, even though they are aimed at affecting collective outcomes. Conversely, participation in small-scale democracy may well involve cooperation with others, for example, others facing the same locally defined situation (e.g. workplace colleagues or fellow students).

Participation in small-scale democracy may involve both voice and exit in Hirschman's (1970) sense. For example, rather than complaining about the conditions at their child's school, parents may decide to move their child to another school. Exit is rooted in a neoliberal tradition of individual choice, where public-service users are seen as a kind of consumers, whereas voice, at least in its collective form, is rooted in republican or social liberal ideals of community and collective decision-making. Therefore, voice and exit could be seen as diametrically opposed alternatives. They may however, also be mutually supportive. The opportunity to exit may serve as a resource for voice. Public agencies as well as private corporations may be more responsive and citizens more confident when both sides know that there is an alternative to which citizens can turn if their voices are not properly heard. Even though the use of exit may more often be associated with small-scale than large-scale democracy, it is by no means confined to the former. For instance, in some countries, 'political consumerism' (Micheletti 2003) has become a common instrument in attempts to improve societal conditions or prevent them from deteriorating (see Chapter 13). What form participation actually takes in small- as well as large-scale democracy is ultimately an empirical question.

Finally, participation in small-scale democracy may certainly be affected by formal institutional opportunities. But it is important to point out that it does not necessarily depend on their existence. Some countries or contexts may provide considerable formal opportunities for participation (e.g. school and work councils where parents and employees are represented), while others provide few or no formal opportunities. This, however, does not rule out the possibility that informal opportunities are used in practice. The measurement instruments we have used take this into account and can be applied regardless of the precise form the actions of citizens actually take or the institutional settings in which they occur.

Background

Before elaborating on the theoretical relevance of the subject, we briefly address a few of the developments in society that have directed attention to small-scale democracy. The concept of small-scale democracy was coined in conjunction with the first of a series of Swedish studies of citizenship, conducted in 1987 (Petersson *et al.* 1989) and replicated in Denmark as well as Norway in the early 1990s (Andersen *et al.* 1993;

Andersen and Hoff 2001). When the concept was launched (with definitions and operationalisations similar to those presented here), it was influenced by Scandinavian debates about the 'activist welfare state' (Hernes 1988) and about the idea of democratising society by strengthening the influence of the users of public services and bringing decisions closer to those affected by them. Another source of influence was debates about workplace democracy, which continued in the aftermath of the aborted attempts to establish economic democracy in Sweden and Denmark.

Thus, the fact that the concept was first applied in a Scandinavian context is not so surprising. Although it is not inherently linked to the 'mature' welfare state, it is certainly at home there. In the classical night-watch state, citizens' encounters with state bureaucracy were largely limited to the core activities of taxation and the maintenance of law and order. With the modern welfare state, contacts with the state apparatus have become a significant part of everyday life, and citizens have been granted ever more social rights, including formal rights of participation. Nowhere have social rights proceeded further than in the Scandinavian welfare states, especially in the domain of welfare services, which have been given extraordinarily high priority.

However, these developments are certainly not limited to the Scandinavian context. The welfare state has grown everywhere and mechanisms strengthening citizens' influence in everyday life has been nourished by several other changes of a much more general nature – basically changes related to continuing processes of modernisation. Looking at the 'demand side' (the citizens) there are reason to emphasise patterns of value change. This includes not only the growth of 'post-materialist' values giving higher priority to participation and co-determination (Inglehart 1997) but also the continuing trend of individualisation (Ester *et al.* 1993). In short, value change among citizens is likely to lead to increasing demand for opportunities to voice as well as exit.

Looking at the 'supply side' (the institutions) we also find significant changes. In line with the transition from an 'industrial' organisation of production to 'post-industrial' forms, authority relations in the workplace have been relaxed. Furthermore, modern management theories call for more autonomy and co-determination and less hierarchy in firms, simply as a means of enhancing productivity. In the public sector, new modes of public administration (often summarised under the heading 'New Public Management') has emphasised 'consumerism' or 'partnership', that is, greater responsiveness to users ('consumers') of public services – not for the sake of democracy, but rather for the sake of consumer sovereignty. Needless to say, such changes are also viewed as politically important in order to ensure the legitimacy of the welfare state.

Thus, on the demand as well as on the supply side, there are strong forces pressing managers and bureaucrats to become more responsive and enhancing citizens' and workers' influence over their own situation, formally and informally. Regardless of whether such changes are motivated by democratic concerns or not, they have the effect of empowering citizens in various domains, that is, providing them with more rights and opportunities to exercise influence. This also means that debates about such empowerment are by no means restricted to the Scandinavian countries. Especially since the 1990s, they have mushroomed in the Anglo-Saxon world (Craig and Mayo 1995; Barnes and Walker 1996; Barnes and Warren 1999). The idea of consumerism has entered (elite) discourses about public governance in most countries; and new management theories have disseminated all over the globe.

Political initiatives in this domain have been concerned mainly with the establishment or strengthening of formal institutions, for example, formal representative bodies (such as school boards), hearing or 'partnership' procedures, freedom-of-choice arrangements, or strengthening of user rights in other regards. Other formal institutions are built from below, for example, patient associations, work councils, local union branches, and shop stewards. However, participation does not only take place through such formal bodies, and does not only rely on formalised rights. Such channels often represent but the tip of the iceberg in instances where there are good opportunities for informal influence. The latter may well be the decisive aspect and, as already indicated, the measures whereby we try to capture the characteristics of small-scale democracy are constructed with that possibility in mind.

The theoretical significance of small-scale democracy

There are at least three central arguments for the theoretical significance of small-scale democracy. First, from a citizenship perspective, small-scale democracy is important in its own right. The extent to which citizens are autonomous in the sense of having a modicum of control over their own situation in central walks of life is an important aspect of citizenship (Rothstein 1998), and the degree to which they are efficacious in this respect should carry weight in an overall assessment of the state of democracy. To an increasing extent, the rights of citizens in the realm of small-scale democracy are also recognised by the law. In various ways and to different degrees, the laws of the countries we study give citizens a right to have a say in their capacity as patients, parents, students, or employees as well as several other significant social roles not covered by our study.

Second, the fact that we have chosen to place participation in small-scale democracy outside rather than inside our definition of political participation should certainly not be taken to mean that we consider the former to fall outside the realm of politics in every respect. To begin with, participation in small-scale democracy often amounts to 'particularised contacts' with the political system as represented by government agencies and personnel. Further, the implementation of political decisions – for example, via meetings between 'street-level bureaucrats' (Lipsky 1980) and 'clients' (e.g. teachers and parents/students and doctors and patients) – has long been regarded an important part of the political process (Pressman and Wildavsky 1973). It is increasingly recognised that there is no such a thing as mechanical rule application even in the tax office (Nielsen 1998), much less so in most other agencies of the welfare state. What is going on is often better described by the concept of negotiation. Finally, even though each of the outcomes we consider in our study of small-scale democracy is of primary importance to only a few individuals, the sum total of such outcomes may well carry weight for the citizenry as a whole. Consequently, it becomes important to consider the potential trade-offs and conflicts that might exist between small-scale and large-scale democracy as well as the character and magnitude of the inequalities we find within each of them.

It is additionally worth mentioning that there is also a methodological link between the study of participation in small-scale versus large-scale democracy. The questions that we would like to ask about the presumed causes and consequences of these two types of participation tend to have much in common. Within the domains of small-scale democracy, however, they can often be posed in much more tangible ways, which considerably increases the prospects of successful measurement. This holds, for instance, for questions about potentially important incentives to take action, such as perceived opportunities to influence (sense of efficacy) and dissatisfaction with the current state of affairs. And it is perhaps even more true for questions about significant consequences, such as whether the attempt to exercise influence was successful and whether the process was perceived as fair and legitimate.

A classical line of reasoning is that a strong democracy must rest on strong citizens. Before universal suffrage was introduced, the decision to exclude parts of the population from the citizenry was justified on precisely that ground. Only those who possessed a certain degree of autonomy and control over their own life situation were considered apt to participate in politics. But as we know, the same line of reasoning can also be used for other purposes. This takes us to the third argument for the importance of small-scale democracy, namely that it may help to prepare and motivate citizens for participation in large-scale democracy.

For reasons similar to those advanced with regard to involvement in voluntary associations, participation in small-scale democracy may increase citizens' sense of efficacy and enhance their civic skills. Further, by participating in decision-making processes focused on relatively narrow and tangible personal concerns, citizens may learn to see that, and how, they form part of a more encompassing whole. They may, for instance, become aware that the personal difficulties they are facing in, say, the educational or healthcare system are due to more general shortcomings. For these reasons, participation in small-scale democracy might be a potent school for democracy on a larger scale.

Within the branch of democratic theory known as 'participatory democracy' (Pateman 1970), workplace democracy has been accorded a particularly prominent role in preparing citizens for participation in politics. It is assumed to equip them with politically relevant skills and orientations with beneficial 'spillover' effects for democracy at large. Similar arguments can of course be developed for other domains of small-scale democracy.

However, questions have been raised about the extent to which learning processes of this beneficial kind can really be expected to take place, particularly as far as civic orientations are concerned. If citizens participate on a purely individual basis and only aim at defending their own private interests – as the 'consumerism' of 'New Public Management' in fact expects them to – they might become more rather than less particularistic in their orientations. In other words, rather than being transformed into 'responsible' citizens, they might be transformed into 'demanding' and narrow-minded consumers (Barnes and Walker 1996; Andersen *et al.* 2000). Such a trend could be reinforced by reforms in the public sector that strengthen elements of individual choice, that is, stimulate exit, possibly at the expense of voice. It is therefore far from obvious that participation in small-scale democracy contributes to the kind of 'civic orientations' Tocqueville was thinking about.

Domains of small-scale democracy

As already indicated, the four roles on which we focus in this study constitute only a sample of those that call for attention within the realm of small-scale democracy. For instance, prior Swedish studies of citizenship (Petersson *et al.* 1989; Petersson *et al.* 1998) include four additional roles not covered here: that of being a resident (housing); a parent of preschool children (childcare); unemployed (another aspect of working life); and a consumer (the goods market). Similar designs have also been used for the purpose of studying the interaction of citizens with social as well as tax authorities (Andersen and Hoff 2001).

Nevertheless, education, healthcare, and working life do constitute some of the most important domains of small-scale democracy. Working life normally accounts for a very substantial part of our existence during a significant portion of our life span. Employees increasingly expect a considerable amount of influence over their working conditions, and workplace democracy has long been regarded as a 'school of democracy'. Much the same can be said about the educational system. The centrality of the healthcare system is subject to more variation. Many patients do not suffer from serious illnesses and have but temporary need for healthcare. Still, it is certainly a domain most people care about. For those who have serious problems with their health over an extended period of time, it is obviously of major importance.

Another reason for selecting these particular domains is that they facilitate cross-national comparisons. In the realm of childcare, for example, such comparisons would be much more difficult due to the large variations in the way such care is organised in different countries. Furthermore, as indicated by some of the hypotheses we present below, the domains selected are sufficiently different in terms of the preconditions for small-scale democracy to make for interesting comparisons between them. Finally, these are domains where we can expect a sufficient number of respondents to be available for analysis (student education being a partial exception). For some other domains, those who qualify for the role represent too small a portion of the population to provide a reasonable reliable basis for empirical conclusions, unless the overall size of the sample is very large or the sample drawn so as to over-represent the target group in question.

Incentives, actions, and consequences

An overview of our study design as well as the order in which we present it is provided by Figure 9.1. The overall purpose of the design is to allow us to assess:

1 the *incentives* citizens may have for taking action in small-scale democracy;
2 whether and how they actually take *action*;
3 what the *consequences* are.

For each of these three general dimensions, we consider two main components. As far as incentives are concerned, we examine:

1 the extent to which citizens express *dissatisfaction* with their situation, and;
2 their perception of the *opportunities* they have to exercise influence.

With respect to the actions themselves, we investigate:

1 the overall propensity of citizens to *take action*, and;
2 the likelihood that they take certain *specific types of actions*.

When it comes to the consequences of action, we assess:

1 the direction of the *outcome*, that is, the extent to which citizens got their wishes satisfied, and;
2 procedural *fairness*, that is, the extent to which they feel that they have received a fair hearing.

The first three of the six properties in the far right column of Figure 9.1 were assessed for all respondents who qualified for the role in question. For child education, this implies parents of children undergoing

Incentives	Perceived opportunities to influence Dissatisfaction with one's situation
Actions	Probability of taking action Probability of taking specific types of actions
Consequences	Direction of the outcome: success versus failure Procedural fairness: perceptions of having received a fair hearing

Figure 9.1 Incentives, actions, and consequences in small-scale democracy.

compulsory education; for healthcare those who, during the past 12 months, had received medical treatment or been in contact with the medical system because a close relative needed medical treatment; for working life those who were employed; and for student education those who were studying. The remaining three properties in the far right column of the figure were assessed only for those who provided a positive reply to the question of whether they had taken action.

Incentives for action

Opportunities

Perceptions regarding opportunities to exercise influence is not only a potentially significant determinant of action (see Chapter 10), but also important in its own right as a quality of life indicator in the same way, and for the same reasons, as measures of political efficacy. Our survey design includes a multiplicity of items designed to provide a fairly comprehensive view of these perceptions across substantively important conditions in each domain. Responses were in all cases obtained on an 11-point graphical scale ranging from 'no possibilities at all' to 'very large possibilities'. For the purposes of our analyses, the scale was rescored to range from 0 to 1. The items themselves, with the simple average across countries[1] (all countries carry equal weight) indicated in parentheses, are presented below. Items focusing on exit- as opposed to voice-based opportunities are prefaced by '(E)'.

Child education

'With regard to your child's schooling, how large possibilities do you think you have to:

- influence the ways and content of the teaching (0.46);
- influence the school environment (0.47);

- influence the ways pupils interact with each other at school (0.48);
- (E) move the child to another school if you want (0.60)'

Healthcare

'With regard to the medical treatment of you or your relative, how large possibilities do you think you have to:

- influence the type of medical treatment you or your relative get (0.51);
- obtain a sufficient amount of medical treatment (0.61);
- (E) choose the doctor you want (0.65);
- (E) change to another medical practice or hospital if you want (0.61)'

Working life

'How large possibilities do you think you have to:

- decide when your work will begin and end for the day (0.42);
- decide how your own daily work will be organised (0.59);
- influence your own working environment (0.55);
- influence decisions about the general direction of your work (0.51);
- change to other working tasks for your current employer if you want (0.39);
- (E) change to another employer if you want (0.52);
- (E) start your own business if you want (0.36)'

Student education

'With regard to your school or university education, how large possibilities do you think you have to:

- influence the ways and content of the teaching (0.44);
- influence the school/university environment (0.42);
- influence the way pupils/students interact with each other at school/university (0.54);
- (E) move to another school/university if you want (0.61)'

As long as voice- and exit-based opportunities are considered separately, the countries tend to order themselves in a similar fashion regardless of which specific item within a domain we look at. For this as well as other reasons, we created three summary indices for each of the four domains, a voice index, an exit index, and a combined index. The reliability coefficients (Cronbach's alpha) are presented in Table 9.1. As expected, the coefficients are typically higher for the voice scales than for

Table 9.1 Index for perceived opportunities to influence by domain (reliability as indicated by Cronbach's alpha)[a]

Measure	Child education	Healthcare	Working life	Student education
Voice	0.81 (3)	0.76 (2)	0.85 (5)	0.69 (3)
Exit	–	0.76 (2)	0.67 (2)	–
Combined	0.74 (4)	0.79 (4)	0.84 (7)	0.56 (4)
Valid number of cases for index as per cent of maximum possible[b]				
Voice	95.7	95.0	95.2	96.5
Exit	–	93.5	93.6	–
Combined	93.5	91.0	91.5	95.3

Notes
a Entries in the upper-part of the table are Cronbach's alpha coefficients with number of items in parentheses. The table is based on the first ten countries that delivered complete data sets.
b Maximum possible is the number of respondents who answered at least one of the questions asked of those to whom the domain applies. Cases were treated as missing if one of the variables included in the index was missing.

the combined scales, in spite of the fact that the latter are based on a greater number of items. Although the voice and exit measures are positively related (r is typically above 0.25), the pattern confirms that they constitute two separate dimensions.

Averages for the scales across domains and countries are presented in Table 9.2. Turning first to the variations across domains, it might be hypothesised that the amount of knowledge required, as well as the capacity of users to cooperate, could have an effect on the perceived opportunities to influence. Both factors would lead us to expect the ranking:

1 working life;
2 child education;
3 healthcare,

as far as the voice dimension is concerned. Working life typically provides rather good preconditions for establishing cooperation with others in the same situation while the healthcare sector is at the opposite end in this respect. As far as knowledge is concerned, few patients are likely to think that they can match the expert knowledge of their doctors. However, many might think that they can match that of their boss, particularly when it comes to knowledge about their own working conditions. In both respects, child education is likely to fall in between.

Based on the opportunities for cooperation and the knowledge requirements, we would thus expect to see the highest level of perceived opportunities in the domain of working life and the lowest in the domain of healthcare. Such is not the case, however. Beginning with the last column of Table 9.2, that is, the average per domain across countries, we find that

Table 9.2 Mean perceived opportunities to influence by domain and country[a]

Measure and domain	NO	DK	SE	CH	NL	WG	EG	ES	PT	SI	RO	MD	Average
Voice													
Child education	0.48	0.58	0.43	0.46	0.55	0.37	0.34	–	0.45	0.39	0.45	0.51	0.46
Healthcare	0.61	0.62	0.57	0.65	0.65	0.54	0.47	–	0.36	0.48	0.46	0.39	0.53
Working life	0.58	0.64	0.55	0.58	0.58	0.40	0.33	0.38	0.37	0.48	0.44	0.35	0.47
Student education	0.47	0.62	0.45	0.47	–	0.44	0.51	–	0.46	0.44	0.43	0.35	0.46
Average[b]	0.56	0.61	0.52	0.56	0.59	0.44	0.38	–	0.39	0.45	0.45	0.42	0.49
Exit													
Child education	0.50	0.88	0.67	0.52	0.77	0.54	0.53	–	0.51	0.58	0.53	0.53	0.60
Healthcare	0.61	0.55	0.57	0.78	0.66	0.67	0.67	–	0.42	0.69	0.53	0.37	0.59
Working life	0.49	0.53	0.57	0.50	0.62	0.39	0.26	0.32	0.39	0.38	0.33	0.23	0.42
Student education	0.55	0.72	0.61	0.58	–	0.65	0.59	–	0.59	0.67	0.50	0.48	0.59
Average[b]	0.53	0.65	0.60	0.60	0.68	0.53	0.49	–	0.44	0.55	0.46	0.38	0.54
Combined													
Child education	0.48	0.65	0.49	0.47	0.61	0.41	0.39	–	0.47	0.44	0.47	0.52	0.49
Healthcare	0.61	0.58	0.56	0.72	0.65	0.61	0.57	–	0.39	0.59	0.49	0.38	0.56
Working life	0.56	0.61	0.56	0.56	0.59	0.40	0.31	0.36	0.37	0.44	0.41	0.31	0.46
Student education	0.49	0.65	0.50	0.50	–	0.50	0.53	–	0.49	0.50	0.44	0.39	0.50
Average[b]	0.55	0.61	0.54	0.58	0.62	0.47	0.42	–	0.41	0.49	0.46	0.40	0.50
Number of cases													
Child education	599	347	233	391	405	296	181	–	239	180	316	395	3,582
Healthcare	1,427	985	999	1,485	1,021	1,066	609	–	412	744	531	358	9,637
Working life	1,331	872	732	1,214	802	814	406	1,550	531	431	413	454	9,550
Student education	186	99	67	37	–	104	48	–	62	170	24	59	856

Notes
a Entries are means of additive indices scored 0–1. The data are weighed so as to be representative of the respective populations but the number of cases refer to unweighted data. Averages across domains and countries are simple averages of the table entries for the individual countries and domains.
b Because of the small number of student respondents, the figures for student education are not included when calculating averages across domains.
c In Spain, data are available for the domain of working life only.

voice opportunities are perceived as greater in the domain of healthcare (0.53) than in that of child education (0.46) and working life (0.47), although we acknowledge that the measures may not be strictly commensurable. For student education, the value is slightly higher than for child education and working life but slightly lower than for healthcare (0.49).

Exit-based opportunities are generally perceived to be greater than voice-based. Thus we note average scores for child education, student education, and healthcare between 0.59 and 0.60. The exception is exit-based opportunities in working life (0.42), but it should be kept in mind that this measure is somewhat different from the others. First, it includes an item about the opportunity to start one's own business, which tends to generate particularly negative assessments. Second, the perception of opportunities to find another job is higher, but strongly related to country differences in unemployment rates.

In the case of country differences, we would expect, based on a 'demand-side perspective', a division between a group of rich countries (the Nordic countries, the Netherlands, Switzerland, and Germany), an in-between group (Spain, Portugal, Slovenia) and a group of poor countries (Romania and Moldova). Democratic tradition follows almost the same division, with the exception of Germany which comes closer to the in-between group. We find the same grouping with respect to involvement in voluntary associations (see Chapter 6).

However, this is not quite the pattern we find when it comes to perceived opportunities. Calculating country averages for voice and exit opportunities across all domains except student education (where the number of cases is quite limited), we find a marked division between one group of countries whose citizens perceive considerable opportunities to influence and another group whose citizens are clearly more pessimistic (see Table 9.2). The former group includes the Netherlands (0.62), Denmark (0.61), Switzerland (0.58), Norway (0.55), and Sweden (0.54). Averages for other countries range from 0.49 in Slovenia to 0.40 in Moldova. There is no systematic division between Romania and Moldova on the one hand and Slovenia, Portugal, and Spain on the other (provided that we extrapolate based on the figure for working life in the Spanish case). Notably, Germany falls into this group as well (average 0.47 for the western part, 0.41 for the eastern part).

The German deviation from the expected pattern is most pronounced for voice-based opportunities. With respect to the average across domains, eastern Germany has the lowest value of all countries (0.38) while the value for western Germany (0.44) is on the same level as that for Slovenia, Romania, and Moldova. There is no overlap between the five countries ranking highest and the other seven. Of the countries in the top group, Sweden comes in last with an average of 0.52 – significantly below Norway and Denmark – whereas Slovenia and Romania (0.45) take the top position among the countries with relatively low scores.

When it comes to exit opportunities, the differences are less clearly marked. As in the case of voice, the Netherlands (0.68) and Denmark (0.65) are at the top but Slovenia (0.55) and West Germany (0.53) score about as high as Norway (0.53) and Sweden (0.54). The lowest level is found in Moldova (0.38) whose average for exit is even below that for voice.

These cross-national differences based on averages across domains are smaller than those we may find within particular domains. We note some dramatically deviant figures exactly where we would expect them. The Danish figure for opportunities to change to another school is as high as 0.88, reflecting an almost completely free choice of school – including private schools with very low fees.[2] In the same country, a marked deviation upwards is also found for the domain of student education (with regard to voice as well as exit). This reflects the unusually strong formal influence of students at the time of interviewing (manifested, for example, by parity between students and teachers on the board deciding about university courses). Similar institutional explanations can be provided for some of the significant variations within healthcare (Dixon and Mossialos 2002; country reports from the European Observatory on Health Care Systems 1996–2000, www.euro.who.int/observatory/Hits/TopPage) where the values for exit opportunities are very high in Switzerland, Germany, the Netherlands, and Slovenia but below average in countries like Denmark and Sweden. The perceptions of exit opportunities also exhibit great variation with respect to child education, with scores far below average in Norway and Switzerland, and close to average in West Germany and Slovenia.

As far as voice opportunities in the domain of child education are concerned, we find above average levels for Denmark, the Netherlands, Norway, and – surprisingly – Moldova (between 0.48 and 0.58) but very low in Germany (0.37 for the western and 0.34 for the eastern part). In line with previous studies (Andersen and Hoff 2001), we find a significant difference between Denmark and Sweden in the domain of child education, which corresponds to a difference in the degree to which decision-making power is delegated to the individual school.

Formal structures however, do not always make a difference. Contrary to expectations, the strong emphasis on worker co-determination in German and Dutch companies does not seem to affect perceived voice opportunities. The Netherlands (0.58) belongs to the cluster of countries with high values, but not more so in the domain of working life than in other domains. East Germany (0.33) has the lowest value of all countries, and West Germany (0.39) ranks lower than Slovenia and Romania.

Overall, perceived opportunities to exercise influence in working life are surprisingly small, considering discourses about things like changing workplace relations and human resource management. Only Danes show high values for this domain (0.64) – higher than any other country, and higher than for other domains in Denmark. As we shall see below, the propensity to take action reveals even larger cross-national variations.

Contrary to expectations, the perceived opportunities to exercise influence in the domain of healthcare, even in terms of voice, are of respectable magnitude in most countries. The highest values are recorded for the Netherlands and Switzerland (0.65). Here we find West Germany (0.54) in a slightly better position, in-between the high-scoring and the low-scoring group, where Moldova and Portugal arc at the bottom (0.39 and 0.36, respectively).

In all domains, the values for Germany are surprisingly low. This deviation is difficult to explain.[3] One might even suspect that, due to translation problems, the question wording is not fully comparable. However, this suspicion is ruled out by the fact that the wording used in Germany was identical to that used in the German-speaking parts of Switzerland. Further, as already observed, we do find some fairly high values for Germany as far as exit opportunities are concerned, in particular in the domain of healthcare. The figure for working life is low even for the exit dimension, but this most likely reflects the high level of unemployment.

Combining voice and exit opportunities, we find Denmark and the Netherlands far above average in the domain of child education, while West Germany has a higher score in the domain of healthcare than Denmark and Sweden. Like Germany, Switzerland seems to get some value for money in its very expensive health sector (OECD 2003):[4] Its score of 0.72 is much higher than in any other country. As far as working life is concerned, Denmark and the Netherlands are at the top of the list (0.61 and 0.59, respectively), whereas East Germany (0.31) ranks alongside Moldova (0.31). Finally, as far as the perceived opportunities of students are concerned, the cross-national differences tend to be relatively small. Only the high scores in Denmark deviate markedly.

Dissatisfaction

Alongside resources and perceived opportunities, dissatisfaction is hypothesised to be of considerable importance for the purpose of explaining citizens' propensity to take action in small-scale democracy (see Chapter 10). While there is certainly nothing that prevents satisfied citizens from taking initiative to influence their situation in the domains under study, those who are dissatisfied obviously have stronger incentives to invest the energy required (Petersson *et al.* 1989). Consequently, we asked respondents to indicate to which extent they had encountered reasons to be dissatisfied with their situation in the four domains under study during the past 12 months. Responses were obtained on an 11-point graphical scale ranging from 'not at all dissatisfied' to 'very dissatisfied', scored to range from 0 to 1 in the analyses presented here. More specifically, the questions asked were:

'During the last 12 months, to what extent have you had reason to feel dissatisfied with:

- conditions at your child's school?
- conditions related to the medical treatment of you or your relative?
- conditions related to your work or work-place?
- conditions at your school or university?'

It is difficult to formulate any clear-cut hypotheses about differences across nations as well as domains as far as dissatisfaction is concerned. Economic development should lead to better services and better working conditions in objective terms, but this does not necessarily reduce dissatisfaction. Dissatisfaction reflects not only the objective living conditions of individuals but also their expectations. If expectations rise with affluence, dissatisfaction does not necessarily decline. Level of spending relative to GDP may provide a better basis for theorising about expected levels of dissatisfaction since it says something about the priority given to a particular area, for example healthcare. However, even in this case, the effect is questionable.

One might imagine that good opportunities for exit should reduce dissatisfaction since those dissatisfied are free to choose an alternative. At least this is what would happen if the public sector would function like a market. However, such is unlikely to the case: parents will most likely prefer a school in their neighbourhood, patients often find it difficult to make a qualified decision (except with regard to the choice of a general practitioner, which is not measured separately), and the workplace is traditionally not regarded as a matter of choice. In short, no firm predictions are possible.

The results are presented in Table 9.3. Beginning with differences between domains, as measured by the cross-national average, dissatisfaction turns out to be most widespread in working life (0.38) and student education (0.40), whereas the level in child education and healthcare is somewhat lower (0.32 and 0.31, respectively).

Turning to country differences (as measured by averages for child education, healthcare, and working life), we do find the highest level of dissatisfaction in the two poorest countries, Moldova (0.38) and Romania (0.43). Possibly, Spain fits this pattern too, with an intermediate position in economic terms and a level of dissatisfaction in working life only slightly below that of the aforementioned countries. However, we have but a single domain to go by in the Spanish case, and with both Portugal and Slovenia temporarily out of the picture (since the measure of dissatisfaction used in those two countries is not fully comparable with that employed elsewhere) it is difficult to say whether the observed tendency represents more than a coincidence. Yet, it is worth mentioning one additional result that support the suggestion of a relationship between objec-

Table 9.3 Mean dissatisfaction by domain and country[a]

Domain	NO	DK	SE	CH	NL	WG	EG	ES	RO	MD	Average
Child education	0.35	0.37	0.34	0.29	0.31	0.28	0.30	–	0.34	0.40	0.32
Healthcare	0.31	0.33	0.30	0.23	0.30	0.28	0.29	–	0.37	0.48	0.31
Working life	0.41	0.41	0.39	0.37	0.39	0.31	0.33	0.41	0.44	0.42	0.38
Student education	0.43	0.42	0.36	0.38	–	0.37	0.37	–	0.44	0.44	0.40
Average[b]	0.35	0.37	0.34	0.30	0.33	0.29	0.31	–	0.38	0.43	0.34

Notes

a Entries are means on a scale ranging from 0 (not dissatisfied at all) to 1 (very dissatisfied). Averages across countries and domains are simple averages of the table entries for the individual countries and domains. Portugal and Slovenia are excluded from this analysis since the measure of dissatisfaction used in these two countries is not fully comparable to that used elsewhere.

b Because of the small number of student respondents, the figures for student education are not included when calculating averages across domains.

tive economic conditions and dissatisfaction, namely the uniquely low level of dissatisfaction shown by the Swiss with regard to their extremely expensive healthcare system (0.23).

If we consider the differences between the countries of northern and central Europe, we find that the Germans, the Swiss, and, to a lesser extent, the Dutch tend to be less dissatisfied than the Scandinavians. However, the differences are small. Overall, the figures are likely to reflect expectations more than objective characteristics, which of course does not diminish the importance of dissatisfaction as a potential motive for taking action (see Chapter 10).

Actions and action types

Actions

If country differences in dissatisfaction tend to be rather small, we find remarkable variations as far as the propensity to take action is concerned. To measure that propensity, respondents were asked to answer 'yes' or 'no' to the following questions:

'During the last 12 months, have you done anything to try to bring about improvements or counteract deterioration:

- with respect to the conditions at your child's school?
- related to the medical treatment of you or your relative?
- with regard to your working conditions or work-place?
- with respect to the conditions at your school or university?'

The results are presented in Table 9.4. Beginning with the overall averages, we notice that participation in small-scale democracy is actually quite a widespread activity. Across all countries and all domains, the average participation rate amounts to 33 per cent. Next, we find significant differences between domains: participation reaches the highest level in working life (a cross-national average of 40 per cent) followed by child education (35 per cent). These results are in line with the hypotheses presented above that it is easier to form networks and establish cooperation with others in the same situation in these two domains than in healthcare (22 per cent). Surprisingly, students in most countries seem rather passive (23 per cent), even though they are among the most dissatisfied and have good opportunities for cooperation.

The most remarkable findings, however, are the cross-national differences. Again, we find the same five countries at the top as in the analysis of perceived opportunities above: Norway (52 per cent), Denmark (47 per cent), Sweden (43 per cent), Switzerland (42 per cent), and the Netherlands (39 per cent). Also as expected, we find low values in Moldova and Romania (26 per cent), with Slovenia in-between (35 per cent). The

Table 9.4 Probability of taking action by domain and country (percentages)[a]

Domain	NO	DK	SE	CH	NL	WG	EG	ES	PT	SI	RO	MD	Average
Child education	52	51	48	41	43	19	17	–	22	32	30	28	35
Healthcare	37	21	18	28	24	11	14	–	5	33	24	28	22
Working life	66	69	61	57	49	12	12	35	23	39	33	23	40
Student education	34	44	31	42	–	16	15	–	13	15	0	15	23
Average[b]	52	47	43	42	39	14	14	–	17	35	29	26	33

Notes

a Entries indicate the percentage of respondents in the respective domain who, in the course of the past 12 months, had taken action in order to improve their situation or prevent it from deteriorating. Averages across countries and domains are simple averages of the table entries for the individual countries and domains.

b Because of the small number of student respondents, the figures for student education are not included when calculating averages across domains.

figure for Portugal is surprisingly low (17 per cent), but the most remarkable outlier is Germany with an average of only 14 per cent participants. The German deviation is found in all domains except for students where several other countries show equally low levels. However, the most dramatic illustration is no doubt working life, where only 12 per cent of the Germans show signs of activity, compared to 61 to 69 per cent in the Scandinavian countries.

Germany is an outlier in healthcare as well (11 to 14 per cent), this time in the company of Portugal. In this domain however, the order of the countries differs from the one typically found. The figures for Sweden and Denmark are remarkably low (18 and 21 per cent, respectively), whereas Norway tops the list with 37 per cent, followed by Slovenia (33 per cent) and Switzerland (28 per cent). We also observe above-average figures for Romania and Moldova (24 and 28 per cent respectively).

The German figures are the lowest the case of child education as well, but here the discrepancy is somewhat less radical (17 to 19 per cent, compared to a country average of 35 per cent). As in the domain of working life, the Scandinavian countries reveal the highest figures (from 48 to 52 per cent), and, the German case aside, we find almost the expected rank order between countries.

The German deviation is an intriguing one. As it is consistent across domains, it seems to suggest a cultural interpretation. It coincides with low perceived opportunities for influence and low levels of dissatisfaction. To what extent this provides an explanation in terms of immediate causes will be examined in the next chapter.

Action types

As a follow-up to the question of whether they had taken an initiative or not, respondents who answered yes were additionally asked what more specifically they had done. This follow-up question allows us to find out precisely what types of actions are involved, which is an important contribution to the interpretation of participation in small-scale democracy.

The question allows us to measure the relative importance of voice and exit within different domains and across countries. Exit and voice serve partly different purposes, but exit can also act as compensation where voice opportunities are limited, as expected, for example, in healthcare.

Among voice options, there are several possibilities. We would assume that contacting the person in charge would be the most obvious thing to do – the default option, so to speak. However, the questionnaire also measures to what extent action involves:

- cooperation with others in the same situation (e.g. workplace colleagues);
- contacts with government agencies;

- contacts with organisations;
- contacts with political parties, solicitors, or the media;
- involvement of social network (e.g. family, relatives, and friends).

The extent to which action is purely individual or involves cooperation with others is important for the interpretation of small-scale democracy. If it is purely individual, it might lead to the development of more particularistic orientations; if it involves cooperation with others, it comes closer to the classical 'school of democracy' situation where people may not only become more skilled in defending their interest but also learn civic skills and orientations. It is also interesting to see to what extent small-scale democracy involves 'particularised contacts' with government officials, and contacts with traditional representative bodies like associations and parties. Finally, people may use their social networks as a resource for action.

Whereas we have some assumptions about what may determine voice, exit, and overall action, we do not have any clear expectations about country differences in patterns of action. We expect cooperation with others to take place mainly at the workplace and in schools; and expect most contact to associations in these places. However, an important question is to what extent wage-earners manage to solve their problems at the workplace themselves, without involving unions or shop stewards.

The question asked for the purpose of specifying the characteristics of the action(s) taken is presented below. This particular version is the one used in the domain of child education. With slight adaptations of the question wording and response alternatives 1, 2, 7 and 9, the same question was asked in the other domains as well.

'More specifically, which of the things on this card did you do to influence the conditions at your child's school? Please indicate all alternatives that apply (Was there anything else that you did?):

1 Turned to a teacher or other member of staff at the school.
2 Turned to an official or agency in central, regional or local government (other than members of the school staff).
3 Turned to a politician or political party.
4 Turned to an organisation or association.
5 Turned to a solicitor or other legal advisor.
6 Turned to the media.
7 Turned to other parents with children in the same class or school as mine.
8 Turned to family, relatives or friends.
9 Changed to another class or school.
10 Other'.

As patterns are reasonably similar across countries, and as the number of cases for some countries is rather small, we begin by presenting the figures for the pooled sample (see Table 9.5). Not surprisingly, action in small-scale democracy involves, most importantly, contacts with the person(s) in charge, for example, the teacher, the doctor, or the manager. Of those who had taken action in the domain of child education, 87 per cent had contacted the teacher or other members of the school staff. Similar figures apply to healthcare and working life, whereas the figure for student education is slightly lower. However, this is clearly the default option. The question is what complementary forms of action people take.

To begin with, we must note that exit is typically used as a supplement to voice, not as an alternative (see also Table 9.6). Except in healthcare, exit is used rarely – by only 6 to 10 per cent of those who report that they have taken an initiative. As expected, exit is much more widely used in the domain of healthcare (23 per cent), where opportunities for cooperation with others in the same situation are limited.

In the domains of child education, working life, and student education, citizens often turn to other citizens in the same situation: 48 per cent in child education; 57 per cent in working life; and 60 per cent in student education. This is important as an indication that, even though participation in small-scale democracy is basically about personal concerns, it is not always a completely individual action. It may well involve collective actions

Table 9.5 Probability of different types of actions by domain (percentages)[a]

Type of action	Child education	Healthcare	Working life	Student education
Turned to person in charge (e.g. teacher, doctor, employer)	87	84	84	78
Turned to government agency	14	11	10	11
Turned to politician or political party	4	1	3	2
Turned to association	18	7	13	19
Turned to solicitor or other legal advisor	1	2	3	1
Turned to the media	6	1	2	6
Turned to others in the same situation (parents, patients, colleagues, fellow students)	48	13	57	60
Turned to family, relatives, friends	22	37	25	26
Exit (e.g. changed to another school, doctor, employer)	5	23	10	7
Other action	11	15	10	16
Number of cases	1,331	2,269	4,210	212

Note
a This table is based on a pooled sample. Entries indicate the percentage of those who took action who performed an action of the specific type described. Note that the results for the pooled sample do not weigh the countries equally. The weight of each country is indicated by the Ns reported in Table 9.6.

on a small-scale where a limited group of people unite and work together. In the domain of healthcare, however, the individual is much more isolated: only 13 per cent have turned to others in the same situation. This also makes exit a much more obvious option. An alternative explanation for the relatively widespread use of exit in the case of healthcare, however, may be that it is less costly and difficult in that case than in the domains of child education and working life.

Participation in small-scale democracy may also involve particularised contacts with government officials (other than those primarily responsible for delivering the service in question). Such is the case in slightly more than 10 per cent of the cases, even if we exclude contacts with a politician or a political party. The results for the latter – once very strong mass organisations in some countries – indicate that the likelihood that they get involved in personal conflicts between citizens and authorities is quite low nowadays. Only 1 to 4 per cent report that they have been in touch with politicians or parties. Even contacts with the media are slightly more frequent.

Associations, on the other hand, often become involved in the activities of small-scale democracy. Figures range from 18 per cent for child education (and 19 per cent for student education) to 7 per cent in healthcare. Surprisingly, contacts with unions related to concerns within working life do not top the list: even though the response alternative extends to contacts with shop stewards, only 13 per cent report having used this option. Furthermore, country variations in this respect are small. In the most unionised country of the world, Sweden, only 9 per cent of those employees who had taken action had contacted a union or shop steward (see Table 9.6).

By contrast, people often seem to draw on support from their social network: family, relatives, and friends. Not surprisingly, this is particularly true for healthcare (37 per cent). Social networks also prove to be important in the domains of child education, working life, and student education, where 22 to 26 per cent have turned to family, relatives, and friends for support. Not least in relation to working life, these are surprisingly high figures.

Country variations in these patterns are presented in Table 9.6. The first rows indicate averages across domains for the use of voice, exit, cooperation with others, contacts with associations and requests for support from family, relatives, and friends. The lower part of the table shows figures for each domain separately.

Voice includes all types of actions except exit and requests for support from family, relatives, and friends. As expected, voice is the typical course of action. On average, 95 per cent of those who have tried to exercise influence have used voice. Country variations are small – the lowest figures are those for Slovenia, Romania, and Moldova (91 to 93 per cent).

Among those who have taken action, the use of exit does not follow the typical dividing lines. The Scandinavian countries cluster together with a

Table 9.6 Probability of different types of actions by domain and country (percentages)[a]

Type of action and domain	NO	DK	SE	CH	NL	WG	EG	ES	PT	SI	RO	MD	Average
Average across domains													
Voice	97	97	96	97	95	97	94	–	96	93	91	92	95
Exit	8	11	8	17	20	19	18	–	4	9	14	17	13
Turned to													
Others in same situation	39	44	20	46	41	44	38	–	22	44	47	52	40
Association	16	7	6	12	25	17	14	–	18	7	4	4	12
Family, relatives, friends	16	16	8	50	32	33	24	–	10	29	51	47	29
Within each domain													
Exit													
Child education	2	6	2	4	6	5	10	–	2	0	13	15	6
Healthcare	15	22	18	28	37	32	34	–	5	13	20	23	22
Working life	7	6	4	18	21	11	11	6	5	13	10	13	10
Others in same situation													
Child education	53	61	22	53	35	61	51	–	26	46	45	50	46
Healthcare	6	8	3	19	15	18	10	–	15	11	22	26	14
Working life	58	62	36	67	72	52	52	37	25	74	73	81	57
Association													
Child education	29	5	8	18	33	23	21	–	40	7	0	0	17
Healthcare	3	3	2	8	24	12	9	–	5	2	2	2	7
Working life	15	14	9	10	17	15	13	17	9	11	11	9	13
Family, relatives, friends													
Child education	11	14	6	43	27	35	13	–	9	19	–	41	22
Healthcare	21	23	15	56	38	43	37	–	10	47	56	54	36
Working life	17	12	6	51	32	21	22	24	10	22	45	47	26
Number of cases													
Child education	310	175	113	164	166	56	30	–	53	57	96	110	1,331
Healthcare	530	204	179	426	255	109	80	–	21	249	125	101	2,269
Working life	878	601	448	696	413	90	42	526	123	167	137	106	4,210

Note

[a] Entries indicate the percentage of those who took action who performed an action of the specific type described. The data are weighed so as to be representative of the respective populations but the number of cases refer to unweighted data. Averages across countries and domains are simple averages of the table entries for the individual countries and domains.

low frequency of exit (on average 8 per cent in Sweden and Norway, 11 per cent in Denmark) compared to most other countries. However, equally low figures are found in Portugal and Slovenia (4 and 9 per cent, respectively), whereas the Germans and the Dutch reveal proportions of around 20 per cent followed by Switzerland and Moldova with 17 per cent.

The German use of exit is particularly high in healthcare (32 per cent in the West, 34 per cent in the East). In the Netherlands and Switzerland, the corresponding figures are 37 and 28 per cent, respectively, whereas the remaining countries reach levels of around or below 20 per cent. In the case of working life, the exit option is used by 11 per cent in Germany, around 20 per cent in the Netherlands and Switzerland, but only 4 to 7 per cent in Scandinavia (despite high job mobility, especially in Denmark). The Scandinavian figures for exit are low in all domains, but in child education and healthcare, the use of the exit option is more widespread in Denmark than in Sweden and Norway. The only countries where exit exceeds 10 per cent in the domain of child education are East Germany, Romania, and Moldova.

Interestingly, small-scale democracy is not as individualised as one might think. Cooperation with others in the same situation is widespread in all countries except Sweden and Portugal. Furthermore, the average figures for healthcare reflect the infrequent contacts with other patients. For child education and working life, the figures are substantially higher. Thus, for parents of school children, the figures are around 60 per cent in West Germany and Denmark, and above 50 per cent in Norway and Switzerland. For initiatives in working life, the corresponding figures are above 70 per cent in the Netherlands, Slovenia, Romania, and Moldova, and around 60 per cent or more in Switzerland, Norway, and Denmark, followed by 52 per cent in West and East Germany. Spain, Sweden, and Portugal are outliers, with only 42, 36 and 25 per cent contacting colleagues, respectively.

Contacts with associations are most widespread in the Netherlands. This holds for all areas including healthcare (24 per cent). In West Germany, the corresponding figure is 12 per cent; 8 per cent in Switzerland, and negligible in Scandinavia. Even in child education, Danish and Swedish figures for contacting associations are as low as 5 to 8 per cent, about the same level as in Slovenia. In the Netherlands, the corresponding figure is 33 per cent, and in both parts of Germany, as well as in Switzerland, it is above 20 per cent. In working life, the figures for contacts with trade unions and shop stewards are surprisingly low in all countries – from 9 per cent in Sweden, Portugal, and Moldova, to 17 per cent in Spain, West Germany, and the Netherlands. Not surprisingly, the two countries with a long tradition of works councils top the list, but Danish and Norwegian figures rank only slightly lower.

Finally, the significant country difference with regard to involving family and friends is characteristic of all domains. Apart from the

Portuguese, Scandinavians are the most reluctant to involve family and friends in their attempts to exercise influence in child education, healthcare and working life. Only 6 per cent of the Swedes turned to friends or family in the domain of child education, compared to 43 per cent in Switzerland. Similar discrepancies are found for healthcare and working life. Apparently, Scandinavian users and employees are on their own, when they try to exert influence. They seldom seek support from associations or social networks but are inclined to turn to others in the same situation, that is, fellow parents or workplace colleagues.

In summary, small-scale democracy involves, most importantly, contacts with the person in charge (teacher, doctor, manager), but especially in child education and working life, it often involves cooperation with others as well. In the healthcare system, the possibilities to exploit this opportunity are weak. Instead, people make more use of the exit option. Finally, attempts to exercise influence frequently involve support from family and friends, especially in healthcare, but in this case, cross-national differences are unusually large. Associations and other ways of action do not play a major role, not even in the domain of working life. In both respects, Scandinavians reveal a more individualised pattern than people from most other countries.

Consequences of action

Outcomes

The next question is whether initiatives in small-scale democracy are efficient: do people obtain what they want? To assess the outcome of their efforts, respondents who had taken an initiative were asked: 'were your wishes essentially satisfied?' The response alternatives offered were 'yes', 'no', and 'still uncertain'. An overview can be provided by comparing success rates between countries and across policy domains. Student education is omitted from the country-by-country analyses since the number of cases is too small.

As is shown in Table 9.7, success rates are generally high: it typically pays off to take action. Success rates are a little higher in healthcare than in child education and working life but otherwise fairly similar, with about three out of four obtaining what they wanted. Only students reveal a markedly lower success rate (64 per cent; not shown).

Country averages do not follow any clear-cut pattern. Within Scandinavia, Swedes appear to be the least and Norwegians the most successful. Moldovans are significantly less successful than anyone else. The highest figures are obtained for Slovenia, but it is impossible to trace any interpretable division of countries. Moving to individual areas, we observe rather low success rates for Swedes in schools, for Danes in healthcare, for Spaniards at work, and for Moldovans in all domains. The Dutch, the Germans, and the Norwegians show high values for healthcare, and the

Table 9.7 Probability of success (percentages)[a]

Domain	NO	DK	SE	CH	NL	WG	EG	ES	PT	SI	RO	MD	Average
Child education	78	78	66	77	62	69	55	–	70	83	81	66	71
Healthcare	84	66	72	86	69	82	89	–	68	89	77	60	77
Working life	78	78	75	74	73	71	73	63	81	79	67	53	72
Average	80	74	71	79	68	74	72	–	73	84	75	59	73
Number of cases													
Child education	310	175	113	164	166	56	30	–	53	57	96	110	
Healthcare	530	204	179	426	255	109	80	–	21	249	125	101	
Working life	878	601	448	696	413	90	42	526	123	167	137	106	

Note

a Entries indicate the percentage answering yes to the question of whether their wishes had essentially been satisfied. The percentage base consists of those who answered either yes or no. The question was asked of those who had taken action. The data are weighed so as to be representative of the respective populations but the number of cases refer to unweighted data. The number of cases also include 'still uncertain' and 'don't know/no answer', which are omitted when calculating the percentages. Unweighted averages for 'still uncertain' are 25 per cent in schools, 18 per cent in healthcare, and 19 per cent for work. 'Don't know/no answer' account for a negligible number of respondents. Averages across countries and domains are simple averages of the table entries for the individual countries and domains.

Slovenians appear to have a high success rate everywhere. The remaining variations are uncertain due to small numbers of cases.

Pathways of citizen action

We may combine information on dissatisfaction, action, and outcome as described in Figure 9.2. Based on the combination of dissatisfaction and action, we can distinguish between various patterns:

- *active discontent* (dissatisfied and trying to do something about it);
- *active promotion* (not dissatisfied but taking action nevertheless);
- *silent contentment* (not dissatisfied and seeing no reason to act);
- *silent resignation* (dissatisfied but unable or unwilling to act).

For those who take action, we can further distinguish between:

- *power* (successful action);
- *powerlessness* (unsuccessful action).

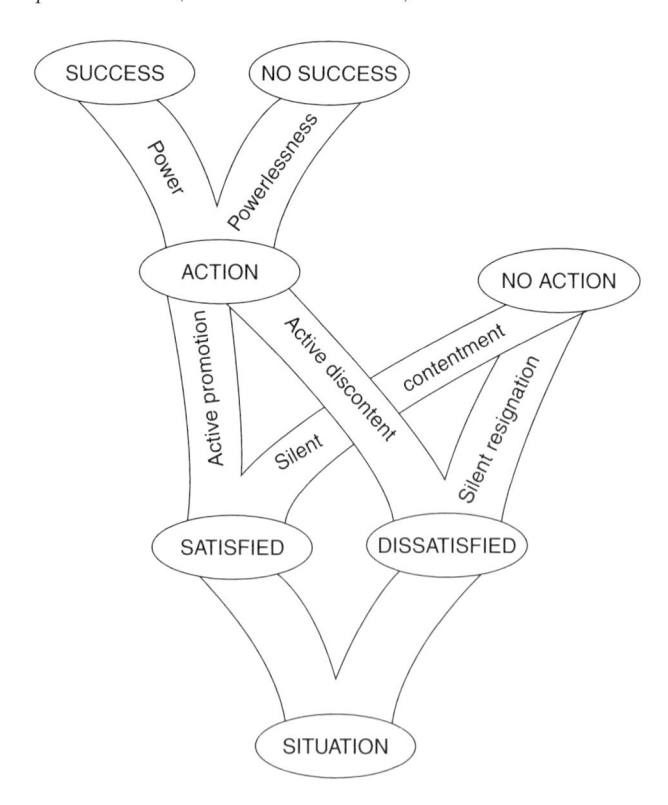

Figure 9.2 Pathways of citizen action in small-scale democracy (source: adapted from Petersson, Westholm, and Blomberg (1989: Figure 2.2)).

Especially the category of silent resignation is interesting from a citizenship perspective: how often does it happen that people abstain from doing anything even if they have reasons to be dissatisfied – how widespread is this feeling of lack of efficacy in various countries and across policy domains?

Operationally, we have dichotomised the dissatisfaction scale, originally scored 0 to 10, using 3 as the cut-point. Scores 0 to 3 are taken to indicate low dissatisfaction and 4 to 10 high dissatisfaction (which brings the median into the low dissatisfaction category in most cases). For the sake of simplicity, we have also dichotomised outcomes by combining 'still uncertain' with 'yes' (wishes essentially satisfied).

The findings are summarised in Table 9.8. Again, we notice the association between dissatisfaction and action: the proportion of dissatisfaction is much higher among those who act. What is particularly interesting, however, is the category that we have labelled 'silent resignation'. Beginning with aggregate figures for the four domains, we note that this figure varies from 18 per cent for child education, over 23 per cent for working life, and 26 per cent for healthcare. For student education, the figure is 41 per cent (not shown), but N's are small.

The most interesting question is how this figure varies across countries. From the averages for child education, healthcare and working life, three groups of countries emerge: among the five old democracies (Scandinavia, the Netherlands, and Switzerland), we find rather small proportions of silent resignation – from 13 to 17 per cent – and relatively high proportions of active discontent and active promotion. The proportion of silent contentment is above average in Switzerland and the Netherlands. With high participation, there are also bound to be some losers (between 8 and 10 per cent) but the proportion of winners – those who have done something and are satisfied with the result – is much higher: from 30 per cent in the Netherlands to 44 per cent in Norway (on all measures, small-scale democracy is more successful in Norway than in Sweden and Denmark).

For Romania and especially for Moldova (but also for Spain, if we extrapolate based on the results for working life), we find the opposite pattern: high proportions of silent resignation (no less than 41 per cent in Moldova) and rather low proportions of successful action – with a proportion of losers (powerlessness) almost as low as in the small democracies. Among Germans, there are few losers – only 3 per cent. This is caused partly by high satisfaction and high success rate, but the main explanation is that most refrained from taking action. The average proportion of silent resignation (26 and 29 per cent, respectively) is as high in Romania as in West and East Germany (see also Chapters 10 and 11 for closer scrutiny of the German deviation).

These country differences are similar across domains, but a few variations within the groups are revealed. There seems to be slightly more silent resignation among Scandinavian (especially Norwegian) parents of

Table 9.8 Pathways of citizen action by domain and country (percentages)[a]

Domain and pathway	NO	DK	SE	CH	NL	WG	EG	ES	RO	MD	Average
Child education											
Active promotion	26	21	19	18	19	7	3	–	12	10	15
Active discontent	26	30	30	23	24	12	14	–	18	18	22
Silent resignation	14	12	12	12	10	22	24	–	21	36	18
Silent contentment	34	37	39	47	47	59	59	–	49	36	45
Powerlessness	8	9	14	8	12	4	6	–	4	8	8
Power	44	42	35	34	31	15	11	–	26	20	29
Healthcare											
Active promotion	21	8	6	15	8	6	6	–	12	9	10
Active discontent	16	12	12	13	16	5	9	–	12	19	13
Silent resignation	17	28	26	15	19	28	28	–	30	45	26
Silent contentment	46	52	56	57	57	61	57	–	46	27	51
Powerlessness	5	6	3	4	6	2	1	–	5	10	5
Power	32	14	15	25	19	10	13	–	19	18	18
Working life											
Active promotion	27	29	25	23	16	4	4	13	12	5	16
Active discontent	39	40	36	34	33	8	8	22	21	18	26
Silent resignation	12	11	13	13	15	27	35	32	29	42	23
Silent contentment	22	20	26	30	36	61	53	33	38	35	35
Powerlessness	11	13	12	12	11	3	3	11	10	9	10
Power	55	56	49	45	40	9	10	24	27	16	33
Average											
Active promotion	25	19	17	19	14	6	4	–	12	8	14
Active discontent	27	27	26	23	24	8	10	–	17	18	20
Silent resignation	14	17	17	13	15	26	29	–	27	41	22
Silent contentment	34	37	40	45	47	60	57	–	44	33	44
Powerlessness	8	9	10	8	10	3	3	–	6	9	7
Power	44	37	33	35	30	11	11	–	24	18	27

Note

a The percentages for 'active promotion', 'active discontent', silent resignation', and 'silent contentment' sum to 100 for each country. Averages across countries are simple averages of the table entries for the individual countries. Portugal and Slovenia are excluded from this analysis since the measure of dissatisfaction used in these two countries is not fully comparable to that used elsewhere.

schoolchildren than in Switzerland and the Netherlands, and there is a higher proportion of losers in Sweden. However, the main difference is found in healthcare where the proportion of silent resignation is above average in Denmark (28 per cent) and Sweden (26 per cent) – the same level as in Germany – and twice as high as in Switzerland. The Danes and Swedes are not only less satisfied; they are more reluctant to do anything about it. Unlike the German deviation, which is a general one, the Danish and Swedish deviation is largely limited to this single domain. Based on the situation at the time of interviewing, it is difficult to come up with explanations in terms of institutions, expenditures or change in expenditures. Budget constraints may have been slightly tighter in Denmark and Sweden than in Norway, but in all three countries, healthcare expenditure was lowered, relative to GDP, so it is hard to believe that this could explain the difference.

Procedural fairness

The consequences of participation in small-scale democracy include two aspects of which the first, the outcome, has already been covered. The second focuses on the procedural side: to which extent do citizens feel that they have been fairly treated in their encounters within small-scale democracy? Obviously, their impressions in this regard may be strongly influenced by whether or not the outcome matched their expectations. Nevertheless, we should not take for granted that their view of the process is merely an echo of how they fared in material terms. Nor should we underestimate the importance of procedural impressions for building legitimacy (see Chapter 11).

Citizens perceptions of the extent to which they had been given a fair hearing were measured by means of the question: 'aside from the outcome, to what extent do you think you were treated fairly in your attempt to influence the situation?' Responses were obtained on an 11-point scale with the one end-point marked 'not at all' and the other 'to a very large extent'. As in earlier cases, the scale was scored to range from 0 to 1.

The results are presented in Table 9.9. In this case, differences between domains are negligible. In fact, averages for all countries are almost the same for child education, healthcare and working life. The cross-national differences that do exist are relatively small. Again, we find the characteristic difference between Scandinavia, the Netherlands, and Switzerland on the one hand and the remaining countries on the other – although on this question, Slovenia joins the top group. The highest average figure is found in Switzerland (0.78 on a scale from zero to one), closely followed by Slovenia and the Scandinavian countries. For the Netherlands, the figure is 0.70, but German and even Romanian figures do not deviate much from this level. Only Portugal and in particular Moldova stand out as countries where people feel they are rather badly treated in small-scale democracy.

Table 9.9 Mean perception of procedural fairness by domain and country[a]

Domain	NO	DK	SE	CH	NL	WG	EG	ES	PT	SI	RO	MD	Average
Child education	0.71	0.76	0.77	0.80	0.75	0.68	0.63	–	0.58	0.79	0.67	0.53	0.70
Healthcare	0.71	0.69	0.68	0.80	0.68	0.69	0.74	–	0.51	0.78	0.69	0.52	0.68
Working life	0.70	0.76	0.74	0.74	0.66	0.67	0.69	0.69	0.72	0.70	0.65	0.51	0.69
Average	0.71	0.74	0.73	0.78	0.70	0.68	0.69	–	0.60	0.76	0.67	0.52	0.69

Note

a Entries are means on a scale ranging from 0 to 1. Averages across countries and domains are simple averages of the table entries for the individual countries and domains.

Breaking down by country and domain simultaneously does not reveal much more information. We note, however, that Sweden and Denmark have relatively low figures for healthcare, especially in comparison with their very high figures for child education and working life. Apparently there is room for democratic improvements in the healthcare sector in these two countries.

Conclusions

From a theoretical point of view, the notion of small-scale democracy contributes to a more satisfactory delineation of political participation by excluding actions aimed at outcomes of primary importance to but a limited number of people from the definition of the concept while maintaining that such actions are relevant in their own right from a democratic (citizenship) point of view. Prior to the present study, however, participation in small-scale democracy had been systematically studied in the Scandinavian context only, and one might have conjectured that the phenomenon was so strongly linked to this particular context that it would not make much sense to look for it in a broader European settings. Perhaps the most important finding of the present chapter is that this hypothesis turned out to be unfounded. On the contrary, participation in small-scale democracy is fairly widespread in many European countries. Overall, about one-third of those who qualified as a potential actor within any one domain under study had made an attempt to influence their situation in that domain during the past 12 months.

We also found that such participation often makes a difference: more than two-thirds of those who had taken action reported that their wishes had essentially been satisfied. Additionally, we found that participation in small-scale democracy is not quite as individualistic as it might seem. Apart from addressing the person(s) in charge (e.g. the teacher, the doctor, or the manager), a substantial percentage also turned to others in the same situation (i.e. fellow parents, students, patients, or employees) for support. Even though exit plays a substantial role, especially in healthcare, we found that it is typically used as a supplement rather than an alternative to voice, as indicated by the fact that the percentage who had tried at least one voice-based option as part of their efforts to exercise influence approached 100 per cent in many countries.

We observed significant country differences in the propensity to take action, as well as in the perceived opportunities to exercise influence. Beginning with the latter, we observed a substantial difference between the Scandinavian countries, Switzerland, and the Netherlands, on the one hand, and two clusters of new democracies on the other. While this is not so surprising, given the differences in socio-economic development, democratic tradition and popular mobilisation, the extraordinary pessimistic perception of opportunities – in particular voice opportunities –

in Germany came as a surprise. We also measured the degree of dissatisfaction among users and employees, based on the assumption that dissatisfaction breeds participation. Even though Germans stand out as relatively satisfied, the extraordinary low participation came as a surprise. However, the resemblance between Switzerland, the Netherlands, and the Scandinavian countries is so profound that it invalidates speculations about a possible 'Scandinavian bias' in the concept of small-scale democracy.

The ability to influence one's personal situation in everyday life is an important aspect of citizenship. This type of influence also comes close to participation in large-scale democracy – perhaps even to the extent, as some have suggested, that it will partly serve as a functional equivalent for some people. If this is the case, it could lead to more particularised orientations to politics. However, there need not be any contradiction between having strong citizens able to control their immediate surroundings in everyday life and having a strong democracy with collectively oriented citizens. On the contrary, it would seem more likely that small-scale democracy may serve as a 'school of democracy' in the more classical sense, especially if it involves cooperation with others, as our data show. In this case, we expect a positive spillover effect on political participation and civic orientations.

Notes

1 Questions on small-scale democracy were not asked in Russia and Spain (except for working life in Spain). For Portugal and Slovenia, data on dissatisfaction are not included since they are not fully comparable with those from other countries.
2 For some countries, the questionnaire included an additional question about the possibility of changing to a private school. For other countries, this possibility is covered by the first question about exit opportunities, which makes cross-national comparisons difficult.
3 One might speculate that country differences in the size and composition of workplaces could play a role. Germany still has a larger industrial sector than most countries, and a larger plant size in manufacturing companies than, for example, Denmark. However, as services is the dominant sector in all countries, and as this sector is probably less heterogeneous in terms of plant size, this cannot explain very much of the difference.
4 The figures are 10.7 (Switzerland) and 10.6 (Germany) per cent of GDP as compared to a range from 7.3 to 8.3 per cent for the other countries where data are available. Alongside Spain, Portugal, and the United Kingdom, Germany and Switzerland are also the countries with the highest increase in healthcare expenditures during the period 1990–2000. In the Nordic countries, healthcare expenditures even declined, relative to GDP. Even though it is often difficult to compare expenditures across countries, the difference between Switzerland, Germany, and the other countries in the survey is so substantial that it is without doubt reliable. When it comes to disaggregated information about spending for basic education, comparisons are too uncertain.

10 Small-scale democracy
The determinants of action

Hanspeter Kriesi and Anders Westholm

Introduction

In the literature on *large-scale social movements*, three approaches are typically distinguished – the so-called classical model, the resource mobilisation model and the political process model (e.g. McAdam 1982). The classical model puts the accent on discontent in order to explain the mobilisation of social movements. Popular discontent, in turn, has different sources according to different variants of the classical model – structural strain, social isolation, status inconsistencies, system strain.

This model has been severely criticised. Most importantly, it has been pointed out that discontent is at best a necessary, but certainly not sufficient cause of social movements. It is more fruitful, as Jenkins and Perrow (1977: 266) suggest, to assume that grievances are relatively constant and pervasive. McCarthy and Zald (1977) state the same point even more forcefully: they are willing to assume that 'there is always enough discontent in any society to supply the grass-roots support for a movement if the movement is effectively organised'. The resource mobilisation model insists that, in order to mobilise collectively, a discontented group of individuals needs some sort of organisation – formal organisations or informal networks – allowing them to voice their discontent.

For some purposes, McCarthy and Zald suggest that we take one step further: grievances and discontent may be defined, created, and manipulated by issue entrepreneurs and organisations. This idea is prominent in the analysis of framing processes – the social construction of grievances and discontent by movement actors (Snow *et al.* 1986; Snow and Benford 1988). While the resource mobilisation model emphasises the indigenous organisational strength of the discontented group, the political process model (see McAdam 1982; Tarrow 1994) puts the group into its political context and focuses on the political opportunities and constraints structuring the way it interacts with its adversaries.

Today, discontent, resources, and opportunities constitute the basic components of the programme for the analysis of the mobilisation by social movements (McAdam *et al.* 1996). The same three components also figure more or less prominently in current as well as past micro-level studies of political participation. Resources, as indicated by socio-economic status, occupy centre-stage already in the first systematic studies of political action on the individual level (see Milbrath and Goel 1977) and continue, in more elaborate form, to dominate subsequent research in the field (as exemplified by the Civic Voluntarism Model of Verba *et al.* 1995; see also Chapters 14 and 15, this volume). Perceived opportunities are intimately related to the notion of political efficacy (Campbell *et al.* 1954; see also Abramson 1983 and Chapters 14 and 15, this volume), a concept which has received almost as much attention as objective resources in attempts to explain political participation. By contrast, discontent – in the sense of dissatisfaction with one's personal situation or specific policies or policy domains – occupies a much less prominent place in research on political participation than in the social movement literature (although occasional counter-examples can be found, e.g. Barnes *et al.* 1979).

Apart from the stronger emphasis on dissatisfaction, the literature on social movements has also to a greater extent been concerned with the way the three components interact. According to the 'logic of value added' that Smelser (1962) recommended for the analysis of collective action 40 years ago, each component is a necessary condition for the mobilisation to take place, that is, collective action requires a combination of discontent, resources, and opportunities. 'Each determinant', said Smelser (1962: 382), 'is a necessary condition for the next to operate as a determinant of an episode of collective action'. In other words, only if discontent is sufficiently widespread will resources become relevant, and only if resources are sufficiently numerous, will opportunities matter. The combination of the three components according to this perspective is multiplicative: all three have to be present for collective action to take place (see Goertz and Starr 2001).

Alternatively, we may conceive of each one of the three components as a facilitating condition, which contributes its share to the emergence of collective action. The combination of the three components according to this perspective is additive and, accordingly, variable combinations of the three may account for collective action. According to this perspective, a high level of discontent may compensate for lack of resources and opportunity and vice versa: collective action may, for example, be forthcoming, if the opportunity presents itself, even if discontent is only moderate. In theory, although not in practice, social-movement analysis has tended to neglect this alternative.

Small-scale democracy focuses neither on large-scale social movements nor on political participation as conventionally understood but on the small-scale efforts undertaken by individual citizens to control their personal situation in areas like working life, child education and healthcare. Nevertheless, in analysing these small-scale efforts, we can benefit from the insights of the two literatures we have briefly discussed. If the way discontent, resources, and opportunities accumulate and combine have proven helpful in understanding the strength of social movements as well as political participation, they should provide a useful starting point also for the less well charted terrain of action within small-scale democracy.

Discontent may provide a motivation not only for the participation in collective action, but also for the efforts of individuals to control their personal situation. But just as in large-scale contexts, discontent may not suffice to bring about action in small-scale situations. Dissatisfied citizens may also need the resources to do what needs to be done. In the case of collective action, these resources basically refer to mobilising structures, that is, organisations. In small-scale situations, organisations may help as well. Membership in formal organisations or informal networks may facilitate the articulation of individual discontent. Other types of resources should also be taken into account: individual resources – such as skills, know-how, and information – may be indispensable for the articulation of grievances. Finally, discontent and resources may not be sufficient for individuals to take initiatives to redress their situation. The circumstances may be such that individuals see no way of influencing their situation. Specific opportunities in a given situation may greatly facilitate the articulation of individual grievances, while situation-specific constraints may prevent them from being articulated.

In addition to the situation-specific opportunities, the country-specific context determines the more general opportunity structure. This larger context is likely to influence the readiness of individuals to act upon their discontent in more specific situations. We have, in the set of countries at our disposal, six well-established democracies – Denmark, the Netherlands, Norway, Sweden, Switzerland, and West Germany – four new democracies from eastern and central Europe – East Germany, Slovenia, Romania, Moldova – and two new democracies from southern Europe – Portugal and Spain.

The impact of old and new democracies on the readiness to take small-scale initiatives to redress unsatisfactory situations is, however, ambiguous. On the one hand, we may expect the citizens of new democracies to have greater objective reasons to be dissatisfied with their situation than those of established democracies due to lower levels of material well-being and less well-functioning institutions. Greater discontent might imply a higher propensity to take action. On the other hand, we may expect the citizens in established democracies to have generally more experience with articulating their discontent as well as greater resources and opportunities to do so. They are, therefore, more likely to take action to redress a situation they consider unsatisfactory.

In other words, we expect the rate of transformation of discontent into action to be higher in old democracies than in new ones. As far as the eastern European countries of the former communist regimes are concerned, they were notorious for the use of so-called 'passive forms of resistance', such as absenteeism, tacit boycotting, or general disengagement. These 'weapons of the weak' (Scott 1985) are not captured by the proactive kind of questions we used in our study. We do not know to what extent the people in eastern Europe are still practising these forms of passive resistance under the changed economic and political circumstances. But to the extent that they do, their rate of transformation of discontent into the kinds of actions we do measure in our study will be lower than the corresponding rates in the old democracies or in the new democracies in southern Europe.

Our theoretical discussion centres on the potential significance of three factors in accounting for individual as well as collective action: discontent, resources, and opportunities. In this chapter, we shall use this triad of factors in an attempt to explain the efforts of individuals to control their own personal situation in three important domains: working life, child education, and healthcare. The 12 country-specific contexts at our disposal imply that we are in a position to consider three sources of variation: the individual, the domain, and the country.

We begin by examining the impact of discontent, opportunities, and resources separately. We then consider their joint impact based on the additive logic of facilitating conditions. Finally, we test if the multiplicative logic of necessary conditions improves the understanding obtained through additive models.

The impact of discontent

Discontent arises as a result of a discrepancy between the demands of individuals and their perception of their objective situation. It is thus a measure of *subjective* deprivation. Consequently, those who are dissatisfied need not be identical to those who are worst off in more objective terms. According to the theories we try to test, it is the discrepancy between expectations and reality that provides the driving force required for action.

Prior research on Scandinavia and Switzerland has already demonstrated that this force is indeed a vital part of the explanation for participation in small-scale democracy (Petersson *et al.* 1989; Petersson *et al.* 1998; Andersen and Hoff 2001; von Erlach 2001). As shown by the logistic functions (with unstandardised logistic regression coefficients in parentheses) in the left half of Figure 10.1, this finding undoubtedly generalises to the larger set of countries considered here.

The curves show how the predicted probability of taking action depends on the level of dissatisfaction within each domain and country. The measures used correspond to those introduced in the previous chapter. For each domain, the dependent variable thus indicates whether or not the respondent has taken any initiative to improve his or her personal situation, or prevent it from getting worse, during the past

Probability of Action as a Logistic Function of Dissatisfaction

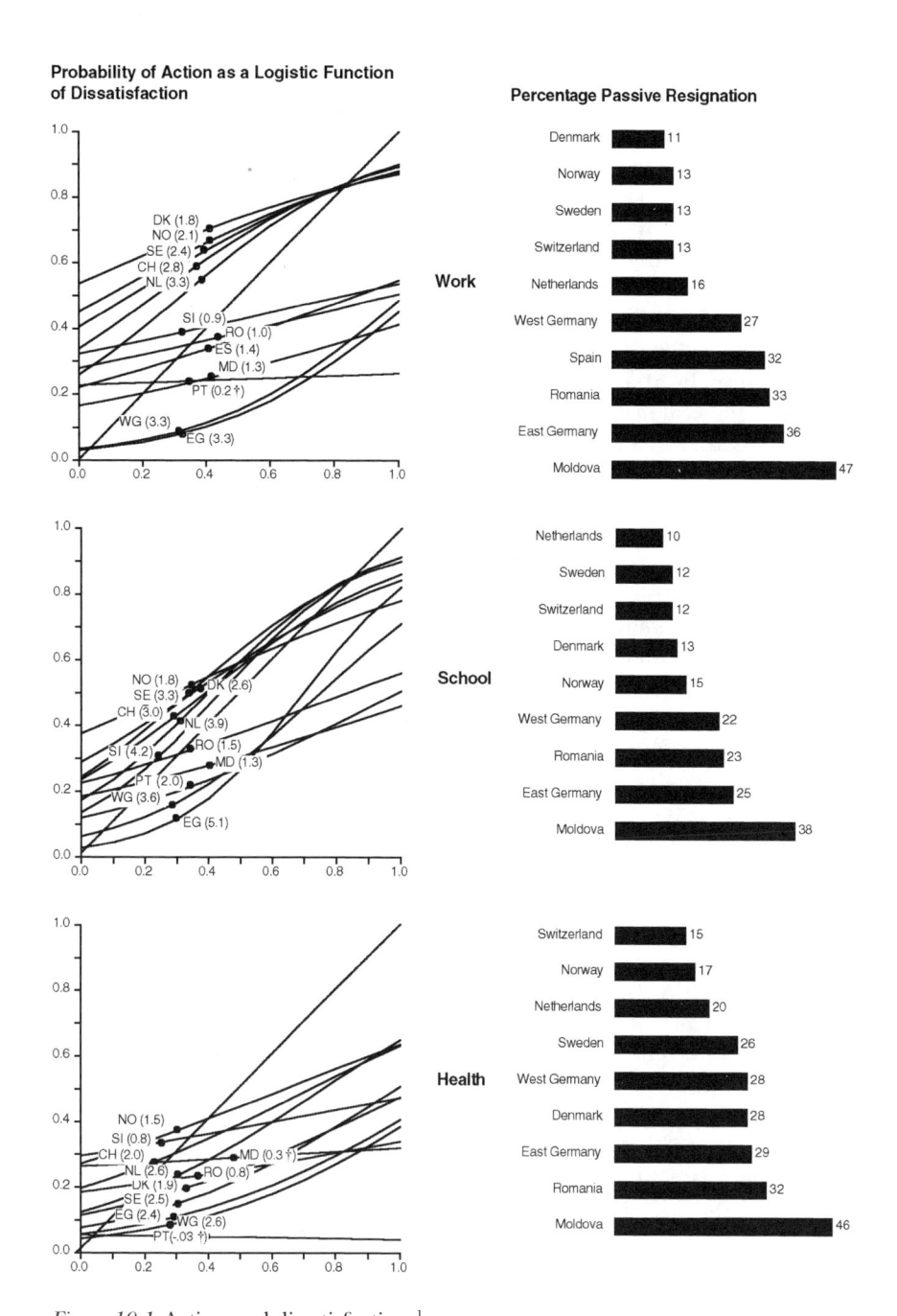

Percentage Passive Resignation

Work

Denmark	11
Norway	13
Sweden	13
Switzerland	13
Netherlands	16
West Germany	27
Spain	32
Romania	33
East Germany	36
Moldova	47

Work graph labels: DK (1.8), NO (2.1), SE (2.4), CH (2.8), NL (3.3), SI (0.9), RO (1.0), ES (1.4), MD (1.3), PT (0.2 †), WG (3.3), EG (3.3)

School

Netherlands	10
Sweden	12
Switzerland	12
Denmark	13
Norway	15
West Germany	22
Romania	23
East Germany	25
Moldova	38

School graph labels: NO (1.8), DK (2.6), SE (3.3), CH (3.0), NL (3.9), SI (4.2), RO (1.5), MD (1.3), PT (2.0), WG (3.6), EG (5.1)

Health

Switzerland	15
Norway	17
Netherlands	20
Sweden	26
West Germany	28
Denmark	28
East Germany	29
Romania	32
Moldova	46

Health graph labels: NO (1.5), SI (0.8), CH (2.0), NL (2.6), MD (0.3 †), RO (0.8), DK (1.9), SE (2.5), EG (2.4), WG (2.6), PT (-.03 †)

Figure 10.1 Action and dissatisfaction.[1]

Note

1 Figures in parentheses in the leftmost set of graphs are unstandardised, bivariate logistic regression coefficients. Figures followed by a † are not statistically significant at the 0.05-level. The dots indicate mean dissatisfaction along with the expected rate of activity at the mean.

12 months. Similarly, the independent variable is a domain-specific measure of the extent to which the respondent feels that he or she has had reason to be dissatisfied with that situation during the past 12 months.

As shown by the graphs, the relationship between dissatisfaction and the propensity to take action is uniformly positive, often strong, and statistically significant at the 0.05 level in all but three cases (Portugal in working life and Moldova and Portugal in healthcare). In other words, the motivating force of dissatisfaction is crucial for taking action. This is the essential message of the classical model of social movement theory – a message which has not been forgotten, but which has been given much less attention by the two more recent approaches to collective action. Here, the classical model is confirmed for small-scale settings of individual action – whether in a collective context or not.

Beyond that general observation, however, there are considerable variations across countries as well as sub-systems (but hardly any sign of an interaction between the two). Three distinct groups of countries are readily discerned based on the levels of the two variables (indicated by the dot on each curve, which shows mean dissatisfaction along with the expected rate of activity at the mean) as well as their relationship with each other. The first consists of five of the established democracies – Denmark, Norway, Sweden, the Netherlands, and Switzerland – where the level of activity is high, the level of dissatisfaction intermediate, and the relationship between the two quantities strong. The second group consists of the new democracies – Moldova, Romania, Slovenia, Portugal, and Spain[1] – where the propensity to act is lower, dissatisfaction higher, and the relationship between the two weaker. The third group consists of East and West Germany where the activity rate (much to our surprise) tends to be considerably lower than anywhere else, the level of dissatisfaction also somewhat lower than elsewhere, but the relationship between the two the very strongest.

Note that the particularly strong association between dissatisfaction and action in the German case becomes visible only if we consider it in logistic terms (as we should as long as we take a causal point of view). Were we to index it by ordinary linear regression or percentage differences, Germany would merely be on a par with the first group of countries with respect to schools and on the lower side in the other two realms. However, logistic analysis reveals that the moderate variation in raw activity rates is due entirely to the unexpectedly low level of activity in the population as a whole.[2]

As we turn to the variation across domains of small-scale democracy rather than nations, we find rather small differences in the overall strength of the relationship as long as we index it in logistic terms (see the unstandardised coefficients in parentheses). Child education has a slight edge followed by working life with healthcare at the bottom. The relationship is visibly weaker in the realm of healthcare than in the other two domains, but this is due primarily to a lower overall rate of activity. A tentative interpretation of this pattern is that the three settings for small-scale democracy differ primarily in the extent to which they generally facilitate action rather than in their ability to channel dissatisfaction. Not surprisingly, working life shows the highest activity rate followed by schools with healthcare at the bottom. This fits nicely with the extent to which we would expect codetermination to be firmly institutionalised across the three realms as well as with their expected centrality in the life of most respondents.

The rightmost column of Figure 10.1 allow us to examine the net implications of these patterns from a normative point of view. The diagrams show the percentage of the combination labelled passive resignation in the previous chapter (i.e. passivity combined with a dissatisfaction level of 0.4 or greater on a zero to one scale) for each small-scale democracy and country. We omit here the two countries (Portugal and Slovenia) for which the dissatisfaction measure (see footnote 2) might not be fully comparable to that used in other countries.

Turning first to the cross-national differences, we find that the three groups visible in the diagrams to the left are largely reduced to two. In Denmark, Norway, Sweden, the Netherlands, and Switzerland, small-scale democracy tends to function considerably better than in other countries as judged by this criterion of evaluation. The reasons why the remaining five perform worse remain distinct however. For Moldova, Romania, and Spain, the lower rate of activity, the higher level of dissatisfaction, and the weaker relationship between the two all contribute to the outcome. For Germany, the sole reason is the very low rate of activity.

If we consider the variation across the three realms, we find schools at the top with working life and healthcare worse off although for entirely different reasons. For working life, the outcome is mainly due to higher levels of dissatisfaction. This increases the amount of passive resignation primarily for those five countries in which dissatisfaction is less well channelled. For healthcare, by contrast, the outcome is largely due to lower overall rates of activity. This makes the distinction between the four countries at the top and those at the bottom somewhat less distinct in this case than in the others.[3]

Turning finally to the question of whether the overall rate of dissatisfaction can help us understand the overall rate of activity across countries and small-scale democracies, the answer is largely negative. While the two show some co-variation across countries, the relationship is weak and not statistically significant. The cross-national variation in activity levels is considerable whereas that in dissatisfaction is relatively modest. Similar observations can be made with regard to the comparison between the three realms.

The impact of perceived opportunities

While discontent constitutes a very important motive for participation in small-scale democracy, the subjective need to improve the situation, or prevent it from getting worse, may not suffice to bring about action if citizens do not perceive any opportunity to act. As described in the previous chapter, we therefore asked respondents to which extent they thought they had opportunities to influence a number of potentially important conditions within each domain.

As shown by the bivariate logistic functions in Figure 10.2, perceived opportunities – operationalised by the summary indices (one for each domain) introduced in the previous chapter[4] – do have a positive, and in many cases relatively strong, impact on the propensity to take action. Unlike discontent, however, opportunity fails to produce a statistically significant relationship in at least some cases: in Sweden, the Netherlands, Switzerland, and West Germany in the realm of child education, and in Denmark, Norway, Sweden, the Netherlands, Switzerland, and East Germany in the realm of healthcare.

A closer look reveals that the strength of the relationship shows a distinctive pattern across countries in this case as well, but that the pattern is in many ways the opposite of that observed in the previous section. The five countries with the highest level of participation, the highest conversion rate between dissatisfaction and action (in probabilistic rather than logistic terms) and the lowest amount of passive resignation tend to display a weaker relationship between opportunity and action than the others. For these five countries – Denmark, Norway, Sweden, the Netherlands, and Switzerland – the effect of opportunity also tends to be weaker than that of dissatisfaction whereas the opposite holds for Moldova, Romania, Slovenia, Portugal, and Spain. The five established democracies are thus closer to the normative ideal of furthering participation on the basis of subjectively felt needs. In the words of Dworkin (1981: 311), they are 'ambition sensitive' rather than 'endowment sensitive'.

Another noticeable tendency is that the relationships tend to be generally stronger in the domain of working life than in the other two spheres. In working life, both 'ambition' and 'endowment' matter a great deal. In the other two domains, the effect of 'endowment' is more restricted, particularly in the established democracies. Possibly, the welfare-state regimes of these countries help to put a lid on the participatory power of the well-endowed in the realm of child education and healthcare (cf. Verba *et al.* 1978).

As shown by the scatter plots in the rightmost half of Figure 10.2, perceived opportunities are also of somewhat greater help in understanding the cross-national variation in activity rates than is dissatisfaction. The correlations between the mean level of opportunities and the level of activity are generally higher in this case (although only the first two are

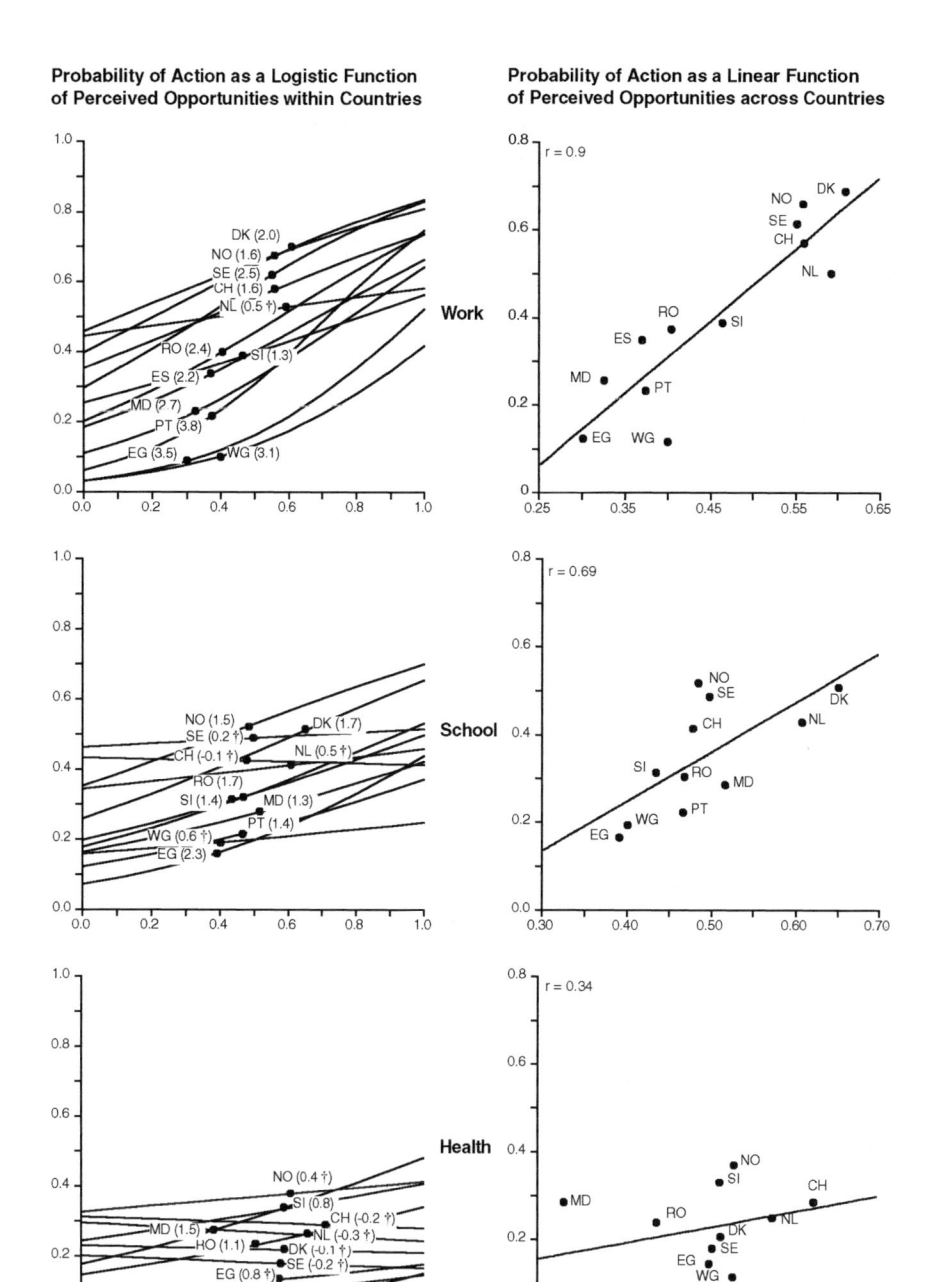

Figure 10.2 Action and perceived opportunities.[1]

Note
1 Figures in parentheses in the leftmost set of graphs are unstandardised, bivariate logistic regression coefficients. Figures followed by a † are not statistically significant at the 0.05-level. The dots indicate mean perceived opportunities along with the expected rate of activity at the mean.

statistically significant). Note in particular the low level of perceived opportunities for Germany in the realm of working life and child education, which provides at least a partial explanation for its remarkably low levels of activity.

At the same time, the curves for the individual-level relationships in the leftmost half of the diagram are far from perfectly coincident. This indicates that we remain quite some distance away from a perfect micro-level account of the cross-national variation in activity. Note also that a comparison of the level of perceived opportunities across the three small-scale democracies does not help us understand their varying degree of activity. If anything, the relationship is in this case contrary to the one we would expect.[5]

The impact of resources

Resources constitute the third and final element in the theory of action we try to test. According to that theory, neither dissatisfaction nor opportunities may suffice to bring about action unless the individual also has the requisite resources.

The relevant resources may be of many different kinds. In the multivariate models presented later in this chapter, we therefore include several types of resource measures. Initially, however, we restrict our attention to the kind of analytical, organisational and communication capabilities known as civic skills (Verba *et al.* 1995). Such skills – indexed by the extent to which respondents take part in decision-making, plan and organise meetings, make public presentations, and write documents as part of their work (four items) or associational life (four items)[6] – have already proven to be of considerable importance in research on political participation (see, for example, Verba *et al.* 1995 and Chapter 14 below) and we have every reason to conjecture that they are equally significant in the context of small-scale democracy. Furthermore, civic skills can for many purposes be regarded as one of the most proximate resource predictors, their magnitude being dependent, in turn, on causally prior resource types, for example, education and organisational involvement.

As shown by the results presented in Figure 10.3, the impact of civic skills closely resemble that of perceived opportunites. In the realm of working life, all relationships are positive and statistically significant at the 0.05 level. In the other two realms, there are some exceptions to the general rule: Denmark and West Germany in child education and Denmark, Norway, Slovenia, and Portugal in healthcare fail to pass the significance test. However, in all but one case (Norway in healthcare), the relationship remains positive.

As in the case of opportunities, the relationship tends to be stronger in the newer democracies than in the established ones. If anything, this is seen with even greater clarity as we turn from the 'subjective resources'

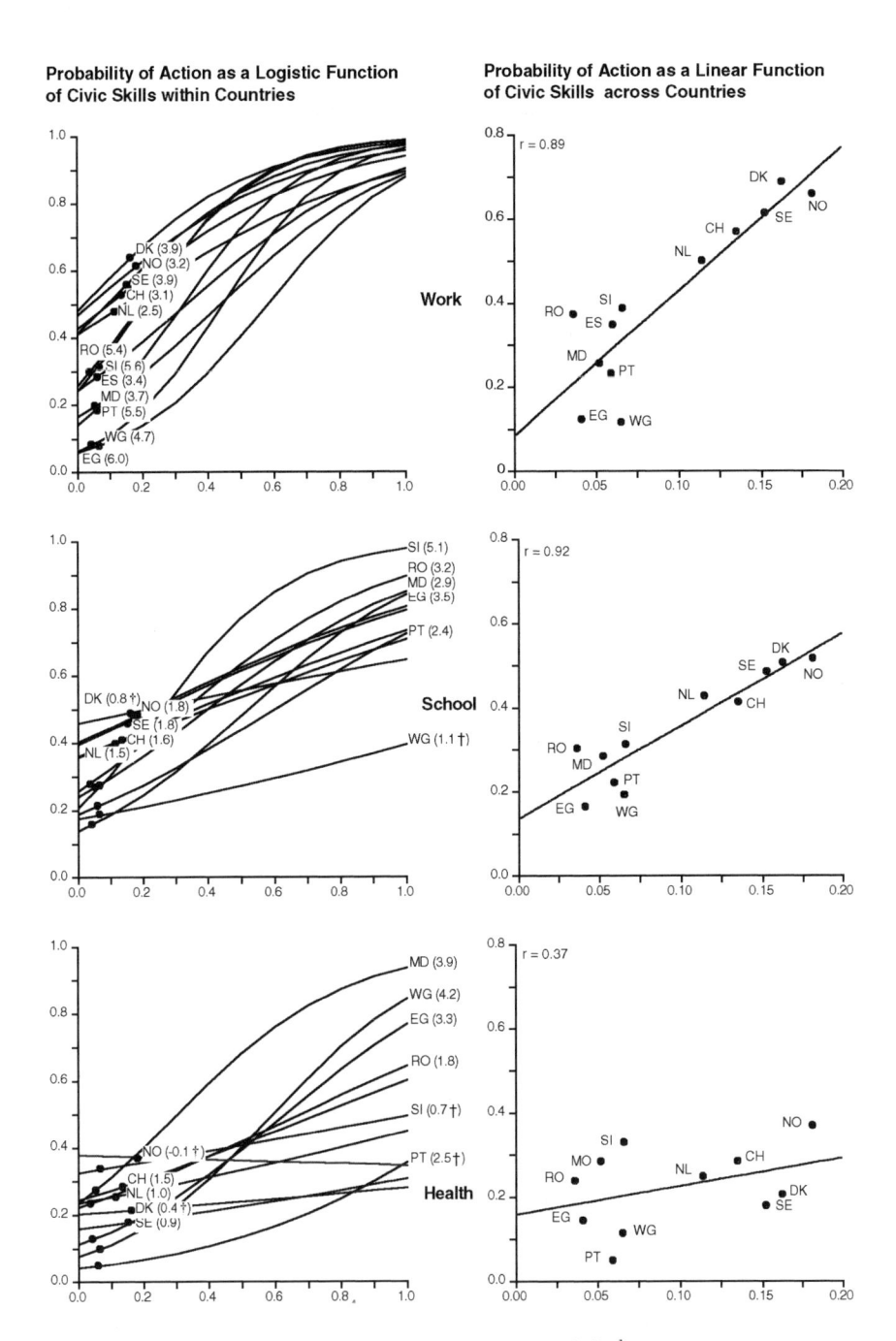

Figure 10.3 Action and resources in the form of civic skills.[1]

Note
1 Figures in parentheses in the leftmost set of graphs are unstandardised, bivariate logistic regression coefficients. Figures followed by a † are not statistically significant at the 0.05-level. The dots indicate mean resources in the form of civic skills along with the expected rate of activity at the mean.

provided by perceived opportunities to the objective ones provided by civic skills. Note that as we approach the maximum level of the skills variable, the predicted values for the newer democracies reach those of the established ones in the domain of working life and tend to surpass them in the other two domains.

With respect to the comparisons across domains as well as the aggregate comparisons across countries, the results largely echo those for perceived opportunities. The individual-level effect tends to be generally stronger in working life than in the other two domains, and the effects, along with the cross-national variation in the magnitude of civic skills, provide at least some help in accounting for the cross-national variation in the dependent variable.

Combined additive models: working life

Let us now consider how the three types of determinants that we have so far considered separately combine when we put them in a multivariate framework. Table 10.1 presents combined models for working life based on the additive logic. Our modelling efforts proceed in several steps. We begin with a model (model 1) based solely on social position as indexed by gender, age, and education.[7]

To that model we then add two resource predictors – general and domain-specific organisational involvement, respectively – that may depend on social position but can be considered causally prior to the triad of factors examined in prior sections. General organisational involvement offers an opportunity to practice civic skills but may also promote attempts to exercise influence in a variety of other ways.[8] Involvement in an organisation within the particular domain – trade unions in the case of working life – may provide individuals with more targeted information and support.[9]

The three predictors previously introduced – discontent, perceived opportunities, and civic skills – are added in a third step which gives us our complete model (model 2). As a final step we include a measure, participation in large-scale democracy – or political participation – whose exogeneity with respect to our dependent variable is less than perfectly clear, but whose potential impact we would nevertheless like to consider.

The table presents unstandardised logistic regression coefficients, levels of significance and a pseudo-R^2 for each country. In terms of presentation order, the countries are divided into two groups based on the length of their democratic history, each of which further subdivided based on geographic proximity (which in turn is consequential for similarities in terms of history and culture). From left to right, we thus have Scandinavia (Denmark, Norway Sweden), central Europe (Switzerland, Netherlands, and West Germany), eastern Europe (East Germany, Moldova, Romania, Slovenia), and the Iberian Peninsula (Spain and Portugal). The pooled

Table 10.1 Predicting action in working life (multivariate logistic regression)[a]

Model and predictor	DK	NO	SE	CH	NL	WG	EG	MD	RO	SI	ES	PT	Pooled
Model 1													
Constant	−2.9**	−2.8**	−3.0**	−2.2**	−3.2**	−4.2**	−6.8**	−4.0**	−2.9**	−1.1	−2.5**	−2.7**	–[b]
Gender (female)	0.1	−0.2	−0.2	−0.3**	−0.4**	−0.2	−0.1	−0.1	−0.1	−0.5**	−0.5**	−0.9**	−0.3**
Age	8.4**	16.7**	9.6**	9.4**	9.4**	6.2	10.0	7.7	−2.9	0.4	8.7**	3.0	7.8**
Age squared	−9.7**	−18.9**	−9.9**	−14.3**	−10.8**	−10.4	−7.3	−9.4	6.6	−2.4	−12.7**	−4.5	−9.7**
Education	3.6**	0.4	2.8**	2.8**	2.9**	2.9**	3.7**	2.8**	4.8**	2.3**	1.3**	4.0**	2.2**
Pseudo-R^2	0.041	0.015	0.028	0.045	0.038	0.038	0.053	0.023	0.071	0.052	0.028	0.083	0.150
Additions to model 1													
Trade union	0.4*	0.6***	0.4	0.2	0.7**	0.0	−0.4	−0.0	0.1	−0.0	0.5*	0.3	0.4**
Org. involvement	2.7**	3.9**	4.8**	3.0**	4.0**	6.1**	10.9**	10.0**	16.2**	4.7	10.8**	11.1**	5.4**
Model 2													
Constant	−2.2**	−2.5**	−1.8	−1.9**	−4.3**	−3.8**	−9.3**	−4.2**	−3.2**	−0.9	−2.2**	−2.2**	–[b]
Gender (female)	0.1	0.0	−0.2	−0.2	−0.2	−0.0	−0.0	−0.1	−0.2	−0.3	−0.4**	−0.7**	−0.1**
Age	0.5	7.1*	−3.5	0.1	9.0**	−2.4	7.4	5.6	−3.9	−5.1	2.9	−5.3	0.7
Age squared	−1.3	−8.9**	4.2	−3.1	−11.6**	−0.1	−2.9	−7.6	6.5	3.3	−7.4	5.2	−2.2
Education	1.4**	−1.4**	0.2	0.9	1.5**	0.1	2.2	0.7	2.2**	1.1**	−0.4	2.0**	0.5**
Trade union	0.5*	0.6**	0.5*	0.2	0.6**	−0.0	−0.8	−0.3	0.4	0.4	0.5*	0.3	0.4**
Org. involvement	−1.1	2.0	0.1	1.4	2.5	1.9	7.5	5.5	5.2	−0.3	6.9**	4.5	1.9**
Civic skills	3.1**	2.7**	2.6**	2.0**	1.5**	4.6**	2.5	2.4**	3.5**	5.3**	2.4**	2.6**	2.7**
Opportunities	1.1**	1.4**	2.1**	1.4**	0.7	1.2**	3.3**	1.9**	2.0**	0.4	1.7**	2.8**	1.6**
Dissatisfaction	1.9**	2.4**	2.6**	3.1**	3.4**	3.5**	4.1**	1.5**	1.9**	1.8**	1.7**	0.7	2.3**
Pseudo-R^2	0.139	0.128	0.174	0.170	0.205	0.218	0.306	0.140	0.206	0.139	0.146	0.202	0.255
Additions to model 2													
Pol. participation	2.5**	2.7**	2.3**	1.8**	3.8**	2.0**	0.2	1.6	0.8	3.3**	1.9**	2.7**	2.2**
Minimal N	949	1,198	712	892	766	762	380	398	361	426	1,446	490	8,780

Notes
a Entries are unstandardised logistic regression coefficients. Levels of statistical significance: ** = 0.05, * = 0.1.
b The pooled models include a separate intercept for each country.

analyses in the rightmost column provides a summary of the general pattern for all the country-specific samples combined. These analyses include a separate intercept for each country so that the variance analysed is that within countries only.

Since all predictors are scored so as to range from zero to one (save for age which is number of years divided by 100), the unstandardised logit coefficients express the expected change in the log odds of the dependent variable as we move from the minimum to the maximum value that each predictor might take on. The coefficients are in that specific sense fully comparable across predictors.

Note, however, that the amount of variation actually observed for our particular samples and operationalisations may differ significantly from one predictor to another in spite of the fact that logical extremes of the scale (zero and one) are the same. Consequently, there is no one-to-one correspondence between the magnitude of the coefficients and the extent to which they are statistically significant or contribute to the variance explained.

Model 1 shows how action is distributed across three social cleavage lines: gender, age, and education. As expected, women are somewhat less likely than men to voice their concerns at work but the difference is generally slight. It reaches statistical significance in only five of 12 countries, headed by Portugal, Spain, and Slovenia. Age differences are somewhat more clearly marked. The positive coefficients for age combined with the negative coefficients for age-squared imply that the curve has the familiar bow-shaped form, peaking among the middle-aged. The coefficients for the pooled sample indicate that the top is reached at an age of about 40 years when level of education (and gender) is held constant. This result strongly suggests that the pattern is primarily due to life-cycle rather than generational effects. Cross-nationally, the relationship tends to be somewhat stronger in the five countries in the leftmost part of the table, that is, Denmark, Norway, Sweden, Switzerland, and the Netherlands. In all five cases, the coefficient for age is above, and that for age-squared below, the estimates for the pooled sample. The effect of education, finally, is fairly strong everywhere except in Norway. While the coefficients for age may at first look more impressive than those for education, one must keep in mind that the two age coefficients (age and age-squared) have opposite signs so that the net age differences are in fact less pronounced than their educational counterparts.

Additions to model 1 in the form of domain-specific (trade unions) as well as more general organisational involvement show that both types of resources contribute perceptibly to our ability to predict action. The results also show, however, that general involvement is a considerably stronger predictor than its domain-specific counterpart (although one must keep in mind here that the trade union measure has greater variance). The cross-national pattern reveals interesting differences as well. Among the newer democracies in the rightmost part of the table, the effect of union involvement is virtually nil (Spain and Portugal excepted) but the effect of general organisational involvement very pronounced. As we move to the five countries in the leftmost part, the effect of union involvement increases while that of general involvement declines. We will soon find reason to return to the mechanisms behind this pattern.

Model 2 adds the three predictors that we have already considered on a bivariate basis: dissatisfaction, perceived opportunities, and resources as indexed by civic skills. Let us note to begin with that all three have a considerable effect even in a multivariate framework. The 36 coefficients have the expected sign in all cases and all but five are statistically significant at the 0.05 level. Furthermore, the impact is strong enough to be of substantive importance in virtually all instances.

Note also that many of the measures that we entered in model 1 now show far weaker effects than they originally did. If we look at the model 2 estimates for the pooled sample in the rightmost column of the table, we can see that the age differences have all but disappeared, that less than one quarter of the educational effect remains, and that the impact of general organisational involvement is reduced to about one third. This shows that a large proportion of the effect of these variables is mediated by the three proximate causes on which we focused in our bivariate analyses.

One notable exception to this pattern, however, is domain-specific resources in the form of union involvement. In this particular case, the effect remains more or less unchanged. This indicates that the impact of being unionised is not mediated by individual characteristics like civic skills, opportunities or dissatisfaction but by furthering the ability to act collectively through the channels provided by the union. The fact that the effect tends to be more visible in countries with relatively strong unions support such an interpretation.

Turning finally to the cross-national differences in the impact of dissatisfaction, perceived opportunities and resources, the results largely confirm those obtained on a bivariate basis. The effect of discontent tends to be highest in the seven countries in the leftmost part of the table. By contrast, the combined impact of perceived opportunities and resources (other than the domain-specific ones), tends to be highest in the seven countries in the rightmost part. This reinforces the picture previously obtained. The older democracies are more ambition sensitive whereas the newer ones are more endowment sensitive.

The addition to model 2 in the form of political participation shows that there is a significant relationship between participation in large- and small-scale democracy even with many significant predictors of small-scale action held constant. The coefficient has the expected sign in every country and is statistically as well as substantively significant in nearly all cases. In view of the difficulties we face when we try to establish the causal direction between the two types of action, we cannot conclude with certainty that the one causes the other. Rather, the results show that we cannot at present reject the claim that political participation increases the propensity to take action in the small-scale setting of working life.

Before we consider how the multivariate results for working life compare with those for child education and healthcare, we would like to examine in somewhat greater detail how our model works across different types of action. As indicated in the previous chapter, where the descriptive contours of our dependent variable are presented, we have the opportunity to distinguish between many different types of initiatives. Based on Hirschman's (1970) well-known distinction, these can be grouped under two major headings: voice and exit. Voice, in turn, may be individual or collective. If someone turns to the boss with a request, we take it as an indication of individual voice. If someone turns to his or her coworkers for help, we take it as an indication of collective voice. If someone tried to change jobs, we take it as indication of exit.

As discussed in the previous chapter, there are many other steps people can take in their attempts to control their personal situation (e.g. turning to government agencies, politicians or the media). Here, however, we will only consider the three significant options indicated, each of which representing one more general class of actions: turning to the boss (individual voice), turning to coworkers (collective voice), and change jobs (exit). Obviously, these are not mutually exclusive alternatives. A certain respondent may have taken all three courses of action and our questionnaire allowed him or her to indicate that such was the case.

Since discriminating between different types of action entails a loss of variance in the dependent variable (i.e. fewer instances of action of any specific kind), it becomes more difficult to distinguish cross-national variations with much reliability. In this particular case, we therefore present the results for the pooled sample only. Table 10.2 shows the impact of all measures included in model 2 for each specific type of action as well as for the generic action measure used in Table 10.1.

We also include two additional types of resource – supervisory position and strength of domain-specific networks – which are available for working life only (and therefore not employed in Table 10.1, where we try to maintain full comparability with the results for child education and healthcare presented below).[10] These two types of resources are of particular interest in the present context since their importance is likely to vary with the type of action chosen. A supervisory position at the place of work is likely to enhance the prospects of individual voice but less likely to promote collective voice and exit. A strong social network at the workplace should facilitate collective voice. However, it may also encourage individuals to speak up on their own even when the network is not explicitly mobilised. By contrast, strong social ties at the place of work is unlikely to facilitate exit.

The results reveal that our three most proximate causes – dissatisfaction, perceived opportunities, and civic skills – strike with roughly similar

Table 10.2 Predicting specific types of action in working life (multivariate logistic regression)[a]

Predictor	Any action	Talk to boss	Turn to co-workers	Change jobs
Gender (female)	−0.2**	−0.1**	0.0	0.0
Age	0.8	1.9	1.9	3.3
Age squared	−2.1	−3.9*	−3.7*	−8.5
Education	0.3*	0.2	0.9**	1.1**
Supervisory position	0.2**	0.2**	−0.0	−0.0
Strength of workplace network	1.3**	1.4**	1.8**	0.1
Involvement in trade union	0.4**	0.2**	0.3**	−0.4
Organisational involvement	2.5**	2.7**	2.8**	−0.2
Civic skills	2.1**	1.6**	1.3**	1.2**
Perceived opportunities	1.6**	1.4**	0.8**	1.0**
Dissatisfaction	2.4**	2.1**	2.0**	1.7**
Pseudo-R^2	0.264	0.254	0.207	0.135

Note

a Entries are unstandardised logistic regression coefficients. All models include a separate intercept for each country. In the model predicting change of job, the general index for perceived opportunities is replaced by a single item specifically asking about the perceived opportunities to change to another employer. The effect of the general index is statistically insignificant once this specific item is included separately. Levels of statistical significance: ** = 0.05, * = 0.1. N equals 7,561 (change jobs) or 7,813 (all other models). The Danish data are not included in this analysis since they do not provide a measure of the strength of workplace networks.

force across the three different types of action. The age pattern is also rather similar. In other respects, however, noticeable differences emerge. Four of the resource measures – supervisory position, trade-union involvement, general organisational involvement, and strength of workplace networks – have a positive impact on individual and (with one exception) collective voice but none on exit. If anything, respondents with a high level of organisational involvement are less likely to opt for exit (i.e. the coefficients for the organisational indicators are negative rather than positive, albeit not significantly different from zero). In addition, the small gender difference is visible only with respect to the propensity to talk to the boss while the direct effect of education is largely confined to the two more demanding (and therefore much less frequent) types of action: that of seeking help from coworkers and that of changing jobs.

Combined additive models: child education and healthcare

Let us now consider the extent to which the results for working life can be generalised to the domains of child education and healthcare. Tables 10.3 and 10.4 present findings for the latter two domains comparable to those presented in Table 10.1 for working life. Turning first to the general

Table 10.3 Predicting action in child education (multivariate logistic regression)[a]

Model and predictor	DK	NO	SE	CH	NL	WG	EG	MD	RO	SI	PT	Pooled
Model 1												
Constant	−2.5	−7.5**	3.8	−5.5**	−4.0	−7.7**	−6.4	−2.3*	2.2	−6.9*	−11.0**	−[b]
Gender (female)	0.3	0.1	0.3	0.2	0.5**	0.2	0.8	−0.0	0.2	−0.0	0.1	0.2**
Age	3.8	30.0**	−23.3	18.4	8.6	29.1	−0.7	−2.0	−0.1	26.2	45.0**	8.7**
Age squared	−4.7	−33.3**	23.1	−20.5	−5.3	−35.0	9.3	2.1	−0.4	−33.9	−57.3**	−9.4**
Education	3.0**	1.8**	3.0**	2.3**	1.5**	0.4	5.8**	3.6**	3.0**	2.6**	2.1**	2.3**
Pseudo-R^2	0.027	0.023	0.037	0.021	0.026	0.011	0.127	0.027	0.028	0.061	0.047	0.071
Additions to model 1												
Parent organisation	0.2	0.7*	0.8*	−0.0	0.4	0.7	−0.3	0.9	0.9	4.1**	0.8	0.6**
Org. involvement	1.0	4.3**	3.9	1.8	4.9**	8.0**	15.0**	10.8**	8.0	7.6	10.7**	4.2**
Model 2												
Constant	−2.4	−7.5**	4.0	−8.0**	−4.9*	−6.5	−18.3**	−3.3**	−1.8	−9.1*	−11.3**	−[b]
Gender (female)	0.4	0.1	0.3	0.2	0.6**	0.2	0.6	0.1	0.4	0.3	0.3	0.3**
Age	−7.1	20.0	−30.2	27.6**	1.7	15.1	34.2	−1.3	−3.7	19.2	40.7*	3.7
Age squared	6.9	−22.3	31.8	−31.8**	1.8	19.1	−22.5	1.7	2.7	−23.0	−53.3**	−4.0
Education	2.1**	1.4**	1.1	0.9	0.7	0.7	4.4**	2.1	0.5	2.9**	2.3**	1.5**
Parent organisation	0.1	0.5	1.1**	0.0	0.7	0.6	0.2	0.7	0.7	5.2**	0.9	0.5**
Org. involvement	2.0	4.1**	2.0	0.7	4.2**	8.8**	9.4	10.2	4.9	−3.9	10.9**	3.5**
Civic skills	0.5	1.1**	1.4**	1.4**	1.3**	−0.6	1.2	0.9	1.4	2.6	−0.9	1.0**
Opportunities	2.1**	2.0**	0.4	0.4	1.4	−0.2	0.8	1.0*	1.6**	2.7**	0.8	1.3**
Dissatisfaction	2.9**	2.3**	3.7**	3.0**	4.1**	3.7**	7.4**	1.6**	1.7**	5.3**	2.4**	2.9**
Pseudo-R^2	0.170	0.115	0.243	0.139	0.273	0.170	0.442	0.106	0.108	0.311	0.163	0.192
Additions to model 2												
Pol. participation	4.1**	0.9	3.8**	3.2**	1.5	4.8**	9.4**	3.0**	2.2	3.9	2.6	2.5**
Minimal N	393	555	228	293	397	273	169	375	282	176	228	3,369

Notes
a Entries are unstandardised logistic regression coefficients. Levels of statistical significance: ** = 0.05, * = 0.1.
b The pooled models include a separate intercept for each country.

Table 10.4 Predicting action in healthcare (multivariate logistic regression)[a]

Model and predictor	DK	NO	SE	CH	NL	WG	EG	MD	RO	SI	PT	Pooled
Model 1												
Constant	−3.0**	−1.3**	−5.3**	−1.6**	−2.1**	−2.9**	−1.6	−2.8**	−2.1**	−1.5**	−6.4**	−[b]
Gender (female)	0.3**	0.3**	0.7**	0.1	0.0	0.2	−0.3	0.1	0.1	0.0	0.5	0.2**
Age	4.6	4.4**	14.0**	3.4	3.1	0.4	−4.2	3.2	0.6	4.6*	12.7	4.8**
Age squared	−4.3	−3.7	−13.6**	−4.4*	−4.2	−1.5	2.1	−3.4	−1.6	−5.3**	−13.6	−5.3**
Education	0.8	−0.9**	0.2	0.4	1.3**	1.7**	2.7**	2.5**	2.5**	0.1	1.5	0.6**
Pseudo-R^2	0.009	0.011	0.041	0.008	0.014	0.021	0.050	0.029	0.044	0.006	0.018	0.060
Additions to model 1												
Patient organisation	0.7**	0.6*	0.4	1.0**	0.9**	0.9*	1.0	–	–	0.9	–	0.8**
Org. involvement	0.1	2.8**	3.0**	0.9	4.0**	9.6**	6.8**	7.5**	4.8	1.8	9.0**	2.8**
Model 2												
Constant	−4.4**	−2.7**	−7.4**	−2.3**	−4.1**	−4.4**	−2.6*	−3.6**	−3.9**	−2.5**	−5.4**	−[b]
Gender (female)	0.2	0.2*	0.7**	0.2	0.0	0.5*	−0.3	0.1	0.1	0.0	0.6	0.2**
Age	5.9**	4.5*	15.2**	2.3	2.9	−3.4	−6.8	3.6	2.4	4.7**	6.2	4.6**
Age squared	−5.4	−3.5	−14.7**	−2.7	−4.0	2.8	4.7	−3.2	−3.3	−5.3**	−6.6	−4.9**
Education	1.0	−1.0**	−0.3	0.0	0.9	0.4	1.7*	1.5	2.6**	0.1	−0.4	0.4**
Patient organisation	0.6*	0.6	0.5	1.2**	0.8*	1.0*	1.3*	–	–	0.9	–	0.8**
Org. involvement	−0.6	3.1**	4.0**	−0.6	4.7**	7.3**	4.5	2.7	5.2	2.3	5.5	2.4**
Civic skills	0.2	−0.5	0.2	1.0**	−0.3	3.3**	1.8	2.5**	−0.3	−0.1	1.4	0.2
Opportunities	0.5	1.0**	1.0**	0.3	1.1**	1.3**	1.4**	1.3**	1.4**	1.1**	1.5	1.1**
Dissatisfaction	2.1**	1.9**	2.9**	2.0**	2.8**	2.9**	2.6**	0.6	1.2**	1.0**	−0.2	2.0**
Pseudo-R^2	0.092	0.068	0.175	0.079	0.156	0.158	0.162	0.077	0.093	0.022	0.059	0.125
Additions to model 2												
Pol. participation	1.6**	0.9**	4.6**	2.4**	1.2*	0.1	1.9*	2.8**	3.4**	2.1**	4.8**	2.0**
Minimal N	936	1,240	975	1,109	950	978	540	345	493	722	391	8,679

Notes

a Entries are unstandardised logistic regression coefficients. Levels of statistical significance: ** = 0.05, * = 0.1.
b The pooled models include a separate intercept for each country.

patterns for all countries combined, the pooled estimates in the rightmost column reveal three broad lines of similarity across all three domains.

First, nearly all measures have a statistically significant impact and the size of that impact does not differ very much by domain. The only partial exceptions from this rule are age, where the effect drops to insignificance in model 2 for child education as well as working life, and education plus civic skills, where the effect is noticeably weaker in the realm of healthcare than in the other two domains.

Second, the direction of the impact is also the same in all but one instance. The one exception is gender. While women are slightly less likely to take action in working life, they are slightly more likely to do so in the domains of child education and healthcare. Traces of the traditional division of labour between men and women thus remain visible, but only weakly so.

Third, the three most proximate causes – dissatisfaction, perceived opportunities, and civic skills – mediate the effect of the more distant ones to at least some extent. In working life, they do so to a very large extent with but one exception: domain-specific organisational involvement. In the other two domains this exception extends to gender. Furthermore, the extent to which the effect of age, education, and general organisational involvement is mediated by more proximate causes is generally lower.

The pattern of cross-national differences also displays several important similarities across domains. In all three areas, dissatisfaction tends to have a stronger impact in the five more established democracies in the leftmost part of the table and East and West Germany in the middle than in the five less-established democracies to the right. With respect to the combined impact of perceived opportunities and resources (other than the domain-specific ones), it is the other way around. The seven countries in the rightmost part of the table tend to show stronger effects than the five to the left. In the realm of child education, however, this pattern is somewhat less visible in the multivariate coefficients than it was in our bivariate graphs.

Combined multiplicative models

In our introductory section, we noted that the theoretical literature on social-movements has paid considerable attention to the way in which discontent, resources, and opportunities combine into collective action. The theoretically dominant hypothesis is that the effect depends on the product rather than the sum of the three components. The impact of each factor should be stronger if the others take on high values than if not. As a final step, we therefore test if the additive approach on which our empirical analyses hitherto rest needs to be revised along the lines suggested by social-movement theory. More specifically, we examine whether the predictive power of our three key factors – dissatisfaction, perceived opportunities, and resources (as indexed by civic skills) – can be improved by moving to a multiplicative framework.

An appropriate way of testing for that possibility is to add interaction effects in the form of products to the logistic regressions previously employed. Each such product is by definition highly correlated with the variables from which the product is formed, which in turn imply problems of multicollinearity. This problem is compounded by the fact that we would like to enter several products simultaneously (one for each pair of factors plus one for all three combined) and also that the samples at our disposal are of rather limited size. We are therefore forced to restrict our test of the multiplicative theory to the pooled sample.

For each domain and variable combination, we can form one product. This gives us four products per domain: DO (dissatisfaction × opportunity), DS (dissatisfaction × skills), OS (opportunity × skills), and DOS (dissatisfaction × opportunity × skills). We then entered these products into the logistic regressions for model 2 in Tables 10.1, 10.3 and 10.4.

The results are largely negative and we therefore abstain from presenting them in numerical detail but only describe the sequence of analyses whereby we arrived at our general conclusion. Already our first step, in which we entered each interaction term separately without the others, indicated that little in the way of a systematic pattern could be discerned. If the multiplicative logic suggested by social-movement theory were correct, the interaction effects should generally be positive. Our initial results, however, returned as many negative as positive coefficients. In working life, DS was positive, OS negative and the other two statistically insignificant (at the 0.05-level, two-sided test). In child education, DO and DOS were both negative and the others statistically insignificant. In healthcare, DS and DOS were both positive and the others statistically insignificant. Additional, more correct but also – with an eye to multicollinearity – more demanding tests, in which we included a) all three two-way interactions and b) all four interactions simultaneously did nothing to resolve the unsystematic pattern first revealed. Furthermore, those effects that passed the criterion of statistical significance were typically just beyond the border in spite of the large sample size obtained by pooling all countries. Consequently, while we cannot rule out the possibility that there are some interaction effects between our key predictors, we can say with some confidence that there is no general pattern of the kind expected on the basis of social-movement theory.

Conclusions

In this chapter, we have tried to model the determinants of the initiatives taken by citizens in order to influence their personal situation in three important domains: working life, child education, and healthcare. At the outset, we conjectured that the three components identified as crucial predictors by the literature on large-scale social movements, and partly by that on political participation as well, would further our understanding of the less well-charted terrain of small-scale democracy. That conjecture is generally vindicated by our analyses. In all three domains, dissatisfaction, perceived opportunities, and objective resources contribute significantly to our understanding of why citizens choose to take action in order to control their own situation.

In another important respect, however, the conjectures we borrow from social-movement theory fare less well. The theory posits that the three components combine in a multiplicative fashion. We therefore tried two different logics – the additive logic of facilitating conditions, and the multiplicative logic of necessary conditions posited by social movement theory. While our additive models confirmed the importance of all three components, we could not confirm the relevance of the multiplicative logic. In the final analysis, the additive logic of facilitating conditions turns out to be more adequate for modelling the impact of dissatisfaction, opportunity and resources on the probability of taking action in small-scale democracy. No systematic evidence of interactions that fit the pattern suggested by social-movement theory could be found in these data.

In an attempt to further specify the impact of the three components, we examined in one domain (working life) how their effect varied depending on the type of action taken: individual voice, collective voice, or exit. Our findings show that several of the resources we consider – organisational involvement inside as well as outside the domain, domain-specific networks and domain-specific status – are important with respect to voice but not exit. This squares nicely with theoretical expectations and helps corroborate the causal assumptions on which our models rest.

With respect to the domain of working life, we also found that the three predictors we consider to be most causally proximate to the dependent variable – dissatisfaction, perceived opportunities, and resources as indexed by civic skills – mediate much of the effect of social position as well as that of more causally distant resource indicators. While there is some evidence of such mediation in the domains of child education and healthcare as well, it is clearly less pronounced than in the case of working life.

In general, our three-component model fares better in the realm of working life and child education than in healthcare, where the impact of some resource indicators as well as perceived opportunities tend to be less pronounced. One conceivable explanation is that the domain of healthcare provides a tighter 'institutional lid' (in the form of strict regulations and professional judgements) that limits the impact of individual endowments evidenced in the other two domains.

Our results with respect to the first of the three components, dissatisfaction, deserve special emphasis on several grounds. Although discontent has received less attention in later versions of social-movement theory than in the classical approach, and although it has never been prominent (as conceived here) in individual-level research on political participation, it has a pronounced impact on the propensity to take action in small-scale democracy.

Whether this is due to a substantive difference between various forms of participation or merely to the way they have hitherto been analysed is obviously hard to tell at this point. What is clear, however, is that the strong relationship between dissatisfaction and action is welcome from a normative point of view. It implies that participation in small-scale democracy depends on the subjectively felt needs of citizens. In Dworkin's (1981: 311) terminology, it is 'ambition sensitive' rather than merely 'endowment sensitive'.

Our most significant finding as far as country differences are concerned is that the degree of ambition sensitivity follows a specific cross-national pattern. Characteristic of the five established democracies of Denmark, Norway, Sweden, Switzerland, and the Netherlands is their greater openness for small-scale action. In these countries, where relevant opportunities and resources are relatively abundant, the propensity to take action depends strongly on the amount of dissatisfaction. In the new democracies of southern and eastern Europe, where citizens generally see fewer opportunities and are less resourceful, action is more dependent on capacity and less on subjectively felt needs.

One country, or pair of countries, that is, the eastern and western parts of Germany, do not fit neatly in either category. Germany resembles the first group of countries in that the impact of dissatisfaction is high and the second in that the effect of opportunities and resources is also high. In a third respect, the overall rate of activity, Germany is more or less *sui generis*. The propensity of Germans to take action within our three domains of small-scale democracy is with one partial exception (Portugal in healthcare) lower than for residents of any other country. Compared to countries like Denmark, Norway, Sweden, Switzerland, and the Netherlands, it is far lower.

To some extent, our findings do contribute to our understanding of why such is the case. For example, Germans are considerably more pessimistic about their opportunities to have a say about their personal situation than are citizens of the five countries just mentioned. They also exercise civic skills far less frequently. At the same time it is perfectly obvious that these explanations are insufficient in at least two respects. First, Germany remains clearly below the expected level even when these two factors, as well as all others examined in this chapter, are taken into account. Second, the rather low scores on perceived opportunities and civic skills, merely beg the question of why, after more than 50 years of democracy and prosperous economic development, western Germany does not distinguish itself from the new democracies in eastern and southern Europe.

Furthermore, the generality of our findings imply that the phenomenon cannot be explained by conditions peculiar to a particular domain. We cannot, for example, invoke the fact that Germany has an especially elaborate systems of co-decision-making ('Mitbestimmung') at the workplace, not only because this would seem likely to promote rather than inhibit the type of activities we have studied but also because the picture is essentially the same in child education and healthcare.[11] The German case thus remains an unresolved puzzle. We are pleased to note in conclusion, however, that in this regard it constitutes an exception rather than a norm.

Notes

1 We should note here that the Portuguese and Slovenian dissatisfaction measures may not be fully comparable to those of other countries. The coefficients for these two countries should therefore be regarded with caution.
2 We have of course checked the question wording of the activity questions for the German case but have not found any reason to suspect problems of comparability.
3 It might at first be suspected that the results in the rightmost half of Figure 10.1 are sensitive to the exact way in which dissatisfaction is dichotomised. We therefore computed a dissatisfaction-passivity-score (DPS) that bypasses this complication. The DPS is simply the product of dissatisfaction (scored 0–1) and passivity (scored 1 for the passive and 0 for the active). The mean DPS-levels confirm the percentage-based pattern in Figure 10.1 in all vital respects.
4 With one exception (the 'change jobs' model in Table 10.4 below; see table note) we rely throughout on the overall index of perceived opportunities in each domain, i.e. the one that includes perceived opportunities with regard to voice as well as exit.
5 Comparisons of perceived opportunities across domains are complicated by the fact that the indicators are (and to some extent must be) domain-specific (see the previous chapter for details). On the other hand, the indicators have been carefully chosen in order to provide as comprehensive a picture as possible of the aspects we deem likely to be most important in each particular domain.
6 The measure we use is the mean of the two indices tapping civic skills practiced at work and in associational life. Respondents who were not gainfully employed or not active in any organisation, and consequently not asked about their activities in either area, are scored zero on the respective index.
7 Education is measured as the number of years of full-time education with the few respondents who report more than 25 years, coded 25. For Slovenia, where years of education are not available, education is measured by six discrete levels. Both measures were eventually scored to range from 0 to 1.
8 General organisational involvement is indexed by the total number of associational types (see Chapter 6, this volume) in which the respondent is a member and the total number of associational types in which he or she is active. Membership and activity are the crucial determinants as far as action in small-scale democracy is concerned. The index we use has greater predictive power than one based on a count of all four indicators of involvement that we have at our disposal (membership, activity, volunteer work, and donations).

9 For working life, domain-specific organisational involvement is indexed by membership and activity in trade unions. For the domains of child education and healthcare, it is indexed by membership and activity in parent and patient organisations, respectively.
10 A supervisory position is operationalised as a dichotomy indicating whether or not the respondent has a supervisory position at his or her place of work. Domain-specific social networks is operationalised by means of three items indexing the extent to which the respondent and his or her co-workers help each other with practical matters outside working life, visit each other privately, and talk about problems at the workplace.
11 It might be argued that the German system of co-decision-making makes employees less dependent on their own personal initiatives for resolving problems at the workplace since they already have representatives acting on their behalf. On the other hand, these representatives provide a channel through which individual employees can act as well as a source of potential support for initiatives taken through other channels. Furthermore, several other countries, e.g. the Scandinavian ones, have systems of co-decision-making similar to that in Germany but nevertheless display very high activity levels.

11 Small-scale democracy
The consequences of action

Anders Westholm and Emanuel von Erlach

Introduction

The first of the preceding two chapters describes the elements of small-scale democracy covered by our research design. The second examines the interrelationship between these elements in an attempt to explain why people do or do not take action in order to influence their personal situation. These two chapters, however, intentionally leave some significant descriptive as well as explanatory questions unanswered. The purpose of this third, and final, chapter on small-scale democracy is to tie up these loose ends, a common denominator of which is that they call attention to the consequences of the actions citizens take in their attempts to exercise influence.

More specifically, we will consider these consequences from five different points of view. First, actions have outcomes. People succeed or fail in their efforts to accomplish what they want. When we consider, as we did in the previous chapter, why people take action, we are thus examining a condition which is often necessary but rarely sufficient for the exercise of power. Consequently, we have reasons to extend previous analyses by asking whether and why some people are more successful than others in having the system respond to their requests.

Second, previous analyses of how small-scale democracy operates in a Scandinavian context – such as those of Petersson *et al.* (1989) and Andersen and Hoff (2001) – have called attention to the potential feedback of the experiences citizens make in their attempts to exercise influence. The general premise of such feedback is that citizens learn from their encounters with the public institutions and private organisations whose decisions shape their lives. A responsive system is likely to strengthen citizens' perceptions that they do have opportunities to exercise influence whereas an unresponsive one is likely to have the opposite effect. As shown in the previous chapter, the extent to which citizens feel they have opportunities to influence is in turn an important determinant of their propensity to take action. Consequently, exogenous changes in system responsiveness may potentially generate positive spirals of empowerment or negative ones of alienation.

In this chapter, we will extend the analysis of such feedback mechanisms to a much broader cross-national setting than that provided by earlier Scandinavian studies. However, we will widen the scope in a more theoretical respect as well. The initiatives a citizen takes give rise to an outcome but also to a process. Regardless of whether citizens ultimately succeed or fail to accomplish what they want, the process allows them to form an impression of whether or not they got a fair hearing. The possibility that the feedback effect is based not only on the direction of the outcome but also on the quality of the process obviously merits investigation. This is so not only because we have positive reasons to expect the impact of the latter to be at least as significant as the former but also because of the normative implications for institutional design. Consequently, we have double incentives to take proper account of both factors.

Third, prior studies of small-scale democracy in Scandinavia examine but one potential target of feedback effects: the citizens' perceptions of their opportunities to exercise influence. We find it motivated to consider yet one possibility. The experiences citizens have when attempting to exercise influence might also affect the extent to which they remain dissatisfied with their situation in the three domains on which we focus (working life, child education, and healthcare). If citizens are fairly treated and their wishes accommodated, the discontent that may have fuelled their actions is likely to be reduced. A fair and responsive system may thus potentially increase its legitimacy in two different ways: by strengthening citizens' feelings of efficacy and by weakening their feelings of discontent.

Fourth, the analyses presented here, as well as in the previous chapter, establish a number of micro-level linkages between the key components of small-scale democracy. The previous chapter examines the impact of discontent and perceived opportunities on citizens' propensity to take action. In the initial sections of this chapter, we examine how the consequences of action in terms of outcome and procedural fairness in turn affect perceived opportunities and the level of discontent. The results we reach in our micro-level analyses makes it meaningful to inquire into the macro-level consequences: are the key components so strongly related to each other that we can form a single scale whereby we can evaluate the performance of small-scale democracy across nations as well as domains?

Finally, the extent to which citizens act and succeed have consequences for the degree of inequality between them. In important respects, we have considered these consequences already in the previous chapter and the first section of the present one. The degree to which activity, as well as success rates, are endowment sensitive (i.e. dependent on the social position, resources and opportunities of individual citizens) or ambition sensitive (i.e. dependent on the motivations provided by discontent) obviously bears on the question of inequality.

Yet, there are other ways in which we can consider that question. A complementary view, which finds a particularly clear expression in Walzer's

(1983) treatise on spheres of justice, is that equality is realised to the extent that inequalities do not cumulate across spheres. Differences within a particular realm may be acceptable, even desirable, to the extent that an inferior position in one domain is compensated by a superior position in another. When seen from this perspective, positive relationships between various types of participation are a discouraging sign since it implies the presence of a cumulative pattern. Our concluding section examines the extent which evidence of such a pattern can be found across the three different domains of small-scale democracy included in our study as well as across the divide between democracy on a smaller and larger scale.

The determinants of system responsiveness

If democracy is the process through which citizens try to exercise influence over their lives, then citizen action is an essential part of that process. Consequently, it becomes of great importance to know whether and why citizens do or do not participate. If citizens do not take action in spite of having incentives to do so, they stumble already on the first step on the path to power and democracy remains unrealised. This is the reason why an understanding of participation is central to our understanding of democracy. This is also the reason why several chapters in this book, including the previous one, are exclusively devoted to the task of furthering that understanding.

However, participation is at best a necessary condition for the exercise of citizen power, not a measure of power itself. Nevertheless, few studies take the step logically implied by this obvious fact: that of investigating how successful the participants are in their attempts to exercise influence. Surely, the reason is not that social scientists find such investigations to be superfluous or uninteresting. Rather, the explanation is that they find them difficult to carry out. Questions like 'Did you get what you wanted?' or 'Did you manage to influence the outcome?' are obviously rather difficult to answer for, say, a participant in a demonstration for women's rights. As far as large-scale democracy is concerned, an inquiry into the consequences of participation typically requires a completely different design rather than additional survey questions and is exceedingly difficult even with the best of tools in hand. Therefore, it is hardly surprising that so few have tried to follow the good example set already by Verba and Nie's (1972) path-breaking study, which includes a heroic attempt to examine not only the causes but also the impact of political participation.

For the type of actions and decisions at issue in small-scale democracy, by contrast, it is reasonable to believe that citizens often have rather firm ideas of whether or not they were successful in their attempts to exercise power. Consequently, our surveys included questions asking those who did take an initiative whether or not they essentially had their wishes satisfied (see Chapter 9).

This puts us in a position to repeat the analysis of the previous chapter but with another dependent variable. Rather than asking why citizens do or do not take action, we are now asking why those who do try succeed or not. The motivations for our choice of predictors are in some respects obvious. For each and every one of the measures of social position and resources previously examined, we have reasons to suspect that the impact extends from the propensity to act to the efficiency of the action. Social position, as indexed by age, sex, and education, and resources, as indexed by organisational involvement and civic skills, may well affect the ability to present one's case in a convincing manner and to exert pressure if necessary. The social status of citizens may also influence the general willingness of the other party to accommodate their requests.

Table 11.1 presents a partial replication of the analyses in Chapter 10 (Tables 10.1, 10.3, and 10.4) with the direction of the outcome (success versus failure) rather than action (active versus inactive) as the dependent variable. Our operationalisation of the predictors is the same as in the previous chapter. Since the respondents we examine must by now qualify for analysis in no less than three ways – by entering one of the three roles we consider, by having taken an initiative in that role, and by knowing the outcome – the samples at our disposal are rather small. Since, furthermore,

Table 11.1 Predicting the success rate of attempts to exercise influence (multivariate logistic regression)[a]

Model and predictor	Working life	Child education	Healthcare
Model 1			
Gender (female)	−0.0	0.0	0.1
Age	−4.3*	2.2	1.1
Age squared	4.9	−1.2	0.8
Education	0.8**	0.1	1.5**
Pseudo-R^2	0.020	0.021	0.064
Model 2			
Gender (female)	0.0	0.0	0.0
Age	−5.7**	1.9	0.6
Age squared	6.2**	−1.0	1.2
Education	0.2	−0.0	1.4***
Domain-specific organisational involvement (trade union/parent org./patient org.)	−0.3**	0.3	0.6*
General organisational involvement	0.6	1.2	1.2
Civic skills	1.4***	0.2	−0.0
Pseudo-R^2	0.032	0.025	0.068
Minimal N	3,259	981	1,719

Note

a Entries are unstandardised logistic regression coefficients. All models includes a separate intercept for each country. Levels of statistical significance: *** = 0.01, ** = 0.05, * = 0.1.

our initial analyses indicated that the association was in many cases weak or absent, we present, in this particular case, the results for a pooled sample only (with a separate intercept for each country) rather than for each country separately.

As in Chapter 10, our analysis proceeds in two steps. In model 1 we include only social position as indexed by gender, age, and education. In model 2, we add the three resource indicators available across all three domains, that is, domain-specific organisational involvement (trade union/parent organisation/patient organisation), general organisational involvement, and civic skills.

In this case, however, we do not include dissatisfaction and perceived opportunities as predictors since we find it more reasonable to regard them as consequences rather than causes of the outcome. While we cannot rule out the possibility that the relationship runs partly in the opposite direction (e.g. that the more disgruntled are more likely to fail because they have stronger demands or that those who are more pessimistic about their prospects are less successful because they make less of an effort), we do not think we have reliable instrumental variables for the use of non-recursive estimation techniques. We are therefore forced to proceed on the basis of a unidirectional assumption.

The results shows that only two of the 12 coefficients in model 1 – those for education in the domains of working life and healthcare – are statistically significant at the 0.05-level in spite of the fact that the pooled samples are fairly large (see the last row of Table 11.1). If we compare the effect estimates with their counterparts in Chapter 10, we also find the impact on the outcome to be considerably weaker on average than the impact on the propensity to take action.

The same pattern is evident as we proceed to model 2. Civic skills make a difference in working life and mediate much of the effect of education whose direct impact is no longer statistically significant. There are also some indications of other effects, two of which have unexpected signs (those for union involvement and age in the domain of working life). One might add that having a supervisory position on the job has a statistically significant effect of 0.5 when added to model 2 for working life but that the 0.3 estimated for strength of workplace network is insignificant (cf. Table 10.2).

All in all, our conclusion must be that there are few signs of major inequalities in outcomes with respect to the dimensions we have examined. This is particularly true of the domain of child education where not a single effect attains statistical significance in spite of the fact that the sample is reasonably large ($N=981$). Although the results for the other two domains are not quite as extreme, the general pattern provides far less evidence of unequal success rates than might have been expected.

The feedback on perceived opportunities

Already in the first analyses of small-scale democracy, Petersson *et al.* (1989: 54–6) find that the experiences Swedish citizens have in their attempts to influence have considerable repercussions on their sense of opportunity and hence on their propensity to try again. Andersen and Hoff (2001: 152–4), in a comparative study of Sweden and Denmark, proceed further along the same line and find that the perceived opportunities to influence one's own situation is less a function of personal resources than of citizens' firsthand experiences with the institutions in question. They conclude that citizens' perceptions of their opportunities are largely shaped by their own encounters with the system.

Those who have analysed small-scale democracy using our particular framework are not the only ones to stress the importance of the feedback resulting from personal experiences. Klosko (2000: Chapter 8) provides a summary of the findings of research focusing on the impact of citizens' personal encounters with the public institutions as well as private organisations whose decisions shape their lives. Like the two Scandinavian teams, he concludes that there is considerable evidence of feedback effects.

Interestingly, however, several studies have found indications that the outcome is not the most decisive factor. While the material result certainly matters, the extent to which people are fairly treated may matter more (e.g. Thibaut and Walker 1975). Obviously, these results are of great interest to students of democracy. No matter how well-behaved a system is in democratic terms, the wishes of citizens cannot always be satisfied, for example, because available resources are insufficient or because the preferences of one citizen conflicts with those of another. If, however, citizens are treated with due respect and come away with a reasonable explanation of why their requests were turned down, the negative decision need not necessarily undermine perceived legitimacy. Good democracy fosters good losers (cf. Esaiasson 2005).

Since our cross-national data sets contain measures of the direction of the outcome as well as the perceived fairness of the process,[1] we are in a position to test this hypothesis across three important domains as well as a wide variety of polities. Table 11.2 presents a set of regression analyses with the index for overall perceived opportunities to influence in the respective domain as the dependent variable and outcome and fairness as independent variable.[2] The regressions also include a set of potentially relevant controls (see table note).

As indicated by our estimates, the evaluation of the outcome as well as the process matter. Virtually all effects are positive, and in the few cases where they are not, the sample size is very limited and the result therefore not statistically significant. Whenever the sample reaches reasonable size, the estimated impact of both variables is uniformly positive and substantively as well as statistically significant in most cases.

Table 11.2 Perceived opportunities as a function of experiences from attempts to exercise influence[a]

Country	Working life			Child education			Healthcare		
	Outcome	Process	N	Outcome	Process	N	Outcome	Process	N
Denmark	0.05***	0.18***	652	0.04	0.23***	197	0.16***	0.34***	203
East Germany	0.03	0.01	42	−0.03	0.14	27	0.15	0.39***	67
West Germany	0.10*	0.06	85	0.12	0.14	52	0.08	0.14	90
Moldova	0.03	0.19*	102	0.16***	0.19**	104	0.08	0.31***	92
The Netherlands	0.03	0.16***	402	0.04	0.23***	163	0.05	0.27***	238
Norway	0.08***	0.18***	808	0.10***	0.26***	295	0.07**	0.27***	456
Portugal	−0.05	0.30***	119	−0.09	0.47***	50	0.04	0.31	19
Romania	0.06	−0.04	132	0.13*	0.18**	90	0.11	0.34***	116
Slovenia	0.06	0.10	159	0.37***	−0.01	54	0.01	0.21***	237
Spain	0.09***	0.00	465	–	–	–	–	–	–
Sweden	0.04	0.12***	441	−0.01	0.33***	111	0.02	0.39***	171
Switzerland	0.09***	0.09**	543	0.10**	0.17*	131	0.04	0.31***	334
Pooled sample	0.07***	0.12***	3,950	0.07***	0.24***	1,274	0.07***	0.31***	2,023

Note

a Entries are unstandardised regression coefficients. Apart from the respondents' evaluation of the outcome and the process, each model includes the following control variables: Gender, age, age-squared, education, domain-specific organisational involvement, general organisational involvement, and civic skills. The pooled models also include a separate intercept for each country. The Spanish survey provides data on working life only. Levels of statistical significance: *** = 0.01, ** = 0.05, * = 0.1.

A closer look reveals, however, that the perceived fairness of the process is of greater importance than the direction of the outcome. A movement from one extreme to the other on the scale of procedural fairness has a greater effect than the transition between success and failure as far as the outcome is concerned. One should keep in mind, however, that the variation on the continuum of procedural fairness is more limited. Few respondents place themselves at its extremes whereas most respondents are at either extreme of the outcome measure. Nevertheless, the difference between the two effects is big enough to hold up even if we consider it in standardised rather than unstandardised terms. As one might expect on substantive as well as psychological grounds, the perceived fairness of the process is fairly strongly correlated with the outcome (on the order of 0.50 on average). But to the extent that the two do not converge, fairness is the more decisive factor.

This implies that perceived opportunities are not only a cause of *action*, as shown in the previous chapter, but also an effect of the *consequences of the action*. Those who take action and succeed gain confidence, and are hence more likely to try again than those who failed. But even more important in this regard is whether the citizen came away from the process with a sense of having been fairly treated. The responsiveness as well as the procedural fairness of the system thus has clear repercussions on the way citizens expect it to respond to future input.

As far as the direction of the outcome is concerned, the magnitude of this feedback effect is fairly constant across the three domains. For procedural fairness, by contrast, it varies somewhat. Interestingly, the order is reversed compared to the one we typically found in the previous chapter. The impact is most pronounced for healthcare and least for working life. No clear country patterns distinguishable from the variation we would expect on the basis of sampling error can be discerned.

The feedback on dissatisfaction

The impact of responsiveness and procedural fairness on perceived opportunities for future action is one important aspect of system feedback. Another is the effect on dissatisfaction. By accommodating the wishes of citizens, the discontent that fuelled their actions can potentially be reduced. While the relationship between dissatisfaction and action indicates the extent to which grievance is channelled into action, that between responsiveness and dissatisfaction reflects the extent to which system can actually absorb discontent. In this case as well, the impact of procedural fairness is worthy of consideration. Even when the system fails to satisfy citizens in material terms, discontent may well be reduced if they felt they got a fair hearing and a reasonable explanation of why it was impossible to satisfy their wishes. As previously noted, discontent results from a discrepancy between realities and expectations. While a better understanding of the preconditions do not alter the realities citizens face in working life, child education or healthcare, it may well modify their view of what they can justifiably expect.

Admittedly, our design is not ideal for testing these hypotheses regarding the feedback on dissatisfaction. Ideally, one would want to observe the level of discontent before as well as after the process. Our measure of dissatisfaction is intentionally retrospective. The question asks about the extent to which the respondent *has had* any reason to feel dissatisfied with his or her conditions within the domain at issue (working life, child education, or healthcare) during the past 12 months. If the question works as intended, respondents who have been dissatisfied but no longer are will indicate their past discontent, thus suppressing the conjectured relationship. In spite of these imperfections, however, it is worth giving the matter a first try.

To that end, we regressed dissatisfaction with one's situation in the respective domain on respondent evaluation of the outcome as well as the process, again including a set of control variables (the same as in our previous analysis; see table note). In spite of the less than perfect analytical circumstances, both hypotheses gain support (see Table 11.3). Although many of the individual estimates are imprecise due to small Ns, the coefficients for the direction of the outcome have the expected negative sign (indicating a reduction of discontent) in nearly all cases. The same is true for procedural fairness.

Note, however, that the coefficients for the procedural factor tend to be larger than those for the outcome in this case as well. Even with respect to dissatisfaction, it matters more how the citizen was treated when he or she took action than whether or not the outcome conformed to the initial ambitions. Just as in our previous analysis, the effect of procedural fairness is on average more prominent in healthcare than in child education and working life. However, the estimated impact of the outcome is in this case slightly greater in working life than in healthcare and child education. As to the cross-national differences, the sample sizes at our disposal again prevent us from drawing any firm conclusions.

Evaluating small-scale democracies

In this as well as the previous chapter, we have so far examined small-scale democracy primarily from a micro-level, causal, and positive point of view. We have been concerned mainly with understanding the way dissatisfaction, opportunity, action, responsiveness, and fairness bear on each other on the individual level. In many cases, we have found evidence of rather firm links. This raises the question of whether and to what extent they covary on the macro level as well. While previous chapters have occasionally touched upon that question, a more systematic view has still to be provided. Do the five central components of our design – dissatisfaction,

Table 11.3 Dissatisfaction as a function of experiences from attempts to exercise influence[a]

Country	Working life			Child education			Healthcare		
	Outcome	Process	N	Outcome	Process	N	Outcome	Process	N
Denmark	-0.13***	-0.28***	648	-0.07	-0.20	196	0.01	-0.58***	201
East Germany	-0.14	-0.24	40	0.14	-0.61**	27	-0.20	-0.30	66
West Germany	-0.22***	-0.21	84	-0.03	-0.46***	52	-0.16	-0.47***	90
Moldova	-0.08	0.02	102	0.15**	-0.24***	105	0.09	-0.29**	94
The Netherlands	-0.14***	-0.44***	402	-0.17***	-0.36***	162	0.01	-0.59***	238
Norway	-0.20***	-0.32***	805	-0.19***	-0.30***	296	-0.24***	-0.41***	456
Romania	-0.20**	-0.28**	131	-0.00	-0.62***	90	-0.16*	-0.32**	121
Portugal	-0.12	-0.06	120	-0.07	-0.06	52	-0.00	-0.29	19
Slovenia	-0.19***	-0.46***	159	-0.21*	0.25	54	-0.12**	-0.50***	237
Spain	-0.21***	-0.21***	465	–	–	–	–	–	–
Sweden	-0.12***	-0.48***	438	-0.18**	-0.28***	112	-0.14**	-0.41***	172
Switzerland	0.12***	-0.45***	542	-0.07	-0.30**	131	-0.09	-0.54***	334
Pooled sample	-0.16***	-0.34***	3,936	-0.13***	-0.29***	1,277	-0.11***	-0.45***	2,028

Note

[a] Entries are unstandardised regression coefficients. Apart from the respondents' evaluation of the outcome and the process, each model includes the following control variables: Gender, age, age-squared, education, domain-specific organisational involvement, general organisational involvement, and civic skills. The pooled models also include a separate intercept for each country. The Spanish survey provides data on working life only. Levels of statistical significance: *** = 0.01, ** = 0.05, * = 0.1.

action, opportunity, outcome, and fairness – in fact allow us to form a single scale whereby we can evaluate the performance of small-scale democracy in a comparative perspective?

Three of the five characteristics we have considered – fairness, responsiveness, and a sense of efficacy (i.e. perceived opportunities to exercise influence) – are in and by themselves desiderata of democratic systems. Citizens should be fairly treated and, insofar as it is possible and impose little or no externalities, successful in their attempts to exercise influence. A sense of efficacy can also be regarded as quality-of-life indicator quite apart from its effects (Campbell and Converse 1972). To be subjectively deprived of the opportunity to exercise influence implies a loss of freedom.

With respect to the other two characteristics, dissatisfaction and action, we have argued that the situation is somewhat more complicated. While neither satisfaction nor action are out of the way from a democratic point of view, the lack of the two becomes a democratic problem primarily when they combine into what we have termed passive resignation, that is, considerable dissatisfaction but a lack of action.

We have hitherto expressed the magnitude of this combination in terms of percentages, which makes it necessary to decide on a somewhat arbitrary basis how to dichotomise the dissatisfaction scale. This complication can be bypassed by instead computing a dissatisfaction-passivity-score (DPS). The DPS is simply the product of dissatisfaction (scored zero to one) and passivity (scored one for the passive and zero for the active). However, we would also prefer to have a scale where, as in other instances, a high score indicates a positive rather than negative state of affairs. If we try to formulate the opposite of passive resignation, we can say that either satisfaction or action suffices. In operational terms, this implies that the relevant quantity is the inverse of the DPS score. A well-functioning system should thus have a high satisfaction-or-action score, SAS, defined as 1 – DPS.

We are thus left with four desiderata of small-scale democracy, namely, a high level of SAS, opportunities, responsiveness, and fairness. These four criteria allow us to raise the question of how they combine. Is one desideratum independent or even contradictory to another or do they in fact converge into a single scale?

The answer is provided in Table 11.4, which shows the per-country levels for the four criteria and the corresponding rank orders.[3] The entries for SAS, opportunities, and fairness are all mean values on a 0–1 scale. Responsiveness is the probability difference between success and failure and can therefore vary from −1 to +1. In practice, however, all values fall within the zero to one range.

The correlations between the four criteria, displayed below each series, clearly indicate that there is a good deal of communality between them. Although factor-analytic techniques are not strictly appropriate in this case (because a good deal of the covariance between the criteria are likely to be due to causal relations between them rather than to a common latent source), a principal-component analysis yields a single dimension based on Kaiser's criterion in every instance.

This makes it meaningful to combine the four into a single scale. For the time being, we have chosen to do so by computing the average rank across the four criteria and then placed the countries in the order given by that rank.

In large part, the cross-national pattern already observed with regard to SAS (or rather its inverse) and efficacy is confirmed when we add responsiveness and fairness to the picture. The four countries found at the top based on the first two criteria are typically close to the top based on the other two as well. In Denmark, Norway, Sweden, the Netherlands, and Switzerland, small-scale democracy tends to operate relatively well in all four respects and across all three realms. The table also reveals, however, that we need to add one country, Slovenia, to that set. While we have some difficulties judging Slovenia's performance with respect to SAS and while its efficacy levels are only intermediate, it does remarkably well in terms of responsiveness and fairness.

Since the top six countries are uniformly the same, save for the German advance in the realm of healthcare, it follows that the same holds for the other extreme. East and West Germany, Moldova, Romania, Portugal, and Spain are with one exception always located in the lower half. Within each group, the order is more variable. Switzerland, however, is uniformly close to the very top and Moldova to the very bottom.

While the cross-national differences are systematic and pronounced, those between the three domains of small-scale democracy show much less of a pattern. As indicated by the figures in bold (overall mean per realm and rank across realms), child education does best overall, followed by healthcare and working life. In this case, however, the order is strongly dependent on which criterion we look at and the differences on which the order is based sometimes small.

The cumulation of participation

As indicated at the outset, we conclude our tour of small-scale democracy by examining the extent to which it satisfies Michael Walzer's (1983) ideal of compensatory rather than cumulative patterns of participation. To what degree do the sets of active citizens overlap across the three domains we have investigated: that of working life, that of child education, and that of healthcare? Is it the same individuals who make their voices heard across all spheres or is a passive role in one domain compensated by an active role in another?

The answer is provided by Table 11.5, which shows the intercorrelations between the action measures for the three domains. Three patterns

Table 11.4 Summary evaluation of small-scale democracy[a]

Domain and country	Absolute level (mean)				Rank order				Mean rank
	Satisfaction-or-action score (SAS)	Opportunities	Responsiveness	Fairness	Satisfaction-or-action score (SAS)	Opportunities	Responsiveness	Fairness	
Working life									
Denmark	0.81	0.46	0.36	0.69	2	3	2	2	2.25
Switzerland	0.90	0.61	0.48	0.76	1	1	2	1	1.25
Sweden	0.89	0.56	0.41	0.74	4	3	4	2	3.25
Norway	0.90	0.55	0.39	0.74	2	5	5	3	3.75
Slovenia	0.90	0.56	0.44	0.70	2	4	3	6	4.00
The Netherlands	0.81	0.46	0.38	0.70	6	6	6	5	5.75
Portugal	0.87	0.59	0.37	0.66	5	2	7	10	6.00
West Germany	0.74	0.37	0.60	0.72	11	9	1	4	6.25
Spain	0.75	0.40	0.34	0.67	9	8	9	9	8.75
Romania	0.76	0.37	0.22	0.69	7	10	11	7	8.75
East Germany	0.75	0.40	0.29	0.65	8	7	10	11	9.00
Moldova	0.74	0.31	0.34	0.69	10	12	8	8	9.50
	0.71	0.33	0.05	0.51	12	11	12	12	11.75
Correlations									
Opportunities	0.96	—			0.86	—			—
Responsiveness	0.47	0.47	—		0.52	0.58	—		—
Fairness	0.60	0.53	0.82	—	0.64	0.50	0.81	—	—
Child education									
Denmark	0.84	0.49	0.32	0.70	1	2	3	1	1.75
Switzerland	0.88	0.65	0.46	0.76	4	1	3	4	3.00
Sweden	0.89	0.48	0.44	0.80	3	6	4	1	3.50
Slovenia	0.90	0.50	0.26	0.77	1	4	8	3	4.00
	0.87	0.43	0.49	0.79	5	9	1	2	4.25

The Netherlands	0.89	0.61	0.17	0.75	2	10	5	4.75
Norway	0.87	0.48	0.38	0.71	6	5	6	5.50
Romania	0.81	0.47	0.47	0.67	8	2	8	6.25
West Germany	0.81	0.41	0.27	0.68	7	7	7	7.75
Moldova	0.74	0.52	0.25	0.53	11	9	11	8.50
Portugal	0.76	0.47	0.28	0.58	10	6	10	8.50
East Germany	0.79	0.39	0.09	0.63	9	11	9	10.00
Correlations								
Opportunities	0.40	—	—	—	0.43	—	—	—
Responsiveness	0.32	0.15	—	—	0.13	—	—	—
Fairness	0.96	0.24	0.45	—	0.88	0.45	—	—
Healthcare	*0.78*	*0.56*	*0.44*	*0.68*	*3*	*1*	*3*	*2.00*
Switzerland	0.87	0.71	0.66	0.80	1	1	1	1.00
Slovenia	0.84	0.59	0.60	0.78	3	6	2	3.25
Norway	0.84	0.61	0.52	0.71	2	3	4	3.50
East Germany	0.78	0.58	0.60	0.74	6	8	3	5.00
The Netherlands	0.83	0.66	0.32	0.68	4	2	8	5.50
West Germany	0.77	0.61	0.55	0.69	8	4	6	5.50
Denmark	0.78	0.59	0.29	0.69	7	5	10	6.75
Sweden	0.80	0.58	0.29	0.68	5	7	9	7.50
Romania	0.74	0.51	0.45	0.69	9	9	7	7.75
Portugal	0.63	0.39	0.35	0.51	11	10	11	9.75
Moldova	0.67	0.38	0.16	0.52	10	11	10	10.50
Correlations								
Opportunities	0.94	—	—	—	0.80	—	—	—
Responsiveness	0.59	0.58	—	—	0.54	0.42	—	—
Fairness	0.91	0.88	0.77	—	0.74	0.58	0.78	—

Note
a Within each domain, countries are ordered by their mean rank.

Table 11.5 The cumulation of participation in small-scale democracy[a]

Country	Working life and child education	Working life and healthcare	Child education and healthcare	Average
Denmark	0.31 (261)	0.07 (507)	0.07 (223)	0.15
The Netherlands	0.17 (252)	0.23 (494)	0.10 (229)	0.17
Switzerland	0.25 (293)	0.15 (854)	0.11 (292)	0.17
Sweden	0.17 (170)	0.12 (571)	0.25 (187)	0.18
East Germany	0.20 (160)	0.13 (218)	0.23 (116)	0.19
Norway	0.18 (468)	0.14 (842)	0.25 (372)	0.19
Portugal	0.31 (129)	0.24 (202)	0.04 (104)	0.20
Romania	0.14 (154)	0.27 (152)	0.18 (129)	0.20
Slovenia	0.33 (129)	0.14 (299)	0.25 (126)	0.24
West Germany	0.16 (279)	0.44 (394)	0.27 (192)	0.29
Moldova	0.36 (185)	0.31 (127)	0.28 (120)	0.32
Average	0.23	0.20	0.18	0.21

Note
a Entries are product-moment correlations with weighted Ns in parentheses. Within each domain, countries are placed in ascending order based on the average strength of association.

are immediately apparent. First, the overlap is neither paramount nor nonexistent but intermediate. The correlations hover slightly above 0.20 on average. Second, there is not much difference with respect to how strongly the three spheres are related to one another. The link is strongest between working life and child education and weakest between child education and healthcare. But the distinction is barely discernible. Finally, the association is generally somewhat stronger in the new democracies than in the old. The difference in this regard is likely to be somewhat under- rather than overestimated since the marginal distributions are often severely skewed for the former set of countries, thereby increasing the attenuation due to measurement error.

The fact that participation tends to cumulate more strongly in countries with a shorter democratic history and lower overall rates of participation matches the patterns already uncovered in two respects. To begin with, it fits the evaluation provided in the previous subsection. Had we added the dispersion of participation as yet an indicator of how close these democracies are to the normative ideal, it would have presented no problems for the conclusions drawn in any respect. The result also fits the causal patterns uncovered in the previous chapter, where we found a tendency for action to be more strongly contingent on capacity in countries where participation is less frequent (as it is in the newer democracies) and more sensitive to subjectively felt needs, that is, dissatisfaction, in countries where participation is more common (as in Denmark, Norway, Sweden, the Netherlands, and Switzerland). Capacity is in turn more likely to cumulate across spheres than is discontent.

Before we leave the stage to democracy on a larger scale, we will conclude our analysis of small-scale democracy by considering a question that bridges the two domains: to what extent are the citizens that take action in order to influence their own situation also those who take action in order to influence the situation of the entire polity?

The vigour of what we have termed small-scale democracy is sometimes portrayed as a threat to people's willingness to engage in political activities with broader aims. If citizens get preoccupied with their own personal situations, they will, according to this line of argument, neither have the time nor the motivation to be concerned with the problems facing the community. However, conjectures to the contrary are equally frequent. Activities for local ends, for example at the place of work, are often regarded as a way of preparing citizens for participation directed toward more global concerns (e.g. Pateman 1970). In a causal and developmental perspective, a positive association between participation in the two spheres would thus be an encouraging sign inasmuch as it would indicate the absence of a competitive relationship and the presence of synergetic one.

However, the causal issue is, to the extent that we can deal with it, reserved for other chapters (10 and 14) in this book and the developmental perspective one that our data do not allow us to take. Hence, our point of view here will be descriptive and static rather than causal and dynamic. The positive justification for looking at the data from that end is that the static pattern of association has consequences for the *equality of participation at the present time* quite irrespective of what it implies for the *level of participation at some future time*.

Our question regarding the cumulation of participation can thus be widened to encompass the relationship between attempts to influence one's own situation and the type of activities with which the rest of this book is concerned: those aimed at influencing more encompassing outcomes. Table 11.6 shows the intercorrelation between participation in the three domains of small-scale democracy and the five dimensions of political participation whose defining characteristics will be elaborated in Chapter 13: voting, party activity, contacting, consumer participation, and protest activity.

Again, three patterns are readily visible. First, the overlap between participation in small- and large-scale democracy is on average weaker than the degree of cumulation within small-scale democracy. Second, that conclusion is strongly contingent on which of the five dimensions of political participation we consider. For contacting and consumer participation, the correlations approach the internal overlap between the three domains of small-scale democracy. For the two forms of participation that form the nucleus of representative democracy, by contrast, the association is virtually zero. Activities that have similar behavioural expressions thus tend to cluster together irrespective of whether they are narrowly or more broadly aimed. Where there is little in the way of such similarity, however, we find

Table 11.6 Relationship between participation in small- and large-scale democracy[a]

Domain and country	Voting	Party activity	Contacting	Consumer participation	Protest activity	Average
Working life						
East Germany	−0.11	−0.05	0.36	0.17	−0.08	0.06
West Germany	−0.01	0.02	0.19	0.17	0.12	0.10
Sweden	0.05	0.00	0.21	0.25	0.02	0.11
Switzerland	0.02	0.05	0.23	0.19	0.07	0.11
Denmark	0.05	0.04	0.23	0.20	0.06	0.12
Norway	0.06	0.07	0.23	0.18	0.09	0.13
Romania	−0.05	0.06	0.24	0.28	0.21	0.15
Moldova	0.13	0.09	0.19	0.23	0.10	0.15
The Netherlands	0.12	0.01	0.29	0.28	0.05	0.15
Portugal	0.02	0.14	0.27	0.21	0.12	0.15
Slovenia	0.12	0.09	0.23	0.24	0.10	0.16
Spain	0.05	0.12	0.30	0.30	0.21	0.20
Average	0.04	0.05	0.25	0.22	0.08	0.13
Child education						
The Netherlands	0.01	−0.04	0.18	0.13	−0.02	0.05
Norway	0.08	0.05	0.18	0.15	0.00	0.09
Romania	0.07	0.01	0.13	0.16	0.14	0.10
Denmark	−0.03	0.02	0.22	0.23	0.11	0.11
Switzerland	0.06	0.03	0.19	0.23	0.10	0.12
Sweden	0.10	−0.01	0.27	0.20	0.07	0.13
Moldova	0.14	0.01	0.23	0.20	0.07	0.13
West Germany	0.04	0.03	0.30	0.25	0.05	0.13
Portugal	−0.02	0.07	0.31	0.20	0.17	0.15
Slovenia	0.13	0.12	0.26	0.30	0.12	0.19
East Germany	0.10	0.05	0.31	0.42	0.12	0.20
Average	0.06	0.03	0.23	0.22	0.08	0.13
Healthcare						
Norway	−0.00	0.02	0.10	0.06	0.05	0.05
Denmark	0.04	0.02	0.13	0.09	0.01	0.06
Slovenia	0.05	0.06	0.14	0.05	0.06	0.07
Switzerland	0.00	0.04	0.13	0.15	0.08	0.08
East Germany	−0.07	−0.03	0.21	0.27	0.15	0.11
West Germany	0.03	0.06	0.19	0.16	0.12	0.11
Portugal	0.03	0.09	0.19	0.15	0.12	0.12
Sweden	0.03	0.12	0.21	0.15	0.08	0.12
Romania	0.01	0.02	0.18	0.25	0.14	0.12
Moldova	−0.04	0.16	0.22	0.16	0.11	0.12
The Netherlands	0.09	0.01	0.20	0.19	0.17	0.13
Average	0.02	0.05	0.17	0.15	0.10	0.10

Note

a Entries are product-moment correlations. Within each domain, countries are placed in ascending order based on the average strength of association.

little overlap but no signs of a directly competitive situation either. Finally, the pattern of cross-national differences is similar to that for the cumulation of activity within small-scale democracy, albeit less clearly marked. The newer democracies tend to display a slightly stronger relationship between the two types of participation than do those with a longer democratic history.

Conclusions

The idea that employees should have a say about their working conditions, parents about the education of their children, and patients about the healthcare they are given is ultimately rooted in the belief that such a solution increases the joint amount of citizen power. According to Coleman (1973), the power of an actor can be defined as his or her amount of control over certain events multiplied by his or her interest in those events. Consequently, the power of citizens can potentially be increased by allowing each of them more control over events of great individual concern in exchange for less control over events that they do not care so much about. Presumably, employees, parents, and patients care more about conditions related to the particular places to which they or their children go for work, schooling, or healthcare than do most other citizens. Hence, they should, according to this line of argument, have more of a say about these conditions than other citizens.

The relevance of this logic is of course not restricted to the domains included in our notion of small-scale democracy but applies in a variety of other contexts as well. For example, the idea that the inhabitants of a municipality, region, or country should have a greater say about events pertaining to these particular entities than inhabitants of other geographic areas follows from exactly the same logic.

The major objections commonly levelled at that logic are fairly well summarised by the reaction of social democratic politicians in Sweden when first confronted with the idea of extending the participatory rights of public-service users. As noted by Andersen and Hoff (2001: 137), many of them were 'sceptical, fearing the manifestation of particular interest, and the possible inegalitarian consequences of such rights'. While the evidence presented in this and earlier chapters on small-scale democracy certainly does not allow us to conclude that such fears are generally misplaced, it does allow us to make some empirical observations of potential importance to anyone interested in assessing the virtues and vices of small-scale democracy.

A first such observations is that participation in small-scale democracy is undeniably endowment sensitive, that is, clearly dependent on the social position, resources, and opportunities enjoyed by individual citizens. Hence, the evidence at our disposal gives us no basis for claiming that such participation is exempt from the general rule already formulated by

Verba *et al.* (1995: 1–2) with respect to large-scale democracy: 'no democratic nation ... lives up to the ideal of participatory equality' since 'citizen activists tend to be drawn disproportionately from more advantaged groups'.

On the other hand, this general conclusion should by no means be taken to imply that the prospects of realising egalitarian or other democratic ideals are universally hopeless. While it may well be true that full equality will always remain unrealised, our results demonstrate that the discrepancy between ideal and reality varies significantly depending on where and how we examine it.

As shown already in the previous chapter, participation in small-scale democracy does not depend on endowment alone but is also sensitive to variations in ambitions or incentives as indexed by discontent. Furthermore, the balance between endowment and ambition sensitivity varies systematically across the countries included in our study. Countries in which the propensity of citizens to take action is relatively high, such as Denmark, the Netherlands, Norway, Sweden, and Switzerland, tend to be closer to the ideal of equality than those in which citizens are less active. Preconditions conducive to high levels of participation thus seem to promote participatory equality as well.

This conclusion receives further support by the results added in the present chapter, where we examine the extent to which participation cumulates across different types of action. In this respect too, countries with high participation rates tend to display a more egalitarian pattern.

Another significant finding, which in some ways serves to mitigate pessimism about the prospects of equality, is that the signs of inequality are not echoed with equal force as we move from participation to the outcomes it generates. Resourceful citizens are only marginally more successful in their attempts to exercise influence than those who are less well-equipped. While this by no means eliminates the inequality of power implied by unequal participation rates, it indicates that the situation gets marginally rather than dramatically worse when we do not stop short at participation but follow the exercise of citizen power to its logical end.

If, as our results indicate, fewer obstacles to participation also imply a greater amount of participatory equality, we have dual incentives to ask ourselves what those obstacles might be so that we have the option of reducing them. In this regard, our analyses of feedback mechanisms provide at least a partial answer. As V.O. Key once remarked, voters are not fools. Nor do they become more foolish when they reflect upon their prospects as potential participants in small- rather than large-scale democracy. Consequently, they learn from their encounters with the system. If the latter turns out to be responsive to their requests and to give them a fair hearing, they are more likely to try again.

Interestingly, the procedural quality of fairness turns out to be more important in this respect than material responsiveness. From the point of view of democratic theory and practice, this is an important finding. No matter how well a system functions in democratic terms, it is unlikely to be able to accommodate the wishes of every citizen every time. However, this need not necessarily undermine legitimacy if the system is so designed that citizens find themselves to be treated with due fairness and respect.

One common implication of virtually all observations we have made so far is that the evaluation of how well small-scale democracy operates in the various countries included in our study is remarkably independent of precisely which criterion we apply. The analyses presented in this chapter confirm that impression. The various characteristics of small-scale democracy are rather strongly related not only on the micro- but also on the macro-level. An optimistic interpretation of that fact is that the operation of small-scale democracy turns out to be reasonably intelligible, which in turn enhances our prospects of reducing its shortcomings.

Notes

1 See Chapter 9 for a presentation of these measures.
2 The outcome variable takes the values 0 for failure, 0.5 for uncertainty, and 1 for success. Analysis with dummy variables for the three possible outcomes shows that it is reasonable to treat responses indicating that the outcome is not yet known as intermediate between failure and success.
3 Due to differences in the question format, the SAS scores for Portugal and Slovenia may not be fully comparable to those of other countries. The results for these two countries should therefore be treated with caution as far as the SAS score is concerned.

Part IV
Large-scale democracy

12 Political involvement

Irene Martín and Jan W. van Deth

Introduction

Involvement with politics is one of the ways in which citizens connect with their communities. The need for a minimum level of political interest is generally accepted, whereas a lack of political involvement is considered destructive for democracy. Without a minimum level of curiosity about politics citizens would not even be aware of the political process or of the opportunities to defend their well-being and to contribute to collective decisions. In democratic systems citizens have to express their demands, wishes, expectations, conceptions, and interests, and these expressions require at least some minimum level of engagement. But even if curiosity or awareness are certainly necessary, they are not sufficient conditions for democracy according to various theoretical models of democracy. Authors such as Benjamin Barber (1984 and 1995) urged for a much more 'participatory' democracy, as an alternative for liberal 'thin democracy' or 'politics as zoo keeping'. Interest in public affairs is a 'key sign of civic virtue' (Walzer 1980: 64; see also Putnam 1993: 87) as well as a critical precondition for more active and collective forms of involvement (Verba *et al.* 1995: 334; Putnam 2000: 31–7). 'If you don't know the rules of the game and the players and don't care about the outcome, you're unlikely to try playing yourself' (Putnam, 2000: 35).

Political involvement has been defined and operationalised in several ways and concepts like *interest in politics, psychological political involvement, political engagement* and, in negative terms, *political apathy* or even *political disaffection* are used to cover more or less the same phenomenon.[1] We will operationalise political involvement as a combination of the degree of people's *interest in politics* and *the importance they attribute to politics in their lives*. Political interest is defined here as the 'degree to which politics arouses a citizen's curiosity' (van Deth 1990: 278) or 'attentiveness to politics' (Zaller 1992: 18). It is not a mode of political behaviour nor is it a synonym of positive feelings towards politics. A person may be very interested in politics and still reject the actual political world when asked how he or she feels about politics. In this sense, political interest is just equivalent to 'paying attention', which is 'a prerequisite for learning anything' that might give citizens the opportunity to participate in democratic decision-making processes' (Lupia and McCubbins 1998: 22). Our concern here is with the willingness of citizens to take notice of politics as a basic prerequisite for democratic citizenship. The second aspect of political involvement we consider is the importance people assign to politics. Here, it is not relevant how important politics is in one's life when compared to other aspects such as the family, friends, one's job, or religion, but whether people perceive politics as important or not.[2]

One of the central ideas of this chapter is that the degree of political involvement on the one hand, and the concepts of democracy and of democratic citizenship that lay behind it on the other, are closely related. Therefore, we analyse the *relationships between theoretical models of democracy and empirical findings regarding political involvement*. In line with classical studies such as Dahl's (1956) and Almond and Verba's (1963), we also want to know whether underlying political cultures in terms of political involvement are consistent with the actual kinds of *political participation* they foster. Following some of the literature on social capital (Putnam 2000) we explore, furthermore, the relationships between different kinds of political involvement and *social participation*. For these analyses we first develop four ideal types of citizenship based on democratic theory: a decisionist, a liberal-representative, a participatory, and a unitary type. Then, we operationalise these distinct types in terms of the forms and levels of political involvement. Third, we turn to the question of whether the four kinds of citizenship can be validated according to their relationship to modes of political behaviour intimately related to political involvement, such as the frequency of political discussions and media exposure.

After developing and validating these four types of citizenship, the second part of this chapter addresses the relationship between distinct types of political involvement and participation. Are the different types of citizens involved in different kinds of political activities? Are some of them more involved than others? And what about the implications of the different kinds of political involvement for social participation? In the last part we concentrate on the explanation of cross-national differences in citizenship. Are the same resources, skills, and orientations related in similar ways to the different types of citizenship? Do we observe the same pattern in every country?

Two main conclusions follow from our explorations. In the first place, different kinds of political involvement should be empirically distinguished in consonance with the postulates of the different theoretical models of democratic citizenship. Second, two distinct groups of countries can be easily traced in cross-national analyses of the distributions of the four types of citizenship. This clear picture disappears, however, when we turn to socio-demographic, cultural, and political antecedents of citizenship in various countries and to the relationship between different kinds of political involvement on the one hand, and social and political participation on the other.

A typology of involvement and citizenship

In the history of political thought several paradigms, models or conceptual maps have been brought to the fore as to how to organise political life.[3] Paradigms or models of 'the good political life' exist, the first of which is represented by the funeral speech of Pericles as recorded by Thucydides. Ever since the days of Pericles, democratic political theory has been concerned with the requirements of individual citizens to facilitate democracy. In his famous speech, Pericles declared 2,400 years ago that the unique character of democracy lies in the fact that a person who does not take an interest in public affairs is considered 'not as a harmless, but as a useless character'.[4] The echo of this verdict can be traced easily in many theories on democracy and citizenship. Yet these theories differ widely in their postulates about how much and in what way individuals should be involved in politics.

Different concepts of democracy have been subject to several systematisation attempts (cf. Constant [1819] 1986; Berlin [1969] 1988; Macpherson 1977; Barber 1984; Held 1987; Sartori 1987; Walzer 1991). In order to obtain a systematic comparison between the ideals of citizenship as formulated in democratic theory, on the one hand, and the attitudes of citizens as we know them through empirical research on the other, a typology of political involvement and citizenship is constructed here. However, due to the very broad scope and the nuances of the theoretical works mentioned, there is no single typology of democratic citizenship accepted by each and every author. For instance, what some of them consider description is classified by others under the realm of prescription, and vice versa. Besides, it is not always easy to characterise the work of a single author as representative of just one of the different models. Since our typology intends to be a purely normative one that helps us analyse real citizens' political attitudes we will not go into these discussions. Given the objectives of this chapter, we will use a simplified version of the different models of democracy that will help us clarify relationships between theoretical and normative notions and the real world. This means that our typology will not be exactly coincident with any of the above-mentioned classification attempts, although it is inspired by all of them. Finally, when constructing our typology, we will not focus on every single aspect of the different models, but only on the differences in the degree and kind of political involvement of the ideal citizen that characterises each of them. As we will see, this depends mainly on the different assumptions about human nature that are reflected in each of the ideal types of citizenship.[5]

We classify all respondents into four groups according to the nature of their political involvement. The ideal models we use as reference models for the empirical analyses are:

1   a type based on strong authority and decision-making;
2   a liberal-representative type;
3   a participatory type;
4   a unitary type.[6]

According to the various perceptions of politics among citizens, each citizen can be considered to be closer to one or the other type of ideal citizen. These types are characteristic of each of the four theories or models of democracy and they can be briefly described as follows.

The decisionist model

According to this model, the political field is not the 'sphere of real interests' of the typical citizen (Schumpeter cit. Sartori 1987: 107) and therefore politics is restricted to the elite. Expressed in terms of the Hobbesian social contract, citizens, fearful of each other, agree to pass on power to a strong authority that can protect them from the consequences of their own nature. This type represents the more extreme kind of protective – in Held's (1987) terms – and elitist models of democracy. In a decisionist democracy there is a strong executive government and decisive leadership. Political parties monopolise representation (Held 1987: 155–6) without trying to reach a consensus with intermediate actors of the civil society which, in this model, play no role at all (Morlino and Montero 1995: 253). It is similar to a technocracy or government of experts. In Margolis's words when describing Schumpeter's concept of democracy, it 'involved the free choice of leaders to do the governing, not the free participation of citizens in the policy-making process. Moreover, the success or failure of a democracy depended by and large upon the quality of its leadership, not upon the rationality of its ordinary citizens' who should exercise self-control and suppress their desires to pressure their representatives to pass specific policies (1979: 108).[7] Citizens, according to this model – and more specifically according to Weber and Schumpeter – *are naturally passive and emotional.* That is why their participation should be limited to voting and only as a way to eschew inefficient leaders (Held 1987: 158).

The liberal-representative model

This model shares several characteristics with the previous one such as the prominent role of the elite[8] and the non-political character of citizens. However, what makes it different is its pluralist character and the role citizens play in politics in a defensive or counterbalancing way. As expressed by Dahl in his definition of a polyarchy, we are in front of a government of 'minorities' which go beyond a few political parties (1956: 84; 1971). Politics is about governing with the consensus of the non-political, civil society. The role of intermediate actors such as non-political associations in the Tocquevillian sense is, therefore, crucial for this concept of democracy.

In this approach, individuals are not spontaneously political. Liberal-representative theories mainly emphasise the need for protection from the excesses of absolutist systems, usually in the form of a constitution conferring rights to individual citizens against the state and against each other – 'negative freedom' – that mainly protects individual rights such as private property (Berlin [1969] 1988). Individuals provide themselves with a government that creates a peaceful environment so that they can dedicate their efforts to their private lives. At the same time, they protect themselves from a strong ruler by limiting its powers. A liberal citizen should only periodically be involved in politics as a way to control those who rule. Politics is perceived as not particularly good but necessary in order to preserve that negative freedom: 'For liberty is to be free from restraint and violence from others, which cannot be where there is no law' (loc. cit. Goodwin 1997: 273). Individuals are primarily motivated by the maximisation of their self-interest, which lies mainly in the private sphere. This is where the consecution of individual freedom will take place – mainly the market, but also the family and religion – and not in the political or public sphere. Margolis synthesises the liberal-representative argument in the following way:

> citizens ought not participate directly in policy formulation, except to vote. Indeed studies of public opinion and voting behaviour show that most citizens do not possess the competence to govern directly. They should *participate indirectly through membership in interest groups or through identification with groups which support their interests and values.*
> (1979: 101; italics added)

Barber (1994) opposes the liberal-representative paradigm as a model of democracy that is representative, weak, 'non-democratic', and apolitical. In his opinion, in any kind of 'representative democracy' the role of the elite replaces citizens' involvement and compromises by definition what is – or should be – democratic politics. In these systems politics is 'what politicians do' and not what 'citizens do'. This model is best represented by liberal democracies as they have existed in the western world over the past two centuries.[9]

The participatory model

The contemporary version of this model shares several aspects with the previous two models, since it does not challenge the idea of a representative system at the national level. However, it does emphasise the *importance of citizens' participation beyond voting and being part or just identifying with intermediate associations* (Sartori 1987: 156). This is the model of democracy defined – and defended – by Barber as direct, 'strong', and political democracy (1984). Also, Sartori considers this as the only strictly political kind of involvement in the long term since it emphasises 'taking part in person' instead of just 'being part' of the political process (1987: 8, 111). Both this and the next model of democracy emphasise 'positive freedom' or, in other words, the real capacities of individuals to be able to choose freely, as opposed to 'negative freedom' that plays a core role in the liberal-representative model (Berlin [1969] 1988).

'Strong democracy' is based in the consideration that citizens are at the same level as the elite. One needs not be an 'expert' to practice politics; a mere 'amateur' is the natural protagonist of politics. Another important difference with the previous two models is that it is based on the idea of the existence of public interests[10] – besides private interests – that are defined in the process of deliberation and that allow the transformation of conflict (Barber 1984). Walzer identifies the participatory model as one of the two responses for the development of the good life that have come from the left and considers it as the model that characterises politics as 'a way of life' (1991).[11]

The unitary model

As in the case of the participatory model, the unitary model is based on the idea of the existence of public interests, but here the emphasis is on the interests of the community instead of those of individual citizens.[12] In fact, politics is not 'a way of life', but an instrument to protect and to promote the interests of the community. This implies that political involvement of citizens is considered good in the short or medium term, but depends upon the achievement of what is considered the most important objective. Barber calls 'unitarian' a model in which citizens are *involved and compromised, but not in a participatory nor political (conflictive) way*. The citizen merges with the community (nation, race, and voluntary will) and it is the public will and not the individual will that guides political involvement (Barber 1984: 153).

Several sub-models such as the Marxist, the Fascist, and the Nationalist fit in the unitary model contributing to the great internal heterogeneity of this group. All of them have in common that politics plays a crucial role in people's life, but it is not the individual that defines this role. Held does not take into account a unitarian model, although he does contemplate the Marxist model as a classical model that looks for 'the end of politics' once classes, and thus conflict, disappear (1987: 121–31). In this sense, the Marxist model can be included in our unitarian model because, first, politics is instrumental and, second, society – in other words, the community – is the protagonist of history and not the individual. Walzer also contemplates two different responses to the development of the good life that can be included in the unitarian model (1991). These are both the Marxist and the Nationalist responses. As in the case of the Marxist (and the Fascist) response, the Nationalist response subordinates the interests of the individual to those of the community.[13] The kind of political involvement expected by the Fascist model, according to Margolis, would also fit in this group. Even when politics will be very important for a fascist individual 'the fascist wants the state to decide for him' (1979: 72).

Obviously, several aspects of this typology of four ideal models of citizenship are controversial. For example, in the participatory model the meaning of participation at a national level is not as clearly defined as in smaller communities. Also, as we have seen, some characteristics are not exclusive of just one model. This is the case with the elitist elements common to both the decisionist and the liberal model, or the belief in the existence of public interests shared by the participatory and the unitary models. The internal heterogeneity of the unitary model establishes one of the most problematic aspects of our typology. Furthermore, non-democratic models can be included both in the decisionist and in the unitary model. Our main objective here is not to elaborate normative theories of democracy, but to analyse to what extent normative elements can be found in real life. The four models, then, might help us to understand the distribution of political involvement in several countries in spite of several contentious aspects just mentioned.

The main characteristics of the four types of citizenship in terms of political involvement and other related characteristics are summarised in Figure 12.1. The upper-part of this overview contains the two crucial aspects of political involvement – importance of politics and interest in politics – that define the different types. In addition, other aspects of each type (political discussion frequency, media exposure) are listed in the lower part of this overview. We will use this fourfold typology for an empirical analysis of citizens' involvement in several countries, defining each type on the basis of the two main aspects of political involvement and using the additional political behaviours to validate the distinction between the four types.

Our typology has been inferred from the description of the four models of citizenship and their expectations about the political involvement of individuals.[14] Decisionist citizens will leave politics up to authorities and are expected to have no interest in politics at all. The apolitical nature of these citizens also explains why politics is not important in their lives. The same apolitical nature applies to the typical liberal citizen.

	Type of citizenship:			
	(i) decisionist	(ii) liberal-representative	(iii) participatory	(iv) unitary
Involvement:				
Importance of politics	Politics is not at all important	Politics is not very important	Politics is clearly important	Politics is important
Interest in politics	Interest in politics is absent	Interest in politics is moderate but present	Citizens are very interested in politics	Citizens are not interested in politics
Behavioural expression of political involvement:				
Discussion of politics	Politics is not at all or rarely discussed	Politics is discussed, but not too much	Politics is discussed often	Politics is discussed often
Political media exposure	Media exposure will be particularly low in what regards political contents	Media exposure will be moderate in what regards political contents	Media exposure will be particularly high in what regards political contents	Media exposure will be high in what regards political contents

Figure 12.1 A typology of citizenship.

Liberal citizens do not consider politics as an important sphere of their lives. On the contrary, the private sphere has priority for them. But, in spite of this, and contrary to the decisionist citizen, a liberal one will be attentive and interested in politics since 'eternal vigilance is the price of liberty' (Margolis 1979: 75). A participatory citizen, as already mentioned, is the most politically involved of all four groups. He or she will consider politics important in absolute terms since politics is 'a way of life'. For the same reason they will be interested in following what goes on in politics, because then they can personally participate in the decision-making process. Finally, the unitary citizen will also consider politics important, since that is the way to protect and promote the interests of the community to which his/her own interests are subordinated. However, the fact that citizens have no say at all in the political objectives to be achieved and that politics is just an instrument to an end, make it reasonable to think that they will not be especially interested or attentive to what goes on in politics. They will just leave it to those who represent the community and the 'public interest'.

With regard to the frequency of political discussion and media exposure we can expect the following. Participatory and unitary citizens are expected to discuss politics quite frequently. Yet, the purpose, the nature, and the result of those discussions will be different in one case or the other as can be inferred from the description of each of the models above. Decisionist citizens will discuss politics least frequently, since politics is not important in their lives nor are they interested in following what goes on. Media exposure in general is difficult to foresee: the contents vary widely and the usage of specific media might depend more on socio-economic resources than on political involvement. Some expectations with regard to political contents can be advanced in the same sense as with the frequency of political discussion: participatory and unitary citizens will expose themselves more often to the political contents of the media followed by the liberal citizens.

Citizenship in Europe

As mentioned in the introduction, our typology of political involvement is the result of combining the individual's interest in politics with their perception of the importance of politics in their lives. The four types of citizenship should be operationalised on the basis of their various degrees of political involvement or, more specifically, on the basis of how important one considers politics to be in one's life and of the various degrees of political interest. The two attitudes are clearly related, but they cannot be considered to be one and the same thing. Theoretically, the perception that politics is important for one's life is relevant for those who presume the existence of a public good to be achieved through politics – either instrumentally or not (unitary and participatory models). This is different

312 *Martín and van Deth*

from considering politics as something intrinsically bad that should be left in the hands of a few, of an elite (decisionist model), as well as from considering politics as something inevitable and necessary to preserve economic and social life and, therefore, something one should be interested in (liberal-representative model).

The two aspects of political involvement are measured in a straightforward way in our data set with a question on the importance of politics in one's daily life and a question on the level of subjective political interest. The wording of these questions is:

- Importance of politics: how important is 'politics' in your life? Here I have a card with a scale going from zero to ten where ten means 'very important' and zero means 'not important at all'.
- Interest in politics: in general, how interested in politics are you? Would you say you are very interested, fairly interested, not very interested, or not at all interested? (1–4)

A first impression of the distribution of political involvement in several European countries can be obtained from Figure 12.2. This graph presents the average levels of political interest and the importance of politics in several countries as measured with the straightforward questions mentioned. From this presentation it is clear, first, that political interest and the importance of politics are closely related at the aggregate level. If the level of political interest is high in a certain country, then we will find

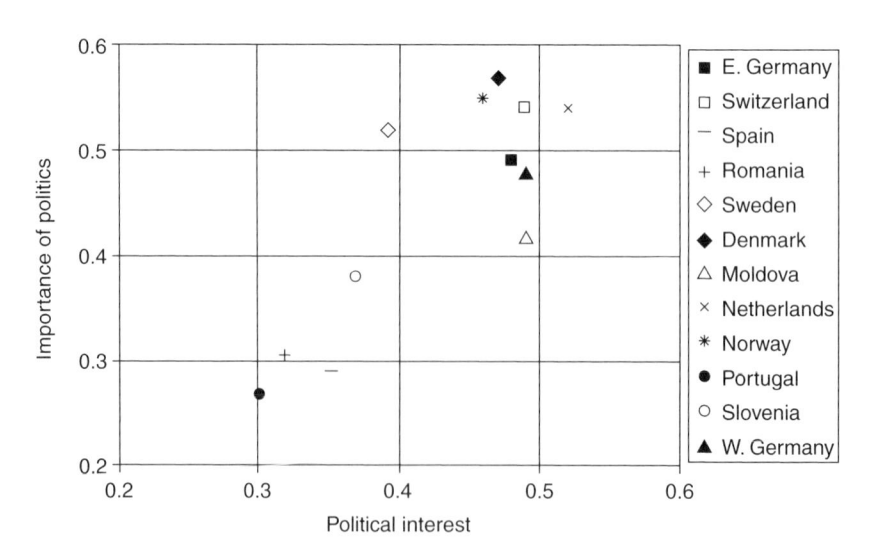

Figure 12.2 Political interest and importance of politics.[a]

Note
a Averages per country.

relatively high levels of the importance of politics in that country – and vice versa. Second, we can already identify two broad clusters of countries, with more recent democracies (Portugal, Spain, Slovenia, and Romania) showing low levels of political involvement on the one hand, and another cluster with established democracies like Denmark, the Netherlands, Switzerland, and Norway showing high levels of political involvement on the other hand. Within the group of more recent democracies it is interesting to notice that it is the oldest among these (Portugal) that shows the lowest levels of both political interest and importance of politics. Besides, Moldova and, even more clearly, East Germany, are much closer to the old democracies than the rest.

The more or less clear distinctions in political involvement at the aggregate level raise the question about the relationships between political interest and the importance of politics at the individual level. The correlation coefficients in Table 12.1 show that – despite the cross-national distinction in the levels of political involvement – the relationship between interest and the importance of politics is very strong at the individual level too.

Combining the two characteristics of political involvement and relating the various combinations to the types of citizenship presented in Figure 12.1, we obtain for categories as summarised in Table 12.2.[15]

Table 12.1 Relationships between political interest and importance of politics[a]

Country	Pearson correlation	Tau-b correlation
Denmark	0.59	0.53
East Germany	0.65	0.57
West Germany	0.53	0.45
Moldova	0.56	0.49
The Netherlands	0.55	0.49
Norway	0.54	0.48
Portugal	0.47	0.41
Romania	0.56	0.49
Slovenia	0.54	0.48
Spain	0.60	0.52
Sweden	0.58	0.52
Switzerland	0.65	0.58

Note
a Figures are bivariate correlations per country. All correlations are significant at $p<0.01$.

Table 12.2 A typology of political involvement

Political interest	Importance of politics	
	High	Low
High	Participatory type	Liberal-representative type
Low	Unitary type	Decisionist type

According to this typology, three types of involvement (participatory, liberal, and unitarian), as opposed to one type characterised by a complete lack of involvement (decisionist), can be discerned. The distributions of these four types in the various countries are summarized in Table 12.3. The results show that the correlation between these two variables at the individual level is far from perfect and that an important number of citizens declare to be interested in politics, but do not consider politics important in their lives (liberal citizens). In every country, except for the Netherlands, the decisionist type of citizenship is the predominant one, and in every country the unitarian type of citizenship is a minoritarian phenomenon, although Moldova seems to be an exception in this sense. Furthermore, there are notorious differences in the presence of each type in each of the countries. Between 60 and 70 per cent of the citizens in Portugal, Spain, Romania, and Slovenia (more recent democracies) can be characterised as decisionist citizens, while this percentage is less than 40 in Denmark, the Netherlands, Norway, and Switzerland. In fact, the countries seem to belong to two broad groups that were already visible in the aggregate results presented in Figure 12.2. On the one hand, we have Portugal, Spain, Romania, and Slovenia with about two-thirds of the population supporting the decisionist model. At the same time, in these countries, the liberal and participatory types together make up for about one-fourth of the population only. The other countries all have a less skewed distribution of the four types, with about 40 per cent decisionists, and much larger proportions of citizens of the liberal and the participatory types than in the first group of countries. In this group especially the very similar distributions obtained for the Scandinavian countries attract the attention. The former East Germany and Moldova are the only new democracies where the spread of the decisionist type is relatively low, but this last country does show a very high number of unitarians. Clearly, the distributions vary across countries and the results suggest the existence of two major groups of democracies.

In order to validate the four types of citizenship in the various countries we return to the additional characteristics listed in the second part of Figure 12.1. Do the differences between the mean scores of these variables – political discussion and political media-exposure – reveal distinctions that are in line with our characterisations? Before we turn to that question, a brief inspection of the levels of political involvement, political discussion, and media exposure in various countries might be helpful. A first look at Figure 12.3 confirms the results presented in Figure 12.2: political interest and the importance of politics are particularly low in Portugal, Romania, Slovenia, and Spain. Yet the citizens of these countries are not characterized by low levels of media exposure. For instance, in Portugal and Spain the attentiveness to political news on radio or television is higher than in both parts of Germany or in Switzerland. Besides, the levels of political discussion vary among the countries and do not show a clear

Table 12.3 Distributions of the four types of citizenship (in percentages)

Type of citizenship	CH	DK	EG	WG	ES	MD	NL	NO	PT	RO	SE	SI	Mean
Decisionist	39	36	44	42	69	47	30	37	70	65	43	61	49
Liberal	20	28	13	17	9	10	15	32	12	11	33	12	18
Participatory	36	32	33	30	14	24	44	27	9	14	22	16	25
Unitarian	5	4	9	11	8	18	11	3	8	10	2	10	8
N	2,136	1,635	1,008	1,966	4,135	1,161	1,645	2,196	992	1,180	1,237	981	20,272

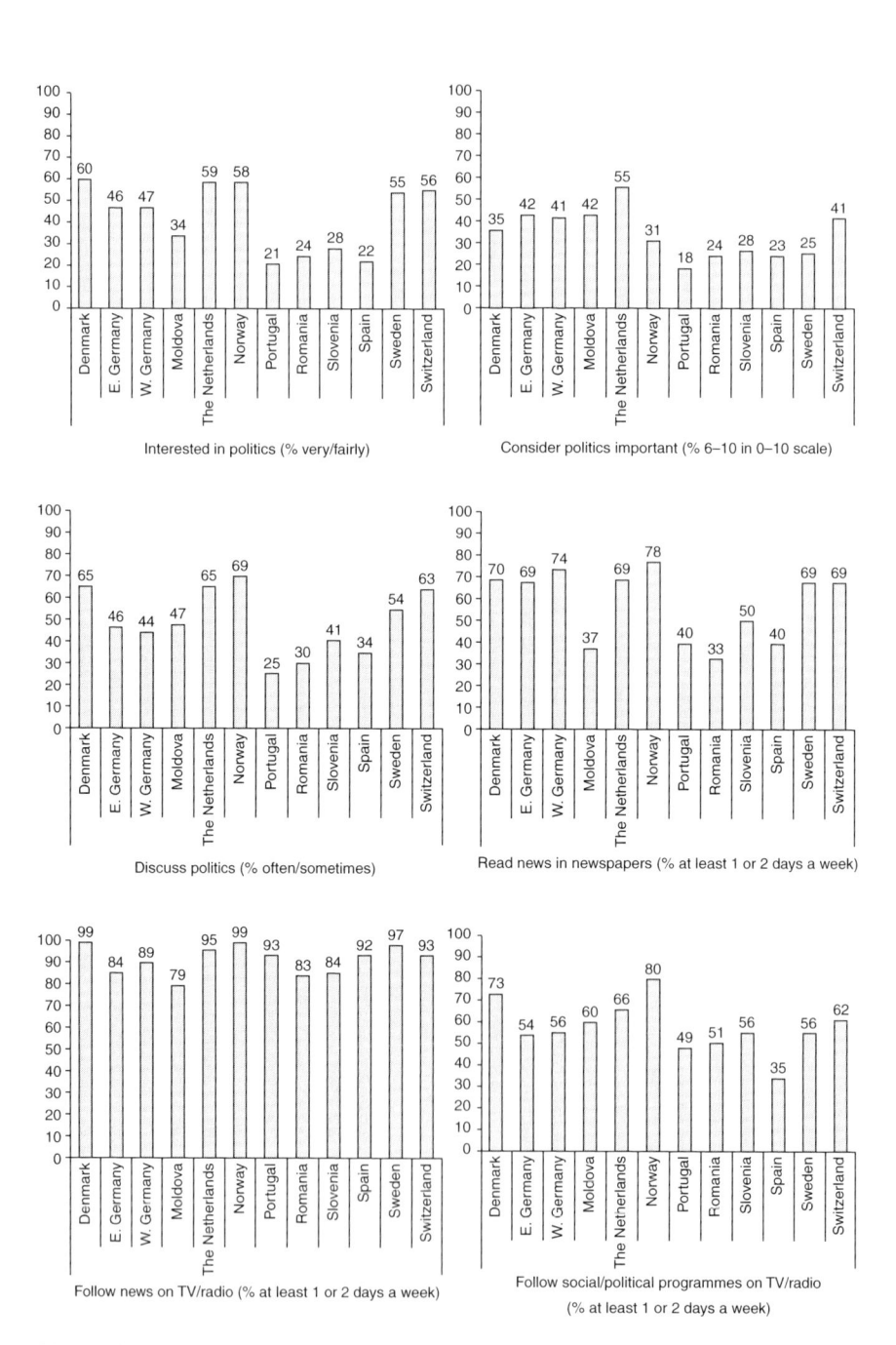

Figure 12.3 Political involvement, political discussion, and media exposure (in percentages).

pattern related to political involvement or to media exposure. Our expectations about the different types of citizenship, however, are concerned with the relative levels of involvement, political discussion, and media involvement and not with the level of these variables in specific countries. In fact, the lack of clear cross-national patterns as illustrated in Figure 12.3 provides a clear challenge for our expectations and a strong test for the use of the citizenship typology.

Table 12.4 shows the mean scores for each of the four types of citizenship in each country separately.[16] These results indicate that there is a

Table 12.4 Behavioural expressions of political involvement related to the four types of citizenship[a]

Country	Type of citizenship	Discussion	Media exposure		
			Newspapers	News on radio and television	Politics on radio and television
Denmark	Decisionist	0.37	0.37	0.91	0.43
	Liberal	0.66	0.66	0.95	0.57
	Participatory	**0.79**	**0.77**	**0.97**	**0.68**
	Unitarian	0.50	0.47	0.93	0.52
East Germany	Decisionist	0.33	0.45	0.67	0.29
	Liberal	0.64	0.81	0.94	0.53
	Participatory	**0.67**	**0.88**	**0.96**	**0.65**
	Unitarian	0.39	0.53	0.69	0.33
West Germany	Decisionist	0.32	0.48	0.73	0.31
	Liberal	0.53	0.80	0.89	0.51
	Participatory	**0.64**	**0.86**	**0.91**	**0.59**
	Unitarian	0.41	0.53	0.72	0.43
Moldova	Decisionist	0.31	0.24	0.60	0.42
	Liberal	0.64	0.49	**0.90**	0.74
	Participatory	**0.74**	**0.53**	0.89	**0.76**
	Unitarian	0.46	0.32	0.66	0.51
The Netherlands	Decisionist	0.32	0.37	0.86	0.32
	Liberal	0.62	0.69	0.92	0.63
	Participatory	**0.75**	**0.80**	**0.96**	**0.71**
	Unitarian	0.43	0.52	0.88	0.39
Norway	Decisionist	0.45	0.45	0.90	0.48
	Liberal	0.66	0.77	0.96	0.67
	Participatory	**0.81**	**0.84**	**0.97**	**0.70**
	Unitarian	0.55	0.46	0.94	0.48
Portugal	Decisionist	0.21	0.30	0.87	0.40
	Liberal	0.54	0.55	**0.95**	0.59
	Participatory	**0.73**	**0.75**	**0.95**	**0.71**
	Unitarian	0.25	0.33	0.78	0.43

continued

Table 12.4 Continued

Country	Type of citizenship	Discussion	Media exposure		
			Newspapers	News on radio and television	Politics on radio and television
Romania	Decisionist	0.22	0.24	0.72	0.40
	Liberal	0.60	0.50	0.91	0.69
	Participatory	**0.76**	**0.58**	**0.97**	**0.80**
	Unitarian	0.39	0.37	0.77	0.47
Slovenia	Decisionist	0.29	0.35	0.70	0.39
	Liberal	0.67	0.64	0.87	0.59
	Participatory	**0.80**	**0.74**	**0.94**	**0.75**
	Unitarian	0.39	0.47	0.74	0.48
Spain	Decisionist	0.25	0.25	0.83	0.24
	Liberal	0.65	0.62	0.94	0.53
	Participatory	**0.74**	**0.68**	**0.96**	**0.59**
	Unitarian	0.44	0.40	0.87	0.34
Sweden	Decisionist	0.35	0.46	0.89	0.34
	Liberal	0.62	0.76	**0.96**	0.55
	Participatory	**0.74**	**0.84**	0.95	**0.65**
	Unitarian	0.51	0.49	0.89	0.40
Switzerland	Decisionist	0.40	0.37	0.75	0.37
	Liberal	0.73	0.67	0.89	0.58
	Participatory	**0.85**	**0.77**	**0.91**	**0.61**
	Unitarian	0.56	0.58	0.83	0.52

Note
a Figures are means; highest levels are emphasized in bold. All F-tests for between-group differences are significant at $p<0.01$.

rather homogeneous pattern among the countries: it is the participatory type that is the most 'involved'. Usually, the decisionist type shows the least involvement, whereas the liberal type shows higher levels of involvement than the unitary type. This last type was rather difficult to define in theoretical terms, since it is the most heterogeneous internally. This theoretical ambiguity is reflected in the minor violations of the expected positioning of the unitarians in several countries.

We turn, first, to the average levels of political discussion among the four types of citizenship. The four types are validated in almost every country. As expected, and in spite of the differences in the aggregate levels of political discussion in the various countries, in all of them it is the participatory type of citizens that discusses politics most often and the decisionist type that discusses the least. After the participatory type, it is the liberal type of citizen who discusses politics most frequently. The differences between countries in the aggregate levels of political discussion are not always reflected in the differences between participatory citizens. Participatory citizens in Portugal,

Romania, Slovenia, and Spain discuss politics more often than German citizens classified in the same group even though the aggregate level of political discussion in Germany is higher than in any of those countries. Among the decisionists – the group that discusses politics the least – we find the opposite: they discuss much less in the first group of countries than in both East and West Germany. This points to a higher distance between participatory and decisionist citizens in their degree of political involvement in the four more recent democracies than in other countries.

The second antecedent of citizenship is media exposure, for which we use three distinct variables: reading about politics in newspapers, watching or listening to news programmes on radio or television, and watching or listening to political and social programmes on radio or television. The results obtained for following these programmes as well as for reading about politics in newspapers validate the four types of citizenship. More deviations and cross-national differences appear when we turn to news broadcasts on radio and television. For example, in Portugal, Moldova, and Sweden it is not the participatory type that watches or listens to the news more often, but the liberal type. Both in West Germany and in Portugal it is the unitary group and not the decisionist group that watches or listens to the news less often. This is probably due to the fact that the content of these programmes is not especially political. In general, however, the expected differences between the four types are validated by the results on media exposure. The results presented in Table 12.4 corroborate the major expectations about the relationship between the four types of citizenship and other political behaviours we distinguished before. This is especially clear in the case of political discussion and following political or social programmes on radio or television and not so evident with regard to listening and watching news on radio or television.[17] These results underline the usefulness of our distinction between different types of citizenship in terms of political involvement, although we allowed for overlap and peculiarities. The types seem to be promising concepts for further analyses of the differences and similarities in political involvement in democratic countries.

Consequences of differences in citizenship

Political involvement and participation are related in a trivial way: people showing interest in a specific topic or theme are more likely to become active in this area than other people. This relationship can, of course, also be specified in the other direction, presuming that interest develops after people have become active. Both causal relationships are not incompatible with each other. Here we will focus on the participatory consequences of belongingness to one of the four types of citizenship developed. Almost by definition, different levels of participation are expected from the four types. We will use the typology of political participation elaborated in

Chapter 13 to distinguish the kinds of political participation that are influenced by different modes of political involvement. Our expectation is that participatory citizens will be the most politically active, followed by the liberals. Decisionists are expected to show the lowest levels of participation. This means that participatory citizens, in general, will be the most active, but, especially so in the most demanding, most active, most informational, voice-based activities such as party activity, protest, and contacts. This difference will be less evident in the case of voting or political consumer activities.

What about social participation? Should we expect, as Putnam does when introducing his argument, that those who perceive the 'dysfunctional ugliness of contemporary politics and the absence of large, compelling projects' redirect their energies 'away from conventional politics into less formal, more voluntary, more effective channels' (2000: 47)?[18] If the relationship between political and social participation is depicted as a zero-sum game, participatory citizens will be more active in politics, but not necessarily in other organizations. Hirschman (1982) used the phrase 'shifting involvements' to characterise this mutual exclusion of involvement in private and public spheres of society. However, we expect the relationship between political and social participation to follow a positive-sum game. This is, of course, not the same as saying that social capital leads to political participation.[19] What we suggest is that those who are politically active are also more active in social groups. Participatory citizens, then, will be more active both in political and in social modes of participation, followed by liberals and, finally, by decisionists. For the purpose of testing this argument we rely on a slightly modified version of the organisational involvement typology developed in Chapter 6.[20]

As the results in Table 12.5 indicate, the relationships between the different kinds of political involvement and political participation show a consistent pattern in most countries. Our hypothesis holds as well for liberal and decisionist citizens. Participatory citizens show the highest rates of political activity for every mode of participation, followed by liberal citizens. This is especially so in the case of participation related to political parties, as well as of contacts.[21] In general, the results for participatory citizens follow the same pattern as the rest of citizenry. They participate, most of all, through voting followed by political consumer activities. They participate more than any other group in the most demanding activities but, again like for the rest of citizens, these are the activities they practice the least. Only in Moldova and Spain participatory citizens are more likely to participate in protest activities than in party activities, but this is a reflection of what happens in these societies and not a peculiarity of this specific group. The only country where participatory citizens show a different pattern is Portugal, where they appear to be the only group that participates more often through contacts than through consumer-like activities.

Participatory citizens also participate considerably in social organisations. This pattern, though, is not as consistent as in the case of political participation. In several countries participatory citizens participate in social organisations with the same or even less intensity as liberals do. In any case, the average scores for social participation clearly show that, in each country, liberal and participatory citizens are more involved than decisionist or unitarian types.

With this brief analysis of the participatory consequences of citizenship, we have, once more, demonstrated that two different kinds of involvement – a participatory and a liberal kind – need to be distinguished. Although both participatory and liberal citizens are interested in politics, a clear difference between the two exists with respect to their actual level and mode of participation. Both types of citizens participate in social organisations to a higher degree than the decisionist and the unitarian citizens do, but no big differences can be identified between the two in this sphere. The differences between participatory and liberal citizens become evident when we look at the level of activity in all the different modes of political participation.

Explaining citizenship

A number of individual characteristics determine the level of political involvement of citizens and many studies have confirmed the relationship between involvement and socio-economic status, occupation, education, age, gender, and income.[22] A first factor taken into account in many approaches at the individual level is *sex* or *gender*. To the well-established results of empirical research belongs the observation that women are less likely to be interested in politics than men. *Age* and *year of birth* are a second factor of political involvement. Usually, age is seen as a surrogate variable for social and psychological aging (life-cycle or age effects), and, when date of birth is used, for the experience with specific historical events (birth cohort effects). Here we will concentrate on the impact of the life cycle.[23] Given that the relationship between age and political involvement is often curvilinear – the youngest and the oldest groups being often less involved than the middle-aged groups – we introduce a quadratic measure of the age variable in our analysis.

A third candidate for explaining political involvement is the level of *education* as an indicator of the level of (political) knowledge and of (political) skills that people possess, and an indicator of the capacity people have to comprehend political phenomena. Another individual resource that is expected to influence the level and kind of political involvement is *time pressure*. One of Putnam's findings when analysing the decline of social capital is that those who have time to develop social networks beyond the place of work are more likely to contribute to the creation of social capital (2000: 189–90, 283, 407). There is no reason why the same

Table 12.5 Impact of political involvement on social and political participation by country and type of citizenship[a]

Country	Type of citizenship	Social participation	Political participation					
			Voting	Party activity	Contacting	Consumer participation	Protest activity
Denmark	Decisionist	0.77	0.87	0.00	0.10	0.22	0.02
	Liberal	**0.87**	**0.97**	0.03	0.18	0.37	0.03
	Participatory	0.84	0.96	**0.09**	**0.23**	**0.39**	**0.05**
	Unitarian	0.80	0.92	0.01	0.08	0.27	0.01
East Germany	Decisionist	0.37	0.79	0.00	0.04	0.12	0.02
	Liberal	0.52	0.82	0.02	0.12	0.26	0.06
	Participatory	**0.64**	**0.91**	**0.07**	**0.19**	**0.34**	**0.10**
	Unitarian	0.35	0.77	0.00	0.05	0.13	0.06
West Germany	Decisionist	0.54	0.77	0.00	0.05	0.22	0.03
	Liberal	0.74	**0.95**	0.02	0.12	0.31	0.05
	Participatory	**0.77**	**0.95**	**0.06**	**0.19**	**0.43**	**0.07**
	Unitarian	0.61	0.81	0.00	0.05	0.21	0.03
Moldova	Decisionist	0.13	0.76	0.00	0.04	0.05	0.04
	Liberal	**0.23**	0.91	0.04	0.09	0.06	0.07
	Participatory	0.22	**0.94**	**0.05**	**0.14**	**0.11**	**0.10**
	Unitarian	0.16	0.82	0.01	0.05	0.06	0.03
The Netherlands	Decisionist	0.65	0.66	0.01	0.15	0.29	0.02
	Liberal	**0.81**	0.86	0.02	0.20	0.45	0.03
	Participatory	0.76	**0.89**	**0.06**	**0.26**	**0.48**	**0.04**
	Unitarian	0.66	0.86	0.01	0.15	0.30	0.01
Norway	Decisionist	0.76	0.84	0.01	0.14	0.35	0.03
	Liberal	0.82	0.95	0.04	0.22	0.49	0.04
	Participatory	**0.83**	**0.96**	**0.11**	**0.28**	**0.53**	**0.07**
	Unitarian	0.77	0.90	0.01	0.13	0.39	0.05

Country	Type					
Portugal	Decisionist	0.42	0.74	0.00	0.07	0.09	0.02
	Liberal	0.53	0.86	0.03	0.17	0.18	0.04
	Participatory	**0.67**	**0.93**	**0.16**	**0.30**	**0.22**	**0.10**
	Unitarian	0.38	0.85	0.00	0.06	0.07	0.00
Romania	Decisionist	0.12	0.90	0.01	0.04	0.07	0.04
	Liberal	**0.28**	0.95	0.03	0.07	0.11	0.06
	Participatory	0.22	0.95	**0.08**	**0.12**	**0.13**	0.06
	Unitarian	0.15	0.94	0.04	0.04	0.05	0.03
Slovenia	Decisionist	0.44	0.69	0.01	0.05	0.15	0.02
	Liberal	**0.58**	**0.87**	0.02	0.11	0.19	0.02
	Participatory	**0.58**	0.86	**0.07**	**0.14**	**0.24**	**0.04**
	Unitarian	0.52	0.72	0.01	0.05	0.12	0.02
Spain	Decisionist	0.34	0.81	0.00	0.08	0.13	0.05
	Liberal	0.54	0.89	0.03	0.21	0.29	0.14
	Participatory	**0.57**	**0.94**	**0.10**	**0.25**	**0.31**	**0.16**
	Unitarian	0.41	0.86	0.01	0.12	0.16	0.07
Sweden	Decisionist	0.77	0.86	0.01	0.08	0.31	0.01
	Liberal	0.84	0.95	0.03	0.16	0.44	0.02
	Participatory	**0.87**	**0.96**	**0.12**	**0.23**	**0.51**	**0.05**
	Unitarian	0.77	0.89	0.00	0.10	0.40	0.01
Switzerland	Decisionist	0.73	0.44	0.01	0.08	0.26	0.02
	Liberal	0.79	0.76	0.05	0.17	0.41	0.03
	Participatory	**0.80**	**0.85**	**0.08**	**0.23**	**0.46**	**0.04**
	Unitarian	0.75	0.65	0.01	0.11	0.31	0.03

Note

a Entries are means with the highest level boldfaced. All F-tests for between-group differences are significant at $p<0.05$, except for voting in Romania and protest activity in Romania and Slovenia.

should not apply to political involvement. Therefore, we expect that those who spend less time at work to be more politically involved than other people.[24]

In addition to socio-demographic factors and resources, political involvement also depends on several other factors. One of the cultural aspects that have most often been associated with social capital is the level of *trust* in other people (Putnam 1993 and 2000: 147). Trust has been considered one of the main products of social participation but it is also supposed to favour interpersonal contacts and the creation of social networks in the first place. If we consider political involvement as a kind – or as a prerequisite for some kinds – of social capital, then trust can be expected to have a positive impact on political involvement as well. For this reason, we use the so-called question on interpersonal trust (see Chapter 2) as an indicator of the relevant level of trust here. A second factor that, at first sight, could be thought to foster interconnectedness is the *size of the locality* where one lives. As Putnam recalls, some have shown certain nostalgia for 'small, close-knit, premodern societies' and see in their gradual disappearance one of the sources of the decline of social capital. Although he finds that in some cases this kind of communities are not associated with civic communities (1993: 114), his argument about the negative impact of travelling and commuting in big metropolitan areas implies a similar argument in favour of small communities that offer more 'humane' distances and places where people can relate to each other (2000: 214–15, 408).

We consider a third group of factors that we have termed 'political', because they do not depend on social position nor on social capital. To represent a group of factors based on the evaluation of political results or performance of a political system we use two indicators. One is the level of *satisfaction* with the way democracy works, and the other one is the degree of *political efficacy* one feels. Lastly, we are concerned with the impact of ideology on the various types of citizenship in two senses. On the one hand, we want to know to what extent a *left ideology* is linked to participatory citizenship, as political discourse and theory would make us expect. In the conventional depiction of Lipset *et al.* the urge for 'social change in the direction of greater equality' characterises left-wing ideologies (1954: 1135). Since these demands are usually not in line with the status quo, people with left-wing orientations are expected to be more heavily involved in politics than other people. We are also interested in the impact of ideological polarisation.[25] Once more, it is Putnam's argument that those that place themselves towards the extremes of the left-right scale are more engaged in both civic and political life whereas moderates or 'middle-of-the-roaders' have tended to drop out (2000: 342).[26]

Studies of political involvement present socio-demographic, social-capital related, and political factors in order to explain the various modes and levels of political involvement. The aim of the present analyses is to explain the various types of citizenship defined and validated in the previous sections. Since these types are characterised on the basis of the levels of importance of politics and political interest, the conventional factors to explain political involvement are likely to explain these four types of citizenship as well.

The results of multinomial regression analyses for the three most important types of citizenship are summarised in Table 12.6.[27] Both the decisionist and the liberal citizens are compared with the participatory group, which has been chosen as the base category in the models. In this way the analyses are focused on the impact of the different individual factors on both the totally uninvolved and those relatively involved when compared to the most involved in each of the countries. Cross-national differences are inferred from the levels of significance of the impact of those individual variables in each of the countries when compared to the rest.

In spite of the modest fit of the models the coefficients reveal a few clear patterns that, once more, validate the distinction between different types of political involvement according to our theoretical models of democracy and citizenship. Since our main focus here is not on the level of variance explained, but on the theoretical relevance of the variables included in the models estimated, several important conclusions can be derived from the results in Table 12.6.

First of all, when comparing the two 'most different' groups of citizens – decisionist vs. participatory – we find that those who have studied for a short period of time, as well as women in most countries, are more likely to be decisionists. Beyond social and resource-based differences two purely political factors seem to increase the probability of being a decisionist kind of citizen in almost every country. These are the feeling of political inefficacy, and placing oneself towards the centre of the ideology scale instead of near one of the two poles. Of all the remaining factors we expected to have an impact on being a decisionist citizen when compared to being a participatory citizen, some appear to be significant in just a few countries. In seven of the 12 countries – Denmark, East Germany, West Germany, the Netherlands, Romania, Slovenia, and Spain – young people are more likely to be decisionists than other people are. The size of the locality where one lives also has a significant influence on political involvement in Denmark, the Netherlands, Norway, Spain, Sweden, and Switzerland. We expected that the increased possibilities for social contacts, which are easier in smaller communities, would have a positive impact on participatory types of political involvement and that bigger communities would foster the kind of decisionist citizen that is not involved in politics. Our results, however, point exactly in the opposite direction: as the size of the locality where one lives grows, so does the likelihood of being a participatory citizen. One explanation could be that political involvement indicates the existence of social capital of the

Table 12.6 Antecedents of three types of citizenship (multinomial logistic regressions, log-odds ratios)[a]

Pair of types and predictors	CH	DK	EG	WG	ES	MD	NL	NO	PT	RO	SE	SI
Decisionist vs. participatory												
Gender (male)	−0.34*	−0.58***	−0.82***	−0.93***	−0.17	−0.68**	−0.43**	−0.25*	−0.75**	−0.21	−0.59***	−0.93***
Age	0.46	−6.07*	−8.54**	−8.89***	−5.19**	−3.57	−9.64***	−3.98	−6.22	−13.40**	−1.38	−8.20*
Age square	−4.23	3.50	5.94	7.04***	3.49	3.05	6.18**	2.41	2.09	10.08*	−2.36	4.83
Education	−3.38***	−3.33***	−1.15*	−1.92***	−2.71***	−4.50***	−3.30***	−0.95*	−4.86***	−3.32***	−3.92***	−2.57***
Work[b]	0.00	0.46**	0.13	0.01	0.05	0.00	0.34	0.29	−0.29	0.13	0.43	0.41
Size of locality[c]	−0.97*	−0.72**	−0.63	−0.48	−0.56**	0.52	−1.85***	−0.84***	0.69	0.03	−0.70*	−0.43
Trust	−0.14	−1.12**	0.42	−0.69**	−0.88**	−0.74	−0.42	−0.71*	0.65	−0.57	−0.72*	0.16
Satisfaction with democracy	−0.22	−0.23	−1.63***	−0.66*	−0.42	−0.90	−1.39***	0.44	−0.61	−1.28**	0.10	−0.41
Efficacy	−2.63***	−3.27***	−0.37	−2.17***	−2.65***	−1.08**	−1.44***	−3.21***	−2.48***	−0.12	−3.28***	−1.64***
Ideology	0.11	0.05	0.56	0.57	1.11***	−0.75*	0.52	1.35***	0.06	−0.64	1.78***	0.04
Polarization	−0.66***	−0.49**	−0.45	−0.61**	−0.80***	−0.62**	−0.73**	−0.81***	−0.91***	−0.51	−0.75***	−1.04***
Constant	3.91***	6.70	4.42	5.69***	5.98***	5.11***	6.80***	3.28	6.89***	7.82***	5.41***	6.41***

Liberal vs. participatory

Gender (male)	0.13	−0.16	−0.00	−0.35*	0.33*	0.14	0.17	0.24	−0.44	0.06	−0.10	−0.16
Age	0.25	1.82	−4.41	−1.14	4.58	10.39	0.03	1.63	0.80	−5.17	0.35	2.41
Age square	−1.35	−2.71	3.26	1.41	−4.33	−10.99	−0.78	−0.96	−3.37	3.92	−1.69	−3.13
Education	−1.69*	−0.02	1.13	0.31	−0.64	−0.67	−0.30	0.73	−0.87	0.84	−0.42	−1.29
Work[b]	0.17	0.23	−0.15	0.26	−0.04	−0.14	0.20	0.15	−0.51	0.28	0.23	0.11
Size of locality[c]	−0.53	−0.46*	−0.73	−0.94**	−0.23	−0.15	0.15	−0.24	0.72	−0.62	−0.01	0.56
Trust	0.20	−0.17	0.22	−0.21	−0.18	−0.20	−0.60	−0.22	−0.12	−0.47	−0.77*	−0.06
Satisfaction with democracy	−0.16	−0.48	−1.73***	−0.00	−0.02	0.94	−0.43	0.80*	0.51	0.51	0.26	−0.03
Efficacy	−0.51	−1.70***	0.24	−0.96**	−1.46***	−0.53	−1.05*	−1.19***	−1.57*	0.08	−1.73***	−1.91**
Ideology	0.32	0.77*	−0.88	0.05	0.65	−0.42	0.15	0.92***	−0.13	−1.14	1.14**	−0.08
Polarization	−0.36	−0.46**	−1.28***	−0.95**	−0.38*	−0.45	−0.26	−0.08	−0.41	−0.09	−0.26	−0.79**
Constant	0.56	0.96	1.52	0.47	−0.76	−2.48	0.09	−1.16	1.74	1.72	1.59	0.91
Pseudo R^2	0.08	0.09	0.07	0.08	0.10	0.10	0.07	0.07	0.10	0.09	0.09	0.11
N	1,092	1,343	718	1,341	2,570	501	1,071	1,703	642	525	1,067	556

Notes

a Levels of statistical significance: *** = 0.001, ** = 0.01, * = 0.05.
b Indicates the amount of time occupied by work: 0 = unemployed, 0.5 = employed part-time, 1 = employed full-time.
c The minimum value is 0 for rural, and the maximum is 1 for big city of more than 500,000 inhabitants.

'bridging' kind (Putnam 2000) since it is often related with concern for public issues and public interest.[28] Social capital in small communities, on the other hand, is more likely to be of a 'bonding' kind given its relationship with personal and local interests. Therefore, it is not surprising that participatory citizens are more likely to be found in bigger communities where, once the obstacles for social interaction are overcome, social networks are more likely to be concerned about broader issues than in smaller communities.

The impact of interpersonal trust on the different kinds of political involvement deserves special attention. We find that the relationship between trust and political involvement, where it exists, reveals the expected direction. Trusting people increases the probability of political involvement and decreases the probability of being a decisionist citizen. The problem we encounter here is that the expected impact can be traced in only five of the 12 countries. Only in Denmark, West Germany, Norway, Spain, and Sweden does trust increase the likelihood of political involvement.

We have seen that there are several aspects that distinguish decisionist citizens from participatory citizens. But what distinguishes participatory from liberal citizens? The comparison between these two types of 'politically involved citizens' is one of our main concerns. Although no general pattern distinguishes these two groups in every country, it is clearly not the same factors that influence political involvement of liberal and participatory citizens. In fact, there are only two countries (Moldova and Romania) where, according to our model, there are no significant differences between liberal and participant citizens. In all other countries we find that some factors increase the probability of belonging to one of them as opposed to the other. This is especially the case for those citizens that feel politically efficacious. In eight of the 12 countries those who feel that 'people like them have greater possibilities than others to make politicians take account of their opinions' are more likely to be involved in a participatory than in a liberal way. This implies that participatory political involvement is directly related to a sense of being able to change something. In other words, we find that if citizens feel that politicians consider people's opinions relevant, they will consider politics to be relevant as well. Otherwise, citizens will consider politics 'interesting but unimportant'.[29] Extending our findings to the creation of social capital in general we expect that social capital, of the 'political' kind, will grow easier if citizens have the perception that they will be heard by politicians.

A second factor that seems to foster political involvement of a participatory kind is ideological polarization. The likelihood of being involved in a participatory way increases with the degree of polarization in five countries. In line with Putnam's findings we observe that those citizens who place themselves near the poles of the ideological scale – no matter whether on the left or on the right side – are more inclined to be participatory citizens, while those who place themselves towards the centre are more likely to be of the liberal type. This is the case in Denmark, in both East and West Germany, in Slovenia, and in Spain.

Apparently resources such as education, time, responsibilities, or social contacts (in smaller communities) do not have the expected impact on fostering participatory citizenship instead of a liberal one. Surprisingly, too, gender does not seem to affect the likelihood of belonging to the liberal group as opposed to the participatory group in most countries either. Moreover, in one of the four countries where this relationship is significant, Spain, it turns out to be contrary than expected: women are more likely to be participatory citizens than men.

The variable that is linked par excellence to the existence of social capital, trust, does not seem to contribute to a more participatory citizenship. Being satisfied with the way democracy works does not make a difference either.

Finally, our analyses show that no clustering or systematic distinctions between groups of countries are identified. The evident distinctions between Portugal, Spain, Slovenia, and Romania on the one hand, and the other countries on the other hand, that appeared so clearly in the previous sections, are not as clearly observed here. In other words: the distinction between recent and old democracies is not as clearcut as our initial analyses suggested.

Summarising the results of the regression analyses it is clear that, in almost every country, the political and socio-demographic factors that increase the probabilities of being a decisionist or a liberal citizen, differ from those that increase the likelihood of being a participatory citizen. Therefore, our findings once more validate the distinction between these three kinds of citizens and, as expected, between liberal and participatory types of involvement. Political involvement is traditionally analysed in a dichotomised way by making a distinction between those interested and those not interested in politics. Here we have emphasized a distinction *within* the first group of citizens; that is, between those who consider politics important and those who do not. The distinctions between these two groups as they appear from our empirical analyses, seem to justify the conceptual separation of the two types in most countries.

Conclusions

In this chapter we studied the opportunities to develop an empirical typology of citizenship based on (normative) democratic theories. The four ideal types of citizenship distinguished – a decisionist, a liberal-representative, a participatory, and a unitary type – are characterised in terms of the forms and levels of political involvement. Two major conclusions can be obtained by using this typology for cross-national empirical analyses of citizenship and involvement.

The first conclusion is that – at the aggregate level – two distinct groups of countries can be traced, with the newer democracies (Portugal, Spain, Romania, and Slovenia) on the one hand, and older democracies (like Denmark, the Netherlands, and Switzerland) on the other. In the first group, more than two-thirds of the populations belong to the decisionist model. The countries in the second group have about 40 per cent decisionists and much larger proportions of citizens of the liberal and the participatory types than the first group of countries. This clear picture of two clusters disappears when we turn to socio-demographic, social-capital related, and political antecedents of citizenship in various countries. Cross-national differences are mainly differences in the distributions of the four types of citizenship. In other words: since similar relationships exist, similar explanations for citizenship and involvement are valid in spite of the clear distributional differences between the countries. Structural differences at the individual level are much less apparent, but they also exist in some countries.

The second conclusion points to the remarkable distinctions between the liberal and the participatory types of citizenship. Both types are characterised by high levels of political interest. Contrary to more conventional approaches, we introduced a distinction *within* this group of interested citizens by adding the importance of politics as an additional feature. The distinctions between participatory and liberal citizens are clearly observable if we look at the differences in political antecedents. Furthermore, clear differences exist between the two in their actual levels and modes of participation. In each and every country, participatory citizens appear to participate more frequently in political activities than citizens belonging to any of the other types of citizenship.

Combining normative approaches and empirical evidence in this chapter, we could show that political involvement and the concepts of democracy and of democratic citizenship that lay behind them, are closely related. From the status quo identified here – especially the predominance of the decisionist type of citizenship in many countries – the conclusion should not be that things couldn't be otherwise. The more established democracies show a less-skewed distribution of the four types of citizenship than the newer ones. Since the structural relationships presented in this chapter are much more similar than the actual distributions of types of citizenship, we might expect a decline in the decisionist type in the newer democracies in the near future as the general level of education grows and as the gender gap decreases. Democracy can be strengthened if the popularity of the decisionist type declines and the unitarian type remains a minority phenomenon. In other words: democracy can be strengthened if the share of participatory and liberal types of citizenship increases. Political involvement of the participatory kind is clearly linked to 'political' activities. Those we have termed liberal citizens are, in some countries, the most involved in 'social' activities. Both liberal and participatory citizens seem to be related to the existence of social capital. However, as has been shown here, participatory citizens are especially qualified for the creation of 'political' social capital. This will mainly depend on whether citizens feel politically efficacious, as well as on whether they cling on to clear left/right positions.

Notes

1 For distinct definitions and demarcations of the concept of political interest and related concepts, see Sigel and Hoskin 1981: Chapters 3–6; Bennett 1984: 31–9; Gabriel 1986: 179–82; van Deth 1990: 276–82; and Zaller 1992: 43 and 333–6.
2 The importance of politics in people's lives is measured here in absolute terms. This differs from other analyses in which a relative measure (political saliency) is used (van Deth 2000).
3 According to Macpherson (1977: 2–9), models in the social sciences are theoretical constructions that intend to explain real relationships between the phenomena we study. Besides, he points out two additional dimensions: the fact that models also try to advance possible future developments of those relationships, as well as to justify them in ethical terms according to what different authors consider 'good' or 'desirable'. In other words, models do not only try to explain phenomena.
4 This quotation from Thucydides' famous account is taken from Sabine and Thorson (1973: 28). A number of other translations are available, many of them presenting slightly different wordings.
5 Notice that – even though our theoretical references are to 'models of democracy' – it is not only 'democratic' political involvement we want to analyse. That is why, from a normative point of view, it is not correct, strictly speaking, to say that we are dealing with four models of *democratic* citizenship.
6 Similar fourfold typologies appear, in a more or less modified form, in most of the literature on models of democracy (see, for instance, the texts edited by Águila *et al.* 1998).
7 The oldest references to this model of democracy, based on the claims of a group of experts, are Socrates' 'philosopher king' and Plato's 'pilots' or 'guardians' (cf. *The Republic*). Our description is inspired by the contemporary competitive-elitist model as defined by Held (1987: Chapter 5). See Sartori 1987: 152 ff. for a critical view.
8 Even J.S. Mill and A. de Tocqueville, in spite of valuing democracy for producing active, public-spirited individuals, had an elitist element in their theories that justifies their consideration as precursors of this model of democracy. Both authors feared the social consequences of the power of the majority and that is why, although considering political activity good for every citizen, they held the idea that the educated minority knows best (Goodwin 1997: 276).
9 This model is basically what Held (1987) has called the 'pluralist model'. Walzer (1991) has also included it as one of the different responses to what would be an appropriate environment for the development of the good life, and has referred to it as the 'capitalist' response. Sartori (1987: 131) also mentions a representative type of democracy that puts more emphasis on the vertical dimension of politics as distinct from a participatory type that puts more emphasis on the horizontal dimension.
10 As Pericles indicated, the interests of citizens do not only lie in their private sphere but also, to a large extent, in the public sphere (Sabine and Thorson 1973: 26–31).

11 This model has also been contemplated by Held (1987: 254), who mentions Macpherson, Pateman, and Poulantzas as three of its main representative authors. Habermas (1994) refers to this model as the 'republican' one, as opposed to the 'liberal' one. Sartori (1987: 111–20) points out the difficulties he finds in defining the participatory model and in differentiating it from similar concepts such as 'direct democracy' and 'referendum democracy'. To these we could add the term 'deliberative democracy', which, in the words of Goodwin (1997: 300–1): 'turns on the quality of the debate of political participants rather [than] on the mechanics of participation'.

12 The label 'communitarian' could be used for this type of citizenship too but because it can be understood as implying 'participatory' we use the label 'unitarian' in order to avoid confusion with the participatory model. Besides, this terminology is not uncommon in the literature and is used in similar ways by, for instance, Benjamin Barber.

13 Some differences can also be observed depending on the specific variant of the unitary type considered. For example, it is in the sphere where the relations of production take place that 'Marxist citizens' will mainly be involved. On the other hand, 'nationalist citizens' will focus on local, community issues.

14 Similar typologies have been developed by Margolis (1979: 74), by Morlino and Montero (1995), and by Offe (2006).

15 These four types are obtained by recoding the two original variables in the following way:

1 Importance of politics in one's life (recoded into 2 categories: 0 for citizens who do not consider politics important or do not have a clear opinion (0–5), 1 for citizens who consider politics important (6–10);

2 Interest in politics (recoded into 2 values: 0 for citizens who are not very interested in politics or not interested at all, 1 for citizens who are very or fairly interested).

16 The variables in these and further analyses have been recoded so that they range from 0 to 1.

17 These findings have been further corroborated with a comparison of the different pairs of groups and the *post hoc* Tamhane test. These results are not shown here.

18 Putnam (2000: 412) does not seem to conclude that this is a zero-sum relationship. In fact, he explicitly recommends the restoring of 'connectedness, trust, and civic engagement . . . in the now often empty public forums of our democracy'. He seems to consider political involvement as one of the several aspects of social capital that needs to be encouraged. The relevance of the political aspects of social capital for Putnam is clear in that he does not leave its restoration up to the indirect effects of other kinds of social capital.

19 See Putnam (2000: 339) and Newton 2001a for an argument against this relationship.

20 The 'social involvement' typology used here to measure social participation corresponds to 0 ('not involved'), 0.5 ('passively involved'), and 1 ('actively involved' in different kinds of organisations). The only difference with the typology elaborated in Chapter 6 is that we have excluded involvement with political parties, which is, in turn, included under the 'political participation' typology.

21 These results have been corroborated by the Tamhane test not shown here.

22 For an early summary of this research, see Milbrath and Goel (1977: 46–8, 96, 98, 102). Other discussions are provided, among others, by Bennett (1984 and 1986), Verba *et al.* (1995), and van Deth and Elff (2000: 7).

23 Since we only have cross-sectional data available, the distinction between age and date of birth has no implications for our empirical analyses including that variable.

24 The way we have operationalised this variable focuses only on the amount of time available outside of work. Another possible way to introduce work-related factors in our model would be to compare those who are employed full-time and those who are unemployed, on the one hand, with those who are employed part-time, on the other. This operationalisation would take into account not only time pressure but 'psychological distress' as well and it would assume that those who are unemployed are amongst the least politically involved for that reason.
25 See also Putnam (1993: 116–17) for a similar argument referring to the political context instead of individual attitudes.
26 In a previous model we included additional variables that, according to Putnam's (2000) study of the explanations for the evolution of social capital, could also be expected to influence political involvement. These variables are 'having children living in the household' and 'church attendance'. The first is understood as a measure of time pressure that has been found to have a negative influence on political involvement (Putnam 2000: 278–9). Church attendance is used as an indicator of an alternative to political involvement. In southern Italy, Putnam (1993: 107–9) found a negative relationship between organised religion and a civic community. In our case, the influence of these two variables on the different types of political involvement is not significant in most cases. But the ultimate reason to exclude these factors from our analyses is the high number of missing cases they introduce into the model for several countries. The same applies to a variable measuring whether the respondent works in the public sector or not.
27 The unitarian group has not been included in the causal analysis for two reasons. First, its theoretical definition is not as clear as in the other three cases. As we have mentioned, this is a rather heterogeneous type containing different versions of 'unitarianism' such as Nationalism, Marxism, and Fascism. Second, the number of citizens that belong to this group is clearly a minority in every country.
28 We are aware of the fact that this is not always the case. See, for example, Putnam (1993: 99, 109) and Tarrow (1971) for a further discussion of the relationship between political involvement and clientelistic networks.
29 See van Deth (2000) for the related expression 'interesting but irrelevant'. The difference between 'irrelevant' and 'unimportant' is that, according to the first, even if politics is considered irrelevant when compared to other spheres of one's life, it may still be considered important in absolute terms. However, if it is considered unimportant, it is not very likely that it will be considered relevant.

13 Political participation
Mapping the terrain

*Jan Teorell, Mariano Torcal, and
José Ramón Montero*

Introduction

Political participation is one of the most central topics for understanding contemporary representative democracy. In the very first sentences of their book, Verba *et al.* (1995: 1) correctly state that 'Citizen participation is at the heart of democracy. Indeed, democracy is unthinkable without the ability of citizens to participate freely in the government process'. Through participation citizens voice their grievances and make their demands heard to the larger public; they also make governments accountable and politicians responsive. The venues open for such activities are multiple. Citizens may vote on election day, write letters to their public representatives, or campaign for a political party. They may sign a petition, put a bumper sticker on their car, or join a protest march. Sometimes the expression of their will is more subtle, such as when they donate money to non-profit organisations or even boycott certain products in the supermarket. As noted by Huntington and Nelson (1976: 14), 'the concept of political participation is nothing more than an *umbrella concept* which accommodates very different forms of action constituting differentiated phenomena, and for which it is necessary to look for explanations of different nature'.

This chapter is a descriptive effort to explore the participatory actions taken by citizens in the 13 societies under study. We will address four basic questions: is there a common pattern of modes of political action across societies with such vast differences in cultural, institutional and political settings? Are some venues for political participation more common than others? Are some countries more politically active than others? Finally, are some modes of participation more tightly linked together, indicating that political activity is more concentrated in the hands of fewer participants?

We shall thus not address the question of what individual and socio-political processes might explain political participation. In the following pages, instead, we first lay out the conceptual foundations for the study of political participation and provide a broad overview of the multiple participatory venues. Next, we propose a new typology of different 'modes', or types, of participation, and explore the interconnections between political acts in order to determine whether they respond to the proposed typology. We then compare the amount of activity in each of these 'modes', and explore the associations among them on the aggregate level. Finally, we look at the individual-level patterns of correlations among different types of political action in order to assess the amount of participatory concentration. The purpose is thus first and foremost descriptive, although we will hint at some causal interpretations. The causal roots of political participation will, however, primarily be traced in the chapters to come.

Defining political participation

According to the classical definition given by Verba and Nie (1972: 2), 'Political participation refers to those activities by private citizens that are more or less directly aimed at influencing the selection of governmental personnel and/or the actions they take'. This view has been held by most large-scale participation studies to date, including the two most influential comparative studies conducted in the seventies (Verba *et al.* 1978: 46; Kaase and Marsh 1979: 42).[1] Defining participation in this way was an important contribution at the time, since it widened the scope of activities democratic citizens may undertake to make their wishes heard. Before the seminal study of Verba and Nie (1972), attention had been almost exclusively directed towards *electoral* participation, 'the selection of governmental personnel' (for instance, Milbrath 1965; Milbrath and Goel 1977). Now the action repertoire available to citizens was made explicitly multidimensional and entailed non-electoral paths of influence as well, including efforts to affect the 'actions' taken by elected officials.

Yet this definition is in one important respect still too narrow. Underlying the classical view was the assumption that 'political outcomes' are always determined by 'governmental personnel', be they elected officials or civil servants. As a matter of fact, Verba and Nie (1972: 2) were themselves aware that this implied a very restrictive notion of what counts as politics:

> Actually, we are interested more abstractly in attempts to influence the authoritative allocations of values for a society, which may or may not take place through governmental decisions. But, like most political scientists who start out with such an abstract concern, we shall concentrate on governmental decisions as a close approximation of this more general process.

The view of political participation we adhere to goes beyond this 'approximation'. We concur with the view that what makes a particular act of participation *political* is 'the act's relation to the authoritative allocation of values for a society' (Easton 1953: 134). However, the kinds of activities we have probed for in our CID surveys are not restricted to activities that target the incumbent political authorities. Some attempts by ordinary citizens to influence politics simply are not directed towards 'governmental personnel' at all. Most importantly, they may equally well be directed towards corporate actors within the non-profit or private sector (Norris 2002: 193). After all, all selected countries in our study subscribe to the principles of a modern, capitalist, market economy. As opposed to the socialist economies of the former communist bloc, the essence of these economic systems is that 'the authoritative allocation of values' is *not* the sole responsibility of state or actors of the public sector. As a result these non-governmental institutions may be targeted by citizen attempts to influence 'political outcomes'. Such is the case, for example, when ordinary people deliberately buy or boycott certain products, not in order to express their views to the government but to directly affect the behaviour and production methods employed by large-scale companies.

Thus, rather than the classical view, we subscribe to the definition of political participation given by Brady (1999: 737): '*action* by *ordinary citizens* directed toward *influencing* some *political outcomes*' (cf. McClosky 1968: 253). This definition consists of four crucial components, all of which have been italicised. First, political participation entails action: observable behaviour undertaken by individuals. Second, those individuals are non-elites. We do not consider the actions taken by political professionals, be they elected officials or paid lobbyists. Third, the action is directed by an intention to influence – to assert demands. This excludes from our definition such activities as to discuss politics among relatives, friends, and peers, or simply being attentive to current affairs in the news media. To count as participation, something more is required: the willingness to affect decisions taken by someone else. Fourth, and finally, this 'someone else' need not by government personnel, not even a state agent. What is required is that the target of the act is any 'political outcome', that is, any decision over the authoritative allocation of values for society. It is this fourth criterion that most clearly distinguishes our view from the classical definition proffered by Verba and Nie (1972) and even from the more nuanced description of the definition provided by Brady (1999).[2]

It should be noted at the outset that this view of participation is more congruent with some versions of democratic theory than with others (Teorell 2006). Most importantly, the definition entails a representative system, where one set of political actors (the elite) makes decisions and others (citizens) try to influence those decisions. As a result, we shall not concern ourselves with the kinds of citizen activity that are primarily advocated by the participatory model of democracy, that is, when citizens themselves *directly* take part in the making of decisions (Nagel 1987: 19). Participation conceived of in our way, by contrast, is to assert *indirect* influence over decisions taken by others. Neither shall we be concerned with the pet activities of deliberative democrats, which most of all concern themselves with the process through which citizen opinions are formed (see, for example, Elster 1998).

In operational terms, as will soon become clear, our approach comes closer to the list of participatory acts elicited in the survey tradition initiated by the *Political Action* research project (Kaase and Marsh 1979; Jennings *et al.* 1990; Marsh 1990; Parry *et al.* 1992; Topf 1995a; Thomassen and van Deth 1998; Dalton 2002), rather than that of Sidney Verba and his colleagues (Verba and Nie 1972; Nie and Verba 1975; Verba *et al.* 1978; Verba *et al.* 1995). By including what they called 'unconventional' forms of participation, the former approach moved beyond the institutional, the 'legal', or at least 'legitimate' forms of behaviour analysed by the latter. For some reason, however, the wider set of action types thus introduced by the Political Action Study never incurred a reconceptualisation of the defining characteristics of political participation.[3] We now hope to have contributed to that end. Nevertheless, for reasons developed below we will not adopt the conventional/unconventional distinction as a way of distinguishing among different forms of political participation.

Mapping political participation

Some recent contributions on political participation have stressed the relevance of both the accuracy of definitional attempts and the quality of empirical measures. For Schlozman (2002: 436), for instance, 'The fuzziness of the borders that surround the domain of voluntary political activity implies that, no matter how sophisticated the conceptualization of this terrain, what really matters are the actual measures'. Table 13.1 displays the large set of items measuring various forms of participation included in the CID survey, and gives their distribution across countries. First, the table includes in the first row the officially reported level of electoral turnout, that is, the percentage of the population who voted in the last parliamentary election. This is followed on the second row by a less-commonly studied side of electoral 'activity': the percentage who declared in the survey whether they had 'ever abstained from participating in a general election out of protest'. Moreover, the table includes information on the involvement in political parties – whether the respondent is a member of a party, has during the past 12 months participated in activities arranged by the party, donated money to the party, and/or done voluntary and thus unpaid work for the party. Finally, the table contains a number of other forms of participation undertaken by respondents in the last 12 months as 'ways of attempting to bring about improvements or counteract deterioration in society'. To keep track of the latest technological advancements we have also reported the percentages that have used the Internet in connection with any of these activities.

Table 13.1 Levels of Political participation (in percentages)[a]

Type of activity	DK	EG	WG	MD	NL	NO	PT	RO	RU	SI	ES	SE	CH	Mean
Voting[b]														
Vote in parliamentary elections	85.9	80.2[c]	82.8[c]	67.5	73.3	78.3	61.8	65.3	61.7	70.1	68.7	80.1	43.3	70.6
Abstain from voting out of protest	10	14	15	8	16	17	9	5	16	10	8	11	18	12
Involvement in political parties														
Have membership	7	3	3	2	6	10	2	4	2	3	2	8	9	5
Participate in party activities	5	3	3	2	3	5	2	3	1	1	2	4	5	3
Donate money	2	1	1	1	1	3	1	2	0	1	1	2	5	2
Do voluntary work	2	2	2	1	2	2	1	1	1	1	1	3	2	2
Attempts to influence society														
Contact a politician	14	8	7	6	11	15	5	4	4	6	7	13	13	9
Contact an organisation	26	13	16	5	33	28	19	4	3	11	17	20	18	16
Contact a civil servant	20	11	10	17	24	29	14	11	7	10	17	22	21	16
Work in a political party	3	5	4	3	3	5	4	2	1	3	3	3	6	3
Work in a political action group	1	5	7	2	2	6	1	1	2	3	6	2	6	3
Work in other organisation	21	13	17	5	34	29	11	5	1	9	17	14	18	15
Wear or display badge/sticker	5	7	7	4	7	7	2	2	1	3	9	5	7	5
Sign a petition	25	31	31	7	35	37	6	6	3	16	23	41	36	23
Take part in a public demonstration	5	14	9	7	5	9	3	6	2	5	13	6	7	7

Activity														
Take part in a strike	5	2	4	8	3	5	4	5	1	2	8	0	2	4
Boycott certain products	21	11	24	2	16	30	2	2	1	3	6	27	26	13
Buy certain products	45	12	27	3	33	44	4	3	4	10	12	48	39	22
Donate money	36	32	36	12	75	66	33	20	10	38	26	42	43	36
Raise funds	7	4	6	4	15	13	5	3	2	6	9	4	5	6
Contact/appear in the media	6	6	5	3	9	10	2	3	2	4	4	9	11	6
Contact solicitor/judicial body	9	11	8	6	13	9	10	4	6	4	9	5	9	8
Participate in illegal protest activities	1	1	1	2	1	0	0	1	0	1	1	1	1	1
Attend a political meeting/rally	11	12	9	13	7	9	4	4	1	3	6	7	13	8
Other	14	2	7	4	12	25	0	3	1	1	3	8	7	7
Use Internet to influence society[d]	10	6	6	4	19	21	3	2	–	5	7	18	16	10

Notes

a All entries have been weighted to adjust for unequal selection probabilities.

b The percentage base for the item on *abstaining from voting out of protest* are those who (according to their self-report) are eligible to vote. Figures for *voting in parliamentary elections* are actual results of turnout in the 1997 parliamentary elections in Norway; 1998 in Denmark, Germany (both West and East), and the Netherlands; 1999 in Portugal, Russia, and Switzerland; 2000 in Romania, Slovenia, and Spain; 2001 in Moldova, and 2002 in Sweden. The sources are www.essex.ac.uk/elections for Moldova, Romania, and Russia, and various issues of the 'Political Data Yearbook', *European Journal of Political Research*, for all countries except the two Germanies, for which the source is Emmert *et al.* (2001).

c The total turnout for Germany was 82.2 per cent.

d The percentage base for this item on Internet use are those who have performed any of the aforementioned activities to influence society; this question was not asked in Russia.

A first look at the table reveals a huge amount of variation both among countries and within each country. For all countries, voting in parliamentary elections is obviously by far the most common participatory activity in terms of percentages; and, as should be expected, participating in illegal protest is the least. Other acts of protest, such as taking part in strikes and demonstrations, are – together with different forms of party activism – also among the least frequent acts in all countries. The act of protest abstention is a bit more common, but it should then be remembered that the timespan for this particular item is not restricted to the last 12 months (or the last election), but concerns whether the respondent has *ever* abstained. Besides the institutionalised act of voting, the most frequent activities in the set of countries taken as a whole are money donations, signing petitions, and the act of 'deliberately buying certain products for political, ethical or environmental reasons'. These particular acts, however, also display a wide range of variation across countries. Whereas they are very common in the Scandinavian countries, the Netherlands, and Switzerland, they are comparatively rare in Moldova, Russia, and Romania. Most participatory acts show a similar pattern of cross-country variation, which also goes for the use of Internet. With the conspicuous exception of Germany, where Internet participation is still comparatively rare, people living in the more economically developed countries in northern Europe are more prone to use the Internet as a channel of political influence as compared to both southern and eastern Europe.

How could we make order out of these variations? In the two following sections we propose a classificatory attempt in order to find some general patterns underlying the distinct levels shown by our set of countries. This typology deals with 'modes' of political participation, and aims at discovering what specific activities cluster together to form more coherent action forms.

Modes of political participation: a typology

The question of whether political participation comes in certain bundles, or 'modes', has attracted considerable scholarly interest over the years. Of course, at the most disaggregated level of analysis each and every activity included in Table 13.1 constitutes a separate action form. The question usually asked, however, is whether there is a systematic pattern underlying people's choice of actions from such a list. The idea, then, is that specific kinds of activities cluster together to form a distinct dimension of political participation. As Dalton (2002: 33) put it, 'a person who performs one act from a particular cluster is likely to perform other acts from the same cluster, but not necessarily activities from another cluster'.

Our expectations as to how the activities elicited in Table 13.1 should cluster are summarised in Figure 13.1. It is primarily based on two distinctions along two dimensions, the first pertaining to the channel of expres-

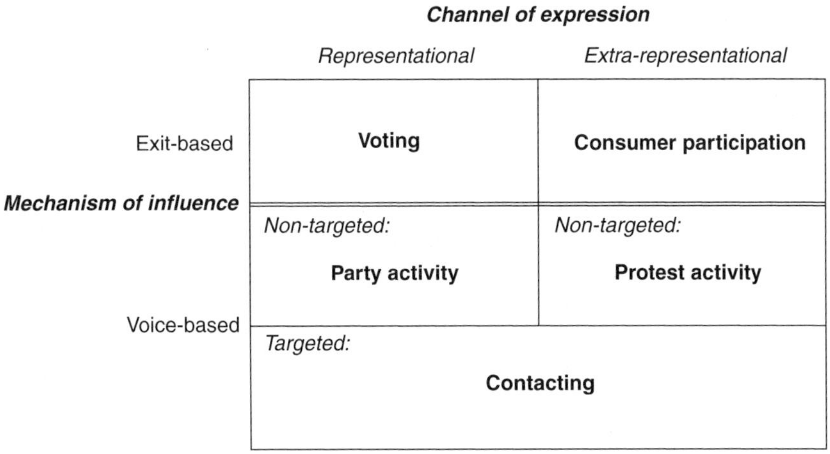

	Channel of expression	
	Representational	Extra-representational
Exit-based	**Voting**	**Consumer participation**
Voice-based — Non-targeted: **Party activity**	Non-targeted: **Protest activity**
Targeted: **Contacting**		

(Mechanism of influence, rows: Exit-based / Voice-based)

Figure 13.1 A typology of the modes of political participation.

sion, the second to the mechanism of influence. The first distinction is straightforward: the difference between political action taking place within the framework of representation and those activities taking place through the extra-representational channels of expression. This distinction should not solely be understood as the typical electoral/non-electoral one. Of course, elections are the key events in the democratic chain of representation. But activities occurring in between elections could be driven by the representational 'logic' as well; for example, when citizens contact and try to influence elected representatives, or work in a political action group with that aim. The representational modes thus include a wider set of activities, the distinguishing feature of which is that they are directed towards the formal channels of representation available in liberal democracies: the political parties and the elected representatives, as well as government personnel and civil servants. The extra-representational modes, by contrast, do not have representative officials as their primary targets of influence. They may instead be directed towards firms, getting attention by the mass media, or even directly aimed at influencing public opinion.

In order to capture the second and horizontal dividing line of Figure 13.1, differentiating among two mechanisms of influence, we shall make use of Hirschman's (1970) well-known distinction between 'exit' and 'voice'. To start with the representational modes, as Hirschman himself asserted there are two ways of expressing party preferences: one can vote for parties, or one can work for them. *Voting* is an 'exit'-based mechanism for political influence. It works by the same dynamics that govern consumers and firms on a competitive market. Once quality deteriorates, some customers stop buying the product – which is tantamount to the situation where voters fail to turn out or vote for another party. *Party activity*, by contrast, is a 'voice'-based mechanism of influence. When disgruntled, party activists try to affect the party platform, not usually by leaving the ship but by protesting through channels of influence internal to the party. Equally important, when the tidings are good they use the very same channels to express their support (Hirschman 1970: 70–5).

We deliberately use the term exit-*based* in order to stress that there are various ways to 'exit' the political system. Rather than abstaining from voting, one may vote for an extremist party with an agenda to subvert the democratic system. One may even leave the country. Voting is thus not the sole 'exit'-option available to citizens, but it is an exit-*based* option in that it shares some common distinguishing features with the other 'exit'-options mentioned. The first such feature is that the casting of ballots is impersonal or even *anonymous*. The preferences expressed are never made public. Moreover, the message sent out is fairly *vague*: it transmits a pro or a con, unreasoned and unconditional. Finally, the process through which preferences are transmitted by the vote is *self-regulatory*. Like the market mechanism, the pressure for change works by counting numbers, be they heads or euros. In all these respects, the voice-*based* activities differ.[4] They work by making preferences and demands *manifest* to the public (or to other members of the party). These demands contain a *specific* piece of information, and their pressure is exercised by the *intensity* of threats or arguments.

The same distinction among exit- and voice-based mechanisms could also be made with respect to the *extra-representational* modes of activity. Outside the confines of the party system and the logic of representation, the exit-based activity par excellence would of course be the politically motivated boycott of certain goods (Hirschman 1970: 86). When citizens want to object to French nuclear policies in the South Pacific, for instance, they stop buying French wines. As the fast evolution of 'environmentally friendly' household products makes clear, there is of course another side of this coin: when citizens deliberately choose certain products to show expressions of support rather than distaste or resistance. There is nowadays a growing interest for these forms of political action, summarised under the heading 'political consumerism' (Micheletti *et al.* 2003). But money donations for political purposes in many ways work similarly. They also use the self-regulatory market mechanism to send anonymous and vague political messages. They thus also share some of the core characteristics of the exit option used by customers in the market. This is why we have labelled these type of political activities *consumer participation*.

The voice-based extra-representational modes of participation, by contrast, are characterised by sending specific demands to the public (or to public elites, be they political or not), the outcome of which is regulated by threats or arguments. As the lower part of Figure 13.1 makes clear, however, we must make a third distinction in order to separate two fundamentally different forms of voice-based, extra-representational political action. Sometimes such action may be *targeted* towards specific institutions within the democratic polity. *Contacting* epitomises these kinds of activities.[5] At other times, taking to the streets is the only viable alternative for those who want to voice their grievances. Public demonstrations and other forms of *protest activity* are thus in this sense non-targeted, a feature they actually share with party activism, which could rather be described as contained *within* one of the central representational institutions.

To sum up, we hypothesise the presence of five different modes of political participation: voting, party activity, consumer participation, contacting, and protest activity. This typology in some ways resembles the classification of participation modes once proffered by Verba and his colleagues; the dimensions underlying both typologies are also similar. In their seminal study of participation patterns in seven nations, they found support for a fourfold typology: voting, campaign activity, communal activity, and particularised (or citizen-initiated) contacts (Verba and Nie 1972: 73; Nie and Verba 1975: 9–12; Verba *et al.* 1978: 55). Our act of 'voting' is obviously exactly equivalent to theirs. The term 'campaign activity' mostly reflects the specific characteristics of American political parties, but is otherwise very similar to our 'party activity' – as a matter of fact, the latter extends beyond the electoral campaign *stricto sensu*, and is thus more inclusive and more in accordance with the reality of political parties in Europe. 'Particularised contacts', that is, contacts on personal matters leading to particularised benefits, are excluded from our conceptual space due to the formulation of the survey question (i.e. the restriction to acts performed in order to bring about changes *in society*). Finally, their 'communal activity' is in many ways similar to our 'contacting', although the choice of terminology to some extent may hide this fact.[6]

However, our typology goes beyond the Verba-typology by also incorporating the extra-representational channels of political expression, including the modes of consumer participation and protest activity. Moreover, our typology provides a more fine-grained set of distinctions than the 'conventional'/'unconventional' dichotomy introduced by the Political Action Study. Conceptually, we reject this dichotomy on two grounds. First, it obscures the two crucial distinctions we make between voice- and exit-based participation, on the one hand, and representational and extra-representational participation, on the other. Second, it is too historically relative (Brady 1999: 768; Topf 1995a: 52). As Table 13.1 makes perfectly clear, what might have appeared as 'unconventional' in the 1970s, such as the acts of boycotting and buying certain products for political reasons, today stand out as some of the most frequently used venues for citizen influence in western Europe.

Modes of political participation: empirical results

Let us now explore whether the fivefold typology presented in Figure 13.1 survives empirical testing. In Table 13.2 we present first of all a 'global' test, including all respondents in all 13 societies under study (but where the data have been transformed and weighted so that each society exerts an equal influence on the results).[7] The table entries are the factor loadings from a principal component factor analysis. Since we expect our modes of activity to be distinct, but not necessarily uncorrelated, we use an oblique rotation method. Standard criteria for the retention of factors (i.e. eigenvalues no smaller than 1) have been used.[8]

As can readily be seen, all items included in Table 13.1 have not been subject to this dimensional analysis. First of all, we have excluded the question on turnout in the last parliamentary election. Since it is the sole item

Table 13.2 Principal component analysis of participatory activities for all 13 societies[a] (pattern matrix with oblimin rotation)

Type of activity	Modes of participation			
	Contacting	Party activity	Protest activity	Consumer participation
Have membership in a political party	0.00	**0.81**	−0.03	−0.00
Participate in party activities	−0.00	**0.86**	0.01	0.00
Donate money to a party	−0.07	**0.67**	−0.01	0.02
Do voluntary work for a party	−0.01	**0.81**	0.02	−0.01
Contact a politician	**0.59**	0.23	−0.02	−0.02
Contact an organisation	**0.69**	0.03	−0.05	0.07
Contact a civil servant	**0.70**	0.01	−0.08	0.03
Work in a political party	0.14	**0.71**	0.07	−0.03
Work in other organisation	**0.57**	0.02	−0.02	0.10
Sign a petition	0.11	0.01	0.22	**0.48**
Take part in a public demonstration	0.03	0.06	**0.69**	0.14
Take part in a strike	−0.06	−0.01	**0.74**	0.02
Boycott certain products	−0.09	−0.02	−0.02	**0.79**
Buy certain products	−0.06	0.01	−0.05	**0.83**
Donate money	0.21	0.01	−0.01	**0.42**
Contact/appear in the media	**0.58**	0.01	0.09	−0.04
Contact solicitor/judicial body	**0.53**	−0.11	0.06	−0.04
Participate in illegal protest activities	0.01	−0.01	**0.61**	−0.08
Eigenvalues	4.0	2.3	1.4	1.2
Variance (in per cent)	22	13	8	7

Note
a Entries are factor loadings from a principal component analysis with oblique rotation of all 21,482 respondents who have responded to each of the 18 items. Before analysis, all variables have been transformed to deviations from country means, and each country is weighted equally (see footnote 7). Loadings equal to 0.30 or larger are in bold. In cases where all loadings with absolute values greater than 0.30 on one component are negative, the signs of the loadings have been reversed for ease of interpretation.

representing the voting mode of activity, we cannot test the dimensionality of this mode on the basis of inter-item correlations with other acts of the same type. In addition, four of the excluded items deserve special mentioning: wearing badges, attending meetings/rallies, raising funds, and working in 'political action groups'.[9] They were each hypothesised to fall into one particular mode of activity. In dimensional analyses preceding the ones presented in Table 13.2, however, their loadings appeared to be too unstable when compared across countries: they simply moved from dimension to dimension in an erratic pattern. Hence, they could not be safely classified as belonging to one or the other of the modes of activity in a way that achieved cross-national comparability. We shall return to the findings for these four items later in this chapter.

With these exclusions in mind, Table 13.2 nevertheless lends strong support for the dimensional pattern we hypothesised. Together with the act of voting, all four modes of activity are clearly present: contacting, party activity, protest activity, and consumer participation. Equally important, each of the 18 types of acts included loads on one, and only one, of the hypothesised dimensions. In most cases, these loadings present few surprises. Thus, all actions including 'contacts' of various sorts load on the 'contacting' dimension, whereas all items relating to parties belong to the 'party activity' dimension. Moreover, attending public demonstrations, taking part in strikes, and reverting to illegal protest activities cluster together into the hypothesise mode called 'protest activity'. Boycotts and the purchase of goods for 'political, ethical or environmental reasons', finally, cluster together with money donations into the market-like, non-electoral mode of activity termed 'consumer participation'.

The location of two items, signing petitions and working in organisations (other than parties and 'political action groups'), is of particular interest since it was not easily predicted beforehand. Signing petitions could, by its nature, equally well have been located in the protest activity mode. After all, petitions share some of the voice-based features: they generally are richer in information content than market behaviour and money donations, and they are less anonymous. This notwithstanding, it makes sense that petitions empirically cluster together with the exit-based action forms. It is less manifest than the protest activities, and it exerts pressure in proportion to numbers in a way similar to money donations and boycotts. Theoretical sense can also be made out of the fact that working in organisations cluster together with the contacting activities. This is simply a reminder that these contacts are in many instances collectively organised and form part of both the representational and extra-representational channels of political expression.

As an illustration of the persistence of this dimensional pattern across our societies under study, Table 13.3 also displays the results from an exactly similar analysis conducted in three groups of countries. We have simply divided the countries into those located in 'Continental Europe'

Table 13.3 Principal component analysis of the participation items by groups of countries (pattern matrix with oblimin rotation)[a]

Type of activity	Modes of participation[b] in Continental Europe[c]				Modes of participation[b] in Scandinavia[d]				Modes of participation[b] in Eastern Europe[c]				Modes of participation[b] in Portugal			
	1	2	3	4	1	2	3	4	1	2	3	4	1	2	3	4
Have membership in a political party	0.02	**0.79**	−0.05	−0.01	0.02	**0.77**	−0.06	−0.01	−0.05	**0.88**	0.01	0.02	−0.05	**0.91**	−0.09	0.03
Participate in party activities	0.01	**0.83**	0.03	−0.01	0.02	**0.83**	0.04	0.01	−0.04	**0.93**	−0.01	0.01	−0.02	**0.89**	−0.04	0.05
Donate money to a party	−0.06	**0.59**	−0.02	0.05	−0.06	**0.62**	−0.00	0.02	−0.06	**0.81**	0.00	−0.04	−0.06	**0.72**	−0.07	−0.09
Do voluntary work for a party	−0.03	**0.76**	0.03	−0.03	0.00	**0.80**	0.04	0.00	0.01	**0.87**	−0.01	−0.00	0.00	**0.92**	−0.08	−0.05
Contact a politician	**0.58**	0.26	0.02	−0.03	**0.61**	0.25	0.02	−0.05	**0.57**	0.14	−0.09	0.10	**0.48**	0.35	0.13	−0.18
Contact an organisation	**0.68**	0.02	−0.03	0.11	**0.68**	0.03	0.02	0.07	**0.66**	0.08	−0.13	0.05	**0.69**	−0.01	0.18	−0.05
Contact a civil servant	**0.69**	0.04	−0.06	0.03	**0.70**	0.02	−0.07	0.05	**0.69**	−0.01	−0.08	−0.01	**0.70**	0.03	0.01	0.04
Work in a political party	0.11	**0.76**	0.04	−0.03	0.07	**0.80**	−0.02	−0.02	0.22	**0.61**	0.14	−0.06	0.21	**0.52**	0.25	0.01
Work in other organisation	**0.56**	0.01	−0.05	0.18	**0.56**	0.03	0.04	0.08	**0.56**	0.05	−0.01	0.04	**0.56**	−0.03	0.25	0.15
Sign a petition	0.09	0.00	0.19	**0.53**	0.11	−0.04	0.24	**0.47**	0.21	0.03	0.25	**0.38**	0.19	0.22	0.23	0.21
Take part in a public demonstration	0.01	0.04	**0.75**	0.17	0.03	0.05	**0.64**	0.13	0.08	0.06	**0.64**	0.11	−0.02	**0.59**	0.21	0.14
Take part in a strike	−0.10	0.03	**0.75**	0.09	−0.01	−0.08	**0.66**	−0.06	−0.08	0.02	**0.76**	0.02	−0.08	0.03	**0.65**	0.11
Boycott certain products	−0.06	−0.00	0.03	**0.74**	−0.08	−0.02	−0.01	**0.79**	−0.04	−0.03	−0.00	**0.80**	0.03	−0.07	−0.07	**0.70**
Buy certain products	−0.02	−0.01	−0.02	**0.80**	−0.08	0.03	−0.08	**0.83**	−0.00	−0.02	−0.00	**0.82**	0.19	0.09	−0.32	**0.75**

Donate money	0.15	0.02	−0.07	**0.56**	0.15	0.01	−0.04	**0.47**	**0.33**	0.01	0.05	0.20	**0.51**	−0.04	−0.01	0.01		
Contact/appear in the media	**0.61**	−0.00	0.06	−0.06	**0.56**	0.06	0.09	−0.03	**0.58**	−0.04	0.12	−0.05	0.23	−0.01	**0.69**	−0.06		
Contact solicitor/judicial body	**0.54**	−0.10	0.05	−0.04	**0.54**	−0.15	−0.05	−0.04	**0.53**	−0.10	0.14	−0.11	**0.61**	−0.01	−0.25	0.03		
Participate in illegal protest activities	0.08	−0.03	**0.55**	−0.13	−0.02	0.04	**0.65**	−0.06	−0.02	0.01	**0.65**	−0.04	−0.17	0.01	0.22	**0.52**		
Eigenvalues	4.0	2.3	1.4	1.2	1.4	3.8	1.2	2.2	4.3	2.5	1.3	1.1	2.2	4.7	1.1	1.4		
Variance (in per cent)	22	12	8	7	8	21	6	12	24	14	7	6	12	26	6	8		

Notes

a Entries are factor loadings from a principal component analysis with oblique rotation of all respondents within each groups of countries who have responded to each of the 18 items. N = 6,610 for Continental Europe, 4,957 for Scandinavia, 8,262 for Eastern Europe, and 1,652 for Portugal. Before analysis, all variables have been transformed to deviations from country means, and each country is weighted equally (see footnote 7). Loadings equal to 0.30 or larger are in bold. In cases where all loadings with absolute values greater than 0.30 on one component are negative, the signs of the loadings have been reversed for ease of interpretation.

b The *modes of participation* are the following:

1 Contacting;
2 Party activity;
3 Protest activity;
4 Consumer participation.

c Continental Europe includes West Germany, the Netherlands, Spain, and Switzerland.
d Scandinavia includes Denmark, Norway, and Sweden.
e Eastern Europe includes East Germany, Moldova, Romania, Russia, and Slovenia.

(West Germany, the Netherlands, Spain, and Switzerland), those located in 'Scandinavia' (Denmark, Norway, and Sweden), and those being former members of the communist bloc in 'Eastern Europe' (East Germany, Moldova, Romania, Russia, and Slovenia); Portugal has been classified separately due to its peculiar results in the factor analysis. The fact that the dimensional pattern is almost identical in all these otherwise distinctive set of political, economic, and cultural spheres is a strong argument for the measurement equivalence of our four modes of activity. This result supports the argument that the multidimensionality of political participation is embedded in the distinctive nature of each mode of participation, and do not respond to nation-specific institutional settings.

One of the small deviations that does occur is that money donations to some extent appear in the contacting dimension in Eastern Europe. Far more important, however, is the fact that the dimensional structure in the former communist bloc is almost an exact replicate of that in the western European countries. As the rightmost column of Table 13.3 makes clear, however, Portugal emerges as an anomaly among our 13 societies. Although something fairly similar to the contacting and party activity dimensions appear in Portugal, this cannot be said about protest activity and consumer participation. From what appears in Table 13.3 it is difficult to make any theoretical sense at all of the third and fourth mode of activity appearing in Portugal. We shall be returning to this anomaly below.

Levels of political participation

After identifying the modes of political participation, we will now compare the different levels of these activities cross-nationally. Table 13.4 presents the average participation in each mode on a zero to one additive scale.[10] As can be seen, the ordering of the countries by participation levels roughly corresponds to the cluster of countries in the preceding dimensional analysis. Although there is some overlap in the rank orders of the first two groups, the Scandinavian countries present the highest levels of political participation in most of the modes, followed by the Continental cluster and the countries of east Europe, with Portugal located somewhere in between. The partial exception to this ordering concerns protest activity, where the Continental groups precedes over the Scandinavian countries. To highlight the more general pattern, we have for each country computed the average of all the non-electoral modes of participation (that is, all modes except voting). According to this non-electoral index, Norway is the most politically active country under study, followed by the Netherlands and Sweden. Moldova, Romania, and Russia are on the other end of the scale.

Table 13.4 makes clear that it proves difficult to assert that specific institutional settings in different countries favour 'voice-based' over 'exit-based' activity. The ranking of the participation modes is quite similar for

Table 13.4 Levels of political participation in 13 societies[a]

Country	Contacting	Party activity	Protest activity	Consumer participation	Non-electoral average	Voting
Norway	0.20	0.05	0.05	0.44	0.18	0.78
The Netherlands	0.21	0.03	0.03	0.40	0.17	0.73
Sweden	0.14	0.04	0.02	0.40	0.15	0.80
Switzerland	0.15	0.06	0.03	0.36	0.15	0.43
Denmark	0.16	0.04	0.04	0.32	0.14	0.86
West Germany	0.11	0.02	0.05	0.30	0.12	0.83
East Germany	0.10	0.03	0.06	0.21	0.10	0.80
Spain	0.12	0.02	0.08	0.17	0.09	0.69
Slovenia	0.07	0.02	0.03	0.17	0.07	0.70
Portugal	0.10	0.02	0.03	0.11	0.06	0.62
Moldova	0.07	0.02	0.05	0.06	0.05	0.68
Romania	0.05	0.02	0.04	0.08	0.05	0.65
Russia	0.04	0.01	0.01	0.05	0.02	0.62

Note

a Entries are means of the respective participation indices, ranging from 0 to 1, except for voting, which reflects the official turnout rates for the last parliamentary election (see Table 13.1, note b). All means have been weighted to adjust for unequal selection probabilities. Countries are ordered by the average level of non-electoral participation.

all the countries, showing that, after voting, the most frequent form of participation is consumer activities (probably the political activity incurring the lowest cost), followed by contacting (with the exception of Moldova) and protest activity. The least frequently used mode is in almost all countries party activity (the exceptions being Sweden and Switzerland, where party activity is next to least frequent, after protest activity) – an accurate reflection of the cross-national reluctance on behalf of the citizenry to use this representational channel to voice their demands.

This consistency of the ranking of modes within countries also suggests that patterns of participation along different modes usually come together. It is *not* the case that low levels of some modes of participation in a country come with high levels in the other modes. In other words, it is difficult to observe at this aggregate level that citizens in some democracies decide to reject the representational modes of participation in favour of the extra-representational ones. This general pattern can be most clearly observed by studying the aggregate level correlations between modes of participation in Table 13.5. In no case are there any strong or even moderate negative correlations. On the contrary, three of the modes – contacting, party activity, and consumer participation – are strongly positively correlated, implying that countries high in one of these modes are also high in the others. The two remaining modes – voting and protest activity – do not systematically correlate with the others and thus present a distinct cross-national pattern of variation. Thus, Spain is, for example,

Table 13.5 Country-level correlations between modes of political participation[a]

Mode of political participation	Contacting	Party activity	Protest activity	Consumer participation	Non-electoral average	Voting
Party activity	0.72	–	–	–	–	–
Protest activity	0.11	−0.03	–	–	–	–
Consumer participation	0.90	0.79	−0.03	–	–	–
Voting	0.27	−0.08	0.28	0.33	0.32	–
GDP per capita	0.86	0.71	0.09	0.92	0.91	0.32
Democratic legacy	0.90	0.81	−0.02	0.94	0.94	0.23

Note

a Entries are country-level correlation coefficients ($N=13$). Data on *GDP per capita* at purchasing power parity, expressed in current international US dollars as of 2000, are taken from the World Development Indicators online (www.publications.worldbank.org/WDI/). GDP per cap for East and West Germany has been computed by using the fraction of GDP per cap in the 'new' (including Berlin) and the 'old' Bundesländer, over Germany as a whole, as given on www.vgrdl.de/Arbeitskreis_VGR/tab02.asp#tab7. *Democratic legacy* is measured as the mean Polity score for each country, ranging from −10 to +10, since the year 1900, available on the Polity IV homepage (www.cidcm.umd.edu/inscr/polity).

the country with highest levels of protest activity, followed by East Germany. Whereas Denmark is the country with the highest reported turn out, Switzerland has the lowest. Interestingly, however, and again in line with the general pattern, these two modes are not negatively correlated but even show a weak positive association.

What factors may explain the differences in levels of participation across countries? Although, as we have stressed, this chapter is first and foremost descriptive in nature, in the two bottom rows of Table 13.5 we test two interpretations of a more explanatory nature. The first is that the cross-country pattern is a reflection of different levels of economic modernisation, measured as GDP per capita at the turn of the century. The second interpretation instead asserts that higher levels of political participation are a product of more years under democratic rule. As should be clear, both interpretations fit fairly well the pattern of cross-national variations in the non-electoral modes. The correlations are around 0.90 for the non-electoral average, a result that seems mostly to be driven by the consumer mode of participation. Although not quite as strongly, both interpretations also fit the contacting and party activity modes. As before, however, voting and protest activity present distinct patterns of cross-national variations that are weakly associated with economic modernisation and democratic legacy.

Which one of these explanatory interpretations fits better? We can give no clear answers. Most correlations are somewhat stronger for the measure of democratic legacy, but the difference is minuscule. Moreover, both explanatory factors are very strongly correlated among themselves ($r=0.92$). Thus, with as few as 13 cases at hand there is hardly any

Associations among types of political action

Table 13.6 presents the *individual*-level correlations among modes of participation in the three groups of countries, plus Portugal. The relationships between contacting, on the one hand, and party activity, protest activity, and consumer participation, on the other, are moderate to high and quite similar across all countries. This confirms again, as we observed briefly in the dimensional analysis above, that contacting taps both the representational and extra-representational dimensions of participation. The relationship between consumer participation and protest activity is also quite constant across countries, confirming the interconnections between these two extra-representational modes of activity.

There is a difference, however, with respect to the correlations between party activity, on the one hand, and protest activity and consumer participation, on the other. It seems that in Eastern Europe and Portugal all the extra-representational activities are linked to party activity. This could reflect the fact that in new democracies, despite its low presence, party activity is the major mobilising force behind most other kinds of political activity. Political parties still appear to be playing the dominant mobilising role for most political activities in new democracies, but not in the old ones. As a result, political activity in these countries is more concentrated in the hands of fewer party activists. This is especially the case in Portugal, and might even be what explains the Portuguese anomaly. Most political mobilisation in Portugal during and after the transition from authoritarian rule took place through the major political parties (Morlino 1998: Chapter 4). Today, party activity is still the dominant underlying dimension of political participation in Portugal, concealing some of the differences between participation modes that would otherwise have been present.[12] In Scandinavia and Continental Europe, party activity does not constitute this mobilising force. This also means there is less concentration of political activity in these countries. Political participation is thus spread on the hands of more people.

These cross-national variations notwithstanding, a general pattern present is the fact that all modes of participation are positively correlated at the individual level. With the exception of voting, which is by and large weakly (but never negatively) associated with the other modes, this pattern is even more consistent than the aggregate-level correlations presented in Table 13.5. This lends behavioural support for the index of non-electoral activities presented in Table 13.4. Underlying the four modes not directly related to the election day (contacting, party activity, protest activity, and consumer participation) is a more general inclination to

Table 13.6 Individual-level correlations between modes of participation by groups of countries[a]

Type of activity	Contacting	Party activity	Protest activity	Consumer participation	Voting
Continental Europe[b]					
Party activity	0.32**	—	—	—	—
Protest activity	0.20**	0.09**	—	—	—
Consumer participation	0.41**	0.15**	0.23**	—	—
Voting	0.12**	0.09**	0.04**	0.11**	—
Abstain from voting out of protest	0.09**	0.01	0.06**	0.15**	−0.12**
Use Internet to influence society	0.32**	0.17**	0.07**	0.16**	0.04*
Work in a political action group	0.30**	0.20**	0.25**	0.22**	0.07**
Raise funds	0.27**	0.09**	0.15**	0.24**	0.07**
Wear or display badge/sticker	0.24**	0.20**	0.34**	0.25**	0.05**
Attend political meeting/rally	0.37**	0.46**	0.27**	0.24**	0.09**
Scandinavia[c]					
Party activity	0.31**	—	—	—	—
Protest activity	0.17**	0.09**	—	—	—
Consumer participation	0.32**	0.09**	0.19**	—	—
Voting	0.08**	0.06**	0.01	0.09**	—
Abstain from voting out of protest	−0.01	−0.06**	−0.00	0.04**	−0.19**
Use Internet to influence society	0.33**	0.11**	0.09**	0.19**	0.03
Work in a political action group	0.24**	0.14**	0.22**	0.17**	0.03*
Raise funds	0.24**	0.14**	0.11**	0.16**	0.03*
Wear or display badge/sticker	0.29**	0.26**	0.24**	0.20**	0.04**
Attend political meeting/rally	0.40**	0.52**	0.21**	0.18**	0.07**

Eastern Europe[d]					
Party activity	0.30**	—	—	—	—
Protest activity	0.30**	0.18**	—	—	—
Consumer participation	0.44**	0.18**	0.31**	—	—
Voting	0.06**	0.06**	0.02	0.06**	—
Abstain from voting out of protest	0.06**	−0.03*	0.03*	0.07**	−0.15**
Use Internet to influence society	0.21**	0.16**	0.09**	0.12**	0.04*
Work in a political action group	0.36**	0.29**	0.21**	0.26**	0.04**
Raise funds	0.25**	0.15**	0.20**	0.23**	0.03**
Wear or display badge/sticker	0.26**	0.29**	0.26**	0.26**	0.04**
Attend political meeting/rally	0.39**	0.31**	0.37**	0.28**	0.06**
Portugal					
Party activity	0.34**	—	—	—	—
Protest activity	0.24**	0.39**	—	—	—
Consumer participation	0.41**	0.23**	0.27**	—	—
Voting	0.08**	0.08**	0.01	0.04**	—
Abstain from voting out of protest	0.13**	−0.01	0.07**	0.16**	−0.13**
Use Internet to influence society	0.29**	0.10**	0.14**	0.19**	0.06
Work in a political action group	0.34**	0.30**	0.22**	0.24**	0.06*
Raise funds	0.34**	0.24**	0.19**	0.22**	0.03*
Wear or display badge/sticker	0.28**	0.50**	0.29**	0.19**	0.05
Attend political meeting/rally	0.40**	0.48**	0.37**	0.22**	0.06*

Notes

a Levels of statistical significance: ** = 0.05, * = 0.1. Each country has been weighted equally (see footnote 7). For convenience, we have set this weight to sum to the average sample size in each country (disregarding variations in item non-response), that is, 1,725.15.
b *Continental Europe* includes West Germany, the Netherlands, Spain, and Switzerland.
c *Scandinavia* includes Denmark, Norway, and Sweden.
d *Eastern Europe* includes East Germany, Moldova, Romania, Russia, and Slovenia.

participate in political affairs.[13] This means that citizens in all 13 societies under study see no trade-off in their choice of mode of participation. It is not the case, as is commonly held, that some citizens continue to use the traditional channels of participation, such as contacting officials and working for a political party, whereas others favour the less conventional modes such as protest or consumer participation. On the contrary, activists within one mode of activity tend to be activists within the others as well.

Table 13.6 also contains information on how the five modes of participation correlate with some of the political activities from Table 12.1 which has until now been left out of the discussion. The first concerns the act of abstaining from the vote out of protest, a kind of political activity which has only ever been undertaken by some 10 per cent of the eligible voters on average. Is this a political act that citizens tend to perform together with some of the other modes of participation? The somewhat surprising finding is that, apart from the expected negative correlation with voting (which in any case is not very strong), there are hardly any substantial correlations with the other modes at all. A partial exception is consumer participation in Portugal and Continental Europe, which tends to go hand-in-hand with protest abstention. But apart from that, the deliberate act of staying home on election day seems to be an isolated political phenomenon.

A second relationship displayed is that with the Internet. Which mode of activity is primarily connected to the use of Internet? Contrary to some expectations in the literature (Norris 2002: 207–11), the Internet has *not* primarily triggered the acts of collective protest activity. It is instead the more mainstream acts of contacting that occur in the first place with help of the new information technology. This pattern is consistent across all countries under study. Thus, the Internet has at this time-point done more to foster the vertical communication *between* masses and the elite than it has strengthened the horizontal networks promoting political action *within* the citizenry. There is, however, a moderate correlation between Internet use and consumer participation, perhaps indicating a future potential of the new information technology.

Finally, Table 13.6 includes the correlations between the fives modes of participation and those four political acts which, as mentioned before, did not fit into any distinct dimensional pattern. The first is working in a 'political action group'. Although this item consistently displays its highest correlation with the contacting mode, its associations with the other modes – in Scandinavia and Continental Europe with protest activity, in Eastern Europe and Portugal with party activity, in particular – are strong enough to perturb that pattern. Raising funds seems to fit the same description. Its strongest correlation is with contacting, but in both Continental and Eastern Europe this is almost on par with the association with consumer participation. Wearing or displaying a campaign badge or sticker is an even clearer case of ambivalence. This activity shows its strongest correlation with different modes in different groups of countries: with protesting in Continental Europe, contacting in Scandinavia, and party activity in Portugal; it correlates roughly the same with *all* non-electoral modes in Eastern Europe. In a similar vein, attending a political meeting or rally is most strongly associated with party activity in all countries except Eastern Europe, where its strongest correlations are with contacting and protest activity. This means that these four items cannot be located in the conceptual typology of participation modes elicited above. Their connections to the other modes vary from country to country. Thus, activity in these particular forms must be studied separately, and can only be explained with reference to nation-specific institutional settings.

Conclusions

In this chapter we have drawn a map over the landscape of political participation in some Western and Eastern European countries. Conceptually defined as deliberate acts by ordinary citizens to influence political outcomes, we have provided descriptive data on some 25 types of political activities in 13 societies. We have shown that these activities cluster into five more generic modes of participation: contacting, party activity, protest activity, consumer participation, and voting. This pattern has been found in all countries except Portugal, where party mobilisation appears to obstruct the presence of distinct dimensions of protest activity and consumer participation. The Portuguese exception notwithstanding, the ample evidence presented in favour of our fivefold typology represents significant progress in this field. Despite the differences in the socio-political processes in these countries, there are similar modes of participation in all of them, that is, there is group of actions sharing the same characteristics across contemporary democracies regardless of the institutional setting, the age of democracy, the level of economic modernisation, and the political, social, and cultural context.

There are, however, cross-national differences in the levels of participation in all five modes. The comparative description of the data has shown that the Scandinavian countries by and large are the most politically active countries. When it comes to non-electoral activities, this goes for the Netherlands and Switzerland as well. The country with lowest levels of political participation in all modes except voting is Russia; with respect to voting, Russia is next to last (only Switzerland has lower turnout). With the exception of East Germany, there are in general lower levels of political participation in the Eastern European countries. In these countries, together with Portugal, political activity is also more concentrated in the hands of fewer activists.

We have suggested that either the age of democracy or the level of economic development might explain why people in some countries are more politically active than in others. In all countries, however, there is a general participatory propensity underlying particularly the non-electoral modes of activity, implying that political activists face no trade-off in their choice of mode of participation. Thus, the difference between newer and older democracies, or between highly and poorly developed countries, is a question of the number of people involved and the level of concentration of political activity. But it would be wrong to conclude that with respect to political participation these two sets of countries constitute two different models of democracy.

Notes

1 In a later definition, Nie and Verba (1975: 1) added the word 'legal' to the activities undertaken by citizens, a qualification much discussed and generally disregarded; see Huntington and Nelson (1976: 6).
2 For Brady (1999: 738), the authoritative allocation of values can only be undertaken by the government, and therefore political activity is the one that attempts to affect governmental action: 'political participation, then, must be directed at some government policy or activity'. Among other broad definitions of participation in this regard, Rosenstone and Hansen (1993: 4) and Booth and Seligson (1978: 6), for instance, link political actions with attempts to influence the distribution of social goods or social values, or the distribution of public goods, respectively.
3 The one objection Kaase and Marsh (1979: 42ff.) raised with regard to Verba's and Nie's classical definition was *methodological*. They argued that when employing sample surveys in the study of rare political acts, one had to include *attitudes* towards the acts – not only actual behaviour – in order to increase statistical variance.
4 Hirschman (1970: 30) himself defined voice:

> as an attempt at all to change ... whether through individual or collective petition to the management directly in charge, through appeal to a higher authority with the intention of forcing a change in management, or through various types of actions and protests, including those that are meant to mobilise public opinion.

5 Theoretically speaking there should be two types of contacting. On one hand, a contact might be targeted toward elected representatives or other public officials and thus is based on the *representational* 'logic'. On the other hand, a contact could be oriented toward some social or economic organisation and thus be *extra-representational*. However, due to insufficient indicators of these different targets of contacting in the survey we will not be able to test this distinction. Instead, we have left contacting as a generic mode of participation that includes both representational and extra-representational targets.
6 Verba and Nie (1972: 64–71) and Verba *et al.* (1978: 317–22) reached the mode 'communal activity' by collapsing two other sets of activities: on the one hand, 'cooperative acts', which they operationalised as various forms of activity in local groups or organisations; on the other hand, 'contacts on social issues', that is, with broader referents than the respondent himself and/or his immediate family. As can be seen, the latter of these two is exactly equivalent to our definition of 'contacting'. Moreover, as shall be clear from the empirical analysis below, one item similar to the 'cooperative acts' – 'worked in an organisation or association' – appears in the same dimension as the contacting acts.

7 First, all variables have been transformed to express each respondent's deviation from the country mean. This levels out all variation across countries, and thus ascertains that only inter-individual variation *within* countries may influence the results. Second, each society is weighted equally. For the sake of convenience we have set this weight to sum the average sample size after listwise deletion in each country, that is, 1,652.5.

8 For the sake of clarity, only the pattern matrix is displayed in the table; the structure matrix yields similar, but somewhat less intelligible results. In addition to principal components, we have tested the dimensional structure with principal axis factoring and maximum likelihood confirmatory factor analysis (using LISREL). The results are very similar to the ones presented here.

9 The other excluded items are protest abstention, the 'other' category, and the use of Internet. The timeframe for the first of these items differs from all the others in that it asks whether the action has *ever* been undertaken, as opposed to the timeframe 'within the last 12 months'. Moreover, the category 'other activity' has been excluded since it by definition measures different things in the different societies under study. Finally, the use of Internet has been excluded since the reference frame of this item is whether it has been used in connection with *any* of the aforementioned activities – it is thus only asked of those who participate in some form of activity.

10 The scale has been constructed to reflect the proportion of all type of activities within each mode the respondent has performed, regardless of item non-response. Only respondents with non-response for all items within a certain mode have been assigned the value of non-response for the entire scale.

11 The partial correlations with the non-electoral average are around 0.30 for both GDP per capita and democratic legacy, controlling for the other factor, which again suggests that we cannot distinguish among the two interpretations.

12 More specifically, what appears to be peculiar about Portugal is the fact that taking part in demonstrations only loads on the party activity dimension (see Table 12.3). With only two items remaining – taking part in strikes and illegal protest activities (the latter almost lacking any variance to begin with) –, this means that the protest dimension collapses. This interpretation is supported by the fact that when the three protest items are left out of the analyses, the three other modes of participation – contacting, party activity, and consumer participation – behave almost perfectly in the dimensional analysis.

13 This more general inclination can be confirmed by a so-called second-order dimensional analysis, that is, a principal component analysis of the four non-electoral participation indices presented in Table 13.4. With conventional criteria for the retention of factors (eigenvalues no less than one), such an analysis results in a clear unidimensional solution within all 13 societies under study

14 Political participation and associational involvement

Klaus Armingeon

Introduction

Democracy as 'government of the people, by the people, for the people' (Abraham Lincoln) requires both that government action is in accordance with the general interest of the people, and that the people determine government action. Political participation is therefore a *conditio sine qua non* of a democratic order. In this chapter I analyse five modes of partaking in politics that are arguably the most important political actions by citizens in modern societies: voting, party activities, contacting decision-makers or the media, political activities as a consumer, and protest activities. Normative democratic theory demands that democratic citizenship be associated with a substantial amount of political participation. Voting based on political knowledge and information should constitute a basic activity performed by nearly all citizens; and more demanding forms of participation should be exercised by a considerable share of the citizens (see the discussion in Chapter 12).

As demonstrated in Chapter 6 associational involvement is widespread in modern democracies although there is considerable variation across countries. We know that this involvement in organisations and informal networks is correlated with a higher level of political participation (Verba *et al.* 1978; Verba *et al.* 1993). If we compare the level of political participation among citizens involved in either of the two largest types of voluntary associations – trade unions and sports clubs (see Chapter 6) – with that of citizens lacking organisational involvement, we find substantial differences (see Table 14.1). In western Europe, as represented in our sample, the electoral turnout of trade union members is 14 percentage points higher than that of citizens without organisational membership; and even for members of an entirely non-political type of organisation such as sports clubs the level is 11 percentage points higher. Similar or even greater differences can be found in other fields of political participation (cf. van Deth 1996, 2001b). These differences are not limited to western Europe. In eastern Europe – that is, East Germany, Moldova, Romania, Russia, and Slovenia – a similar, albeit less pronounced rift can be demonstrated

Table 14.1 Levels of political participation by organisational involvement[a]

Involvement	Voting		Consumer participation		Contacting		Party activity		Protest activity	
	Western Europe	Eastern Europe	Western Europe	Eastern Europe	Western Europe	Eastern Europe	Western Europe	Eastern Europe	Western Europe	Eastern Europe
No involvement	0.77	0.81	0.14	0.07	0.00	0.04	0.00	0.00	0.00	0.02
Sports clubs	0.88	0.83	0.39	0.22	0.16	0.11	0.05	0.04	0.05	0.06
Trade unions	0.91	0.84	0.41	0.20	0.16	0.12	0.05	0.05	0.05	0.08

Note

a Entries are means on a scale ranging from 0 to 1. *Involvement* implies that the respondent is a member, participates in activities or does voluntary work in an organisation of the type described. *No involvement* refers to respondents who are not members, active or volunteering in any of the 28 types of organisations on which we have data. Eastern Europe includes the eastern part of Germany. The national samples are weighted so that the effects of different sample sizes are eliminated.

(see Table 14.1). Provided these differences represent a causal effect in the sense that membership in formal and informal associations enables, helps or stimulates citizens to participate in politics, voluntary associations may be considered as a major precondition for a working democratic order (cf. van Deth 1997).

The statistical relationship between organisational involvement and political participation should not be overstated, however. On the one hand there are very substantial differences between citizens within and outside of organisations. But on the other hand the median trade unionist or an insider of a sports club is far from meeting the criteria of a 'model' participating citizen. Most members of voluntary associations do not reach the maximum level of political participation (i.e. 1 on the scales of participation).[1] In addition, political participation varies greatly within the two groups of citizens considered: those with and without organisational involvement. Regressing our measures of political participation on a dummy variable, scored 1 for those involved in any of the 28 organisations on which we have data, yields coefficients similar in size to the differences of means in Table 14.1. But the proportion of variance explained is very low. The R^2 ranges from less than 1 per cent (for voting in the east and protest activity in the west) to a maximum of 9 per cent (for consumer participation in both parts of Europe). Nevertheless, it remains true that citizens involved in organisations tend to be significantly more active politically than their organisationally uninvolved fellow citizens.

How can we explain this covariation between political participation and organisational involvement? This is the guiding question of this chapter. I focus on three different answers suggested in the literature. According to the first, organisations are 'schools of democracy', which impart skills, values, and attitudes favourable to participation in democratic politics. The classical statement of the idea is given in Tocqueville's *Democracy in America*:

> Feelings and ideas are renewed, the heart expands, and the human spirit develops only through the reciprocal action of human beings on one another. I have shown that this action is almost nonexistent in democratic countries. Hence it must be created artificially, and only associations can do it.
> (Tocqueville [1835, 1840] 2000: 598; see also Warren 2001)

This idea is at the centre of an argument labelled 'social capital' theory (Putnam 2000).

A second answer points to associations as organisers of societal conflicts. If a citizen feels attached to a societal segment – for example a social class or an ethnic group – he or she can be represented by an organisation focused on that segment. The organisation mobilises and guides its members in political affairs without placing much demand on the political interest or knowledge of the individual (cf. Pollock 1982). A classical statement is Lenin's definition of trade unions as transmission belts of overarching political goals administered by a political vanguard. Another rendition is Lipset's and Rokkan's (1967) idea of stable coalitions between organisations and societal groups. In the perspective of this theory of cleavage politics, parties and interest groups organise societal segments. They do not expect strong political activity by citizens in the segment. Rather the willingness to follow the leaders of organisations suffices.

According to the third answer the correlation between organisational membership and political participation is spurious. The individual characteristics that favour organisational involvement also promote participation in politics. In that sense associations are self-selective. They do not educate citizens. Rather, politically educated citizens tend to join organisations to a much stronger extent than citizens without much interest in, or knowledge about, politics (Newton 1997, 1999b).

There is also a fourth response, which denies the premise of the question I am asking, and which can therefore be rejected on the basis of the evidence already presented at this early stage. According to that response, associational involvement is negatively or not at all correlated with political participation. One reason may be limited time budgets crowding out political activity once a citizen has become active in an association. Another reason is gradually shifting involvements between private, social, and political activities caused by frustrations in the present domain of participation (see van Deth 1997: 10–13).

In this chapter I will show that most of the co-variation between organisational involvement and political participation can be explained by the self-selectivity of voluntary associations, whereas the mobilising function of the organisational elite is near zero. The Tocquevillian logic may work reasonably well in the case of consumer participation and contacting, but it is hardly a prominent cause of any of the other modes of political participation.

Theories, variables, and research design

Self-selectivity

What testable hypotheses can be deduced from the three competing theories? Let us start with the theory of individual attributes accounting for organisational involvement as well as political participation (Newton 1997, 1999b; Uslaner 2002; Hooghe and Stolle 2003a). According to this theory of self-selectivity, citizens with resources and values favouring political participation are overrepresented in formal organisations and informal networks, without being affected by their interaction with the association. Consequently, the correlation between organisational memberships and political participation is spurious, and will disappear once the individual attributes promoting involvement in the organisational as well as the political domain are taken into account.

What are the characteristics of citizens who are participating in politics and may simultaneously be overrepresented in organisations? We know that the causes of political participation vary with the mode of participation. For example, voting is less demanding in terms of skills and curiosity about politics than partisan activity. And political protest activity depends more on dissatisfaction with the way democracy is working than conventional strategies like contacting decision-makers. Hence, although there is a list of attributes that have proven to possess explanatory power for at least one mode of participation, there is no reason to expect that each of these attributes are of similar importance for all forms of political participation.

The following enumeration of these independent variables builds on a huge literature in which a large number of causal assumptions are specified and elaborated. For the purpose of answering my guiding question, however, it is not necessary to detail all these assumptions and their sources.[2] Rather I will itemize the attributes and give some selected prominent arguments regarding the way they are thought to affect political participation.

A first group consists of structural characteristics like education, income, age, civil status, and gender. Education helps citizens to understand and evaluate politics and political options, facilitates deliberation, clarifies the importance of a working democracy for their own lives, and helps them handle frustrations in the domain of politics. Income is related to education – better education increases the likelihood of enjoying a high income – and exerts an independent impact on participation. For example, money may be used for political endeavours.

Age has turned out to be of central importance in explaining political participation. According to a large number of studies, its effects on participation are due to variations in social integration. Young people are less socially integrated. They are in a period of life in which questions of identity and self-realisation are typically of much greater salience than politics – in particular politics within the established institutions of the political system. After adolescence, integration into family life as well as working life becomes stronger and the likelihood of being drawn into politics increases. Paying taxes as well as enjoying the benefits of the welfare state provide lessons about politics and demonstrate its relevance; and family members or workplace colleagues may provide a stimulus or social pressure towards increased political participation. Therefore the likelihood of such participation increases with age. When reaching the point of retirement from working life, the age curve flattens or even declines. Decreasing social integration and the physical and psychological correlates of age contribute to stagnant or declining political participation. Whilst the above argument focuses on life-cycle effects, political participation may vary by generation too. A well-known example is provided by theories of value change, where the particular historical events experienced during childhood and adolescence are assumed to result in values more or less favourable to political participation in general as well as particular modes of participation (see Inglehart 1977; Inglehart and Norris 2000).

Civil status may be related to political participation as well. Those who remain single are less exposed to social control and the benefits of reduced information costs. They do not risk critical questions if they stay in bed instead of going to the ballot box on election day, and they cannot avoid the burden of decision-making by adopting the choice of a trustworthy partner. Being married or cohabiting increases the likelihood of political participation due to social integration and the social control and positive incentives for political participation that it provides. For parents, decisions on school fees are obviously linked to their private budget, and the relevance of politics for the needs of private life is self-evident.

In addition to these structural variables, psychological predispositions and attitudes affect the likelihood of political participation. Political interest is a major personal characteristic causing a switch from passivity to participation in many cases (Lane 1965: 144; van Deth 1990). Lack of interest does not, however, exclude all political activity – in particular if they are not very demanding – and great political interest may even result in passivity (van Deth 1996). But in general, researchers agree that political interest is favourable to participation.

The same applies to the feeling of being personally capable to change something in politics and the feeling that politicians are responsive to citizens' demands. A sense of efficacy – both internal ('I can affect something') and external ('they are responsive') – increases the likelihood of political participation. Similarly, the belief that a particular mode of political action is effective should increase the likelihood that it is used.

Another reason why some citizens are active in politics may be a sense of civic duty. This argument has become prominent in rational choice analyses. Since material gratifications have shown little explanatory power, the concept has been stretched to include psychological gratifications, such as fulfilling a duty (Clarke *et al.* 2002). In fact, such civic duties have turned out to be the most important predictor when rational choice models of electoral turnout have been tested empirically. Hence, during their political socialisation some individuals acquire norms of civic duty. To the extent that they do so, their likelihood of political participation increases. Such norms include the duty to vote, the duty to show solidarity with others, and the duty to form one's own opinion.

Social trust (see Chapter 2) should be favourable to political activities, in particular if they depend on cooperation, as for example party activity, protest movements, and consumer participation.

For some modes of participation, ideology may be important. Unconventional modes of political participation – like consumer participation or protest activity – may be more attractive for leftists or those at the extremes of the political spectrum, while those who are middle-of-the-road in ideological terms may feel little temptation to demonstrate, go on strike or use illegal means for political ends. Protest activity, in particular, is also likely to depend on the degree of satisfaction with life and with the way democracy works.

Party identification – that is, the psychological attachment to a specific political party – has been found to be an important explanation for participation in many studies (cf. Finkel and Opp 1991). Strong identifiers are more likely to vote for their party, to be mobilised into other types of political action by its appeals, and to contact its politicians.

As shown in prior studies, church attendance is another important predictor of participation. Those who go to church regularly receive politically relevant information and interpretations by church elites who they trust. This reduces information costs in, for example, electoral decisions.

A major contribution of recent research on political participation concerns the strong positive effect of skills – such as the capability to give a speech or chair a meeting – on political participation (Brady *et al.* 1995; Verba *et al.* 1995). In my analysis, however, I have to omit these skills from the set of predictors. Since we have data on politically relevant skills only for those who are involved in organisations and for those who are gainfully employed, there is no sensible way of controlling for skills when analysing the impact of organisation. And if I were to include civic skills acquired in the course of earning a living, the analysis would be restricted to those gainfully employed and hence not representative of the citizenry as a whole. As will be shown, however, the model has sufficient explanatory power even without a measure of civic skills.

Cleavage politics

A competing hypothesis about the relation between involvement in associations and political participation focuses on mobilisation effects by sociocultural milieus, their organisations and their elites (Leighley 1996). Although Leninist organisations like the communist trade unions of the interwar period are a very illustrative example, the effect can be found in other groups as well. In scholarly debate, the classical work in this area is Rokkan's analysis of cleavage formation (Lipset and Rokkan 1967; Rokkan 1977; see also Bartolini and Mair 1990). In the perspective outlined by Rokkan and others, citizens feel attached to a specific segment of society, which has specific interests. Occupational, religious, and ethnic groups are the most prominent examples. Since these groups are in continuous conflicts with one another, political entrepreneurs start building organisations of interest representation, in the form of associations as well as political parties. Those who feel attached to a segment join its organisations and are willing to follow the lead of the elites representing them. For instance, belonging to the socialist, catholic, protestant, or peripheral segment of a country has become a byword for electoral choices. As Richard Rose put it in the mid 1970s, 'to speak of the majority of voters at a given election as choosing a party is nearly as misleading as speaking of a worshipper on a Sunday "choosing" to go to an Anglican rather than a Baptist or Catholic church' (quoted in Gallagher *et al.* 2001: 252).

In the process of modernisation some of these attachments may have weakened, such as attachments to religious groups. Others may have strengthened, like the attachment to one's gender group. However strong these attachments are, recent research concurs in the observation that belonging to a societal subgroup does not carry as much implication for political behaviour as it did 50 or 100 years ago (Franklin *et al.* 1992; Mair 2002). This does not exclude the possibility that these feelings of belonging still have some effect on the various modes of participation, albeit less so than has previously been the case.

An illustrative example are workers in interwar Europe joining socialist trade unions and parties, not because they were particularly interested in politics, but because they felt that these were the organisations which represented their societal segment and its interests (see the important analyses by Lepsius 1979). Mobilisation occurs through leaders who reduce information costs of their members by telling them what the ordinary member of the segment should do in politics. This type of political mobilisation through organisational membership takes place if two crucial conditions are fulfilled: one has to be attached to a certain societal segment and one has to be a member of an organisation. If both conditions are met, a top-down mobilisation can take place. In my empirical analyses, I construct an interaction term based on the involvement in organisations and the strength of attachment to groups defined by religion, ethnicity, gender, and social class. This interaction term should have a strong effect if the theory of top-down mobilisation by organisational elites applies.

This can be the case only in nations in which there is a tradition of cleavage politics. Since stable coalitions between societal groups and organisations do not form instantly, it takes some time for cleavage-based politics to develop. For that reason we cannot expect such mechanisms in the new eastern democracies. Rather they should be observable only in the western nations, in particular in those having a long democratic history.

As in the test of the self-selectivity model, structural variables, like income, gender, age, and education, are included in this model of cleavage politics as controls.

Social capital

In recent years, neither the theory of self-selectivity nor that of top-down mobilisation of societal segments has been at the centre of the debate on the relationship between voluntary associations and political participation. Rather, the stage has been dominated by the Tocquevillian theory, which has gained great renewed interest in scholarly discourse. In a path-breaking analysis, Verba and co-authors (Brady *et al.* 1995; Verba *et al.* 1995) showed that organisational membership is conducive to the acquirement of skills, which in turn facilitates political participation, in particular if it is more demanding than just casting a ballot. In his works on social capital Putnam (1993, 1995a, 2000) proceeds along a similar line. He maintains that associations and informal networks are favourable to political participation on four grounds:

1   They 'instil in their members habits of cooperation and public spiritedness, as well as practical skills necessary to partake in public life'.
2   They are 'schools of democracy, where members learn how to run meetings, speak in public, write letters, organise projects, and debate public issues with civility'.
3   They 'serve as forum for thoughtful deliberation over vital public issues'.
4   They serve as 'occasion for learning civic virtues, such as active participation in public life' (Putnam 2000: 338–9).

From this perspective active involvement in formal and informal associations generally has favourable effects on political participation. This is mainly, but not exclusively, due to the skills, attitudes, and values imparted to the individual in the course of interaction within the organisation. For the organisation to socialise the individual member, he or she must be actively involved. It does not suffice to be a passive member. Rather, participation in the organisations or volunteering is a crucial precondition for triggering a process of political socialisation. As long as this face-to-face interaction takes place, the type of organisation does not matter. Skills useful for political activity and a sense of duty towards society can be acquired in sports clubs as well as in interest organisations (see Olsen 1972; van Deth 1996). Hence we expect similar effects of active involvement in organisations with and without political goals.

In order to test this hypothesis I distinguish between voluntary associations, such as political organisations (e.g. parties and human right groups) and interest groups (e.g. pensioners' and employers' organisations) on the one hand, and non-interest groups, that is, clubs and societies on the other hand. Interest groups such as trade unions, farmers' organisations, professional organisations, and, as a matter of course, political parties, have direct or indirect political goals. Hence a positive effect of active involvement in these associations may simply be due to the political convictions and interests the members already had before joining the organisation. A positive effect of involvement in 'non-political' associations, by contrast, can more readily be attributed to a process of political socialisation. Therefore I split the sample in four groups:

1   Those who are not actively involved;
2   those who are actively involved exclusively in clubs and societies;
3   those who are actively involved exclusively in interest groups and political organisations;
4   those who are actively involved in interest groups and political organisations as well as clubs and societies.

It will take some time for associations that are able to perform socialising roles of the kind described to develop, and it will take some time for citizens to be socialised in such associations. In established democracies, the odds that the associational system shows a positive effect due to socialisation are therefore much better than in newer democracies. Hence, as for the model of cleavage politics, we expect an east–west divide with the socialising effect more clearly visible in the western nations than in the eastern.

As in the case of top-down mobilisation of societal segments, direct effects of structural variables on participation are to be expected. Therefore they are included as controls. Figure 14.1 gives an overview of how the three competing models specify the causal relationship between involvement in formal and informal networks and modes of political participation.

Research design

The dependent variables are operationalised as described in Chapter 13, except for contacting which excludes working in, and contacting, organisations. In models where the dependent variable is party activity, the independent variable of organisational involvement excludes involvement in political parties, in order to avoid entering the same data on both sides of the regression equation.

Four dimensions of involvement in organisations and networks are considered at various stages in the analysis:

1   'Involvement in organisations': whether the respondent is currently a member of at least one of 28 possible types of organisations, and/or has taken part in activities in, and/or done voluntary work for, at least one of them during the past 12 months.
2   'Member network': whether this involvement is associated with other contacts to co-members outside organisational life. Examples are mutual help with practical matters or private visits.
3   'Informal network': whether the respondent is involved in informal networks outside organisational life that imply contact on a regular basis.

Self-selectivity: the correlation between involvement in associations and political participation is spurious

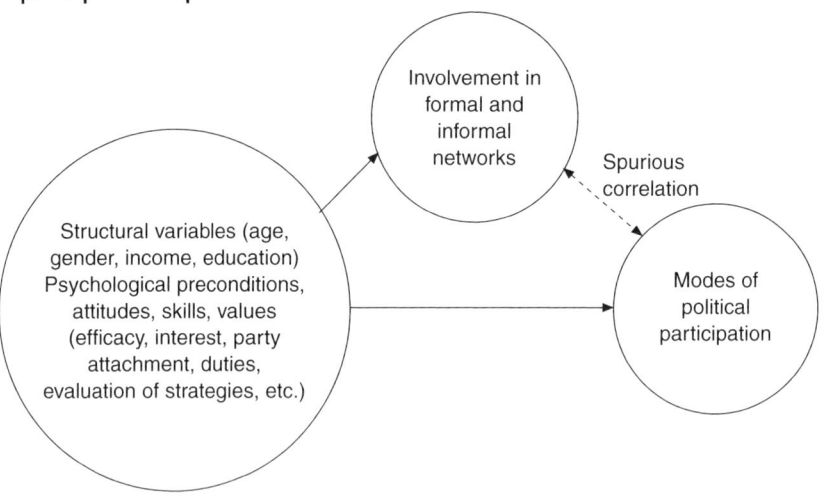

Political mobilisation through organisational elites: members of societal segments are politically mobilised by the elites of their organisations and by social control of their socio-cultural milieu

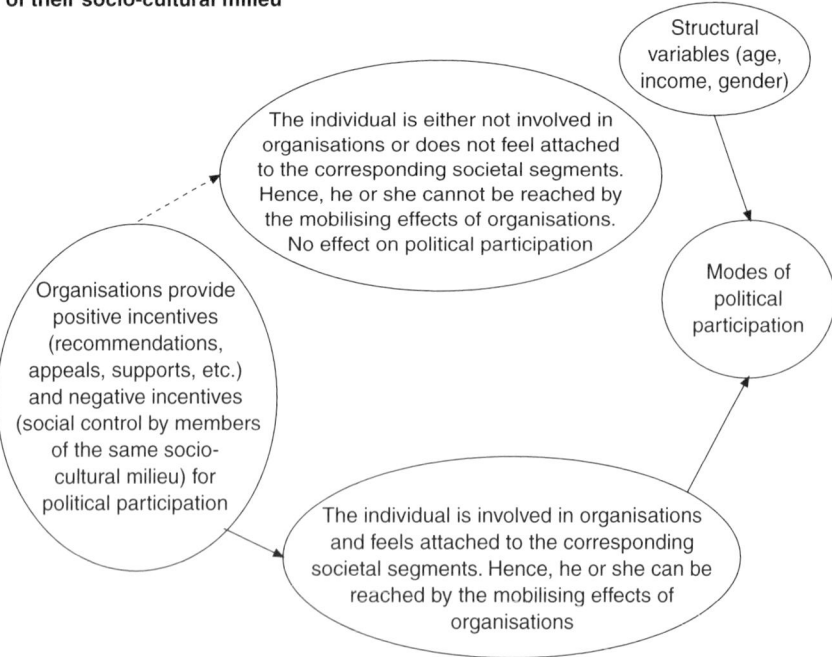

Figure 14.1 Causal relationship between organisational involvement and political participation.

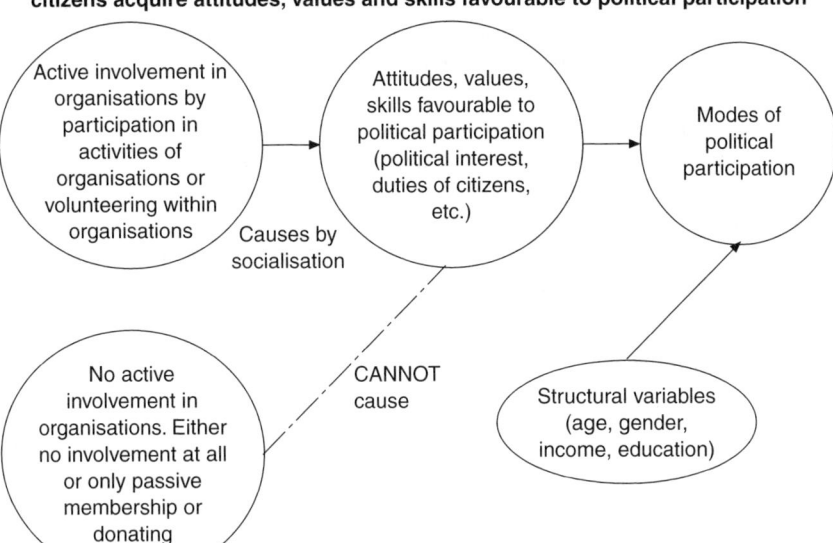

Political participation and associational involvement 369

Political socialisation by organisations: by active involvement in organisations citizens acquire attitudes, values and skills favourable to political participation

```
┌─────────────────┐         ┌─────────────────┐
│ Active involvement│        │ Attitudes, values,│
│ in organisations  │        │ skills favourable │      ┌──────────┐
│ by participation  │───────▶│ to political      │─────▶│ Modes of │
│ in activities of  │        │ participation     │      │ political│
│ organisations or  │        │ (political interest,│    │participation│
│ volunteering within│       │ duties of citizens,│     └──────────┘
│ organisations    │         │ etc.)             │
└─────────────────┘ Causes by└─────────────────┘
                   socialisation
```

Figure 14.1 continued.

4 'Participation in small-scale democracy': whether the respondent has taken an initiative during the past 12 months to improve his or her personal situation in important social domains (see Chapter 9) or prevent it from becoming worse.

As in all other analyses in this volume, the variables have been scored so as to range from a minimum of 0 to a maximum of 1. Generally 1 denotes the extremes of very much, strongly, etc., while 0 denotes none, not, not at all, etc. For purposes of summarising information and in order to test the assumption of different effects due to experience of a long period of democratic rule and associational freedom, the western and the eastern European societies have been pooled into two samples (with West Germany in the western part and East Germany in the eastern). Within the pooled samples, the data have been weighted so that the size of each national sample does not affect the results. Although my interpretations are informed by analyses conducted country by country, only the summary information for the two regional groups will be shown due to space limitations.

In all models, I control for structural variables like gender, income, age, civil status, and education. There is no reason to assume that these variables are affected by organisational involvement, and we know from previous research, that they are likely to have a systematic influence on participation. In order to keep the number of such variables small, I first estimated models with the dependent and the structural variables. If a structural variable was significant in at least five out of 13 societies, I included it in the general model. The results are presented in Table 14.2.

The explanatory power of these general models is very modest, although significant effects in the expected direction clearly show up. The likelihood of voting, for example, increases if the respondent ranks high in terms of income, age, and education and if he or she is cohabiting or married, whilst the likelihood of protest activities grows if the respondent is young and well-educated.

Cleavage politics

The fascinating idea of cleavage politics is that political participation does not presuppose individual resources or motivations, such as an interest in politics or a sense of political efficacy. Rather if a citizen is integrated into a socio-cultural milieu, he or she will follow the leads of that milieu due to positive incentives. For example, information costs are low because trustworthy elites of the milieu tell their constituents what to do. And there may be sanctions too. If one belongs to a group that is in conflict with other groups, abstention from group politics may be taken as a sign of insufficient solidarity, as in the case of strike breakers.

There is ample evidence that the cohesion of socio-cultural milieus have dwindled in the course of societal modernisation (Lepsius 1979; Franklin *et al.* 1992). This does not imply that the institutions representing the cleavages are being dismantled. They may well continue to exist. But they can no longer rely on a stable coalition with a coherent societal segment and its resources, such as a 'guaranteed' share of the votes largely independent of competing organisations and their achievements (cf. Bartolini and Mair 1990; Mair 2001; Mair 2002). The milieus once associated with the organisations have vanished and so has the directive power of organisations over individual political behaviour.

The analyses reported in Table 14.3 support such an interpretation. Apart from the variables of the general model, three additional variables are included: extent of attachment to socio-cultural groups; involvement in organisations; and the product between the two (labelled 'integration into societal segments'). If the theory of mobilisation by cleavage organisations holds true, there should be a strong effect of the product (interaction) term, particularly in western Europe, but not for its components taken alone. The hypothesis is not borne out, however. Generally, the interaction effect in country-by-country analyses is statistically insignificant. The idea of top-down mobilisation of societal segments turns out to be of little help in understanding political participation in Europe.[3]

Table 14.2 A general model for explaining political participation[a]

Predictor	Party activity		Contacting		Consumer participation		Protest activity		Voting	
	Western Europe	Eastern Europe	Western Europe	Eastern Europe	Western Europe	Eastern Europe	Western Europe	Eastern Europe	Western Europe	Eastern Europe
Education	0.05***	0.01*	0.15***	0.03***	0.41***	−0.07***	0.04***	0.03***	0.72***	0.48***
Gender (male)	0.02***	0.02***	0.04***	0.02***	−0.04***	0.00	–	–	–	–
Age	0.06***	0.01*	–	–	–	–	−0.08***	−0.06***	2.44***	1.35***
Income	–	–	0.53***	0.45***	0.48***	0.59***	–	–	4.24***	1.78
Partner	–	–	–	–	–	–	–	–	0.58***	0.43***
Adjusted/Nagelkerke R^2	0.02	0.01	0.05	0.02	0.09	0.02	0.02	0.02	0.08	0.04
N	7,983	4,974	6,185	3,732	6,188	3,730	7,936	4,968	11,281	4,605

Note

a Entries are unstandardised coefficients from OLS or (for voting) logistic regressions. Levels of statistical significance: *** = 0.01, ** = 0.05, * = 0.1. *Education* is operationalised as described in Chapter 1. *Gender* is a dummy variable scored 1 for male. In order to take account of the curvilinear relationship between age and political participation, *age* has been logged and afterwards transformed to range from 0 to 1. *Income* is operationalised as household income, standardised to have a standard deviation of 1 for each country. After this standardisation, the values were transformed by adding the minimum value and dividing by the maximum value so that the variable ranges from 0 to 1. *Partner* is a dummy variable scored 1 for those who are married or cohabiting.

Table 14.3 Top down (cleavage politics) model for explaining political participation[a]

Predictor	Party activity		Contacting		Consumer participation		Protest activity		Voting	
	Western Europe	Eastern Europe	Western Europe	Eastern Europe	Western Europe	Eastern Europe	Western Europe	Eastern Europe	Western Europe	Eastern Europe
Education	0.04***	0.02***	0.12***	0.04***	0.33***	−0.01	0.04***	0.04***	0.58**	0.71***
Gender (male)	0.01***	0.02***	0.04***	0.02***	−0.06***	−0.02*	–	–	–	–
Age	0.06***	0.02*	–	–	–	–	−0.08***	−0.07***	2.34***	0.85***
Income	–	–	0.51***	0.41***	0.42***	0.40***	–	–	4.59***	1.43
Partner	–	–	–	–	–	–	–	–	0.54***	0.49***
Attachment to socio-cultural groups	0.00	0.00	0.00	0.02	−0.09*	−0.09***	0.00***	0.00	0.60	1.24***
Involvement in organisations	0.01	0.01	0.07***	0.04	0.13***	0.15***	0.00	0.02	0.22	1.18***
Integration into societal segments	0.03	0.03*	0.01	0.06*	0.09*	−0.02	0.01	0.02	0.55	−1.10*
Adjusted/Nagelkerke R^2	0.02	0.02	0.06	0.07	0.13	0.13	0.02	0.04	0.10	0.06
N	7,759	3,925	6,041	2,784	6,044	2,782	7,722	3,919	10,992	3,028

Note

[a] Entries are unstandardised coefficients from OLS or (for voting) logistic regressions. Levels of statistical significance: *** = 0.01, ** = 0.05, * = 0.1. *Attachment to socio-cultural groups* is in additive index based on four items indicating how attached the respondent feels to people with the same religion, the same cultural background, the same gender, and a particular social class; *Involvement in organisations* is a dummy variable scored 1 if the respondent is a member of, has taken part in activities in, and/or volunteered in at least one of 28 possible types of organisations. *Integration into societal segments* is operationalised as the product between involvement in organisations and attachment to socio-cultural groups. For other variables, see Table 14.2.

Two additional tests support that conclusion. The first is based on an alternative specification of the interaction term (number of memberships × attachment to socio-cultural groups). Again, the general conclusion is that the interaction effect in country-by-country analyses is statistically insignificant. In the pooled samples it does not have the expected relative magnitude and sometimes not even the expected sign. This does not fully apply to voting, where we find some weak evidence in support of the cleavage hypothesis. And it does not apply to partisan activity in western Europe. But considering the very little additional explanatory power gained by adding these three variables to the general model, even in the case of voting and partisan activities, political mobilisation as understood by the cleavage model is not important in the societies studied.

As a final test, I split the pooled sample by the dichotomous variable 'involvement in organisations' and compared the coefficients for 'attachment to socio-cultural groups' in the two sub-samples. Once again, I found only weak effects in the expected direction: in the case of voting in the west and in the case of partisan activity in both the east and the west.

Social capital

From a normative point of view, the weak support enjoyed by the cleavage model of mobilisation for participation comes as a relief. In this model interest in politics, political knowledge or democratic deliberation does not play any role. Organised members of societal segments are seen as docile followers of their respective elites. On normative grounds the view of organisational involvement as a precondition for participation in democratic politics is far more exciting. Active organisational involvement is conceived of as social capital yielding returns in terms of the attitudes and skills that serve as a precondition for political participation, in particular demanding forms like partisan activity.

In technical terms this is a hierarchical model that can be estimated by techniques like path analysis. Since the analysis covers five different modes of political participation and since there are a large number of intervening variables between organisational involvement and political participation, a parsimonious path model can hardly be estimated. In addition, even in the presence of strong path coefficients between organisations and intervening variables, one could argue that this is due to the political character of some voluntary associations. Therefore the direction of causality remains unclear.

An alternative approach starts from the claim that the socialising effect of organisations can be observed in all types of voluntary associations as soon as individuals participate or volunteer (Olsen 1972). Sheer passive membership or chequebook-participation does not bring about these socialising effects. Non-political clubs and societies instil civic virtues in their members as do local trade unions or party groups: 'Taking part in a choral society or a bird-watching club can teach self-discipline and an appreciation for the joys of successful collaboration' (Putnam 1993: 90).

The estimates for the models in Table 14.4 do not support such a view, however. Out of the 65 coefficients for active membership in non-political associations generated by country-by-country analyses, only about one-third are significant and in the expected direction. The explanatory power of the models is very modest. It rarely exceeds 10 per cent of the variance, is usually only slightly above that of the corresponding cleavage model in Table 14.3, and weaker than that of the cleavage model using the alternative specification. If there is a systematic effect of social capital as based on active organisational involvement, it does not make a huge difference. For reasons specified above, we would also expect a weaker effect in eastern than in western Europe. However, such a difference is hardly visible in the results. There is little difference between east and west, and the variation within the two groups of countries is as impressive as the variation between them.

Probably the most challenging finding for proponents of social capital theory is the magnitude of the coefficients for involvement in non-political organisations relative to those for active involvement in interest groups and political organisations. The coefficients for the non-political associations are generally much lower (and less frequently significant) than those for the political associations. When controlling for structural variables and involvement in interest groups and political organisations, bird watchers and members of soccer clubs are hardly more prone to participate politically than are citizens without any active associational involvement.

However, if those who are active in non-political associations are active in political organisations as well, their propensity to participate politically increases. Generally, the level of participation is highest for those who are actively involved in both types of organisations. In the perspective of social capital theory, one could argue that this represents 'layered' effects of social capital and the self-selectivity of political groups. The data fit another, more parsimonious explanation: some citizens are more sociable and outward directed than others. Due to their individual characteristics they are more active in political as well as associational life. Their political participation is not caused by the socialising effects of active involvement in associations. Instead, both are caused by their individual traits.

Before turning to the empirical evidence for that line of reasoning, we may want to consider the possibility that the disappointing results for social capital theory may be explained in another way. In a recent contribution, it is argued that the socialisation whereby associational involvement instils civic virtues mainly takes place in the formative phase of life: 'the search for the socialising effects of adult participation will result in the discovery of relative minor changes if primary socialisation experiences are not

Table 14.4 Social capital model for explaining political participation[a]

Predictor	Party activity		Contacting		Consumer participation		Protest activity		Voting	
	Western Europe	Eastern Europe	Western Europe	Eastern Europe	Western Europe	Eastern Europe	Western Europe	Eastern Europe	Western Europe	Eastern Europe
Education	0.01*	0.01**	0.11***	0.04***	0.34***	−0.05***	0.03***	0.03***	0.30	0.56***
Gender (male)	0.01***	0.01***	0.04***	0.02***	−0.05***	−0.01	–	–	–	–
Age	0.04***	0.01	–	–	–	–	−0.09***	−0.06***	2.22***	1.42***
Income	–	–	0.46***	0.35***	0.36***	0.40***	–	–	3.99**	0.97
Partner	–	–	–	–	–	–	–	–	0.54***	0.44***
Active involvement in clubs and societies only	0.02***	0.02***	0.03***	0.05***	0.06***	0.12***	0.00	0.02***	0.08	0.54***
Political organisations and interest groups only	0.07***	0.12***	0.06***	0.05***	0.00	0.08***	0.04***	0.04***	0.56*	0.51*
Both types of associations	0.07***	0.11***	0.10***	0.13***	0.17***	0.23***	0.02***	0.08***	0.92***	0.57***
Adjusted/Nagelkerke R^2	0.06	0.12	0.09	0.07	0.14	0.13	0.03	0.04	0.11	0.05
N	7,983	4,974	6,185	3,732	6,188	3,730	7,936	4,968	11,281	4,605

Note

a Entries are unstandardised coefficients from OLS or (for voting) logistic regressions. Levels of statistical significance: *** = 0.01, ** = 0.05, * = 0.1. Active involvement (i.e. participation in activities and/or voluntary works) is a set of dummy variables indicating whether the respondent is actively involved in clubs and societies only, in political organisations and interest groups only, in both types of organisations or not actively involved (reference category). For other variables, see Table 14.2.

included in the study' (Hooghe and Stolle 2003a: 50). For instance, the civic virtues of a socially isolated 75-year-old citizen may have been brought about by his experiences as a Boy Scout and teenage soccer player.

A provisional test of this hypothesis can be conducted via a separate analysis of the youngest portion of our samples, that is, those below 30 years of age. Due to the relatively small number of such respondents, the analysis is confined to the pooled samples (western vs. eastern societies). The results indicate that there are no substantial difference between the results for the sub-samples of young citizens and the total samples. Probably this attempt to salvage the theory on organisational involvement, socialisation, and political participation is not the most promising one.

Self-selectivity versus social capital

Is the co-variation between organisational membership and political participation due merely to a common origin, that is, to a set of individual characteristics that further political participation as well as organisational involvement? The results of the regression analyses presented in Table 14.5 support such a claim to a large extent. For all five modes of participation, the explanatory power of the self-selectivity models is superior to those of the previously estimated models.

However, the effect of involvement in formal and informal networks on participation does not disappear entirely. Using the criteria that a coefficient for a variable has to be significant in the expected direction in at least five out of 13 societies, the results for the social capital variables in the self-selectivity models can be summarised as follows: for voting, social capital does not make any difference. This comes as no surprise, since voting is one of the least demanding forms of political participation. The socialising effects of active involvement in networks should be the more powerful, the more difficult the participatory acts are. If there is an organisational effect on voting, it is more plausible that it works via social control and reduced information and decision cost, as in the model of cleavage politics. That model performs best, relatively speaking, with respect to voting.

For consumer activities, like boycotting certain products or writing petitions, integration in networks carries much more weight. Some form of involvement in formal and informal associations, starting with passive membership, as well as involvement in informal groups, and participation in small-scale democracy do increase the likelihood of participation, even after controlling for a large number of individual traits. The effect is moderate, however. If we exclude these variables from the model, the proportion of variance explained drops by four percentage points for western societies and seven percentage points for eastern.

Similar conclusions apply to contacting. Significant effects are produced by the frequency of informal contacts between members of associations, inclusion in informal networks and participation in small-scale democracy. Without these variables, the proportion of variance explained is five percentage points lower for western societies and six for eastern.

Social capital has less of an impact on partisan activity. The most important contribution comes from the density of member networks (frequency of contacts with co-members). Without social capital variables, the proportion of variance explained drops by two percentage points in western societies and four in eastern.

Finally, hardly any impact of social capital can be found for protesting. This is remarkable since protests depend on some forms of informal networks. But these are not prominent in the regression results. In a similar vein, social trust, often equated with social capital, does not contribute to our understanding of why some people protest more often than others.

Although for three out of five modes of political participation, the effect of involvement in informal and formal networks remains significant in the models of self-selectivity, the explanatory power of these social-capital variables is quite modest in view of the claim that social capital is of utmost importance for the working of a democarcy. The effect may be smaller still if another crucial variable is included into the model, namely civic skills. Brady *et al.* (1995; see also Verba *et al.* 1995) argue convincingly that skills such as being able to give a speech or to organise a meeting are a crucial precondition of demanding political activities. Since our data provide information on the extent to which the respondent practices such skills only for those involved in at least one organisation and for those who are gainfully employed, I cannot control for them in the sample as a whole. When the analysis is restricted to those who are gainfully employed, the results reveal that civic skills have no impact on voting, nor on partisan and protest activities. For contacting and consumer participation, the magnitude of the regression coefficient is greater than for formal as well as informal networks, although the latter remains statistically significant in most cases.

What lessons can be drawn from these results? Comparing the explanatory power with those of the two previous models, self-selectivity fares better. However, it does not reduce the effect of social capital to insignificance. This may be due to the omission of important control variables. But it may also be that formal and informal networks have the expected socialising consequences for consumer participation, contacting, and party activity, albeit on a modest scale. In no case is the effect very prominent.

Comparing the 'social capital' models with those that test for self-selectivity poses the problem that the variables of involvement in formal and informal networks are not identical for the two models. This is due to my attempt to find a specification of the models which takes into account both the theoretical arguments put forward by the social-capital theorists and the need to partial out the effects of self-selectivity inherent in any involvement in a interest group or a political organisation. However, rerunning the self-selectivity models after replacing the four aspects of network involvement (involvement in organisations, density of member

Table 14.5 Self-selectivity model for explaining political participation[a]

Predictor	Party activity		Contacting		Consumer participation		Protest activity		Voting	
	Western Europe	Eastern Europe	Western Europe	Eastern Europe	Western Europe	Eastern Europe	Western Europe	Eastern Europe	Western Europe	Eastern Europe
Education	−0.01	0.00	0.03	0.07***	0.20***	0.02	0.02	0.04***	−0.13	0.74**
Gender (male)	0.00	0.01	0.02***	0.02	−0.05***	−0.03**	−0.09***	−0.10***	1.28***	—
Age	0.02*	0.02	—	—	—	—	—	—	2.14	0.82
Income	—	—	0.26***	0.28*	0.08	0.07	—	—	0.53***	−0.27
Partner	—	—	−0.01	—	—	—	—	—		0.32
Involvement in organisations	−0.01**	−0.04***	−0.01	0.01	0.08***	0.07***	−0.01	0.00	−0.03	0.35
Organisational networks	0.06***	0.15***	0.12***	0.09***	0.09***	0.07*	0.03***	0.06***	0.27	−0.52
Informal network	0.00	−0.01	0.03***	0.04***	0.04***	0.05**	0.01**	0.00	−0.11	−0.22
Participation in small-scale democracy	0.00	−0.01	0.06***	0.07***	0.09***	0.07***	0.00	0.02**	−0.12	0.12
Political interest	0.07***	0.03**	0.15***	0.06***	0.20***	0.12***	0.04***	0.03*	0.62**	−0.33
Party identification	0.09***	0.07***	0.02*	0.03*	0.02	0.02	0.03***	0.03***	2.00***	1.77***
External efficacy	0.01	0.00	−0.04*	−0.01	−0.05*	0.03	−0.02	0.04	0.26	−2.02***
Internal efficacy	0.08***	0.04**	0.21***	0.11***	0.08***	0.00	0.01	0.00	0.22	1.13*
Church attendance	0.01*	−0.01	0.03**	−0.04*	0.03*	−0.03	0.00	0.00	0.57***	0.64
Satisfaction with democracy	−0.03***	−0.04**	−0.07***	−0.05*	−0.03	−0.07**	−0.03***	−0.02	−0.01	0.64
Satisfaction with life	0.00	0.00	−0.07***	−0.02	−0.05	0.08**	−0.01	−0.02	0.04	0.03
Duty to vote	−0.03**	0.00	−0.01	−0.03	0.03	−0.01	−0.01	−0.02	3.54***	3.09***
Duty to solidarity	0.00	0.01	0.02	0.03	0.09***	−0.04	0.02*	−0.02	−0.55	−1.01*
Duty to form own opinion	0.00	−0.02	0.02	0.00	0.09***	0.02	−0.02*	0.00	−0.29	−0.13
Effectiveness of unconventional participation	−0.04***	−0.02	−0.06***	−0.01	0.29***	0.12***	0.06***	0.07***	−0.49	0.34

Effectiveness of conventional participation	0.07***	0.05**	0.07***	0.07**	−0.09**	0.00	−0.04**	0.03		0.29
Social trust	0.00	−0.02	−0.06***	−0.02	0.05*	0.07*	−0.02	−0.01	0.20	0.76
Ideology	−0.02*	−0.01	−0.02	−0.01	−0.15***	−0.11***	−0.08***	−0.03*	−0.15	−0.33
Extremism	0.02*	0.00	0.00	0.03	0.04*	0.01	0.03***	0.03*	0.21	0.57
Adjusted/Nagelkerke R^2	0.17	0.15	0.20	0.17	0.26	0.21	0.08	0.09	0.34	0.28
N	5,881	2,144	4,760	1,618	4,762	1,618	5,870	2,144	8,591	1,727

Note

[a] Entries are unstandardised coefficients from OLS or (for voting) logistic regressions. Levels of statistical significance: *** = 0.01, ** = 0.05, * = 0.1. *Involvement in organisations* is a dummy variable scored 1 if the respondent is a member of, has taken part in activities in, and/or volunteered in at least one of 28 possible types of organisations. *Organisational networks* is an additive index based on the frequency of doing the following with other members of the organisations or clubs to which the respondent belongs: Helping each other with practical matters outside organisational life; visit each other privately; talk about problems concerning the organisation or its goals; argue or quarrel. If the respondent is not involved in organisations, density of networks is scored 0. *Informal network* is a dummy variable scored 1 if the respondent belongs to any group or network of friends or acquaintances (outside organisational life) with whom he/she has contact on a regular basis. *Participation in small-scale democracy* is a dummy variable scored 1 if the respondent has done anything to try to bring about improvements or counteract deterioration as a patient/relative of a patient in the health system, as a parent in the child's school, or as gainfully employed at the workplace. If the respondent is neither a patient/relative of a patient, nor a parent of school children, nor gainfully employed, the value is missing. *Political interest* reflects the respondent's interest in politics (not at all, not very, fairly, or very interested). *Party identification* is based on answers to questions regarding the extent to which the respondent is a supporter of a particular political party or feels close to it. *External efficacy* is an additive index based on answers to the following two questions (11-point scales): 'How large possibilities do ordinary people have to present their opinions to politicians', and 'How much weight do politicians attach to opinions presented to them by ordinary people'. *Internal efficacy* is an additive index based on answers to the following two questions (11-point scales): 'Do people like you have greater or smaller possibilities than others to present their opinions to politicians' and 'Do people like you have greater or smaller possibilities than others to make politicians take account of your opinions'. *Church attendance* is a seven-point scale ranging from never to several times per week. 'Don't knows' are coded as never. *Satisfaction with democracy* indicates whether the respondent is not at all, not very, fairly, or very satisfied with the way democracy works in his country. *Satisfaction with life* reflects the extent to which the respondent is satisfied with his life as a whole these days (11-point scale). *Duty to vote* reflects the extent to which the respondent thinks it important for a good citizen to vote in public elections (11-point scale). *Duty to solidarity* reflects the extent to which the respondent thinks it important for a good citizen to show solidarity with people who are worse off than him-/herself (11-point scale). *Duty to form own opinion* reflects the extent to which the respondent thinks it important for a good citizen to form his own opinion independently of others (11-point scale). *Effectiveness of unconventional participation* is an additive index of the effectiveness (11-point scales) of boycotting certain products, participating in public demonstrations, and participating in illegal protest activities. *Effectiveness of conventional participation* is additive index of the respondent's view of the effectiveness (11-point scales) of working in a political party, in voluntary organisations, of voting in elections, and of personally contacting politicians. *Ideology* is the respondent's position on an 11-point left-right scale (see Chapter 2 for details). *Extremism* is the same left-right scale modified so that 0 is the middle point and the values squared (with increasing scores indicating a movement to the right). *Social trust* is an index measuring interpersonal trust (i.e. this variable reflects the degree of left- as well as right-wing extremism). For other variables, see Table 14.2.

networks, informal networks, participation in small-scale democracy) by the three dummy variables of the social capital model brings about the expected changes: the proportion of variance explained increases, and the magnitude and statistical significance of the coefficients for the dummy variables decreases compared to models without the control variables of the self-selectivity model. However, the effect of the social capital variables is not generally reduced to statistical insignificance. This lends further support to the hypothesis that even after controlling for individual traits there is a very limited, but non-spurious impact of social capital on participation.

Shifting the focus of interpretation from the role of social capital to the major determinants of various forms of political participation, some findings stand out. The determinants of political participation vary by type of participation as well as by country. I cannot discuss the cross-national differences here because they have to be dealt with in a theory-guided comparative analysis that relates macro characteristics of the national political system to individual-level data. Rather, I point to some similarities across all societies and within the west and the east. The following summary remarks are based on the magnitude of the regressions coefficients, their statistical significance, and their cross-national consistency with regard to direction (positive versus negative effect).

Voting is the least demanding of the political activities under study. The two major explanatory variables are the sense of citizen duty to vote and party identification. Consumer participation is mainly dependent on political interest, the feeling that unconventional political activity is effective and an ideological leaning to the left. In the western societies a high level of formal education is also conducive to this form of political participation.

Contacting is more likely to be undertaken by politically interested citizens who have the feeling that they can bring about changes in politics, are active in small-scale democracy, and have private contacts with their co-members in associations. The strength and consistency of the effect the density of informal networks and the sense of political efficacy is less pronounced in the eastern than in the western societies.

Partisan activity is most widespread among those with dense private networks, strong political interest and party identification, and a sense of political efficacy. In addition, party activists believe in the effectiveness of conventional political participation. This applies more to the west than to the east. In the newer democracies of the east, party activity is less contingent on political interest and a positive evaluation of conventional participation.

Protesters in the western countries tend to be young, convinced of the efficacy of unconventional political participation, and lean to the left ideologically. In the eastern societies, by contrast, only age has a clear effect, while the impact of sense of efficacy and ideological self-placement is less readily visible.

Comparing the explanatory power of the various models on the basis of the results of the pooled samples, three findings stand out:

1 The models explain a greater proportion of the variance in the west than in the east, pointing to less idiosyncratic determinants of political participation in established democracies.
2 The model of self-selectivity is clearly superior to that of cleavage politics and social capital. In addition, variables within the self-selectivity model, which are significant and refer to aspects of social capital, have at best a moderate explanatory power.
3 In the east as well as the west, the models explain the decision to take part in elections relatively well. Consumer participation comes next, followed, at some distance, by contacting and partisan activity. The models perform very poorly with regard to protest activity. The latter seems to be highly contingent on contextual factors, like institutional and strategic conditions, so that models built on individual characteristics including social integration do not explain much (Kriesi *et al.* 1995; Norris *et al.* 2002).

Conclusions

How can we explain the co-variation between organisational involvement and political participation? Three competing arguments have been put forward in the discussion. According to the first line of reasoning, societies are segmented into socio-cultural groups represented by organisational networks. Mobilisation into political participation occurs within these networks through leaders of organisations. Citizens within these segments just follow the lead of their elites. The data do not provide much support for this theory. This is not surprising inasmuch as citizens' identification with socio-cultural segments as well as their docility tends to decline with the process of modernisation and individualisation, while the coherence of socio-cultural milieus and their organisational substructure dwindles.

More promising are theories of social capital. In this perspective, active involvement of citizens in formal and informal networks leads to a political socialisation in favour of political participation. Organisations are schools of democracies, and the more schools there are and the more frequently they are attended, the better the democracy in terms of participation. Hence social capital makes societies and polities 'healthy, wealthy and wise' (Putnam 2000: 287). Although I found some weak evidence for such an effect, it is far from prominent. Its explanatory power is similar to that of the cleavage politics model. The beneficial effects of social capital on political participation are overstated. If there is a collapse of communities in democratic nations, as feared by Putnam for the United States, it is not very likely that this will be a major cause of declining political participation.

How then should we explain the fact that in the 13 societies under study there is a higher propensity among those involved in voluntary associations to partake in politics, although there are no strong causal effects flowing from such involvement to political participation? The answer given in this chapter is that organisations are to a large extent self-selective. Citizens with a propensity to participate politically have a similar propensity to join other formal and informal networks.

In this regard it supports some earlier research, such as that of Newton (1997). In comparison with prior analyses, however, the results presented here rest on a much better empirical basis, in particular with regard to the operationalisation of the theoretical concepts. Another contribution is the attempt to specify the underlying theoretical ideas more adequately in the statistical models and to compare the explanatory power and the significance of the effects included in the competing models. Based on this direct comparison of competing theories, we have been able to show in considerable detail that the participation-enhancing effects of cleavage politics and of social capital are – if they have ever existed – largely gone. Rather, the co-variation between social and political participation in modern democracies is due in large part to the fact that both are explained by the same individual characteristics.

This analysis is based on a data set covering 13 societies. The aim has been to identify patterns of causation with respect to political participation in these nations. One important result is the similarity between the newer democracies in the east and the older democracies in the west. Although the models generally work better in the west than in the east, the difference is more of a quantitative than a qualitative one. Another important finding concerns variation between societies. The political socialisation of the overwhelming majority of citizens in the western countries has taken place under democratic rule, Portugal and Spain excepted. Nevertheless the impact of the independent variables and the explanatory power of each model as a whole vary between nations. For that reason, differences in macro constellations – socio-economic conditions, institutions, policy traditions, and cultural outlooks – have to be taken into account in explaining political participation in a comparative perspective.

Finally, this study points to major differences in the causes of different forms of political participation. Conditions favourable to electoral turnout do not increase partisan or protest activity. And while the feeling of internal efficacy is crucial for contacting decision-makers, it explains much less in the case of consumer participation. Hence, the analyses in this chapter show not only that social capital fails to be the master cause of political participation. They also indicate that such a cause is still found wanting.

Notes

1 The dependent variables are operationalised as described in Chapter 13, except for contacting which excludes working in and contacting organisations. Since the major independent variable of this analysis is organisational involvement, it would be tautological to include aspects of organisational involvement in the dependent variable.
2 For helpful overviews, see Brady *et al.* 1995; Verba *et al.* 1995; Topf 1995a, 1995b; van Deth 2001b; and Norris 2002.
3 The presence of interaction effects causes multicollinearity due to the fact that the product term is a non-linear function of its two components. This decreases the statistical precision of the estimates but does not distort them:

> The changes occur because the coefficients in an interactive model describe the relationship between the variables in different terms than do the coefficients in an additive model – as conditional relationships rather than general relationships ... Similarly, the standard errors of the interactive model describe the variability of estimates ... not as general but as conditional ones.
>
> (Friedrich 1982: 803)

15 Participation and political equality

An assessment of large-scale democracy

Jan Teorell, Paul Sum, and Mette Tobiasen

Introduction

Democratic citizenship entails equal rights to participate in the governing process. Equal opportunities to express one's opinions are bestowed upon citizens in all spheres of political activity. This is, in theory, the normative requirement of political equality. In this chapter we shall assess the extent to which our 13 societies under study deviate from this norm. We will make this assessment with regard to the same five modes of political activity as presented in Chapter 13: contacting, consumer participation, protest, party activity, and voting. Following Verba *et al.* (1978), we will adopt the characteristics of 'participatory systems' as our dependent variable. This requires, first of all, a more refined set of evaluative criteria as a framework for empirical analysis. We shall then assess more specifically the extent to which individuals with certain attitudinal preferences are more participatory than others, the degree to which particular social groups are over- or under-represented, and the causal roots of this over- and under-representation. We portray the overall levels of political equality in each country under study, and finally conclude by summing up our results.

Participation and political equality: an analytical framework

Modern democratic theory presents several normative perspectives from which we may evaluate the level of equality through political participation (Teorell 2006). In this chapter we shall restrict our attention to one of the most established perspectives, at least among political scientists during the last decades (Dahl 1956; Downs 1957; Riker 1982; Miller 1992). Following Dahl (1971: 2), we adopt the normative conception of democracy as 'a political system one of the characteristics of which is the quality of being completely or almost completely responsive to all its citizens'. We call this model *responsive democracy*. According to this normative perspective, political participation – be it voting, party activity, or protest behaviour – channels citizen demands to the decision-makers. Although it is seldom recognised, there are in effect two fundamentally different notions of political equality implied in this model of democracy: an outcome-oriented and a procedural interpretation (Teorell 2006). According to the outcome-oriented, or consequentialist, interpretation of the model, the normative requirement of democracy is that citizen participation should influence those responsible for the authoritative allocation of values in society. However, more is expected of governing officials than simply responding to demands or articulated orientations. The requirement of *democratic* responsiveness requires that all citizens should be treated equally in the process of representation. Thus, this first principle of political equality is simply the slogan 'one man – one vote' carried across to the spheres of non-electoral participation. Each citizen preference should be weighted equally in the authoritative procedure for allocating values in society.

This principle of equality has been the prime normative force behind the empirical studies of political participation conducted by Sidney Verba with colleagues (Verba and Nie 1972; Verba *et al.* 1978; Verba *et al.* 1995). The normative ideal of their model is that 'elected officials should give equal consideration to the needs and preferences of all citizens' (Verba 1996: 1). Although we widen the set of potential recipients of participatory input to include other actors in society, possibly even market forces – the basic empirical question involved remains the same: is the active public representative of the population at large? Our focus is thus on distortion of participatory input – the extent to which participation affects politics in ways that are not consistent with the principle of equal respect and consideration.[1]

As Verba's statement makes clear, however, the outcome-oriented principle of equality actually comes in two guises. According to Verba *et al.* (1995: 171) equal consideration should not only be given to the expressed *preferences* of the public, but also to the *needs* implicit in their social characteristics. 'We cannot dismiss demographic characteristics from the list of characteristics that are potentially politically relevant ... Apart from the explicit demands made by activist publics, there is implicit information in their social characteristics'. Admittedly the posited link between 'implicit needs' and 'social characteristics' could be questioned. It certainly adds complexity to the task of empirical measurement. Nevertheless, including 'needs' among the characteristics to which a political system should respond is an important contribution. It makes the evaluative standard sensitive to what Lukes (1974) termed the 'third face of power': the fact that a group of individuals might possess a common interest for some government policy or social outcome even if it is not reflected in their manifest preferences.

In this chapter we shall make use of both versions of the outcome-oriented principle of equality. Thus, we first explore the relationship between participation and explicit stands on political issues and value dimensions. The aim here is to assess the extent to which equality exists between participant and non-participant preferences and attitudes. Our second aim is to explore the inequalities of participation among categories of four social groupings: gender, age, education, and urban/rural locality.

Our third aim is to evaluate the causal roots of group based inequalities. We base this analysis on a *procedural*, as opposed to the consequentialist, interpretation of the responsive model of democracy. According to this perspective we should pay no attention to the outcome of participation. What matters is instead the idea that 'the *terms* of participation in democratic procedures should themselves be fair' (Beitz 1989: 22, our italics). To identify the conditions under which the terms of participation can be regarded as fair, an analogy with theories of justice is useful (Teorell 2006).

We can think of the factors that enable citizens to participate as a distributive mechanism – an allocation scheme according to which some are entitled to participation, considered as a 'social good', while others are not. Thus, 'fairness in the terms of participation' requires parameters or constraints on the design of this distributive mechanism (Beitz 1989: 17). Following Dworkin (1981: 311), we could say that ideally the mechanism generating political participation should not be 'endowment-insensitive', but 'ambition-sensitive'. That is, whether people end up as participants or not should 'depend on their ambitions (in the broad sense of goals and projects about life) and not on their natural and social endowments (the circumstances in which they pursue their ambitions)' (Kymlicka 1990: 75). If this requirement is fulfilled, there is freedom to choose whether to become involved in politics or not.

Due to varying ambition, this freedom might be exercised to a different degree by different individuals or groups in society. In Sen's words, the 'freedom to achieve' need not be congruent with the 'actual achievement' (Sen 1992: 31). Thus, there might still be unequal rates of participation among individuals. There might even be unequal rates of participation across social groups with different policy stands or interests otherwise understood. But as long as the freedom to choose is equally distributed, the procedural principle of political equality is not compromised. We adopt a model that assesses the extent to which differences in participation rates across social groups can be explained by the 'endowment' and 'ambition-sensitive' mechanisms.

Attitudes and political inequality

We begin our analysis with an evaluation of participatory distortion among individuals who hold different political attitudes. We concentrate on two sets of attitudes, namely: left–right placement (as a measure of ideological orientation) and tolerance. Left–right placement carries specific ideological connotations related to social class and resource distribution. Conceptually, tolerance is less straightforward as an indicator of individual preferences since it includes the willingness 'to consider and debate the view of others, even unpopular or unorthodox views' (Verba et al. 1995: 500). Expressions of tolerance do not simply convey preferences to political authorities; they bring democratic values into politics. Distortion that shows that participants are more tolerant may thus be preferable for democracy in a wider sense: first, it heightens the quality of democracy since it may 'enhance the quality of political discourse and democratic governance' (Verba et al. 1995: 507). Second, to the extent that values of tolerance are transmitted to political authorities it may 'counterbalance' other forms of political inequality. Nevertheless, we will only evaluate the participatory distortion of tolerance in the more restricted sense entailed by our consequentialist criterion. According to this view more tolerant activists are no better than intolerant activists; in both instances the general outlook of the public is distorted by the participatory input.

Operationally, the left–right measurement represents respondents' self-placement on a scale running from zero to ten, where zero represents the extreme left and ten represents the extreme right. In practice the scale is recoded to run from zero to one. Tolerance is measured by a summary (simple additive) index computed from respondents' opinions about whether 11 different groups:

1 should be allowed to hold public meetings (political tolerance); and
2 would be desirable as neighbours (social tolerance).

A zero to one scale is created, averaging across these two forms of tolerance, where zero equals intolerant attitudes towards all 22 groups and one represents tolerance for all 22 groups.[2]

To assess distortion, we compare differences in attitudes between the politically active and non-active parts of the population. To that end we compute unstandardised regression coefficients from a model predicting attitudes with the summary participation scales ranging from zero to one. Thus, these coefficients represent differences in mean left/right placement and tolerance, respectively, between the theoretically most active and most passive parts of the population in each country. A higher coefficient indicates larger participatory inequality among individuals holding divergent attitudes, whereas a smaller coefficient indicates little distortion.

As regards political participation and *left–right placement*, Verba and Nie show that conservative – i.e. rightist – preferences are 'more frequently represented because of the greater command of resources conservatives are said to have' (in Jennings and van Deth 1990: 364). From a different perspective, Jennings and van Deth (1990: 364) argue that unconventional activity (which in the present context refers to consumer participation and protesting) in contrast to conventional participation (voting, party activism, and contacting) is associated with leftist orientations. We shall hold these expectations in mind when interpreting the results that follow.

Table 15.1 shows the amount of participatory distortion in terms of left–right placement. The largest distortion possible is one – where a positive coefficient indicates that all participants are extreme rightists. A negative coefficient indicates that activists are more to the left than non-activists are, the theoretical minimum being negative one. If there is no distortion the coefficient equals zero.

Overall, ideological bias is modest. Typically the differences approximate ±0.10 or below, and for voting, differences are almost non-existent. Apart from an extreme case of −0.49 (see footnote 3), the largest difference on political orientation between activists and non-activists is −0.27. In a majority of instances activists are more leftist leaning than

Table 15.1 Distortion of left–right placement through participation (OLS estimates)[a]

Country	Contacting	Consumer participation	Protesting	Party activity	Voting	Mean of absolute values
Sweden	−0.03	−0.10	−0.49	−0.04	0.01	0.13
Russia	−0.08	0.07	−0.16	−0.22	0.00	0.11
Spain	−0.08	−0.11	−0.19	−0.10	0.03	0.10
Moldova	0.21	0.10	0.11	−0.07	0.02	0.10
Switzerland	−0.02	−0.12	−0.27	0.08	0.02	0.10
East Germany	−0.08	−0.12	−0.17	−0.09	−0.01	0.09
Denmark	−0.04	−0.11	−0.20	0.04	0.05	0.09
Norway	−0.03	−0.10	−0.23	−0.06	0.02	0.09
Romania	0.06	0.09	0.06	0.16	0.00	0.07
Portugal	−0.06	−0.01	−0.10	−0.14	−0.02	0.07
Slovenia	0.06	−0.03	−0.16	0.07	−0.00	0.06
The Netherlands	−0.03	−0.10	−0.15	0.03	0.01	0.06
West Germany	−0.05	−0.07	−0.10	−0.04	0.02	0.06
Mean of absolute values	0.06	0.09	0.18	0.09	0.02	

Note

a Entries are the unstandardised regression coefficients resulting from regressing left–right placement on each index of participation. Countries are ordered by the absolute mean distortion across modes of participation. Percentages of missing data per country (on the left–right scale) are as follows: SE 7; RU 34; ES 21; MD 38; CH 11; EG 13; DK 8; NO 4; RO 43; PT 21; SI 31; NL 7; WG 13. In a few instances (including the extreme case of protesting in Sweden) there are no respondents who have participated in the maximum number of activities that make up the respective indices. The extreme value, then, is not 1, but the second-highest score on the single participation index. In those instances where there are substantial differences between activists and non-activists, this means that the difference may be artificially high. However, running an analysis excluding the extreme value 1 in all countries does not alter the relative difference between countries in any significant way. Therefore scales have not been changed for the countries in question.

non-activists. However, some interesting variations across modes of participation and countries are present.

First, disregarding the direction of distortion and looking at the average absolute distortion across countries (last row in Table 15.1), protesters are on average more different from non-protesters (mean of absolute values: 0.18) in comparison with differences between activists and non-activists in other modes of participation. The differences between party-activists/non-activists (0.09), political consumers/non-political consumers (0.09) and between people who have contacted and those who have not (0.06) are smaller. In contrast, there is no difference in regard to political leaning between voters and non-voters (0.02).

The general tendency among protesters is that they are on average more leftist. The average differences are largest in the Scandinavian countries, Switzerland and Spain (between −0.19 and −0.49).[3] There are, however, some interesting exceptions to the leftist bias of active protesters: Moldovan and Romanian activists are on average slightly more *rightist* than non-protesters in the respective countries. Differences between citizens who have engaged in consumer participation and people who have engaged in contacting – and their respective counterparts – follow a similar pattern as protesting. Only the differences are smaller. The exception for consumer participation is the Russian, Moldovan, and Romanian cases: consumer activists in these countries are on average more rightist (0.07–0.10). As regards contacting, the exceptions are Moldova, Slovenia, and Romania; people who are employed in contacting in these countries lean marginally to the right in comparison with those what have not been active (0.06–0.21).

Looking at differences between participants engaged in party-activities and those who are not, the leftist bias of activists is less consistent. In the majority of countries party-activists are more leftist than non-activists but party-activists in Switzerland, Denmark, Romania, Slovenia, and the Netherlands lean marginally towards the right in comparison with non-activists.

Summing up, the analysis suggests that distortion in left–right orientations is at best modest, and non-existent for voting. One evident tendency across the remaining modes of participation is that activists are marginally leaning toward leftist sentiments in comparison with non-activists – a tendency which is strongest for protesting. Consequently, the analysis in part supports the expectation, derived from Jennings and van Deth (1990), that activists in unconventional modes of participation have leftist sentiments in comparison with non-activists. But there are exceptions, where activists on average have slightly more rightist attitudes. In fact, eastern European countries account for the majority of instances where a rightist bias in activists' attitudes is identified. Care must be taken in interpreting the results for left–right placement among these countries, however, since the legacy of the communist regimes has altered the conventional meaning of left and right resulting in, among other things, party systems that do not conform to traditional left–right dynamics (Kitschelt *et al.*

1999). This indicates that left–right placement could make less sense for the respondents in some eastern European countries – a point which also is supported by the very high percentage of missing data on left–right placement in these countries, which is between 31 and 43 per cent (see note to Table 15.1). Having said this, the data from these countries might just as well be interpreted as giving support to Verba and Nie's finding that activists are more rightist due to greater command of participatory resources among the rightist part of the population.

Looking next at *tolerance*, Verba et al. (1995: Chapter 16) show that participants in the US tend to be slightly more tolerant than nonparticipants. This is exactly what we should expect from the perspective of participatory democracy. Through participation citizens learn to tolerate other people with markedly different social and political outlooks (Pateman 1970). Table 15.2 shows (unstandardised) regression coefficients indicating the distortion in tolerance for each participatory index. The largest distortion possible is one and a positive coefficient indicates that all activists are absolutely tolerant. A negative coefficient indicates

Table 15.2 Distortion of tolerance through participation (OLS estimates)[a]

Country	Contacting	Consumer participation	Protesting	Party activity	Voting	Mean of absolute values
West Germany	0.18	0.09	0.13	0.02	0.05	0.09
Moldova	−0.08	−0.10	−0.10	−0.17	0.01	0.09
Slovenia[b]	0.07	0.03	0.10	−0.12	−0.06	0.08
Portugal	−0.12	−0.09	0.06	−0.05	−0.05	0.07
Romania	−0.13	0.04	0.03	−0.12	−0.02	0.07
Switzerland	0.02	0.07	0.10	−0.06	−0.01	0.05
Russia	−0.02	−0.11	0.09	0.01	−0.02	0.05
Sweden	0.08	0.05	0.05	0.01	−0.00	0.04
Norway	0.00	0.03	0.03	0.05	−0.03	0.03
Spain	−0.00	0.01	0.06	−0.03	−0.03	0.03
The Netherlands	−0.02	−0.04	0.04	−0.00	−0.02	0.02
East Germany	0.02	0.01	0.03	−0.01	0.05	0.02
Denmark	0.00	0.01	0.01	−0.01	0.01	0.01
Mean of absolute values	0.06	0.05	0.06	0.05	0.03	

Notes

a Entries are the unstandardised regression coefficients resulting from regressing tolerance on each index of participation. Countries are ordered by the absolute mean distortion across modes of participation. Percentages of missing data per country (on the tolerance-index) are as follows: WG 10; MD 43; SI 21; PT 14; RO 28; CH 47; RU 11; SE 8; NO 0; ES 24; NL 6; EG 10; DK 1. Regarding the participation indices and their extreme values, see the note to Table 15.1.

b In Slovenia, only a subset of groups are included in the tolerance measure (for *meetings:* Christian fundamentalists, Islamic fundamentalists, left-wing extremists, immigrants, homosexuals, racists, other race, right-wing extremists; for *neighbours:* immigrants, homosexuals, criminals, racists, other race, AIDS patients, drug addicts).

that activists are less tolerant than non-activists, the theoretical minimum being minus one. Again, zero indicates no distortion.

Overall the bias in tolerance from participatory input is even more modest than was the case for political orientation. The means of absolute values for different modes of participation range between 0.03 and 0.06. The largest difference between activists and non-activists is 0.18 but most typically differences are about ±0.10 or less. There are, however, at least three interesting tendencies across modes of participation. First, the pattern for protesting is almost perfectly consistent across countries. Protesters are on average slightly more tolerant than non-protesters (mean of absolute values: 0.06). In particular this is the case in West Germany (0.13), whereas differences are negligible in many other countries. The main exception is Moldovan protesters, who on average are slightly more intolerant than people who have not engaged in protesting (−0.10).

Second, turning to consumerism and contacting differences between activists and non-activists are negligible in many countries (mean of absolute values 0.05 and 0.06, respectively). Moreover, the pattern is mixed, that is, in some countries there is a tendency for people who engage in contacting and consumerism to be slightly less tolerant than non-activists, whereas in other countries they are more tolerant. Third, even though differences among party-activists and non-activists (mean of absolute values: 0.05) and voters/non-voters (0.03) are small, it is interesting that the tendency in the majority of countries is the opposite than was the case for protesting. In nine out of the 13 countries included in the analysis, party-activists are marginally *less* tolerant than non-activists. However, only in a few countries do party-activists differ substantially from non-activists: Moldova (−0.17), Romania (−0.12) and Slovenia (−0.12). Turning to voting the tendency is the same, but differences are even smaller, the highest difference being −0.06.

Taken together, distortions of participatory equality in terms of tolerance are minor. The main tendency is that in particular protesters tend to be slightly more tolerant than their counterparts. On the contrary, party-activists in some cases – especially east European countries – tend to be slightly less tolerant, relative to non-activists. To some extent, this tendency is also reflected in voting – but differences are negligible. With respect to contacting and consumerism, there is no consistent pattern. Thus, in contrast to the expectation that activists are more tolerant (Verba et al. 1995: 501–3), the analysis suggests that participation – maybe except for protesting – is not encouraging for tolerant attitudes in any conclusive manner. Even though the objective is not to take a stand on the causal relationship between participation and tolerance, this is in fact a somewhat disturbing result seen from the perspective of theories that stress that participation fosters tolerance. The positive version of the story is that, in general, non-participation is not biased towards intolerance in any significant sense across countries.

Social groups and political inequality

Equality among participants extends beyond attitudes such as ideological orientation and tolerance. Social characteristics endow individuals with different resources and are associated with contexts, which lead to varied abilities and opportunities to participate. If such social characteristics signal lines of divergent political needs and interests, then participatory inequality across categories diminishes distinct voices and preferences from political discourse. Thus, rates of inequality may mirror social divisions, which in turn can reduce the effectiveness of responsive democracy.

To what extent does social group inequality exists cross-nationally? With this question in mind, we consider levels of inequality within four social categories: gender, age, education, and locality type (urban and rural). This choice of social groups is by no means straightforward (cf. Verba *et al.* 1978: 164–5), but we argue that the four dividing lines we have singled out fulfil two crucial criteria. First, they are expected to reflect important social categories in each society under study. People holding common social characteristics are thus assumed to share some common need, or interest in political outcomes. Second, the selected categories are amenable to statistical analysis. This implies that the groups are fairly large, and that their defining characteristics are measurable as well as comparable across nations.

To evaluate the variance of participation across groups, we compute the average level of participation for the subsets of our four social categories on a scale of zero to one. We then divide the subgroup mean by the sum of mean participation rates across all groups of that social category. This produces a relative figure of proportionality, which represents a subgroup's 'share' of the total level of participation.[4] The proportionality figures range from zero to one, and the sum of all subgroups within a social category equals one. For gender and locality type, which are dichotomous, perfect equality is achieved at the 0.5 level of proportionality for each subgroup. For age and education, which have threefold categories, 0.33 represents perfect equality among subgroups.

We also calculate a summary measure of the amount of inequality pertaining to each social category. Conceptually this measure can be conceived of as the Euclidean distance in a *k*-dimensional space between the observed proportionality scores for k subgroups to the 'equality point', that is, the allocation that would be obtained if all shares were equal. This distance is 'normed' to range from zero (perfect equality) to one (perfect inequality), and is thus called the '*N*ormed *D*istance to the *E*quality *P*oint' (NDQP).[5]

The graphs in Figure 15.1 show subgroup inequality for our four social categories in columns for the five forms of political participation. The horisontal axis displays the cases according to their individual country NDQP measure (greatest to least inequality). The vertical axis reflects the proportionality figure for each subgroup (whose sum equals one).

Gender as a social category represents key differences in political interests that may be distorted within the context of political participation (Burns *et al.* 2001). Long deprived of basic rights and liberties women have gained formal recognition and status as political equals in the twentieth century. The proliferation of women's groups has helped to articulate these interests and maintain them on the political agenda. However, as a result of historical relationships and the persistence of social and economic inequality, gender continues to be a relevant social, and thus political, category.

In terms of contacting, males engage in this activity more often than females. In Slovenia, Switzerland, Romania, and the two parts of Germany, men comprise more than 60 per cent of the share of contacting. The exception to this pattern appears in Russia where we find nearly perfect equality with a slightly higher proportionality figure for women at 0.504. For consumer participation, women tend to engage in this activity more often than men with the exceptions of Slovenia and East Germany. However, the discrepancy between men and women, as reflected in the NDQP score, is relatively small. A male bias appears among those taking part in protests with the exceptions of Russia and Norway. Party activism shows the largest gender bias in favour of men among the five forms of participation. Except for Sweden, the male share for party activity exceeds 0.57 and reaches as high as 0.77 in Romania. In sharp contrast, voting approximates equality in all countries. The exception to this is Switzerland where women were disenfranchised until 1971.

In assessing aggregate levels of inequality for gender, the overall NDQP measures (located next to the title of each graph of Figure 15.1) show that the largest gender discrepancy appears within party activity (0.312). Voting reflects the least overall difference (0.015) followed closely by consumer participation (0.052). Thus, the impact of gender varies somewhat depending on the act but with the exception of consumer participation, men tend to be more participatory than women.

When considering participatory inequality among age groups, life-cycle effects account for some variance (Nie *et al.* 1974; Verba *et al.* 1978: 265–6). Although sensitive to the type of participatory act, younger people tend to participate less often than middle-aged individuals who are more settled into their communities and probably have developed a larger stake in political outcomes. As people continue to age, they become less physically able to participate, or perhaps less interested, resulting in lower rates. The result is a curvilinear relationship between age and participation with middle-aged individuals participating most frequently.

Accumulated life-experience adds to our explanation of the effects age has on political participation. Differences in the accumulated experiences over time shape needs, priorities, and attitudes of a particular age group in a more linear fashion. In addition, generational differences account for different participation rates among different age groups. That is, due to

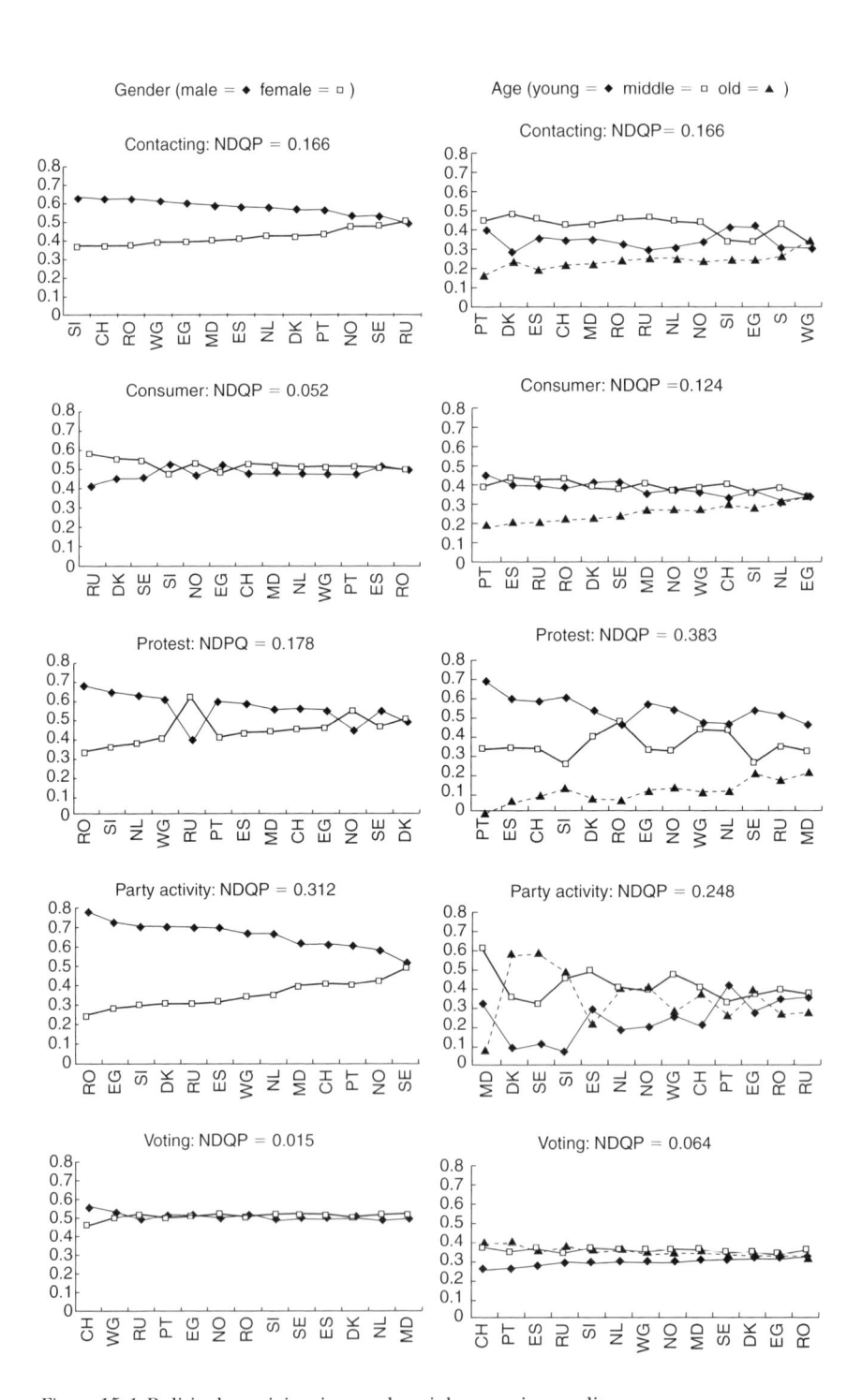

Figure 15.1 Political participation and social group inequality.

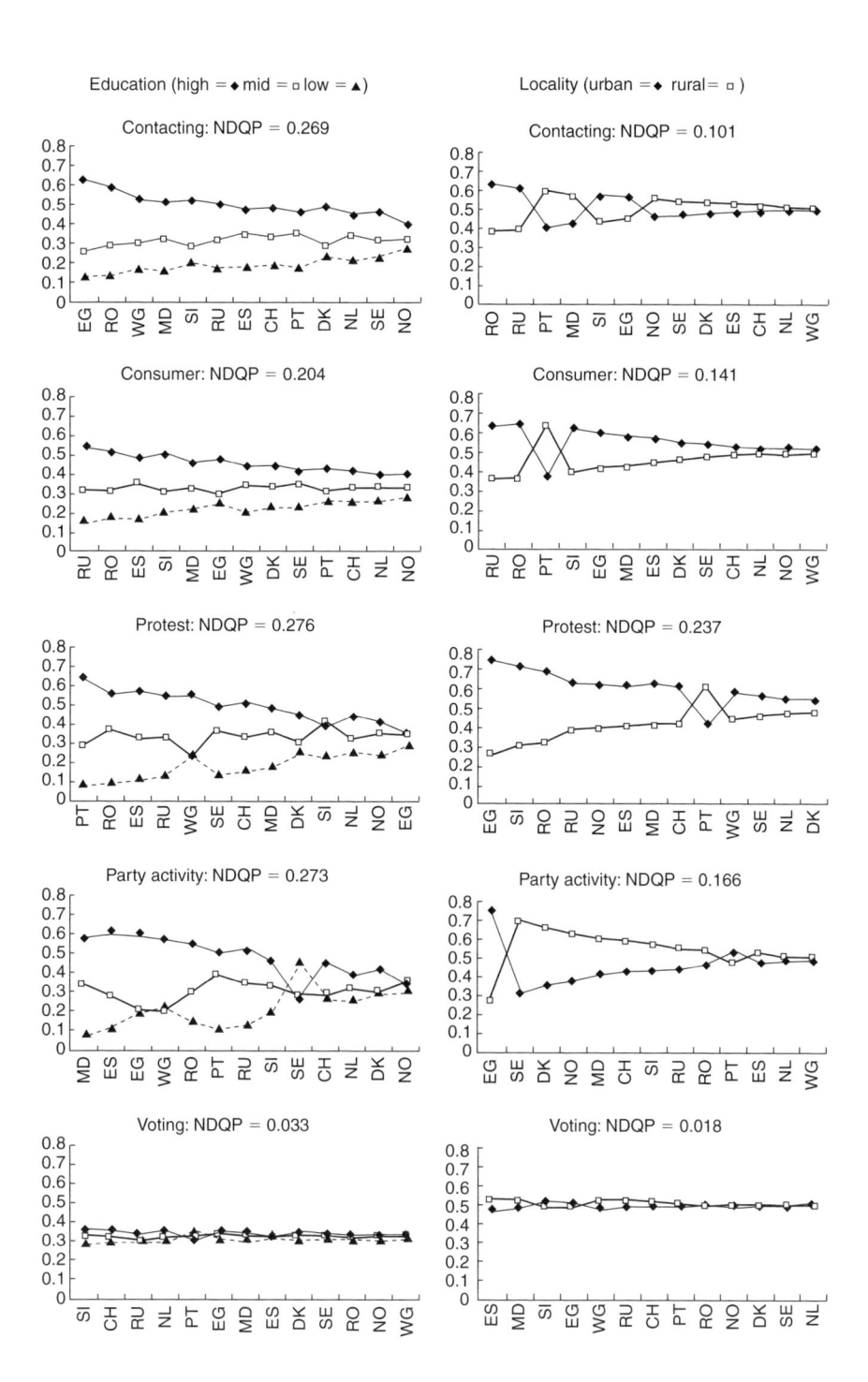

Figure 15.1 continued.

particular circumstances pertaining to the time at which one grew up, different generations display different dispositions to take political action (Rosenstone and Hansen 1993: 139–40).

We make a threefold distinction among age groups: the young, middle-aged, and old.[6] According to Figure 15.1, the relationship between contacting and age reflects a curvilinear pattern of inequality. Middle-aged individuals are the most likely to engage in contacting, followed by younger people, although West Germany approximates equality (0.33) among the age groups. With regard to consumer participation, older people are under-represented in most cases. The difference between the younger and middle-aged categories is mixed but generally small with East Germany approaching equality. Among those engaged in protesting, younger people tend to be the most active although the difference between the young and middle-aged categories varies according to the case. Once again, older people are uniformly under-represented among protesters. Age and party activity demonstrates considerable variance among the age groupings but generally younger people tend to be under-represented. In Moldova, the middle-age group dominates party activity. In Denmark, it is the older generation who are more active in parties. Participatory inequality across age groups among voters is minimal though younger individuals tend to be slightly under-represented.

Referring to the NDQP measures for age, protesting shows the greatest level of aggregate inequality at 0.383 in which younger people are most active. Younger individuals are the least active in political parties, which is reflected in a relatively high NDQP score of 0.248. Voting shows near equality across age groups with an NDQP measure of 0.064.

There is ample evidence to show a strong relationship between education and rates of political participation (for example, Verba *et al.* 1978; Rosenstone and Hansen 1993; Verba *et al.* 1995). Higher levels of education serve as a resource from which people draw to assist in navigating through the political system. In addition, as people become more educated, they may acquire a stronger sense of civic duty, which contributes to higher levels of political participation. Individuals who have different levels of education are likely to carry different political attitudes and interests. If we assume that people from different education categories have different political demands, to what extent are these demands advanced equally through political participation?

Education is divided into three groups: the lower, middle, and higher third of the educational range within each country.[7] The analysis shows that for contacting and consumer participation, the association between participation and education groups is linear. For all countries, the highest education group is proportionally more active, and the lower education group is the least active. The middle education group approximates its 'equal' share of participation with proportionality measures near 0.33 for both contacting and consumer participation. More highly educated individuals also tend to protest more than other education groups although East Germany approximates equality in protesting. The pattern of more highly educated individuals participating at higher rates extends to party activity with the exception of Sweden where individuals with lower education are the most active in parties. Education has a minimal effect on voting but in cases where distinctions exist, the higher education group tends to participate at slightly higher rates.

With regard to overall inequality among education categories, the NDQP measures show that protesting (0.276), party activity (0.273), and contacting (0.269) reflect pronounced levels of inequality. Consumer participation is also relatively high at (0.204). In most cases, the most highly educated individuals participate at levels higher than others.

Locality type is the last social category under analysis. We divide type of locality into two groups: urban and rural.[8] Verba et al. (1978: 270–1) consider two models which explain the effect of locality type on participation. The 'mobilisation model' suggests that individuals in urban areas participate at higher rates than those in rural communities primarily because of greater opportunities (Milbrath 1965: 113–14). The 'decline-of-community model' predicts the opposite. In smaller communities, citizens are more connected socially to each other and have closer personal relationships to political leaders, both of which lower the threshold to participate (Verba and Nie 1972: 231). Since forms of participation vary in terms of the resources required, it is plausible that both models apply depending on the type of participatory act.[9] We expect people who live in different locality types to have different political interests and needs, and thus contribute to our cross-national understanding of political participation inequalities.

Inequality in contacting based on locality type produces mixed results. Some cases reflect nearly equal participation: West Germany, the Netherlands, and Switzerland. In cases such as Romania and Russia urban-dwellers have a higher propensity to contact. Portugal and Moldova, alternatively, shows that contacting is more prevalent in rural communities. For consumer participation, where inequality exists, rural inhabitants tend to be under-represented. Protesting reflects a similar result to consumer participation with urban-dwellers clearly more active in all cases except for Portugal. According to the NDQP measure, protesting exhibits the highest level of inequality between locality types (0.237). For party activity, rural-dwellers tend to be more participatory relative to those in cities although East Germany, and to a lesser extent Portugal, show party activity higher in urban areas. Voting appears to approach equality (0.33) in all cases for locality type.

To summarise, social groups influence levels of inequality in political participation. Our analysis suggests that an outcome-oriented model of democracy, where public officials are responsive to political inputs through citizen participation, faces distortions since certain interests and needs, derived from social categories, may not be heard equally.

The NDQP measures, which evaluate aggregate levels of inequality for each social group across the five forms of participation, support this general finding. According to the NDQP measures, the greatest inequality appears in age/protest (0.383), gender/party activity (0.312), education/protest (0.276), education/party activity (0.273), education/contact (0.269), age/party activity (0.248), locality/protest (0.237), and education/consumer participation (0.204). In other words, age and education stand out as the most relevant sources of inequality and protesting and party activity are the forms of participation most susceptible to equality distortions from social categories.

Levels of inequality are lowest for gender/vote (0.015), locality/vote (0.018), education/vote (0.033), gender/consumer participation (0.052), and age/vote (0.064). Thus, each of our four social categories produces some level of inequality. Voting appears to be greatly insulated from inequalities based on social groupings while protesting and party activity are the least insulated forms of participation.

Explaining political inequality

Thus far we have been looking at the two sides of the consequentialist interpretation of responsive democracy. We now turn to the procedural conception, which maintains that inequalities in political participation may be accepted in so far as they are driven by varying ambitions, but not if they are the result of differing endowments. In other words we shall assess the causal factors that explain why inequalities in political participation come about. First, we shall consider a set of factors working as *motivation* to act. To the extent they drive participation, political action may be said to be 'ambition-sensitive'. Second, following Sen (1992), we shall look at a set of factors affecting the *capability* to take part in political action. They shall work as our operationalisation of whether or not the mechanisms leading to participation are 'endowment-sensitive'.

Starting with the motivating factors, our theoretical point of departure is a simple 'calculus of participation' (Nagel 1987: 26), based on the traditional 'calculus of voting' (Riker and Ordeshook 1968; Aldrich 1993) and an extension of that into other forms of participation (Muller and Opp 1986; Finkel *et al.* 1989; Whiteley 1995). According to this logic, the motivation to engage in political activity is first of all a function of each individual's perceived stake in the issue at hand, or inversely: his or her level of dissatisfaction. Moreover, motivation is derived from selective incentives, such as the entertainment value of participation, from expressive incentives such as ideological attachment, and from norms that instil a sense of duty to take part. Finally, the cost of participation needs to be discounted, in particular information costs. Thus, the set of explanatory variables we employ under this 'motivational' umbrella are:[10]

- Life satisfaction and satisfaction with the way democracy works (represents the stake in the issues).
- General political interest (represents the entertainment value of participation and reduces information costs).
- Frequency of discussing politics with others (reduces information costs).
- Political media exposure (reduces information costs).
- Party identification (represents expressive incentives).
- Participatory norms (represents the sense of citizen duty to take part).

With respect to factors improving the capacity to participate, we focus on resources and a certain psychological predisposition mediating the link between resources and action. First and foremost among the resources enabling political action is involvement in voluntary associations. Most evidently, being active in organisations yields returns in human capital. Ample evidence supports the contention that organisations – much like the workplace – develop 'civic skills' that can be employed for political purposes (Verba *et al.* 1995). Yet even passive members receive a boost in their participatory activity, which by and large can be explained in terms of social capital: they are solicited into action through the weak ties generated in organisational networks (Teorell 2003). Adding household income to this equation implies that we have measures of all of three generic types of resources: physical, human, and social capital (Coleman 1990). Among the psychological factors crucial to capability, the 'sense of political efficacy' is of course of paramount importance. In terms of the classical distinction, we shall only be looking at the 'internal' side of efficacy (perceptions of the self), thus excluding 'external efficacy' (perceptions of the system) (Balch 1971; cf. Westholm and Niemi 1986: 61–2).[11]

Thus, the variables we employ under the 'capacitating' umbrella include:[12]

- Household income (represents physical capital).
- The habit of practising 'civic skills' within voluntary organisations and/or at the workplace (represents human capital).
- Membership in 28 types of voluntary associations (represents social capital).
- Internal efficacy (represents perceived capability).

We will concentrate on explaining political inequalities across social groups.[13] The question, then, is whether the participation gaps across social groups diminish when we control for these two general sets of variables. The more they do, the better we can explain social inequalities in political participation from the perspective of procedural democracy. This test will be performed on a country-by country basis, and proceeds in four steps. As a baseline model, we will look at each social category individually using the measures developed earlier in the chapter. As a second step, we will look at each social category when controlling for the other group variables. Thus, the gender gap will be explored after controlling for age, education, and locality, and so on. This will enable us to partial out the potential overlaps in participatory inequalities between our particular set of social groups. Third, we will control for the motivation factors. If they are unevenly distributed across the social groups in a way that matches the uneven participation patterns, we will have positive evidence for 'ambition–sensitive' mechanisms driving participation. That is, the model will work as hypothesized and the activity gap will narrow. Finally, we will introduce the capacitating factors into the model.[14] If they contribute to an additional narrowing of the participation gap – even when the motivational factors are controlled for – we will receive support for 'endowment-sensitive' mechanisms at work. If this turns out to be the case, the patterns of inequality are rooted in unfair terms of participation.[15]

The results from these four models applied to the four social groups, on a country-by-country basis, are presented in Figure 15.2. For purposes

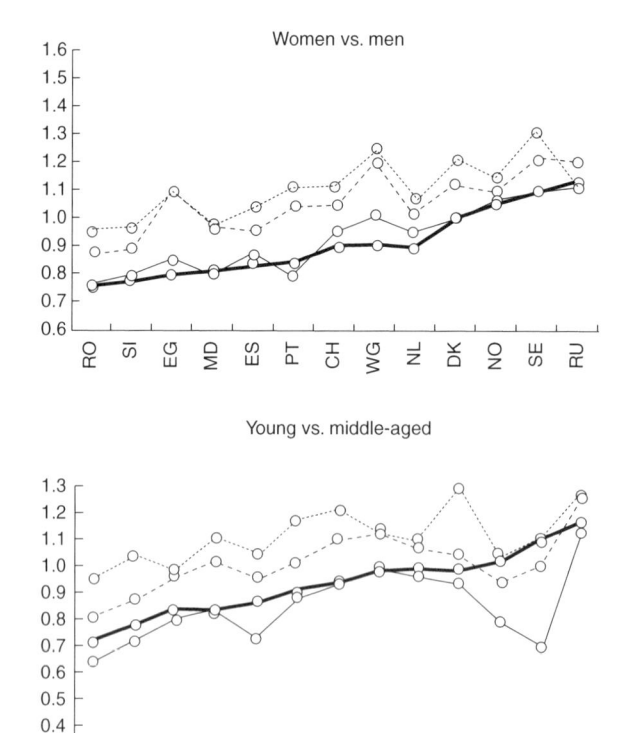

Figure 15.2 Explaining participatory inequalities.

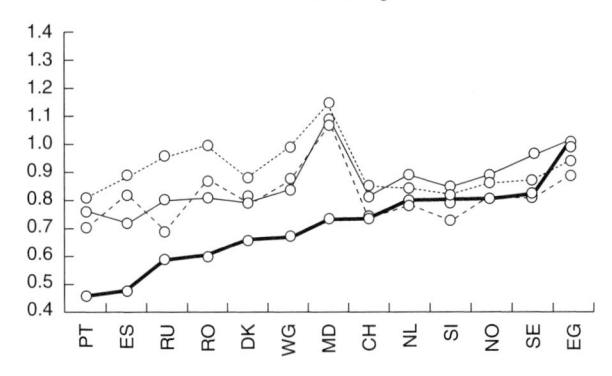

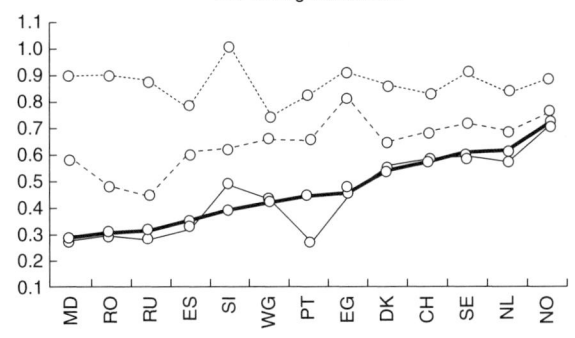

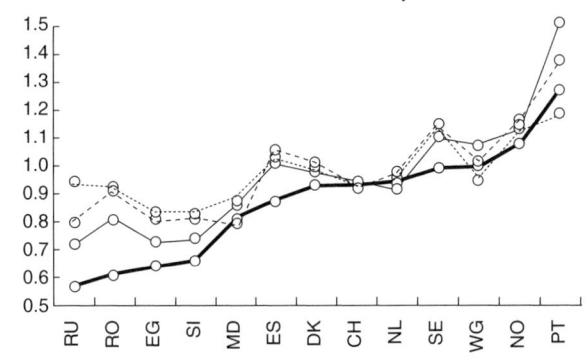

Figure 15.2 continued

of presentational clarity, we make no distinction among the four different non-electoral modes of political activity – that is, contacting, consumer participation, protesting, and party activity. Instead an 'overall non-electoral activity index' has been constructed, which simply summarises the mean participation rate across these four modes of participation (excluding voting), giving each mode equal weight.[16] This overall index of course masks important differences among the four modes, differences that were conjectured and tested in Chapters 13 and 14, and that has been dealt with earlier in this chapter. Nevertheless, the composite index enables us to reveal the most general patterns in order to avoid being unable to see the forest for the trees (cf. Verba *et al.* 1995: 188–9). The results for voting are by and large less interesting, since there is so little group inequality to be explained. Nevertheless, we shall return to voting later in this chapter.

Entries in the figure are ratios of the predicted amount of overall participation in one social group over another, taking the different sets of control variables into account.[17] Thus, perfect equality in this case occurs when each group participates to the same extent; that is, when the ratio equals one. Ratios smaller than one indicate that the first group along each category line is under-represented: women, the young, the elderly, those with low education, and people living in the countryside. Ratios larger than one indicate, by contrast, that these groups are over-represented. The countries are entered in descending order according to the amount of inequality in each social category according to the baseline model, that is, with no control variables applied.

We first look at the gender gap. As can readily be seen, in all countries except the Scandinavian countries and Russia, women are systematically under-represented among political activists. And in no case can this under-representation be explained in terms of the other social groups. This is indicated by the fact that the line representing model 2, with the social controls applied, almost concur with the baseline model. Thus, women are not less politically empowered due to their age or their level of education. Women are however held back due to their smaller stock of motivational factors: the gap between the line for model 3 and the two former models is more substantial in almost every country. By and large, then, women are less psychologically involved in politics, and as a result they take less action than men. But on top of that, women have less access to the factors capacitating political action. Apart from Russia, where it is actually *men* who are incapacitated for political action, the exceptions to this rule are East Germany and Moldova (in these two countries the lines for models 3 and 4 concur). But in all other countries we find support for the notion that opportunities to take part in politics are not evenly distributed among men and women. Over and above the 'ambition-sensitive' factors at work, there is 'endowment-sensitivity' in the terms regulating the gender gap.

In terms of age, the analysis has been split in two contrasts with the middle-aged, focusing on the young and the elderly respectively. To begin with the former the young are in most countries under-represented, but there are quite a few exceptions to this rule. In Portugal and Slovenia younger individuals are actually more active than the middle-aged, whereas in East Germany, Moldova, Spain, and Sweden, there is hardly any discernible gap between the two groups. Again this pattern cannot be explained in terms of the other social group attributes. On the contrary, in most countries (and especially in Russia, Portugal, and Spain) the participation gap between the young and the middle-aged widens when we control for the other social groupings. This pattern is of course mostly due to education. The young are on average more highly educated than the middle-aged, and when that comparative advantage is being controlled for their degree of under-representation is exaggerated. But then again, a lack of motivation is a very strong factor behind this under-representation. In most countries a substantial amount of the gap can be explained in terms of varying levels of motivation. However, even to a greater extent than for gender (as reflected in the larger distances between lines 3 and 4), there are also incapacitating mechanisms at work. In all countries except Switzerland, East Germany, and Slovenia, the young are held back by 'endowment-sensitivity' in the terms regulating political participation.

With respect to the elderly this 'endowment-sensitivity' operates more consistently throughout all of the countries. Over and above the controls for other social groups and motivation, the capacitating factors explain parts of the participatory gap separating the elderly from the middle-aged. Generally speaking the pattern for the elderly is rather similar to the representation of the young, with two important exceptions. The first is that there is a clear and consistent under-representation of older individuals to begin with in all countries except East Germany. The second is the fact that the other social groupings, most importantly education, explain a substantial amount of this gap. Thus, in this case the gap closes when the other social factors are held constant, whereas for the young it widens.

When we next turn to education, we find the clearest and most serious case of 'endowment-sensitivity'. In all countries without exception those with lower education are held back due to incapacitation. Although motivational factors are also an important part of the story, the capacitating factors with regard to the education gap in many instances are on par with motivational ones. This clearly separates the mechanism driving the under-representation of the less educated from the mechanisms behind both the gender and the age gaps, where motivation plays the most crucial role.

Finally, we saw in the last section that urban/rural locality is, together with gender, the social grouping least conducive to participatory inequality. We can now add to this the finding that the locality gap is hardly driven at all by incapacitation. In most cases in the graph the lines for the motivational and the capacitating factors run parallel to each other. There are, however, two groups of countries where some 'endowment-sensitivity' takes place. The first is Russia and Moldova, where the under-representation of the rural population can in part be explained in terms of incapacitation. The second group, interestingly, are the countries located above the equality line – in the countries where people living in the countryside are more active than city- and town-dwellers. This is the case in West Germany, Norway, and Portugal. In these three countries the under-representation of urban-dwellers can to some extent be accounted for in terms of incapacitation. The general pattern, however, is that capacity plays an insignificant role in explaining the locality gap.

In conclusion, by looking at the change in slope of the lines within each of the five graphs in Figure 15.2, we can say something about our model's overall ability to explain the country differences in representational gaps. Since the countries are ordered in terms of the amount of under-representation present in the baseline model (without any control variables applied), the degree of country-level variation for each social grouping is larger, the steeper the slope of this baseline model. If we account for these country-level differences by adding the control factors, the result should be that the slope levels out. A horizontal line thus represents a case where there are no country differences in the amount of under- or over-representation.

With this simple (and, admittedly, crude) yardstick in mind, we can say that the model performs best in terms of explaining differences in participatory inequality across countries with regard to education. We can infer that the stronger the relationship between education and participation, the more the motivational and the capacitating factors grow in importance. Thus, when these factors are taken into account the country differences level out. In terms of the gender and age gaps, our model also works fairly well in terms of explaining country-level variation, although not quite as well as in the case of education. With respect to the locality gap, by contrast, the two operating mechanisms do not perform as well in contributing to our understanding of country differences. The slope of the baseline model is in this case not very different from the model that applies the full set of control variables.

Comparing political inequality across nations

We are now in a position to take stock and compare our assessment of the state of political inequality across countries. A summary look at country-level differences in the three facets of inequality we have studied – attitudinal distortion, social group inequality, and incapacitation – is presented in

Table 15.3. We present one set of results for the four non-electoral modes of activity added together, and one for voting. Entries in absolute levels are drawn from the earlier tables and figures presented in this chapter, but we have now added rank-orders of countries in terms of the overall amount of each form of political inequality. As can be seen, the rankings of the countries vary considerably across the three evaluative standards. The correlations among the rankings both between the two consequentialist perspectives (attitudinal distortion and social group inequality) and between those and the procedural criterion (incapacitation) are weak (below 0.30), or at best modest (between 0.30 and 0.50). This applies both for voting and the non-electoral modes of participation.

In terms of the non-electoral modes of participation, the three countries highest on attitudinal distortion are Moldova, Russia, and Sweden, whereas Romania, Slovenia, and East Germany rank highest on social group inequality. In terms of incapacitation the picture is again different, with Russia, Romania, and Slovenia at the bottom. If we look at the other side of the spectrum, the Netherlands, Denmark, Norway, Spain, and East Germany rank low in terms of attitudinal distortion, whereas the Netherlands, Norway, and Sweden rank lowest on social group inequality. From the consequentialist perspective, thus, the Netherlands and Norway are the countries displaying the highest levels of political equality. However, in terms of the procedural perspective both parts of Germany and Portugal exhibit the most equality. The countries that on average show the lowest rates of equality across the three dimensions are – with the important exception of East Germany – the post-communist countries of eastern Europe: Russia, Romania, Moldova, and Slovenia. The two countries most consistently equal are Norway and the Netherlands.

With respect to voting, the most conspicuous result is how little inequality there is compared to the non-electoral modes. Both in terms of attitudes and social group characteristics, people turning up at the electoral booth differ little from those who stay at home. Moreover, the small amount of group inequality that does exist can hardly be explained in terms of incapacitation. Group inequalities in voter turnout are mostly driven by 'ambition-sensitivity', not 'endowment-sensitivity'.[18] The one country that proves to be an exception to this rule is Switzerland, where some incapacitation drives the gaps in turnout.

When we contrast the rates of inequality in voting with those in the non-electoral modes, the results speak to the long-standing debate on the desirability of high levels of political participation. Since citizens turn out to vote at rates much higher than the percentage of individuals engaged in non-electoral forms of participation, the message seems to be that higher levels of participation reduces the amount of political inequality. But of course, this is a crude comparison. To test the conjecture more systematically, Table 15.3 also includes figures at the country level of the overall *level* of political participation (that is, apart from turnout rates, the

Table 15.3 Summary evaluation of participation and political equality[a]

Country	Absolute level				Rank order				
	Attitudinal distortion	Group inequality	Incapacitation	Level of participation	Attitudinal distortion	Group inequality	Incapacitation	Mean rank	Level of participation
Non-electoral modes									
Norway	0.07	0.14	0.06	0.18	4	1	4	3.00	1
The Netherlands	0.05	0.14	0.08	0.17	1	2	7	3.33	2
East Germany	0.07	0.24	0.03	0.10	3	11	1	5.00	7
West Germany	0.09	0.18	0.05	0.12	8	5	3	5.33	6
Denmark	0.05	0.19	0.11	0.14	2	6	9	5.67	5
Portugal	0.08	0.23	0.05	0.06	6	10	2	6.00	10
Switzerland	0.09	0.18	0.06	0.15	10	4	5	6.33	3
Spain	0.07	0.23	0.08	0.09	5	8	6	6.33	8
Sweden	0.11	0.17	0.11	0.15	12	3	10	8.33	4
Moldova	0.12	0.22	0.11	0.05	13	7	8	9.33	11
Slovenia	0.08	0.25	0.11	0.07	7	12	11	10.00	9
Russia	0.10	0.23	0.17	0.02	11	9	13	11.00	13
Romania	0.09	0.28	0.15	0.05	9	13	12	11.33	12
Mean	*0.08*	*0.21*	*0.09*	*0.10*	–	–	–	–	–
Correlation									
Group inequality	0.22	–	–	–	0.12	–	–	–	–
Incapacitation	0.34	0.34	–	–	0.41	0.22	–	–	–
Level of participation	−0.45	−0.86	−0.48	–	0.46	0.83	0.41	0.80	–

Voting									
Romania	0.01	0.01	0.00	0.65	2	1	7	3.33	10
Sweden	0.01	0.02	0.01	0.80	1	3	8	4.00	4
East Germany	0.03	0.02	0.00	0.80	10	4	2	5.33	3
Norway	0.03	0.02	0.00	0.78	7	5	4	5.33	5
Spain	0.03	0.04	0.00	0.69	8	9	3	6.67	8
Slovenia	0.03	0.04	0.00	0.70	9	11	1	7.00	7
The Netherlands	0.02	0.03	0.01	0.73	4	7	10	7.00	6
Denmark	0.03	0.02	0.01	0.86	11	2	9	7.33	1
Moldova	0.02	0.03	0.01	0.67	5	6	11	7.33	9
Russia	0.01	0.04	0.01	0.62	3	10	12	8.33	12
West Germany	0.04	0.05	0.00	0.62	12	8	5	8.33	2
Portugal	0.04	0.03	0.00	0.83	13	12	6	10.33	11
Switzerland	0.02	0.08	0.02	0.43	6	13	13	10.67	13
Mean	*0.02*	*0.03*	*0.00*	*0.69*	—	—	—	—	—
Correlation									
Group inequality	0.09	—	—	—	0.30	—	—	—	—
Incapacitation	−0.49	0.53	—	—	−0.48	0.08	—	—	—
Level of participation	0.31	−0.82	−0.61	—	−0.33	0.58	0.43	0.41	—

Note

a Countries are ordered by their mean ranks. The figures for *attitudinal distortion* are based on data presented in Tables 15.1 and 15.2, averaged across all relevant modes and the two forms of attitudinal distortion. The figures for *group inequality* are based on the overall means in NDQP, averaged across all relevant modes and all social groups, computed from Figure 15.1. The figures for *incapacitation* are based on the differences in participation ratios predicted by model 4 and model 3 in Figure 15.2 (or, for voting, by separate analyses), averaged across social groups. The *level of participation* is for the non-electoral modes based on the summary participation measure, taking the average across all four modes, presented in section 15.4, weighted to adjust for unequal selection probabilities. The levels for *voting* are actual turnout figures (For sources, see Table 13.1).

country means of all four non-electoral modes). Do the countries that exhibit higher levels of participation more generally show more political equality? As the table demonstrates, the answer varies across the different types of inequality, and to some extent between voting and the non-electoral modes of participation. In terms of the non-electoral modes, the level of participation is related to attitudinal distortion and incapacitation, suggesting that more participation leads to more equality. However, the strength of these relationships is questionable (r is between 0.41 and 0.48). By contrast, with respect to social group inequality the country-level correlation with level of participation is rather impressive, both in absolute ($r = -0.86$) and rank order ($r = 0.83$) terms. And the simple message is: the more participants, the less political inequality among social groups.

When it comes to voting, the picture is clouded by the fact most correlations are weaker in terms of rank orders than in absolute terms. This in turn can mostly be explained by the Swiss case. Since Switzerland is the only country with any voting group inequality and incapacitation of consequence, the absolute correlations with the level of turnout ($r = -0.82$ and -0.61) are mostly driven by this extreme case. Expressing the country differences in terms of rank orders instead, which implies that each country is assumed to be at equal distances from each other, suppresses the effect of the Swiss outlier ($r = 0.58$ and 0.43). Having said this, the overall pattern is the same: more electoral participation implies less inequality. Only the relationship is somewhat weaker for group inequality and somewhat stronger for incapacitation. With respect to attitudinal distortion, by contrast, the level of turnout in elections does not seem to matter.

How should we interpret the relationship between level and equality of participation? Is it generally the case that as the level of participation rises, people's voices are more equally heard? To be sure, the general methodological dictum applies: correlation does not prove causation. It might very well be the case that both the low levels of participation and the high rates of inequality in the countries under study are due to some underlying confounding factor. One such factor is alluded to by the cross-country pattern mentioned above, namely the post-communist legacy. Maybe the recently experienced transition from communism, or the communist legacy itself, is what explains both the low levels of participation and equality in these countries?

There are however two reasons why this seems implausible. First, the relationship between level and equality of participation holds also among the non-communist countries in Scandinavia, western and southern Europe (results not shown). This implies that whatever is driving the correlation cannot be solely attributed to a post-communist legacy. Moreover, the two Germanies might be thought of as a real-world micro-experiment testing the legacy of communism. And the fact that the eastern part of

Germany resembles the western part to such a surprising extent, particularly in terms of the mean ranks in non-electoral inequality, again lends weak support for an explanation in terms of post-communism.

A more tenable proposition would be to view the relationship between the level and equality of political participation in the light of either modernisation theory or the age of democracy. According to the first view, modernisation precipitates rising levels of participation by lowering the barriers of entry into politics, both in terms of providing motivation and capacity to act. As was mentioned in Chapter 13 (Table 13.5), the simple correlation between the level of non-electoral participation and GDP per capita in the countries under study is an impressive 0.91. Equally important, as the amount of socio-economic resources accumulate they tend to spread among the populace of a country. Thus, with modernisation follows increased political equality as well: the country-wise correlation between GDP per capita and group inequality is −0.77. Taken together these patterns indicate that the level of participation does not cause participatory equality, neither does equality cause the level of participation. Instead, modernisation causes both.[19]

However, much as in Chapter 13, a story told in terms of the age of democracy fits the data equally well. According to this view, as citizens gain experience with democratic politics over time they become better able to navigate the political system and they internalise motivations to participate. As a result, when democracy matures the level of participation rises (the correlation between the level of non-electoral participation and the age of democracy is 0.94). Apparently this learning process then disseminates gradually through different groups of the population. Accordingly, as the democratic institutions grow older the amount of group inequality decreases (the correlation is −0.84). Thus, both the level and equality of participation may be caused by the age of democracy.[20] Our data is too limited to enable us to discriminate between these two causal stories. What they do indicate, however, is that the relationship between the level and equality of participation is not causal in itself.

Either the modernisation or learning theory also helps explain why the post-communist countries rate much lower on most forms of political equality. Apparently, their common communist past does not have a direct impact on the equality of participation. It is instead a reflection of their comparatively low levels of economic modernisation, or with their comparatively short experience of having democratic institutions.

Conclusions

In this chapter we have applied three evaluative standards to assess the extent to which there is inequality in political participation in the countries under study. The first two standards deal with the extent to which participants differ from the population at large; first in terms of political attitudes (left–right placement and tolerance), second in terms of social characteristics (gender, age, education, and locality). Since participants are assumed to have a stronger impact on the allocation of values for a society, the more they differ from the population at large the less equal will be the resulting political discourse and allocation.

Our results indicate that there is not much distortion of explicit attitudes or value orientations present in the participatory process. Political activists do differ in their ideological outlooks from the population at large, giving certain opinions stronger voice than others. This is particularly so in the case of left–right placement, with activists in most countries being more leftist than the general public. By and large, however, these differences are small. The tendency among participants to differ in their level of tolerance from the population at large is even weaker.

In terms of social characteristics the difference between participants and the general public is more sizeable. With one major exception, namely the act of voting, certain groups of people are more represented in the political process than others based on their participation rates. Generally speaking, participants speak with the accent of highly educated middle-aged male urban-dwellers. The widest gulf between activists and non-participants are in terms of educational attainment, followed by age composition. Participants are more representative in terms of gender and urban–rural locality, with two important exceptions: the gender difference is consistently wide in terms of party activity, and the urbanites by and large out-perform the rural dwellers in terms of protest activity.

Our third evaluative criterion turns attention to the mechanisms generating participation at the individual level. By distinguishing between the factors that motivate action and those that induce the capacity for action, we assess the extent to which the *terms* of participation are equally distributed. In this procedural sense, the more prominent the role capacitating factors play over motivation effects in accounting for participation, the more inequality there is. As it turns out, the gender and age gaps in participation can to the largest extent be explained in terms of differing levels of motivation. On top of that, however, women, the young, and the elderly are excluded from politics due to their lack of capacitating factors. This impact is even stronger for differences in education levels where we find the most substantial amounts of incapacitating mechanisms at work. On the other hand, variation in motivation or capacity for action does little to explain urban–rural distinctions.

Turning to the general country profiles depicted, our results are multi-faceted. Equality is highly dependent on the evaluative standard chosen as well as the distinction between voting and non-electoral modes of activity. Results vary in terms of which participatory systems can be labelled more equal or more unequal. Nevertheless, we can extract two common threads based on our analysis. The first is that the countries of northern Europe, particularly Norway and the Netherlands, achieve most in all forms of political equality, whereas the nascent democracies in eastern Europe, particularly Russia and Romania, suffer most consistently from all forms of inequality.

Second, and related to this, there are indications of a positive relationship between the level and equality of political participation. This relationship is strongest between the level and group equality of the non-electoral modes of participation. But to some extent it also applies to attitudinal distortion and incapacitation, and in terms of voting as well. We suggest two interpretations of this relationship: either it is the product of economic modernisation or the result of the age of democracy. Apparently it is not rising levels of participation in itself that strengthens political equality.

Yet, whether causal or not, the fact that there is a positive relationship between levels and equality of participation has an optimistic implication. Since the more politically active parts of the population are not representative of the general public, it is a commonly held belief that more participation will only incur more inequality by giving those non-representative activists even more say over government decisions. However, our results indicate no such trade-off between the amount and equality of participation. On the contrary, in societies with more activists the differences between the active and non-active parts of the population are generally smaller. In other words, in societies with higher levels of participation there are better prospects for responsive democracy.

Notes

1 It could of course be argued that under certain circumstances the intensity of preferences held should entitle some to have a larger say over public policies than others. This is, however, a complication we are unable to address in this chapter.
2 More specifically, the summary index is computed from political and social tolerance towards the following groups: Christian fundamentalists, Islamic fundamentalists, left-wing extremists, immigrants, homosexuals, persons who have a criminal record, racists, people of a different race, right-wing extremists, people who have AIDS, and drug addicts. Only respondents who have answered *all* items that make up the index are included in the index. Correlations (country wise) between an index composed of political and social tolerance respectively, justify composing an overall tolerance-index: Pearson's r is between 0.40 and 0.83, except in Sweden, where $r=0.31$. More fine-grained analyses show that in some cases the relationship between the participation indices and tolerance goes in opposite directions for specific groups. Consequently, since all groups enter into the summary index, some differences between activists and non-activists are 'artificially' small and the nuances are lost. However, for reasons of simplicity and due to space-limitations, we present only analyses with the summary index. Moreover – and most importantly – these analyses will reveal that the distortion effects of tolerance are modest, and this conclusion was also upheld in the more detailed analysis not presented.
3 Sweden seems to be an exceptional case (-0.49). One reason for this could be that in Sweden no-one receives the maximum score of 1 on the protest index (i.e. no-one has both taken part in a strike, a public demonstration, and an act of illegal protest). The regression coefficient might thus be artificially high due

to the fact that it makes an out-of-sample prediction. However, examining the degree of left–right distortion individually for each of the three protest items does not change the overall country ordering, nor the fact that Sweden is an extreme case.

4 Thus, in Rae's (1981: 110–11) terminology, we measure inequality according to the 'ratio criterion'.

5 The formula for computing NDQP for k subgroups is:

$$\sqrt{\left(\sum_{g=1}^{k}(P_g - (1/k))^2\right) * (k/(k-1))}$$

where Pg is group g's share of the total amount of participation.

6 Our age breakdown is as follows: young = 18–30; middle-age = 31–64; old = 65 plus.

7 Cases are based on individual 'years of education' with the exception of Slovenia, which is collapsed into seven education levels. Due to differences in the cross-national distribution of years of education, breaking points among the cases vary. Respectively, the subgroup means, medians, and standard deviations for the remaining twelve countries are as follows: low = 7.30, 8.00, 2.30; middle = 11.61, 12.00, 0.89; high = 16.18, 16.00, 2.48. This threefold distinction was in its turn based on a more fine-grained sixfold categorisation. In terms of cross-national comparisons the sixfold categorisation yields results almost identical to the threefold distinction (and both yield very similar results to an even more fine-grained grouping of the years of education into deciles).

8 Locality type is categorised according to the number of inhabitants in a community. Urban ≥5,000, and rural <5,000. Romania adds 'villages' of more than 5,000 (7.2 per cent of the sample) to the rural group. For Norway: urban ≥10,000 and rural <10,000.

9 For example, the higher population density of urban areas and the presence of more mobilising agents lower the 'costs' of effective protests. The absence of many mobilising agents and the more intimate settings of rural communities facilitate party activism (Zuckerman and West 1985; Sum and Badescu 2004).

10 *Life satisfaction* is measured on a 0–10 scale responding to the question, 'All things considered, how satisfied are you with your life as a whole these days?' *Political interest* and *frequency of discussing politics* are both based on fourfold self-classifications, the former from 'not at all' to 'very interested in politics', the latter from 'never' to 'often' responding to the question, 'How often would you say you discuss political matters with others?' *Political media exposure* is the average frequency with which the respondents 'read the political content of a newspaper', 'listen to or watch news programmes on radio or television', and 'listen to or watch other programmes about politics and social affairs on radio or television'. *Party identification* distinguishes among:

1 those who do not 'usually think of themselves as a supporter of a particular political party';
2 those who agree that there is 'still some party that they feel closer to than the others';
3 those who 'usually think of themselves as a supporter of a particular political party', but who do not 'consider themselves a strong supporter of this party', and;
4 those who *do* 'consider themselves a strong supporter of this party'.

Two kinds of *participatory norms* are used, measured on a 0–10 scale: the mean perceived importance for being a good citizen of 'to vote in public elections' and 'to be active in organisations'.

Participation and political equality 413

11 The reason behind our exclusion of 'external efficacy', together with measures of trust for political institutions, is a theoretical ambiguity as to whether these perceptions gauge capacity or motivation. A certain social group may feel incapacitated by its negative perceptions of institutions, but at the same time that negative perception might be fuelling the motivation to act (see, for example, Norris 2002: 30).

12 *Household income* was measured in different ways in different countries. Some surveys asked about income after taxes, some before tax deductions; some asked about yearly, others about monthly income. Most importantly, in some countries exact figures were given in the national currency, whereas other countries used predetermined response categories. This makes it impossible to construct any cross-nationally comparative measure of income other than a simple threefold distinction: being in the lower third, in the middle third, or in the higher third of the income range within each national sample. *Civic skills* are measured as the average frequency of which respondents 'participate in decisions at a meeting', 'plan or chair a meeting', 'prepare or give a speech before a meeting', and 'write a text other than a private letter at least a few pages long', on the one hand within voluntary organisations, on the other at work. The index on *membership in voluntary associations* is the average number of memberships the respondents claim to hold from a standardised list of 28 types of organisations applied in all countries under study. *Internal efficacy* is the mean response of two 0–10 scales responding to the questions, 'Do people like you have greater or smaller possibilities than others to present your opinions to politicians?' and 'Do people like you have greater or smaller possibilities than others to make politicians take account of your opinions?'

13 The reason why we refrain from explaining attitudinal distortion is that there is, overall, not much to explain (as was made clear early on in the chapter).

14 For two reasons, we had to exclude income from the final analyses presented here. First, there is too much missing data on this variable, in some countries excluding around 50 per cent of the sample. But second, and more importantly, the threefold income grouping in all countries only displayed a small and insubstantial effect on the overall participation index, when controlling for all other factors.

15 The direction of causality operating between motivation and capacity can be assumed to be reciprocal (Teorell 2006). This complicates tests of the model on cross-sectional data. Should the variance common to the two sets of explanatory factors be attributed to one or the other general mechanism? We try to solve this by adding the motivating factors before the capacitating ones. This should make it less likely that the participation gap diminishes when the latter is controlled for. As a result, our test of the capacitating factors is at least a conservative one.

16 The pooled mean of this index is 0.10, the standard deviation 0.13 ($N = 22,426$, each country weighted equally). A second-order principal component analysis of the four participation indices, using the conventional criteria for retention of factors (that is, an eigenvalue larger than 1), results in one factor accounting for 44 per cent of the variance ($N = 21,785$ each country weighted equally.) In a country-by-country analysis, this unidimensional solution holds up in all 13 societies under study.

17 The estimates are based on a series of analyses of covariance, using country and the four social groupings as categorical factors. In the baseline model, each factor representing a social grouping (gender, the threefold age-grouping, the threefold educational grouping, and the rural/urban dichotomy) is entered independently. In the second model, all four social groupings are entered. In the third and the fourth models all motivational and capacitating variables,

respectively, are added as continuous covariates (scaled from 0 to 1). Each model includes the interaction effect between country and all other variables. The predicted amount of participation in each social group is based on the least square means (using the LS Means option in the SAS GLM procedure). Finally, the ratio of the relevant contrast groups is computed for each social grouping and model. Cases have been deleted if they are missing values for any pertinent variable in the fourth model, leaving a pooled $N = 16,315$.

18 The results on incapacitation in voting have been computed from the same explanatory factors as those for the non-electoral modes, but using the predicted probabilities from logistic regressions instead of OLS estimates.

19 The country-wise partial correlation between the level and amount of group inequality of non-electoral participation, once GDP per capita is controlled for, is -0.25, that is, almost non-existent. We use the same measure of GDP per capita as in Table 13.5 of Chapter 13.

20 The country-wise partial correlation between the level and amount of group inequality of non-electoral participation, once the age of democracy is controlled for, is -0.12. We base our measure of the age of democracy on the mean Polity scores since 1900; see Table 13.5 of Chapter 13 for details.

16 Conclusion

The realisation of democratic citizenship in Europe

José Ramón Montero, Anders Westholm, and Jan W. van Deth

Introduction

The point of departure for this book, as formulated in Chapter 1, falls back on T.H. Marshall's (1950) notion of *effective citizenship*. In his analysis of the historical development of citizen rights, Marshall proceeds beyond citizenship as a legal concept and introduces it as a sociological one. In his view, citizenship can be seen as an ideal 'against which achievement can be measured and towards which aspirations can be directed' (1950: 28). This conception, in turn, allows us to describe our endeavour as a cross-national inquiry into the realisation of citizenship.

The time has now come to summarise what we have learned through that inquiry. We take on this task in three steps: by briefly reminding the reader of some significant characteristics of our research design and the purposes it is intended to serve (pages 415–19), by spelling out what we consider to be some of the most important contributions of the individual chapters in each part of the book (pages 419–37), and by highlighting certain themes and patterns that transcend chapter divisions (pages 437–8).

Components of citizenship

Studies sharing our concern about the realisation of democratic citizenship have in many cases been rather narrowly focused. We have chosen to cast our nets more widely. By giving due attention to no less than four major components – civic orientations, involvement in associations and social networks, participation in small-scale democracy, and participation in its large-scale counterpart – we emphasise the multidimensional nature of the notion of citizenship.

There are several reasons why we have opted for that route. One of them, to which we will return shortly, is that the four components are potentially interrelated in many important ways. The fact that we include all four puts us in a privileged position when it comes to examining these relationships empirically.

Before we consider that point in further detail, however, we would like to emphasise that this is not the only reason. Each of the four components deserves attention as an important part of democratic citizenship aside from its effects on other components. The extent to which citizens are tolerant towards one another, for example, is certainly important for their quality of life, even if it would turn out not to affect their propensity to participate politically. Their ability to cooperate in voluntary organisations matters even if it would not generate increasing levels of social trust. The capacity of citizens to influence their own personal situation so as to satisfy their subjective needs in significant social roles – as an employee, a student, a patient, or a parent – makes a difference irrespective of whether it also stimulates their interest in public affairs. And their propensity to participate politically clearly merits attention, regardless of whether or not it promotes confidence in the institutions of government.

In short, while the interrelationships between the four components are of great importance, the status of each component as a part of the notion of democratic citizenship does not stand and fall with the presence or absence of those relationships. Since there is no guarantee that the different components behave in perfect accord with one another, and since each of them merits attention in its own right, the fact that we include all four allows us to provide a considerably more complete and comprehensive picture of the realisation of citizenship than we had otherwise been able to offer.

A complementary reason is that such an inclusive picture has, to our knowledge, not been provided by any prior cross-national study. Aside from the Scandinavian studies that have served as a source of inspiration for our endeavour (Petersson *et al.* 1989; Andersen *et al.* 1993; Petersson *et al.* 1998; Andersen and Hoff 2001), the same holds for country-specific studies. Even if we consider each of the four components separately, the empirical data at our disposal, especially on a cross-national basis, left much to be desired when our surveys entered the field about the turn of the millennium. At that point, more than 25 years had passed since the last major cross-national study of political participation was conducted (Barnes *et al.* 1979). For reasons detailed in Chapter 6, the cross-national (and, in most cases, national) information on involvement in voluntary associations was far thinner than the one we can provide. And, until recently, few outside Scandinavia had probably heard much about the phenomenon we refer to as small-scale democracy.

As a result of the international cooperation within the CID network, we are in a position to offer not only cross-nationally comparable information but also what we consider to be new and better concepts and indicators. Our extensive measure of social participation covers four different forms of associational involvement (membership, donations, participation in activities, and voluntary work) across 28 different types of associations, and has additionally been extended to include social networks of various kinds. Political participation has been revisited, both in its definition and its operationalisation to include new elements such as political consumption. The concepts and measures of small-scale democracy have escaped from their Scandinavian confines and had their wings tested in a wider European context. And improved indicators of significant civic orientations, such as social trust, have been made available.

Links of citizenship

As indicated in the previous section, one important reason for our study to cover all four components of citizenship is that they are held, according to a large number of prominent ideas in social and political theory, to be related to one another. A significant motive for our choice of research design was our desire to examine these relationships empirically, and analyses to that end make up a very significant portion of this book.

While it would certainly have been tempting to try to impose a general hierarchical order on the relationships between the four components by designating one of them (say, political participation) as the ultimate effect, another (say, civic orientations) as the ultimate cause, and the other two as mechanisms mediating the impact of the cause on the effect, we have resisted that temptation. Neither the theoretical universe in which we are interested nor our own judgement gives us much reason to think it is that simple. In many instances, a case can be, and has been, made for a reciprocal rather than unilateral relationship between elements belonging to different components. One of several pertinent examples appearing in this book is the link between associational involvement and social trust (see Chapters 2, 6, and 7). The face-to-face interaction with others through active forms of involvement in associations may generate trust, but those who are initially trusting may also be more likely to engage in such interaction.

We are well aware of the difficulties to which such reciprocal relationships give rise as far as our statistical analyses are concerned. In many cases, the contributors to this volume therefore either abstain entirely from attempts to sort out the direction of causality (as in Chapter 6) or caution the reader that the direction assumed by their model is not the only conceivable alternative and that this must be kept in mind when interpreting the results.

We are also well aware of the availability of statistical techniques (e.g., two-stage least squares regression) that, given certain assumptions and at the expense of statistical precision, can eliminate the endogeneity bias created by reciprocal relationships and disentangle the two possible directions of causality, even on the basis of static data like ours. Regrettably, instances where there are strong reasons to believe that the assumptions are valid are rarely encountered, and the techniques not very robust against discrepancies between assumptions and reality. For this and other reasons, we have abstained from using these techniques in this book.

Since we have not found it justifiable to impose a hierarchical causal order on the four components and the elements of which they consist, we have been forced to find another way to organise and present our analyses. The strategy we have chosen is to single out a specific phenomenon as the focal point of each chapter. In some cases, the main purpose of the chapter is to define and describe the phenomenon in question, for example associational involvement in Chapter 6, central features of small-scale democracy in Chapter 9, political participation in Chapter 13, and political equality in Chapter 16. In other cases, the task of describing the phenomenon is accompanied or replaced by the task of explaining it, such as for social trust in Chapter 2, confidence in institutions in Chapter 3, norms of good citizenship in Chapter 4, tolerance in Chapter 5, associational involvement in Chapter 7, participation in small-scale democracy in Chapter 10, and political participation in Chapter 14. In still others, the analytic task is still more variegated, covering causes, effects, as well as descriptive contours, such as for social networks in Chapter 8, consequences of participation in small-scale democracy in Chapter 11, and political involvement in Chapter 12.

But although we are not willing to elevate one of the four components of citizenship to a higher status than the others, although we refrain from ordering them hierarchically, and although the focal point and analytic tasks of the various chapters show considerable variation, it is still possible to distinguish one factor that, more than any other, serves as a hub around which the others spin, namely social participation in the form of involvement in associations and/or social networks. Whether as a phenomenon to be described as a cause, or as an effect, this particular component of citizenship plays a prominent role in all but a few of the chapters in the book.

That such is the case is neither surprising nor unjustified. Inspired by the work of Robert Putnam (1993, 1995a, 1995b, 2000), the research community has, over the past decade, witnessed a strong revival of interest in the ideas about social involvement and social capital that trace their roots back to Alexis de Tocqueville's *Democracy in America* (published as two volumes in 1835 and 1840). This interest has received additional fuel with the observation that involvement in voluntary associations, a form of social involvement that is considered to be of particular relevance for the well-being of society and democracy, may be on the decline in those mature democracies where it has reached relatively high levels, and more or less absent in many newly established democracies.

A relationship of particular interest for our purposes is that between social involvement and political participation. Many different theories have been advanced with respect to this linkage. The theories target on three different properties of the relationship. The first concerns its direction and magnitude. While the most common conjecture is that the relationship is positive, a case can also be made for a zero or negative association. For example, van Deth (1997), in a review of models of the linkage between social involvement and political participation, points out that disappointment or saturation with regard to the one sphere may lead people to turn to the other in a pattern of shifting involvement similar to that suggested by Hirschman (1982). Another possibility is that the one type of involvement competes with the other for scarce resources in terms of time.

A second theoretical focal point concerns the extent to which the relationship is causal. One prominent hypothesis is that social involvement promotes political participation. But it is also possible to argue that the statistical association between the two is spurious, that is, due to the fact that they have common antecedents (see, e.g., Newton 1997, 1999b), for example, in the form of education or other indicators of socio-economic status.

A third theoretical consideration focuses on the mechanisms whereby social involvement tends to increase the propensity to participate in politics. One possibility in this regard is that social involvement fosters certain civic orientations favourable to political participation, for instance, social trust or norms stressing the obligation to participate. Another significant alternative, however, is that social involvement provides an opportunity to develop civic skills that facilitate political action, takes place on an arena where potential participants can be recruited through personal requests as well as broader appeals, or even becomes more or less indistinguishable from political participation, as, for example, activity within a voluntary organisation directly concerned with political issues.

We will find reason to return to these theoretical considerations on several occasions in the course of summarising the empirical results of our study.

Part I: Civic orientations

The first part of the book focuses on civic orientations with a particular emphasis on social trust, confidence in governmental institutions, norms of good citizenship, and political as well as social tolerance. As indicated in the introductory chapter, we do not claim that the orientations we have singled out exhaust the set of dispositions that would merit investigation in a study like ours. What we do argue is that these are among the most prominent candidates for an inquiry into the realisation of democratic citizenship.

In Chapter 2, Sonja Zmerli, Ken Newton, and José Ramón Montero revisit a central theme in classical as well as current political thought: the part played by mutual trust in shaping political processes. More specifically, the authors set out to re-examine the relationship between the faith citizens have in one another (social trust) and the faith they have in the institutions by which they are governed (confidence in institutions). An important starting-point for that analysis is the fact that the theoretically expected association between these two dimensions of trust – the horizontal and the vertical – has stubbornly refused to manifest itself in most empirical investigations on the individual level. In contrast to virtually all prior studies, however, Zmerli, Newton, and Montero find the two to be quite strongly and consistently related. Furthermore, they also show precisely why their results differ from those obtained by others. The culprit turns out to be poor measurement. Once the two concepts (in particular social trust) are appropriately operationalised – by means of more as well as better indicators – the theoretical expectations are borne out.

In a second step, Zmerli, Newton, and Montero consider the relationship between the two dimensions of trust and satisfaction with the way democracy works in the countries studied. While initial bivariate analyses show satisfaction with democracy to be consistently associated with both dimensions of trust, the strength of the relationship matches the degree to which the first factor is conceptually proximate to the other two. Hence, satisfaction with democracy is more strongly related to confidence in governmental institutions than to social trust. In addition, further multivariate analyses indicate that the weaker of the two relationships is indirect or spurious. While confidence in governmental institutions is directly linked to social trust as well as satisfaction with democracy, there is not much direct association between the latter two.

In line with these results, as well as prior expectations, the three factors also turn out to be related on the aggregate level. In all three instances, the more established democracies are found at the top and the newer ones at the bottom. Notably, three Eastern European countries – Moldova, Romania, and Russia – trail all others regardless of which of the three orientations we consider.

If the results go some way towards rehabilitating current theory with regard to the internal relationships between the three orientations, they continue to cast doubt on the part played by organisational involvement in generating social trust and confidence in institutions. Although the measures of such involvement included in our cross-national survey are considerably richer than those employed in prior studies, none of them shows much of an individual-level effect on any of the three orientations studied. This, in turn, makes it increasingly difficult to dismiss the outcome as merely an artefact of poor measurement. Hence, as far as the impact of organisational involvement is concerned, the findings presented by Zmerli, Newton, and Montero strengthen the suspicion that the discrepancy between theory and data should be blamed on the former rather than the latter.

In Chapter 3, Bas Denters, Oscar Gabriel, and Mariano Torcal proceed to an in-depth examination of one of the three civic orientations introduced in the previous chapter: that of vertical trust. Although, as shown in Chapter 2, it is empirically legitimate to treat this orientation as a single construct, Denters, Gabriel, and Torcal demonstrate that it can, for some purposes, be profitably divided into three components: confidence in the actors of representative democracy (parties and politicians), in its institutions (parliament and cabinet), and in the institutions embodying the rule of law (civil service, courts, and police).

In a first step, they confirm that the cross-national pattern evidenced in Chapter 2 holds for each of the three components separately. In all three instances, the more established democracies generally show higher levels of confidence than the newer ones. In addition, however, they find that the level of confidence varies systematically with the target. In virtually all countries, it is higher for the institutions of the rule of law than for those of representative democracy, and higher for the institutions of politics than for its actors.

In a second step, Denters, Gabriel, and Torcal pit two general types of explanations for the development of confidence in actors and institutions against each other. The first is the socio-cultural approach, which stresses the importance of long-term socialisation processes. This type of explanation is divided into two subcategories: that of social capital (as indexed by factors such as social trust and organisational involvement) and that of modernisation and value change (as indexed by factors such as age or generation, education, and materialist versus post-materialist values). The second major type of explanation instead emphasises shorter-term political experiences and perceptions (as indexed by, for example, the perceived responsiveness of the political system, satisfaction with the way democracy works in one's own country, and the extent to which the current cabinet mirrors one's own political outlooks).

The authors conclude that, for all three components of confidence, both major types of explanations as well as both subcategories within the first type enjoy some empirical support, but that the politically oriented explanations have a certain edge. When trying to explain the difference observed between confidence in the institutions of representative democracy, on the one hand, and those embodying the rule of law, on the other, they find political factors to be of major importance, whereas indicators of social capital have little effect. With regard to macro-level differences, finally, they find that micro-political factors explain a considerable part of the cross-national differences in confidence initially observed but also that the impact of such factors tends to be stronger in countries where the overall level of confidence is low.

In Chapter 4, the same author team turns to another set of orientations of considerable interests to students of democratic citizenship: the way ordinary citizens themselves think about the norms of good citizenship. Based on the theoretical literature as well as data from our survey, the authors identify three basic notions of citizenship: a traditionalist-elitist notion emphasising law-abidingness, a liberal notion stressing the value of deliberation, and a communitarian notion underscoring the importance of solidarity. Two main questions guide the subsequent analysis of citizen support for these norms of good citizenship, the first of which focusing on the degree of value fragmentation and the second on the impact of social capital.

With respect to the first question, the authors find that, although the three notions are distinct enough to surface in a dimensional analysis, this does not imply that they represent mutually exclusive belief systems in the minds of citizens. On the contrary, the degree of support for any one of the three norms tends to be positively and fairly strongly correlated with the degree of support for the others. Furthermore, a majority of citizens in all countries, typically a large majority, express a fair amount of support for all three norms.

A noteworthy and theoretically unexpected finding is that the cross-national differences in the degree of support for the three norms do not repeat the familiar divide between more established and newer democracies. If anything, the pattern suggests that support for all three norms tends to be stronger in the countries belonging to the Northern and Eastern parts of Europe than in those belonging to the Central or Southern parts. This pattern tends to be slightly more pronounced for law-abidingness than for the other two dimensions. In virtually all countries, support for the norm of solidarity tends to be slightly weaker than for the other two. In six of the countries (Moldova, Romania, Russia, Portugal, Spain, and Sweden) – all but one of which belonging to the set of newer democracies – law-abidingness has the edge. In the remaining seven, the norm of deliberation enjoys the highest level of support.

As far as the second question is concerned, the authors point out that the theoretical literature gives us reasons to expect that social capital (as indexed by organisational involvement and social trust) should be of considerable importance for the development of civic virtues such as the norms of good citizenship considered here. Yet, they find only moderate support for that hypothesis in most cases. The addition of a set of control variables considered relevant in prior research (education, age, church attendance, left–right self-placement, and television exposure) substantially improves the explanatory power, although it generally remains fairly low in absolute terms.

The impact of social capital (particularly in the form of social trust) tends to be somewhat more pronounced in those countries where it is more prevalent, that is, in the more established democracies. Yet, support for the norms of good citizenship is not generally weaker in those countries where democracy was late to arrive. The authors suggest that this may be due to alternative mechanisms associated with the past dictatorships. Since these mechanisms may now be withering away and the amount of social capital remains low, Denters, Gabriel, and Torcal conclude by pointing to the risks such a situation implies with respect to the maintenance of public support for key norms of democratic citizenship.

In the last of the four chapters on civic orientations, José Manuel Leite Viegas considers yet one significant norm of democratic citizenship: that of tolerance. The concept of tolerance has a political as well as a social side. Our cross-national survey captures both aspects, in the former case as the willingness of citizens to allow certain others to hold public meetings and in the latter as their readiness to accept them as neighbours. In both cases, the potential targets cover eleven different groups, including ideological extremists ('left-wing extremists', 'right-wing extremists', and 'racists'), religious extremists ('Christian fundamentalists' and 'Islamic fundamentalists'), stigmatised groups ('people with a criminal record', 'drug addicts', 'people with AIDS', and 'homosexuals'), and ethnic minorities ('immigrants' and 'people of a different race').

A first analysis reveals that the degree of tolerance varies significantly across countries. It also shows that the differences tend to match the distinction between newer and more established democracies to a considerably greater extent than is the case for the norms of good citizenship covered in the previous chapter. The pattern is not without exceptions, however. As far as political tolerance is concerned, Denmark, the Netherlands, Norway, Portugal, and Sweden form the most tolerant group, East and West Germany, Spain, and Switzerland are in the middle, and Moldova, Romania, and Russia at the bottom. The corresponding grouping for social tolerance is similar, save for the fact that the Netherlands, Norway, and Sweden now fall in the intermediate rather than the top category.

A comparison of the two aspects of tolerance indicates that citizens tend to be more tolerant in a political than in a social sense. This tendency is clearly evident in all of the established democracies, where the overall level of tolerance is relatively high, but is slight or invisible in the newer ones, where the overall level of tolerance is usually lower. An examination of the results for individual target groups additionally reveals that the propensity of citizens in established democracies to be more tolerant politically than socially is particularly pronounced for groups such as 'drug addicts' and 'people with a criminal record'. With regard to 'homosexuals', 'immigrants', and 'people of a different race', by contrast, citizens in these countries tend to display equally high levels of tolerance in both regards.

In Leite Viegas's view, this pattern reflects a structural distinction. In some countries, there is a fair amount of 'principled' tolerance. Where such is the case, the tendency to exclude is highly selective and manifests itself primarily with respects to groups that are perceived as an immediate threat, such as 'drug addicts' and 'people with a criminal record' in the social domain, and various types of extremist groups in the domain of politics, as well as social life. In other countries, where intolerant attitudes are prevalent, citizens tend to make less of a distinction based on the perceived characteristics of the specific situation. Consequently, differences across target groups as well as domains are less apparent.

In the analyses that conclude the chapter, Leite Viegas turns to microlevel explanations of tolerance with a primary focus on two selected components: political tolerance with regard to ideological and religious extremists on the one hand and stigmatised groups and ethnic minorities on the other. On the basis of prior research, he puts forth a set of hypotheses primarily representing three more general types of factors: those related to the level of modernisation (such as age or generation, level of education, religiosity as indexed by church attendance, and a rural versus urban environment), those reflecting social attitudes and identities (such as social trust and attachment to people sharing one's own culture and religion), and those that are more explicitly political (such as confidence in governmental institutions, ideological position, political involvement, and degree of support for the norms of law-abidingness, deliberation, and solidarity).

The results display a considerable amount of variation across countries, in terms of the overall amount of explanatory power as well as with regard to the impact of individual predictors. Nevertheless, some patterns can be distinguished. First, as theoretically expected, the results indicate that the combined explanatory power tends to be somewhat greater for the second of the two tolerance measures (stigmatised groups and ethnic minorities) than for the first (ideological and religious extremists). Second, the three general types of factors included in the regression models all contribute some explanatory power, although the strength of the effects varies considerably across countries, across the two dependent variables, and across the individual predictors within each general type of factor. The predictors that show the strongest and most consistent effects on the degree of tolerance are age or generation (negative), social trust (positive), cultural attachment (negative), confidence in governmental institutions (positive), law-abidingness (negative), deliberation (positive), and left–right ideological position (negative).

Part II: Voluntary organisations and social networks

The second part of the book focuses on social participation in the form of involvement in voluntary organisations and social networks. In view of the particular prominence of organisational involvement in the literature to which we relate – that on social capital and political participation – we have made a special effort to capture this aspect of social participation in a considerably more comprehensive way than most prior studies. Consequently, our treatment extends over two chapters, the first of which focuses on the task of describing the many faces of organisational involvement and the second on the task of explaining its magnitude. For social networks, by contrast, the descriptive and explanatory sides are combined in a single chapter.

As pointed out by Laura Morales and Peter Geurts when they embark on their empirical analysis in Chapter 6, the information on organisational involvement included in the CID surveys improves on that available in prior cross-national studies in two significant ways. First, the measurement instrument systematically probes for involvement in no less than 27 different types of organisations plus a residual category. Second, for each type of organisation, it provides data on as much as four different forms of involvement: membership, donations, participation in activities, and voluntary work. This allows Morales and Geurts to provide a more detailed as well as a more accurate picture of organisational involvement than earlier cross-national studies.

After first letting the results illustrate some of the pitfalls to which cruder measures of organisational involvement may fall prey, the authors turn to a systematic examination of the cross-national pattern. As far as the level of involvement is concerned, they find sizeable variations across countries for all four forms of involvement. The differences are particularly dramatic when considered in terms of the breadth of involvement, that is, the number of organisations of different types in which any one citizen tends to engage. For all four forms of involvement as well as for a combined measure, the figures are roughly ten to 20 times higher for the country at the top of the distribution than for that at the bottom.

Regardless of which involvement measure we look at, the newer democracies in the Eastern and Southern parts of Europe tend to trail the established democracies in the Northern and Central parts. The levels of involvement are particularly low in Moldova, Romania, and Russia, while East Germany, Slovenia, Portugal, and Spain form an intermediate group. As the authors note, the extent to which citizens tend to progress from less to more active forms of involvement is slightly higher in those countries where the overall level of involvement is low. However, this tendency is by no means sufficient to close the gap in the cross-national distribution even for the most active forms of involvement. Rather, it implies that for these particular forms, the differences are reduced from immense to merely large.

Since the measures employed in the CID surveys do not presume any fixed relationship between different forms of involvement (e.g. that membership is universally a precondition for participation in activities), it becomes meaningful to test empirically for the extent to which they can be combined into a single scale. The authors find that three of the four forms – membership, participation in activities, and voluntary work – generally satisfy the requirements of cumulative scaling. For the fourth – donations – the picture is slightly less clear. First, this form of involvement does not scale with the others in every country. Second, unlike the other three forms, its position on a scale ranging from more common (less demanding) to less common (more demanding) forms of involvement varies across countries. In some cases, for example Norway and Switzerland, donating money is the second most common form of involvement (after membership). In other cases, such as East and West Germany, it is the least common of all four types of involvement.

While organisational involvement may vary with the individual attributes of citizens (as exemplified by the analyses of Chapter 7), it may also vary with the characteristics of the organisation. Since the CID surveys provide information on such a wide range of different types of organisations, Morales and Geurts are in a position to test this general idea. To that end, they introduce a distinction based on the nature of the primary (or constitutive) goals of various organisations: private goods on the one hand versus public goods on the other. Their hypothesis is that organisations that primarily seek private goods (e.g. hobby associations and sports clubs) should stimulate more active forms of involvement (participation in activities, voluntary work) to a greater extent than those focusing on public goods (e.g. organisations concerned with human rights or environmental issues) since, in the former case, activity appears to be a direct precondition for the acquisition of the good. Their conclusion is that the data provide a fair amount of support for such a proposition.

The final empirical section of the chapter furnishes a set of tests of the hypothesis – prominent in social-capital theory – that organisational involvement and social trust form a virtuous circle of mutual reinforcement. These tests, which complement those presented in Chapter 2, do nothing to dispel the doubts raised by earlier analyses. First, the strength of the statistical relationship remains weak. Second, the authors find little evidence that the causal mechanism suggested – the face-to-face interaction between citizens generated by active forms of organisational involvement – is indeed responsible for that relationship.

In Chapter 7, Gabriel Badescu and Katja Neller proceed to the task of explaining why individual citizens do or do not become involved in associations. Based on a thorough review of prior research, they develop a model focusing on five different types of individual characteristics: socio-economic resources, level of social integration, social orientations, political orientations, plus a residual category for factors that do not unambiguously belong to any one of the aforementioned types. To these micro-level determinants, they add a macro-level distinction based on prior regime type, that is, established democracies versus post-communist and other post-authoritarian regimes. Their central idea is that the impact of the micro-level determinants is at least partly contingent on macro-level characteristics, such as the extent to which voluntary associations are 'naturally grown' or 'imported' from abroad (for the purpose of supporting the transition to democracy) and the extent to which associational involvement can be assumed to serve private versus public ends.

In a first step, Badescu and Neller examine the impact of these factors on a summary measure combining all forms of involvement across all types of associations. In so doing, however, they keep their eyes open for the possibility that the effect of the predictors is contingent on the particular form of involvement considered. The results indicate that all five types of individual characteristics considered by the authors have at least some systematic impact: socio-economic resources in the form of education and income; social integration as indexed by conditions and habits pertaining to family, friends, residence, religion, working life, and public affairs; social orientations in the form of social trust and civic norms of solidarity and activism; political orientations in the form of interest in politics, political efficacy, and satisfaction with democracy; and the residual type in the form of age and gender. While these factors certainly do not strike with equal force across all countries, the effects are sufficiently consistent for the authors to conclude that there is a fair amount of cross-national homogeneity as far as the pattern of individual-level effects is concerned.

That said, Badescu and Neller still find at least some support for their ideas regarding the impact of macro-level conditions. To begin with, and as hypothesised, the explanatory power of the model as a whole tends to be lower in Eastern than in Western Europe. In line with that observation, a number of the individual predictors – for example, church attendance, social trust, and the norm of activism – have less of an effect (sometimes none) in the post-communist societies. In addition, the authors find that at least three of the Eastern European countries – Moldova, Romania, and Russia – are quite similar overall with respect to the pattern of individual-level effects.

In a second step, Badescu and Neller additionally consider the extent to which explanations of associational involvement are contingent on the type of association to which the involvement pertains. To that end, they distinguish between four different types of associations: spare time and sports associations (e.g. hobby clubs), interest groups (e.g. trade unions), socio-cultural organisations (e.g. charity and social-welfare organisations), and religious associations. While the authors find a good deal of homogeneity in the way and extent to which the individual determinants affect the level of involvement across different types of associations, there are several interesting exceptions to that rule. The organisations that deviate most clearly from the general pattern are the religious ones. In this case, a considerable number of predictors that otherwise have a noticeable impact, for example many of the measures of social integration and socio-economic resources, have little or no effect.

In Chapter 8, Hajdeja Iglič and Joan Font Fábregas move the spotlight to a less formally regulated arena of social participation: social networks. The authors focus on three aspects that, in their view, are crucial for understanding the political implications of such networks: their multiplicity, defined as the number of networks in which an individual is involved, the strength of the social ties that serve as their constitutive elements, and the extent to which they act as vehicles for the exchange of political views and information.

In some important respects, the cross-national patterns uncovered by Iglič and Font Fábregas turn out to be remarkably similar to those evidenced by Morales and Geurts in Chapter 6. Not only do citizens in the established democracies of Northern and Central Europe show considerably greater breadth in their associational involvement than those in the newer democracies of Southern and Eastern Europe; they are also involved in a significantly larger number of informal social networks. And not only do citizens in the latter set of countries opt for more intense forms of associational engagement, when at all involved, than those in the former; they also tend to form stronger ties within the smaller number of informal networks in which they appear. By implication, the structure of social interaction is in the former case predominantly marked by a relatively large number of fairly weak ties and in the latter by a relatively small number of fairly strong ties.

Interestingly, the multiplicity of networks and the strength of ties are not inversely related on the individual level, as one might guess. On the contrary, the individual-level relationship turns out to be consistently positive. Consequently, it is of no help in accounting for the pattern of cross-national differences. Iglič and Font Fábregas instead suggest an explanation in terms of sociability style. In their interpretation, social ties in Northern and Central Europe tend to be formed on a highly individualised and selective basis. In other words, people tend to form strong ties with only a few selected others in each of several different social settings (working life, associational life, residential life, and so forth). In Southern and Eastern Europe, by contrast, the formation of social ties is more group-oriented. People tend to form strong ties with multiple others encountered in a more limited number of settings.

Beyond the cross-national picture of network multiplicity, strength of ties, and the interrelationship between the two, Iglič and Font Fábregas also contribute several valuable insights regarding the causes of network characteristics as well as their consequences, particularly with regard to patterns of political communication. One of many noteworthy findings is that social trust is positively and systematically related to involvement in social networks, and, just as in the case of associational involvement, more so in the Western than in the Eastern parts of Europe. While it is debatable whether the relationship is generally stronger for involvement in social networks than for involvement in voluntary associations, it does reach respectable strength in one particular instance, namely when the two aspects of social participation are combined and we consider the extent to which social networks are formed within the social setting provided by voluntary associations.

Part III: Small-scale democracy

The third part of the book focuses on the characteristics of small-scale democracy. Our treatment of this phenomenon is divided into three chapters. The first presents the concept itself and associated measures, the second tries to explain why citizens do or do not take action in small-scale democracy, and the third considers the consequences of those actions.

In Chapter 9, Jørgen Goul Andersen and Sigrid Roßteutscher define participation in small-scale democracy as the actions taken by individual citizens to control their own personal situation in important roles of everyday life. The roles (and associated domains) singled out for empirical investigation in the CID study are those of being gainfully employed (working life), being a student (student education), being a parent of school children (child education), and being a patient or relative of a patient (health care). As pointed out by Andersen and Roßteutscher, these particular roles and domains constitute examples rather than the universe of relevant roles and domains. The actions taken by citizens in order to control their personal situation in any of these roles may be quite variegated. They may be carried out individually or in cooperation with others; they may take place through informal as well as formal channels; they may involve contacts with government officials but may also be directed toward other targets; they may take the form of voice as well as exit; and they may depend on both informal and institutional opportunities.

Andersen and Roßteutscher begin their empirical analysis by assessing the incentives citizens may have for taking action. To that end, they present a set of measures focusing on the perceived opportunities to exercise influence within each domain. Although there are theoretical reasons to expect that the values for voice-based opportunities would be highest for working life and lowest for health care, such is not the case. While the overall differences across domains are rather small, health care is at the top, followed by student education, working life, and child education. With respect to exit-based opportunities, working life deviates in a negative direction while the other three domains are more or less on a par. As far as cross-national differences are concerned, the theoretical arguments advanced by the authors give us reasons to expect higher values for the countries in Northern and Central Europe than for those in the Eastern and Southern parts. By and large, this hypothesis turns out to be correct with one noticeable exception: not only the Eastern but also the Western part of Germany sides with the latter rather than the former group of countries.

A second significant type of incentive is the extent to which citizens are dissatisfied with their situation. In this case, the authors find it more difficult to derive theoretical expectations inasmuch as the degree of discontent is not only a matter of objective conditions but also of subjective expectations. The actual results show dissatisfaction to be somewhat more pronounced in the domains of working life and student education than in those of child education and health care. The cross-national differences are relatively small, but do point to slightly higher levels of dissatisfaction in the poorest countries.

With respect to action itself, an important result is that participation in small-scale democracy turns out to be relatively widespread. On average, no less than one-third of those respondents who qualified for the domain in question had taken action within the past 12 months. The percentages tend to be considerably higher for working life and child education than for the other two domains. The cross-national differences resemble those for perceived opportunities, with the German deviation from the expected pattern being still more pronounced for actual participation is concerned. As far as the type of action is concerned, voice clearly dominates over exit. Only in the domain of health care is exit a relatively frequent phenomenon. Further, participation in small-scale democracy turns out to be less individualistic than one might think: a substantial share of those who chose to take action did so on a cooperative basis.

Andersen and Roßteutscher conclude by presenting two measures focusing on the consequences of action. The first assesses whether those who took action felt that their wishes had been satisfied. The second gauges the extent to which they felt they got a fair hearing. In both cases, the values are generally high. For example, no less than two-thirds considered themselves successful in their attempts to exercise influence. The differences between domains and across countries, by contrast, are relatively small.

In Chapter 10, Hanspeter Kriesi and Anders Westholm proceed to the question of why citizens do or do not take action in order to influence their situation. Inspired by social-movement theory, they build a model based on three major components: discontent, perceived opportunities to exercise influence, and resources. Whereas perceived opportunities (efficacy) and resources also figure prominently in the literature on political participation, discontent plays a much more significant role in the study of social movements. Kriesi and Westholm raise the question of whether these three elements, which have already proven their usefulness in the study of large-scale phenomena, can be similarly useful in the much less familiar terrain of small-scale democracy.

They also raise the question of how the three components combine in promoting action. According to some theorists, for example Smelser (1962), the combination should be multiplicative rather than additive. In his view, each of the three components is a necessary condition for the next to operate as a determinant. In other words, only if discontent is sufficiently widespread will resources become relevant, and only if resources are sufficiently large, will opportunities matter. Alternatively, one may conceive of each component as a facilitating condition, which contributes its share to the propensity to take action. In this case, the components would combine in an additive rather than multiplicative fashion.

The empirical analysis shows that each of the three main components of the model – dissatisfaction, perceived opportunities, and resources – does contribute significantly to an understanding of why citizens choose to take action to control their own situation in the domains under study. However, the hypothesis of social-movement theory, that the three components combine in a multiplicative rather than additive fashion, does not find much empirical support. No systematic pattern of interactions of the kind conjectured could be identified.

Following Dworkin (1981: 311), the mechanism generating action in small-scale as well as large-scale democracies should ideally be 'endowment-insensitive', but not 'ambition-sensitive'. From this point of view, there is an important distinction between dissatisfaction on the one hand and the other two components on the other. The more action turns out to depend on subjectively felt needs as indexed by discontent, and the less it is contingent on capacity as indexed by opportunities and resources, the closer the correspondence with Dworkin's ideal.

The authors find that the countries included in our study differ systematically in this regard. In most of the established democracies (Denmark, the Netherlands, Norway, Sweden, and Switzerland), where opportunities and resources are relatively abundant, and participation levels relatively high, the propensity of citizens to take action depends more on subjectively felt needs and less on capability than in the newer democracies of Southern Europe (such as Portugal and Spain) and Eastern Europe (such as Moldova, Romania, Russia, and Slovenia), where both opportunities and resources are more scarce, and the level of participation lower. The case of Germany is once again exceptional. Neither East nor West Germany fits in either category.

In Chapter 11, Anders Westholm and Emanuel von Erlach examine the consequences of participation in small-scale democracy from several different points of view. More specifically, they raise five different questions with regard to these consequences. The first is an extension of one of the questions asked in the previous chapter. While Kriesi and Westholm ask about the extent to which resources determine the propensity to take action, Westholm and von Erlach ask about the extent to which they determine the outcome of the action (i.e. whether citizens manage to get their wishes satisfied or not). In general, the results indicate that the relationship is weaker in the latter case than in the former. Consequently, the degree of inequality between more or less privileged citizens is more pronounced with regard to participation itself than with regard to the response it produces.

The next two questions concern the feedback effects of the outcome as well as the perceived fairness of the process on the perceived opportunities to influence and the level of dissatisfaction. Westholm and von Erlach conclude that both factors have an impact in the expected direction on each of the two dependent variables, but that the extent to which citizens consider themselves fairly treated in procedural terms has a stronger effect than the material outcome. As the authors point out, this finding is highly relevant for democratic theory and practice, since democratic regimes, although unable to accommodate the preferences of every citizen all the time, nonetheless have the capacity to strengthen their legitimacy by treating citizens in a fair and respectful manner. In short, as Westholm and von Erlach put it, 'good democracy fosters good losers'.

The fourth question focuses on the macro-level consequences of the micro-level processes previously examined. To that end, the authors focus on four properties: opportunities, responsiveness, fairness, and the relationship between dissatisfaction and action. They find that these four components can be combined into a single scale for the purpose of evaluating the overall performance of small-scale democracy across countries. With few exceptions, the results repeat the familiar divide between newer and older democracies. The countries that occupy the top positions are Denmark, the Netherlands, Norway, Sweden, and Switzerland along with Slovenia. At the other end of the spectrum, we find Moldova, Romania, Portugal, and Spain together with East and West Germany.

The fifth question, finally, concerns the degree of inequality based on Walzer's (1983) ideas about spheres of justice. In Walzer's perspective, equality is realised to the extent that inequalities do not cumulate across spheres. Differences within a particular realm may be acceptable, even desirable, as long as an inferior position in one domain is compensated by a superior position in another. On the basis of this perspective, Westholm and von Erlach examine the extent to which participation shows a cumulative pattern across the three different domains of small-scale democracy as well as across the divide between small- and large-scale democracy. In this case, too, the cross-national pattern repeats the familiar division between old and new democracies. A shorter democratic history and lower levels of participation imply a stronger tendency for participation to cumulate.

Part IV: Large-scale democracy

Political involvement and political participation are sometimes taken to be more or less synonymous. In this book, however, they are regarded as conceptually distinct entities. In Chapter 12, Irene Martín and Jan W. van Deth define political involvement on the basis of two different dimensions: the *importance* citizens attribute to politics on the one hand and their *interest* in (or attentiveness to) politics on the other.

By means of these two dimensions, Martín and van Deth develop a typology of citizenship inspired by democractic theory. The typology includes a decisionist type (where politics is neither important nor interesting), a liberal-representative type (where it is of little importance but at least moderately interesting), a participatory type (where it is of considerable importance as well as interest), and a unitary type (where it is of considerable importance but little interest). In developing their typology, Martín and van Deth explain how it relates to behavioural expressions of political involvement such as frequency of political discussions and media exposure. They also develop hypotheses about the way the various types can be expected to correlate with political as well as social participation.

The application of this typology to the 13 societies included in our survey yield interesting results. First, the prevalence of the four types differs considerably between newer and older democracies. In the former set of countries, more than two-thirds of the citizens belong to the decisionist type. In the latter, by contrast, the majority belong to the liberal and participatory types.

Second, the difference between the two sets of countries disappears when Martín and van Deth turn to the relationships linking political involvement to its social, cultural, and political antecedents. The explanations of why citizens belong to one type rather than another are fairly similar for newer and older democracies. Instead, the explanatory pattern turns out to vary with the pair of types considered. With respect to the distinction between decisionist and participatory citizens, social position (as indexed by gender, age, and education), social capital (as indexed by social trust), political efficacy, and ideological position all have a systematic impact. With respect to the distinction between liberal and participatory citizens, by contrast, only the last two predictors have a clear effect.

Finally, the various types have systematic implications for both social involvement and political participation. Consequently, the results confirm the hypothesis that the statistical association between the latter two is at least partly due to the fact that they have common antecedents. At the same time, the findings reject the idea that the relationship between social involvement and political participation amounts to a zero-sum game (e.g. because of mechanisms of shifting involvements of the type suggested by Hirschman 1982). Instead, engagement in the one sphere tends to go hand-in-hand with engagement in the other.

Martín and van Deth conclude by pointing out that the cross-national distribution across the four types is not set in stone. The fact that the conditions explaining why citizens belong to one type rather than another are similar across different countries implies that we can hope for the newer democracies to catch up with the more established ones as the social and other preconditions for the development of political involvement improve.

The concept of political participation certainly deserves just as careful consideration as that of political involvement. In Chapter 13, Jan Teorell, Mariano Torcal, and José Ramón Montero therefore begin their analysis of how much and in what ways citizens take part in politics by examining the definition of the phenomenon they set out to study. Although they concur in several important respects with Verba and Nie's (1972: 2) classical definition (where 'political participation refers to those activities by private citizens that are more or less directly aimed at influencing the selection of governmental personnel and/or the actions they take'), they take issue with one of its elements. According to Easton (1953: 134), the extent to which an act is political depends on its 'relation to the authoritative allocation of values for a society'; and (as recognised by Verba and Nie 1972: 2) that allocation is not in all respects decided by government personnel but also by non-governmental institutions within the non-profit or private sector. Consequently, not only the former but also the latter may be targeted by attempts to influence 'political outcomes', such as when citizens deliberately buy or boycott certain products to influence market actors.

Once the general definition has been settled, Teorell, Torcal, and Montero consider how the long list of indicators it subsumes might be reduced into a more limited set of dimensions. To that end, they develop a typology based on three criteria: the channel of expression (representational versus extra-representational), the mechanism of influence (exit-based versus voice-based), and the scope (targeted versus non-targeted). While the typology shows several similarities with that previously developed by Verba and Nie (1972), one advantage is that it includes the extra-representational channels of political expression, and thereby consumer participation (deliberate purchases or boycotts of products for political reasons) as well as protest activity. It also offers a more fine-grained set of distinctions than the 'conventional' versus 'unconventional' dichotomy introduced by Barnes *et al.* (1979).

Based on this typology, Teorell, Torcal, and Montero hypothesise that the long list of indicators of political participation included in our surveys can be reduced to five dimensions: voting, party activity, consumer participation, contacting, and protest activity. When they consider the dimensional pattern in different parts of Europe, they also find that such a generalisation fits the data relatively well. Aside from the dimensional structure, another important similarity between countries is that the ranking of the various modes tends to follow the same pattern, with voting as the most common activity followed (in the order listed) by consumer participation, contacting, protest activity, and party activity. A third similarity is that in all countries the modes of participation tend to be positively rather than negatively correlated, implying that they do not constitute alternatives in a strict sense but often go hand-in-hand with one another.

If the dimensional structure and the rank-order of the five modes turn out to be similar across countries, the levels of participation are in many cases widely different. The level turns out to be highest in the Scandinavian countries, with the Netherlands and Switzerland more or less on a par except in the case of voting. The authors suggest that either the age of democracy or the level of economic development might account for the cross-national pattern with respect to levels of participation.

In Chapter 14, Klaus Armingeon proceeds to the question of how we can explain the statistical relationships between the various modes of political participation on the one hand and involvement in voluntary organisations on the other. To that end, he presents three alternative models suggested by the literature. The first is based on cleavage politics as defined by Lipset and Rokkan (1967), where the relationship between social involvement and political participation arises as a result of processes of mobilisation by political entrepreneurs representing different social segments. The second draws on ideas from social-capital theory (e.g. Putnam 2000). According to this model, organisations function as 'schools of democracy', providing their members with resources, values, and attitudes that encourage political participation. The final model, suggested, for example, by Newton (1997), posits that the correlation between associational involvement and political participation is due to self-selectivity. In other words, it is not due to a causal impact of the one on the other but is spurious and will disappear once we control for the individual attributes that serve as common antecedents of social involvement as well as political participation.

According to the results obtained by Armingeon, support for the cleavage-politics model is quite limited. The social-capital model fares somewhat better but is hardly well-supported either. These conclusions are reinforced by the fact that neither model enjoys much more support in the Western than in the Eastern parts of Europe. As observed by Armingeon, cleavage politics is much more developed in the West than in the East. The amount of social capital is also higher and has been given due time to realise its potential through various type of socialisation processes. Nevertheless there is little evidence of the interaction effects we would expect to see on these grounds.

The explanatory power of the self-selectivity model, by contrast, is relatively high. This means that the correlation between social involvement and political participation is only to a limited extent due to a causal relationship between the two. Instead, the observation that socially involved citizens are more likely to participate in politics can, in Armingeon's analysis, mainly be attributed to the fact that the two have common antecedents.

In Chapter 15, finally, Jan Teorell, Paul Sum, and Mette Tobiasen examine to what extent political participation deviates from the normative requirement of political equality. To that end, they apply three evaluative standards, a common denominator of which is that they are all based on the ideal of responsive democracy (Dahl 1971).

The first two standards are rooted in an outcome-oriented principle of equality; that is, they concern the extent to which the input provided by participants is biased. One focuses on expressed preferences, the other on the needs implicit in social characteristics. In the former case, Teorell, Sum, and Tobiasen choose to examine ideological (left–right) orientation and tolerance. In the latter, the characteristics analysed include gender, age, education, and rural versus urban residence.

The third standard, by contrast, is rooted in a procedural perspective on equality and focuses on the extent to which differences in participation across social groups can be explained by differences in motivations rather than capabilities. To the extent that such is the case, Dworkin's (1981) norm as applied to political participation – that it should be ambition-sensitive but endowment-insensitive – is satisfied. Based on the classic 'calculus of participation' (Nagel 1987), the motives depend on the perceived stake in the issue at hand as well as various forms of selective incentives (operationalised by factors such as life satisfaction, satisfaction with democracy, interest in politics, frequency of political discussion, political media exposure, party identification, and participatory norms) while the capabilities depend on various resources and psychological predispositions mediating the impact of these resources on the propensity to act (operationalised as income, civic skills, organisational membership, and internal political efficacy).

As far as the first evaluative criterion is concerned, Teorell, Sum, and Tobiasen find modest distortions for ideological orientation across all modes of participation except voting. Political activists tend to be drawn disproportionally from the left in most countries, but the differences are small. For tolerance, the bias is even smaller and its direction depends on the mode of participation.

With respect to the second criterion, the differences between participants and non-participants are more clearly pronounced and more consistent across countries across all modes of participation (except, once again, voting). In line with prior research in this area, citizens with certain social attributes are considerably better represented than others in the political process. The distortion is greatest for education, followed, in descending order, by age, gender, and rural versus urban residence.

When it comes to the third criterion, finally, the results indicate that part of the differences in participation with respect to age and gender can be explained by differences in motivations. However, women, the young, and the elderly are also excluded from political life due to a lack of capacitating factors. This holds to an even greater extent for citizens with low levels of education.

When the three criteria are employed for a general assessment of political inequality across countries, the results are not so easily summarised. The pattern varies with the evaluative criterion and mode of participation considered. Nevertheless, a general tendency can be discerned. Countries in the North-Western corner of Europe, particularly Norway and the Netherlands, tend to be the most egalitarian. At the other end, the most consistent expressions of political inequality are found in the new Eastern European democracies, particularly Russia and Romania.

Higher levels of political participation thus tend to be accompanied with higher levels of equality. In the authors' view, this is not because the one causes the other. Rather, they find reasons to think that both are due to economic modernisation and/or the age of the democratic regime. Yet, regardless of the way it comes about, the positive correlation between the amount of participation and the degree of equality has positive implications. It indicates that we do not face a trade-off between a participatory democracy and an egalitarian one but that both can be achieved simultaneously.

Conclusion

In conclusion, there are two general patterns in our findings that we would like to highlight. The first concerns the individual-level effects of social involvement on participation in small-scale and large scale democracy on the one hand and on civic orientations on the other. In both regards, there are many instances in which the hypothesis of a positive effect does turn out to enjoy a modicum of empirical support. On the other hand, the impact is rarely strong and clear. On the contrary, it is often weak and uneven. Even in cases where the statistical relationship is plainly visible in bivariate terms, such as between social involvement and political participation, the analyses presented here suggest that it is largely due to common antecedents rather than a causal impact of the first factor on the second. It is therefore difficult to escape the conclusion that the faith placed in associational and other forms of social involvement as a prime engine of the realisation of democratic citizenship is stronger than the empirical evidence warrants.

At the same time, it is important to emphasise that we have found no evidence whatsoever that the different forms of involvement and participation we have analysed directly compete with one another for the time and attention of citizens. On the contrary, the bivariate statistical relationships are uniformly positive. This holds for the link between social involvement and participation in small-scale as well as large-scale democracy. It also holds for the relationships between different modes of political participation, between different domains of small-scale democracy, and across the divide between small-scale and large-scale democracy.

The second general pattern concerns the cross-national differences. The analyses in this book have ratified again and again the existence of systematic differences between newer and older democracies. What is surprising about this pattern is not its mere existence but how consistent it is across the many facets of citizenship we have analysed. Regardless of whether we consider civic orientations, involvement in voluntary associations and social networks, the various qualities of small-scale democracy, or political involvement and political participation, the picture repeats itself. While our analyses show that there are exceptions to this rule, they are indeed very few. Furthermore, the exceptions typically amount to the observation that there is not much of a difference, rather than a reversal of the typical pattern.

In addition, the gaps between newer and older democracies are not only systematic but also of considerable magnitude. Such is the case with respect to the level of social involvement as well as participation in small-scale and large-scale democracy. The same holds for several of the civic orientations that we have considered.

Finally, it is noteworthy that the pattern extends not only to univariate distributions of various kinds but also to a set of particularly important relationships: those that tell us something about the degree of inequality. In small-scale and large-scale democracies alike, there appears to be no trade-off between the level of participation and the degree of equality. On the contrary, the most participatory societies also tend to be the most egalitarian ones.

As indicated in several chapters, it is difficult to separate the effect of the age of the democratic regime from other factors, for example the level of economic development. On the other hand, it certainly seems plausible that the position of the newer democracies with respect to economic wealth as well as other aspects of modernisation might have been better, perhaps vastly better, if they had become democracies at an earlier stage. It therefore remains possible to argue that the age of democracy remains the vital, if not necessarily the immediate, cause.

An obvious question raised by our results is how the differences between newer and older democracies that we have observed will develop in the future. As pointed out by several of the authors, the picture we have collectively drawn is by no means chiselled in stone. On the other hand, it is certainly not easy to provide a reliable forecast. We conclude by expressing a hope for convergence in the best of the many possible forms it can take.

Bibliography

Abramson, Paul R. 1983. *Political Attitudes in America: Formation and Change*. San Francisco: W.H. Freeman.
Águila, Rafael del, Fernando Vallespín, Ángel Rivero, and Elena García Guitián, eds. 1998. *La democracia en sus textos*. Madrid: Alianza Editorial.
Ajzen, Icek. 1988. *Attitudes, Personality, and Behavior*. Milton Keynes: Open University Press.
Aldrich, John H. 1993. Rational choice and turnout. *American Journal of Political Science* 37 (1): 246–78.
Almond, Gabriel A. 1980. The intellectual history of the civic culture concept. In *The Civic Culture Revisited. An Analytic Study*, ed. Gabriel A. Almond and Sidney Verba. Boston: Little, Brown & Co., pp. 1–36.
Almond, Gabriel A. and Sidney Verba. 1963. *The Civic Culture: Political Attitudes and Democracy in Five Nations*. Princeton: Princeton University Press.
Andersen, Johannes, Ann-Dorte Christensen, Kamma Langberg, Birte Siim, and Lars Torpe. 1993. *Medborgerskab: Demokrati og politisk deltagelse*. Herning: Systime.
Andersen, Jørgen Goul. 1996. Membership and Participation in Voluntary Associations in Scandinavia in a Comparative Perspective. Aalborg University: Department of Economics, Politics and Public Administration. The Democratic Citizenship in the Nordic Countries. Project paper no. 8.
Andersen, Jørgen Goul and Jens Hoff. 2001. *Democracy and Citizenship in Scandinavia*. New York: Palgrave Macmillan.
Andersen, Jørgen Goul, Lars Torpe, and Johannes Andersen. 2000. *Hvad folket magter*. Copenhagen: Jurist- og Økonomforbundets Forlag.
Anderson, Christopher J. 1998. Political Satisfaction in Old and New Democracies. Working Paper 98.4. Institute for European Studies. Cornell University.
Anderson, Christopher J. and Christine A. Guillory. 1997. Political institutions and satisfaction with democracy: a cross-national analysis of consensus and majoritarian systems. *American Political Science Review* 91 (1): 66–81.
Anderson, Christopher J. and Andrew J. LoTempio. 2002. Winning, losing, and political trust in America. *British Journal of Political Science* 32 (2): 335–51.
Anderson, Christopher J. and Yuliya V. Tverdova. 2001. Winners, losers, and attitudes about government in contemporary democracies. *International Political Science Review* 22 (4): 321–33.
Ash, Timothy G. 2000. Conclusions. In *Between Past and Future: The Revolutions of 1989 and Their Aftermath*, ed. Sorin Antohi and Vladimir Tismaneanu. Budapest: Central European University Press, pp. 395–402.

Babchuk, Nicholas and John N. Edwards. 1965. Voluntary associations and the integration hypothesis. *Sociological Inquiry* 35 (Spring): 149–62.

Badescu, Gabriel. 2003. Social trust and democratization in the post-communist societies. In *Social Capital and Democratic Transition*, ed. Gabriel Badescu and Eric M. Uslaner. London: Routledge, pp. 120–40.

Badescu, Gabriel, Paul Sum, and Eric Uslaner. 2004. Civil society development and democratic values in Romania and Moldova. *East European Politics and Societies* 18 (2): 316–42.

Balch, George. 1971. Multiple indicators in survey research: the concept 'sense of political efficacy'. *Political Methodology* 1: 1–43.

Barber, Benjamin. 1984. *Strong Democracy. Participatory Politics for a New Age*. Berkeley: University of California Press.

Barber, Benjamin. 1995. *Jihad vs. McWorld*. New York: Times Books.

Barnes, Marian and Alan Walker. 1996. Consumerism versus empowerment: a principled approach to the involvement of older service users. *Policy & Politics* 24 (4): 375–93.

Barnes, Marian and Lorna Warren. 1999. Introduction. In *Paths to Empowerment*, ed. Marian Barnes and Lorna Warren. Bristol: Policy Press, pp. 1–10.

Barnes, Samuel H., Max Kaase, Klaus R. Allerbeck, Barbara G. Farah, Felix Heunks, Ronald Inglehart, M. Kent Jennings, Hans O. Klingemann, Alan Marsh, and Leopold Rosenmayr, ed. 1979. *Political Action: Mass Participation in Five Western Democracies*. Beverly Hills: Sage Publications.

Barry, Brian. 2001. *Culture and Equality: An Egalitarian Critique of Multiculturalism*. Cambridge: Polity Press.

Bartolini, Stefano and Peter Mair. 1990. *Identity, Competition, and Electoral Availability. The Stabilisation of European Electorates 1885–1985*. Cambridge: Cambridge University Press.

Baumgartner, Frank R. and Beth L. Leech. 1998. *Basic Interests: The Importance of Groups in Politics and Political Science*. Princeton: Princeton University Press.

Baumgartner, Frank R. and Jack L. Walker. 1988. Survey research and membership in voluntary associations. *American Journal of Political Science* 32 (4): 908–28.

Beitz, Charles. 1989. *Political Equality. An Essay in Democratic Theory*. Princeton: Princeton University Press.

Bennett, Stephen Earl. 1984. Apathy in America, 1964–1982: a new measure applied to old questions. *Micropolitics* 3 (4): 499–545.

Bennett, Stephen Earl. 1986. *Apathy in America 1960–1984: Causes and Consequences of Citizen Political Indifference*. Dobbs Ferry, New York: Transnational Publishers.

Berlin, Isaiah. [1969] 1988. *Four Essays on Liberty*. Oxford: Oxford University Press.

Berman, Sheri. 1997. Civil society and the collapse of the Weimar Republic. *World Politics* 49: 401–29.

Blais, André, Louis Massicotte, and Antoine Yoshinaka. 2001. Deciding who has the right to vote: a comparative analysis of election laws. *Electoral Studies* 20: 41–62.

Bobo, Lawrence and Frederick Licardi. 1989. Education and political tolerance. *Public Opinion Quarterly* 53 (3): 285–308.

Bock, Gisela. 2002. *Women in European History*. Oxford: Blackwell.

Boix, Carles and Daniel N. Posner. 1996. Making Social Capital Work: A Review of Robert Putnam's Making Democracy Work: Civic Traditions in Modern Italy. Working Paper Series, vol. 96, no. 4. Cambridge: Center for International Affairs, Harvard University.

Booth, John A. and Patricia Bayer Richard. 2001. Civil society and political context in Central America. In *Beyond Tocqueville: Civil Society and the Social Capital Debate in Comparative Perspective*, ed. Bob Edwards, Michael W. Foley, and Mario Diani. Hanover, New Hampshire: University Press of New England.

Booth, John A. and Mitchell A. Seligson. 1978. Images of political participation in Latin America. In *Political Participation in Latin America, vol I: Citizen and State*, ed. John A. Booth and Mitchell A. Seligson. New York: Holmes and Meier.

Bouckaert, Geert and Steven van de Walle. 2001. Government Performance and Trust in Government. Presented at the annual conference of the European Group on Public Administration. Vaasa, Finland.

Bourdieu, Pierre. 1980. *Le Sens Pratique*. Paris: Minuit.

Brady, Henry. 1999. Political participation. In *Measures of Political Attitudes*, ed. John P. Robinson, Phillip R. Shaver, and Lawrence S. Wrightsman. San Diego: Academic Press.

Brady, Henry E., Sidney Verba, and Kay Lehman Schlozman. 1995. Beyond SES: a resource model of political participation. *American Political Science Review* 89 (2): 271–94.

Braithwaite, Valerie and Margaret Levi. 1998. *Trust and Governance*. New York: Russell Sage Foundation.

Brehm, John and Wendy Rahn. 1997. Individual-level evidence for the causes and consequences of social capital. *American Journal of Political Science* 41 (3): 999–1023.

Brewer, Marilynn B. and Roderick M. Kramer. 1986. Choice behavior in social dilemmas: effects of social identity, group size, and decision framing. *Journal of Personality and Social Psychology* 50: 543–9.

Buchanan, James M. 1965. An economic theory of clubs. *Economica* 3: 1–14.

Burns, Nancy, Kay Lehman Schlozman, and Sidney Verba. 2001. *The Private Roots of Public Action: Gender, Equality, and Political Participation*. Cambridge: Harvard University Press.

Campbell, Angus and Philip E. Converse. 1972. *The Human Meaning of Social Change*. New York: Russell Sage Foundation.

Campbell, Angus, Gerald Gurin, and Warren E. Miller. 1954. *The Voter Decides*. Evanston, Illinois: Row, Peterson.

Christensen, Tom and Per Laegreid. 2002. Trust in Government: The Relative Importance of Service Satisfaction, Political Factors and Demography. Presented at the annual conference of the European Group on Public Administration, Potsdam, Germany.

Christiansen, Peter Munk. 1993. *Det frie marked – den forhandlede økonomi*. Copenhagen: Jurist- og Økonomforbundets Forlag.

Citrin, Jack. 1974. Comment: the political relevance of trust in government. *American Political Science Review* 68 (3): 973–88.

Claibourn, Michele and Paul S. Martin. 2000. Trusting and joining? an empirical test of the reciprocal nature of social capital. *Political Behavior* 22: 267–91.

Clarke, Harold D., Nitish Dutt, and Allan Kornberg. 1993. The political economy of attitudes toward polity and society in western European democracies. *Journal of Politics* 55: 998–1021.

Clarke, Harold D., David Sanders, Marianne C. Stewart, and Paul F. Whiteley. 2002. Downs, Stokes and modified rational choice: modelling turnout in 2001. In *British Elections & Parties Review, Volume 12: The 2001 General Election*, ed. Lynn

Bennie, Colin Rallings, Jonathan Tonge, and Paul Webb. London: Frank Cass Publishers, pp. 28–47.
Cohen, Jean. 1999. Trust, voluntary association and workable democracy: the contemporary American discourse of civil society. In *Democracy and Trust*, ed. Mark E. Warren. Cambridge: Cambridge University Press, pp. 208–48.
Cohen, Joshua and Joel Rogers. 1992. Secondary associations and democratic governance. *Politics and Society* 20 (4): 393–472.
Coleman, James S. 1973. *The Mathematics of Collective Action*. Chicago: Aldine.
Coleman, James S. 1988. Social capital in the creation of human capital. *American Journal of Sociology* 94: 95–120.
Coleman, James S. 1990. *Foundations of Social Theory*. Cambridge: The Belknap Press of Harvard University Press.
Conover, Pamela Johnston, Ivor M. Crewe, and Donald D. Searing. 1991. The nature of citizenship in the United States and Great Britain: empirical comments on theoretical themes. *Journal of Politics* 53: 800–32.
Conover, Pamela Johnston and Donald D. Searing. 2002. Expanding the envelope: citizenship, contextual methodologies, and comparative political psychology. In *Thinking about Political Psychology*, ed. James H. Kuklinski. Cambridge: Cambridge University Press, pp. 89–114.
Constant, Benjamin. [1819] 1986. De la liberté des anciens comparée à celle des modernes. In *L'esprit de conquête et de l'usurpation*, ed. Ephraïm Harpaz. Paris: Garnier-Flammarion.
Converse, Philip E. 1964. The nature of belief systems in mass publics. In *Ideology and Discontent*, ed. David Apter. New York: The Free Press.
Craig, Gary and Marjorie Mayo, eds. 1995. *Community Empowerment. A Reader in Participation and Development*. London: Zed Books.
Craig, Stephen. 1993. *The Malevolent Leaders: Popular Discontent in America*. Boulder, Colorado: Westview Press.
Crozier, Michel, Samuel Huntington, and Joji Watanuki. 1975. *The Crisis of Democracy: Report on the Governability of Democracies to the Trilateral Commission*. New York: New York University Press.
Curtis, James E., Edward G. Grabb, and Douglas E. Baer. 1992. Voluntary association membership in fifteen countries. *American Sociological Review* 57: 139–52.
Curtis, James E., Douglas E. Baer, and Edward G. Grabb. 2001. Nations of joiners: explaining voluntary association membership in democratic societies. *American Sociological Review* 66 (4): 783–805.
Dahl, Robert A. 1956. *A Preface to Democratic Theory*. Chicago: University of Chicago Press.
Dahl, Robert A. 1971. *Polyarchy: Participation and Opposition*. New Haven: Yale University Press.
Dalton, Russell J. 1988. *Citizen Politics in Western Democracies. Public Opinion and Political Parties in the United States, Great Britain, West Germany, and France*. Chatham, New Jersey: Chatham House.
Dalton, Russell J. 1994. Communists and democrats: attitudes towards democracy in the two Germanys. *British Journal of Political Science* 24: 469–93.
Dalton, Russell J. 2002. *Citizen Politics: Public Opinion and Political Parties in Advanced Industrial Democracies*. 3rd edn. New York: Seven Bridges Press.
Dasgupta, Partha and Ismail Serageldin, eds. 2000. *Social Capital. A Multifaceted Perspective*. Washington, DC: The World Bank.

Davis, James A. 1975. Communism, conformity, cohorts and categories: American tolerance in 1954 and 1972–73. *American Journal of Sociology* 81: 491–513.

Dekker, Paul and Andries van den Broek. 1995. Citizen Participation in Civil Societies. Presented at the annual meeting of the International Society of Political Psychology, Washington, DC.

Dekker, Paul and Andries van den Broek. 1996. Volunteering and politics: involvement in voluntary associations from a 'civic culture' perspective. In *Political Value Change in Western Democracies: Integration, Values, Identification, and Participation*, ed. Loek Halman and Neil Nevitte. Tilburg: Tilburg University Press, pp. 125–51.

Dekker, Paul and Eric M. Uslaner, ed. 2001. *Social Capital and Participation in Everyday Life*. London: Routledge.

Delhey, Jan and Kenneth Newton. 2003. Who trusts? the origins of social trust in seven societies. *European Societies* 5 (2): 93–137.

Denters, Bas. 2002. Size and political trust: evidence from Denmark, the Netherlands, Norway and the United Kingdom. *Government and Planning C: Environment and Planning* 20: 793–812.

Denters, Bas and Peter Geurts. 1998. Opvattingen over politieke machteloosheid tegenover de gemeentelijke en de nationale overheid. In *Lokale democratie in Nederland: burgers en hun gemeentebestuur*, ed. Bas Denters and Peter Geurts. Bussum: Coutinho, pp. 55–108.

Diani, Mario. 2000. Capitale Sociale, Partecipazione Associativa e Fiducia Istituzionale. *Rivista Italiana di Scienza Politica* 30 (3): 475–511.

Di Palma, Giuseppe. 1970. *Apathy and Participation. Mass Politics in Western Societies*. New York: The Free Press.

Dixon, Anna and Elias Mossialos, ed. 2002. *Health Care Systems in Eight Countries: Trends and Challenges*. London: European Observatory on Health Care Systems.

Dogan, Mattei. 1997. Erosion of confidence in advanced democracies. *Studies in Comparative International Development* 32: 3–29.

Döring, Herbert. 1992. Higher education and confidence in institutions: a secondary analysis of the 'European Values Survey' 1981–83. *West European Politics* 15: 126–46.

Downs, Anthony. 1957. *An Economic Theory of Democracy*. New York: Harper & Row.

Dunn, John. 1993. Trust. In *A Companion to Contemporary Political Philosophy*, ed. Robert E. Goodin and Philip Pettit. Oxford: Blackwell.

Dworkin, Ronald. 1981. What is equality? *Philosophy and Public Affairs* 10 (3–4): 185–246, 283–345.

Eastis, Carla M. 1998. Organizational diversity and the production of social capital. One of these groups is not like the other. *American Behavioral Scientist* 42 (1): 66–77.

Easton, David. 1953. *The Political System: An Inquiry into the State of Political Science*. New York: Alfred A. Knopf.

Easton, David. 1965. *A Systems Analysis of Political Life*. Chicago: University of Chicago Press.

Easton, David. 1975. A re-assessment of the concept of political support. *British Journal of Political Science* 5: 447–53.

Easton, David and Jack Dennis. 1969. *Children and the Political System*. New York: McGraw-Hill.

Edwards, Bob, Michael W. Foley, and Mario Diani, eds. 2001. *Beyond Tocqueville:*

Civil Society and the Social Capital Debate in Comparative Perspective. Hanover, New Hampshire: University Press of New England.

Elster, Jon, ed. 1998. *Deliberative Democracy*. Cambridge: Cambridge University Press.

Emmert, Thomas, Matthias Jung, and Dieter Roth. 2001. Das Ende einer Ära – Die Bundestagswahl vom 27 September 1998. In *Wahlen und Wähler: Analysen aus Anlass der Bundestagswahl 1998*, ed. Hans-Dieter Klingemann and Max Kaase. Wiesbaden: Westdeutscher Verlag.

Encarnación, Omar. 2003. *The Myth of Civil Society: Social Capital and Democratic Consolidation in Spain and Brazil*. New York: Palgrave Macmillan.

Erbe, William. 1964. Social involvement and political activity: a replication and elaboration. *American Sociological Review* 24 (2): 198–215.

Erickson, Bonnie H. and Terry A. Nosanchuk. 1990. How an apolitical association politicizes. *Canadian Review of Sociology and Anthropology* 27 (2): 206–19.

Esaiasson, Peter. 2005. Will Citizens Take No For An Answer? On the Relationship between Fair Procedures and Legitimate Authorities. Presented at the third ECPR conference, Budapest.

Esping-Andersen, Gøsta. 1991. *The Three Worlds of Welfare Capitalism*. London: Polity Press.

Ester, Peter, Loek Halman, and Rud de Moor. 1993. *The Individualising Society: Value Change in Europe and North America*. Tilburg: Tilburg University Press.

Farah, Barbara G., Samuel H. Barnes, and Felix Heunks. 1979. Political dissatisfaction. In *Political Action. Mass Participation in Five Western Democracies*, ed. Samuel H. Barnes *et al*. Beverly Hills: Sage Publications.

Feldman, Stanley and Marco R. Steenbergen. 1996. Beyond self-interest, toward other-directedness: prosocial orientations and political behavior. In *Research in Micropolitics, Volume. 5: New Directions in Political Psychology*, ed. Michael Delli Carpini, Leonie Huddy, and Robert Y. Shapiro. Greenwich, Connecticut: JAI Press, pp. 61–93.

Finkel, Steven E., Edward N. Muller, and Karl-Dieter Opp. 1989. Personal influence, collective rationality and mass political action. *American Political Science Review* 83 (3): 885–903.

Finkel, Steven E. and Karl-Dieter Opp. 1991. Party identification and participation in collective political action. *Journal of Politics* 53 (2): 339–71.

Fiorina, Morris P. 1999. Extreme voices: a dark side of civic engagement. In *Civic Engagement in American Democracy*, ed. Theda Skocpol and Morris P. Fiorina. Washington, DC: Brookings Institution Press, pp. 395–425.

Fisher, Claude S. 1982. *To Dwell Among Friends: Personal Networks in Town and City*. Chicago: University of Chicago Press.

Fishman, Robert. 2004. *Democracy's Voices. Social Ties and the Quality of Public Life in Spain*. Ithaca: Cornell University Press.

Foley, Michael W. and Bob Edwards. 1996. The Paradox of Civil Society. *Journal of Democracy* 7: 38–52.

Franklin, Mark N., Thomas T. Mackie, Henry Valen, Clive Bean, Ole Borre, Harold Clarke, Papayote Dimitras, Cees van der Eijk, Tom Lancaster, Michael Lewis-Beck, Brad Lockerbie, Ian McAllister, Renato Mannheimer, Michael Marsh, Arthur Miller, Peter Much, Anthony Mughan, Kees Niemöller, Maria Oskarson, Franz Pappi, Giancomo Sani, Andrew Skalaban, and Marianne Stewart, eds. 1992. *Electoral Change. Responses to Evolving Social and Attitudinal Structures in Western Countries*. Cambridge: Cambridge University Press.

Freitag, Markus. 2003. Social capital in (dis)similar democracies: the development of generalized trust in Japan and Switzerland. *Comparative Political Studies* 36 (8): 936–66.
Friedrich, Robert J. 1982. In defense of multiplicative terms in multiple regression equations. *American Journal of Political Science* 26 (4): 797–833.
Fuchs, Dieter and Hans-Dieter Klingemann. 1995. Citizens and the State: a changing relationship? In *Citizens and the State*, ed. Hans-Dieter Klingemann and Dieter Fuchs. Oxford: Oxford University Press, pp. 1–23
Fuchs, Dieter, Giovanna Guidorossi, and Palle Svensson. 1995. Support for the democratic system. In *Citizens and the State*, ed. Hans-Dieter Klingemann and Dieter Fuchs. Oxford: Oxford University Press, pp. 323–53.
Gabriel, Oscar W. 1986. *Politische Kultur, Postmaterialismus und Materialismus in der Bundesrepublik Deutschland*. Opladen: Westdeutscher Verlag.
Gabriel, Oscar W. 1995. Political efficacy and trust. In *The Impact of Values*, ed. Jan W. van Deth and Elinor Scarbrough. Oxford: Oxford University Press.
Gabriel, Oscar W. 2002. Neue Köpfe – bessere Stimmung? Eine Analyse der Implikationen des Regierungswechsels 1998 für die Einstellungen der Bevölkerung zum politischen System der Bundesrepublik. In *Wahlen und Wähler. Analysen aus Anlass der Bundestagswahl 1998*, ed. Hans-Dieter Klingemann and Max Kaase. Wiesbaden: Westdeutscher Verlag, pp. 163–203.
Gabriel, Oscar W. and Volker Kunz. 2000. Soziale Integration und politische Partizipation. Das Konzept des Sozialkapitals – Ein brauchbarer Ansatz zur Erklärung politischer Partizipation? In *Kontext, Akteur und strategische Interaktion*, ed. Ulrich Druwe, Stefan Kühnel, and Volker Kunz. Opladen: Leske + Budrich, pp. 47–74.
Gabriel, Oscar W. and Volker Kunz. N.d. *Engagement in Freiwilligenorganisationen*. Wiesbaden: VS Verlag für Sozialwissenschaften. Forthcoming.
Gabriel, Oscar W., Volker Kunz, Sigrid Roßteutscher, and Jan W. van Deth. 2002. *Sozialkapital und Demokratie. Zivilgesellschaftliche Ressourcen im internationalen Vergleich*. Vienna: Wiener Universitätsverlag.
Gallagher, Michael, Michael Laver, and Peter Mair. 2001. *Representative Government in Modern Europe. Institutions, Parties, and Governments*. 3rd edn. New York: McGraw-Hill.
Gambetta, Diego, ed. 1988a. *Trust: Making and Breaking Cooperative Relations*. Oxford: Blackwell.
Gambetta, Diego. 1988b. Can we trust trust? In *Trust: Making and Breaking Cooperative Relations*, ed. Diego Gambetta. Oxford: Blackwell.
Gamson, William A. 1968. *Power and Discontent*. Homewood, Illinois: The Dorsey Press.
Gaskin, Katharine and Justin Davis Smith. 1995. *A New Civic Europe? A Study of the Extent and Role of Volunteering*. London: Volunteer Centre UK.
Gensicke, Thomas. 2001. Das bürgerliche Engagement de Deutschen. Image, Intensität und Bereiche. In Bürgerengagement in Deutschland. Bestandsaufrahmen und Perspektiven, ed. Rolf G. Herinze and Thomas Olk. Opladen: Leske + Budrich, pp. 283–304.
Gibson, James L. 1992a. The political consequences of intolerance: culture conformity and political freedom *American Political Science Review* 86 (2): 338–56.
Gibson, James L. 1992b. Alternative measures of political tolerance: must tolerance be 'least-liked'? *American Journal of Political Science* 36 (2): 560–77.

Gibson, James L. 2003. Social networks, civil society, and the prospects for consolidating Russia's democratic transition. In *Social Capital and the Transition to Democracy*, ed. Gabriel Badescu and Eric M.Uslaner. London: Routledge.
Gibson, James L. and Amanda Gouws. 2000. Social identities and political intolerance: linkages within the South African mass public. *American Journal of Political Science* 44 (2): 278–92.
Giddens, Anthony. 1990. *The Consequences of Modernity*. Stanford: Stanford University Press.
Goertz, Gary and Harvey Starr. 2001. Necessary Conditions: Theory, Methodology, and Applications. Manuscript.
Goodwin, Barbara. 1997. *Using Political Ideas*. Chichester: Wiley.
Gould, Carol. 1988. *Rethinking Democracy: Freedom and Social Cooperation in Politics, Economy, and Society*. Cambridge: Cambridge University Press.
Granovetter, Mark S. 1973. The strength of weak ties. *American Journal of Sociology* 78: 1360–80.
Gunther, Richard and José Ramón Montero. 2004. Attitudes toward democracy in seven countries: dimensional structure and behavioral correlates. *Studies in Public Policy 385*. Glasgow: University of Strathclyde.
Habermas, Jürgen, 1961. *Student und Politik*. Neuwied am Rhein: Luchterhand.
Habermas, Jürgen. 1994. Human rights and popular sovereignty: the liberal and the Republican versions. *Ratio Juris* 7: 1–13.
Hall, Peter. 1999. Social capital in Britain. *British Journal of Political Science* 29: 417–59.
Hardin, Russell. 1991a. Hobbesian political order. *Political Theory* 19 (2): 156–80.
Hardin, Russell. 1991b. Trusting persons, trusting institutions. In *The Strategy of Choice*, ed. Richard J. Zeckhauser. Cambridge: MIT Press.
Hardin, Russell. 1993. The street-level epistemology of trust. *Politics and Society* 21 (4): 505–29.
Hardin, Russell. 1996. Trustworthiness. *Ethics* 107: 26–42.
Hardin, Russell. 1998. Trust in government. In *Trust and Governance,* ed. Valerie Braithwaite and Margaret Levi. New York: Russell Sage Foundation.
Hardin, Russell. 1999. Do we want trust in government? In *Democracy and Trust*, ed. Mark E. Warren. Cambridge: Cambridge University Press.
Hardin, Russell. 2000. The public trust. In *Disaffected Democracies: What's Troubling the Trilateral Countries?*, ed. Susan Pharr and Robert D. Putnam. Princeton: Princeton University Press.
Hardin, Russell. 2002. *Trust and Trustworthiness*. New York: Russell Sage Foundation.
Hart, Vivien. 1978. *Distrust and Democracy. Political Distrust in Britain and America*. Cambridge: Cambridge University Press.
Held, David. 1987. *Models of Democracy*. Cambridge: Polity Press.
Hernes, Helga. 1988. Scandinavian citizenship. *Acta Sociologica* 31 (3): 199–215.
Hirschman, Albert O. 1970. *Exit, Voice, and Loyalty: Responses to Decline in Firms, Organizations, and States*. Cambridge: Harvard University Press.
Hirschman, Albert O. 1982. *Shifting Involvements: Private Interests and Public Action*. Princeton: Princeton University Press.
Hirst, Paul. 1994. *Associative Democracy*. Oxford: Polity Press.
Hollis, Martin. 1998. *Trust within Reason*. Cambridge: Cambridge University Press.
Holmberg, Sören. 1999. Down and down we go: political trust in Sweden. In

Critical Citizens. Global Support for Democratic Government, ed. Pippa Norris. Oxford: Oxford University Press, pp. 103–22.
Hooghe, Marc. 2003. Voluntary associations and democratic attitudes: value congruence as a causal mechanism. In *Generating Social Capital: Civil Society and Institutions in Comparative Perspective*, ed. Marc Hooghe and Dietlind Stolle. New York: Palgrave Macmillan.
Hooghe, Marc and Dietlind Stolle. 2003a. Age matters: life cycle and cohort differences in the socialisation effect of voluntary participation. *European Political Science* 2 (3): 49–56.
Hooghe, Marc and Dietlind Stolle, ed. 2003b. *Generating Social Capital: Civil Society and Institutions in Comparative Perspective*. New York: Palgrave Macmillan.
Howard, Marc. 2003a. *The Weakness of Civil Society in Post-Communist Europe*. Cambridge University Press.
Howard, Marc. 2003b. Why post-communist citizens do not join voluntary organisations. In *Social Capital and Democratic Transition*, ed. Gabriel Badescu and Eric M. Uslaner. London: Routledge, pp. 165–84.
Huckfeldt, Robert and John Sprague. 1991. Discussant effects on vote choice: intimacy, structure, and interdependence. *The Journal of Politics* 53: 122–58.
Huckfeldt, Robert and John Sprague. 1995. *Citizens, Politics, and Social Communication: Information and Influence in an Election Campaign*. Cambridge: Cambridge University Press.
Huntington, Samuel P. and Joan M. Nelson. 1976. *No Easy Choice: Political Participation in Developing Countries*. Cambridge: Harvard University Press.
Inglehart, Ronald. 1977. *The Silent Revolution: Changing Values and Political Styles Among Western Publics*. Princeton: Princeton University Press.
Inglehart, Ronald. 1979. Political action. The impact of values, cognitive level, and social background. In *Political Action: Mass Participation in Five Western Democracies*, ed. Samuel H. Barnes *et al.* Beverly Hills: Sage Publications, pp. 343–80.
Inglehart, Ronald. 1990. *Culture Shift in Advanced Industrial Society*. Princeton: Princeton University Press.
Inglehart, Ronald. 1997. *Modernization and Postmodernization: Cultural, Economic and Political Change in 43 Societies*. Princeton: Princeton University Press.
Inglehart, Ronald. 1999. Postmodernization erodes respect for authority, but increases support for democracy. In *Critical Citizens. Global Support for Democratic Governance*, ed. Pippa Norris. Oxford: Oxford University Press, pp. 236–56.
Inglehart, Ronald and Pippa Norris. 2000. The developmental theory of the gender gap: women's and men's voting behavior in global perspective. *International Political Science Review* 21 (4): 441–63.
Jenkins, J. Craig and Charles Perrow. 1977. Insurgency of the powerless: farm worker movements (1946–1972). *American Sociological Review* 42: 249–68.
Jennings, M. Kent and Jan W. van Deth. 1990. Some consequences for systems and governments. In *Continuities in Political Action: A Longitudinal Study of Political Orientations in Three Western Democracies*, ed. M. Kent Jennings, Jan W. van Deth *et al.* Berlin: Walter de Gruyter.
Jennings, M. Kent, Jan W. van Deth, Samuel H. Barnes, Dieter Fuchs, Felix J. Heunles, Ronald Inglehart, Max Kaase, Hans-Dieter Klingemann, and Jacques J.A. Thomassen, 1990. *Continuities in Political Action: A Longitudinal Study of Political Orientations in Three Western Democracies*. Berlin: Walter de Gruyter.

Jones, Emma and John Gaventa. 2002. *Concepts of Citizenship: A Review*. IDS Development Bibliography 19. Brighton: Institute of Development Studies.

Jordan, Grant and William A. Maloney. 1997. *The Protest Business? Mobilizing Campaign Groups*. Manchester: Manchester University Press.

Kaase, Max. 1999. Interpersonal trust, political trust and non-institutionalised political participation in western Europe. *West European Politics* 22 (3): 1–23.

Kaase, Max and Alan Marsh. 1979. Political action. A theoretical perspective. In *Political Action: Mass Participation in Five Western Democracies*, ed. Samuel H. Barnes *et al*. Beverly Hills: Sage, pp. 27–56.

Kaase, Max and Kenneth Newton. 1995. *Beliefs in Government*. Oxford: Oxford University Press.

Kalb, Don. 2002. Afterword: globalism and postsocialism perspective. In *Postsocialism. Ideals, Ideologies and Practices in Eurasia*, ed. Chris Hann. London: Routledge, pp. 317–35.

Katz, Daniel and Paul F. Lazarsfeld. 1955. *Personal Influence: The Part Played by People in the Flow of Mass Communications*. New York: The Free Press.

Katzenstein, Peter J. 2000. Confidence, trust, international relations and lessons from smaller democracies. In *Disaffected Democracies: What's Troubling the Trilateral Countries?*, ed. Susan J. Pharr and Robert D. Putnam. Princeton: Princeton University Press, pp. 121–48.

King, Anthony. 1975. Overload: problems of governing in the 1970s. *Political Studies* 23: 284–96.

Kitschelt, Herbert, Zdenka Mansfeldova, Radoslaw Markoski, and Gabor Toka. 1999. *Post-Communist Party Systems: Competition Representation and Inter-Party Cooperation*. Cambridge: Cambridge University Press.

Klages, Helmut. 1984. *Wertorientierungen im Wandel*. Frankfurt am Main: Campus.

Klages, Helmut. 2000a. Engagement und Engagementpotential in Deutschland. In *Die Zukunft von Arbeit und Demokratie*, ed. Ulrich Beck. Frankfurt am Main: Suhrkamp, pp. 151–70.

Klages, Helmut. 2000b. Engagementpotenzial in Deutschland. In *Freiwilliges Engagement in Deutschland. Ergebnisse der Repräsentativerhebung zu Ehrenamt, Freiwilligenarbeit und bürgerschaftlichem Engagement. Band 2: Zugangswege zum Freiwilligen Engagement und Engagementpotenzial in den neuen und alten Bundesländern*, ed. Joachim Braun und Helmut Klages. Stuttgart: Kohlhammer, pp. 114–98.

Klages, Helmut and Thomas Gensicke. 1999. *Wertewandel und bürgerschaftliches Engagement an der Schwelle zum 21. Jahrhundert*. Speyerer Forschungsberichte 193. Speyer: Forschungsinstitut für öffentliche Verwaltung.

Klingemann, Hans-Dieter. 1999. Mapping political support in the 1990s: a global analysis. In *Critical Citizens. Global Support for Democratic Government*, ed. Pippa Norris. Oxford: Oxford University Press, pp. 31–56.

Klingemann, Hans-Dieter and Dieter Fuchs, ed. 1995. *Citizens and the State*. Oxford: Oxford University Press.

Klosko, George. 2000. *Democratic Procedures and Liberal Consensus*. Oxford: Oxford University Press.

Knack, Stephen and Philip Keefer. 1997. Does social capital have an economic payoff? A cross-country investigation. *Quarterly Journal of Economics* 112 (4): 1251–88.

Knoke, David. 1982. Political mobilization by voluntary associations. *Journal of Political and Military Sociology* 10 (Fall): 171–82.

Knoke, David. 1986. Associations and interest groups. *Annual Review of Sociology* 12: 8–9.
Kohn, Melvin L. and Carmi Schooler. 1982. Stratification, occupation, and orientation. In *Work and Personality: An Inquiry into the Impact of Social Stratification*, ed. Melvin Kohn and Carmi Schooler. Norwood: Ablex, pp. 5–53.
Kollock, Peter. 1998. Transforming social dilemmas: group identity and cooperation. In *Modeling Rational and Moral Agents*, ed. Paul Danielson. Oxford: Oxford University Press.
Kornberg, Allan and Harold D. Clarke. 1992. *Citizens and Community. Political Support in a Representative Democracy*. Cambridge: Cambridge University Press.
Kornhauser, William. 1960. *The Politics of Mass Society*. London: Routledge and Kegan Paul.
Kriesi, Hanspeter, Ruud Koopmans, Jan Willem Duyvendak, and Marco G. Giugni. 1995. *New Social Movements in Western Europe. A Comparative Analysis*. London: UCL Press.
Krosnick, Jon A. and Leandre R. Fabrigar. 1997. Designing rating scales for effective measurement in surveys. In *Survey Measurement and Process Quality*, ed. Lars E. Lyberg, Paul Biemer, Martin Collins, Edith de Leeuw, Cathryn Dippo, Norbert Schwartz, and Dennis Trewin. New York: Wiley.
Kuechler, Manfred. 1991. The dynamics of mass political support in western Europe: methodological problems and preliminary findings. In *Eurobarometer. The Dynamics of European Public Opinion*, ed. Karlheinz Reif and Ronald Inglehart. London: Macmillan.
Kymlicka, Will. 1990. *Contemporary Political Philosophy: An Introduction*. Oxford: Clarendon Press.
Kymlicka, Will and Wayne Norman. 1995. Return of the citizen: a survey of recent work on citizenship theory. In *Theorizing Citizenship*, ed. Ronald Beiner. Albany: State University of New York Press, pp. 283–322.
Lane, Robert E. 1965. *Political Life. Why and How People Get Involved in Politics*. New York: Free Press.
Lawrence, David. 1976. Procedural norms and tolerance: a reassessment. *American Political Science Review* 70 (1): 70–80.
Lazarsfeld, Paul F., Bernard Berelson, and Hazel Gaudet. 1944. *The People's Choice: How the Voter Makes Up His Mind in a Presidential Campaign*. New York: Duell, Sloan and Pearce.
Leighley, Jan. 1996. Group membership and the mobilization of political participation. *The Journal of Politics* 58 (2): 447–63.
Lepsius, M. Rainer. 1979. Parteiensystem und Sozialstruktur: zum Problem der Demokratisierung der deutschen Gesellschaft. In *Deutsche Parteien vor 1918*, ed. Gerhard A. Ritter. Köln: Kiepenheuer und Witsch.
Lerner, Daniel. 1958. *The Passing of Traditional Society: Modernizing the Middle East*. Glencoe: The Free Press.
Levi, Margaret. 1996. Social and unsocial capital: a review essay of Robert Putnam's making democracy work. *Politics and Society* 24 (1): 45–55.
Levi, Margaret and Laura Stoker. 2000. Political trust and trustworthiness. *Annual Review of Political Science* 3: 475–508.
Lewis, J. David and Andrew Weigert. 1985. Trust as a social reality. *Social Forces* 63: 967–85.
Linde, Jonas and Joakim Ekman. 2003. Satisfaction with democracy: a note on a

frequently used indicator in comparative politics. *European Journal of Political Research* 42 (3): 391–408.
Linz, Juan. 1988. Legitimacy of democracy and the socioeconomic system. In *Comparing Pluralist Democracies*, ed. Mattei Dogan. Boulder: Westview Press.
Lipset, Seymour Martin. 1960. *Political Man: The Social Basis of Politics*. New York: Doubleday.
Lipset, Seymour Martin. 1994. The social requisites of democracy revisited. *American Sociological Review* 59 (1): 1–22.
Lipset, Seymour Martin and William Schneider. 1983. *The Confidence Gap*. New York: The Free Press.
Lipset, Seymour Martin, Paul F. Lazarsfeld, Allen H. Barton, and Juan Linz. 1954. The psychology of voting: an analysis of voting behavior. In *Handbook of Social Psychology, Volume 2*, ed. Gardner Lindzey. Reading, Massachusetts: Addison-Wesley, pp. 1124–75
Lipset, Seymour Martin and Stein Rokkan. 1967. Cleavage structures, party systems, and voter alignments: an introduction. In *Party Systems and Voter Alignments: Cross National Perspectives*, ed. Seymour Martin Lipsert and Stein Rokkan. New York: The Free Press.
Lipsky, Martin. 1980. *Street Level Bureaucracy*. New York: Russell Sage Foundation.
Listhaug, Ola. 1995. The dynamics of trust in politicians. In *Citizens and the State*, ed. Hans-Dieter Klingemann and Dieter Fuchs. Oxford: Oxford University Press, pp. 261–97.
Listhaug, Ola. 1998. Confidence in Political Institutions: Norway 1982–96. Manuscript.
Listhaug, Ola and Matti Wiberg. 1995. Confidence in political and private institutions. In *Citizens and the State*, ed. Hans-Dieter Klingemann and Dieter Fuchs. Oxford: Oxford University Press.
Lowndes, Vivien. 2000. Women and social capital: a comment on Hall's social capital in Britain. *British Journal of Sociology* 30: 533–40.
Luhmann, Niklas. 1979. *Trust and Power*. New York: Wiley.
Luhmann, Niklas. 1988a. Trust: a mechanism for the reduction of social complexity. In *Trust and Power*, ed. Niklas Luhmann. New York: Wiley.
Luhmann, Niklas. 1988b. Familiarity, confidence, trust: problems and perspectives. In *Trust: Making and Breaking Cooperative Relations*, ed. Diego Gambetta. Oxford: Blackwell.
Lukes, Steven. 1974. *Power: A Radical View*. London: Macmillan.
Lupia, Arthur and Mathew D. McCubbins. 1998. *The Democratic Dilemma. Can Citizens Learn What They Need to Know?* Cambridge: Cambridge University Press.
McAdam, Doug. 1982. *Political Process and the Development of Black Insurgency, 1930–1970*. Chicago: University of Chicago Press.
McAdam, Doug. 1988. Micromobilization contexts and recruitment to activism. In *From Structure to Action*, ed. Bert Klandermans, Hanspeter Kriesi, and Sidney Tarrow. Greenwich, Connecticut: JAI Press.
McAdam, Doug and Ronnelle Paulsen. 1993. Specifying the relationship between social ties and activism. *American Journal of Sociology* 99: 640–67.
McAdam, Doug, John D. McCarthy, and Mayer N. Zald, ed. 1996. *Comparative Perspectives on Social Movements. Political Opportunities, Mobilizing Structures, and Cultural Framings*. Cambridge: Cambridge University Press.
McAllister, Ian. 1999. The economic performance of governments. In *Critical*

Citizens. Global Support for Democratic Governance, ed. Pippa Norris. Oxford: Oxford University Press, pp. 188–203.

McCarthy, John D. 1996. Mobilizing structures: constraints and opportunities in adopting, adapting, and inventing. In *Comparative Perspectives on Social Movements*, ed. Doug McAdam, John D. McCarthy, and Mayer N. Zald. Cambridge: Cambridge University Press.

McCarthy, John D. and Mayer D. Zald. 1977. Resource mobilization and social movements: a partial theory. *American Journal of Sociology* 82: 1212–41.

McClosky, Herbert. 1964. Consensus and ideology in American politics. *American Political Science Review* 58: 772–81.

McClosky, Herbert. 1968. Political participation. In *International Encyclopedia of the Social Sciences, Volume XXI*, ed. David L. Sills. Glencoe: The Free Press.

McClosky, Herbert and Alida Brill. 1983. *Dimensions of Tolerance*. New York: Russell Sage Foundation.

Macpherson, Crawford Brough 1977. *The Life and Times of Liberal Democracy*. Oxford: Oxford University Press.

McPherson, Miller J. and Lynn Smith-Lovin. 1987. Homophily in voluntary organizations: status distance and the composition of face-to-face groups. *American Sociological Review* 52: 370–9.

Magalhães, Pedro C. 2006. Confidence in parliaments: performance, representation and accountability. In *Disaffected Citizens in Contemporary Democracies: Social Capital, Institutions and Politics*, ed. Mariano Torcal and José Ramón Montero. London: Routledge.

Mair, Peter. 2001. The freezing hypothesis: an evaluation. In *Party System and Voter Alignments Revisited*, ed. Lauri Karvonen and Stein Kuhnle. London: Routledge.

Mair, Peter. 2002. In the aggregate: mass electoral behaviour in western Europe, 1950–2000. In *Comparative Democratic Politics*, ed. Hans Keman. Thousand Oaks: Sage Publications.

Mansbridge, Jane. 1980. *Beyond Adversary Democracy*. New York: Basic Books.

Mansbridge, Jane. 1999. Altruistic trust. In *Democracy and Trust*, ed. Mark E. Warren. Cambridge: Cambridge University Press.

Marcus, George E., John L. Sullivan, Elizabeth Theiss-Morse, and Sandra L. Wood. 1995. *With Malice Towards Some: How People Make Civil Liberties Judgments*. Cambridge: Cambridge University Press.

Margolis, Michael. 1979. *Viable Democracy*. New York: St. Martin's Press.

Marsh, Alan. 1977. *Protest and Political Consciousness*. Beverly Hills: Sage Publications.

Marsh, Alan. 1990. *Political Action in Europe and the USA*. London: Macmillan.

Marsh, Alan and Max Kaase. 1979. Measuring political action. In *Political Action: Mass Participation in Five Western Democracies*, ed. Samuel H. Barnes *et al.* Beverly Hills: Sage Publications.

Marshall, Thomas Humphrey. 1950. Citizenship and social class. In *Citizenship and Social Class and Other Essays*. Cambridge: Cambridge University Press.

Marshall, Thomas Humphrey. [1963] 1973. *Class, Citizenship and Social Development*. Wesport, Connecticut: Greenwood Press.

Meulemann, Heiner. 1996. *Werte und Wertewandel. Zur Identität einer geteilten und wieder vereinten Nation*. Weinheim: Juventa.

Micheletti, Michele. 2003. *Political Virtue and Shopping*. New York: Palgrave Macmillan.

Micheletti, Michele, Andres Føllesdal, and Dietlind Stolle, ed. 2003. *Politics, Prod-*

ucts, and Markets. Exploring Political Consumerism Past and Present. New Brunswick, New Jersey: Transaction Publishers.
Milbrath, Lester W. 1965. *Political Participation. How and Why Do People Get Involved in Politics?* Chicago: Rand McNally.
Milbrath, Lester W. and Madan Lal Goel. 1977. *Political Participation: How and Why Do People Get Involved in Politics*. 2nd edn. Chicago: Rand McNally.
Miller, Arthur H. 1974a. Rejoinder to 'comment' by Jack Citrin: political discontent or ritualism. *American Political Science Review* 68: 989–1001.
Miller, Arthur H. 1974b. Political issues and trust in government: 1964–1970. *American Political Science Review* 68: 951–72.
Miller, Arthur H. and Ola Listhaug. 1990. Political parties and confidence in government: a comparison of Norway, Sweden and the United States. *British Journal of Political Science* 29: 357–89.
Miller, Arthur H. and Ola Listhaug. 1999. Political performance and institutional trust. In *Critical Citizens: Global Support for Democratic Governance*, ed. Pippa Norris. Oxford: Oxford University Press, pp. 204–16.
Miller, David. 1992. Deliberative democracy and social choice. In *Prospects for Democracy. North, South, East, West*, ed. David Held. Oxford: Polity Press.
Miller, Warren E. 1979. Misreading the public pulse. *Public Opinion* 2: 9–15.
Minkoff, Debra C. 2001. Producing social capital: national social movements and civil society. In *Beyond Tocqueville: Civil Society and the Social Capital Debate in Comparative Perspective*, ed. Bob Edwards, Michael W. Foley, and Mario Diani. Hanover, New Hampshire: University Press of New England.
Mishler, William and Richard Rose. 2001a. Political support for incomplete democracies: realist vs. idealist theories and measures. *International Political Science Review* 22 (4): 303–20.
Mishler, William and Richard Rose. 2001b. What are the origins of political trust? Testing institutional and cultural theories in post-communist societies. *Comparative Political Studies* 34 (1): 30–62.
Misztal, Barbara A. 1996. *Trust in Modern Societies*. Oxford: Blackwell.
Montero, José Ramón, Richard Gunther, and Mariano Torcal. 1997. Democracy in Spain: legitimacy, discontent, and disaffection. *Studies in Comparative International Development* 32 (3): 124–60.
Morales, Laura. 2001. Citizens in Polities: The Individual and Contextual Determinants of Political Membership in Western Countries. Estudios/Working Papers, Vol. 164. Instituto Juan March de Estudios e Investigaciones, Madrid.
Morales, Laura. 2002. Associational membership and social capital in comparative perspective: the problems of measurement. *Politics and Society* 30 (3): 497–523.
Morales, Laura. 2004. Institutions, Mobilisation and Political Participation: Political Membership in Western Countries. Ph.D. Thesis. Instituto Juan March de Estudios e Investigaciones, Madrid.
Morales, Laura and Peter Geurts. 2004. Associational Involvement in Europe. Manuscript. Department of Political Science. University of Murcia.
Morlino, Leonardo. 1998. *Democracy Between Consolidation and Crisis. Parties, Groups, and Citizens in Southern Europe*. Oxford: Oxford University Press.
Morlino, Leonardo and José Ramón Montero. 1995. Legitimacy and democracy in southern Europe. In *The Politics of Democratic Consolidation*, ed. Richard Gunther, P. Nikiforos Diamandouros, and Hans-Jürgen Puhle. Baltimore: The Johns Hopkins University, pp. 231–60.

Morlino, Leonardo and Marco Tarchi. 1996. The dissatisfied society: the roots of political change in Italy. *European Journal of Political Research* 30: 41–63.
Muller, Edward N. and Karl-Dieter Opp. 1986. Rational choice and rebellious collective action. *American Political Science Review* 80 (2): 471–87.
Muller, Edward. N. and Mitchell A. Seligson. 1994. Civic culture and democracy: the question of causal relationships. *American Political Science Review* 88: 635–52.
Münkler, Herfried. 1997. Der kompetente Bürger. In *Politische Beteiligung und Bürgerengagement in Deutschland. Möglichkeiten und Grenzen*, ed. Ansgar Klein and Rainer Schmalz-Bruns. Baden-Baden: Nomos, pp. 153–72.
Nagel, Jack. 1987. *Participation.* Englewood Cliffs: Prentice-Hall.
Newton, Kenneth. 1997. Social capital and democracy. *American Behavioral Scientist* 40 (5): 575–86.
Newton, Kenneth. 1999a. Social and political trust in established democracies. In *Critical Citizens. Global Support for Democratic Government*, ed. Pippa Norris. Oxford: Oxford University Press, pp. 169–87.
Newton, Kenneth. 1999b. Social capital and democracy in modern Europe. In *Social Capital and European Democracy*, ed. Jan van Deth, Marco Maraffi, Kenneth Newton, and Paul Whiteley. London: Routledge, pp. 3–24.
Newton, Kenneth. 2001a. Trust, social capital, civil society, and democracy. *International Political Science Review* 22 (2): 201–14.
Newton, Kenneth. 2001b. Social Trust and Political Disaffection: Social Capital and Democracy. Presented at the EURESCO conference entitled Social Capital: Interdisciplinary Perspectives, Exeter, UK.
Newton, Kenneth and Pippa Norris. 2000. Confidence in public institutions: faith, culture, or performance? In *Disaffected Democracies: What's Troubling the Trilateral Countries?*, ed. Susan Pharr and Robert D. Putnam. Princeton: Princeton University Press, pp. 52–73.
Nie, Norman H. and Sidney Verba. 1975. Political participation. In *Handbook of Political Science, Volume 4: Nongovernmental Politics*, ed. Fred I. Greenstein and Nelson W. Polsby. Reading: Addison-Wesley.
Nie, Norman H., Jane Junn, and Kenneth Stehlik-Barry. 1996. *Education and Democratic Citizenship in America.* Chicago: University of Chicago Press.
Nie, Norman H., Sidney Verba, and Jae-on Kim. 1974. Political participation and the life cycle. *Comparative Politics* 6 (April): 319–40.
Nielsen, Hans Jørgen. 1998. Forvalterne og loven. In *Borgerne og Lovene*, Jørgen Goul Andersen, Hans Jørgen Nielsen and Marie Louise Hultin. Aarhus: Aarhus University Press, pp. 396–432.
Nisbet, Robert. 1969. *The Quest for Community.* Oxford: Oxford University Press.
Noelle-Neumann, Elisabeth. 1978. *Werden wir alle Proletarier? Wertewandel in unserer Gesellschaft.* Osnabrück: Edition Interfrom.
Norris, Pippa. 1996. Does television erode social capital? A reply to Putnam. *PS: Political Science and Politics* 29: 474–80.
Norris, Pippa. 1999a. The growth of critical citizens. In *Critical Citizens: Global Support for Democratic Governance*, ed. Pippa Norris. Oxford: Oxford University Press, pp. 1–27.
Norris, Pippa. 1999b. Institutional explanations for political support. In *Critical Citizens: Global Support for Democratic Government*, ed. Pippa Norris. Oxford: Oxford University Press, pp. 217–35.

Norris, Pippa. 1999c. Conclusions: the growth of critical citizens and its consequences. In *Critical Citizens: Global Support for Democratic Governance*, ed. Pippa Norris. Oxford: Oxford University Press, pp. 257–72.

Norris, Pippa. 2000. The impact of television on civic malaise. In *Disaffected Democracies: What's Troubling the Trilateral Countries?*, ed. Susan J. Pharr and Robert D. Putnam. Princeton: Princeton University Press, pp. 231–51.

Norris, Pippa. 2002. *Democratic Phoenix. Reinventing Political Activism.* Cambridge: Cambridge University Press.

Norris, Pippa, Stefaan Walgrave, and Peter van Aelst. 2002. Who Demonstrates? Anti-State Rebels, Conventional Participants, or Everyone? Manuscript. Harvard University and Universiteit Antwerpen.

Nozick, Robert. 1974. *Anarchy, State, and Utopia.* New York: Basic Books.

Nunn, Clyde Z., Harris Crockett, and Allen Williams. 1978. *Tolerance for Nonconformity.* San Francisco: Jossey-Bass.

Nye, Joseph S., Jr. 1997. Introduction: the decline of confidence in government. In *Why People Don't Trust Government*, ed. Joseph S. Nye Jr., Philip D. Zelikow, and David C. King. Cambridge: Harvard University Press, pp. 1–18.

Nye, Joseph S., Jr. and Philip D. Zelikow. 1997. Conclusion: reflections, conjectures and puzzles. In *Why People Don't Trust Government*, ed. Joseph S. Nye Jr., Philip D. Zelikow, and David C. King. Cambridge: Harvard University Press, pp. 253–81.

OECD. 2003. *OECD at a Glance.* Paris: OECD.

Offe, Claus. 1999. How can we trust our fellow citizens. In *Democracy and Trust*, ed. Mark E. Warren. Cambridge: Cambridge University Press, pp. 42–87.

Offe, Claus. 2006. Political disaffection as an outcome of institutional practices? Some neo-Tocquevillean speculations. In *Political Disaffection in Contemporary Democracies: Social Capital, Institutions and Politics*, ed. José Ramón Montero and Mariano Torcal. London: Routledge, pp. 23–45.

Offe, Claus and Susanne Fuchs. 2002. A Decline of social capital? The German case. In *Democracies in Flux. The Evolution of Social Capital in Contemporary Society*, ed. Robert D. Putnam. Oxford: Oxford University Press.

Oldfield, Adrian. 1990. *Citizenship and Community.* London: Routledge.

Olsen, Marvin E. 1972. Social participation and voting turnout: a multivariate analysis. *American Sociological Review* 37: 317–33.

Olsen, Marvin E. 1982. *Participatory Pluralism: Political Participation and Influence in the United States and Sweden.* Chicago: Nelson-Hall.

O'Neill, Onora. 2002. *A Question of Trust: The BBC Reith Lectures 2002.* Cambridge: Cambridge University Press.

Orren, Gary. 1997. Fall from grace: the public's loss of faith in government. In *Why People Don't Trust Government*, ed. Joseph S. Nye, Philip D. Zelikow, and David C. King. Cambridge: Harvard University Press.

Parry, Geraint. 1976. Trust, distrust and consensus. *British Journal of Political Science* 6: 129–42.

Parry, Geraint, George Moyser, and Neil Day. 1992. *Political Participation and Democracy in Britain.* Cambridge: Cambridge University Press.

Pateman, Carole. 1970. *Participation and Democratic Theory.* Cambridge: Cambridge University Press.

Paxton, Pamela. 1999. Is social capital declining in the United States? A multiple indicator assessment. *American Journal of Sociology* 105 (1): 88–127.

Paxton, Pamela. 2002. Social capital and democracy: an inter-dependent relationship. *American Sociological Review* 67: 254–77.
Peffley, Mark A. and Robert Rohrschneider. 2003. Democratization and political tolerance in seventeen countries: a multi-level model of democratic learning. *Political Research Quarterly* 56 (3): 243–57.
Pérez-Díaz, Víctor M. 1993. *The Return of Civil Society. The Emergence of Democratic Spain.* Cambridge: Harvard University Press.
Petersson, Olof, Anders Westholm, and Göran Blomberg. 1989. *Medborgarnas makt.* Stockholm: Carlsson Bokförlag.
Petersson, Olof, Jörgen Hermansson, Michele Micheletti, Jan Teorell, and Anders Westholm. 1998. *Demokrati och medborgarskap. Demokratirådets rapport 1998.* Stockholm: SNS Förlag.
Pharr, Susan J. and Robert D. Putnam, ed. 2000. *Disaffected Democracies. What's Troubling the Trilateral Countries?* Princeton: Princeton University Press.
Pitkin, Hanna F. 1967. *The Concept of Representation.* Berkeley: University of California Press.
Pollock, Philip H., III. 1982. Organizations as agents of mobilization: how does group affinity affect political participation? *American Journal of Political Science* 26 (3): 485–503.
Pressman, Jeffrey L. and Aaron Wildavsky. 1973. *Implementation: How Great Expectations in Washington Are Dashed in Oakland.* Berkeley: University of California Press.
Prior, David, John Stewart, and Kieron Walsh. 1995. *Citizenship: Rights, Community and Participation.* London: Pitman Publishing.
Protho, James W. and Charles W. Grigg. 1960. Fundamental principles of democracy: bases of agreement and disagreement. *Journal of Politics* 22: 276–94.
Putnam, Robert D. 1993. *Making Democracy Work: Civic Traditions in Modern Italy.* Princeton: Princeton University Press.
Putnam, Robert D. 1995a. Bowling alone: America's declining social capital. *Journal of Democracy* 6: 65–78.
Putnam, Robert D. 1995b. Tuning in, tuning out: the strange disappearance of social capital in America. *PS: Political Science and Politics* 29: 664–83.
Putnam, Robert D. 1998. Democracy in America at the end of the twentieth century. In *Participation and Democracy. East and West. Comparisons and Interpretations,* ed. Dietrich Rueschemeyer, Marilyn Rueschemeyer, and Björn Wittrock. New York: M.E. Sharpe, pp. 233–65.
Putnam, Robert D. 2000. *Bowling Alone. The Collapse and Revival of American Community.* New York: Simon & Schuster.
Putnam, Robert D., ed. 2002. *Democracies in Flux. The Evolution of Social Capital in Contemporary Society.* Oxford: Oxford University Press.
Putnam, Robert D., Susan J. Pharr, and Russell J. Dalton. 2000. Introduction: what's troubling the trilateral democracies? In *Disaffected Democracies: What's Troubling the Trilateral Countries?,* ed. Susan J. Pharr and Robert D. Putnam. Princeton: Princeton University Press.
Rae, Douglas. 1981. *Equalities.* Cambridge: Harvard University Press.
Richter, Rudolf. 1985. *Soziokulturelle Dimensionen freiwilliger Vereinigungen.* München: Minerva.
Riker, William H. 1982. *Liberalism against Populism: A Confrontation between the Theory of Democracy and the Theory of Social Choice.* Prospect Heights: Waveland Press.

Riker, William H. and Peter C. Ordeshook. 1968. A theory of the calculus of voting. *American Political Science Review* 62 (1): 25–42.

Robinson, Michael. 1976. Public affairs television and the growth of political malaise: the case of 'the selling Pentagon'. *American Political Science Review* 70: 409–32.

Rogers, David L., Ken H. Barb, and Gordon L. Bultena. 1975. Voluntary association membership and political participation: an exploration of the mobilization hypothesis. *Sociological Quarterly* 16 (Summer): 305–18.

Rogers, Joel and Joshua Cohen. 1995. *Associations and Democracy*. London: Verso.

Rohrschneider, Robert and Rüdiger Schmitt-Beck. 2003. Trust in democratic institutions in Germany: theory and evidence ten years after unification. *German Politics* 11: 35–58.

Rokkan, Stein. 1977. Towards a generalized concept of 'verzuiling': a preliminary note. *Political Studies* 25: 563–70.

Rose, Lawrence E. and Per Arnt Pettersen. 2002. *The Good Citizen. Democratic Theory and Political Realities among Norwegians*. Presented at the annual meeting of the Midwest Political Science Association, Chicago.

Rosenberg, Morris. 1956. Misanthropy and political ideology. *American Sociological Review* 21 (6): 690–5.

Rosenberg, Morris. 1957. Misanthropy and attitudes toward international affairs. *The Journal of Conflict Resolution* 1 (4): 340–5.

Rosenstone, Steven J. and John Mark Hansen. 1993. *Mobilization, Participation, and Democracy in America*. New York: Macmillan.

Roßteutscher, Sigrid and Jan W. van Deth. 2002. Associations Between Associations. The Structure of the Voluntary Association Sector. Arbeitspapiere-MZES 56.

Rothstein, Bo. 1998. *Just Institutions Matter*. Cambridge: Cambridge University Press.

Rothstein, Bo. 2002. Social capital in the social democratic state. In *Democracies in Flux. The Evolution of Social Capital in Contemporary Society*, ed. Robert D. Putnam. Oxford: Oxford University Press.

Rothstein, Bo. 2004. Social capital and quality of government: the causal mechanism. In *Creating Social Trust: Problems of Post-Socialist Transition*, ed. Janos Kornai, Susan Rose-Ackerman, and Bo Rothstein. New York: Palgrave Macmillan.

Rothstein, Bo and Dietlind Stolle. 2001. Social Capital and Street-Level Bureaucracy: An Institutional Theory of Generalized Trust. Presented at the EURESCO conference entitled Social Capital: Interdisciplinary Perspectives, Exeter, UK.

Rothstein Bo and Dietlind Stolle. 2003. Social capital, impartiality, and the Welfare State: an institutional approach. In *Generating Social Capital: Civil Society and Institutions in Comparative Perspective*, ed. Marc Hooghe and Dietlind Stolle. New York: Palgrave Macmillan.

Sabine, George H. and Thomas L. Thorson. 1973. *A History of Political Theory*. 4th edn. Hinsdale, Illinois: Dryden Press.

Sampson, Steven. 1996. The social life of projects. Importing civil society to Albania. In *Civil Society: Challenging Western Models*, ed. Chris Hann and Elisabeth Dunn. London: Routledge, pp. 120–38.

Saris, William E. and Irmtraud Gallhofer. 2003. Report on the MTMM Experiments in the Pilot Studies and Proposals for Round 1 of the ESS. (Available at www.europeansocialsurvey.org).

Sartori, Giovanni. 1987. *The Theory of Democracy Revisited. Part I: The Contemporary Debate.* Chatham, New Jersey: Chatham House.

Schlozman, Kay Lehman. 2002. Citizen participation in America: what do we know? Why do we care? In *Political Science: The State of the Discipline*, ed. Iva Katznelson and Helen V. Milner. New York: W.W. Norton.

Schlozman, Kay Lehman, Sidney Verba, and Henry E. Brady. 1999. Civic participation and the equality problem. In *Civic Engagement in American Democracy*, ed. Theda Skocpol and Morris P. Fiorina. Washington, DC: Brookings Institution Press, pp. 427–59.

Schmitt, Hermann. 1983. Party government in public opinion: a European cross-national comparison. *European Journal of Political Research* 11: 353–75.

Schweisguth, Étienne. 1999. L'affaiblissement du clivage gauche-droit. In *La démocracie à l'épreuve*, ed. Gérard Grunberg, Nonna Mayer, and Paul M. Sniderman. Paris: Presses de Science Po.

Scott, James 1985. *Weapons of the Weak: Everyday Forms of Peasant Resistance.* New Haven: Yale University Press.

Sears, David O. 1993. Symbolic politics: a socio-psychological theory. In *Explorations in Political Psychology*, ed. Shanto Iyengar and William J. McGuire. Durham: Duke University Press, pp. 113–49.

Seeman, Melvin. 1972. Alienation and engagement. In *The Human Meaning of Social Change*, ed. Angus Campbell and Philip E. Converse. New York: Russell Sage Foundation, pp. 467–527.

Seligman, Adam B. 1997. *The Problem of Trust.* Princeton: Princeton University Press.

Seligson, Amber L. 1999. Civic association and democratic participation in Central America. *Comparative Political Studies* 32 (3): 342–62.

Sen, Amartya. 1992. *Inequality Reexamined.* Oxford: Clarendon Press.

Sigel, Roberta S. and Marilyn B. Hoskin. 1981. *The Political Involvement of Adolescents.* New Brunswick, New Jersey: Rutgers University Press.

Skocpol, Theda. 1999. Advocates without members: the recent transformation of American civic life. In *Civic Engagement in American Democracy*, ed. Theda Skocpol and Morris P. Fiorina. Washington, DC: Brookings Institution Press, pp. 461–509.

Smelser, Neil 1962. *Theory of Collective Behavior.* New York: The Free Press.

Smith, David H. 1975. Voluntary action and voluntary groups. *Annual Review of Sociology* 1: 247–70.

Smith, John C. 1957. Membership and participation in voluntary associations. *American Sociological Review* 22: 315–26.

Smith, Tom W. 1990. Trends in voluntary group membership: comments on Baumgartner and Walker. *American Journal of Political Science* 34 (3): 646–61.

Smolar, Aleksander. 1996. Civil society after communism: from opposition to atomization. *Journal of Democracy* 4: 24–38.

Sniderman, Paul M., Joseph F. Fletcher, Peter H. Russell, and Philip E. Tetlock. 1996. *The Clash of Rights: Liberty, Equality, and Legitimacy in Pluralist Democracy.* New Haven: Yale University Press.

Sniderman, Paul M., Philip E. Tetlock, James M. Glaser, Donald Philip Green, and Michael Hout. 1989. Principled tolerance and the American mass public. *British Journal of Political Science* 19 (1): 25–45.

Snijders, Tom and Roel Bosker. 1999. *Multilevel Analysis: An Introduction to Basic and Advanced Multilevel Modeling.* London: Sage Publications.

Snow, David A. and Robert D. Benford. 1988. Ideology, frame resonance, and participant mobilization. In *From Structure to Action: Social Movement Participation across Cultures*, ed. Bert Klandermans, Hanspeter Kriesi, and Sidney Tarrow. Greenwich, Connecticut: JAI Press.

Snow, David A., Louis A. Zurcher, and Sheldon Ekland-Olson. 1980. Social networks and social movements: a microstructural approach to differential recruitment. *American Sociological Review* 45: 787–801.

Snow, David A., E. Burke Rochford Jr., Steven K. Worden, and Robert D. Benford. 1986. Frame alignment processes, micromobilization, and movement participation. *American Sociological Review* 51: 464–81.

Staub, Ervin. 1989. Individual and societal (group) values in a motivational perspective and their role in benevolence and harmdoing. In *Social and Moral Values: Individual and Societal Perspectives*, ed. Nancy Eisenberg, Janusz Reykowski, and Ervin Staub. Hillsdale: Erlbaum, pp. 45–61.

Steenbergen, Marco R. and Bradford S. Jones. 2002. Modeling multilevel data structures. *American Journal of Political Science* 46: 218–37.

Stolle, Dietlind. 1998. Bowling alone, bowling together: the development of generalized trust in voluntary associations. *Political Psychology* 19 (3): 497–526.

Stolle, Dietlind. 2001a. Getting to trust: an analysis of the importance of institutions, families, personal experiences, and group membership. In *Social Capital and Participation in Everyday Life*, ed. Paul Dekker and Eric M. Uslaner. London: Routledge.

Stolle, Dietlind. 2001b. Clubs and congregations: The benefits of joining an association. In *Trust in Society*, ed. Karen S. Cook. New York: Russell Sage Foundation.

Stolle, Dietlind. 2002. Trusting strangers: the concept of generalized trust in perspective. *Österreichische Zeitschrift für Politikwissenschaft* 31: 397–412.

Stolle, Dietlind. 2003. The sources of social capital. In *Generating Social Capital: Civil Society and Institutions in Comparative Perspective*, ed. Marc Hooghe and Dietlind Stolle. New York: Palgrave Macmillan, pp. 19–42.

Stolle, Dietlind and Thomas R. Rochon. 2001. Are all associations alike? In *Beyond Tocqueville: Civil Society and the Social Capital Debate in Comparative Perspective*, ed. Bob Edwards, Michael W. Foley, and Mario Diani. Hanover: Tufts University/University Press of New England.

Stouffer, Samuel. 1955. *Communism, Conformity and Civil Liberties*. New York: Wiley.

Sullivan, John L., James Pierson, and George E. Marcus. 1982. *Political Tolerance and American Democracy*. Chicago: University of Chicago Press.

Sum, Paul E. and Gabriel Badescu. 2004. An evaluation of six forms of participation. In *Romania since 1989: Politics, Economics and Society*, ed. Henry F. Carey. New York: Lexington Press.

Sztompka, Piotr. 2000. *Trust: A Sociological Theory*. Cambridge: Cambridge University Press.

Tarrow, Sidney. 1971. The urban–rural cleavage in political involvement: the case of France. *American Political Science Review* 65: 341–57.

Tarrow, Sidney. 1994. *Power in Movement: Social Movements, Collective Action and Mass Politics in the Modern State*. Cambridge: Cambridge University Press.

Teorell, Jan. 2003. Linking social capital to political participation: voluntary associations and networks of recruitment in Sweden. *Scandinavian Political Studies* 26 (1): 49–66.

Teorell, Jan. 2006. Political participation and three theories of democracy: a research inventory and agenda. *European Journal of Political Research* 45 (5): 787–810.
Tetlock, Philip E. 2002. Coping with trade-offs: psychological constraints and political implications. In *Elements of Reason. Cognition, Choice, and the Bounds of Rationality*, ed. Arthur Lupia, Mathew D. McCubbins, and Samuel L. Popkin. Cambridge: Cambridge University Press, pp. 239–63.
Thalhammer, Eva, Vlasta Zucha, Edith Enzenhofer, Brigitte Salfinger, and Günther Ogris. 2001. *Attitudes towards Minority Groups in the European Union*. Vienna: European Monitoring Centre on Racism and Xenophobia.
Thibaut, John and Laurens Walker. 1975. *Procedural Justice: A Psychological Analysis*. Hillsdale, New Jersey: Lawrence Erlbaum.
Thomassen, Jacques. 1995. Support for democratic values. In *Citizens and the State*, ed. Hans-Dieter Klingemann and Dieter Fuchs. Oxford: Oxford University Press.
Thomassen, Jacques and Jan van Deth. 1998. Political involvement and democratic attitudes. In *The Postcommunist Citizen*, ed. Samuel H. Barnes and Janos Simon. Budapest: Erasmus Foundation and Institute for Political Science of the Hungarian Academy of Sciences.
Tocqueville, Alexis de. [1835, 1840] 2000. *Democracy in America*. New York: Library of America (Penguin Putnam).
Tönnies, Ferdinand. [1887] 1955. *Community and Association*. London: Routledge and Kegan Paul.
Topf, Richard. 1995a. Beyond electoral participation. In *Citizens and the State*, ed. Hans-Dieter Klingemann and Dieter Fuchs. Oxford: Oxford University Press.
Topf, Richard 1995b. Electoral participation. In *Citizens and the State*, ed. Hans-Dieter Klingemann and Dieter Fuchs. Oxford: Oxford University Press.
Torcal, Mariano. 2002. Disaffected but Democrats. The Origin and Consequences of the Dimensions of Political Support in New Latin American and Southern European Democracies. Manuscript.
Torcal, Mariano. 2003. Political Disaffection and Democratization History in New Democracies. Working Paper 308. Kellogg Institute, Notre Dame University.
Torcal, Mariano. 2006. Political disaffection and democratization history in new democracies. In *Political Disaffection in Contemporary Democracies: Social Capital, Institutions and Politics*, ed. Mariano Torcal and José Ramón Montero. London: Routledge, pp. 157–89.
Torcal, Mariano and José Ramón Montero. 1999. Facets of social capital in new democracies: the formation and consequences of social capital in Spain. In *Social Capital and European Democracy*, ed. Jan W. van Deth, Mario Maraffi, Kenneth Newton, and Paul Whiteley. London: Routledge.
Torcal, Mariano and José Ramón Montero. 2006. Political disaffection in comparative perspective. In *Political Disaffection in Contemporary Democracies: Social Capital, Institutions and Politics*, ed. Mariano Torcal and José Ramón Montero. London: Routledge, pp. 3–19.
Uslaner, Eric M. 1999. Democracy and social capital. In *Democracy and Trust*, ed. Mark E. Warren. Cambridge: Cambridge University Press.
Uslaner, Eric. M. 2001a. Producing and consuming trust. *Political Science Quarterly* 115 (4): 569–90.
Uslaner, Eric M. 2001b. Volunteering and social capital: how trust and religion

shape civic engagement in the United States. In *Social Capital and Participation in Everyday Life*, ed. Paul Dekker and Eric M. Uslaner. London: Routledge.

Uslaner, Eric M. 2002. *The Moral Foundations of Trust*. Cambridge: Cambridge University Press.

Uslaner, Eric M. 2003. Trust and civic engagement in east and west. In *Social Capital and European Democracy*, ed. Gabriel Badescu and Eric M. Uslaner. New York: Routledge, pp. 81–95.

van Deth, Jan W. 1990. Interest in politics. In *Continuities in Political Action: A Longitudinal Study of Political Orientations in Three Western Democracies*, ed. M. Kent Jennings *et al.* Berlin: Walter de Gruyter, pp. 275–312.

van Deth, Jan W. 1996. Voluntary associations and political participation. In *Wahlen und politische Einstellungen in westlichen Demokratien*, ed. Oscar W. Gabriel and Jürgen W. Falter. Frankfurt am Main: Lang, pp. 389–411.

van Deth, Jan W. 1997. Introduction. Social involvement and democratic politics. In *Private Groups and Public Life. Social Participation, Voluntary Associations and Political Involvement in Representative Democracies*, ed. Jan W. van Deth. London: Routledge, pp. 1–27.

van Deth, Jan W. 2000. Interesting but irrelevant: social capital and the saliency of politics in western Europe. *European Journal of Political Research* 37 (2): 115–47.

van Deth, Jan W. 2001a. Soziale und politische Beteiligung: Alternativen, Ergänzungen oder Zwillinge? In *Politische Partizipation in der Bundesrepublik Deutschland. Empirische Befunde und theoretische Erklärungen*, ed. Achim Koch, Martina Wasmer, and Peter Schmidt. Opladen: Leske + Budrich, pp. 195–219.

van Deth, Jan W. 2001b. The Proof of the Pudding: Social Capital, Democracy, and Citizenship. Presented at the EURESCO conference entitled Social Capital: Interdisciplinary Perspectives, Exeter, UK.

van Deth, Jan W. 2002. Sozialkapital/Soziales Vertrauen. In *Handwörterbuch zur politischen Kultur der Bundesrepublik Deutschland*, ed. Martin and Sylvia Greiffenhagen. Wiesbaden: Westdeutscher Verlag, pp. 575–9.

van Deth, Jan W. 2003. Measuring social capital: orthodoxies and continuing controversies. *International Journal of Social Research Methodology* 6 (1): 79–92.

van Deth, Jan W. and Martin Elff. 2000. *Political Involvement and Apathy in Europe 1973–1998*. Mannheim: Mannheimer Zentrum für Europäische Sozialforschung.

van Deth, Jan W. and Frauke Kreuter. 1998. Membership of voluntary associations. In *Comparative Politics. The Problem of Equivalence*, ed. Jan W. van Deth. London: Routledge, pp. 135–55.

van Deth, Jan W., Mario Maraffi, Kenneth Newton, and Paul Whiteley, ed. 1999. *Social Capital and European Democracy*. London: Routledge.

van Gunsteren, Herman. 1994. Four conceptions of citizenship. In *The Condition of Citizenship*, ed. Bart van Steenbergen. London: Sage Publications, pp. 36–48.

von Erlach, Emanuel. 2001. Moving to a Smaller Scale: Explaining Participation at Work. Presented at the ECPR first general conference, September 6–8, Canterbury, U.K.

von Erlach, Emanuel. 2002. Measures of Associational Involvement: The Impact of Different Interview Techniques, Question Wordings and Missing Values. Manuscript. Institute of Political Science. University of Bern.

Verba, Sidney. 1996. The citizen as respondent: sample surveys and American democracy. *American Political Science Review* 90 (1): 1–7.

Verba, Sidney and Norman H. Nie. 1972. *Participation in America: Political Democracy and Social Equality*. New York: Harper & Row.
Verba, Sidney, Norman H. Nie, and Jae-On Kim. 1978. *Participation and Political Equality: A Seven-Nation Comparison*. Chicago: Chicago University Press.
Verba, Sidney, Kay Lehman Schlozman, and Henry Brady. 1995. *Voice and Equality: Civic Voluntarism in American Politics*. Cambridge: Cambridge University Press.
Verba, Sidney, Kay Lehman Schlozman, Henry E. Brady, and Norman H. Nie. 1993. Citizen activity: who participates? What do they say? *American Political Science Review* 87 (2): 303–18.
Volker, Beate and Henk Flap. 2001. Weak ties as a liability: the case of East Germany. *Rationality and Society* 13: 397–428.
Walzer, Michael. 1980. Civility and civic virtue in contemporary America. In *Radical Principles: Reflections of an Unreconstructed Democrat*. New York: Basic Books.
Walzer, Michael. 1983. *Spheres of Justice: A Defence of Pluralism and Equality*. Oxford: Basil Blackwell.
Walzer, Michael. 1989. Citizenship. In *Political Innovation and Conceptual Change*, ed. Terrence Ball. Cambridge: Cambridge University Press, pp. 211–19.
Walzer, Michael. 1991. The idea of civil society. *Dissent* Spring: 293–304.
Walzer, Michael. 1995. *Toward a Global Civil Society*. Providence: Berghahn Books.
Warren, Mark E., ed. 1999a. *Democracy and Trust*. Cambridge: Cambridge University Press.
Warren, Mark E. 1999b. Democratic theory and trust. In *Democracy and Trust*, ed. Mark E. Warren. Cambridge: Cambridge University Press.
Warren, Mark E. 2001. *Democracy and Association*. Princeton: Princeton University Press.
Wattenberg, Martin P. 1986. *The Decline of American Political Parties*. Cambridge: Harvard University Press.
Weil, Frederick, D. 1989. The structure and sources of legitimation in western democracies: a consolidated model tested with time-series data in six countries since World War II. *American Sociological Review* 54: 682–706.
Weisberg, Jacob. 1996. *Defense of Government: The Fall and Rise of Public Trust*. New York: Scribner.
Wellman, Barry. 1979. The community question: the intimate networks of East Yorkers. *American Journal of Sociology* 84: 1201–31.
Wessels, Bernhard. 1997. Organizing capacity of societies and modernity. In *Private Groups and Public Life*, ed. Jan W. van Deth. London: Routledge.
Westholm, Anders and Richard Niemi. 1986. Youth unemployment and political alienation. *Youth & Society* 18: 58–80.
Whiteley, Paul F. 1995. Rational choice and political participation: evaluating the debate. *Political Research Quarterly* 48: 211–33.
Whiteley, Paul F. 1999. The origins of social capital. In *Social Capital and European Democracy*, ed. Jan W. van Deth, Mario Maraffi, Kenneth Newton, and Paul Whiteley. London: Routledge, pp. 25–44.
Wilson, Thomas C. 1994. Trends in tolerance towards rightist and leftist groups, 1976–88. *Public Opinion Quarterly* 58 (4): 539–56.
Wirth, Louis. 1938. Urbanism as a way of life. *American Journal of Sociology* 44: 3–24.
Wright, James D. 1976. *The Dissent of the Governed*. New York: Academic Press.
Wuthnow, Robert. 1999. Mobilizing civic engagement: the changing impact of reli-

gious involvement. In *Civic Engagement in American Democracy*, ed. Theda Skocpol and Morris P. Fiorina. Washington, DC: Brookings Institution Press, pp. 331–63.

Wuthnow, Robert. 2002. United States. Bridging the privileged and the marginalized? In *Democracies in Flux. The Evolution of Social Capital in Contemporary Society*, ed. Robert D. Putnam. Oxford: Oxford University Press.

Yamagishi, Toshio. 1988. The provision of a sanctioning system in the United States and Japan. *Social Psychology Quarterly* 51 (3): 265–71.

Yamagishi, Toshio. 2001. Trust as a form of social intelligence. In *Trust in Society*, ed. Karen S. Cook. New York: Russell Sage Foundation.

Zaller, John R. 1992. *The Nature and Origins of Mass Opinion*. Cambridge: Cambridge University Press.

Zmerli, Sonja. 2004. Politisches Vertrauen und Unterstützung. In *Deutschland in Europa*, ed. Jan W. van Deth. Wiesbaden: Verlag für Sozialwissenschaften, pp. 229–55.

Zuckerman, Alan S. and Darrell M. West. 1985. The political bases of citizen contacting: a cross-national analysis. *American Political Science Review* 79 (1): 117–31.

Index

Page numbers in *italics* denote figures or tables where these are separated from their textual references

absenteeism 258
action: collective 165, 242–3, 256; consequences 287; democracy, small-scale 238, *239*, 240–3, *244*, 245–6, 280–2; discontent 257–8; dissatisfaction *259*, 260, 290; feedback effects 281; opportunities *263*, 268, 274–5; outcomes 246–53; resources *265*; working life *249*, *291*; *see also* citizen action; political activism
age 31; associational involvement 159–60, 168–9, 173; decisionist citizenship 325; discrimination 123–3; inequality 396; modernisation 73; opportunity for action 268; party activity 396; political activism 403; political equality 392; political involvement 321; political participation 362–3, 410; protest activity 396; resources 271; social capital 103; social networks 193, 196; tolerance 109–10, 126, 131
AIDS sufferers 119, 122, 125, 131
Almond, Gabriel A. 90, 304
altruism 164
Andersen, Jørgen Goul 13–14, 280, 297, 429, 430
andrarchy 2
animal rights groups 144
aristocracy 2
Armingeon, Klaus 15–16, 435
associational involvement 65n24, 75, 103, 147, 168–9, 427; activism 140–3, *148*, 150, 153, 158; age 159–60, 168–9, 173; breadth of *141*; CID 137–9; civic virtue 173; degrees of 137, *138*, 139, *146*, 150; democracy 135–7, 153, 158–9; gender 159–60, 168–9, 173; institutions 165; locality 168–9, 182; measuring 137–9, 167; overview 139–40, 159–67; political orientations 164–5; Putnam 54, 140, 142, 153; regime types 165–7; social networks 197–8, 207; social participation 416–17; social trust 12, 54, *55*, *56*, 149–55, 162–4, 172, 182; solidarity 164, 172, 185; tolerance 163, 164, 172, 182; voice/exit 245; *see also* organisational involvement
associations, types 13, 143–9, *170–1*, 173, *174–81*, 182
authoritarianism 125
automobile organisations 144
autonomy 6–7

Badescu, Gabriel 13, 172, 187n11, 187n15, 426–7
badge wearing 345, 354–5
Barber, Benjamin 303, 307, 308
Barry, Brian 4
bicameral parliament 25–6
Bismarck, Otto von 24
Blomberg, Göran *248*
Bock, Gisela 23–4
Boix, Carles 145
boycotting 258, 334, 336, 345, 376
Brady, Henry 336, 356n2, 377
Brehm, John 163
Brill, Alida 124

capitalism 112

464 *Index*

charities 144, 145
child education: action efficacy 249, 291; citizen action 229–30, 231, 270, *272*, 275–6; combined additive models 271–4; democracy, small-scale 8, 13–14, 234, 240, 241–3, 429; dissatisfaction 236, 260–1; gender 274; opportunities 262–4; participation *296*; voice/exit 231, 233, 245, 276
childcare 227–8
church attendance 32n2, 216n14, 333n26; civic virtues 103–4; organisational involvement 182–3; social networks 197; tolerance 126, 131
CID (Citizenship, Involvement, Democracy) survey 17; associational involvement 137–9; characteristics *28*; citizenship 92–5; common core questions 27, 29, 155n6; confidence 11, 41, 43; social networks 12–13; trust 37
citizen action 14, 140, 275–6, 284, 297, 298, 336; child education 229–30, 231, 270, *272*, 275–6; democracy 282, 334–5; Germany 277–8, 279n11; pathways 248–51; responsiveness 280–1; working life 227, 230–1, 233, 275–6
citizenship 32n1, 90–2, 311–19, 417–19, 421–2; communitarian 5, 89, 96, 422; components of 415–17; democracy 112, 226; explanations 321, 324–5, 328–9; good 11–12, *94*, 95–7; involvement 305–11; liberal-representative 304, 306–7, 312, 433; Marshall 23, 415; normative theories 4, 88, 92–5; rights 1–2, 12, 22, 92, 225–7; social capital 99, 101; solidarity *94*, 363; typology 304–5, *310*, *315*, *317–18*, 319, *322–3*, 324–5, *326–7*, 329–31, 432–3; unitary 304, 308–9, 311, 433; *see also* decisionist citizenship; liberal citizenship; participatory citizenship
citizenship studies, Swedish 27, 32n5, 92, 223–5, 281
civic duty concept 163, 183, 185, 363
civic norms 89, 95, 97–106
civic orientations 6, 9, 10–12, 419–24, 437
civic republicanism 91–2
civic skills: action *265*; efficacy 284; political participation 9, 270–1, 275, 278n6, 377, 399; political party 364; resources 264, *265*; social involvement 418, 419
civic virtues 88, 92, 376; associational involvement 173; church attendance 103–6; non-political associations 373–4; social capital 422; social trust 102, 103; Tocqueville 106; voluntary associations 91
cleavage politics 364–5, 370, 373, 376, 435
client-type involvement 140, 142, 225–6
Cohen, Joshua 136
Coleman, James S. 297
communism 26, 66, 408–9, 427
communitarian tradition 5, 91, 93, 95, 96, 98, 332n12
community: attachment 52, 54, 62, 65n24; citizenship 5, 89, 96, 422; decline of 397; involvement 61; membership 4; participation 35; size 161; social capital 328; trust 60–1
Comparative Study of Electoral Systems 27
confidence 78–9; CID 11, 41, 43; collective action 165; education 73; institutions 66, 131, 182, 184–5, 420; political institutions 35–6, 37, 39–43, *42–3*, *58*, 61, 131; public sphere 40–1; socio-cultural approach 421; voluntary associations 57; *see also* political confidence
conflict 118, 123, 360
Conover, Pamela Johnston 90, 91
consumer organisations 144
consumer participation 342; gender 393; ideology 363–4; political interest 380; political participation 349, 351, 354, 355, 389
consumerism 223, 224, 225, 227, 340
contacting 343, 356n5, 380; fundraising 354; gender 393; participation 15; party activity 351; political equality 397
cooperation 147, 189
criminal records, people with 119, 423
critical attitudes 66, 90–3, *94*, 95–6, 100
critical/deliberative principles 11, *100*, 125, 129; *see also* deliberative values
Cuba 23
cultural traits 124, 129, 193, 304–5
Curtis, James E. 161

Index 465

Dahl, Robert A. 304, 307
Dalton, Russell J. 340
decentralisation of state 82
decisionist citizenship 304, 306, 309, 328, 329, 330, 432, 433; age 325; elite 312; political participation 320
Dekker, Paul 164–5
deliberative values 107n3; citizenship 11, 89, 92, 93, *94,* 95–6, 100, 129; social capital *100;* tolerance 125
democracy 7, 15, 305–6; associational involvement 135–7, 153, 158–9; citizen action 282, 334–5; citizenship 112, 226; endowment/ambition sensitive 262, 277, 281, 386, 402, 403–4, 431; equal rights 384; freedom 23; institutions 11, 68; integration 153; large-scale 6, 7–8, 15–16, 432–3; law-abidingness 422; liberal view 4, 90–1, 93–4, 109; Lincoln 358; new/old 96–7, 329, 330, 355–6, 369, 409, 420, 421, 425, 438; opportunity for action 264, 266; organisational involvement 425; participatory 15, 91–2, 226–7, 303; political confidence 70–1; political involvement 15, 303–5; representation 11, 68; responsiveness 384–5; satisfaction with 35–6, 43–5, 51–60, 182, 324, 399, 420; tolerance 118, 423; traditional-elitist view 91; *see also* CID; democracy, small-scale
democracy, small-scale 221, 225–7, 227–8, 429–32, 437–8; actions 238, *239,* 240–3, *244,* 245–6, 280–2; child education 8, 13–14, 234, 240, 241–3, 429; dissatisfaction 228, 235–8, 288, *289,* 290; efficacy of activism 246–53; evaluating 288–91, *292–3;* Germany *239,* 240, 254; healthcare 226, 235, 240, 429; incentives to participate 228–38; individual citizens 256–7; measures 417; opportunities 228, 229, *232;* participation 8–9, 222–3, *294,* 295, *296,* 297, 369, 431–2; social networks 243; Swedish studies 223–5, 281; voice/exit 234, 235, 240–1, 243, 245; working life 234–5, 429
Denmark 6, *17, 20–1;* associational involvement 103, 140, 150; child education 234, 264; citizen action 298; citizenship dimensions 93, 95; consumer organisations 144; decisionist citizenship 325; democracy 23, 24, 43, *44;* democracy, small-scale 233, 238, *239,* 240; discontent 258–61; dissatisfaction *259,* 260, 261; drug addicts 119; efficacy of activism 249, 251; EU 25; exit opportunities 234, 245; family involvement 246; gender factors 169, 402; GNI per capita 18; healthcare 240, 264; language 32n1; law-abidingness 101; locality 169; monarchy 25; NATO membership 25; opportunities 285; parenthood 169; party activity 389, 396; political confidence 83; political exclusion 114–15, 130–1; political involvement 313, 314; political participation 340, 348; procedural fairness 251, *252,* 253; recreational associations 182; residency 169; satisfaction-or-action score 291; social discrimination 114–15; social groups inequality 405; social trust 150; solidarity 101; tolerance 423; trust 39, 328; voice/exit choice 235; voluntary work 139; voting 117, 350; welfare state 26; working life 13–14, 234–5, 429
Denters, Bas 11–12, 57, 420–1, 422–3
dictatorships 24
discontent 255, 257–61, 276–7, 287–8, 429–31
discrimination 114–15, 123–4
dissatisfaction 14; action *259,* 260, 290; child education 236, 260–1; democracy, small-scale 228, 235–8, 288, *289,* 290; discontent 429–30; efficacy of activism 256; feedback 287–8; healthcare 236; opportunities for action 269, 270–1, 284, 431–2; predicting action 274–5; resignation, silent 249; resources 269; student education 236; working life 236, 261
dogmatism 125
donations 12, 139–40, 144, 150, 334, 340, 342
drug addicts 119, 125, 423
Dunn, John 35
Dworkin, Ronald 14, 262, 277, 386, 431, 436

Easton, David 44, 336, 434
economic development 66, 355–6
education 2, 19, 31, 103; associational involvement 160, 168–9; confidence 73; democracy, small-scale 8, 226;

466 *Index*

education *continued*
  opportunity for action 268; political activism 403; political discussions 209, 212; political equality 392; political involvement 321; political participation 362–3, 396–7; religious associations 173, 182; social networks 193; tolerance 109–10, 123–4, 126, 131; trust 52
efficacy of activism 249, *283*, 290–1; civic skills 284; democracy, small-scale 246–53; dissatisfaction 256, 324; political involvement 182; politics 165, 399
elites 336, 381
employment 8, 13–14, 161–2, 168–9, 172, 182, 193
Encarnación, Omar 166
environmental organisations 144
environmentally friendly buying 340, 342
equality 4, 384–6, 408, 435–6; *see also* political equality
Erlach, Emanuel von 14, 431–2
Esping-Andersen, Gøsta 114
ethnic minorities 114–15, 122, 125, *128*, 423
ethnicity 19, 22
Eurobarometer survey 39, 41, 118
European Union 25, 41
European Values Survey 118, 139
exclusion: *see* political exclusion
exit/voice: *see* voice/exit
extremism 114–15, 119, *127,* 130, 131, 423–4

fairness 251–3, 287, 290, 298–9, 432
Fascism 308–9
feedback 281, 287–8, 431–2
Finland 2, *20–1*
Flap, Henk 205
Font Fábregas, Joan 13, 427–8
France 2, 4, *20–1,* 23–4
fraternity 4
freedom 4, 23, 369, 386
Freedom House 23
French Revolution 4
Friedrich, Robert J. 383n3
friendship ties 99, 173, 183, 198, 215n4
Fuchs, Susanne 54
fund raising 345, 354

Gabriel, Oscar 11–12, 163, 167–8, 420–1, 422–3

Gambetta, Diego 38
gender: associational involvement 159–60, 168–9, 173; child education 274; consumer participation 393; contacting 393; healthcare 274; opportunity for action 268; participatory citizenship 329; political activism 402, 403–4; political discussions 209; political equality 392, 393; political involvement 321; political participation 362–3, 410; social networks 193, 196, 216n10; Spain 329; suffrage 2; tolerance 124, 126, 131; voting 393, 398
generational differences *see* age
Germany 6, 10, *17, 20–1*; associational involvement 147; child education 240; citizen action 277–8, 279n11; democracy 24; democracy, small-scale *239,* 240, 254; dissatisfaction 261; electoral system 25, 26; ethnicity 22; EU 25; exit opportunities 245; GNI per capita 18; healthcare 240; NATO 25; opportunities 264; political participation 340; population 18; social discrimination 122; suffrage 24; trust question 38–9; voluntary work 139; *see also* Germany, East; Germany, West
Germany, East 6; associational involvement 103, 167; church attendance 172–3; citizenship dimensions 93; civic values 102; communist past 165; consumer participation 393; critical/deliberative principles 99, 101; decisionist citizenship 325; dissatisfaction *259,* 260; efficacy of activism 249; gender 196, 393, 402; law-abidingness 101; leftist views 106; media exposure 173; opportunities 257; political activism/age 403, 431; political confidence 45, 47, 70–1, 83; political discussion 205, 212, 319; political equality 396; political involvement 313, 314; political orientations 172; political participation 348; protest activity 350, 397; satisfaction-or-action score 291; social attitudes 172; social groups inequality 405; social networks 192; social trust 45, 47, 102; socio-cultural associations 182; solidarity 101; tolerance 423; trust 39, 198; voice/

exit choice 235; workplace networks 193
Germany, West 6; age 169; associational involvement 54, 103, 150; child education 264; church attendance 172–3, 182–3; citizenship 93, 325; critical/deliberative principles 99, 101; decisionist citizenship 325; democracy, satisfaction with 43, *44*; democracy, small-scale 233; dissatisfaction/action *259*, 260; drug addicts 119; education/religious associations 173; friendship ties 183; gender 196, 393; healthcare 235; law-abidingness 101; locality 169, 404; media exposure 173; opportunities 257; political action 431; political confidence 69, 83; political discussion 212, 319; political equality 397; political exclusion 114–15; political orientations 172; political participation 348; recreational associations 182; residency 169; satisfaction-or-action score 291; social discrimination 115; social networks 192, 199; social trust 150; solidarity 101; tolerance 423; trust 39, 328; voice/exit 234, 235
Geurts, Peter 12–13, 425, 428
Gibson, James L. 189
GNI per capita 18–19
goods: collective 149; common 88; constitutive 145; private 147, 149, 426; public 311–12
Grigg, Charles W. 124

habitocracy 3
habitus 111
Habsburg, House of 19, 24
Hardin, Russell 38, 147
healthcare: action efficacy 249, 291; citizen action 230, 231, 233, 235, 275–6; combined additive models 271–4; democracy, small-scale 8, 13–14, 226, 235, 240, 429; dissatisfaction 236, 261; dissatisfaction/action 260–1; gender 274; opportunities 262–4; participation *296*; predicting action 270, *273*; procedural fairness 253; voice/exit 242, 245, 276
Held, David 306, 308–9, 331n9, 332n11
Hirschman, Albert O. 14, 223, 270, 320, 341, 419

Hirst, Paul 136
Hoff, Jens 280, 297
Holmberg, Søren 74
Holy Roman Empire 19, 24, 25
homosexuals 119, 122, 423
Hooghe, Marc 36
housing 8, 227
Howard, Marc 165
human capital 399
Human Development Index 114, 117–18
humanitarian organisations 144
Huntington, Samuel P. 334

ideology: consumer participation 363–4; distorted 436; extremism 119; left–right 106, 129, 386–7; liberalism 125; participatory citizenship 324; political participation 363–4; Putnam 328–9
Iglič, Hajdeja 13, 427–8
immigrants 119, 131, 423
immigrants' organisations 144
incapacitation 16
income factors 160, 168–9, 362–3, 399
individual/society 90
inequality 14–15, 16, 112, 396; *see also* political inequality
information costs 125–6, 398–9
Inglehart, Ronald 73, 89
insecurity 110–11, 118, 131
institutions: associational involvement 165; confidence 66, 131, 182, 184–5, 420; democracy 11, 68; judicial 182, 184–5; non-governmental 336; public confidence 66; trust 125; *see also* political institutions; *Rechsstaat*
integration 89, 114, 184; democracy 153; social networks 113, 161–2, 192; strength of social ties 204
interest organisations 168, *176–7*, 366–7
Internet 340, 354
intolerance: *see* tolerance
involvement 12, 125; citizenship 305–11; family 245–6; organisational 13, 16; political participation 418–19, 433–4; social 437; social networks 190, *191*, 192–3, 196–200; typology 305–11; *see also* associational involvement; organisational involvement; political involvement
Iraq 23
Islamic fundamentalists 119, 130

Jenkins, J. Craig 255
Jennings, M. Kent 387–8, 389
Jordan, Grant 142
judicial institutions 182, 184–5
justice 282, 432

Kaase, Max 36
Key, V.O. 298
Klages, Helmut 106, 107n1
Klosko, George 285
Korea, North 23
Kriesi, Hanspeter 14, 430–1
Kunz, Volker 163
Kymlicka, Will 90–2

language 19, 22
law-abiding behaviour 107n3; citizenship 11, 89, 92, 93, *94*, 95–6, 99, 101; democracy 422; social capital 100; tolerance 125, 129
left–right ideology 106, 129, 386–90, 410
legitimacy 44
Leite Viegas, José Manuel 12, 423–4
Lenin, V.I. 361
Leninist organisations 364
Levi, Margaret 41
liberal citizenship 89, 309, 311, 320–1, 330–1, 422, 4328
liberal democracy 4, 90–1, 93–4, 109
liberalism 112, 125
liberal-representative citizenship 304, 306–7, 312, 433
liberty 4, 82
life expectancy 19
life experience, accumulated 393, 396
life satisfaction 52, 54, 57, 60, 62, 65n24
Lincoln, Abraham 358
Lipset, Seymour Martin 324, 361, 435
Listhaug, Ola 57
locality factors: associational involvement 168–9, 182; decisionist citizenship 325, 328; political equality 392; size of 131, 169, 324; social networks 197; urban/rural 126, 397, 403–4
lodges 144, 147
loyalty 214–15
Lukes, Steven 385

McAllister, Ian 79
McCarthy, John D. 255
McClosky, Herbert 124

macro-political explanations 11, 79–83, 421
Maloney, William A. 142
Margolis, Michael 307
marital status 168–9, 182, 363
Marshall, T.H. 1–2, 3–4, 23, 415
Martin, Irene 15
Marxism 5, 308–9
Mayakovsky, Vladimir 2
media exposure 161–2, 173, 183, 184, *316*, 319, 399
micromobilisation contexts 188
micro-political explanations 11, 73–5, 78, *80*, 82, 85, 122–30, 421
Mill, J.S. 331n8
Miller, Arthur H. 74
mobilisation 188, 365, 370, *372*, 397
modernisation: attachments 365; economic 110, 350, 438; individual 72–3; learning theory 409; societal 88–9, 110, 370
Moldova 6, *17, 20–1*; age 169, 396, 403; associational involvement 105, 139–40, 147, 166–7; child education 234; citizenship dimensions 93, 328; civic values/social trust 102; democracy 24, 43, *44*; democracy, small-scale 233, 238, *239*, 240; dissatisfaction 236, *259*, 260, 261; drug addicts 119; education 19; efficacy of activism 249; freedom 23; gender 196, 402; GNI per capita 18; healthcare 235, 240; languages 22; law-abidingness 101, 422; leftist views 106; life expectancy 19; locality 404; opportunities 257; parenthood 169; participatory citizenship 320; party activity 391, 396; political activism 402, 403; political confidence 47, *49*, 71, 83; political discussions 212; political equality 397; political exclusion 131; political involvement 313, 314; political orientations 172; political participation 340, 348; procedural fairness 251, *252*, 253; protest activity 389, 391; *Rechtsstaat* institutions 69; republic 25–6; satisfaction-or-action score 291; social groups inequality 405; social networks 192, 196, 199; strength of social ties 200–5, 204; tolerance 423; trust, generalised 198; two-party systems 26; value orientations 78;

voice/exit 234, 235, 243, 245; workplace networks 193
monarchies 25
Montero, José Ramón 7, 10–11, 12, 15, 419–20, 433–4
Morales, Laura 12–13, 425, 428
multi-party systems 26
mutuality 35, 60–1

Nagel, Jack 436
natiocracy 2–3
Nationalism 308–9
NATO (North Atlantic Treaty Organisation) membership 25
NDQP (Normed Distance to the Equality Point) 392, 393, 396, 397, 398
Neller, Katja 13, 426–7
Nelson, Joan M. 334
neo-Conservatives 66
neo-Liberals 66
neo-Marxists 66
neo-pluralism 97
Netherlands 6, *17*; associational involvement 103, 147; bicameral parliament 25–6; child education 234; citizen action 298; citizenship dimensions 93; country characteristics *20–1*; decisionist citizenship 325; democracy 23, 24, 43, *44*; democracy, small-scale 233, 238, *239*, 240; dissatisfaction *259*, 260, 261; drug addicts 119; efficacy of activism 249, 251; environmental organisations 144; ethnicity 22; EU 25; friendship ties 183; gender factors 169, 196; GNI per capita 18; languages 22; law-abidingness 101; monarchy 25; NATO membership 25; opportunities 257; party activity 389; political confidence 69, 83; political discussion 205, 213; political equality 397, 410–11; political exclusion 114–15; political involvement 313, 314; political orientations 172; political participation 340, 348; procedural fairness 251, *252,* 253; recreational associations 182; residents' associations 144; satisfaction-or-action score 291; social discrimination 114–15; social groups inequality 405; social networks 192, 196, 199; socio-cultural associations 182; tolerance 423; trust 39; voice/exit 234, 235, 245; welfare state 26; women's voting rights 117
New Public Management 224, 227
Newton, Kenneth 10–11, 12, 41, 72, 107, 382, 419–20, 435
Nie, Norman H. 7, 8, 282, 335, 336, 356n6, 387, 390
Noelle-Neumann, Elisabeth 10, 38–9, 47
non-governmental institutions 336
non-political associations 307, 373–4
Norman, Wayne 90–2
normative political theories 4, 88, 92–5
Norris, Pippa 41, 72, 75, 78, 82
Norway 6, *17*; associational involvement 105, 137–9, 139–40; bicameral parliament 26; child education 234; citizen action 298; citizenship dimensions 93; consumer participation 393; country characteristics *20–1*; critical/deliberative principles 99, 101; data collection 29–30; decisionist citizenship 325; democracy 23, 24; democracy, small-scale 233, 238, *239,* 240; discontent 258–61; dissatisfaction *259,* 260, 261; donations 140; drug addicts 119; education/religious associations 173; efficacy of activism 249; exit opportunities 234, 245; family involvement 246; gender factors 169, 196, 402; GNI per capita 18; healthcare 240, 264; humanitarian organisations 144; independence 24–5; languages 22; law-abidingness 101; locality 169, 404; monarchy 25; NATO membership 25; opportunities, situation-specific 257; political confidence 83; political discussion 205, 213; political efficacy 182; political equality 410–11; political exclusion 114–15; political involvement 313, 314; political orientations 172; political participation 340, 348; procedural fairness 251, *252,* 253; professional organisations 144; satisfaction-or-action score 291; social discrimination 115; social groups inequality 405; social networks 192, 199; solidarity 101; tolerance 423; trust 39, 328; welfare state 26; women's voting rights 117

Nozick, Robert 4

Offe, Claus 54
opportunities 262–4, *286*; action *263*, 268, 274–5; child education 262–4; democracy 264, 266; democracy, small-scale 228, 229, *232*; discontent 257, 430–1; dissatisfaction 269, 270–1, 284, 431–2; exit 233; feedback 285–7; grievances 255–6; resources 257; social networks 193, 196–200
organisational involvement 86n13, 99, 102, 103; church attendance 182–3; democracy 425; dimensions of 367, 369–70; explanations of 167–73, 182–3; membership 257; political equality 137; political participation 16, 61, *359*, 360, 361, *368*, 373–7, 376, 380–1, 435; social trust 36, 416, 420, 426; types of 167–8, 425–8; *see also* associational involvement
Ottoman Empire 24

parenthood 161, 168–9, 182, 363
participation 15–16, 107n3; by chequebook 144; child education *296*; citizen 334–5; community 35; compensatory 291; cumulation 291–7; democracy 294; democracy, small-scale 8–9, 222–3, 228–38, *294*, 295–7, *296*, 297, 369, 431–2; equality of 295; impacts of 282; political 15, 304, 334–5, 335–7; political involvement 12, 319–20; social 9, 304, 320, 416–17; social movements 277; voting 15, 340, 362; *see also* political participation
participatory citizenship 304, 308, 311, 318–19, 433; gender 329; ideology 324, 328–9; Portugal 320–1; social capital 330–1
participatory democracy 15, 91–2, 226–7, 303
partnership initiatives 225
party activity 15, 342, 349, 351, 389–90, 396
passivity 257–8, 290, 306, 373
Peffley, Mark A. 112–13
Pérez-Díaz, Víctor M. 166
Pericles 305, 331n10
Perrow, Charles 255
Petersson, Olof *248*, 280, 285
petition-signing 334, 340
Pettersen, Per Arnt 93, 96

pluralism 90, 106
plutocracy 2
political action groups 345, 354
Political Action Study 8, 337, 343
political activism 431; age 403; associational involvement 99, 158; capability 398; citizenship 140; education 403; gender 402, 403–4; left–right ideology 387–8, 410; types 351, 354–5
political actors 68, 78–9
political confidence 9; comparative levels 69–71, 83; crisis in 66; democracy 70–1; explanations of 71–5; influencing factors 83, 85; measuring 67–9; multilevel analysis *84*; multivariate analyses 51–60; social trust 9, 35–7, 45–50, *48*, 54, 56, 60, 62, 420; socio-cultural explanations 67, 75, *76–7*, 78
political discussion 189, 314, *316*, 317; citizenship types 318, 319; education 209, 212; gender 209; regression analysis *210–11*; social networks 205–13
political equality: age 392; attitudes 386–91; contacting 397; education 392; gender 392, 393; Germany, East 396; locality 392; Netherlands 410–11; Norway 410–11; organisational involvement 137; political participation 411, 437, 438; protest activity 397; tolerance 387, 391; voting 397; *see also* political inequality
political exclusion: attitudes 111; Denmark 130–1; ethnic minorities *128*; extremist groups *127*; Portugal 119, 122, 130–1; social discrimination 112–22; stigmatised groups *128*; Switzerland 122
political inequality: assessment 436–7; education 403, 404–5, 408–9; explanations 398–404; gender/vote 398; political participation *400–1*, 409–10; social groups 392–8, 397, 399–400
political institutions 44; confidence 35–6, 37, 39–43, *39–43*, *58*, 61, 131
political interest 162, 303–4, 312, 380
political involvement *313*, 314, *316*; age 321; citizenship types *317–18*, *322–3*, 329–31; cultural 304–5, 324; decisionist 314; degrees of 337;

democracy 15, 303–5; liberal 314; participatory 314, 319–20; political importance 304, 312, *313*; social capital 325, 328; socio-demographic 304–5, 324–5; socio-economic status 321; tolerance 129; trust 328; unitarian 314

political orientations 164–5, 182, 184–5

political participation 7–9, 334–7, *346–7*; age 362–3, 410; civic duty 363; civic skills 9, 270–1, 275, 377, 399; cleavage politics 370, 373; consumer participation 349, 351, 354, 355, 389; economic development 355–6; education 396–7; equality 384–6, 408; exit/voice 434; explanations *371–2*; gender 410; ideology 363–4; individual-level correlations *352–3*; information costs 398–9; involvement 418–19, 433–4; levels of *338–9*, 348–51, 405, *406–7*, 408; mapping 337, 340; modes 341–8, 351, 354, 373, 434–5; non-electoral 355, 405; organisational involvement 16, 61, *359*, 360, 361, *368*, 373–7, 380–1, 435; participatory 91–2; political equality 411, 437, 438; political inequality *400–1*, 409–10; psychological predispositions 363; representational/extra-representational 434; self-selectivity *378–9*; social capital *375*, 381–2, 424–8; social group inequality *394–5*; social trust 363; structural characteristics 362–3; targeted/non-targeted 434; tolerance 390–1; two-step flow model 188; typology 340–3, 355; voice/exit 348–9; voluntary associations 61, 62–3, 382

political parties 207, 364

politics: efficacy of activism 165; loyalty 214–15; meeting attendance 345; politico-historical factors 87n31; trust 35–7, 328

Polity IV database 23

polyarchy 307

populations 18

Portugal 6, *17*; age 169; associational involvement 103, 137–9, 167; citizenship dimensions 93; civic values/social trust 102; client-type involvement 142; consumer participation 354, 355; country characteristics *20–1*; democracy 24;

democracy, satisfaction with 43, *44*; democracy, small-scale 233, *239*, 240; dissatisfaction 236, *259*, 260, 261; donations 139; drug addicts 119; education 19; ethnicity 22; EU 25; exit opportunities 245; extra-representational activity 351; family involvement 246; friendship ties 183; gender/social networks 193, 196; GNI per capita 18; healthcare 235, 240, 264; income 169; law-abidingness 101, 422; leftist views 106; locality 169, 404; NATO membership 25; opportunities, situation-specific 257; parenthood 169; participatory citizenship 320; party activity 351; party mobilisation 355; political activism/age 403; political confidence 69, 71, 83; political discussion 205, 212, 319; political equality 397; political exclusion 119, 122, 130–1; political involvement 313, 314; political participation 348, 350; political socialisation 382; procedural fairness 251, *252*, 253; protest activity 355; regime type 186; republic 25–6; satisfaction-or-action score 291; social groups inequality 405; social networks 192, 199; social trust/associational membership 150; solidarity 101; strength of social ties 200–5; tolerance 115, 117, 423; trust 39; trust, generalised 198; two-party systems 26; value orientations 78; welfare state 26; workplace networks 193

Posner, Daniel N. 145

post-authoritarian regimes 166

post-communist regimes 165–7, 183, 185–6, 257–8

private sphere 40

procedural fairness 251, *252*, 253

professional organisations 144

protest activity 334, 343, 349, 351, 355; age 380, 396; left–right ideology 389; participation 15; political equality 397; social trust 377; types 340, 345

Protestantism 19, 32n2

Prothro, James W. 124

psychological predispositions 363

public agencies 223, 224–5

public engagement 90–1

Putnam, Robert D.: age factors 196; associational involvement 54, 140, 142, 153; citizenship 93, 95; communitarianism 91; community size 161; generational differences 159–60; ideology 328–9; left–right ideology 324; political interest 303; social capital 10, 67, 71–2, 97–8, 149, 150, 321, 324, 333n26, 360, 366, 381–2, 418; social participation 320; social trust 324; television 105; videomalaise 78, 161–2

race factors 119, 131, 423
racists 119, 130
Rahn, Wendy 163
rainmaker hypothesis 37
Rechtsstaat 68, 69, 78–9, 83
reciprocity 35, 60–1, 188–9
recreational associations 144, 168, *174–5*, 182, 426
regime types, prior 165–7, 185–6
religion 19, 32n2, 124, 161; *see also* church attendance
religious associations *180–1*, 185
religious fundamentalism 119, 423
religious groups 54, 144, 168
representation 11, 68, 153, 155
republics 5, 25–6
residency 168–9, 182
residents' associations 144, 145
resignation, silent 249
resources: age 271; allocation 136; citizens 361–2; discontent 430–1; dissatisfaction 269; impact of 264–6; opportunities 257; predicting action 274–5
responsiveness: to citizen action 280–1; democracy 384–5; democracy, small-scale 290; determinants 282–4; political 74; public agencies 223, 224–5
rights: of association 135; citizenship 1–2, 12, 22, 92, 225–7; civil 1–2; cultural 2–3; equality of 384; legal 1–2, 3; political 1–2; realised 5; respect 118–19; social 1–2, 3–4; voting 27
Rochon, Thomas R. 54
Rogers, Joel 136
Rohrschneider, Robert 112–13
Rokkan, Stein 361, 435
Roman Catholicism 19
Romania 6, *17, 20–1*; associational involvement 103, 139–40, 147, 150, 166–7, 172; bicameral parliament 26; citizenship dimensions 93, 95, 328; civic values 102; consumer participation 393; critical/ deliberative principles 99, 101; decisionist citizenship 325; democracy, satisfaction with 43, *44*; democracy, small-scale 233, 238, *239*, 240; dissatisfaction 236, *259*, 260, 261; drug addicts 119; education 19; efficacy of activism 249; ethnicity 22; freedom 23; gender 196, 393; GNI per capita 18; healthcare 240; law-abidingness 101, 422; leftist views 106; life expectancy 19; locality 169; NATO membership 25; opportunities, situation-specific 257; Ottoman Empire 24; party activity 389, 391; political confidence 47, *49*, 71, 82; political discussion 205, 212, 319; political equality 397, 411; political exclusion 131; political involvement 313, 314; political orientations 172; political participation 340, 348; protest activity 389; satisfaction-or-action score 291; social groups inequality 405; social networks 192, 196, 199; social trust 102, 150, 172, 187n15; solidarity 101, 107; strength of social ties 200–5, 204; tolerance 423; trust, generalised 198; value orientations 78; voice options 243; workplace networks 193
Rose, Lawrence E. 93, 96
Rose, Richard 365
Rosenberg, Morris 39, 63n8
Roßteutscher, Sigrid 13–14, 429, 430
rule of law 11, 109
Russia 6, *17, 20–1*; age 169, 403; associational involvement 105, 140, 147, 166–7; church attendance 182–3; citizenship dimensions 93; civic values/social trust 102; client-type involvement 142; communist past 165; consumer participation 389, 393; democracy, satisfaction with 43, *44*; donations 140; drug addicts 119; education 19; electoral system 26; federation 25; freedom 23; gender factors 169, 393, 402; GNI per capita 18; languages 19, 22; law-abidingness 101, 422; leftist views 106; life expectancy 19; locality 169,

404; political activism 403; political confidence 69, 71, 83; political efficacy 182; political equality 397, 411; political exclusion 131; political participation 340, 348; political parties 26; population 18; *Rechtsstaat* institutions 69; republic 25–6; social groups inequality 405; solidarity 101; survey 29; tolerance 423; voter turnout 117, 355; welfare state 26; women's voting rights 117
Russian Orthodox 19

Sartori, Giovanni 332n11
satisfaction-or-action score 290–1
Scandinavia: *see individual countries*
Schlozman, Kay Lehman 337
Schumpeter, Joseph 306
secularisation 19
self-critical 93
self-determination 6–7
self-government 8
self-realisation 164, 172, 182
self-selectivity 361–4, 435; political participation *378–9*; social capital 365–7, 374, 377; social networks 377, 380
Sen, Amartya 386, 398
sensitivity, endowment-/ambition-based 262, 277, 281, 386, 402–5, 431
service clubs 144, 147
Slovenia 6, *17, 20–1*; associational involvement 105, 137–9; bicameral parliament 26; charities 144; citizenship dimensions 93; civic values/social trust 102; consumer participation 389, 393; decisionist citizenship 325; democracy 24; democracy, satisfaction with 43, *44*; democracy, small-scale 233, 238, *239*, 240; dissatisfaction 236, *259*, 260, 261; donations 139; education 31; efficacy of activism 246, 248; EU 25; gender factors 196, 393; GNI per capita 18–19; healthcare 240, 264; income 169; languages 22; law-abidingness 101; locality 169; NATO membership 25; opportunities, situation-specific 257; party activity 389, 391; political activism 403; political confidence 69, 71, 83; political discussion 212–13, 319; political involvement 313, 314; political participation 348;

procedural fairness 251, *252*, 253; recreational associations 182; social groups inequality 405; social networks 173, 192, 196, 199; solidarity 107; trust 39, 198; voice/exit 234, 243, 245; welfare state 26
Smelser, Neil 256
Sniderman, Paul M. 111, 118
sociability style 428
social capital 99, *100*, 101; age 103; civic virtues *104–5*, 422; cleavage politics 373; community size 328; effects of 102, 103; impact 422–3; partisan activity 377; political involvement 325, 328; political participation *375*, 381–2, 424–8; Putnam 10, 67, 71–2, 97–8, 149, 150, 321, 324, 333n26, 360, 366, 381–2, 418; self-selectivity 365–7, 374, 377; social networks 188–9; social trust 324; socio-cultural explanations 11
social capital theory 35–7, 51, 86n9, 426, 435
social discrimination 111, 114–15, 119, *121*, 122, *123*
social groups *123*, 392–8, 399–400, 405
social involvement 65n24, 97–106, 418, 419; *see also* associational involvement; organisational involvement
social movements 255–6, 274–5, 276–7, 430–1
social networks 6, 13, 166; age 193, 196; associational involvement 197–8, 207; CID 12–13; cross-national differences 13; cultural traits 193; democracy, small-scale 243; gender 193, 196, 216n10; integration 72, 161–2, 192; involvement 190, *191*, 192–3, *195*, 196–200; multiplicity 189, 190, *191*, 192–3, *194*, 196–200, 213–15; opportunity structures 193, 196–200; political discussion 205–15; political implications 427–8; political potential 189–90; self-selectivity 377, 380; social capital 188–9; social positions 193; social ties 188, 189, 200–5, 209, 213–15; territorial identity 198–9; trust 197; voluntary associations 214, 215n3, 428; voluntary organisations 8, 424–8; workplace 270; *see also* friendship ties
social norms 106, 163–4

social participation 9, 304, 320, 416–17
social positions 193, 283
social trust 10–11, 37–8, *40,* 61;
  associational involvement 12, 54, *55, 56,* 149–55, 162–4, 172, 182; civic norms 97–106; civic virtues 102, 103; multiple regression analysis *53;* multivariate analyses 51–60; organisational involvement 416, 426; political confidence 9, 35–6, 45–50, 54, 56, 60, 62, 420; political participation 363; private sphere 40; protest activity 377; Romania 187n15; satisfaction with democracy 50–1; social capital 324; voluntary organisations 54
socialisation 71, 367, *369,* 382, 421
society/individual 89
socio-cultural approach 11, 73, *81,* 83, 85, 370, 421
socio-cultural associations 168, *178–9,* 182, 381
socio-demographic factors 304–5, 324–5, 329
socio-economic resources 160, 184, 321
solidarity 11, 89, 91, 92, 93, 95–6, *100,* 107n3, 422; associational involvement 164, 172, 185; citizenship *94,* 363; social capital model 99, 101; tolerance 125, 129, 131
Spain 6, *17, 20–1*; associational involvement 54, 103, 137–9, 167; church attendance 182–3; citizenship dimensions 93; civic values/social trust 102; client-type involvement 142; decisionist citizenship 325; democracy 24; democracy, small-scale 233; dissatisfaction 236, *259,* 260, 261; donations 139; drug addicts 119; education 19, 173; efficacy of activism 249; EU 25; gender 329; gender/social networks 193, 196; GNI per capita 18; languages 19, 22; law-abidingness 101, 422; monarchy 25; NATO membership 25; opportunities, situation-specific 257; participatory citizenship 320; political activism/age 403; political confidence 47, *49,* 50, 71, 83; political discussion 205, 207, *208,* 212, 319; political efficacy 182; political involvement 313, 314; political participation 348; political

socialisation 382; prior regime 166; protest activity 349–50, 389; recreational associations 182; regime type 186; republic 25–6; satisfaction-or-action score 291; social attitudes 172; social groups inequality 405; social networks 192, 193, 196, 199; social trust *50,* 102, 150; socio-cultural associations 182; solidarity 101; strength of social ties 200–5, 204; survey 29; tolerance 423; trust 39, 328; two-party systems 26; voluntary work 139; workplace networks 193
sports clubs 144, 168, *174–5,* 426
stigmatised groups 110–11, 114–15, 122, 125, *128,* 131, 423
Stoker, Laura 41
Stolle, Dietlind 54, 163
Stouffer, Samuel 110, 113, 124
student education 13–14, 230, 233, 236, 249, 429
suffrage 2, 23, 115, 117
Sullivan, John L. 109, 110, 124
Sum, Paul 16, 435–6
support networks, informal 215n5
Sweden 6, *17, 20–1*; associational involvement 103, 140; child education 234; citizen action 298; citizenship dimensions 93; consumer organisations 144; consumer participation 393; decisionist citizenship 325; democracy 23, 24; democracy, satisfaction with 43, *44;* democracy, small-scale 233, 238, *239,* 240; discontent 258–61; dissatisfaction *259,* 260, 261; drug addicts 119; efficacy of activism 249, 251; ethnicity 22; EU 25; family involvement 246; gender factors 196, 402; GNI per capita 18; healthcare 240; law-abidingness 101, 422; monarchy 25; opportunities 257, 285; political activism/age 403; political confidence 69; political confidence levels 83; political discussions 213; political efficacy 182; political exclusion 114–15; political orientations 172; political participation 340, 348; procedural fairness 251, *252,* 253; protest activity 397; residency 169; satisfaction-or-action score 291; social discrimination 114–15; social groups

Index 475

inequality 405; social networks 192, 196, 199; socio-cultural associations 182; solidarity 101; tolerance 423; trade unions 243; trust 39, 328; voice/exit 234, 235, 245; welfare state 26; women's voting rights 117
Swedish citizenship studies 6, 27, 32n5, 92, 223–5, 281
Switzerland 6, *17, 20–1*; age 403; associational involvement 103, 137–9, 140, 147; citizen action 298; citizenship dimensions 93, 95; consumer participation 393; data collection 29–30; decisionist citizenship 325; democracy 23, 24; democracy, small-scale 233, 238, *239*, 240; discontent 258–61; dissatisfaction *259*, 260, 261; donations 140; drug addicts 119; education/religious associations 173; efficacy of activism 249, 251; environmental organisations 144; exit opportunities 245; federation 25; gender factors 196, 393; GNI per capita 18; healthcare 235, 240; languages 22; law-abidingness 101; opportunities, situation-specific 257; party activity 389; political activism 403; political confidence levels 83; political discussion 205, 207, *208*, 213; political efficacy 182; political equality 397; political exclusion 114–15, 122; political involvement 313, 314; political participation 340, 348; procedural fairness 251, *252*, 253; professional organisations 144; protest activity 389; republic 25–6; residency 169; satisfaction-or-action score 291; social discrimination 115, 122; social networks 192, 196, 199; social trust 150; solidarity 101; strength of social ties 203; suffrage 2; tolerance 115, 117; trust 39; unemployment 117; value orientations 78; voting 23–4, 117, 350, 355, 408

television 73, 75, 78, 103, 161–2, 173, 187n16
Teorell, Jan 7, 15, 16, 433–4, 435–6
territorial identity 198–9, 217n18
Thucydides 305, 331n4
Tobiasen, Mette 16, 435–6
Tocqueville, Alexis de: civic virtues 106;

democracy 331n8; *Democracy in America* 10, 360, 418; majority principle 109; networks 66–7, 97; non-political associations 307
tolerance 9; age 109–10, 126, 131; associational involvement 163, 164, 172, 182; church attendance 126, 131; critical/deliberative behaviour 129; democracy 118, 423; education 109–10, 123–4, 126, 131; gender 124, 126, 131; individual level 122; insecurity 131; law-abiding behaviour 125, 129; left–right ideology 410; overall levels 114–18; political equality 387, 391; political involvement 129; political participation 390–1; political/social 12, 110, 122–30; Portugal 115, 117; Sniderman 111; solidarity 125, 129, 131; Switzerland 115, 117; voter turnout 117
Torcal, Mariano 7, 11–12, 15, 420–1, 422–3, 433–4
trade unions 144, 243, 245, 268–9, 358, 361, 364–5
trust: CID 37; community 60–1; education 52; generalised 38, 39, 198, 216n16; horizontal/vertical 11, 421; individual level 35; institutions 125; particularised 38; politics 35–7, 328; reciprocity 188–9; social networks 197; voluntary organisations 36–7; *see also* social trust
trustworthy behaviour 63n7
two-party systems 26

unemployment 8, 117, 161, 227, 235
unitarianism 333n27
United Nations 41
United States of America 142, 196, 381–2
Uslaner, Eric M. 36, 39, 163, 197, 198

value orientations 72–3, 78, 89–90, 163
van den Broek, Andries 164–5
van Deth, Jan W. 15, 333n29, 387–8, 389, 419
Verba, Sidney 7, 8, 90, 282, 304, 334–5, 336, 337, 343, 356n6, 384, 385, 387, 390, 397
videomalaise 78, 161–2
voice/exit 15; action 270, 430; associational involvement 245; child education 231, 233, 245, 276;

voice/exit *continued*
  citizen power 14, 230–1, 233, 234, 253–4; democracy, small-scale 234, 235, 240–1, 243, 245; healthcare 242, 276; Hirschman 223, 341; political participation 348–9; voting 341; working life 276
Volker, Beate 205
voluntary activity 61
voluntary associations 6, 52, 97, 166; civic virtues 91; confidence 57; interest groups 366–7; involvement 11, 12–13; membership 52, 54, 360, 399; political participation 61, 62–3, 382; social networks 8, 214, 215n3, 424–8; social trust 54; strength of social ties *201*; trust 36–7; *see also* associational involvement; organisational involvement
voluntary work 12, 139, 145
voting 222–3, 402; gender 393, 398; participation 15, 340, 362; political equality 397; rights 27; Switzerland 408; trade union members 358; turnout 117, 343–4, 350, 358, 405; voice/exit 341; *see also* suffrage

Walzer, Michael 91, 92, 281–2, 291, 308, 331n9, 432
Warren, Mark E. 38, 145, 147

Weber, Max 306
Weimar republic 24
welfare states 26, 113–14, 224, 262
Westholm, Anders 14, *248*, 430–1, 431–2
Wiberg, Matti 57
women's groups 393
women's suffrage 2, 23, 115, 117
work councils 222
working life: action 249, 291; citizen action 227, 230, 231, 233, 275–6; combined additive models 266–71; democracy, small-scale 13–14, 234–5, 429; dissatisfaction 236, 261; opportunities 264; participation 72, *296*; predicting action *267*, 270; voice/exit 276
workplace democracy 227
workplace networks 190, 193, *202*, 207, 215n2, 270
World Values Survey 39, 41, 46, 47, 139
Wuthnow, Robert 161

youth associations 145
Yugoslavia (former) 19

Zald, Mayer D. 255
Zaller, John R. 303
Zimbabwe 23
Zmerli, Sonja 10–11, 12, 67, 419–20

eBooks – at www.eBookstore.tandf.co.uk

A library at your fingertips!

eBooks are electronic versions of printed books. You can store them on your PC/laptop or browse them online.

They have advantages for anyone needing rapid access to a wide variety of published, copyright information.

eBooks can help your research by enabling you to bookmark chapters, annotate text and use instant searches to find specific words or phrases. Several eBook files would fit on even a small laptop or PDA.

NEW: Save money by eSubscribing: cheap, online access to any eBook for as long as you need it.

Annual subscription packages

We now offer special low-cost bulk subscriptions to packages of eBooks in certain subject areas. These are available to libraries or to individuals.

For more information please contact webmaster.ebooks@tandf.co.uk

We're continually developing the eBook concept, so keep up to date by visiting the website.

www.eBookstore.tandf.co.uk